STRATEGIES OF
BRITISH INDIA

BRITAIN, IRAN AND AFGHANISTAN
1798–1850

STRATEGIES OF BRITISH INDIA

BRITAIN, IRAN AND AFGHANISTAN
1798–1850

M. E. YAPP

CLARENDON PRESS · OXFORD
1980

Oxford University Press, Walton Street, Oxford OX2 6DP

OXFORD   LONDON   GLASGOW
NEW YORK   TORONTO   MELBOURNE   WELLINGTON
KUALA LUMPUR   SINGAPORE   JAKARTA   HONG KONG   TOKYO
DELHI   BOMBAY   CALCUTTA   MADRAS   KARACHI
NAIROBI   DAR ES SALAAM   CAPE TOWN

© Malcolm Yapp 1980
Published in the United States by
Oxford University Press, New York

British Library Catalogue Data

British Library Cataloguing in Publication Data

Yapp, Malcolm Edward
  Strategies of British India.
  1. India – Foreign relations
  2. India – Politics and government – 1765–1947
  3. India – National security   4. Great Britain
  – Foreign relations – 19th century
  5. Great Britain – History, Military –
  19th century
  I. Title
  327.54   DS446.5   79–41089

  ISBN 0–19–822481–8

Filmset in 11/12½ point Baskerville
Printed and bound in Great Britain
by W & J Mackay Limited, Chatham

Contents

List of Maps

Abbreviations

SLV Secret Letters Various (India Office Records)

References to the two principal published collections of Russian documents are as follows:
AKAK akty, sobrannye kavkazskoj arkheograficheskoj komissiej
VPR Vneshnyaya Politika Rossii

2 ABBREVIATIONS USED IN REFERENCE TO PERIODICALS

BSOAS Bulletin of the School of Oriental and African Studies
CAR Central Asian Review
CHJ Cambridge Historical Journal
CSSH Comparative Studies in Social History
EHR English Historical Review
HJ Historical Journal
IHRC Proceedings of the Indian Historical Records Commission
IJMES International Journal of Middle Eastern Studies
IZ Istoricheskie Zapiski
JAH Journal of Asian History
JBIPS Journal of the British Institute for Persian Studies
JBS Journal of British Studies
JCAS Journal of the Central Asian Society
JEH Journal of Economic History
JICH Journal of Imperial and Commonwealth History
JIH Journal of Indian History
JMH Journal of Modern History
JPHS Journal of the Pakistan Historical Society
JRAS Journal of the Royal Asiatic Society
JSHS Journal of the Sind Historical Society
MES Middle Eastern Studies
RCAJ Royal Central Asian Journal
RDM Revue des Deux Mondes
RHM Revue de l'histoire moderne
SR Slavonic and East European Review
UZIV Uchenye Zapiski Instituta Vostokevedeniya
ZRGO Zapiski Russkogo Geograficheskogo Obshchestva

Introduction

The subject of this book is the search for a system which would safeguard British India from the dangers of attack from the north-west. Interesting as the problems are, discussion of the northern, eastern, and maritime frontiers of India is excluded, except where events in these areas directly affected decisions related to the north-west. The area examined is that which intervened between the British frontier in northern India and the Caspian Sea; it includes the states of the Indus system together with those of Afghanistan, Iran, and Turkestan. I should like to have extended the examination to have embraced the western parts of the Middle East, that is, the Ottoman Empire, but reasons of space dictate the limitation of this study to the eastern region of Western Asia.

The period investigated extends from 1798, when the possibility of attacks by Afghanistan and France led to the first consideration of a suitable distant defensive system, until 1849, when the annexation of the Panjab brought the frontier of British India into contact with that of Afghanistan. This period may be divided into four parts, corresponding to the four parts of this book. During the first, from 1798 to 1838, Britain experimented with a system of defence in which the central role was played by Iran. In alliance with British India Iran was thought to offer an insurmountable obstacle to any would-be invader of India. The story of the tribulations of the Anglo-Iranian alliance is recounted in the first part of the book. Disappointed with the fruits of the Iranian alliance Britain began in 1830 to investigate alternatives. The search was concentrated on the countries along and beyond the Indus and therefore became connected with the problems of the frontier of British India itself. In the first chapter of Part II the development of this frontier is described, and in the second the development of the new Indus policy is taken to the point when the failure of the Iranian alliance appeared to call for more far-reaching policies. The remainder of Part II is devoted to an examination of how these new policies—which led to the first Anglo-Afghan War—were formed. Part III deals with the Afghan system itself, a novel, extensive system of defence hinged upon Afghanistan, through which country Britain sought to extend her influence into Turkestan. The collapse of the Afghan system in 1842 ushered in the last phase, described in Part IV, when British India abandoned all idea of distant buffer states and focused her attention upon the states immediately adjoining her own frontier. The changed emphasis led to the annexation of Sind in 1843 and of the Panjab in 1849.

Presented in this fashion the subject appears as a simple progression in which policies are devised to meet contingencies and discarded when experience indicates them to be unsuitable. As usual, appearance is deceptive. The difficulties arise from several sources but principally from this: that the defence of British India from attack from the north-west was neither the sole, nor even the principal determinant of the policies pursued in the region during the half-century under consideration. The defence of India was indeed indicated by contemporaries and by subsequent historians as the principal motive underlying British dealings with the countries of the north-west, but it is the contention of this book that both were in error; the external defence of India will not serve as a sufficient explanation of British policy in Iran, Afghanistan, and on the Indus. Now for an author to suggest to his readers first that his book is about the defence of India from an attack from the north-west and then to assert that, after all, it is not about this subject, is behaviour likely to provoke irritation, and the sin is compounded when the book is a large one. Some explanation is plainly required and in this introduction I will display the general views concerning the problems of Indian defence upon which the paradox is founded, indicate certain of the major issues with which the book is concerned, and supply background material which may aid my readers in their journey. It will be convenient to begin with some consideration of the various individuals, groups, and institutions concerned with the formation of British policies in the region. These may be divided into two main bodies: those in Britain and those in India.

Within Britain the British public had little to say about India and for long was uncertain what value it should attach to the possession. The early hopes of great financial support to British revenues from the acquisition of Bengal in 1765 were quickly replaced by worries lest India should prove an actual drain upon Britain's resources or that its wealth, falling into the hands of unscrupulous individuals or into those of the Crown, might be employed to subvert the English constitution. The fading of these fears was succeeded by a period of indifference occasionally disturbed by the hopes and fears of merchants, manufacturers, missionaries, statesmen, and other interested parties. Only very gradually did the idea that India was a valuable possession, not lightly to be sacrificed, percolate into the British consciousness. Even then

most men would have found difficulty in defining India's value. However, we may date the general acceptance of the view that India was
well worth having to the years 1830–1850, that is, in the latter part of
the period of our concern. It is important to observe the implications of
this belated dawning of conviction. Until India's value to Britain
became an axiom of conventional wisdom it was not enough merely to
state that India was in danger in order to call forth the resources
required for its defence; such a statement was likely to provoke a
cost-benefit analysis and a possible verdict that India was not worth
saving. The British view of India, as expressed in Press and Parliament,
was an important constraint upon British Indian policy, or at least
upon the ways in which policies could be discussed; arguments about
the defence of India had to be phrased in a manner which would not
leave room for critics to declare India to be a burden upon Britain.

Public indifference to the possession of India was reflected in the
views of the Cabinet and the Cabinet's lack of interest in, or understanding of the problems of Indian defence is frequently and clearly
exhibited in this book. Two ministers in particular were occupationally
obliged to take some notice of India: these were the Foreign Secretary
and the President of the Board of Control for Indian Affairs, and for
most of the period with which we are concerned these two ministers
were chiefly responsible for forming Cabinet policy on Indian defence.

To consider the role of British Foreign Secretaries requires some
assessment of the place of India in British foreign policy. In the original
draft of this book I devoted much space to this question, but was wisely
advised to defer that discussion to a subsequent work. Here it must
suffice to state the problem and to outline the conclusion. The problem
is to determine whether the pursuit of the European balance of power,
or of commercial gain, or of imperial advantage predominated in
British foreign policy during the period from the middle of the eighteenth to the middle of the twentieth century. It is insufficient to argue
that each played its part; it is agreed that all factors are present, but we
yet wish to know what were the priorities of British statesmen. Nor is it
enough to state that the mixture of motives varied according to area,
period, statesmen, and problem; of course it did, but it remains true
that Britain could have only one foreign policy and each element in that
policy had to be embraced within a hierarchy of values. In practice—if
one excepts the Marxists with their forlorn, unreasoning attachment to
economic motives—most twentieth-century students of British foreign
policy have given the palm to the imperial element and, within that
conglomerate, especially to India, and have seen British foreign policy
in the nineteenth and early twentieth centuries as especially concerned

with the defence of India and of the routes to India; in particular they have seen the Indian factor at the heart of British policy in the Eastern Question. It is my view that this assessment is wrong in relation to the period as a whole and especially so when applied to the half-century under review. It is my contention that Europe always held first place and India and its defence a lowly place in British foreign policy, or, to put it more precisely, that the dispositions of British diplomacy took little account of the problems of India.

British Foreign Secretaries saw India in two ways. First, they saw it as an embarrassment. British Indian interests demanded arrangements which hampered negotiations with other European governments, notably with those of France and Russia. Alternatively, the British Indian Government might adopt some course of action which could become a source of complaint by another European government, or be cited by that government as a justification for an action offensive to British interests. Second, British Foreign Secretaries saw India as a possible aid to British actions in Europe. This was especially the attitude of Palmerston, who observed that the military resources of India could be deployed east of the Cape of Good Hope without undue Parliamentary scrutiny and in a manner which could assist Britain in negotiations which were quite separate. Alternatively, the mere threat of action by British India might serve the same purpose. But, whether it figured as liability or as asset, India occupied a minor position in the balance sheet of British foreign policy and no Foreign Secretary made its security or the security of the routes to India a major objective of his diplomacy.

It was India which was required to accommodate itself to the exigencies of British foreign policy; not Britain to the demands of India. For the first part of the period with which we are concerned Britain was at war with France, a war in which the chief object was to prevent French domination of Europe and in which Britain's principal hope lay in those continental states threatened by the ambitions of Napoleon. Of these powers Russia was seen as Britain's natural ally, and Britain's policy in Western Asia was dictated largely by the position of Russia: when Russia was hostile to Napoleon Britain sought to free Russia from her commitments in the Ottoman Empire and in Iran in order that Russian forces might be free to campaign in Central Europe; when Russia was friendly towards France, Britain sought to prolong the Russian conflicts with the Ottomans and with Iran in order that Russian forces might not be deployed in Europe against Britain's other continental hope, Austria. Beside these European considerations those of the defence of India or of the routes to the subcontinent were given no importance. And in the aftermath of 1815 British policy was directed primarily towards the maintenance of the European concert; in Western Asia Britain was content to follow the Austrian lead and anxious to avoid any appearance of opposition to Russia. Only at the end of the 1820s did fears that Russian ambitions might instigate a partition of the Ottoman Empire and upset the European balance cause a revision of this attitude. Britain's new, still uncertain view of Russia as a menace to British interests was then reinforced by a new perception of Russia as a major threat to those European liberties for which Britain had become the chief spokesman. Only in this new climate of opinion could British Indian fears of Russia, expressed intermittently since the beginning of the nineteenth century, begin at last to make headway. It is an interesting and noteworthy circumstance that the growth of Russophobia in Britain coincided with the enhanced sense of the value of India which was remarked above, and thereby paved the way for the easier acceptance of the idea that there was a Russian threat to India which also menaced Britain. Under the management of Palmerston Britain's European and Asian interests appeared to dovetail neatly together and to produce the impression of a comprehensive and coherent British foreign policy. It will, I hope, be demonstrated in this book that this coherence was an illusion: Palmerston was not anti-Russian, but merely believed that certain Russian ambitions should be restrained in the interest of the European balance of power and he had no intention either of pursuing a policy of unremitting hostility to Russia in deference to supposed British Indian interests or of negotiating an unwanted agreement with Russia concerning the interests of the two powers in Asia. To Palmerston India was a pawn and the Great Game was in Europe, not in Asia; and the only difference between him and his successors was that he used or abused the Indian pawn more vigorously than they did.

The position of the President of the Board of Control was quite different from that of the Foreign Secretary. The President had two roles: to represent or to interpret the views of the Court of Directors of the East India Company and of the Government of India to his ministerial colleagues, and to convey the views of his Cabinet colleagues and others to the Directors and to the Government of India. Strongminded, determined Presidents like Henry Dundas extended these mediatory roles so as to give great prominence to their own views.

In the light of this statement it might be thought that the India Board would be the point at which British and British Indian ideas of how India might be defended would fuse, and where a balance of

British interests would be struck. Only the eyes of faith could detect such a function, however; the Board was a post office rather than a melting-pot. It was not a major Cabinet office; indeed in the early years of the nineteenth century its holders were not always members of the Cabinet. Its Presidents included ambitious politicians like Castlereagh and Canning who took the post as a despised stepping-stone to higher things; men, otherwise unregarded, who were introduced to the Ministry in order to conciliate some faction or interest and who, it was thought, would do less damage at the India Board than in some other department of state—men like Minto, Wynn, and Fitzgerald; and those who made the government of India a serious object of ambition—Buckinghamshire and Hobhouse and to a lesser extent Dundas and Ellenborough. The most striking feature of the behaviour of the first group is the speed with which they sloughed off their Indian experience when once they left their office and how little their knowledge of India influenced their conduct of British foreign policy. The second group was too undistinguished to have much influence. Only the last group might have produced the sort of synthesis contemplated above and they did not do so; Buckinghamshire was too aggressive and Hobhouse too subservient, Dundas operated in a period when Indian affairs were still regarded as partly insulated from those of Europe, and Ellenborough's sweeping fantasies failed to convince anyone. Nor were they very successful as intermediaries. As will be shown, in general the Presidents failed to persuade their Cabinet colleagues of the merits of British Indian views (which they themselves often did not understand) and failed to persuade the Indian Governments that the opinions of the Cabinet had much value. Much of their time was given to mediating between the Court of Directors and the Cabinet and Indian Governments, an activity better suited to producing an understanding of political tactics than of imperial strategy.

The East India Company, particularly the Court of Directors and its officials, represented the last and the most expert element in the British appreciation of the problems of British India. However, the Company's ability to influence British policy was sorely limited by the circumstance that matters relating to external defence were withdrawn from its oversight and nominally confined to its Secret Committee (the Chairman, Deputy Chairman, and one Senior Director) and in practice wholly vested in the Board of Control which wrote the dispatches. The Court's influence was therefore indirect and exercised through the individual force of powerful individuals such as Charles Grant and Henry St. George Tucker and through its ability to create difficulties in linked spheres of activity, notably those of appointments and finance.

The debate about the defence of India which was carried on by Court and Board was commonly one concerned with who should pay for defence: the Court usually argued that the defence of India was an imperial matter and therefore should be paid for by the Crown; the Board that it was an Indian affair and should be paid for out of Indian revenues. Thus a dispute over money led to presentations of the issues in a fashion likely to mislead the student of British foreign policy. Apparent arguments about strategy can rarely be taken at face value. Although the Board usually won such arguments, they had some effect in so far as the Board was restrained from pressing the Company too hard lest the Directors should take their complaints to the Parliament of which several were members. The Company's unwillingness to accept additional financial burdens formed a powerful limitation on the ability of British Governments to employ Indian resources in support of their foreign policy.

To sum up, the relations of the British institutions and individuals concerned with India prevented the emergence of any real appreciation of the requirements of Indian defence or agreement about how the needs of Indian defence could be accommodated within the wider framework of British foreign and defence policy. The elements involved with Indian defence worked on different assumptions in partly insulated compartments; and their communications with one another were conducted in a language calculated to obscure rather than to clarify the issues at stake.

In India the Governor-General was apparently the counterpart of the President of the Board of Control. He was both the head of the Indian Government and also a man who normally possessed extensive experience of British politics and/or diplomacy. In theory he was well placed to mediate between British and British Indian interests. In practice he functioned largely in the capacity of head of the Indian Government; it often seemed as though he packed away his British experience with his British overcoats (and, indeed, apparently reversed the process on his return journey to England). The Governor-Generalship of India provides one of the most singular proofs of the truth of the observation that the office makes the man. To generalize further about the behaviour of Governor-Generals would be both superfluous and dangerous; superfluous because much of this book is concerned with their policies; dangerous because of the great variety of their approaches to Indian problems, from the rationalism of Auckland to the intuitiveness of Ellenborough, from the confidence of Wellesley to the insecurity of Hardinge, and from the silliness of Minto to the genius of Dalhousie. In one respect, however, they did employ their knowledge of British politics; in the presentation of their policies they knew which chords to stress so as to draw out the most favourable resonance from Britain and it was no concern of theirs if in doing so they misled their successors and historians as well.

Within British India the Governor-General presided over a hierarchy of conflicting interests. It is unnecessary to describe here the British Indian system of government; these remarks will be confined to those features which contributed directly to the formation of defence policy. In the latter part of the nineteenth century a vital role in this sphere was played by the Commander-in-Chief and his headquarters staff, but in the first half of the century the Commander-in-Chief was singularly ineffective. Invariably a Queen's (as opposed to a Company's) soldier, commonly enjoying a belated reward for distinguished service during the Napoleonic wars, possessing little or no previous experience of India, and lacking either a capable staff or an intelligence department, the Commander-in-Chief knew too little of the issues under discussion to make an influential contribution to the debate, except in relation to the strength and dispositions of the British Indian army. More influence was enjoyed by the other members of the Supreme Council; apart from the law member, all had considerable experience of India. For many, however, that experience lay chiefly in revenue or judicial services and this limited their effectiveness in political matters. Undoubtedly the greatest influence on the Governor-Generals stemming from their immediate entourage, was exercised by the Secretariat. The Chief Secretary, the secretaries in charge of secret and political matters, and the private and military secretaries of the Governor-Generals were masters of the flow of current information. It was his Secretariat which provided continuity of policy both by its collective memories and habits of response and by its ability to influence the selection of men for key appointments.

Although the Supreme Government in Bengal dominated British Indian policy-making, it was yet obliged to acknowledge the rights of certain institutions outside Bengal to be consulted. The Governors of Madras, although important in relation to Burma, played little part in the making of policy towards the north-west, but the Government of the Bombay Government Presidency was much more significant. The Bombay Government was responsible for the southern section of the western frontier of British India and for the conduct of day to day relations with the countries along that border; it performed a similar office in relation to the Persian Gulf. The Bombay Secretariat was also an important repository of expertise in relation to these areas and this knowledge was deployed to considerable effect by powerful public servants such as Francis Warden and J. P. Willoughby. Furthermore, the comparative poverty and weakness of the Bombay Presidency as it existed before 1818 made it strongly inclined to pursue an expansionist policy through which it might hope to gain the territory and revenues which could guarantee security, employment, and the prospect of promotion for its officers and officials. From the 1830s a new institution of importance in frontier policy-making was the Lieutenant-Governorship of the North-Western Provinces. For Charles Metcalfe, Thomas Robertson, and George Clerk the office provided a platform from which they could advance their distinctive views on British Indian foreign policy with some reasonable claim to be heard; James Thomason, on the other hand made no effort to influence frontier strategy.

Without doubt the greatest influence on British Indian strategic thought was that of the Politicals, by which term I mean to designate the Ministers, Envoys, Residents, and Political Agents. The Politicals with whom we are chiefly concerned are those who dealt with the problems of the north-west, although it should be noted that those in other, more remote areas could also exercise some influence through their authority in the matter of the internal enemies of British India. Of those in the north-west different Residents played leading roles at different times according to the movement of the frontier. On the Bengal frontier it was the Resident at Lucknow who first became the principal repository of information and advice concerning the countries of the north-west; he was subsequently surpassed by the Resident with Sindhia at Ujjain and from 1803 by the Resident in Delhi. In turn the Resident at Delhi lost his pre-eminence to the agent at Ludhiana who was eventually displaced by the Resident at Lahore and his many assistants. On the Bombay frontier it was first the Residents in Baroda who exercised the chief influence before they gave way to the Residents in Cutch and later Sind. Beyond the frontier were other agents. At various times those in the Gulf and in Baghdad helped to mould policy, but the principal sources of influence during the period with which we are concerned are the mission in Tehran, permanently established in 1809 and occupying an ambiguous position between the British Indian and the British systems, and the whole system of Political Agents which functioned in Afghanistan and Upper Sind from 1838 to 1842.

The influence of the Politicals derived from their virtual monopoly of information and from their ability to interpret that information. Their long experience of Indian, Iranian, or other politics was important to them, but it did not compare in magnitude with their possession of the most recent information; the experience of men who had served for years in certain areas was rapidly discounted when it was set against the flow of new information. It is reasonable to make two assumptions about the Politicals: they were anxious for professional advancement which might be secured either by promotion or by the enlargement of their existing spheres of activity; and they had local problems in their existing posts. In order to attract favourable notice and to deal with their local problems it was necessary that they should divert more resources towards themselves and to accomplish this end they were obliged to represent their situation in an appropriate manner. To ask for additional resources merely to deal with a local problem was to invite a refusal, but when they argued that their local problem was directly related to a larger question of imperial strategy which could affect the security of British India they were more likely to achieve their goal. It was the Politicals, therefore, who became the main providers of information, recommendations, and strategic theories within the British Indian system and the study of British defence policy is the tracing of the origin of their ideas, the progress of those ideas through the bureaucratic system, the modification of those ideas in accordance with the different interests and attitudes of superior authorities in India, and the eventual determination of that policy in discussions between Calcutta and London. Most of this book in one way or another deals with that process. British policy in the north-west was mainly the consequence of attempts to support, restrain, or deflect the recommendations of the local agents, and the strategic thinking of British India is the result of the refining and harmonizing of their analyses.

It is now time to turn from this sketch of the institutional framework of policy-making to consider the main elements in the policies themselves. The fundamental question which we have to ask is what did Britons in India believe to be the dangers which threatened their security? In answering that question it will be convenient to divide the dangers under two headings: the internal enemy and the external enemy.

The internal enemy bore two aspects: the threat from Indian states and the threat from within British India. From 1765 until the establishment of paramountcy in 1818 the danger that British India might be attacked by a coalition of other Indian states was seen to be the principal menace to British security. In the south Mysore imperilled the peace of Madras until 1799 and in the north it was the Marathas who were regarded as the main enemy. What was feared was not so much that the British settlements and provinces might be engulfed by the Indian states and the British driven into the sea, but rather that the peace and prosperity of the British territories might be so damaged by the needs of warfare that the territories would not be worth the expenditure required to hold them. It was a matter of profit and loss rather than of life and death, but for an enterprise such as British India the two were not very different. The problem could not be solved by the defensive posture which was enjoined by London; only the elimination of British India's enemies would answer. The subsidiary alliance system, especially favoured by Richard Wellesley, which gave some control over the policies and power of Indian states at no cost to the Company, was a partial solution; and the establishment of paramountcy in 1818 diminished the problem presented by the Indian states much further, although it did not end it—apart from those states such as Lahore, Nepal, and Burma which lay outside the ring-fence created by the 1818 Settlement there remained within the ring powerful Indian states such as Gwalior, Oudh, and Haidarabad which possessed forces which demanded to be watched and thereby required some diversion of British Indian resources. Nevertheless, from 1818 the emphasis shifted from the Indian states towards the enemy within British India.

The enemy within had many faces: a Muslim conspiracy, an outbreak of warlike peoples, a plot by disaffected and dispossessed traditional leaders, popular disturbances in village or town sparked off by some real or fancied infringement of religious, customary, or economic rights, and others. But the greatest danger was usually perceived to be a mutiny of the Company's army. The East India Company had a small number of European infantrymen and artillerymen of its own, hired a larger number of British troops from the Crown, but relied chiefly upon its disciplined Indian sepoy forces. The sepoys were invaluable in campaigns against other Indian states, being cheap and efficient, but their loyalty was never certain, as was proved by a series of mutinies of which those at Vellore in 1806 and in the Bengal Army in 1857 to 1858 were only the most notable.

British India lived in fear of an insurrection which could neither be predicted, nor understood, nor controlled. It may be replied that there was nothing very singular about this situation as fear of internal insurrection was the common experience of most states at the time; from 1789 onwards much of Europe lived in constant apprehension of revolution and Britain itself came within a hair's breadth of a workers' rising on several occasions between 1815 and 1848. Yet there is a difference between the European and the colonial situation. In Europe men knew what the dangers were and by rational policies of conciliation and coercion could hope to diminish or remove the hazards. In India, as Bentinck remarked, Britons were strangers in the land; they did not know what the dangers were and had no confidence that they could be avoided by rational policies. Again and again Britons in India describe themselves as men walking in a powder-magazine; they groped cautiously by the light of experience and intuition. And however weak were the coercive instruments at the disposal of European states, they were a good deal more reliable and effective than the Company's army; in Europe urban workers were crushed by peasant armies; in India the army itself was suspect. Further, in Europe governments commonly rallied to each other's side against popular risings; in India an internal commotion was thought to be the time when the Indian states might attempt to recoup their previous losses and mysterious hordes of tribesmen might descend upon British India from beyond the frontiers.

Whether we are guided by an examination of the objective facts of the British situation in India or by the subjective perceptions of those who lived with the dangers, we must be impressed by the menace of the internal enemy. Before the development of railways no defensive system that the British could afford could provide against the enemy within, no precise rules could be devised nor strategic textbooks written to guide men through the perils. The mysterious foe could be held in check only as the tightrope walker keeps his balance; by a few broad principles, by occasional imperceptible adjustments, by intuition, and by the experience of years. An immense premium was accorded to experience; the mystique of the City banker did not compare with that of British India. One other weapon was thought to be greater even than any of these: this was prestige. When men asserted, as they often did, that the British Empire in India rested on opinion they were not claiming that it was liked by the Indian people; the opinion to which they referred was that of British invincibility. If Indian enemies of British power believed that revolt was foredoomed to failure they would be less inclined to make the attempt. Accordingly, it was vital that the Raj should never be defied and never beaten but should always present an impression of confident, overbearing power. Essentially it was bluff, but it was a bluff which no one could be allowed to call and its maintenance was at the root of most of the wars of British India.

Many bold spirits, particularly those of the new, social-engineering school which flourished in the North-Western Provinces during the twenty years which preceded the Indian Mutiny and who laid great stress on public works and accurate land-settlements, might roundly declare that all this was mere mumbo-jumbo and that what was needed was sound government upon Benthamite or Christian principles, but only the bravest Governor-General would espouse such doctrines and disregard the accumulated wisdom of his Politicals, who were the authoritative interpreters of the internal enemy.

It will be convenient also to subdivide the external enemy of British India. First, were those Asian enemies outside the ring-fence, some of which have already been mentioned: they include Burma, Nepal, Lahore, and Sind; during the period studied some pass, in whole or part, into the fold of British India. Beyond the circle of neighbouring Asian states were others; in particular, on the north-western side there extended for thousands of miles territory which was inhabited by feared, Muslim peoples. Under certain circumstances it was thought, these Muslim peoples of Western Asia might once more descend upon the plains of India and might also appeal to sentiments of their co-religionists within the Indian subcontinent. Second, there were the European enemies of British rule in India. During the eighteenth century the only serious European foe was France. By 1763 French power in India was broken, but the possibility remained that it might be re-established either by the activities of Frenchmen in the service of Indian states, or by a sea-borne attack launched from the French islands in the Indian Ocean, or by a mixed naval and military expedition from France, or by an overland invasion. At various times each of these possibilities was agitated as well as the more mundane threat that the activities of French privateers might threaten the security of British rule be jeopardizing the profitability of the Company's commercial operations. In retrospect it is evident that there was no serious French intention to recover a position in India which had never been profitable. At the most, French statesmen regarded India as a diversionary area: a threat posed to India might draw off British forces from other theatres of operations which were of much greater importance to France. Nevertheless, even if it is granted that the French threat had little substance after 1763, this does not dispose of the possibility that contemporary Britons genuinely believed that France did constitute a serious menace to the security of British India. The opinion of historians and commentators concerning the British reaction to the alleged French threat to British India has always been divided. Did the British rulers in India—Warren Hastings, Richard Wellesley, and Gilbert Elliot, Lord Minto—adopt their different policies in order to combat a danger from France which they thought to be real? Or did they merely profess to be acting in opposition to French designs in order to gain acceptance in England for policies which they were aware would be forbidden to them if the policies were advanced as solutions to purely Indian problems? The arguments for the first proposition are manifest in their public pronouncements; the arguments for the second are more indirect but also persuasive. Britons in London did not share British India's perception of the internal enemy nor did they sympathize with the solutions propounded by British India for its problems. Instead they forbade expansion except under certain conditions. One of those conditions was always a threat from France; furthermore, in resisting French ambitions in Asia the Company could be seen to be fighting the same battle that Britain was fighting in Europe—British India could thus be regarded as a source of strength to Britain. To present expansion in India as dictated by the needs of defence against France could have been an attractive option for British India.

After 1815 the French threat dwindled, to be eventually replaced by that from Russia. The French threat did not disappear entirely from British perceptions and it played some part in British dispositions during the 1840s. And the Russian threat took longer to become established than is sometimes supposed; it was only in the last quarter of the nineteenth century that it assumed dominant proportions. The Russian threat was perceived in a more limited fashion than that of France had been: either in the form of a direct overland invasion of India via Iran or Turkestan, or in the manner of the extension of Russian influence over the countries to the north-west of India and the consequential excitement of feeling against British rule in India. It was this second aspect which was always the more important in British Indian thinking; the notion of an overland invasion, which attracted much attention in England from the late 1820s onwards and which was given some credence in military circles, was almost unknown in serious discussion in British Indian circles from the moment it was discarded by analysts at the beginning of the nineteenth century until its reintroduction at the end.

It is necessary to pose the same questions of authenticity about the Russian threat to British India which we asked about the French threat. We may first note the argument of Soviet writers that there was no threat from Russia to British India and that the British belief in that threat was simulated in order to cloak an ambition to extend British power into Central Asia in order to gain commercial advantages. Soviet writers strongly object to the phrase 'defence of India' which they consider implies a misrepresentation of British and Russian policy. I would agree with the general assertion that there was no Russian intention to invade India. And, with some reservations concerning certain individuals, I would accept the view that official Russian policy was not concerned to take up a position upon the borders of British India with any formed, hostile intent; indeed during the first half of the nineteenth century the Russian Government was not interested in

assuming a dominant position in Afghanistan. Whatever their consequences, the basic impulses of official Russian policy upon their southern frontier during this period seem to me to be defensive. But this is
irrelevant to the British argument. Britons in India did not fear a direct
Russian invasion and it did not matter to them whether the Russian
intent was hostile or not; the British argument was that the mere
presence, however innocent, of Russian agents upon the borders of
British India could be sufficient to invoke the danger of an internal
insurrection. Nevertheless, in the course of this book I shall argue that
there was an element of simulation in the British argument concerning
the alleged Russian threat, although the reason advanced by Russian
writers is quite mistaken; there was little thought of commercial advantage to be obtained from expansion in Central Asia, no significant
pressure from British manufacturers for the enlargement of British
India's frontiers, and if there was imperialism it was bureaucratic, not
economic.

Let me repeat and enlarge upon what was the leading British Indian
formulation of the Russian threat from a very early period. It was that
there was no real danger of a direct Russian invasion. The danger was
that the spread of Russian influence into Iran and Afghanistan would
cause unrest in India. Unrest in India would necessitate higher British
military expenditure and the presence of more, expensive, British
troops, in India. The finances of British India, already precarious,
would become disastrous and India would be in a fair way to becoming
unprofitable to hold and a burden upon Britain itself, both because of
the drain upon resources and because of the constraints which would be
imposed upon British policy in Europe by the need to conciliate Russia
so as to dissuade her from exploiting the dangerous situation, possibly
by encouraging attacks upon India by external Asian enemies. In
short, the external enemy was feared because of his potential effect
upon the internal enemy.

In the situation which obtained after 1818 the relationship of external and internal enemies may be more clearly exhibited because the
completion of the continuous British Indian defensive frontier created a
sharp division between the two enemies. Before 1818 there is an
ambiguity which derives from the position of those powerful Indian
states which lay outside the long, disconnected frontiers of British India
and from the presence of French influence within the Indian subcontinent. Nevertheless, even in that earlier period one may discern in the
presentation of the French threat the outlines of the same formulation
which dominated the presentation of the Russian threat: the danger
from France, declared Wellesley and Minto, was less that of a direct

attack than the prospect that the approach of France and French influence might inspire to active hostility the enemies of British power in India, notably the Maratha powers. Thus, even in that earlier period it is likely that the external enemy was feared chiefly because of his potential effect upon Indian enemies within or without the actual frontiers of British India.

In its developed form in relation to Russia this formulation of the dangers presented by the concatenation of internal and external enemies was largely the work of John Malcolm. The influence of Malcolm upon the strategic thinking of British India during the first half of the nineteenth century was greater than that of any other man and the shadow of his strategic intellect extended to the last days of the Raj. The true brilliance of his formulation lay in the fact that it was almost impossible to refute; everyone accepted the reality of the internal enemy and few would dare to try the experiment of exposing the internal enemy to the abrasive presence of Russia. Thus men were drawn towards the forward policy which Malcolm and others advocated. The forward school argued that it was necessary to pre-empt the advance of Russian influence by extending British influence into the intervening areas. This could be accomplished by alliances with Iraq, Iran, Afghanistan, or the states of Turkestan, or by assuming a commanding position in the Persian Gulf. In one way or another the external enemy should be kept at a distance so that his vexations would exhaust themselves in places remote from British territory.

There remains the nagging doubt whether the advocates of this strategy were wholly sincere. It has been suggested already that the French threat might have served as a cloak for British Indian ambition. Did the Russian threat serve the same purpose? Was Malcolm's theory not a very convenient one for ambitious Politicals who wished to advance their narrower interests? And at different levels of policy-making did the Indian Governments or the Cabinet find the theory a useful device in furthering their own disconnected ambitions? The excellence of Malcolm's theory is revealed also in its comprehensiveness; it accomplished the seemingly impossible task of comprehending within the same vision the internal problems of British India and the European preoccupations of Britain. Talk bawdy, Sir Robert Walpole urged his guests, then we can all join in. In the deepest and truest sense Malcolm's was a bawdy theory; it provided a means by which Britons in Britain and in India could talk to each other about different things while seeming to talk about the same.

Malcolm's was not the only nor even the principal strategic formulation current in British India. A second strategy recommended confining precautions to the British territories. Security could be obtained, it was argued, either by ploughing all resources into military expenditure or by the nineteenth-century equivalent of the policy of winning hearts and minds—attaching the people of India to British rule by conciliation. Conciliation might take one of two forms—either the conciliation of traditional leaders of Indian society who in turn might be expected to exercise their influence in a manner calculated to reconcile their followers to the existence of British rule; or the setting aside of traditional leaders and the attempt to find a new support for British rule in a prosperous and contented peasantry, a flourishing class of artisans, and a wealthy and conservative merchant community. Conciliation could go hand in hand with a forward policy—Malcolm advocated both a forward policy beyond the frontier and the judicious cultivation of a native aristocracy within the British territories and those of their protected allies, and Thoby Prinsep combined aggressive expansionism in Central Asia with an active, levelling policy in India. But conciliation of the internal enemy could also be an alternative to expansion and its adherents argued frequently either that the external enemy was of no consequence, or that he could be made of no consequence if the danger of internal insurrection were removed, or that there was nothing that the Indian Government could do to prevent his approach. Those who adopted this third line of argument claimed that it was the job of the British Government to combat any danger from Russia, either by diplomatic pressure upon the Russian Government, or by a suitable agreement by which both parties would agree to refrain from expansion, or by war, carried on in the Baltic or the Black Sea. Their opponents were quick to point out, however, that it was most unlikely that Britain would be prepared to jeopardize her relations with Russia; still less go to war with that country over a threat to India, let alone over a merely prospective danger.

From these brief comments on some of the strategies of British India it will be observed that the decisive factor in determining strategies calculated to reduce the harm expected from the external enemy was the view taken of the internal enemy. Those who believed the enemy within was ultimately irreconcilable were attracted either to the immobile despair of Charles Metcalfe who believed that British rule could not last and could be prolonged only be concentration on military spending to the exclusion of all else, or to the forward policies of Malcolm who believed that conciliation could alleviate the problem but not eliminate it and that the internal enemy required to be insulated from outside infection by the exclusion of enemies from the regions adjacent to British India. Those who believed that the internal enemy could be controlled and gradually drained of vitality by judicious conciliation (whether of the leaders of India's past or of India's future) were led either to a hostility to any expansion, thinking it to be a gross misuse of resources which could be better employed within India—the view of John Lawrence, or to an expansionism based upon optimism—good government could win over both the people of India and the people of the countries beyond the frontier and, as Charles Napier argued, the expansionism which was recommended by strategy was also indicated by duty.

From London, however, the view of Indian strategies was quite different. To men in Britain the internal enemy rarely had the same reality which it possessed for men in India; the external enemy was more readily comprehensible and more nearly bore upon their European preoccupations. Accordingly, strategists in Britain assessed strategies principally in terms of their appropriateness as devices for dealing with the external European enemy and judged them in connection with other objects of British foreign policy, the achievement of which also required dealings with Russia. In that difference of outlook may be detected the outline of the major misapprehension which has bedevilled the study of the place of India in British foreign policy.

Before we return to the paradox which was set out at the beginning of this introduction it is necessary to touch upon another topic which is not considered in this book. This book is concerned with the ostensible defence of British India from attacks emanating from the north-west and not with the defence of the routes to India, a subject which was discussed in an earlier draft but eventually excluded because its magnitude required separate treatment. The defence of the routes to India has been held to be the point at which British foreign policy was principally affected by the possession of India. British policy in the Eastern Question, that is, in the diplomatic and other problems arising from the situation of the Ottoman Empire, has been considered by many writers to have been largely influenced, even determined, by the need to exclude other European powers from positions which could dominate the routes to India. It might be argued, therefore, that whatever the merits of the thesis of this book concerning the defence of India itself, no disharmony existed in respect of the defence of the routes to India. On this proposition I will limit myself to two observations. First, the evidence that I have seen clearly demonstrates that the Indian Government was unconcerned about the protection of the routes to India, and British policies in the Ottoman Empire and Iran were in no way decided by the Indian Government acting with that object in view. Second, the policies of the London Government in

Western Asia are explicable in terms of European interests alone, even though several Foreign Secretaries found financial, diplomatic, political, or military advantages in linking the presentation of their policies in the area to the needs of India. In short, I do not accept that the so-called problem of the defence of the routes to India constitutes an exception to the general proposition of this book that the strategic interests of Britain and of British India were quite separate; on the contrary I assert that a detailed study of the routes to India question would provide confirmation of the thesis here so briefly and badly stated.

So at last we approach the justification of the statement made near the beginning to the effect that British policies in the regions lying to the north-west of British India were not primarily concerned with the defence of the sub-continent. It is argued that the concerns of British foreign policy were mainly in Europe and Indian strategies were viewed in the light of that preoccupation; the attention of those directly responsible for the security of British India, on the other hand, were focused within India itself. The external enemy, which served to rationalize or legitimize British actions in the north-western regions was primarily a device by which the British and British Indian systems could be linked, through which they could discuss the allocation of resources from a common pool to meet a common danger, but a device which in reality concealed quite different purposes.

To embrace this complex situation we require a new theory of strategy. Strategy may be defined as military economy; the association with the older term for economics emphasizes the element of scarcity. A strategy is simply a way of deploying scarce resources; if resources were in abundance strategies would not be required. A strategic theory, therefore, is a claim upon resources; an assertion that a particular disposition is the most economical and efficient way of dealing with an identified problem or problems. Britain and British India constituted separate systems, each with its own preoccupations. But they also constituted one system in so far as British India was dependent upon Britain for legitimation, for supplies of manpower, and for general underwriting; and Britain came to believe that she could not survive in her existing eminence if she ceased to possess India. Britain and British India required a language in which they could discuss the allocation of resources between them, a language which would mean all things to all men. This language was supplied by the strategy of defence against the external enemy. Accordingly, the discussion of British activities in Central and Western Asia was conducted as though those activities were concerned to protect India or the routes to India against a

European enemy. Under the guise of a common interest Britain and British India could pursue their own designs, and British activities could assist both the European interests of Britain and the internal security problems of British India.

No doubt, in an effort to drive home the point, I have taken it too far in those last two sentences, implying too great a degree of contrivance, reducing policies to rituals, and passing from the world of strategy to the world of Maya. It is not pretended that the strategic intercourse of Britain and British India operated so smoothly or consciously as this brief rehearsal occasionally suggests; indeed, as our drama unfolds, it will be observed that inefficiency is the rule and that the players frequently forgot their lines and many participants in the Great Game came to believe that it was not a game at all. None the less, as we explore formulations and motivations, it should be clear that the traditional view of British policy in the regions to the north-west of India does not accord with the evidence and that we are confronted with at least two distinct systems linked in a single strategic formulation. And, in the last analysis, I do not believe that there is any clear dividing line between the world of strategy and the world of illusion. Strategic theories are not descriptions of the real world, but blueprints for possible worlds. It is the grand error of the historian to regard them as the former.

PART I

THE IRANIAN BUFFER

The Formation of the Anglo-Iranian Alliance, 1798–1810

Under all the circumstances of the present time, I am satisfied that we cannot secure to ourselves that advantage without establishing an independent station of our own from which the Court of Persia on the one hand, and the Pacha of Bagdad on the other cannot expel us; from which we may observe everything, direct and influence many, and be in a position to take advantage of new events, to meet every favourable change of disposition, in a word to embrace fortune if she should turn towards us. Such a station would be a rendezvous and depot, a point of departure, and a point of retreat, as well as a centre of political observation, operations and influence. The post I have in view is the Island of Carrack.

Minto to Hewitt, 27 August 1808.

At breakfast, employed in laughing very heartily at the gross imposture of the missions to and from Persia, which will cost Mr. Bull one or two of his spare millions.

Sir James Mackintosh, 24 January 1811.

Iran formed the meeting-place of European and Indian politics. West of Iran the interests of Britain in Europe predominated over her interests in India. East of Iran British policy was primarily influenced by the strategic situation of British India. In Iran there was a collision, which forms the first theme of this chapter and of the three which follow. The second theme is the role of Iran in relation to British India. How far did men believe that Iran had a positive role to play in the defence of the British territories there? The first two themes provide the setting for the working of the third theme. This is the role of the local agents. In 1798 British policy towards Iran was unformed clay. In skilful hands it could be moulded to form a new diplomatic empire; it could become a road to power and distinction. The less certain that London, Calcutta, and Bombay were of their role in Iran, the more opportunity for their agents to try to convince them of what it should be. The peculiarity of the British position in Iran gave the agents even greater scope than they enjoyed elsewhere.

The division of these four chapters may be quickly explained. Between

1798 and 1809 the initiative was largely in the hands of British India. There was, however, no strong commitment to the Iranian alliance and it was weighed in relation to other British interests within India, and other possible distant defensive systems in Afghanistan and the Gulf. At the end of the period the initiative effectively passed to London, which chose the Iranian alliance, in the Preliminary Treaty of 1809. The period from 1810 to 1815 is concerned with London's attempts to regulate the position which it had taken up in Iran and ends with the Definitive Treaty which marked a decided reduction in that role. By 1815 both London and Calcutta had roughly defined their small concerns in Iran. The third chapter in this group centres on the attempt by London, after a period of indifference, to revive the Iranian alliance, and the last chapter deals with the failure of that attempt.

British political interest in Iran dates from 1798. Before that date her interests had been almost entirely commercial. Under pressure from its Mercantilist critics in England the Company had, from the seventeenth century, sought to foster British exports to Iran, whose climate made it a possible consumer of English woollens. In face of the opposition of the Levant Company, the Company had also endeavoured to divert the raw silk of northern Iran into the holds of its vessels in the Gulf. Lastly, Iran formed a useful adjunct to the Company's 'country' trade, that is the trade in Asian goods between Asian ports. To handle this trade British factories were maintained in Iran. Bandar Abbas was the main factory until the removal of the Company's headquarters to Basra in 1763 when Bushir, further up the Gulf and the principal port for Shiraz and Isfahan, became the centre of British trade in Iran.

In 1798 a new Commercial Resident was appointed at Bushir. This was Mehdi Ali Khan, an Iranian from a distinguished Khurasani family. Mehdi Ali, a man of ability, charm, and, it was said, considerable vanity, owed his appointment to the favour of Jonathan Duncan, Governor of Bombay.[1] His appointment was resented, particularly since he was not British, by the supporters of the man whom he displaced, Nicholas Hankey Smith. The Governor-General, Richard Wellesley, who did not like the appointment, suggested the Basra Resident, Samuel Manesty, as a more suitable choice, but Duncan stood by his protégé.[2] Mehdi's duties were largely commercial, concerned with selling British woollens and forming a commercial treaty with Masqat, but he was also enjoined to counteract French influence in Iran. This last injunction, however, did not betoken a sudden political insight, but was merely a general precaution in view of reports which had been received of French travellers in the area. Similar reports of French interest in Masqat led to Mehdi's visiting that state, under instructions from Duncan, and negotiating, in October 1798, an agreement to exclude the French.

Mehdi now suggested another political function for himself, in relation to the apparent threat to India from Afghanistan. Even before his arrival in India Wellesley had stressed the threat from Afghanistan and the frightening possibilities of a war on two fronts against Tipu Sultan of Mysore, in the south and against Zaman Shah of Afghanistan, in Oudh.[3] Mehdi suggested that he should be authorized to offer the Government of Iran arms and ammunition so that Iranian forces might threaten the western frontier of Afghanistan and divert Zaman from India. Duncan supported this proposal and Wellesley agreed. Wellesley suggested that Britain might also persuade the Ottomans to put pressure on Iran.[4] Orders were sent to Mehdi Ali on 1 November 1798. It is worth noting that it was the Afghan threat, and not that from France with which Mehdi was to deal. Although the news of the French landing in Egypt had been received in Calcutta on 18 October, Wellesley was little concerned about an overland invasion. Right down to February 1799 he continued to see the Afghan diversion as the main object of Mehdi's mission. On 5 February he wrote to Dundas suggesting that Iran might be given a small annual subsidy to keep Zaman occupied: 'This system, well executed, would save us a large proportion of the expense of draining our armies to the frontier of Oude whenever the Shah chooses to cross the Attock.'[5]

Wellesley's ready adoption of the proposal that Iran should be employed to divert Afghanistan from India raises some questions about his policy. An alternative would have been to have sought an agreement directly with Afghanistan, but Wellesley never made any serious effort to reach any arrangement with Zaman. The direct approach to Afghanistan was advocated by Harford Jones, the Resident at Baghdad. Jones also suggested an Anglo–Ottoman embassy to Kabul. He argued that Zaman was misled by false reports emanating from Istanbul of British weakness and Mysorean strength. If Zaman were more correctly informed of the situation he might abandon his aggressive plans and become a useful ally of Britain.[6] The association with the Ottomans, who, like the Afghans, were Sunni and who were now Britain's allies against France, might be expected to have special value. No doubt Jones was not a wholly disinterested party. From the beginning he was uncertain of his newly-created position in Baghdad and was anxious to move on to fresher pastures. But he based his arguments upon a review of the local situation of the Governments of Iran and Afghanistan; Wellesley was wrong to lean upon Afghanistan because Zaman was much stronger: 'The Persian Government is a bubble. The

other is a rock.'[7] As it happened, Jones was wrong. The Qajar dynasty
in Iran was to prove remarkably durable, while the Sadozay dynasty in
Afghanistan was shortly to collapse in anarchy. But at the time his was
a reasonable estimate. The Qajars had only recently fought their way to
an unstable throne, and the partisans of their ousted predecessors, the
Zands of southern Iran, with whom Jones was closely connected, were
still restive and influential; in Afghanistan the Sadozays had been
firmly established for half a century. His argument therefore seemed
more tenable than that of his opponents, and was supported by Manesty and by Dundas himself.[8]

Wellesley did not want an alliance with Afghanistan. Although he
did later consider the possibility that Malcolm might go on to Afghanistan in 1799 or 1800, he never appears to have been serious about the
possibility. His policy was to make Afghanistan weak and disunited
and the results of the anarchy which followed the revolt of Mahmud
against Zaman were eminently satisfying to him.[9] In fact, by 1801
Jones himself had veered round to the view that a divided Afghanistan
was better for Britain than a united state.[10] But by then it was plain that
no danger existed from Afghanistan and Jones was probably already
thinking that he might find employment as Ambassador to Iran. A
question mark still surrounds Wellesley's hostility to the Afghan connection in 1799.

Jones himself thought there was something strange about Wellesley's blank refusal to contemplate an approach to Afghanistan. He
wrote to his supporter, James Willis, at East India House: 'Between
friends, I cannot help thinking somebody or other is interested in
manyfying [*sic*] the danger to be apprehended from Zemaun Shah.'[11]
Wellesley never explained his own reluctance to make overtures to
Zaman beyond suggesting that this might incite Zaman to attack India
again.[12] Malcolm, although admitting that he was not acquainted with
all Wellesley's views, tried to do it for him. He argued that an approach
would suggest weakness, and that there were no existing commercial
links with Afghanistan; with Iran on the other hand, there was, he
claimed unconvincingly, a solid basis of interest.[13] There were, he
wrote, also difficulties in the path of an approach to Afghanistan;
Jones's suggestion of the value of the Sunni link with Istanbul was
treated with majestic sarcasm.[14] But the real key was Oudh and this
was made clear in another letter to Manesty. Malcolm explained: 'an
extensive plan of settlement which the Governor General proposes to
carry into execution in the Vizier's provinces, renders it at this moment
a matter of the highest political importance to prevent *for a period* any
attempts of Zemaun Shah to disturb the Peace of that Country.'[15]

Malcolm's explanation seems straightforward; Wellesley wanted to settle with Oudh and wanted to be free from Afghan threats while he did so. This was indeed, as we shall see, exactly what Malcolm had been told in his instructions. But there was no danger from Zaman after he turned back from Lahore in January 1799 and reason to believe that Wellesley never thought very much of the danger at any time. The truth seems to be that Wellesley did want to settle with Oudh, but Zaman was the excuse not the cause, and an embassy to Kabul would have quickly exposed the truth. Perhaps the problem is suggested in a letter which Wellesley wrote to Henry Dundas: 'The zeal of Mr. H. Jones may possibly lead him to take steps at the Court of Kabul entirely inconsistent with those I deem essentially necessary to the security of the objects which I have in view in Oudh.'[16]

Dundas had in fact supported the suggestion of a direct approach to Afghanistan, but did not press the point in the face of Wellesley's hostility. He believed the Afghan threat had been underestimated in the past and feared a possible connection between Afghanistan and France. Dundas was prepared to support a number of measures of precaution in early 1799.[17] In the autumn he apparently shifted his ground after news of Zaman's retreat had been received. He then claimed that he had never regarded the danger from Afghanistan as formidable without French assistance, and this could not be given unless France acquired control of the sea. Nevertheless Zaman should still be watched in case a connection with France via the Indus was formed, and Dundas maintained his support for various precautionary alliances and advocated the strengthening of the British position on the western coast of India.[18] For Dundas, as ever, France was the key. It could be argued that Dundas never feared an Indian enemy unless supported by France and that Wellesley never feared a French enemy unless he was supported by an Indian.

In 1798–1799 Britain was for the first time asked to choose between an Afghan and an Iranian ally. Clearly there was disagreement before the choice apparently went in favour of Iran. Perhaps, after all, Wellesley may genuinely have thought that this was the safer policy. But there is good reason for inclining to the view of Ingram Ellis that his choice was dictated not by the problems of defending British India against Afghanistan or any other attack from beyond the Indus, but by the needs of his policy within the Indian political system. The British position required a new arrangement with Oudh and that was compatible with an Iranian alliance but not with an Afghan connection. If this is so, Wellesley was not choosing a buffer for the defence of India from the north-west, but a smoke-screen for the improvement of the British position within India. A study of his Iranian policy suggests that this was the case.

The Iranian approach apparently succeeded. Whether it really had any effect, however, seems very doubtful. The timing is suspiciously tight. Mehdi wrote to Tehran on 2 December 1798; Mahmud, the claimant to Zaman's throne, left Tehran on or about 18 December and arrived in western Afghanistan in early January. Zaman retired from Lahore on 4 January 1799. It seems impossible that Mahmud's arrival could have had anything to do with Zaman's withdrawal and unlikely that Mehdi's letter could have influenced Mahmud's departure from Tehran. Neither Jones nor Malcolm believed that Mehdi Ali had worked the trick, although it is true that neither would have willingly granted him credit for anything. Jones suggested that Fath Ali Shah Qajar was preparing an attack on Khurasan before Mehdi wrote to him.[19] Mehdi himself thought that Zaman's retirement was the result of internal troubles in Afghanistan.[20]

Wellesley professed to believe that the threat from Iran had been the decisive factor. His view may have been the result of a distinct change in his policy towards Iran in the early part of February 1799. As late as 5 February he had been content to continue only a modest link with Iran, but on 13 February he declared that he wished to extend relations with Iran 'to the utmost practicable degree'. He wanted a political treaty with Iran both to threaten Afghanistan and to exclude France.[21] In the meantime Iran could be offered an annual subsidy of £20,000 or £30,000.

The reasons for the shift in Wellesley's Iranian policy are unclear. The obvious explanation is that he had suddenly become alive to the French danger. But the French danger was no greater in February than before and as Wellesley's troops began to roll forward towards Mysore the threat was materially diminished. Nor did Wellesley show any urgency in carrying out his new policy. It was not until July that Duncan instructed Mehdi Ali to go to Tehran to persuade the Shah to act against Afghanistan and to keep the French out of Iran.[22] Mehdi did not arrive in Tehran until 4 December 1799. He then secured Fath Ali's agreement to the exclusion of France from Iran and also the offer of an island in the Gulf. To arrange the details an Iranian envoy, Haji Khalil, was to go to India. Haji Khalil, who was given the title Khan for the occasion, was an Iranian merchant who had for many years been engaged in trade between India and the Gulf. He was in fact a business associate of Mehdi Ali and of Jones and Manesty as well. His mission, however, was suspended for the time being, when news arrived that Wellesley was planning to send a new, more imposing mission to Iran, under the leadership of John Malcolm.

Dundas, who never liked Wellesley's Iranian diplomacy, was later critical of his decision to send Malcolm on this very expensive mission. Dundas himself never set any value on the alliance with Iran. In 1796 he had refused a suggestion of an alliance. To meet the Afghan threat he preferred a direct approach to Afghanistan or alliances with the Sikhs and Marathas. Nor did his extensive plans for combating France include an alliance with Iran. Partly he seems to have feared that Iran might turn against Britain, partly his objections were to the expenditure, but his principal worry seems to have been the possibility that an alliance with Iran might lead to difficulties with Russia, the country which he regarded, in true eighteenth-century fashion, as Britain's natural ally.[23]

Wellesley's defence of Malcolm's mission was weak. Partly it was necessary, he wrote, because native envoys were inherently unsuitable. Certainly, when in August 1799 he first notified Malcolm of his decision to send him to Iran, he wrote that Mehdi Ali was too indiscreet. Malcolm's relative and companion, Charles Pasley, later wrote that Mehdi Ali's 'vanity had got the better of his reason',[24] but there is no evidence given to support these allegations. Mehdi Ali had done all that was asked of him. Wellesley's second line of defence was that Malcolm's mission had much more extended objects than that of Mehdi, but a study of the mission shows that this was not so.[25]

The objects of Malcolm's mission were virtually identical with those of Mehdi Ali. According to his instructions, which were not finally drawn up until 10 October 1799, he was to gain the assistance of Iran against France and Afghanistan. The principal objective was to counteract Zaman and the sole purpose was to give Wellesley time to settle with Oudh. Once Wellesley had secured complete civil and military control over Oudh he would no longer fear Zaman. Three years would be enough to settle the Oudh problem, and the political treaty was needed only for that time. It is plain that the French threat was not the main problem. Apart from the wording of the instructions, there is also the fact that Wellesley did not send the mission until the French threat from Egypt was waning. The Afghan threat had also virtually disappeared by October 1799, but an explanation for its continuing significance has already been discussed. Malcolm was instructed to conceal the basically political motives of his mission by making the signature of a commercial agreement the main ostensible issue.[26]

Malcolm's mission achieved nothing of value. He did not hurry to Iran, but delayed to allow Fath Ali time to return to Tehran from his campaign in Khurasan, in eastern Iran. On the way Malcolm visited Masqat, signed a treaty with the Sultan, and found time to consider the problems of the Gulf. At Bushir he conferred with Mehdi Ali who had returned to his post in May 1800, via Baghdad and Basra. Malcolm did not arrive in Tehran until November 1800, by which time the Afghan threat was still more improbable. Malcolm, therefore, chose to concentrate on the threat from France, remote as it was, and upon the commercial treaty. After laborious negotiations he emerged, on 28 January, with two treaties. One was a vague and ill-worded commercial treaty which brought no advantages and the other was a political alliance. By the latter Britain allied with Iran against both France and Afghanistan. Despite Wellesley's instructions Malcolm secured no time-limit on its duration. In the situation of 1801 it served no purpose whatsoever and was little more than an embarrassment. In the negotiations Malcolm had sought to acquire the island of Qishm in the Gulf. The possibility that Iran might cede an island had been raised in Mehdi Ali's mission, but Malcolm had made the proposal his own and secured Wellesley's agreement to press for it. He failed to gain Iranian agreement, however, and the question was left open to further negotiation. On his return Malcolm tried to persuade Wellesley to buy the island. Malcolm had gained nothing that had not already been secured by Mehdi Ali.[27]

Malcolm blamed his difficulties in Iran principally upon problems raised by the status of the Governor-General of India. The Shah objected to negotiating with a subordinate ruler and refused to recognize the existence of the East India Company as a body capable of acting as a sovereign ruler. In return Malcolm endeavoured to establish the reputation of the Company by maintaining a lavish rate of expenditure and by insisting upon his own personal dignity. The Shah's lack of knowledge of or sympathy for European diplomatic practices also proved a handicap to the success of the mission. Fath Ali declined to ratify the treaty in the normal manner because this would have involved placing his seal below the signatures of the actual negotiators and this he held to be derogatory to his position. He also refused to allow an English translation of the treaty to be attached, perhaps a wise manœuvre. In the end Malcolm had to accept his refusal to ratify and to content himself with the issue of a firman by the Shah to give force to the treaties.

The long-term results of Malcolm's mission were bad for Anglo-Iranian relations. As Mehdi Ali had foreseen, the congestion of British missions, queuing to go to Tehran, and their princely scale, led the Iranian authorities to conclude that Britain set a high value on their friendship. The question of the status of the Governor-General was to have further unfortunate consequences in the future, when Minto's dignity was also hurt. Perhaps most important of all was the effect on Malcolm. He had gone to Iran fresh from his successes in Haidarabad and hoped to further his reputation in Iran. But whatever face he might put on it, his performance had been undistinguished. The result was to produce in Malcolm a revulsion against Iran. The Iranian Government, he wrote, was 'the most prejudiced, proud and absolute in the world', and he never lost this view. He helped to communicate it to generations which followed through the hostile and depressing picture which he gave in his *History of Persia* (1815) and in his *Sketches of Persia* (1828) which he wrote during his third mission. Despite its elegant style and the acclaim which it has received from scholars, the *Sketches* is a caricature of Iran, revealing dislike rather than understanding. His view also helped to drive him further towards the Gulf policy (discussed below) which would make Britain independent of the humiliations of the Iranian alliance.

Malcolm, who returned to India via Baghdad and Basra, was followed by Haji Khalil who now resumed his interrupted mission. The frustrations of the start of Khalil's mission were continued during his perilous and uncomfortable voyage to Bombay, during which he lost most of his baggage. But the worst was yet to come. He arrived at Bombay at the end of May 1802 and on 20 July he was accidentally killed in a scuffle in the streets.[28]

Wellesley's reaction was much stronger than might have been expected. Why this should have been so is difficult to understand. He had set little store by the Iranian alliance earlier and nothing in his future policy was to suggest that he thought Iran had any significant role to play in the defence of India. Possibly he felt that his honour and the dignity of his office were involved. Possibly Malcolm's influence prevailed. Ingram Ellis offers the interesting suggestion that Wellesley wanted a justification for his Maratha policy; Afghanistan had gone, the French danger was weakening, but there now arose the possibility that, if he demonstrated sufficient concern for the Iranian alliance, he might persuade London that there was a danger to India from Russia and that this might be held to warrant taking drastic measures against the Marathas.[29] The theory is not wholly improbable, in view of Wellesley's policy in previous years, but unfortunately there is no evidence to support it and indeed no real indication that Wellesley ever placed any importance on any Russian threat. His Maratha policy was after all to be hinged upon the French danger.

Wellesley dispatched Malcolm to arrange matters in Bombay. Malcolm carried out his task with customary extravagance. Khalil's colleagues were consoled with liberal presents and the body sent to the

Shiite holy city of Najf, with an escort under the charge of a Bombay
civil servant named Day. The corpse and its escort found their way to
Baghdad where their arrival coincided with that of the plague. Day
became so terrified that Jones sent him off to Basra. According to Jones,
far from regarding Khalil's last journey as an honour, the local population thought it a humiliation that an infidel should attend the body of a
true believer to the grave. Suleyman Pasha, the Governor of Baghdad,
became quite sarcastic about the affair.[30]

Wellesley also decided that a mission of condolence would be sent to
Iran, under the leadership of the newly-appointed Resident at Bushir,
Jonathan Henry Lovett. Mehdi Ali had been recalled and the Bushir
Residency placed under the direct control of the Governor-General. As
it happened, Lovett was still in India at the time and promptly fell sick
at Poona. In his place Charles Pasley was sent ahead, to prepare the
way. Lovett did not arrive at Bushir to take over until 11 January 1803.
Lovett, a star performer at Wellesley's new training college and
another of Duncan's protégés, was not a good choice for the post.
Nature had not equipped him for it either physically or mentally. He
was fat, sickly, and suffered with his feet; he disliked the climate at
Bushir, which was understandable, and dreaded the thought of the
journey to Tehran. His intellectualism, which no doubt appealed to
Duncan, was combined with lack of self-confidence and poor judgement. He leaned at first on the advice of Mehdi Ali, who did not leave
for India until 11 May, and possibly on Mehdi's advice was led to
assume the character and style of an ambassador rather than that of a
mere messenger, bearing a letter of condolence. Misled by Lovett's
assumed appearance and hopeful of new British offers, the Iranian
authorities urged him to proceed to Tehran. In September a *mehmendar*,
or guide, arrived to escort him to Shiraz, where another waited to take
him on to Tehran. Lovett, however, fearful of his health, did not want to
go. When he had heard of the approach of the *mehmendar* he had been
tempted to flee back to India, but he had stayed on and now was
obliged to make continual excuses to explain his failure to move. In
November he asked if he could send the Governor-General's letter to
Tehran, but the Iranians refused to accept it from anyone but Lovett
himself.[31] Lovett would not entrust it to Pasley, because, he said
mysteriously, he had been entrusted with some financial negotiations.
Eventually the *mehmendar* decided that Lovett's sickness was a mere
pretext. He concluded correctly that Lovett was planning to slip off to
India, and to prevent this happening, ordered all boats leaving Bushir
to be inspected. The Iranians did not wish to be deprived of all the rich
gifts of which they believed Lovett to be the bearer. By now Lovett's

situation was beginning to resemble that of Canetti's orientalist; he was virtually a prisoner at Bushir and terrified for his personal safety. Pasley, whose memorandum is the principal source for these events, was disgusted and wrote that Lovett's conduct was degrading the name of his country.[32]

Lovett sought help from the Resident at Basra, Samuel Manesty, with whom he offered to exchange jobs.[33] 'For God's sake come and save us all', he wrote desperately.[34] Nothing loath, Manesty came down to Bushir on 17 January 1804. As it happened the exchange did not take place. Lovett went not to Basra, but, on 15 February, departed for Calcutta, where he arrived in May. Sadly, his gloom about his health was proved to be justified. He went to sea to try to recover and died on the voyage in 1806. His mission was left in the glad grasp of Manesty.

Manesty was not the most stable of men, as his previous conduct at Basra and his eventual suicide showed. But his unauthorized mission to Tehran in 1804 deserves to rank high even among his remarkable adventures in the service of the Company. Manesty was determined to travel in style. He justified this on the grounds that Lovett's position had become so bad that in order to have any prospect of success it was necessary for Manesty to assume a character superior even to the style which Lovett had adopted without any authority at all. Success in what, since Lovett's task had merely been to deliver a letter of condolence, Manesty did not explain. A more probable explanation of his splendour is simple jealousy of Malcolm. He wrote to Jones that he had affected 'a state not very essentially differing from that which Major Malcolm adopted and by no means inferior to it'.[35] Throughout the course of his mission he carefully exacted all the attentions previously enjoyed by Malcolm. On 25 February he set off for Shiraz in 'the Embassadorial stile [*sic*]' as he explained to a surely bewildered Wellesley.[36] To give further weight to his mission he rounded up all available Europeans, including Pasley, Dr. Andrew Jukes, Lieutenant Edward Tanner, Edward Bellasis, and John Tanner, to make an impressive suite. With the addition of an escort of Indian infantry and Iranian cavalry, a drum and fife band, and a cannon he set off on his journey, 'British flags proudly waving in the wind', as he patriotically announced to Wellesley.[37] After spending six weeks at Shiraz and a month at Isfahan Manesty reached the Shah's camp at Sultaniyah on 2 July 1804, almost two years after poor Haji Khalil had met his doom in Bombay. The following day he presented the letter of condolence. His mission was then officially at an end, but Manesty immediately looked around for fresh fields to conquer. Even before he had left Basra he had been revolving in his mind the possible prospects for some new political *coup* in Iran. At Bushir he had begun to think that he might find a suitable opportunity in the state of relations between Russia and Iran.

A major change in Russo–Iranian relations was encompassed by the Russian annexation of Georgia—or, to be more precise, of the chief principalities of Georgia—in 1800. The reasons for this event do not concern us, but its effects do. Under the direction of the powerful and energetic Commander-in-Chief (1802–6), P. D. Tsitsyanov (1754–1806), Russian power was extended over the neighbouring Georgian principalities and over the various Muslim Khanates of Azerbaijan which formed a belt dividing Georgia from Iran. These Muslim Khanates enjoyed real independence but recognized Iranian suzerainty. The Khanates included the following: in the eastern region between the river Kura and the Caspian—Kuba, Shakeen, Baku, and Shirvan; in the central region between the Kura and the Aras—Ganja, Qarabagh, and Nakhchivan; and in the western region—Erivan. Also in dispute was the independent Khanate of Talish which lay south of the Aras on the Caspian shore. Tsitsyanov turned his attention to these Khanates in 1804 and on 2 January annexed Ganja which was renamed Elizavetpol. Iran, already disgruntled by the appearance of Russia in Georgia, immediately rallied to the defence of the Azerbaijani Khanates, and a long struggle ensued in which fortunes fluctuated, but the Russians made steady progress in the eastern and central regions.[38]

Manesty injected the Russian question into Anglo–Iranian relations. He decided that British interests demanded that Russian encroachments on Iran should be prevented. He hoped to do this by making himself the mediator.[39] He did not regard Russian conquests in Georgia and Armenia as in themselves likely to injure Britain but, as he explained in a letter to the Prime Minister, Addington, Russia and France might ally and attack India through Herat and Kabul.[40] Such an overland invasion he believed could be executed 'without much difficulty'.[41] The danger could be averted, he informed Addington, if he, himself, were appointed permanent minister at Tehran.

Manesty did not allow his lack of instructions to hinder his work. Without instructions he would use his discretion; with them he would attempt: 'to check the Progress of the great Northern Nation, in an Eastern Direction . . . whatever may be its attendant Danger, Difficulty and Responsibility'.[42] Three days after writing this portentous epistle (letter seems too modest a substantive) he received private letters from Wellesley and from the Governor-General's private secretary, Major Merrick Shawe, from which he drew unwarranted comfort.[43] These letters were written merely to approve Manesty's taking over Lovett's original mission and before Wellesley learned how Manesty had chosen to interpret it. Indeed, Wellesley's principal interest in Iran appeared to lie in securing some Persian horses.[44] The fact that they later turned out to be very poor horses may have increased Wellesley's subsequent fury with Manesty.[45]

Manesty decided, after discussing the question with the Shah's minister, Mirza Reza Quli, that it would be necessary for Britain to open direct negotiations with Russia at St. Petersburg. He offered to go to London himself, at once, and to lay the matter before the Cabinet. He expected that he would be sent to St. Petersburg to assist the Ambassador with the negotiations, and felt fairly confident of success; Iran, mainly interested in expansion to the east, would be prepared to make concessions in the north-west; and Russia, provided she was guaranteed possession of Georgia, would, he hoped, be willing to relinquish Armenia. Britain would secure considerable advantages from stopping the progress of Russia. If Russia controlled Iran she would pose an immediate threat to British trade and an ultimate threat to the security of British India. For a Russian-controlled Iran would mean a considerable increase in military expenditure to defend India and might force Britain to advance to the Indus in order to bar the way to an invader.[46] At this interesting point, however, Manesty was obliged to suspend his negotiations. The Shah had decided to move his camp from Sultaniyah to Erivan on 9 July, and Manesty, concerned about his own safety after the royal departure and full of his own plans to go to London, decided to make his way to Baghdad. He left Sultaniyah on 8 July. As he approached the Iraqi border on 9 September, he was horrified to learn that Wellesley had refused to honour the bills which he had drawn to pay his expenses.

It was about the beginning of July that Wellesley first discovered something of the truth concerning Manesty's 'extraordinary and unwarrantable proceeding', in assuming the character of an ambassador. His first impulse was to disown the eccentric Resident promptly, but, feeling this might endanger Manesty's life, he simply wrote to recall him immediately.[47] Further revelations of Manesty's proceedings caused him to order that bills should not be paid, although subsequently he rescinded this order.[48] In his haste, however, Wellesley was the unwitting instrument of yet another disaster to the diplomatic fortunes of Great Britain in the Middle East.

Manesty completed his tale of havoc by administering a fatal thrust to the British position in Baghdad. After receiving the news of his disgrace, he had to beat a hasty retreat from his potentially irate creditors in Iran. On 10 September he arrived in Baghdad, where he encountered his old rival, Harford Jones. Jones seems to have decided that this was a splendid opportunity to humiliate Manesty, for he summoned a public meeting of Baghdad merchants and informed them that Manesty's bills were worthless. In revenge Manesty appears to have informed the Pasha of Baghdad, Ali, that Jones had conspired against him at the time when Ali came to power in Baghdad. From this time onwards, Jones's influence in Baghdad sank to insignificance and Ali did all he could to get rid of him.[49] Manesty then went on to Basra and, after recuperating during the winter, passed on to Calcutta where he arrived in June 1805.

The most serious criticism of Manesty's mission is that it left the Iranian Government with a completely false impression of British interest in Iran. Although Wellesley had over-reacted to Khalil's murder, he had not intended that his generosity should lead to a closer political connection. He had intended no more than a mission of condolence and it was the combined efforts of Lovett and Manesty which had given the mission a quite misleading appearance. The error had been compounded by Manesty's invention of new British political interests, in which no member of the Indian Government had any interest. The Indian Government then completed this diplomatic horror story by omitting to inform the Iranians that all of Manesty's communications on political matters had been made without any authority.

The extent of the Iranian misconception of British interest was revealed by the new mission sent to India by the Shah. The Iranian Government was now becoming seriously concerned about the way in which the Russians were consolidating and expanding their position in Transcaucasia. The previous British missions, and especially the 1801 Treaty and the confident promises of Manesty, had led the Iranians to believe that Britain valued the Iranian alliance against France and would be willing to give aid against Russia. Their unfortunate choice of a representative should not lead us to suppose that they were uninterested in the alliance with Britain; they did in fact choose a man whom they believed had the knowledge and experience of Britons which would enable him to negotiate.

The mission was led by another merchant, named Muhammad Nabi Khan. He was doubly related to the unfortunate Khalil, since he was at once his half-brother and his brother-in-law. Their shared mother had once been the mistress of A. Douglas, the Company's chief factor at Bandar Abbas and subsequently at Basra. Like Khalil, Nabi was closely associated in business ventures with the Company's agents in the Gulf. One such venture had had unfortunate repercussions. This had involved Mehdi Ali. During the Khurasani's absence in the Red

Sea in 1801 Nabi's elder brother, Aga Muhammad Jaffir, had been left in charge of the Bushir factory. Nabi, who normally lived at Basra under the protection of the Company's Resident, had visited Bushir at that time and a rather shady transaction had taken place in which Mehdi sold the Company's stock of broadcloth (valued at £20,000) to Nabi on credit. According to Nabi, Mehdi was to receive half the profits from the deal. After Khalil's death, Nabi attempted to evade paying for the cloth, professing to regard it as blood-money for Khalil. He was Khalil's executor and apparently appropriated the greater part of the dead man's estate. Following Khalil's death he had played an obscure role and one possibly hostile to British interests.[50]

Muhammad Nabi had asked for the Indian mission partly in order to keep control of Khalil's estate. He was reported to have paid £20,000 for the appointment, which, not surprisingly in view of previous displays of British munificence, was believed to be a very lucrative job. Nabi clearly shared this belief. While at Baghdad he asked his old friend Harford Jones, to whom he had once taught Persian, whether he should ask Duncan to 'shoe his horses with gold and silver' 'stating it, at the same time, to be his intention, that these shoes should be so lightly fastened, that they might from time to time drop off, and be scrambled for by the spectators'.[51] William Hickey reported that he was accompanied by elephants and hundreds of servants.[52]

Nabi arrived in Bombay in August 1805 and did not reach Calcutta until April 1806. He left Iran in the company of Manesty, but had lingered on the way at Baghdad and Basra. The delay was unfortunate for him because, after the departure of Wellesley on 5 August 1805, the political climate in Calcutta grew much cooler. Under strong pressure from England to cut down expenses and commitments the new Governor-General, Lord Cornwallis, and his successor, George Barlow, had little time or money to spare for Iran. Barlow was determined to reduce commitments throughout the Middle East. He had abolished the post of Political Agent at Bushir, leaving Lieutenant William Bruce, who had been at Bushir since 1804, as Acting Commercial Resident only, and although he re-established the Political Residency in September 1806, he gave the Resident strict instructions to keep out of political involvements in Iran. In April 1807 Barlow abolished the Masqat Residency and also worked to eliminate one of the Iraqi posts.

The financial situation and his own unsavoury personal reputation ensured a sceptical reception for Nabi's reports of French interest in Iran. In the latter part of 1803 Napoleon had turned his gaze towards that country for the first time, requesting information from the French

Ambassador at Istanbul and from the Consul-General, Jean François Rousseau, at Baghdad. Rousseau opened a correspondence with Iran and when he received an encouraging reply it was decided to send two French envoys to Iran. The first, Alexandre Romieu, the Commissaire Général at Corfu, reached Tehran in September 1805, but fell ill and died before he was able to carry out his orders. The second, Amédée Jaubert (1779–1847) who had previously served as interpreter with the Egyptian expedition of 1798, was delayed *en route* and arrived at Tehran only in June 1806, where he discovered that Fath Ali Shah wanted an alliance with France against Russia. An Iranian envoy, Mirza Reza Khan, was ordered to return to Europe with Jaubert and to negotiate an alliance with France against Russia offering in return collaboration against India or against the Ottomans. Reza was instructed not to offer France a Gulf port, but to hold out hopes in this direction if Napoleon agreed to send a French ambassador to Iran.[53]

The Indian Government had already received some reports of these dealings from Manesty and Jones. In particular Jones, in his constant anxiety to find some justification for his continued political existence in Baghdad, had made himself the principal source of information concerning Iran. He had established a number of informants there including an Armenian named Owannes Pitcairn in Tehran; a Catholic missionary, Dom Leopold Sebastiani; a British traveller, Charles Richard Vaughan (1774–1849), later prominent in diplomacy in the Ottoman Empire and Spain; and Haji Muhsin, an agent of Nabi, who wrote in Persian cypher to his son in Baghdad. Jones also received letters from the prominent Iranian minister and advisor to the Heir Apparent, Mirza Bozorg. These sources provided important information about the mission of Alexandre Romieu. More specifically Mirza Bozorg and his colleague, Reza Quli, wrote asking for British help against Russia, saying that they would prefer a British to a French alliance, but could not wait indefinitely.[54]

Barlow believed neither Jones nor Nabi. Nabi's stories of French influence were dismissed as being merely intended to advance his own interests. Haji Muhsin, as his agent, could also be ignored. Their previous conduct had destroyed their credibility. 'These circumstances', stated Barlow, 'tend greatly to discredit the intelligence related to the intrigues of France.' Correct reports of the mission of Jaubert to Tehran and of Reza Khan to Europe were not believed. It was decided that Nabi's demands would be dealt with 'in a manner to preclude any Embarrassment and any inconvenient obligations between the Court of Persia and the British Government'.[55]

Nabi's mission failed. In January 1807, after receiving instructions from the Shah, Nabi put forward a formal claim for British military assistance against Russia. The claim was based upon a clause in Malcolm's 1801 Treaty which referred to 'mutual aid and assistance between the two states' and upon Manesty's unauthorized promises, which the Iranians held to constitute a gloss upon that clause. At the same time Nabi threatened that if Britain did not give aid, Iran would seek help from France. Barlow refused aid. He took the view that the 1801 Treaty did not involve any obligation to give aid against Russia and that Manesty's promises had no value since they were made without permission. For a final opinion, however, he agreed to refer the question to London.[56] Meanwhile Nabi returned empty-handed to Iran, where, surprisingly, he obtained the post of Governor of Bushir. His reprieve, however, was short; his enemies caught up with him and he was finally cut into small pieces in the presence of the Shah.[57] Fath Ali was, by this time, already committed to France.

Jaubert had returned to Europe accompanied by Mirza Reza, collecting an Ottoman Ambassador on the way. Diplomatic negotiations were conducted at Finkenstein. Napoleon was more interested in an Ottoman alliance than in obtaining an agreement with Iran, but he found Mirza Reza more complaisant than his suspicious Ottoman colleague and the Treaty of Finkenstein was signed on 4 May 1807. The treaty was plainly directed first and foremost against Russia and its application against British India was only of minor significance. France guaranteed the integrity of Iranian territory, including Georgia, agreed to force Russia to evacuate that province, and undertook to supply Iran with military stores and officers. Iran agreed to break her alliance with Britain, declare war on that country, and expel all Britons from Iran. Iran also undertook to persuade the Afghans and 'les autres peuples du Candahar'—whoever they might be—to join in an attack upon India and to give passage if required to a French army marching upon India.[58]

Napoleon had already arranged to send a mission to Iran led by Brigadier Claude Mathieu de Gardane. Gardane was instructed first to obtain Iranian co-operation against Russia and to urge Iran to make greater efforts to expel Russia from Georgia and to co-operate with the Ottomans against Russia. The strengthening of Iran against Russia 'en un mot, de la rendre plus forte, plus redoubtable aux Russes' was the essence of the mission of Gardane.[59] Only second was Gardane instructed to prepare for an expedition against India and it was stressed that the identity of Franco–Iranian views which prevailed with regard to Russia did not obtain in the case of Britain and that the resources of the French mission were insufficient to support a contest in Iran against both Russia and Britain. Third, Gardane was to negotiate a commercial treaty.

No sooner had Gardane departed than Napoleon destroyed the principal reason for his mission. Napoleon's policy towards the Ottomans and Iran had been governed by his problems with Russia in Central Europe. The temporary settlement of his differences with Russia at Tilsit (7 July 1807) meant that there was no longer any question of giving Iran military aid against Russia. Gardane was told that there was now no reason to continue the war between Russia and Iran; instead Gardane was to work for peace between the two states. The treaty was to operate only against Britain.[60] This was to kill his mission at birth, for it was acknowledged that Iran had no quarrel with Britain and evident that Napoleon had no serious intention of attacking India. It was some time, however, before the true implications of Napoleon's shift of policy became evident either to Iran or to Britain and in the meantime Gardane carried on with his castrated mission. He arrived in Tehran on 4 December 1807 and exchanged ratifications of the treaty. The Shah broke off relations with Britain, signed a commercial treaty, and agreed to give France naval facilities in the Gulf. When it came to fulfilling his part of the bargain Gardane was evasive concerning help against Russia. Fath Ali, however, was reluctant to admit that he had made a mistake and continued to hope that French mediation might achieve some advantage for Iran in her struggle with Russia.

The struggle between Iran and Russia had reached a critical phase. During the course of 1805 Russia had made extensive gains; Tsitsyanov had forced the submission of Qarabagh and Shakeen and annexed Shirvan. In February 1806, however, he was murdered while going to receive the submission of Baku. With Iranian support the Khanates which had submitted revolted against Russian rule. But aided by their domination of the waters of the Caspian the reinforced Russian forces under the new Commander-in-Chief, General I. V. Gudevich (1741–1820); Commander-in-Chief (1806–9) recovered their position and by September 1806 the Iranians were inclining towards peace. Peace at that time also seemed attractive to the Russians, committed as their forces were in Central Europe after the defeat of Austria at Austerlitz. Not until Tilsit was this pressure relieved and by then the Russians were also at war with the Ottomans and obliged to divide their forces in Azerbaijan. A French mediation in 1808 therefore had some prospect of success, although formal French mediation was unacceptable to the Russians.

The peace negotiations held during the Russo–Iranian truce of the summer of 1808 failed. The positions of the two sides were still too far apart. Fath Ali wanted Georgia and the Transcaucasian Khanates; Gudevich demanded peace on the basis of acceptance of a frontier along the Kura, Aras, and Arpachaya rivers and would not have accepted less than the *status quo* even as an interim measure. The contest was renewed in the autumn of 1808 when Gudevich attempted to win a decisive victory in the western sector. He failed in his attempt to take Erivan, however, and narrowly escaped a complete disaster during his consequential retreat. Gudevich blamed French intervention for his defeat. He was forced to resign his command and on 14 February 1809 was replaced by General A. P. Tormasov (1752–1819; Commander-in-Chief 1809–11). Tormasov's arrival coincided with the end of French influence at Tehran, however, and its replacement by that of Britain, and we must now return to consider the circumstances of the revolution which had taken place in British policy towards Iran.

Contrary to Iranian belief and also to the judgement of subsequent historians of these events, there had been no change in British Indian policy from the time of Wellesley to that of Barlow. Wellesley, no more than Barlow, had believed that Iran had any significant role to play in the defence of India. Neither had feared a French attack through Iran and neither had any thoughts of quarrelling with Russia about her movements in Transcaucasia. The difference between Wellesley and Barlow was one of presentation and personality, not of policy. Wellesley had found it appropriate to create an illusion of British interest in Iran; Barlow dispensed with the flummery and in a refreshingly rude manner had set out British India's lack of interest as unmistakably as possible. It was not surprising, however, that the Iranians, accustomed to British policy transmuted by the eccentric agents who had been employed in their country, should have felt that British policy had undergone a sudden reversal. The real reversal, however, had yet to come for it was still in process of preparation—not in India, but in London.

The authorities in London became closely concerned with Iranian politics for the first time in 1807; earlier, Henry Dundas had never enthused over Wellesley's policy in Iran. The Cabinet's first involvement in the consideration of British policy towards Iran is significant because it introduced the important new element of European politics into the problems of British relations with Iran and marked the opening of the prolonged conflict over the related questions of whether European or British Indian interests should prevail in the conduct of British policy towards Iran and of who should control that policy. Because of the ramifications of those questions it is necessary to examine closely the sources of the new initiative of 1807 and to disentangle the various arguments which underpinned it.

The first moves in London were made by Harford Jones. In February 1806 Baghdad had at last become too hot for him and he had arrived back in England in December of that year. He set himself to win support in high places, such as might serve either to allow him to recover his post at Baghdad or to enable him to find other suitable diplomatic employment in the East. One way of achieving these ends was to stress the possible danger to British India arising from Russian pressure on Iran. Jones revived Manesty's 1804 proposal, suggesting that he (Jones) should be sent to St. Petersburg to mediate between Russia and Iran. In fact a proposal to mediate had already been made by W. C. Stuart, Secretary to the British Embassy in St. Petersburg.[61] Jones deployed three arguments. The first was the argument that there was a long-term danger to British India arising from Russian control of Iran. This argument had first appeared in 1801, and had then been discussed by Elgin, Malcolm, Manesty, and by Jones himself. It is doubtful if anyone put any weight on this argument in 1807. The second point brought forward by Jones was one which was to become of considerable significance in 1812 to 1813. It was a straightforward derivative of the European balance of power theory. If Russian troops were diverted to war with Iran (or with the Ottomans) they could not be used to oppose French ambitions in Europe. It was therefore in British interests to try to end hostilities between Russia and Iran. Probably it was this argument which weighed most heavily with British statesmen in the post-Austerlitz period, when the fate of Central Europe was at stake. Similar arguments led, ironically enough, first to the British attack upon the Ottoman Empire at the end of 1806 and then to the efforts in 1807 to patch up a peace between Russia and the Ottomans in order to free Russia for operations against France. Jones's third argument was the oldest; it was the familiar threat of a direct French invasion of India. It had never impressed British statesmen; in 1798 to 1801 only Henry Dundas had been strongly influenced by it. The situation had not altered much in 1807; most British statesmen were incredulous or uninterested. But Robert Dundas had apparently inherited his father's fears. Like Holland Rose later, but like few men at the time, he believed that the overthrow of British power in India was central to Napoleon's purposes. As President of the Board of Control from March 1807, he was able to give effect to his views. The fears were shared by Gilbert Elliot, Earl of Minto, who held the Board of Control under Grenville until his appointment as Governor-General of India in June 1806. It was the presence of these two men, with their beliefs, in two of the critical posts, that was a major factor in the development of British policy in Iran in the years which followed. In particular the prospect of a Franco–Russian coalition against Britain, after Tilsit (July 1807), brought their fears to a high point.

The changing international situation and the changing personnel of the ministries during the period 1806 to 1807 led to continual revisions of the plan of action. Jones's first approach had naturally been to his employers, the Court of Directors. The Court had suggested that an Envoy to Russia and Iran should represent the Crown. In his memorandum of 7 January 1807, therefore, Jones made a firm proposal to send a Crown mission to St. Petersburg to mediate between Russia and Iran with a view to combating French aims in Iran.[62] This plan was accepted by the then President of the India Board, George Tierney. The Foreign Office apparently played little part in the matter. Tierney was notoriously anxious for good relations with the Court and Jones had powerful support from certain Directors, including Sir Hugh Inglis, Sir Francis Baring, and especially from his fellow countryman, the Chairman, Edward Parry. Parry's support was apparently gained when Jones agreed to take as Secretary, a Major L. F. Smith, the son of a friend of Parry's, in place of Charles Vaughan, whom Jones and the Foreign Office preferred and who was undoubtedly a far better choice.[63] It was suggested to Jones that if he were successful in his mission he would be made Governor of Bombay. This was the post which above all others Jones had coveted, not least because it would give him an excellent opportunity to get his illegitimate daughters married off. Opposition to Jones came from partisans of John Malcolm, led by Arthur Wellesley, who told Tierney that Jones was 'an improper man'.[64] Wellesley suggested that Malcolm should be sent to Tehran to make a treaty directed against France and that Jones could be Secretary. Tierney, however, stuck to his decision, although when he left office in March 1807 the question was thrown back into the melting-pot.

Robert Dundas changed the purpose of the mission. It was not that he objected to Jones, whom he was prepared to accept on his father's recommendation.[65] It was that he thought that the most serious problem was that of a direct threat to India from France, and gave much less weight to the argument which had appealed to the Whigs, namely that the mission could release troops for use against France in Europe. In the light of Robert Dundas's priorities it was more sensible to send Jones direct to Iran. In his memoirs Jones says that the idea of the mission to St. Petersburg was abandoned at the end of April 1807 and this statement must refer to this decision by Dundas.[66] But Dundas's decision was not the end of the proposal because it was revived by George Canning, who had become Foreign Minister. Sir Hugh Inglis thought that Wellesley was at the bottom of the new delay and was working for Malcolm.[67] In another letter he complained bitterly 'What Ministers are about is not for me to say but if they manage their other business as they have managed this Lord have mercy upon our poor country.'[68] If Inglis was correct then it represents a truly cynical volte-face by Arthur Wellesley. Certainly the idea of the mission to St. Petersburg still appears in a draft of instructions to Jones dated 1 June, and it would seem that a final decision to send Jones direct to Iran via the Cape and not via St. Petersburg was not taken until 20 August 1807, that is, after the news of Tilsit had finally ended the prospects for any immediate approaches to Russia.

Ingram Ellis puts forward an interesting theory to explain the decision to send Jones directly to Iran. According to this, Canning was primarily influenced by the European situation. He saw in the post–Tilsit world the possibility of using Iran as a pawn in the general struggle against the Franco–Russian coalition. Jones should go direct to Iran with a view to persuading the Shah to attack Russia in the Caucasus, so taking pressure off Austria. In other words, Canning supported Robert Dundas's policy but to defend Europe, not India. The theory is attractive and Ellis is certainly right to emphasize the priority which ministers gave to European interests both before and after the decision to send Jones direct to Iran. But the evidence on Canning's motives is too slight and the indications are that the theory probably overstates his interest in Iran at this time and the degree of control which he exercised. On balance it would seem that the vital figures remained Dundas, the Directors, and Jones himself.

Jones wrote his own instructions, of which there are several drafts.[69] In the first in June 1807 it was proposed that he should go to Iran, not as resident Minister, but on a special mission with the express purpose of defeating French intrigues. He was to travel to Iran via St. Petersburg in order to try to adjust Russo–Iranian differences.[70] After the St. Petersburg proposal was dropped a new draft was prepared dated 21 August 1807.[71] In this Jones was instructed to travel directly to Iran via Bombay and Bushir. The purpose of this mission was to negotiate a revision of the 1801 Treaty so as to limit and define the circumstances in which Iran could call upon British aid. If Iran were agreeable to this proposal Jones was to arrange for the supply of military aid to Iran, the establishment of a permanent British representative at Tehran, and the visit of an Iranian Ambassador to London. If, on the other hand, he was unable to persuade the Qajars to honour the treaty he was to consider ways of neutralizing the power of Iran either by encouraging a rising in southern Iran under the leadership of a member of the former Zand dynasty or, as a last resort, by making an agreement with the most revolutionary group in the area—the puritanical Wahhabis of Arabia. Plainly these last two suggestions were contributed by Jones. Through his early experience in the Gulf he had an unrivalled knowledge of both the Zands and the Wahhabis. Both suggestions, and particularly the first, were to become, in the next hundred years and more, part of the stock-in-trade of political discussions about the area. In the final instructions, dated 2 September 1807, these points were repeated and the main aim of the mission was defined as being to counteract French intrigues and to provide aid in return for Iranian assistance in the defence of India.[72]

The final versions of Jones's instructions place his mission in the context of the defence of India against France and not in the context of the European balance of power. This does not prove, however, that the problem of defending India was uppermost in the minds of ministers in the summer of 1807. What it does show is, that the utility of Iran in the European balance had temporarily disappeared after Tilsit and that other influences were allowed to come to the fore. These influences were first, the predominance, in the drafting of the instructions, of Dundas, the Court, and Jones, that is, men whose interest in the situation derived from India; and second, the vital importance of the questions of the financing and control of the mission.

The influence of Robert Dundas and through him that of his still active father are quite clear from the documents. The Dundases' fears of the French danger had been substantially increased by Tilsit. Robert Dundas feared the old bogey of a direct French overland invasion assisted by Iran or Russia. Like his father, he had unbounded confidence in the ability of Britain's enemies to surmount the physical and other problems of the march. France could easily advance on India through either Asia Minor or Syria to Iran and Russia could move from the Caspian to the Indus.

however improbable its execution may appear, the character of the present Ruler of France renders it by no means unlikely that the scheme will be attempted and that every effort of force and intrigue will be employed for the attainment of his object and the destruction of the British power in India.[73]

Apart from sending reinforcements to India, Jones's mission, wrote Dundas, was the only means by which England could assist in frustrating French aims. But Minto, as Governor-General of India, was urged to act to persuade all the countries which intervened between Iran and the British Indian frontier to co-operate with Britain in opposing France. Security was paramount and although Minto was reminded of the prohibition on defensive alliances, he was given permission to disregard it and to annihilate the Marathas if they appear hostile. In fact the situation was identical with that of 1798 to 1800. Once more a Dundas was in power and once more the one thing which reconciled the Board to an interventionist policy was the fear of France. Minto, although he did not take it, was given the same opportunity as Wellesley.

The importance of the questions of finance and control appear repeatedly in the documents. When Charles Grey and Tierney had accepted Jones's original proposal it had been intended that the Crown should pay the costs of Jones's mission and also control it. Robert Dundas also believed that the Crown should accept responsibility, arguing that success in so important a matter was more likely to be achieved by a man who had the prestige of the Crown rather than that of the Company behind him. The Crown should pay because the war with France was a concern of Britain and not merely of British India.[74] Canning later claimed that he had opposed this proposal and although there is no direct evidence from 1807 to support his claim, it would seem that he must have done so because a compromise did emerge. Jones was given certain credentials from the Crown and also the power to sign a treaty in the name of the Crown, but the Company was to pay all expenses, and to be responsible for providing any aid under the treaty. In addition the Company could issue instructions to Jones and Jones was to conform to those instructions and any which he might receive from the Governor-General.[75] Canning was silent on what Jones should do if his instructions from Minto clashed with those from the Crown, an unfortunate omission, which was to cause great difficulties. The justification for making the Company financially responsible was clearly stated in an official letter to Bombay by Robert Dundas, although his explanation contradicted his own previous argument. He wrote: 'as the interests of the British Dominions in India are the object and end of this mission the expense of the embassy is to be defrayed by the Company.'[76] In other words it was necessary in the instructions to Jones to insist upon the primacy of Indian interests because only in this way could the Directors be made to accept the unwelcome financial responsibility. In compensation they claimed and were given the right to appoint all staff apart from the Ambassador. The net effect, however, was further to confuse the question of control. The financial arrangements for the mission caused the venture to become highly unpopular in the Court, so much so that Jones complained that many of the Directors were not even civil to him.[77] The Directors' attitude was hardly surprising in view of the shortage of money in the Company. Still smarting after their experience of Wellesley's expensive wars they did not want to sign another blank cheque, although this is what was implied by Jones's instructions. Nevertheless, their hostility demonstrates also that they were not convinced that the mission was justified on the grounds of Indian defence.

The Crown made one further cheap contribution to the mission by giving Jones a baronetcy. In the first edition of his *War in Afghanistan*, John Kaye stated this fact, but in the absence of positive evidence he was obliged to withdraw the statement when Jones's family protested. In his retraction, however, he made it clear that he still believed his original charge to be true and in revenge added the gratuitous comment that Jones was a man of inferior parts. Although he greatly underestimated Jones's ability, Kaye was right about the baronetcy. Jones's own claim that it was for his alleged services at Baghdad was always unlikely and the correspondence makes it clear that Jones sought and obtained the baronetcy for the mission to Iran. Jones was a man whose life seemed to be a story of continual slights and he craved the warm solace of honours. He had already secured a knighthood and the new mission was his opportunity to take a further step. Henry Dundas supported his claims especially 'as it would add consequence to your mission'.[78] Sir Hugh Inglis wrote to Robert Dundas on Jones's behalf on similar lines; a baronetcy would show that Jones possessed the confidence of Government.[79] The origins of the baronetcy which Jones received in August need not be doubted. But Jones deserves credit for his skill and persistence. In December 1806 he had crept into London, thrown out of Baghdad by the Pasha, and regarded as a nuisance and worse by the Government of India and his own Embassy in Istanbul. His career seemed to be at an end. On 27 October 1807 he sailed from Portsmouth aboard H. M. S. *Sapphire* as Sir Harford Jones, Bart., H. M. Ambassador to Iran, and with hopes of a peerage and the Governor's Mansion at Bombay. Napoleon and Alexander had served him well; it was perhaps poetic justice that Minto and Malcolm were to serve him so badly.

While Jones's mission had been taking shape in London, a separate but similar initiative had been evolved in India where the new Governor-General, Lord Minto, had arrived in July 1807. Minto deserves closer scrutiny, for his personality was to be a significant factor in the development of the situation in Iran and elsewhere along the Indian frontier.

Minto was one of the weakest men to hold the office of Governor-General. His previous career had been spent in law, politics, and diplomacy in which his most prominent post had been that of Ambassador in Vienna. Politically he was what Fortescue called expressively a sentimental Whig, a phrase indicating a disposition to take refuge in cant, a feature of Minto's correspondence. As President of the Board of Control in 1806, he had been well placed to put himself forward as a compromise candidate for the Governor-Generalship when the Ministry and the Court of Directors had reached deadlock over their respective candidates.[80] Minto had no desire to go to India, but needed the handsome salary to salvage his fortunes. In India his situation was unenviable, as the return of the Tories to power in England meant that he lacked support in the mother country and his failure to solve the financial problems of the Company soon cost him the favour of the Court of Directors. Lacking support from England, wanting real qualities of intellect and judgement, and knowing little of India, Minto inevitably looked for guidance to his colleagues in the Indian Government and finding little help from his fellow Councillors who lacked political ability and understanding, the Governor-General fell under the influence of a miscellaneous group of men prominent among whom were former lieutenants of Richard Wellesley including John Adam, Mountstuart Elphinstone, Charles Metcalfe, and John Malcolm.

Like Robert Dundas, but unlike Wellesley, Minto believed in the reality of the French threat to India and came to India imbued with the hope that India might contribute something to Britain's great struggle by means of an expedition to Java.[81] His attention, however, was soon diverted from Java by the alarming reports which reached him from Iran. In September 1807 he was informed that Bandar Abbas had been ceded to France[82] and by the end of the year he was acutely worried by the combination of Tilsit and the spectre of French activities throughout the Middle East.[83] For a long time Minto was held back from taking any action by his belief that relations with Iran should be controlled by the Government in England. He wrote to Dundas: 'The interests of Persia are now so much connected with the politics of Europe that no negotiations of a general nature could be carried on from hence.'[84] The Envoy to Iran, he concluded, must receive his principal instructions from London. Somewhat illogically Minto went on to argue that he should be allowed to choose the Envoy and to give him local instructions.

Minto finally nerved himself for action at the beginning of 1808. Tilsit had already made it certain that British mediation at St. Petersburg was no longer feasible, thus destroying one of the main arguments for launching the mission from London. In January 1808 Minto received a false report that a French army was marching with an Ottoman force towards Iran and that a Franco–Russian invasion of India was threatened.[85] To await the arrival of this force on the British Indian frontier was too dangerous, Minto decided, for its approach would provoke insurrection within British territory and attacks from other Indian states. (The recent Vellore mutiny had made the dangers of internal commotion seem peculiarly vivid in British India.) No force adequate to quell such eruptions existed and the shock to British financial credit would make it very difficult, Minto supposed, to raise more troops. The Governor-General concluded that a forward policy was essential in the circumstances; the French must be stopped before they reached India. To lead a mission to Iran, Minto selected John Malcolm, who he had wanted for the job when he was still at the Board of Control in London. In addition to Malcolm's diplomatic mission Minto proposed to assemble two expeditionary forces—one of four or five thousand men to prevent France seizing a Gulf port and the other of up to twenty-five thousand men for use in Iran against France.[86]

Minto's initiative owed much to the influence of Malcolm, whose position and activities in India bore a striking resemblance to those of Jones in London. Malcolm's brilliant career in diplomacy in Iran and India had suffered a temporary reverse after the departure of the Wellesleys. Under the guidance of Barlow he completed negotiations for a settlement of the Maratha wars and then reluctantly returned to his official appointment as Resident in Mysore where he sulked, complaining that he was a forgotten man to whom advance was denied by his association with the discredited policies of Richard Wellesley. Just as Jones in similar moments of depression longed for his home on the Welsh Borders, Malcolm wrote fondly of retiring to his cottage by the Eske.[87] Barlow's replacement by Minto provided Malcolm with an opportunity to regain the limelight. Malcolm was already friendly with a younger son of Minto who was in the Madras Civil Service. This son does not sound to have been a very attractive personality; the convivial Hickey described him as 'one of the most pert, assuming and forward coxcombs I ever saw'.[88] But to Malcolm he was a lifeline to advancement. Through the medium of the younger Elliot Malcolm sent a remarkable memorandum to Minto in July 1807.[89]

This consisted of a sustained attack upon almost everyone in the Indian Government. Barlow, his Council, and the Secretariat all came under Malcolm's lash. Only his friend, John Adam (1779–1825), then Deputy Secretary in the Political Department, who was later to form a vital link between the policies of Wellesley and those of Hastings, and that remarkable scholar Henry Colebrooke (1765–1837), who served on the Supreme Council from 1807 until 1812, emerged with credit from the memorandum. In it Malcolm also dwelt upon his own prospects. He disclosed that he had hoped (presumably through the Wellesley influence) to be appointed to lead the new embassy to Iran and did not conceal his fury at being passed over in favour of Jones. He wrote indignantly: 'I cannot refrain from stating that it was not possible that I could have suffered a greater mortification than to have the pretensions of that gentleman brought in competition with my own.' A little later he offered his opinion that Jones owed his appointment to intrigue and because he promised to do the work on the cheap.[90] What was needed, wrote Malcolm, was a mission from India and to support his argument produced two additional memoranda on the policies which should be pursued in Iran and Iraq.

Malcolm's arguments were presented with all his characteristic, bold, fertile, and far-reaching strategic insight. They embraced the entire Middle East. He foresaw the establishment of the dominance of France within the Ottoman Empire. With French assistance the Sultan would be able to restore his decayed authority over the Arab provinces, including Syria and Iraq. France would thus gain control over all the strategic approaches to India. When this was combined with the already-formed Franco–Iranian alliance, India would be under a serious threat. To meet it Malcolm proposed new initiatives in both Iraq and Iran. An alliance with Iraq would convert that country into a British protectorate complete with a subsidiary force. Such a state would form a far better buffer state than the Ottoman Empire.[91] An alliance with Iran was also still possible. It was in Britain's interest that Iran should remain a strong independent state; the French connection could be broken if Russia could be persuaded to accept British mediation.[92] Of course Malcolm was wrong in most if not in all of his assumptions. But he demonstrated how he could think on a strategic scale which was unmatched in India and elements of his analysis recur throughout the history of the British connection with India. It is small wonder that his contemporaries found him so persuasive.

Malcolm's analysis showed Minto the way to action. In view of Jones's mission he could not send Malcolm directly to Iran. Instead he sent him on a general mission to Iran, Iraq, and the states of the Gulf in order to warn all rulers who appeared to be contemplating entering into an alliance with France. Malcolm was given control over all other British agents in the area and ambassadorial credentials to employ if Jones did not appear. 'The real and ultimate object of this mission is to obstruct the progress of the French towards India.'[93] Jones might have been forgiven for thinking that it was to obstruct his progress. Minto explained his own views in a private letter which accompanied his official one. He wrote that he would have sent Malcolm on a similar mission in July 1807, but for orders from Britain which arose from the delicate state of Anglo–Russian relations in Europe. He now felt himself free from the limitations imposed by these orders by virtue of Tilsit and 'the growing necessity of the case in Asia'.[94]

Full instructions to Malcolm were not issued until 7 March.[95] A large part of these instructions was occupied by lists of vast tracts of information which Malcolm was to collect. The significant parts, however, show how limited Minto still felt his position to be. Malcolm was to travel as the Envoy of the Governor-General. He was not allowed to make any significant offers of support to Iran, for example, a defensive alliance against Russia or even mediation, without authority from England. He could offer money or military assistance only against France or the Ottomans. The object of his mission was to break the influence of France in Tehran and to exclude France from any islands or ports in the Gulf. For the last purpose a small expedition, large enough to cope with any French threat, was to be sent from Bombay.[96] If Malcolm encountered Jones he was not to proceed to Iran, unless Jones wished him to do so, but to limit his activities to Iraq and the Gulf.

Minto's caution extended to the instructions governing the proposed mission to Baghdad. Malcolm was instructed merely to try to prevent French influence becoming established in Baghdad, but was warned to exercise particular care because of the problems of Anglo–Ottoman relations. (Britain was of course still nominally at war with the Otto-man Empire, although this had not affected the British position in Iraq). In fact the Baghdad element in Malcolm's mission appeared only because of the complications of the existence of Jones's mission to Iran. In the circumstances of 1808 the only diplomatic move which had any immediate relevance was the approach to Iran. Iran therefore had to be the main objective of the Malcolm mission. But Minto dared not send him to Iran alone because this would clash with the mission from England. In effect, therefore, his instructions represent an attempt to smuggle Malcolm into Iran under the camouflage of a vague and general responsibility in the Middle East. But the limitations imposed by the Crown mission's existence meant that Minto could make only limited offers to Iran. Malcolm went to Iran not only camouflaged but hamstrung as well.

The Baghdad mission was given greater emphasis by Minto when he heard formally of the appointment of Jones and that his arrival at

Bombay was imminent. Minto concluded that he might have to abandon Malcolm's Iran mission entirely. He then gave Malcolm permission to operate not only in Iraq but also in Syria and even to proceed to
Istanbul. In Baghdad, Minto argued improbably, Malcolm would be
able to secure more accurate information about French activities than
Jones would find possible in Tehran. Also Malcolm would be a far more
suitable representative than Jones in Baghdad because of Jones's previous career in that capital and his inability to co-operate with Manesty
at Basra (they were 'old, inveterate and irreconcilable rivals'), and
because Malcolm's exceptional stature and ability were the best 'which
either Europe or Asia could afford'.[97] Pleasing as these compliments
must have been, they could not disguise the fact that the Baghdad
mission was a mere consolation prize for Malcolm. Jones's own experience there from 1798 to 1806 had shown that it was a diplomatic blind
alley. Despite his own valiant pleas for an initiative there in 1807,
Malcolm himself always seems to have known this. Baghdad was too
weak to be of much value as an ally, he wrote to Minto, and if the Pasha
became hostile he could easily be ruined by encouraging either Iran or
the Wahhabis to attack him. All Britain really needed was control over
the Shatt al-Arab—in other words a return to the Basra only concept.[98]
For Malcolm it was really Iran or nothing and he was determined to
beat Jones to Bushir.

Malcolm was already working hard to frustrate Jones. As soon as he
had received his first instructions he had set off for Bombay. At the
same time he sought to turn Minto against Jones. He put forward
constitutional arguments in a manner calculated to make Minto feel
that his pride was at stake. Certainly, argued Malcolm, the Envoy
should have credentials from the Crown, but he should be wholly under
the control of the Governor-General. When Malcolm learned that
Jones's instructions apparently made him 'in a great degree independent of the Governor-General's authority' he complained that this was
likely to create confusion and to damage the dignity and power of the
Indian Government.[99] He denied that he had any personal interest in
the matter, claiming, incredible as it sounds, that he had never sought
the post of Envoy. But the tirade of abuse which he directed against
Jones's ability, knowledge, and personal character, indicate how
strongly Malcolm was influenced by his own feelings.

Malcolm was a man who has been much misunderstood by writers
on India. The main reason for this is because he deliberately presented
himself in a deceptive character. The image which he projected was one
consistent with his large, powerful physique. It was of a bluff, straightforward, honest man, filled with zeal for the public service, a good

companion, always ready with a joke. This is the legend of Boy Malcolm, the man who was the inevitable product of the child who promised to cut down Haidar Ali with his sword. He was, wrote Malcolm, a man 'whose only lessons have been learned in the school of experience'.[100] This is the picture which appears in the memoirs of his contemporaries and above all in the magnificent biography of Malcolm which was written by John Kaye, who did not meet him. Kaye speaks of two rooms filled with his papers, but they disappeared after the publication of Kaye's book and it is therefore Kaye's picture which has dominated the vision of later historians. So Edward Thompson summed up Malcolm as 'the typical soldier-sportsman-statesman of the time and of all time', although he also quoted disbelievingly Henry Lawrence's revealing dismissal of Malcolm as 'a clever, fortunate humbug'.[101] In an earlier essay I accepted the traditional view.[102] After more research I have now concluded that this view was completely mistaken.

It will be easiest to begin with what Malcolm was not. He was not a soldier. Most of his career was spent upon non-military duties. In his only major battle—Mahidpur 1817—he nearly lost by leading a charge against enemy guns in a well-prepared position. He was a poor diplomatist. His missions to Iran were all disastrous. In his negotiations with the Marathas he gave way on important points and was strongly criticized by both Wellesley and Hastings. His method was always to try to buy agreement with presents and concessions. He defended this by various arguments, but the truth was he was a poor bargainer, unable to estimate the weaknesses in his adversaries' position and too vain and too susceptible to flattery. As an administrator he showed more talent, especially in his settlement of central India, although there his habitual generosity with government property also led to later difficulties. As Governor of Bombay he was only moderately successful, much less distinguished than his predecessor Elphinstone, and he contrived to entangle himself in a disastrous conflict with his Chief Justice.

Malcolm was not a frank and open man. He was a skilful and merciless intriguer, ready to grasp at any prospect of advance. Anyone reading the history of British India between 1798 and 1830 must be surprised at the number of times that Malcolm's name comes into the most diverse events. His ubiquity was not accidental but was the result of careful manœuvring. At an early age he had seen that the best prospects of advancement lay in the political service and had steadily climbed the ladder, transferring with great judgement from one patron to another—Kennaway, Alured Clarke, General Harris, Wellesley,

Lake, and Minto. He made friends easily and exploited them well—Arthur Wellesley was perhaps his greatest catch. At the same time he could be hard with friends when it was convenient. William Bruce at Bushir was a protégé of his, but when Bruce gave assistance to Jones in Iran he attributed it to Bruce's timidity and limited understanding.[103] With those who stood in his way he could be quite ruthless. His character-assassinations of the Bengal Government and of Jones are good examples. To his own subordinates he was habitually patronizing. Certainly he was both ambitious and extremely vain. Only an excess of vanity could have led him in letters to Minto to blame Jones for doing exactly the same things which he must have known Minto knew were also true of Malcolm. To accuse Jones of owing his position to influence was justified but ridiculous, since Malcolm had always sought advance in the same way and was even then hoping that his Wellesley connections would restore him to favour. His constant stress on his own integrity and his own superiority to pettiness and intrigue begin to look like hypocrisy.

All this is not to say that Malcolm was worthless or that he was very different from his contemporaries in his powerful ambition and in his methods. He entered the British Indian environment at an early age and adopted both the aims and the forms of a highly competitive society. What it is to say is that he was quite different from the admirable figure which Kaye presented as a model for Victorian public servants in India. In making him into a prototype David Blaize, Kaye did Malcolm less than justice. For Malcolm had one superb talent which is obscured in Kaye's book and in the image which he himself projected. He was the ideologue *par excellence* of British India. It is true that Charles Metcalfe and Mountstuart Elphinstone were much more self-consciously intellectual than he was. Both had a foundation of Classical learning on which they could build. Malcolm was a self-made intellectual, but in the end he was much more at home with ideas than were any of his contemporaries. He was a great talker—Canning, who got tired of his arguments, called him Bahadur Jah—and a great writer. He could grasp ideas, reformulate them, put them in new and illuminating patterns, and expound them with matchless conviction. In studying the development of the strategy of Indian defence Malcolm is inescapable. Time and again, as one comes to trace the origin of particular ideas, one comes up against the contribution of Malcolm. His insight, his imagination, his willingness to think outside accepted patterns, and above all his capacity to bring in a range of considerations far beyond that of which others were capable, all mark him out as a man of real intellectual genius. It is the combination of his intellectual power with his personal ambition which gives him true fascination, not the dull and worthy qualities of the conventional schoolboy hero. As with Bulldog Drummond, the true interest lies below the surface. It is only when one understands the real Malcolm that the major clash which now took place over policy towards Iran becomes comprehensible.

Malcolm wasted no time at Bombay. He quickly assembled an imposing mission, added an escort the size of a small army, and sailed hurriedly on 17 April 1808. He was just in time to avoid Jones, who arrived at Bombay on 24 April, and also new instructions from Minto, who, hearing that Jones's arrival was imminent, had finally lost his nerve and suspended Malcolm's mission to Iran, while leaving him free to continue his mission in other countries.

To keep ahead of events Malcolm moved in a hurry. He had no time for careful negotiation; quick results were essential to him. His technique was to overawe others by bluster and a display of force. The first state to experience this procedure was Masqat, where Malcolm arrived on 30 April. The ruler was suspected of dallying with France and had quarrelled with the British Resident, David Seton, who had left in a huff. Minto had condemned Seton for departing on quite inadequate grounds. (The quarrel arose from the Sultan's refusal to make available to Seton land on which the Resident wished to build a house.)[104] Malcolm now decided to force the Sultan's hand He informed his representative that the Sultan could not be allowed to be neutral. 'If he were not found to be decidedly a friend, he would be treated as an enemy.'[105] The Sultan promptly gave way. Vulnerable as he was to attack from the sea and dependent also on the trade with India, he had little choice.

The same threatening tactics were applied by Malcolm in quite different circumstances in Iran and failed completely. The Iranian Government in Tehran was neither vulnerable to an attack by sea nor concerned about the trade of the south. Malcolm arrived at Bushir on 10 May and immediately sent his cousin, Charles Pasley, towards Tehran. Pasley was instructed to demand the expulsion of the French and in return to offer a supply of arms from India.

Malcolm was bluffing. He calculated that the Shah and his ministers wanted the British mission to move slowly towards Tehran but did not want a formal breach with the French mission under Gardane. They wanted to keep both parties in play. Malcolm thought that if he adopted a high tone he could force them to choose. Accordingly he would not move north from Bushir until he received 'those concessions that I deem indispensable for the honour as well as the interest of the Country'.[106] The central demand was for the expulsion of Gardane.

Once that was granted Malcolm would make concessions. He would not object to French officers and artificers being retained for a time. But first the Shah must decide for Britain. Malcolm believed that he had a fair chance of success because he reasoned correctly that the Franco–Russian agreement would make it impossible for France to fulfil her promise to Iran and that therefore in the end the Iranians must turn to Britain.

The fatal weakness of Malcolm's position was that he had no authority to offer much in the way of inducements to Iran. He could neither offer a new treaty nor aid against Russia. As he wrote to Pasley: 'I am at a great loss to instruct you how to answer those demands which I am aware will be made for aid against the Russians.'[107] In fact Malcolm went far beyond what his instructions permitted on this point. He gave Pasley permission to declare that if Britain were at war with Russia 'every aid' would be given to Iran and if the two powers were at peace Britain would offer mediation. In conversations with Nasrullah Khan at Shiraz, Pasley appears to have extended this much further. He spoke of Britain sending an army of twenty-five to thirty thousand men to assist Iran against Russia. Now such a force had been mentioned by Minto only as a force to be sent to Iran for use against a French invasion, and the Governor-General had virtually shelved the proposal on 4 April after discovering the military implications.[108] But in any case the army could not have been offered to Iran for use against Russia. Malcolm also disobeyed his instructions in relation to Jones's mission. The Iranians knew that Jones was arriving from England and were naturally inclined to wait for him in hopes of a better offer. Malcolm, of course, could hardly allow this. He therefore ordered Pasley to say that Jones was entirely under the orders of Minto and as such was no different from Malcolm. This, of course, was untrue.

The Iranians decided to play for time. Malcolm's analysis of their position was broadly correct. They wanted aid against Russia and it was now beginning to appear that France might not produce it. It was sensible to keep open the option of a British alliance in case France did fail. It was also true that the presence of a British mission was more likely to spur France into activity. Accordingly, they decided to try to keep the British agents in the south. Pasley was informed that the Shah had designated Shiraz as the place of negotiation, that he would be detained there, and that no British agent would be allowed to go on to Tehran.

Malcolm's bluff had failed. The purpose of his demand had been to force the Iranians to choose between Britain and France. Instead they had chosen to play for time. Malcolm was therefore hoist with his own petard. If he wanted to negotiate he would now have to withdraw his demand for the expulsion of the French. Even so, if he had had time he might have won when the Shah finally tired of Gardane's procrastination. But Malcolm did not have time. At any moment he expected to be replaced by Jones. Accordingly, he decided to bring matters to a head. When Pasley returned to Bushir and reported that he could not go on to Tehran Malcolm broke off negotiations and, with Nicholas Hankey Smith, sailed direct for Calcutta on 12 July, leaving Pasley in control at Bushir. Subsequently Pasley reported that there was a plot to seize him and, about 24 August, he departed with the military escort for Khurramshahr, leaving William Bruce in charge at Bushir.

Malcolm had not yet given up his hopes of shaping policy in Iran. Instead of returning to Bombay, where his wife was expecting their first child but where he would also have encountered Jones, he sailed directly for Calcutta in the hope of getting hold of Minto at once before his own latest dispatches arrived and before Jones departed. Malcolm anticipated correctly that Minto would disapprove of his own conduct in the negotiations and would attribute his decision to break off negotiations to a fit of private pique.[109] Minto did indeed criticize Malcolm for making the expulsion of the French a precondition of negotiation instead of the ultimate goal to be achieved, as had been intended.[110] But with impressive skill Malcolm had not only prepared his explanations but had formed a new plan of defence for British India.

Malcolm's new plan involved the seizure of a base in the Gulf. The idea of occupying an island base in the Gulf first made its appearance in British thought in the mid-eighteenth century and thereafter repeatedly figured in the recommendations of local agents.[111] Their concern, however, was neither political nor strategic, but purely commercial: their object was to discover some position from which they could conduct their trade free from the inconveniences to which they were subjected in their mainland factories by the political convulsions which periodically racked Iran and Iraq. At various times the islands of Bahrayn, Qishm, and Kharag were considered as possible havens, but nothing was done and the Company's factories remained on the mainland. The first suggestion of a political argument for a Gulf base was made in 1796 by William Eton, the former British Consul at St. Petersburg.[112] The notion was greatly developed by John Malcolm during his first mission to Iran in 1799 to 1800 when he supported the proposal for a base at Qishm with commercial and strategic arguments. Malcolm contended that the real danger to British India was of an attack by a European power—France or Russia—and that such an attack would be delivered through the Gulf. The threat could be

neutralized by denying a base to the European power and by establishing a British base on Qishm from which Britain could mount a block-
ade.[113] In 1800 Malcolm's arguments were opposed by the two British
agents in Iraq, Samuel Manesty and Harford Jones, who presumably
saw the probability that they would be subordinated to the proposed
British agent on Qishm. Wellesley showed no real interest in his agent's
suggestion and Malcolm failed to induce the Iranians to part with an
island when he raised the matter in his negotiations.[114]

Malcolm had resurrected his 1800 proposal in November 1807 when
he had suggested seizure to Minto. He repeated the idea in his instructions to Pasley who was told to threaten the Iranian ministers that
Britain would seize islands in the Gulf to use against the French.
Malcolm now favoured Kharag as a British base and argued that
control of that island would enable Britain to command all the shores of
the Gulf and contemplate with indifference the policies of the rulers of
Tehran and Baghdad.[115] In letters to Minto of 5 and 6 June 1808,
written before he received news of Pasley's disappointment at Shiraz,
he had moved a step further. The best way to gain Iranian co-operation
he then argued, was through fear and fear could be instilled by the
occupation of Kharag with a substantial force. Malcolm's persistent
advocacy of the Gulf Island strategy makes one wonder whether his
tactics in Iran might not have been intended to fail in order to clear the
way for what he clearly believed was a superior system of defence.[116]

Malcolm arrived at Calcutta on 22 August. He immediately set to
work to persuade Minto he had been justified in breaking off negotiations. French influence, he claimed, was too strongly established in
Iran. It could not be broken and success in his mission was 'altogether
impossible and hopeless'. He even added a little colour with a story of
an alleged Iranian plot to seize Pasley and himself at Shiraz. It is
difficult to believe that Malcolm believed his new account which contradicted all the assumptions on which he had acted during his mission.
It served, however, both to extricate himself from trouble and to
predispose Minto towards support of Malcolm's revolutionary new
plan, which could only be acceptable on the assumption that Iran was
inveterately hostile. The gullible Minto accepted both the explanation
and the plan in all its details.

According to the new plan, Malcolm was to return to Iran with an
expedition. Iran was to be given a last chance to accede to British
demands. But Minto had reduced his offers of assistance. He would aid
Iran against a French invasion only with a force of four or five thousand
light cavalry. The main British force would make its stand near the
frontiers of British India. Minto recognized that such limited assistance

was 'incompatible with any plan of permanent defensive alliance with Persia'. But in any case he did not want the alliance. An Iranian alliance was both undesirable on general grounds and on the particular grounds that the Indian Government could not contract such an alliance without authority from England because of the complications of Russo–British relations. It was in fact both hoped and thought more likely that Malcolm would find Iran still inclined towards the French alliance. In this case he was to seize Kharag and convert it into a base from which Britain would control the whole area of the Gulf. If necessary, he was to 'throw the whole Empire of Persia into complete disorder' by encouraging revolts; he was also to control Baghdad and Masqat, cultivate alliances with Bahrayn and the Wahhabis, and check piracy.[117] The Gulf scheme thus offered complete security and independence for the Indian Government, both from local powers and from its own superiors in London. Every desirable object was to be attained by the seizure of Kharag. Small wonder that Jones remarked, 'Sir John had a furious passion for the possession of an island in the Gulf.'[118]

It was the despised and forgotten Jones who brought Malcolm's magnificent edifice tumbling down. Jones was a man who was under-rated both at the time and subsequently. Kaye and other historians saw his obvious failings—his ambition, his intrigues, and his deceits. Unsavoury episodes were sprinkled through his career and were the inevitable concomitants of his struggles for survival and recognition in the jungle that was the Bombay Service. But he has not been given credit for his considerable abilities. Jones was a complex, highly intelligent man. He knew far more of the area, its people, and it languages than did Malcolm. Unlike Malcolm, he liked the Persians and Arabs and was prepared to conform to their standards. Although he lacked Malcolm's range and vision, he was by no means an unoriginal thinker. Above all he possessed one quality which Malcolm lacked; Jones could endure. At Baghdad he had had such a training in bearing indignities that he had learned to put up with them in silence and to persist in his aims. It was this quality of persistence which now allowed him to survive, to defeat the plans of Minto and Malcolm, and to change completely the direction which British policy in the Middle East was taking.

Jones had made a slow passage to India. The *Sapphire* had been obliged to stay at Cape Town to make repairs. He did not arrive at Bombay until 24 April (26, according to Morier), just one week after Malcolm had departed. Although Jones suspected the true reason for Malcolm's departure, he swallowed his pride and disappointment and agreed to postpone his journey to Iran until 1 September.[119] Even when on 25 August he received the news that Malcolm had retired from Bushir, he still waited for Minto's instructions. But on 4 September (Morier, 6) he received a letter from Minto dated 12 August in which he was given permission to proceed with his mission if he heard that Malcolm had failed. He then decided to go to Bushir and try his own fortune.

Jones sailed for the Gulf on 12 September aboard the *Nereide*, whose captain, a man named Corbett, was a memorable disciplinarian. Jones took with him his staff, most of whom he had recruited in Bombay. Of the two men whom he had brought with him from England, one, his unwanted secretary, Major Smith, had gone off to Bengal and the other, James Morier, a member of a family long connected with the Levant, he promoted to fill Smith's place. Thomas Henry Sheridan, a relative of the dramatist, joined him as Political Assistant from the Bombay Civil Service and Captain James Sutherland (Bombay Army) became surveyor. Jones also collected two young soldiers from the Madras Cavalry whom Malcolm had left behind. These were Cornet Henry Willock and Lieutenant Valentine Blacker. When he reached Iran Jones added a surgeon (Dr. D. Campbell) and William Bruce. He also seems to have been accompanied as far as Shiraz by another surgeon, Dr. Andrew Jukes, who was apparently dismissed for disrespect. Almost all the members of his staff were to play a significant part in British relations with Iran in the future and there seems no doubt that their association with Jones both helped to mould their attitudes and labelled them in the eyes of Government as members of a particular faction.

Jones missed by two days the arrival of a further dispatch from Minto, dated 22 August and written after Malcolm had begun to change the Governor-General's mind. In this dispatch Minto asked Jones to suspend his mission once more. Malcolm later claimed that Jones had deliberately hastened his departure in order to avoid possible orders to this effect.[120] There is little doubt that Malcolm had done just this five months earlier, but there is no good evidence to suggest that Jones knew of any change of mind. Jones did not receive Minto's letter until it caught up with him in Bushir just after the middle of October. Jones had landed at that port on 15 October. On 1 November he received a more detailed letter from Minto, written on 29 August after Minto's conversion to Malcolm's new Gulf base scheme. In this letter Minto asked Jones to remain at Bombay. Jones, however, had written to the Iranian Government as soon as he had arrived at Bushir and before he received Minto's first letter. He, therefore, replied announcing that he was already in Iran, and in correspondence with the Iranian Government and that in the circumstances he thought he should go on.[121]

Jones did leave for Shiraz on 17 December (Morier gives 13) and in so doing missed a further letter of recall from Minto. Jones's departure was due to what he considered to be an encouraging letter, written by Mirza Shafi, the Chief Minister of the Shah, which he had received on 20 November. Minto's letter, which was dated 31 October, did not arrive at Bushir until 31 December and was not received by Jones at Shiraz until 4 January 1809. Once more Jones decided to disregard the order. In the first place the situation in Iran was not such as Minto (acting on Malcolm's evidence) believed. Second, Jones thought that he would not be allowed to return to Bushir because the Iranians would detain him as security for Malcolm's good behaviour; rumours of the expedition had apparently reached them. Jones actually signed a bond making himself responsible for Malcolm.[122] But most important of all he took a stand on principle. Minto, he argued, had no power to control his movements because his credentials were from the Crown. As he said to Sheridan, he would not retire: 'principally for this, that by doing so, at this moment, I should proclaim to the Persians, that the Governor General is superior to the King; and this my Welsh blood will never suffer me to do'.[123] Certainly Jones always did his utmost to assert the dignity of his sovereign. George III's letter to the Shah was carried in a special litter, escorted by an officer and ten horsemen. A trumpet blast signalled each occasion on which the letter was withdrawn from or replaced in its resting place. When in camp the letter, covered by a cloth of gold, was placed under guard in the ceremonial tent and no one was permitted to sit with his back to it.[124] Absurd as this flummery was, the letter was the symbol of Jones's independent status. For all his bold front he was now becoming worried by his own disobedience and there may well be truth in Malcolm's comment that Jones 'was marching as fast as he could to get ahead of your Lordship's future orders'.[125] Despite delays caused by snow during a difficult winter march, he made much faster time than any previous Envoy. Refusing Iranian attempts to persuade him to negotiate at Shiraz he marched on to Isfahan where he arrived on 1 February. Two weeks later, on 14 February, like a harried ludo counter scuttling to safety, he reached Tehran.

Malcolm was defeated. He had done his best. He had been obliged to remain in Calcutta until the end of October in order to maintain Minto's new resolution. Returning to Bombay on 1 December he had thrown himself into the task of collecting his Gulf expedition, (which was supposed to have been prepared the previous spring) characteristically complaining bitterly about the lack of help from the Bombay Government. Duncan's 'life is spent in flying from one corner to another to avoid doing his duty', he wrote[126] But the real obstacle was Jones, and for him Malcolm reserved his strongest language. He was sure that Jones would not succeed. He feared, however, that Jones would allow himself to be drawn to Shiraz and held hostage against the abandonment of Malcolm's expedition. He wrote to Minto: 'he appears to consider any civil word as a positive pledge of friendship and to court delusion by a blind credulity.'[127] If Jones did become such a hostage Malcolm was quite prepared to sacrifice him.[128] The expedition was ready at the beginning of January 1809 and in anticipation, on 30 December, Malcolm wrote to Jones peremptorily ordering him to withdraw and announcing that in any event he would seize Kharag twenty days after the arrival of the letter. News from Europe came to Jones's aid. The reports of the risings in Spain and Portugal made it clear that France would have no troops to spare for India. Undaunted, Malcolm still recommended that the expedition should go ahead; a base in the Gulf was still essential for permanent security.[129] But Minto's nerve had failed again. The European news was decisive. He postponed the expedition and at the end of March formally abandoned it.

The same news from Europe which finally dispatched the hopes of Malcolm was a vital factor in ensuring the success of Jones in his negotiations at Tehran. The news of Arthur Wellesley's victory over the French in Spain was received in Tehran in January 1809, at the same time as the news of Britain's reconciliation with the Ottomans. The balance was finally tipped against Gardane. For some time Iranian patience with France had been running short. In November 1808 Fath Ali had given Gardane sixty days to produce results. That period had expired on 20 January 1809 and on 29 January the Iranian ministers had finally decided to receive the advancing Jones. Gardane left the capital on 13 February, the day before Jones entered it. The Iranian decision to part with France was made reluctantly and the ministers were determined to extract the best terms they could from Britain. The negotiations consequently had a rude and colourful vigour, into the spirit of which Jones entered generously. The Iranian negotiators were the Amin al-Dawlah and Mirza Shafi. The latter implied on one occasion that Jones was cheating. Jones lost his temper, called the minister 'a stupid old blockhead', threatened to knock him down, and 'kicked down the shades, overset the palzoozes and kicked the candlesticks about in great style'.[130] The Iranians thought he was mad.

One difficulty which Jones met was a relic of Malcolm's previous visit. Jones had been admitted to Tehran on condition that he agreed to fulfil the promises made by Malcolm and Pasley in 1808. He was disturbed and incredulous when the Iranians informed him that these included an unqualified offensive/defensive alliance; the assistance, without conditions, of twenty-five thousand, or thirty thousand men; one hundred pieces of artillery and artillerymen; twenty thousand muskets; and payment for the expenses of the Afghan campaign of 1800.[131] Jones did not believe that Malcolm and Pasley had made such offers and they were certainly not authorized to do so. One could dismiss the whole story but for the evidence cited above that Malcolm and Pasley had greatly exceeded their instructions and the revelations of their private letters that most of the offers had been discussed in a more limited form. In their desperate eagerness to achieve some quick success it does not seem impossible that they led the Iranian agents to think that some such offers might be forthcoming. Whatever the truth of the matter, Jones's task in 1809 was made more difficult by the need to reduce Iranian expectations.

The so-called Preliminary Treaty was signed on 12 March, although signatures were not exchanged until 15 March. Jones promptly sent it off to England by the hand of his secretary, Morier, who was accompanied by an Iranian Ambassador, Mirza Abu'l Hasan Khan, nephew of the prominent minister, Haji Ibrahim. Jones selected Abu'l Hasan partly because he had already gained some experience of English ways through his previous residence in Calcutta. Morier was to make use of his acquaintance to portray his Iranian companion in his famous character, Haji Baba of Isfahan. The treaty itself will be discussed in detail later. Its main clauses provided that Iran would not allow any European force to pass through Iran on its way to India and that if Iran were invaded by a European force Britain would supply military stores and officers; if Britain made peace with the European country concerned, Britain would offer mediation and if the mediation failed she would continue to pay the subsidy.[132] The principal point to note is that the phrase 'a European power' concealed a fundamental contradiction within the treaty. In 1809 the only European power which it was feared might possibly invade India was France; in this sense the treaty was a bargain for Britain, since without Iranian co-operation France could attempt nothing and Britain would never be called upon to supply any assistance. But the only European power which might invade Iran was Russia, with which Britain had no quarrel, once the brief scare of 1807 had gone. Jones was perfectly well aware that Britain and Iran were talking about two different European powers. His instructions had prescribed avoidance of anything which was likely to make the achievement of peace between Britain and Russia more difficult and he had done his best to draft the subsidy clauses in such a way as to avoid the danger of setting Britain against Russia in Iran. Nevertheless the treaty had, from the beginning, rich potential for misunderstandings.

Jones's troubles with Minto were by no means over and now reached a new peak. Baulked in his efforts to recall Jones, Minto informed the Iranian Government that Jones's mission was suspended.[133] Thinking that Jones might suppress this information, William Bruce, Malcolm's ally with Jones, sent a copy of Minto's letter to the Iranian ministers.[134] This bombshell was received at the end of April 1809. At the same time Minto refused to honour Jones's bills. Jones fought back again. He pursuaded the Iranian ministers to continue to recognize him as the representative of the Crown and raised money by whatever expedients were available. From August 1809 he supported the mission entirely on his own personal credit. One agent he employed was Ja'afir Ali Khan, a former Company newswriter at Shiraz. Ja'afir Ali later claimed that Jones had authorized him to make certain promises to the Iranian ministers which the Envoy had subsequently dishonoured. All Jones gave him for his trouble was an elaborate certificate emblazoned with Jones's coat of arms, by which Ja'afir Ali was appointed 'our true and certain agent' in Shiraz. The unfortunate agent complained in his appeal: 'It is true he granted me a Patent, the benefit I received for it was that whenever I showed it to any Gentleman he burst out laughing.'[135] Minto was unsoftened by the news of the successful negotiation of the treaty. He accepted the treaty while complaining about certain stipulations, but still ordered Jones to withdraw. The only bills which he would pay were those incurred by Jones in making his departure.[136]

Minto still wanted Malcolm as the British representative in Iran. Jones, he claimed, had lowered the importance of the Government of India in Iranian eyes by his 'injudicious and unwarrantable proceedings'. Only Malcolm's speedy arrival in Tehran could restore the Governor-General's prestige. Prestige was now the main issue for Minto. Jones's claim to be able to commit the Indian Government to an agreement on the basis of instructions from London was 'a solecism in the history of diplomatic negotiations' which he refused to believe that the ministers of the Crown had intended. If such had been their intention it must 'involve the annihilation of the powers and responsibility vested in the Supreme Government of India by a formal act of the legislature and by the constitution of the East India Company'.[137]

There seems little doubt that it was Malcolm who had manœuvred Minto into this fatal position. Malcolm had constantly denigrated

Jones, reporting anything to his discredit, including wild stories of bribes given to the Iranian ministers. It was such a man, Malcolm suggested, who had presumed to set himself against Minto. Malcolm and his friends also continually laboured the argument of constitutional impropriety. The embassy from London, wrote Pasley, was 'unnatural, irregular and preposterous'.[138] During his 1800 mission, claimed Malcolm, he had continually argued that Iran had no concern with Europe and had urged the Iranian ministers to limit their relations only to those European powers which had possessions in India.[139] This should still be the policy. He wrote to Minto: 'I can contemplate no revolution that does not place the agent employed in Persia exclusively under the Indian Govt. with common patience.'[140] It was with such feelings that Malcolm set off, on 10 January 1810, on what amounted to his third mission to Iran. He arrived at Bushir on 13 February. His secretary, Pasley, had already written to the Iranian ministers to announce both Minto's acceptance of the treaty and the impending change in the Envoy.

Jones's feelings at his prospective supersession by Malcolm may be imagined, and may partly excuse his subsequent conduct. His bitterness flowed out in abuse of the Company and its servants.[141] Particularly, he complained about the Governor-General. In a passionately indignant and revealing letter to Minto of 1 January 1810, he set out on paper some of his own abiding sense of inferiority because of his background, reiterating that he was only a plain man, appealing to common sense, and accusing Minto of wishing to reduce Jones's family to beggary. With justifiable sarcasm he wrote:

Amidst the singularities which have attended His Majesty's Mission under my charge, the following is, I believe, unique. General Gardanne has been disgraced by his Court for quitting Persia, and Your Excellency has attempted to disgrace me for procuring his Expulsion.[142]

Minto did have the right to give him orders concerning arrangements which involved the Company, but he denied that Minto had the power to dismiss him. It was plain that Jones was weakening under the strain. He wrote to Canning asking to be recalled and informed the Iranian ministers that he would withdraw if they received Malcolm.[143]

Malcolm himself was also beginning to lose confidence in his cause. He had left Bushir about the middle of April 1810, solacing his feelings by a still more mighty and impressive appearance. Like the elder Duke of Omnium, 'a retinue almost Royal, together with an expenditure which Royalty could not rival, secured for him the respect of the

Nation'.[144] But his faith in his mission was greatly reduced both by reports from England that the final decision was likely to go in favour of Jones and by his own total opposition to the Iranian alliance which he was sent to uphold. His old dislike of Iran and the Iranians became still stronger. He complained that they were more avaricious than ever and he bemoaned the cost of his magnificent mission.[145] 'There is', he wrote to Jones:

no country in the universe where truth is so totally disregarded, where the system of rule is at once so despotic and lax, where the ruled are so oppressed and depraved and consequently where the virtues of national faith, patriotism and morality are so little known, or at least so little practised.[146]

The whole system, he considered would soon break up. He wrote to Wellesley: 'it is my lot to be sent to keep this trash in repair, and to bolster and support a system which I have deprecated at every stage of its progress.'[147] By now he would have preferred recall, but he had no choice but to go on to the Shah's camp at Sultaniyah, where he arrived on 15 June. There he enjoyed a last victory over Jones.

Jones was completely taken aback when Malcolm's agent, Andrew Jukes, of all men, arrived to demand an appropriate reception for the mission. Jones had been assured by the Iranian ministers that Malcolm would not be allowed to advance until a decision had been received from England. Possibly the thought of all the rich presents which Malcolm bore was too great a temptation for them. A quarrel ensued between Jones and the ministers in which Jones admitted to using strong language. Foolishly, Jones allowed himself to be induced to try to dictate the form of Malcolm's reception. He presented a list of demands to regulate Malcolm's position at Court, even down to the playing of trumpets, the display of flags, and the position of his tent. His hurt pride was his undoing because the Iranian ministers promptly showed the list to Malcolm, who gleefully sent it on to Minto. By standing firm on his demands Malcolm forced Jones to give way.[148] But it was his last triumph. On 2 July 1810 the verdict of London arrived; the Iranian mission was to remain under Crown control: Jones was to remain in charge until a new Ambassador, Sir Gore Ouseley, arrived. Malcolm had to beat an ignominious retreat.

The final verdict of the Government in London was delivered, ironically enough, by Malcolm's old chief, Wellesley, in March 1810. But Wellesley was only endorsing a line of policy firmly maintained by his predecessors. During 1808 ministers had for once inclined to take the French threat seriously. It was not only Robert Dundas but even a statesman so apparently innocent of thoughts about the East as Addington (now Lord Sidmouth) who believed that the French designs upon India were both serious and practical.[149] Although the Spanish rising had finally ended the fear of invasion, the Iranian alliance was still made desirable by the Franco–Austrian settlement. And Jones had done all that had been asked of him in breaking French influence in Iran and securing the treaty. So, although Dundas originally approved Malcolm's 1808 mission, praised his ability, and urged Jones to co-operate with him, he did not hesitate to condemn Malcolm's subsequent conduct. Malcolm, he thought, had been wrong to make so peremptory a demand for the expulsion of the French, and he shared Jones's scepticism about the alleged plot to seize Malcolm. He also criticized Minto's attempt to prevent Jones's departure for Iran.[150] In a significant move, in November 1809, Dundas ordered Minto to pay Jones's bills, while Bathurst, who had replaced Canning at the Foreign Office after that worthy's duel with Castlereagh, disallowed Minto's recall of Jones and confirmed both Jones's powers and Canning's original instructions. Jones was to obey Minto's orders only when they were compatible with his instructions from England.[151] In his eventual decision Richard Wellesley, who replaced Bathurst, praised Jones's moderation and control under the embarrassing circumstances created by the conduct of the Government of India.[152] Coming from one who had been so anxious to support the authority of the Governor-General when he himself bore that title, this must have been especially galling to Minto and Malcolm.

Minto had already accepted defeat in April 1810 when he received the November dispatches. In a private letter to Dundas, written in the excruciating style of the pompous clerk of a bad solicitor, he agreed to withdraw Malcolm's mission. Jones was not forgiven, and Minto still demanded his removal. He had not only lowered the dignity of the Governor-General but had personally insulted Minto by the 'low and insulting scurrility' of his letter of 1 January.[153] Loyally, Minto still supported Malcolm, whose conduct had been 'marked with peculiar judgement, temper and ability. His general notions of policy in our transactions with that Court [Iran] appear to me at once enlarged and profound.'[154]

Malcolm's third mission had accomplished nothing of real value. The only important outcome was the collection of information about Iran and the surrounding countries. This information was to be of some significance in the future development of British policy in these regions, not least because of its jaundiced presentation of the situation. Malcolm had sent a number of officers by different routes to Iran. Captain

Christie and Lieutenant Henry Pottinger travelled via the Mekran; at
Nushki they separated—Christie went north to Herat to the wealth
and importance of which he was the first Briton to draw attention; and
Pottinger went by the southerly route through Kirman. Pottinger is
best known for his account of Baluchistan; his view of Iran endorsed
that of Malcolm: 'the very fountainhead of every species of tyranny,
cruelty, meanness, injustice, extortion, and infamy, that can disgrace
or pollute human nature; and have ever been found in any age or
nation'.[155] Captain W. P. Grant went by boat to Gwadur and thence
followed the south coast to Bandar Abbas. Lieutenant William Mon-
teith (1790–1864) who subsequently surveyed the Russo–Iranian
boundary, and Lieutenant John Macdonald (later Sir John Macdonald
Kinneir (1782–1830)) later to be Envoy in Iran, explored Khuzistan.
Macdonald produced an account of the geography of Iran.[156] Grant
was also employed, in company with Lieutenant Fotheringham, in
exploring the route to Baghdad, but they were murdered near the Iraq
frontier. The books of Pottinger and Macdonald, together with Malcolm's own *History of Persia*, for the writing of which he was given special
leave, were to become major sources of information about the area until
the next wave of exploration in the 1830s. It may well be that the
discouraging view which they presented of these areas helped to ensure
that Iran and its neighbours would be left alone.

The conflict of jurisdiction over relations with Iran had been to a
considerable extent the product of the personal views and ambitions of
Jones and Malcolm. Both had been able to manipulate the views of
their superiors by the use of their local knowledge. On the whole, Jones
had been the more consistent of the two. Partly no doubt his insistence
upon Crown control had derived from the fact that he owed his
appointments to Baghdad and Iran to the two Dundases and that he
knew that he had nothing to hope from Calcutta. But as early as 1801 he
had suggested that relations with the Ottomans and Russia made it
necessary that there should be a permanent Envoy in Iran, appointed
by the Crown and paid by the Company,[157] and he had taken the same
view consistently since 1805. Malcolm, on the other hand, had already
realized on his first mission that an Envoy needed Crown credentials
and both in 1805 and in 1823 was to take the position that he would not
go without such credentials. But in 1808 to 1810 he had done just the
opposite. His insistence therefore that Iranian diplomacy had nothing
to do with Europe and that the Governor-General's authority should be
untrammelled has a degree of inconsistency and surely derives from the
knowledge that his own personal position depended upon the support
of Minto. It was, of course, arguable that the purpose of Crown

credentials was solely to give additional prestige to the Envoy, but in practice it was impossible to limit the question in this way. This conclusion appeared in the official discussion of the problems that had been raised.

Although Jones and Malcolm had created the problem, they had raised issues of much wider import which were to have great significance in the future course of British relations with Iran. Robert Dundas, through the Secret Committee, set out the argument for control by London in two dispatches of 6 May 1810 and 14 February 1812. In the first dispatch it was admitted that the object of giving Jones credentials from the Crown was 'only to give greater dignity and weight to his mission, and not in any respect to withdraw him wholly from subjection to your authority'.[158]

The complications appeared in the second dispatch.

He derived his appointment directly from the Government at home, and although, in the conduct of his mission, he was referred for further orders and instructions to the Government of India, he was directed to correspond with, and taught to expect occasional instructions from this country, to which he would, of course, be bound to pay the most implicit obedience. His attention therefore was not exclusively directed to the Indian Government; he had conferred with the authorities at home, and was intimately acquainted with their sentiments and wishes regarding the objects of his mission. In proportion as he withdrew, during the progress of his mission from the Seat of Supreme Government in India, he approximated towards his and their common Superiors, and although he was aware that he had adopted a line of policy the wisdom of which you did not recognize, he appears nevertheless, to have entertained a sanguine, and (we must add) a reasonable expectation that he was fulfilling the intentions of those to whom he was ultimately responsible, and to whom he had appealed. Taking all the circumstances of this case into our consideration, we did conceive that it bore sufficient marks of an extra-ordinary character to justify us in deviating from a rule applicable only to ordinary circumstances.[159]

Dundas upheld Jones in his statement to the Iranian ministers that a Crown mission was superior to one from India; that was the whole point of the grant of Crown credentials. It was Pasley's misrepresenta-tion of his position which had forced Jones to make the declaration.

Although injured pride certainly played some part in Minto's viru-lent hostility to Jones and in his assertion of his own prestige, the Governor-General did have a point of more general consequence. The Company's Governor-Generals were always peculiarly anxious to insist upon the dignity of their own position and very quick to resent any reflections upon their sovereignty. The reason was sensible. If their claims were not recognized their powers of decision would be lost and with them, in a crisis, India itself. Minto was consistent in his insistence upon exacting recognition, as a revealing episode arising from Elphinstone's 1809 mission to Kabul demonstrates. Elphinstone had been persuaded to accept a clause in the preamble to his treaty which, by depicting the Governor-General as subordinate to the ministers of the Crown, was held to be derogatory to the dignity of his office. Minto refused to accept the clause, arguing that it was essential to the preservation of the British Empire in India that Asian states should consider British India as a sovereign state.[160] In this he went beyond Wellesley, who had accepted a similar clause in the 1801 Treaty with Iran. In the light of this attitude Minto's reluctance to accept that Jones could be independent of him is understandable and Jones's victory could be seen as damaging to the defence of India.

Although the official discussions arising from the controversy had begun to ventilate some of the issues involved in the struggle for the control of the Iranian mission, they had stopped short of the crucial issue. This was the question of which should prevail in British relations with Iran—the interests of the Indian Government in the defence of India or the interests of Britain in the European balance of power. The question had underlain the discussion which preceded the appointment of Jones, but had not been answered then and it was not answered after the crisis. By treating Jones's mission as a special case within a general constitutional problem the main question had been avoided. The answer, however, was implicit in what had happened.

The appearance of Russia in northern Iran had made it certain that European considerations would ultimately prevail in Iranian diplomacy. Malcolm's assertion that Iran should deal only with European powers who had interests in India was nonsensical in the light of events in Transcaucasia. Malcolm was forced to admit as much in 1810. It was impossible, he wrote, for India to check Russian encroachments in north-western Iran. 'The success or failure of such plans must depend more upon the state of Europe than that of Asia.'[161] Minto's own argument that the cost of the activities in Iran was incurred solely because of European considerations was one which was very damaging to his own case.[162] For the moment the issue was still confused by the war with France. It was one thing to make urgent arrangements to frustrate a possible French invasion of India at a time when Britain was at war with France throughout the world; it was quite another to defend Iran against Russia, when it was still hoped that that country would become once more Britain's ally in Europe. The first could conceivably be left to India; the second certainly could not. As later Governor-

Generals recognized, the latter contingency could be dealt with only by diplomatic representations at St. Petersburg, or by war in the Baltic or the Black Sea. Accordingly, the Cabinet must control British relations with Iran.

The Indian Government had emerged from the crisis with radically different views about the policy to be pursued towards Iran. Under Minto, Malcolm's Gulf policy became the preferred mode of defence for British India. In consequence the Indian Government became indifferent to the state of British relations with Iran. In the future the Indian Government was to adhere fairly consistently to this view, but was never to be allowed to put it into practice. London could not allow the Indian Government to act independently in Western Asia because of the possible repercussions which its actions might have upon Britain's European relations. Control of relations with Iran therefore was retained by London, with only two brief exceptions. By implication the primacy of Europe over India was confirmed.

The last consequence of the jurisdictional clash which remains to be considered is the effect upon Iran. Reference has already been made to the astonishing expenditure on British missions to Iran. Each successive Envoy found good reasons for maintaining a high estate. Malcolm wished to impress the Shah with the power of the Company; Manesty had to disguise the doubts about the status of his mission; and Jones felt obliged to assert the pre-eminence of a representative of the Crown. In fact, despite Malcolm's accusations of lavish expenditure and bribes, Jones's mission was actually the cheapest. The average annual cost was just under forty thousand pounds and Morier recorded how disgruntled the Iranian ministers were with their modest presents.[163] Malcolm had spent at the rate of nearly seventy thousand pounds a year—Jones estimated the total cost of his second and third missions at £262,000. The palm, however, goes to Manesty, who in the course of his unauthorized mission, which had lasted less than one year, had spent no less than £105,791. The mission of Sir Gore Ouseley which followed that of Jones averaged just over forty-one thousand pounds a year.[164] For similar reasons, each Envoy had insisted upon the most elaborate ceremonial. Whatever had been accorded to his predecessors had to be exceeded to mark his own superiority. The imagination boggles at what must have been the net effect of this torrent of wealth, these absurd formalities, and the unedifying series of repudiations and quarrels and their accompaniment of unmeasured abuse, upon the Iranian mind. Spectacular as Malcolm found Iranian history, it held no parallel to a schizophrenic Croesus. The first modern diplomatic contacts of Britain and Iran left impressions which were to cast an evil shadow beyond.

The Consummation of the Alliance, 1810–1815

This treaty is concluded by both parties, in the hope of its being everlasting, and that it may be productive of the most beautiful fruits of friendship between the most serene Kings.

Preliminary Treaty between Britain and Iran,
12 March 1809.

The Preliminary Treaty of 1809 had reflected the peculiar situation which had arisen in relation to Iran by virtue of the threatened invasion of India by France. The disappearance of this threat and the emergence of the problem of relations with Russia made the treaty an embarrassment. The main problems of the years 1810 to 1815 were to modify that treaty so as to remove its more objectionable features and also to carry out its inconvenient obligations in the manner least uncomfortable to Britain. The implications of the new situation, however, took some time to be appreciated and in the meantime the position was to be further confused by the mission of Sir Gore Ouseley.

The resolution of the conflict between London and Calcutta left Jones in charge of affairs in Iran, although he was not to hold his position. In 1811 he was replaced by Sir Gore Ouseley and he went back to England, not to receive the honours which he thought were his due, but to premature retirement. Jones had been right, but he had made the mistake of being too right. Before his withdrawal, however, he did develop important new lines of policy in Iran, both in pledging Britain's assistance to the policy of modernization of the Iranian army and in his work in relation to Russia.

The withdrawal of the French officers had left gaps which Jones had undertaken to fill with British officers, sergeants, and equipment. His work in this respect brought Jones into contact with Fath Ali's eldest son, Abbas Mirza, the Governor of Azerbaijan. For some time Jones lived with Abbas in his provincial capital of Tabriz, so as to be with him during his military operations against Russia. Jones conceived a strong admiration for Abbas, whom he saw, particularly by contrast with his brother, Muhammad Ali Mirza, the Governor of Kirmanshah, who hated European novelties, as a modernizer and an innovator. 'He may', wrote Jones: 'at some future period become the instrument by which great changes will be introduced, not only in Persia, but perhaps in different parts of Asia.'[1] Malcolm for once agreed: 'Abbas Meerza is certainly the first character in the Country and the hope of real and permanent Benefit from the Connexion would appear in a great degree insulated to him.'[2] Jones was particularly impressed by Abbas's recently formed disciplined infantry and artillery regiments, but Abbas Mirza's curiosity about Europe went further than purely military matters. Although his request to have the *Encyclopaedia Britannica* translated into Persian for his information, was beyond the resources of Jones's surgeon, Campbell, some articles on gunnery and fortifications were translated.[3] Students were sent to England for study, mining was begun, a printing press and an arsenal established at Tabriz, and fulling mills were also developed.[4] Abbas's minister, Mirza Bozorg, whom Morier described as 'by far the most superior man whom I saw in Persia',[5] revealed similar, wide interests. He put forward proposals for encouraging the settlement of Armenians in Irán, developing British trade via the Black Sea in order to break the Russian commercial dominance in northern Iran, and for land reform to increase peasant agricultural production.[6]

Jones's main work was in relation to Russia. In his own published account of his mission Jones claimed that he had urged Iran to fight on the defensive and to concentrate upon internal development.[7] His dispatches tell a slightly different story. It appears that Jones frustrated the possibility of peace between Russia and Iran. In 1809 the Iranian ministers had been considering cutting their losses and making peace; the French had already proved a broken reed and they feared correctly that Britain would also desert them when it was convenient. While on his way to Tehran, Jones had intended to encourage Iran to make peace with Russia, in the conviction that the release of Russian troops for the European theatre was still an important objective. Robert Adair, the British Ambassador in Istanbul, instructed him otherwise. Adair believed that British interests would be better served if the Iranians, like the Ottomans, continued their wars with Russia for the time being and thereby diverted Russia from any plan she might have to attack Austria.[8] Jones accepted this view and in May 1809 offered Abbas Mirza six months' subsidy if he would continue the war.[9]

Adair was also responsible for changing Jones's views over another matter. Jones wanted Iran and the Ottomans to form an alliance against Russia and to agree that neither would make a separate peace.[10] This project—essentially one to employ the two Muslim states to divert Russia from Central Europe—bears an eerie resemblance to

Napoleon's strategy of the early part of 1807. But Adair opposed an Ottoman–Iranian alliance for fear that it would make it easier for France to extend her control to Iran if she should recover her position in the Ottoman Empire.[11] No alliance was formed, although in truth neither the Ottomans nor the Iranians wanted one; the Ottomans regarded the Iranians with contempt and were indifferent to whether they made peace or not.

In pursuance of the new policy Jones helped to frustrate attempts to make peace between Iran and Russia during the years 1809 to 1810. During the whole period from 1808 until 1812 the Russians were anxious for peace in Transcaucasia and made repeated attempts to negotiate a settlement. With many of their troops diverted to Europe to meet the threat of France the forces remaining in Transcaucasia were badly stretched to deal with the problems presented by the Ottomans, the Iranians, and the rebels in Georgia itself. To defend adequately the vast front extending from the Black Sea to the Caspian was impossible and the Russians were obliged to relinquish any hope of assembling a field force and to disperse their forces among many fortresses.[12] Gudevich sought peace through the mission of Baron Vrede in 1808 and his successor, Tormasov, made a fresh attempt soon after he assumed command. In July 1809 he sent Vrede to Iran again to renew the offer of peace on the basis of the Kura, Aras, Arpachaya frontier and warned Abbas Mirza that reliance upon Britain would not help Iran.[13] Abbas Mirza's minister replied to the effect that Iran wanted peace, but the two parties found it impossible even to agree on a location for the talks which Russia wanted to take place in St. Petersburg. Jones opposed the peace-move and when war was renewed by the Iranians, Tormasov blamed Britain for the failure. Certainly the British subsidy made it possible for the Iranians to mount their campaigns into Azerbaijan. In February 1810 Tormasov tried again once more through another mission led by Vrede.[14] Vrede hinted that very favourable terms might be obtained by Iran if she would agree to negotiations. On 15 February Mirza Bozorg, Abbas Mirza's minister, informed Jones that the Shah had instructed him to make peace with Russia at once. Although this may have been simply a device for extracting more assistance from Britain, Jones was obliged to take action and he did his best to prevent an armistice.[15] After long discussions the talks failed, seemingly over the question of the Ottoman frontier, and the Iranians launched a new campaign which was thrown back in the summer of 1810.[16]

How far British policy was responsible for the prolongation of the war is uncertain. The weakness of the Russian forces may well have encouraged the Iranians to fight on in hope of better terms, more particularly since the campaigns were fought in Russian-controlled territory. But Jones's pressure and especially his use of the coveted subsidy must have been a factor favouring war. Whether the Iranians might have secured favourable terms if they had made peace during this period must be a matter for conjecture. Seemingly the Russians never wavered in their demand for the acceptance of the Kura, Aras, Arpachaya frontier which would have excluded Iran not only from the central and eastern areas which were uncertainly held by Russia, but also from Erivan which the Russians had failed to take, but which, with its substantial Christian population, they coveted. But it may be that if Iran had entered upon serious negotiations she might have been able to obtain some concessions and at least a recognition of the *status quo* or even the creation of a neutral zone between the two states. By fighting on, however, Iran was to miss a time of Russian weakness and eventually to lose still more.

The negotiation for a Definitive Treaty to replace the Preliminary Agreement which had been signed by Jones began in London during the first half of 1810. The Iranian side was represented by Mirza Abu'l Hasan Khan, who had arrived in London on 4 December 1809, bearing *inter alia* a letter purporting to be from the 'Queen of Persia', no less. Abu'l Hasan's social and amorous triumphs were matched by the respect which was given to him by a reluctant George III. Wellesley had pleaded that he might be given special attentions, including a Public Entrance, in order to demonstrate that Britain would not fall behind Iran in such courtesies. The King grumbled about the inappropriateness of 'Oriental ceremonies' in European courts, but agreed to the arrangements so long as they did not constitute a precedent.[17] Wellesley was less co-operative in the negotiations, however. The Iranians wanted two improvements in Jones's treaty. First, they wanted a firm British commitment to recover Georgia for Iran and secondly, they wanted an increase in the annual subsidy from the 120,000 tomans (£66,000) fixed by Jones to 200,000 tomans (£110,000). Wellesley wanted to avoid the first, awkward commitment, but was prepared to give way on the second, more particularly since the burden would fall upon the Company and not the Crown. The Directors accepted this 'most burthensome charge' with the greatest reluctance, and they stipulated that the salaries of the officers they supplied to Iran should be deducted from the subsidy. In return they asked hopefully if Wellesley would obtain the cession of Kharag or some other island in the Gulf.[18] Wellesley also wanted other changes, however, and for these thought it better that negotiations should be transferred back to Iran. For this purpose he needed a new Ambassador to replace Jones.

To lead the new mission to Iran Wellesley choose Sir Gore Ouseley (1770–1844). Ouseley was, like Wellesley, from an Anglo–Irish Protestant family. He had gone to India in 1787 to seek his fortune and, like many another, had found lucrative employment in Oudh where he had been given a military command, in addition to carrying on private trading ventures. He had become influential as an advisor to the Nawab Vizir and had played a curious part in the negotiations which led to the 1801 Treaty. It was believed that he had encouraged Sa'adat Ali to resist Wellesley's demands and the British negotiator, Henry Wellesley, had threatened to deport him if he gave any trouble. Ouseley 'replied that he felt extremely obliged to me for (what he called) treating him like a gentleman' and promised to try to help.[19] So he did, and there is reason to suppose that his change of allegiance was instrumental in inducing Sa'adat Ali to accept Wellesley's terms. The whole episode, and particularly the quintessential servility, is redolent of the authentic Ouseley as he became revealed in Iran. Ouseley remained in India performing services for Britain, notably in the 1803 Maratha war, until he returned to England in 1805. Henry Wellesley had thought him shrewd and an excellent Persian scholar and strongly recommended him. Richard did what he could. In 1808 he obtained a baronetcy for Ouseley and in 1809 gave him the post of *Mehmendar* (guide) to Abu'l Hasan. But Ouseley's appetite for honours and financial rewards was only whetted and he requested the post of Ambassador to Iran in a confiding letter which he vainly urged Wellesley to burn. 'The consideration', he wrote appealingly, 'of the possibility of my being refused shall not deter me from offering myself as a candidate.'[20] Wellesley's appointment of such a man is curiously revealing. In India Wellesley had acquired a high reputation as a judge of men, although his correspondence reveals frequent alarming swings in his opinions. He may simply have made a mistake with Ouseley, but it seems more likely that he thought Iran had such little importance that even Ouseley could do little damage. If the latter were the case he had made a grievous error, for in all that rich gallery of eccentrics who adorned the British missions in Iran, Ouseley stands supreme for his incompetence, vanity, and absurdity.

Ouseley's instructions were quite straightforward. He was to negotiate a Definitive Treaty and a commercial treaty; to collect information and to frustrate the intrigues of France and Russia. He was to be responsible to the Crown, but was to attend to suggestions by the Indian Government when these were not incompatible with his instructions from London. To avoid the possibility of a recurrence of Jones's financial problems, Ouseley and his first secretary, Morier, were to be paid by the Crown. Ouseley's diplomatic rank was to be superior to that of any previous European minister in Tehran during recent years. (He bore the title of Ambassador Extraordinary and Minister Plenipotentiary). He was to insist upon proper ceremonial.[21]

The one point of his instructions on which Ouseley fastened with unrelenting determination was the last. His biographer explains that it was considered important that he should raise the tone of British representation in Iran from its previous manifestations. Accordingly 'he was resolved to act from the beginning . . . as the representative of a great King, and the ambassador from a powerful state' and, consequently, 'was strict in requiring the honours due to him'.[22] Behind these restrained words lies the story of a memorable Odyssey. Ouseley spent the greater part of his embassy in scrupulously exacting greater deference than anyone had received hitherto; to believe that such dedication was merely in the line of duty is to strain credulity too far.

Ouseley's mission, apart from himself and Morier, included his brother, the scholarly Sir William Ouseley (d.1842), as private secretary; the Honourable Robert Gordon, brother of Lord Aberdeen and later Minister in Vienna and Istanbul, as attaché; two clerks (Price and Sindey); two majors from the Royal Artillery (D'Arcy and Stone); and two Indian army officers who joined at Bombay. These were Lieutenant George Willock, brother of Jones's companion, Henry, and Dr. Sharpe; Willock commanded the escort and Sharpe acted as surgeon. The mission was later supplemented by men from Jones's mission. Ouseley was accompanied on his journey by Mirza Abu'l Hasan Khan.

The leisurely journey soon acquired the irresistible Ouseley patina. The mission sailed aboard the *Lion* on 10 July 1810. No sooner had they left port than Ouseley induced the captain to accord him royal honours. The *Lion* followed the customary route via Madeira to Rio de Janeiro, where Ouseley was well received by the Portuguese authorities. Ouseley observed with insular satisfaction the effect of the reception upon the Iranian Ambassador.

I must also avow that notwithstanding the attention and hospitality I have experienced here I was not sorry to see that the great superiority of the English over the Portuguese in laws, customs, manners, police, arts, sciences, houses, roads, eating, drinking, cleanliness, comfort and real splendour did not escape his observation.[23]

From Rio the mission sailed for Bombay via the Cape. At Bombay, where he arrived on 30 January 1811, Ouseley paused long enough to discuss the situation with Malcolm and others. Ouseley was as impressed by Malcolm as was almost everyone else who met him and was inclined to accept the criticisms of Jones which Malcolm was careful to make.[24] He then sailed for Bushir where he landed on 5 March.

Ouseley's problems began at Bushir. He had previously asked Jones to procure him a *mehmendar* to meet him at Bushir. To his dismay he discovered that Jones had recruited his own former *mehmendar*, Muhammad Zaki Khan, and not a man of higher rank, appropriate to Ouseley's greater dignity. So he promptly rejected Zaki.[25] But this was not the worst. In typical Persian fashion, Zaki had chosen to spend Nawruz at Shiraz and Ouseley had no guide at all, but was left, as he complained, encamped 'on a sandy desert with my Tents constantly blowing down upon me'.[26] In desperation Ouseley decided to advance to Shiraz without a *mehmendar*. In this way, he wrote inscrutably, he 'established our national character and independence on the highest grounds'.[27] Alas, to his chagrin he discovered in the middle of his journey that he could not manage without a guide. In the end he was delighted to receive the despised Zaki and indeed, became so attached to him that when Muhammad Zaki was replaced at Shiraz by Mirza Zaki, the *Mustaufi*, the fourth-ranking minister of the Shah, he was quite disappointed.

There was a long wait at Shiraz, while Lady Ouseley gave birth to a daughter. The members of the mission took the opportunity to make excursions to the nearby Achaemenid ruins at Persepolis. Such visits were indeed one of the few useful products of Ouseley's mission, for they considerably enlarged the stock of information on Iran as well as the lengthy list of British names carved on the entrance arch of the Achaemenid palace.[28] On 10 July the mission set off for Isfahan, where it arrived on 29 July. Here there were further delays, caused by Ouseley's own illness, although his spirits were restored somewhat by the gratifying appearance of yet another guide of still higher status. This was Haji Muhammad Husayn Khan, the *Amin al-Dawlah*, the second-ranking minister of the Shah. Under his care, Ouseley set off for Tehran where he eventually arrived on 9 November, just sixteen months after he had left England. Five miles from the city he was met by a splendid reception committee and he was made the guest of the Shah himself.

At Tehran Ouseley immediately gave his full attention to the problems of ceremonial. He submitted an immense list of the various ways in which greater honours were to be given to him than to any of his predecessors. For example, he demanded to be allowed to sit five or six yards closer to the Shah than any former Ambassador. A long argument took place over what was the appropriate gun salute. Ouseley had carefully scrutinized all the details of the reception of previous Ambassadors and had noted that Jones had mentioned the firing of a gun. The discharge was presumably accidental since gun salutes were at that time unknown in Iran. Nevertheless, Ouseley presented a demand, which was naturally greeted by complete bewilderment, for a bigger and better salute. In the context of such refinements of courtly dignity Ouseley's presents came as something of a disappointment to the Iranians. Mirza Shafi, the *Moatemed al-Dawlah*, the first minister of the Shah, complained that the diamond ring, given by George III to the Shah, weighed only eighteen carats. Indignantly Ouseley replied that his sovereign 'was not a diamond merchant' and that in any case it was bigger than the one the Shah had given George III. He complained to Wellesley: 'In truth, my lord, the meanness and sordid covetousness of these people are quite disgusting.'[29] Ouseley himself was notorious for his parsimony; he spent nothing on his own staff.[30] In such affairs Ouseley spent the early days of his mission; three weeks were consumed as he argued with Mirza Shafi about which dignitary should visit the other first. And so matters went on intermittently throughout the mission. To the Iranians it must have been peculiarly galling to be placed in a position of inferiority which was quite unlike the conduct of relations at Istanbul.[31]

Even before his arrival at Tehran Ousley had had to deal with the question of a proposed Iranian mission to London. In July 1810 the Iranian Government had proposed the establishment of a permanent embassy in London. It had been suggested that the Ambassador, Haidar Ali Khan, should accompany Jones when he returned to England.[32] Wellesley had welcomed the proposal[33] but Ouseley certainly did not agree, reasonably enough, considering that the presence of an Iranian Ambassador in England would hamper his own negotiations at Tehran. Accordingly, Ouseley informed Jones that the Foreign Office agreed with his views and he asked Jones to prevent the departure of the mission.[34] Jones was surprised to learn that Wellesley had changed his mind but he informed the Iranian Government that their Ambassador was not wanted. Shortly afterwards, however, Jones received a letter from the Foreign Office which made it clear that Wellesley was still expecting the Iranian Ambassador, and promptly jumped to the conclusion that Ouseley had no authority to stop the embassy. He immediately made arrangements for a new mission.

Ouseley, who was then at Shiraz, was furious with Jones. All Malcolm's warnings seemed confirmed. He had already complained of Jones's 'spirit of mean jealousy and envy' towards himself.[35] Now

Ouseley concluded that the embassy was a private plan, hatched by Jones and foisted upon reluctant Iranian ministers.[36] He burst out with passionate denunciations of Jones. He had been: 'opposed, threatened and (as far as Sir H. Jones' insinuations could operate) disgraced in a quarter where the most suspicious Person could not have apprehended anything but kindness and assistance'.[37] He freely abused Jones and his policies. By August at Isfahan he had become convinced that all Malcolm's stories were correct. If Jones had not bribed his way to Tehran the Shah would have been forced to seek an alliance with Britain and might now be paying Britain for help instead of receiving a subsidy.[38]

The dispute was resolved by the postponement of the Iranian embassy, but the episode left its mark upon the state of British diplomatic representation in Iran. The division between the supporters of Malcolm and those of Jones has already been remarked. The antipathy which Ouseley now conceived towards Jones and all who were associated with him underlined that division and perpetuated it. Henry Willock escaped Ouseley's wrath because of the Ambassador's liking for the commander of his escort, Henry's brother George. But other associates of Jones were ignored, including Dr. Cormick, an engineer named Armstrong and his assistants who were engaged in developing industries, and most of all Thomas Sheridan. Sheridan, who died shortly afterwards, wrote bitterly of his solitary existence: 'it requires all my philosophy to bear it any longer . . . I am no Robinson Crusoe.'[39] In the short run the work of the mission was impaired; in the long run a pattern of factional disputes was established at Tehran.

Ouseley's first main task was to negotiate the revision of the 1809 Treaty. His breach with Mirza Shafi was now healed; he described the minister as 'the most sensitive and intelligent man I have ever seen in Persia' and hinted that if the Mirza co-operated suitable bribes would be forthcoming.[40] But his main discussions were held directly with the Shah, with whom, Ouseley recorded coyly, he was 'a little bit of a favourite'.[41] Ratifications of the Preliminary Treaty were exchanged at the end of January 1812 and work began on the Definitive Treaty. This was concluded by the middle of March and Ouseley sent his brother William to England with the new treaty on 1 July. Ouseley had not liked the Preliminary Treaty—it would have been better, he said, to have no treaty and he introduced a number of changes into the new one.[42] The most important of these, he claimed, was to make Abbas Mirza, as heir to the throne, a party to the treaty. It was, he wrote, the only way 'to make this (I must call it so) ruinous and unfortunate treaty in any shape secure and permanent'.[43] Otherwise it would die with

Fath Ali Shah. He said little about the rest of the new treaty. This part will be discussed later; it may suffice here to remark that he had conceded several points which went far beyond the Preliminary Treaty and which were to cause considerable alarm in London.

The introduction of Abbas Mirza into the treaty is illustrative of a changing British attitude towards the Iranian alliance. In 1809 the problem had been, essentially, a short-term one—to buy out the French. By 1810 Jones was already beginning to look at the alliance on a longer time-scale and to plan the future with Abbas Mirza. Although Malcolm would have preferred no Iranian alliance, he too came to concede that if there were to be a link with Iran it must be conceived as a prolonged effort by Britain. 'We are,' he wrote to Jones, 'mistaken if we imagine it is only necessary to give the Shah an impulse and that it will do the rest itself.'[44] The subsidy should be permanent so that a body of troops could be created which would ensure that Abbas Mirza succeeded to the throne. Ouseley saw the problem in similar fashion. Like Jones, Malcolm, and Morier, he pinned his faith in Abbas Mirza and long-term modernization; the vital need was to guarantee his succession. Like Malcolm, he thought this could be done by putting him in the treaty and by developing a disciplined army.

The question of the development of European-style forces in Iran is an interesting and complicated one. Apart from such early ventures as that associated with Abbas Shah and the Sherley brothers in the seventeenth century, the process may be dated from the collision with Russia in Transcaucasia after 1800. The first Qajar prince to adopt the fashion was apparently Husayn Ali Mirza, the Governor of the southern province of Fars, who used Russian prisoners to drill Iranian troops at Shiraz, even dressing his men in Russian uniforms, shaving their beards, and replacing their matchlocks with firelocks.[45] Abbas Mirza subsequently took up the idea and employed it systematically. With French assistance, he had, by 1809, raised six thousand disciplined troops and was rapidly developing his artillery. Jones had continued this work and it was greatly expanded under Ouseley. Majors D'Arcy and Stone and European non-commissioned officers from India drilled the troops; Christie worked with the infantry; and Lieutenant Henry Lindsay, (later Sir Henry Lindsay Bethune, Bart. (1787–1851)), who had come with Malcolm in 1810, worked with the artillery.[46] Some fought with their troops, and Christie and at least two sergeants were killed in action. The military effort continued until the officers and sergeants were withdrawn in 1815.

The complication arises when the purpose of the disciplined army is considered. Jones, like Abbas Mirza, saw it as the main army of the future, primarily to repel foreign invasion. Malcolm thought it useless for this purpose and persuaded Minto and later Ouseley to agree with him. Iran could neither be defended by Company forces nor by its disciplined troops; its best defence was 'active predatory warfare' carried out by traditional irregular Horse.[47] Malcolm's view derived principally from his Indian experience and especially from the advice of Arthur Wellesley; the downfall of Tipu and the Marathas, it was argued, was caused by their abandonment of the traditional light cavalry in favour of disciplined infantry and artillery. 'This pursuit [of disciplined and numerous corps of infantry] is, I believe, the mania of the moment.'[48] Malcolm's objection to disciplined troops in Iran was based on his belief that they were incompatible with Iranian institutions and that they would therefore be ineffective against European enemies; his objection did not extend to the formation of a small body of disciplined troops for use as an internal police force and it was such a force which he and Ouseley advocated. He proposed that Britain should give Iran a permanent subsidy tied to the support of seven thousand disciplined troops and artillery under British officers.[49] It was this for which Ouseley worked.[50] Had the policy been continued it must have established firm British control over Iran, driven Britain into opposition to Russia, and hastened the modernization of Iran; it would have done much of what was contemplated by the 1919 Agreement. The abandonment of this policy in 1815 was to have an important influence on the future.

The principal problems with which Ouseley had to deal once the treaty negotiations were finished was that of the Russo–Iranian war which had continued its weary course while Ouseley wound his slow way to Tehran. At his own request Tormasov had been relieved in 1811 and replaced by General Paulucci. Paulucci commanded during a very difficult period. Possibly only the inability of the Ottomans and Iranians to co-operate saved Russia from defeat in Transcaucasia during this period. In April 1812 Paulucci was replaced by General N. F. Rtishchev (1754–1835; Commander-in-Chief, 1812–16) who, like his predecessors, was ordered to seek peace on the basis of the Kura, Aras, Arpachaya frontier. In addition, however, Rtishchev was ordered to bring the Khanate of Talish, lying south of the Kura, under Russian protection.[51] In his task Rtishchev was aided by the conclusion of peace between Russia and the Ottomans at Bucharest in May 1812, an event which enabled him to concentrate additional forces upon the Transcaucasia front against Iran, but severely handicapped by the consequences of the French attack on Russia in June 1812.

The British attitude to the Russo–Iranian war completely changed after the French attack on Russia. Napoleon's onslaught made Russia once more Britain's ally in Europe. In Iran, as in the Ottoman Empire, British diplomats were instructed to contrive a peace which would free Russian troops for the war with France. Despite the claims of his biographer, it seems likely that the efforts of Stratford Canning had little effect upon the settlement at Bucharest which owed much more to the wishes of Russia and the Ottomans than to British intervention.[52] But in Iran Ouseley apparently played a more significant role in achieving peace. In effect Jones had sacrificed Iran to the Ottomans; Iran was to fight on as a support to the Ottomans. Ouseley sacrificed Iran to the Russians; Iran was to make peace with Russia in order once more to fulfil British ends in Europe.

In 1812 Ouseley persuaded the Shah to appoint him as joint negotiator with Abbas Mirza; he was determined, he wrote to Welles-ley in August, to stretch his powers to the utmost in order to procure peace.[53] The main issue in the negotiations which began at Aslandaz in September 1812 was territorial: Russia seemingly wanted the *status quo*; Iran demanded the return of all conquered provinces including Geor-gia, believing that the French invasion of Russia, combined with unrest in Georgia itself, would make the Russians more pliable. Ouseley thought a compromise was possible by which Russia retained Georgia, but returned all the other conquered provinces; he wrongly believed Russia had no power in these latter areas and would be glad to surrender them. In October 1812 he sent Morier to Rtishchev with this proposal.[54] The Russians rejected it, negotiations were suspended, and Ouseley and Morier returned to Tehran. On the night of 31 October the Russians attacked Abbas Mirza's camp at Aslandaz and heavily defeated his forces. In January 1813 General Kotlyarovsky captured the fortress of Lenkoran in Talish.

In the aftermath of Aslandaz, strains began to appear in the Anglo–Iranian alliance. The formation of the Anglo–Russian alliance (July 1812) led to the withdrawal of the British officers from active service with the Iranian troops whom they had trained. Mirza Bozorg, Abbas Mirza's Chief Minister, wanted to dismiss them altogether. Ouseley accused the Mirza of having a vested interest in continuing the war, but this charge seems unwarranted; Mirza Bozorg was worried about the territorial losses in the provinces for which he was respons-ible. There seems little doubt, however, that the French successes in Russia made him look regretfully after the lost French alliance.

The compartmentalization of Iranian government meant, however, that the misgivings of those who were responsible for the government of Azerbaijan were not necessarily shared by ministers in Tehran and

Ouseley found there a greater willingness to continue the effort to make peace. There were several reasons for this. The Russian war had become much less profitable for Iran with the Russians on the offensive than during the preceding period when the Russians had stayed on the defensive; previously plunder had been won on raids and the British subsidy had paid the bulk of the cost. Second, there were fears of internal disturbances and of attacks by the Turkomans and the Ottomans; troops were needed to meet these dangers. Finally, with the collapse of the Sadozay Empire in Afghanistan, new opportunities for expansion opened in the east.[55] In this atmosphere Ouseley was able to secure from the Shah a declaration of loyalty to the British alliance.[56] The declaration concluded with the words 'in short do in Persia exactly as if it belonged to you' and this is precisely what Ouseley sought to do. He pressed for military bases for the East India Company and for peace. He had, however, interpreted the Shah's politeness too literally and his demands led to a quarrel with him in the summer of 1813. Nevertheless the Iranians had little option but to seek peace.

In July 1813 Ouseley was made sole peace negotiator. His attitude was scarcely what might have been expected from a man occupying such a post, for he wrote to congratulate Castlereagh, who had become Foreign Secretary: 'upon the prospects of our being able to assist our good friends and allies the Russians even in this remote quarter'.[57] His policy was to secure peace at any price. In July he sent Dr. Campbell to the Russian camp with a proposal for an armistice to last a year, and in a letter to Rtishchev begged him 'on my Account give up to them some small portion of territory'.[58] Rtishchev, however, was inflexible; he would surrender no territory and grant only a fifty-day armistice to allow peace negotiations to begin. Ouseley persuaded the Shah to accept the *status quo*, providing an extra article was added to the treaty which would allow Iran to plead for the restitution of the conquered provinces. Rtishchev still refused; he would not accept the extra article in the treaty—only in a separate, private form.

Ouseley now came under considerable Iranian suspicion on account of his complaisant attitude towards the Russian demands. Mirza Bozorg accused him of merely wanting to make peace in order to be rid of the obligation to pay the subsidy and prophesied that Britain would refuse to pay the subsidy after the peace even if no provinces were restored. Fath Ali demanded an assurance on this point. Ouseley gave it to him on the spot in the form of a bond written in Persian. This bond was to be the centre of much subsequent controversy; at the time Ouseley merely stated that he had safeguarded the British position by making Britain 'umpires of the degree of restitution to be demanded and acceded'.[59] At the time, however, the bond won back the Shah's confidence. With his consistent support Ouseley superintended the negotiation of the Peace of Gulistan (24 October 1813) on the basis of the territorial *status quo*. Iran abandoned her claim to the Georgian provinces and Russia was confirmed in possession of the central and eastern Khanates of Azerbaijan, with the addition of part of Talish. Ouseley had done well by Russia despite Rumyantsev's suspicions of his role and he reported that Rtishchev had drunk his health and shed tears of gratitude.[60]

Ouseley now decided to return to England. He saw few prospects of further advancement and reward since the resignation of his patron, Wellesley, an event which he described as 'a death blow to my interests'.[61] His health was not good and the daughter born at Shiraz had died the following year. He had developed a strong dislike for Iran and its people and had come round to a view close to that of Malcolm. Britain would be better off without the Iranian alliance and with a weak Iran rather than a strong one. The defence of India could be better served by a base at Kharag or Bushir if a suitable pretext for seizing them could be found.[62] Lastly, he had hopes that he might yet, on his journey home, pull off a great diplomatic *coup*. For he proposed to return to England via St. Petersburg, a journey he claimed 'which is generally admitted to be the most dangerous and fatiguing ever attempted'.[63] At St. Petersburg he proposed to mediate personally between Iran and Russia. If he did not do so Iran might refuse to ratify the Gulistan Treaty and instead ally with the Ottomans against Russia. Also Ouseley thought he had found the key solution. When he read what it was, Castlereagh's blood must have run cold, for it was nothing less than that Britain should buy Georgia from Russia and turn it into an independent state with Britain as guarantor of its independence.[64]

Ouseley's visit to Russia was as absurd as the rest of his diplomatic career. He left Tehran on 23 April 1814 and crossed the frontier on 20 June. Morier was left in charge of the mission. Ouseley was handsomely received wherever he stayed in Russia. At St. Petersburg, however, he found a disappointment. Instructions from Castlereagh forbade him to make Britain the guarantor of any settlement between Russia and Iran, and to do nothing which might delay the ratification of the treaty. After that there was little that he could do in Russia. He met Nesselrode and urged him to restore to Iran the provinces of Karabagh and Talish, and in a private meeting with the Tsar hinted that conciliation would help. Alexander replied that he was always conciliatory, an answer which apparently convinced Ouseley that, but for Castlereagh's veto, he could have been the arbiter of a permanent settlement.[65] But it may well be that Ouseley himself was unwilling to jeopardize his pleasing reception by the Russians; the Tsar had given him 'the Grand Cordon of St. Alexander Nevski in Brilliants and thanked me in the most handsome manner for the services I rendered him in Persia'.[66] So he was not sorry to leave the business of negotiation to the Iranian Ambassador, Mirza Abu'l Hasan Khan, who arrived in St. Petersburg on 10 April 1815. In the meantime Ouseley settled down to enjoy himself for the winter at St. Petersburg, while continuing to draw his pay and allowances as Ambassador. Ouseley's haughtiness to his subordinates was equalled only by his fawning delight in the company of those of high position; he might have been the very model for Jane Austen's Mr. Collins.

His final return to England bore the inimitable Ouseley hallmark. His finely-developed sense of the dignity of his position led him to request a frigate to be sent to fetch him. The Admiralty refused and offered him a horse-transport instead. Much mortified, Ouseley refused this offer and was thereupon told to hire a boat and return to England promptly because the British Government would not pay his salary any longer. The details of Ouseley's diplomatic career were now coming under close scrutiny in England; in particular, the Definitive Treaty was being heavily criticized and the President of the Board of Control, Buckinghamshire, was seriously annoyed about it.[67] Deeply hurt by this criticism Ouseley complained: 'Certainly there never was a man whose unceasing exertions almost at the sacrifice of his life, have been so indifferently received, and whose acts have been so unfortunately misunderstood and hastily condemned.'[68] But he had to return to England where he arrived on 27 July. That was the end of his diplomatic career. In 1819 he was made a Privy Councillor, but his last career was that of Orientalist, in which he won considerable distinction. He was one of the founders of the Royal Asiatic Society in 1823 and of the Oriental Translation Committe in 1828. He became chairman of the latter organization and in 1842, first President of the Society for the Publication of Oriental Texts.

I have given so much space to Ouseley's absurdities not merely because they are entertaining, although that is not a bad reason, but because of their significance in the history of British relations with Iran. It is not only that Ouseley's incompetence was damaging to Anglo–Iranian relations but because his presence there is a revealing commentary on the British attitude to the Iranian alliance. That so fantastic a figure should have been sent to Iran and left so long with virtually no instructions nor any real scrutiny of his actions until too late indicates a profound lack of British interest in Iran. The defence of

India had ceased to be an issue and the Indian Government, which did not want the Iranian alliance, had been squeezed out of control of affairs in Iran. The Company was merely left with most of the bill. As Minto's successor, Lord Hastings complained: 'Without any means of curtailing the prodigality of the ambassador or of determining the propriety of expenditures quite unconnected with the interests of India, we are bound to answer the bills drawn upon us by Sir Gore Ouseley.'[69] Ouseley's policies in Iran were guided principally by European interests and these were very slight—he had only to tie up the loose ends of Jones's mission and to do what little he could in Iran to ensure the victory of Allied arms over Napoleon. What happened to Iran in the process was of little consequence to the Government in London. The notion which Jones and others developed of building up Iran as a permanent strong buffer was never of interest in Whitehall and gradually fell from view.

The grumbles of the Indian Government, of the Company, and the Board of Control about the state of the Iranian alliance focused in an attack upon Ouseley's Definitive Treaty. They thought it too vague, too likely to involve Britain in the internal affairs of Iran, and too expensive; they wanted to get rid of the subsidy as soon as possible.[70] Prodded by Buckinghamshire, the Foreign Office was eventually obliged to investigate the state of Iranian relations. It was then decided to refuse ratification on the perfectly accurate grounds that the treaty introduced new engagements which were not in conformity with the Preliminary Treaty.[71] Further changes were sought with the objects of limiting applications for British help; removing clauses which might excite Russian jealousy (for example that in which Britain agreed to assist in the establishment of an Iranian navy on the Caspian); and modifying articles which threatened to involve Britain in the internal affairs of Iran. This last object involved the elimination of Ouseley's prized Article 11 which made Abbas Mirza a party to the treaty. Article 12 by which Britain agreed to assist Iran to increase her territory, so implying an inintended offensive alliance, was also to go.[72] Finally, the subsidy was to end from the date of the Gulistan Treaty and all the Company's officers and men in Iran were to be withdrawn.[73] In short, the whole policy of British support for Iranian modernization was to be abandoned, together with Ouseley's wilder fancies.

To negotiate the new changes a special agent was sent to Tehran to assist Morier. This was Henry Ellis, Buckinghamshire's illegitimate son and private secretary, who had previously accompanied the mission of Nicholas Hankey Smith to Sind and Malcolm's third mission to Iran and who, through his subsequent service at the India Board and as

Ambassador in Tehran, was to contribute largely to British policy in the Middle East. On his way to Iran, Ellis encountered the Iranian Ambassador in Istanbul and for the first time saw a Persian copy of the written bond which Ouseley had executed in 1813 to persuade the Shah to accept the Gulistan settlement. Suspiciously, Ouseley had not sent a copy to England.[74] Ellis was astonished to discover that in the bond the termination of the subsidy payments was made conditional upon the ratification of the Treaty of Gulistan *and* (و) the restoration of the conquered territories. Ouseley later asserted that in the original draft, made on the back of the letter from Rtishchev in which the Russian Commander had set out his terms, he had written *or* (يا) and it was this which the Shah had approved. The error, he thought had probably crept into the fair copy which he had given to Abbas Mirza and upon which the Iranian claims were based.[75] Without the original draft it is impossible to decide if Ouseley was telling the truth, but the evidence suggests that he was not. The readiness with which the Shah accepted the bond suggests that it met the point on which he was demanding assurances and the *or* version certainly did not do so. Also that a diplomatist and good Persian scholar could make such a blunder on so crucial a point is difficult to believe. There seems little doubt that Ouseley cheated the Iranians. In any case the Iranians were sure that they had a perfectly good claim to the continuation of the subsidy.

The question of the bond left Ellis in a quandary. He was instructed to inform the Iranians that the subsidy had already ended nearly a year before. He put the matter to Morier when they met at the Iranian frontier on 14 August 1814. They then decided that they must take the position that the bond itself was not binding and that Ouseley had exceeded his powers in issuing it. This was a difficult position in view of the title and prestige which had been given to Ouseley's embassy, but they had little alternative, since they knew that their Government would not be bound by Ouseley's action.[76]

The bond remained a stumbling-block throughout the negotiations. The Iranian negotiators, not surprisingly, accused the British of bad faith. But, unlike Ouseley, Morier and Ellis stood firm and the Iranians eventually agreed to accept the proposed modifications in the Definitive Treaty. But they still refused to sign the new treaty without some satisfaction over the question of the bond. Morier and Ellis still refused to recognize the bond and in the end the Britons prevailed in the compromise which was found. The Iranian ministers would sign the treaty, provided that Ellis would return to England with a request for Britain to reconsider her position on the bond.[77] With this obvious escape alley open, Ellis agreed and the Treaty of Tehran of 1814 was born.

The 1814 Treaty formed the basis of British relations with Iran until 1838. The most important articles were numbered 1, 4, 6, and 9. Article 1 contained Iran's major obligations. By it Iran declared all alliances contracted with European powers which were in a state of hostility with Britain to be null and void. She undertook to oppose the passage of any European army into Iran or India and to refuse entry to the nationals of any European country 'entertaining a design of invading India or being at enmity with Great Britain whatever'. Iran also undertook to use her influence to persuade the rulers of Khiva, Tartary, Bukhara, Samarqand, etc., to oppose the passage of any European army preparing to invade India. Britain's major obligations were contained in articles 4 and 6. By article 4 the Governor-General of India agreed, if any European nation invaded Iran, either to send a military force to Iran or to pay an annual subsidy of 200,000 tomans (£110,000). This liability, however, was conditional upon Iran not being the aggressor. By article 6 Britain undertook, in the event of war between Iran and any European power which was at peace with Britain, to offer mediation and, if that failed, to pay the subsidy for the duration of the war. It was unclear whether this obligation was affected by the question of who was the aggressor and the doubt was to cause trouble in 1826.

Little consideration was given to article 9 at the time the treaty was made. By it Britain undertook not to interfere in any war between Iran and Afghanistan unless both parties desired her mediation. In 1838 this article became of great importance and inquiries were then made into its origins, but nothing could be discovered.[78] The article first appears as article 7 in the Preliminary Treaty of 1809, when Britain agreed not to take part in any war between Iran and Afghanistan except to mediate at the request of both parties. At the time Jones commented that the article could be amended if it conflicted with any engagements which were made by the simultaneous mission of Mountstuart Elphinstone to Kabul.[79] The article reappeared as article 6 of Ouseley's Definitive Treaty of 1812. Ouseley then mentioned that the Iranian ministers had raised objections to the article on the grounds that since the treaty specified elsewhere that Iran should assist Britain against Afghanistan (a survival of Malcolm's original 1801 Treaty) it was unreasonable that Britain should refuse to help Iran against Afghanistan. Ouseley, however, did not yield this point since Minto had instructed him to guard against introducing into the treaty any engagements which were inconsistent with the alliance which had been negotiated with Afghanistan.[80] On this evidence it seems possible that the article was introduced as an escape clause by which Britain could evade claims by Iran for help against Afghanistan. This argument is reinforced by the fact that Jones's original treaty was presented for tactical reasons as a modification of the 1801 Treaty which had grown out of the idea of using Iran as a counterbalance to Afghanistan. In this case it would have been sensible to have preserved as much of the old treaty as possible and to have introduced new articles to nullify the less desirable consequences of the old. But against this argument there is the point that Jones had no instructions to put in such an article and to have omitted it altogether would have left Britain greater discretion. On balance, therefore, it seems likely that the article was originally introduced at the request of the Iranian ministers, who in 1809 may have been concerned by reports of Elphinstone's mission to Kabul.

Like Topsy, the 1814 Treaty 'just growed'. It was the result of repeated modifications of the 1801 Agreement carried out under constantly changing circumstances. Wellesley's original purpose in Iran had been to give himself the opportunity to reconstruct the north-western defences of Bengal. Even when it was signed, the 1801 Treaty was out of date. Two quite different impulses had been substituted for the original purpose. One was the defence of India against France and the other was the preservation of the European balance. The first of these new impulses had also disappeared almost before the treaty was signed. The French danger rapidly declined and the Russian threat had never been regarded seriously. Minto himself had decided that for the defence of India he preferred Malcolm's Gulf strategy to the Iranian buffer. The second impulse lasted longer: first Iran was to be kept in the war to support the Ottomans and then she was to be got out to help the Russians. But by the end of 1813 Iran seemed to have very little to do with the European balance of power.

By 1814 the sensible course would have been to have terminated an alliance which no one wanted and which was increasingly an embarrassment. This course was not taken for various reasons. First of all the division of control and finance meant that one major impetus to termination was lost. Also certain vested interests had been built up which were attached to the idea of the alliance—most notably those men who were employed in Iran. But most important of all, Britain had drifted into the assumption of obligations to divest herself of which would have required a greater effort than to drift on. So a compromise was devised by which the re-negotiation whittled down the obligations as far as possible and the cost of the mission was cut down to the minimum. The subsidy was ended, the officers and sergeants withdrawn, and a tiny mission replaced the splendours of Ouseley's embassy.

The consequences of the decision to continue the alliance in this castrated form were damaging to both parties. Britain was left with still extensive commitments and neither the will nor the capacity to fulfil them. Ever since Manesty's mission it had been quite clear both that Iran wanted help only against Russia and that Britain never wanted to provide such assistance. Britain had agreed to do so as a quid pro quo at a time when her hostile relations with Russia made it possible for her to give such help, but now that the older harmony between the two European powers had seemingly been restored, Britain would help Iran no more. Nevertheless, Britain had done enough to rouse Russian suspicions of her intentions in Iran. From the time of Gudevich onwards Russian generals and diplomatists found it convenient to blame malignant French and British influence for their own reverses in Iran. Iranians fostered this belief for their own purposes. Thus, in 1815, the Iranian agent in Istanbul, Mustafa Aga, brother of Husayn Aga, informed the Russian Ambassador, Italinsky, that Britain was opposing closer contacts between Russia and Iran; that Britain had tried to prevent the sending of an Iranian Ambassador to St. Petersburg; and that when obliged to accept the embassy, Britain had forced Mirza Haji to select not the man he wanted, but Mirza Abu'l Hasan Khan, who would not act in accordance with the Shah's wish to give priority to links with Russia.[81] Russians, anachronistically viewing Britain's Indian Empire as essentially a commercial empire, attributed Britain's alleged desire to dominate Iran, to concern for the Indian trade. Enlarging on this, Rumyantsev discerned a British desire to dominate the Caspian trade, a mistaken conclusion, which may be seen to lie at the root of subsequent Russian policy in Turkestan.[82] This erroneous contemporary Russian view of British policy in Iran, seemingly confirmed by the equally mistaken interpretations of British policy in Iran by subsequent British historians, have provided the basis for a false interpretation of British policy by Soviet historians. Much valuable work has been done by Soviet scholars on this period of history, notably that by Professor A. R. Ioannisyan, but comments on British policy have been misleading; a predisposition to a theoretical bias has been emphasized by a failure in the interpretation of archival material.[83] That the principal ingredient of British policy was foolishness and not Machiavellianism seems to have eluded Soviet writers.

For Iran the consequences of her association with Britain were still worse. British promises had inclined her to continue a war she could not win, to miss opportunities to make peace and, finally, to conclude an unsatisfactory peace. Without a study of the Iranian archives it is difficult to be sure how much influence Britain actually had upon these decisions. It was once supposed that Britain had had a large influence on the Ottoman decision to make peace in 1812, but recent research has shown that the Ottomans made up their own minds. It may be that future historians will place more emphasis on internal Iranian factors. But there is one significant difference between the Ottoman and Iranian situations; the terms available to the Ottomans in 1808 to 1809 were materially worse than they obtained in 1812, for the Iranians the terms they might have had before 1812 were probably better than those which they obtained in 1813. Talish could certainly have been saved. Ottoman peace tactics could be said to have been in the Ottoman interest; Iranian tactics were not in the interests of Iran. Until new evidence appears it would seem reasonable to suppose that British influence did play a considerable and maleficent part in Iranian policy during these years. The kindest action in 1814 would have been to have turned Iran loose to digest the lessons of her expensive education in the intricacies of European diplomacy; instead she was encouraged to cherish further hopes of British help and in 1826 to return for a yet more expensive lesson in the same subject.

It will be useful at this point to anticipate some of the material presented in Chapter 5 and to consider British policy in Iran as part of British policy in the whole area from the Mediterranean to the Indian frontier.

During the years 1798 to 1815 British policy in the countries to the north-west of British India resembles a tug-of-war between two diametrically opposed considerations. One of these was the defence of India and the other was the balance of power in Europe. These considerations underlay all the distortions imposed by the contestants, whether they were members of the Cabinet or the executive agents in the countries concerned. At the one extreme, British policy in all those areas which were accessible from the Mediterranean was dominated by European considerations; the Indian Government was neither consulted nor interested. At the other extreme, in those areas directly contiguous with the British Indian frontier, Indian policies were dominant, even if they were formulated in a manner suggestive of a relationship with events in Europe. The true area of conflict is the intervening area. Of this area we can dismiss that part which was of little interest to either party, namely the southern and western coasts of Arabia. On the Arabian shores of the Gulf the Indian Governments were left to dispute about their policies. The crucial conflicts took place over Iraq, Iran, and Afghanistan, and it is possible to distinguish three stages in the problem.

In the first stage, from 1798 until 1806, the Indian Government is dominant and the main consideration is the problem of Indian defence; in London men saw no direct clash between the defence of India and the problems of European diplomacy. Wellesley, however, saw no threat to India from the north-west; the main danger to the security of the British possessions proceeded from within India—from Mysore and from the Marathas. Consequently he took but a perfunctory interest in the countries of the north-west: Iraq he left to Henry Dundas; Afghanistan it was convenient to present as a hostile power; and Iran was useful only as a diversion which would help to endorse the opinion of the threats from Afghanistan and France which he found it convenient to affect. Certainly he appeared uninterested in creating any permanent buffer system, in marked contradistinction to his policy in India, where he always built for posterity.

The second stage is dominated by the effort of Minto to create a system of distant defence in the north-west which would serve the needs of British India. Unlike Wellesley, Minto believed in the danger from France, and he gave his main attention to problems outside India. His Governor-Generalship is notable for the expeditions to Java and Mauritius and for the great surge of diplomatic activity which he directed to the countries of the north-west. Within India he did not seek expansion. Apart from his almost accidental advance to the Satlej, he was content to uphold the Cornwallis and Barlow settlement, and rejected a magnificent opportunity to overthrow it. Whatever judgement may be made upon his estimates of the threat to the security of British India, it is clear that the policy which he evolved in the north-west was shaped primarily by an impression of the needs of Indian defence. What this policy amounted to was a powerful, independent position in the Gulf, a buffer state in Afghanistan, good relations with Lahore which would permit the operation of Company's forces in advance, and, if possible, similar good relations with Sind. This policy was shaped by various officials and most notably by John Malcolm; Elphinstone would have taken it rather further and annexed Sind and the Panjab.[84] The distinctive feature of this basic strategy was that it was all within the capabilities of the Indian Government; by its adoption British India could depend entirely on her own. She would be emancipated from reliance upon other, more distant and uncertain states such as Iraq and Iran. Still more, she would be freed from the besetting complications of European politics. To make Iraq into a buffer state would have involved its separation from the Ottoman

Empire, a move which ran so directly counter to Britain's policy in Europe that Minto could not contemplate such a move. To make Iran into a buffer state involved all the problems attendant upon the question of Russia. In Iraq and Iran London must claim the overriding voice.

The second stage also saw the assertion of the second consideration—that of the balance of power in Europe. The growth of the realization that the problems of British Indian action in Iran could not be divorced from the problems of Europe can be traced from Manesty's suggestion of a mission to Russia, through to the final amendment of the Treaty of Tehran. In that process it is instructive to compare two dispatches which were written by Robert Dundas. In the first, in September 1807, he had made the defence of India the primary consideration and had urged upon Minto a policy of general alliances in the countries of the north-west. In the second, two years later, he renounced this strategy. Minto's policy of creating a general confederacy of all the states between the Jamna and the Caspian in order to defeat the plans of France and Russia was, he argued, based upon the faulty assumption that Iran was hostile. Jones's success in Iran had therefore made the whole system unnecessary. Iran was 'the great hinge upon which the whole system turns'. In addition the confederacy was undesirable because existing conflicts between the states involved made it unstable. Minto should look not to alliances but merely to the collection of information and the acquisition of influence. In the long run alliances might be possible, but for the time being, all that could be hoped was that the states concerned could, by desultory opposition, so weaken an invading army as to give the British forces a better chance of defeating it when it arrived in India.[85] Information and influence thus became a face-saving formula enabling Dundas to withdraw from his previous strategy and were used as such by Minto. The formula could not conceal the fact that Dundas had shifted the basis of his strategic analysis. Instead of a strategy based upon the defence of India he had adopted that policy which maximized the importance of European interests. The consequence of the London intervention in favour of the Iranian alliance and its related policies was to impose upon the Indian Government a defensive strategy which it did not want. British India acquired an undesired alliance with Iran, an unsatisfactory position in Iraq, no real power in the Gulf, and no alliance with Afghanistan. Only in the treaty with Lahore did Indian interests dictate the final form of the settlement.

The third stage, which covers the period 1810 to 1815, saw the loss of any interest in the area. Minto had never been really interested in permanent defensive arrangements; he had always been obsessed by the short-term threat from France. Now saddled with a system which he did not want he made little effort to preserve it. In London the Court and India Board sympathized. Financial claims again reasserted themselves. No dangers either from the north-west, or from the sea, or from within India, which would justify large continuing military expenses, were seen to exist. Accordingly: 'we are convinced of the absolute necessity of an immediate reduction of these (military) expenses, even at the hazard, if unavoidable, of some degree of security.'[86] The Foreign Office was not prepared to stand against this pressure. Ministers had never seen the Iranian alliance as a vital element in Indian defence, but as an adjunct, useful or embarrassing, of the European diplomatic system. After 1812 Iran was certainly an embarrassment and the Foreign Office were therefore willing to listen to the complaints of the East India Company that it was called upon to pay for a system of defence that it did not want and which was irrelevant to its ostensible purpose. It was in the light of these views that the British connection with Iran was brutally hacked down to a more appropriate size.

The consequence of the diplomatic activity of 1798 to 1815 was that no permanent system for the forward defence of India emerged. The apparent triumph of the Iranian buffer system was an illusion. In reality it was founded not upon the needs of Indian defence, but upon those of the European balance. The rival system of forward defence, which was designed in India, failed, partly because it conflicted with European considerations and partly because there was not enough sense of the need for a permanent system of defence to reinforce the short-term problem of France. The effects of the failure to construct a permanent system were to be extremely damaging when a new threat from Russia emerged some years later. When that took place strategists had neither a policy nor a *tabula rasa* with which to work. Instead they had the uncertain fragments of an ancient battlefield.

The Middle Age of an Alliance, 1815–1835

But the Persians are so perverse, so perfidious and so wanting in wisdom that it is difficult to calculate on their procedure. In matters of foreign policy they frequently act more like children than men, being alternately outraged by their fears, their petty dissensions, and their individual interests, to which everything is sacrificed without a scruple.

Macdonald to Ellenborough, 18 June 1829.

Too much kindness on our part has spoiled the Persians, they do not appreciate the friendship and liberality of the British Government towards them, or they would at once be glad to accept any article that promised them protection.

Sir John Campbell, Diary, 21 June 1835.

In 1815 British interest in Iran sank to its lowest point since 1806. The subsidy had ceased and the officers were withdrawn; only a few sergeants on special duties remained. Attempts by Abbas Mirza to recruit British officers directly were discouraged; officers on half pay were advised not to accept posts in Iran because of possible complications in Anglo–Russian relations.[1] Instead Iran was forced to accept French and Italian instructors from the debris of Napoleon's armies. The status of the British mission was also reduced. Morier and Ellis had advised that an agent of lower rank was preferable to a Minister Plenipotentiary with inadequate allowances.[2] Morier did not want the post: 'In Persia,' he wrote, 'there is nothing to attach the heart.'[3] In his place the Foreign Office appointed Henry Willock as chargé d'affaires.

Willock was a former Madras cavalry officer, who had been brought to Iran by Jones. He had served as Persian translator under Ouseley and had been promoted to interpreter by Morier and Ellis. His continuous service in Iran, his excellent knowledge of Persian (he was a fine Persian poet) allied to his abilities gave him more insight into the situation in Iran than that possessed by any of his predecessors and his reports contained much better information, despite the fact that his staff was so tiny. It consisted only of his brother George (another fluent

Persian-speaker) and a surgeon. Willock certainly represented the best bargain Britain had so far had in Iran. Unfortunately no one wanted him. The Indian Government was uninterested in the Iranian alliance and regarded Willock as a Foreign Office man vaguely tarred with the Jones brush. In 1818 Canning instructed Hastings: 'to continue to avoid all interference in the politics of that Kingdom and all interest with the King and Royal Family of Persia, beyond the interchange of civilities and general expressions of good will'.[4] The Foreign Office saw him as a necessary evil. The Prince Regent saw him as the source of an occasional bottle of Shiraz wine.

The main problems of Anglo–Iranian relations arose from the territorial settlement made under the Treaty of Gulistan. Britain had undertaken to mediate on behalf of Iran. Following Ouseley's perfunctory efforts at St. Petersburg, the duty was inherited by the British Ambassador, Lord Cathcart (1812–19), who returned to St. Petersburg with the Tsar in November 1815. Cathcart had no success in his efforts to persuade Russia to make territorial concessions. The Iranian Ambassador to Russia, Mirza Abu'l Hasan Khan, complained that this was because Cathcart did not try hard enough and asked unsuccessfully to be allowed to go to London to plead Iran's case himself.[5] Abu'l Hasan did Cathcart an injustice. In fact Cathcart and his secretary, Walpole, were among the very few Britons who pressed for a policy to contain Russian expansion during this period. In September 1814 Walpole advocated an Ottoman–Iranian alliance against Russia because of the long-term danger to India.[6] In a dispatch written in November 1816 Cathcart also expressed considerable scepticism about Russian assurances. Russia, he argued, aimed at dominating Iran with a view to opening trade with India and the idea of posing a military threat to India which could counterbalance the menace of British naval power in the Baltic. In connection with this theory he mentioned the Russian recruitment of Colonel Drouville, a former member of Gardane's mission.[7] The opposition to any British action came from Castlereagh.

Cathcart opened his discussions with the Tsar and with Nesselrode in February 1816. After some delay Nesselrode stated, in May 1816, that the matter would be referred to General A. P. Yermolov (1772–1861), Governor-General of Georgia (1816–27), for decision. In the meantime he rejected any British claim to offer her good offices, firstly, because the matter had nothing to do with Britain and secondly, because, he claimed, Asiatic states responded to fear, not reason. Russia, he declared, would never admit the mediation of other European powers in her relations with Asian states.[8] Russia had accepted

British mediation in the peculiar situation of 1812 solely for the purpose of concluding the Gulistan Treaty. While reserving the British position in theory, Castlereagh accepted the Russian verdict in practice and British representations were suspended in 1817 for the duration of Yermolov's mission to Tehran.

The announced purpose of Yermolov's mission was to report on the value of the disputed territory. On the basis of Yermolov's judgement Alexander would decide which, if any, districts might be returned to Iran.[9] Yermolov was instructed to do what he could to solace the Shah while surrendering nothing of importance to Iran. In fact, far from discussing possible concessions by Russia, Yermolov appeared to be, as Cathcart had warned, far more interested in extending the Russian frontier to the Aras river. Yermolov decided that all the districts which she held were vital for Russia and recommended that nothing should be given back to Iran. With a mixture of threats and flattery Yermolov gained the partial agreement of Fath Ali to this course of action, but the Governor-General completely alienated Abbas Mirza.[10]

Willock's attempt to intervene in the discussions between Yermolov and the Iranian Government was stopped by Castlereagh who instructed him to 'confine himself to the collecting and transmitting of the most correct intelligence, and to the maintaining to the utmost of his power the most cordial Friendship and good understanding between the Crowns of England and Persia'.[11] Castlereagh himself merely renewed British representations to Russia in 1818 and 1819 and then finally dropped the embarrassing topic. Far from assisting Iran, British intervention may have operated to the detriment of the interests of that state because, by exaggerating the strength of British influence in Iran, Yermolov was able to strengthen his argument that nothing should be returned to the Qajars. As for Willock, he had learned his lesson. Subsequently he wrote that he understood the duties of the British representative at Tehran to be 'to prevent the possibility of any discussion arising with Russia out of the proceedings of their agents in this country'.[12]

The Iranian Government had still not correctly interpreted the clear signals of the direction of Castlereagh's policy and persisted in the belief that the problem lay with the agents of British policy. In 1818 the Iranian Government, despite British objections, decided to send Mirza Abu'l Hasan Khan back to London, both to try to establish exactly what British views were and to seek compensation for the failure to implement Ouseley's bond.[13] Willock also reported that the envoy was instructed to try to persuade the British Government to return control of the mission to India.[14] Probably, however, this last was merely to test

Willock's reaction. The future conduct of Iranian ministers made it clear that they did not want to be returned to the care of an uncaring Indian Government.

Castlereagh politely brushed off the new Iranian approach. Abu'l Hasan's request for clarification of the British Government's attitude was met by a promise that a new British minister would be sent to Tehran 'with full Explanations and friendly Assurances'. But he was neither told the name of the new minister nor when he would come and there is no evidence that Castlereagh ever seriously considered replacing Willock. Nor did Abu'l Hasan obtain further British help against Russia. At Aix-la-Chapelle in 1819 Castlereagh made his last token offer of British good offices to Alexander, but with no result. In fact Castlereagh made it clear to Abu'l Hasan that Britain had no intention of jeopardizing her European interests for the sake of an Asian frontier dispute. The only success that the Iranian envoy could show was a promise that the East India Company would pay a claim of 100,000 tomans for arrears of subsidy.[15] Even this was unsatisfactory since the Company did not want to pay it. The Court did not authorize the payment until 1820 and then Hastings delayed payment. In July 1821 Willock reported that Abbas Mirza was 'becoming excessively impatient and importunate' on the subject[16] and in September Willock succumbed to the continual pressure and agreed to pay the demanded sum in advance of instructions. This promise was in the hope of persuading the Iranians not to attack Baghdad, but he failed in his purpose.[17] War broke out between Iran and the Ottomans and was brought to an end in 1823 only by Anglo–Russian pressure.

The Iranian–Ottoman war has a number of points of interest in the context of Anglo–Iranian relations. The British failure to prevent the war is a sign of the diminution of British influence; Castlereagh's lesson was at last beginning to be understood in Tehran. The war also represents the increase of Russian influence; as the hopes of British mediation declined, so the Iranians came to consider the chances of making the best bargain which they could with Russia. In 1816 Cathcart had suggested that Russia would try to persuade Iran to seek compensation for her losses in the north in a contest with the Ottomans and the evidence suggests that the hope of winning Russian support was one motive in Abbas Mirza's decision. In fact in the end Russia joined Britain in opposing the war. Finally, the war also suggests the distance which British policy had traversed since 1809 when Jones and Adair had contemplated an Ottoman–Iranian alliance against Russia. Now, in 1821, Britain failed to prevent a war between the two countries which earlier had been seen as constituting a barrier to Russia. Still more, after the war, when the possibility of an Ottoman–Iranian alliance against Russia was again brought forward, the British Ambassador at the Porte, Lord Strangford (1821–4), exerted himself to persuade the Ottomans to reject a proposal which might embroil them with Russia.

The crisis in Anglo–Iranian relations came to a head in 1822. Despite his agreement, Willock had not paid the subsidy arrears in 1821, and the Shah tried to extract them by issuing a bill on Willock for the amount, in order to cover a gambling debt. When Willock refused to pay the Shah accused him of having appropriated the money to finance his own private trading ventures and threatened the British representative's life. Willock promptly withdrew from Iran, leaving his brother in charge, and returned to London, in July 1822, hotly pursued by an Iranian Ambassador, Mirza Saleh, who had been sent by Abbas Mirza with a string of complaints.

The new Foreign Secretary, George Canning, decided to get rid of the whole embarrassing relationship by handing Iran back to the charge of the East India Company.[18] Not surprisingly, however, he did not state his true reasons, but disguised them by various arguments purporting to show the advantages of Indian control. Although partly bogus, these arguments are of interest for the light which they shed on the conflict of British interests in Iran. Canning set them out in a long letter to Charles Wynn, the new President of the Board of Control, in which he proposed that the Company should send a new, splendid mission to Tehran:

The objects of the intercourse with Persia are principally, if not purely Asiatick. The mixed character of the Russian Government as a European and Asiatick power, and the projects against India . . . attributed to the Government of France with which Persia was in the year 1809 in close alliance, brought Persia, as it were, within the circle of European politicks; and naturally suggested the consideration whether the Embassy to that Court might be more advantageously an Indian or European mission.

The events which have since occurred and the present state both of European and Asiatick Politicks seem to restore the question to the state in which it originally stood, before Bonaparte's projects of invasion against our East Indian possessions were in agitation.

Whether Russia herself may not have adopted and may not hereafter attempt to put into practice the designs which Bonaparte entertained and abandoned it is not now necessary to discuss. It seems to be sufficient for the present that it is with a view to India chiefly that a good understanding with Persia is matter of importance; and it seems to follow that an Asiatick mission to an Asiatick court would, for objects essentially Asiatick, be more expedient than the maintenance of a chargé d'affaires from London in competition with the Russian Minister of higher rank and allowances.[19]

The apparent belated recognition of the merit of Minto's arguments is misleading; Canning's true reason was disclosed in 1826 when he wrote that his object was 'not to strengthen but to relax the bonds of a most inconvenient compact'.[20] His policy was no different from that of Castlereagh.

The Company's reaction was mixed. The Court of Directors, despite misgivings, accepted the proposal, but the Indian Government, which was not consulted, was strongly opposed. India did not want to control the mission and the Governor-General, Lord Amherst, made a prolonged and determined effort to force the Foreign Office to reverse its decision. He pointed out that the Indian Government could not dare to oppose Russia on its own initiative. At the same time:

So important a subject as the security of the British possessions in the East from invasion through Persia by an enemy possessing the gigantic powers and resources of Russia must ever be an object of permanent consideration to the authorities at home. It must rest with them to determine the justice as well as the policy of dictating to the Court of St. Petersburgh the course she is to pursue with regard to Persia at the risk of war with Great Britain.[21]

His protest and his appeal to the value placed on the possession of India by Britain were in vain. Canning insisted that the Indian Government should accept control of relations with Iran. Amherst was forced to give way, but the Indian Government's views were still more clearly stated:

We would take the liberty of observing in this place that unless we greatly misapprehend the real nature and interests of the British mission at the Court of Persia, our intercourse with that state may be said to have for its object matters much more intimately concerned with European than Asiatic Policy. It is true that the preservation of our Indian Empire from the assumed designs of Russia is the chief if not the only motive which induces us to endeavour to maintain a paramount influence at the Persian Court; but it is equally true that this is an Asiatic object in name only and must in reality be promoted and secured by the measures which in the wisdom of His Majesty's Ministers it may appear to them in communication with your Honourable Committee to adopt. No effectual measure, it is evident, to counteract the hostile designs of Russia, directed from Persia against India, could be undertaken by your Government in this Country, without the previous sanction and authority of the Home Authorities.[22]

In the Indian Government's opposition to the proposed transfer new and important issues are raised. In the first place, there is a clear appeal to Britain's sense of the value of India and the corollary that Britain must be prepared to make some sacrifices for its preservation. Second, there is, reversing Canning's view, the assertion that Britain's European interests must inevitably prevail in relations with Iran and that therefore it would be meaningless to transfer ostensible control of them to India. Third, there is in the arguments of both Canning and Amherst the assumption that any danger proceeds from Russia. Although in their stated views there is an implied disbelief in the alleged designs of Russia, their consideration and employment of the argument shows the change which was beginning to come over discussions of Indian defence. The Russian threat is no longer the preserve of the lonely prophet, but the question has entered the centres of power. Nevertheless, there is still a strong suspicion that the importance which Amherst attached to the Russian threat was the outcome of convenience rather than conviction. For there is a bogus element in the arguments of the Indian Government also. Amherst did not want the Iranian alliance at all. He accepted the assumptions of the Gulf strategy; at the time that he made his protest British Indian forces had recently seized the island of Qishm in the Gulf and Amherst wanted to be allowed to keep it. For him a connection with the Tehran Government was an embarrassment.

The Iranian Government also did not want the transfer and for long refused to accept it. The Iranians were suspicious of the Company's designs in the Gulf; correctly believed that the Indian Government would be even less help than the Foreign Office in the struggle with Russia; and disliked the clear implication of inferior status. The Shah complained that 'he has ridden an elephant too long to submit to their setting me to ride a Jackass'.[23] But in the end he gave way, in the hope, as Willock wrote, 'that the good times of Sir John Malcolm, Sir Harford Jones, and Sir Gore Ouseley were to be renewed, and that H. M. was to receive abundant and frequent presents'.[24]

The chosen Envoy of the Company was Sir John Kinneir Macdonald. Macdonald was a disciple of Malcolm, who had himself been offered the post of Envoy in 1823. Malcolm had refused because Canning would not give him Crown credentials. Macdonald had accompanied Malcolm on his third mission to Iran, was related to him by marriage, and had adopted his political views. Over the years these had come to focus upon the Russian threat to India through Iran as a serious potential danger to the security of British India. It was especially the arguments of Willock and Malcolm which had wrought the change in British views on Russia which was noticed above. Macdonald accepted this view and thought that a real effort to check Russian encroachments on Iran must be made through representations at St. Petersburg, a course which was also implied in Amherst's letters.[25] But this was precisely the course which Castlereagh and Canning had found so embarrassing ever since 1813 and which they had consistently sought to avoid. Canning conceded that in the long run Russia might pose a threat to British interests in India, but thought that the day should be postponed as long as possible. If there were no other political questions in the world it might be advisable to take precautionary measures and to warn Britain and Russia of the danger. 'But it is quite another question whether a war with Russia in Europe would be a proper price to pay for this system of early precautions.'[26] Once again Indian and European interests had come into conflict and once more Canning had asserted the pre-eminence of European interests. His European policy was based upon securing the co-operation of Russia in the settlement of the Greek question and he was not going to endanger that for the defence of India. So much indeed for the argument, advanced by C. W. Crawley and others, that British policy in the Greek question was based upon the defence of the routes to India. It was instead rooted in the balance of European power which for Canning was always of primary concern. He might call in the New World to redress the balance of the Old, but he would never jeopardize the balance of the Old for the prospects of the Third World.

The long argument between London, India, and Tehran consumed so much time that Macdonald did not reach the Shah's camp until 3 September 1826, by which time Russia and Iran were again at war. The war was the outcome of the continued territorial disputes which had arisen from Gulistan. The new frontier had never been defined on the ground and the Iranians accused the Russians of wrongly occupying the district of Gokcheh. Attempts to persuade Russia to withdraw failed; the Russians would not receive an Iranian envoy and gave their own special Envoy to Tehran in 1826, Prince Menshikov, no authority to discuss the question; Willock's attempt to mediate failed. Finally, under strong pressure from religious groups, the Shah was almost compelled to order an attack on the Russian forces.[27]

Macdonald was immediately confronted with a demand for British assistance under the Treaty of Tehran. The Iranians claimed that the Russian occupation of Gokcheh constituted aggression. Under article 4 of the 1814 Treaty this gave them a claim to the subsidy, and under article 6 to mediation. Macdonald promptly temporized. Although he believed the Iranian claim was well founded, yet he foresaw the likelihood that to pay the subsidy would be regarded as an act of outright hostility by Russia.[28] Meanwhile he dissuaded the Shah from sending his own Ambassador to put the Iranian case in London and sent Willock instead.[29]

The question was decided not by the responsible minister, the President of the India Board, Charles Wynn (1775–1850), but by Canning. Wynn, a weak personality, despised by Canning and the Directors, who owed his appointment to his Grenville connections, was inclined to agree that Russia was the aggressor, but Canning brusquely overruled him. 'I am sorry (or rather I am happy) to say that I cannot agree with you in thinking that the *Casus Foederis* has occurred under the last of the incredibly foolish treaties of which I enclose copies.'[30] Russia's occupation of Gokcheh was not aggression, but merely an encroachment to be discussed and which could not justify the Iranian attack. Canning refused either to pay the subsidy or to mediate. He argued that under article 6 the obligation to mediate was dependent upon Iran being the victim of aggression.[31] 'Mr. Canning', wrote Malcolm, 'appears . . . most anxious to shake off Persia.'[32] With justice, Wellington disagreed with Canning's curious interpretation of the treaty and, most reluctantly, Canning was persuaded to broach the subject of mediation with the Russian Ambassador, Prince Lieven, at Brighton in January 1827. Following his usual practice he first showed Lieven the draft of his proposed note and when Lieven appeared unresponsive Canning hastily dropped the subject. He wrote to Wynn: 'My own private opinion is certainly that Russia is right and that if I were in her place, I would when England began to talk of her treaty with Persia, send a General with a name ending in off or oursky to make a treaty with the King of Oude.'[33] Lieven's reply came in a confidential memorandum given to Canning on 26 February 1827 and its contents justified Canning's fears. Russia declined British mediation and stated that it was a principle of Russian policy not to admit the interference of other powers in Russian relations with Asiatic powers. The 1814 Treaty of Tehran and, by implication, Britain were held to be probably responsible for Iranian aggression, as Iran expected to receive the subsidy apparently promised by the treaty. The memorandum concluded with a conventional renunciation of 'aucunes vues ambitieuses'.[34] After this Canning did not again raise the question of British good offices (for to this more humble role had mediation declined) until the summer of 1827. By that time they consisted of no more than an effort, similar to that of Ouseley, to induce Iran to accept Russia's terms. This duty was carried out with considerable devotion so that the terms obtained exceeded even the expectations of Russia.

Iran lost the war which had begun in July 1826 with considerable success for her arms. A strangely nervous Yermolov was replaced by General I. F. Paskevich (1782–1856). In September 1826 the tide turned against Iran and in 1827 Paskevich captured Erivan and Nakhchivan, and another Russian force occupied Abbas Mirza's provincial capital of Tabriz (13 October 1827). The Iranians were obliged to sue for peace which was concluded, with British assistance, at Turkomanchai (9/22 February 1828). By this agreement Iran ceded to Russia the provinces of Erivan and Nakhchivan, thereby firmly establishing the Russian frontier on the coveted Aras. Paskevich would have retained the Iranian province of Azerbaijan as well, but possibly fearing that such an appetite for conquest might provoke a European reaction, his Government overruled him. Had the Iranians continued the war Russian policy was to break Azerbaijan into separate independent Khanates, but not to annex the province.[35] But a continuation of the war would have been an embarrassment to Russia because the forces were needed for the war against the Ottomans which was declared in March 1828. By the Treaty of Turkomanchai Russia also acquired other advantages including the right to nominate Consuls wherever they were required and Iran agreed to pay an indemnity of five million tomans (twenty million roubles or three million, five hundred thousand pounds).[36]

The indemnity imposed upon Iran provided Britain with an opportunity to rid herself of the last of her embarrassing obligations under the 1814 Treaty. The Shah needed money desperately; Russian troops were in occupation of most of Azerbaijan and would not depart until a substantial portion of the indemnity was paid. The idea that this was a chance to purchase the abrogation of the subsidy clauses appears to have occurred to Macdonald and Wynn simultaneously in the autumn of 1827, and in 1828 the Iranian Government accepted an offer of two hundred thousand tomans for that purpose.

No sooner had the Iranians agreed to the disembowelling of the treaty than they regretted it. With what seems a pathetic faith in so obviously ineffective an alliance they sought to keep it in being. The Iranian Government refused to ratify the abrogation agreement and offered to repay the money. Abbas Mirza actually deposited the sum in the British treasury. Further, the Iranians were prepared to agree to a revision of the treaty if Britain found the old subsidy articles unacceptable. They would replace them with a single article taking the form of a general declaration that if Iran were attacked by a European country which was at war with Britain, Britain would assist her with a military force or with money; or, if the European country concerned was not at war with Britain, Britain would offer mediation instead.[37]

Macdonald had a long and often comic battle to obtain his ends. Although he personally favoured the Iranian proposal, he was determined to secure the ratification of the abrogation. He agreed to put forward the proposed new article only if Iran would first abrogate the old. The Shah finally agreed to ratify, but then Abbas Mirza refused to surrender the ratification. When at last Abbas agreed to hand it over Macdonald could not persuade the Iranian ministers concerned to draw up the necessary documents. On one occasion Macdonald arranged a meeting to complete the work. The ministers first asked for food and sat at the British Envoy's table for three hours; Abbas Mirza's principal minister, the *Qa'im maqam*, Mirza Abu'l Qasim Khan, composed poetry. When at last the minister (who was in fact a most distinguished Persian poet) agreed to desist and attend to the transfer, he suddenly discovered that he had forgotten his spectacles. The resourceful Macdonald lent him a pair, and at last the *Qa'im maqam* began to write out the agreement. While he was so engaged Macdonald went out for ten minutes with the other minister, Mirza Abu'l Hasan Khan, to look at some horses. When they returned the *Qa'im maqam* had gone.[38] In the end Abbas Mirza gave up the ratification only when Russian pressure for the payment of the war indemnity forced him to withdraw the money which he had deposited with Macdonald. Needless to say, the British Government did not take up the question of the new article.

The events of 1826 to 1828 had provided further confirmation of the trend which had been visible in British policy towards Iran since 1813. The failure to support Iran in 1826 and the evisceration of the treaty in 1828 had shown that Canning's new basis for relations was a fraud. All that his action had done was to abet the persistent self-deception of the Iranian ministers. But now changes in the style and character of the British mission demonstrated finally that British interest in Iran was minimal.

The first obvious demonstration of British indifference was a drastic reduction in the scale of the mission. In 1823 Canning had not only deceived Iran but also the Court of Directors. Under the impression that the transfer was part of a striking new initiative in Iran the Directors had authorized an establishment equivalent to that of a first-class Residency in India. The subsequent revelation of Canning's true views persuaded the Directors to include the Iranian mission in the general economy drive which preceded the abolition of the China trade monopoly. Between 1809 and 1828 Britain had spent a total of between three and four million pounds in Iran; the level of expenditure was now drastically reduced. In 1827 Macdonald was told to reduce expenses to £1,000 a month. In 1829 members' allowances were reduced and the escort withdrawn. Macdonald protested at the reductions, and particularly at the threat to the detachment of officers and sergeants which he had brought with him to train the Iranian army. If these were withdrawn, he complained, their place would be filled by Russians.[39] In fact Macdonald probably exaggerated the significance of the detachment. Because of the Russo–Iranian hostilities it had scarcely been employed and the sergeants were usually drunk. The only man of influence was Captain Hart, who commanded Abbas Mirza's army and had acquired some personal influence in Azerbaijan. In 1829 there was indeed a proposal that he should become the paymaster of the army, receiving assignments of provincial revenues for this purpose. If this proposal had been accepted no doubt there would have been a considerable increase of British influence, but Ellenborough, now at the Board of Control, rejected it because of the problems of expense and involvement in internal affairs.[40] Hart died in 1830, at the same time as Macdonald, and no British officer inherited his personal influence. Fearing the dispatch of yet another Iranian embassy to London, the Foreign Office sought to stem the economy drive, but although it was briefly halted by Ellenborough, its momentum continued. After Macdonald's death in June 1830 the expenses of the mission were further reduced and the new Envoy was allowed to give none of the traditional presents to mark his appointment. Fath Ali complained bitterly: 'They do what they like now. They think the waters have passed over me.'[41]

The decline of British prestige was accelerated by new troubles within the mission. Macdonald was an indifferent Envoy. His vanity was hurt by his humiliating position. The style of his dispatches was one calculated to infuriate their recipients. His judgement was poor; even as late as January 1830 he still wrote of the unshakeable ascendancy of Britain in Iran and particularly of his own personal influence.[42] This must have puzzled those of his readers who recalled the dispatch of December 1828 in which he wrote of 'the perennial ascendancy of Russia'. But this earlier dispatch had been written primarily with a view to supporting his claim for credentials from the Crown, without which he felt he was greatly handicapped in opposing Russian influence. In fact Macdonald was a victim of what may be called the rational fallacy of British policy in Iran. According to this analysis, Russia was the natural enemy of Iran and therefore Iran would always prefer an alliance with Britain to one with Russia. Consequently, it was unnecessary and even undesirable for Britain to do much in Iran. Macdonald shared Malcolm's convictions concerning the unreliability of Iranians. He constantly complained of their perfidy and foolishness and even included Abbas Mirza—'a wretched devil on whom it would be folly to place dependence'—in his condemnations.[43] All that Britain needed to do was to assist Abbas Mirza to build up a force which would establish internal security and, beyond that, to insert into the 1814 Treaty a general article which would satisfy the Iranian desire for protection. If these measures failed Britain should abandon the Iranian buffer policy and instead neutralize its power by disrupting the south.[44] In other words Macdonald was veering back to the Gulf strategy.

Whatever the deficiencies of Macdonald, they did not compare with those of his successor, John Campbell (1799–1870). Campbell was vain, untruthful, and possessed an ungovernable temper. He insulted and disgusted every Iranian at court and quarrelled with members of the mission including Colonel Passmore, who succeeded Hart as Commander of the detachment. It is true that the full details of Campbell's unsuitability emerged only gradually through the complaints of Iranian ministers, private letters, and the report of a special British agent. But it is also clear that there were grave doubts about his fitness even at the time of his appointment. The circumstances of this appointment and the long duration of his service in Iran shed some light on the nature of British relations with Iran in this period.

When Macdonald died the obvious successor was Henry Willock, who had remained in Iran to serve as first assistant to Macdonald. Willock, who was not a rich man, certainly wanted the post. But although he had some supporters in the Calcutta Secretariat and others in England, including Henry Ellis at the India Board and relatives who were Foreign Office clerks, he was opposed by the influential Malcolm faction. Malcolm, now Governor of Bombay, wrote to the Governor-General, Lord William Bentinck, that Willock 'has neither ability nor manliness, but is a flatterer and an intriguer'.[45] Macdonald had also done his best to get rid of Willock, complaining that their views differed so widely that it was difficult for them to work together.[46] Shortly before Macdonald's death, Willock had been recalled and as a result, although Willock had not left Iran at the time, it was Campbell, the former second assistant, who took charge of the mission, with Dr. John McNeill, the former surgeon to the mission, as his assistant. The two Willocks returned to England in disgust. There seems little doubt that the path had been deliberately cleared for Campbell. Through the Pasley family he was related both to Malcolm and Macdonald and possessed a still more powerful supporter in the person of his father, Sir Robert Campbell, Chairman of the Court of Directors in 1831.

Although Campbell was now in control of the mission, he still needed confirmation of his position. The constitutional position regarding the appointment of a new Envoy was clear; it was a matter for the Governor-General. Bentinck, however, did not propose to exercise his right to make the appointment. Like Amherst, he believed that the appointment should be made from London, because of the connection of Iranian diplomacy with Europe, the facility of more rapid communications between London and Tehran, and the fact that only European intervention could save Iran.[47] His letter to Ellenborough setting out his reasons crossed a similar letter written by Ellenborough, whose views on policy were sharpened by fears that Bentinck might appoint Willock. But Ellenborough's distinguished choices (Mountstuart Elphinstone and Richard Jenkins, both of whom had made their names under Wellesley) refused the post. In addition the Court intervened to point out that constitutionally Bentinck should make the choice. Accordingly, Bentinck offered the post to the able Captain Josiah Stewart who had accompanied Malcolm on his third mission and was then Resident at Gwalior, but he too refused the post because of the reduction in allowances.

Finally, Bentinck appointed Campbell, almost certainly to oblige his father who had induced the new President of the India Board, Charles Grant, to agree. In July 1831 there had been a long debate on the subject of the Iranian mission at India House. There were wide differences of opinion and the upshot was that the decision had been left to Bentinck with a broad hint—'in compliance with your desire to have some information to guide you'—that he should appoint Campbell.[48]

Bentinck had not asked for guidance from the Court and his minute of 13 December 1831 announcing Campbell's appointment made it clear that he was following the Court's advice. This circumstance gave a constitutional basis to the enemies of Campbell and the partisans of Willock and produced a further heated debate in the Court in July 1832. By a majority of one it was agreed that Bentinck should be told that the responsibility was his and if he thought (as it appeared he did) that Campbell was unsuitable he should replace him.[49] Sir Robert Campbell fought back with a note of dissent impugning the motives of Campbell Marjoribanks, the Deputy Chairman, who had led the opposition to Campbell's appointment. Under the standing order of April 1811 Marjoribanks was allowed no rejoinder and the draft dispatch (dated 11 July 1832) and the note of dissent were sent to Grant for approval. Grant substituted a revised version of the dispatch, restating the correct constitutional position but giving Bentinck credit for his disinterested action in forgoing his patronage rights. It was assumed that Campbell was efficient and the suggestion that he should be replaced was omitted from the revised dispatch.[50] The Directors, who had access to private information from India, still believed that Bentinck had doubts, and they rejected this draft and substituted a third.

In the end much careful management was required in order to keep Campbell in his post. The final draft represented a compromise in which the Court restated their view that Bentinck had appointed Campbell in deference to the views of the Court, but assumed that Bentinck did recognize his constitutional responsibilities and would not appoint an unqualified man.[51]

Apart from its constitutional interest, the debate illuminates two aspects of British relations with Iran. In the first place it shows the absurd consequences of Canning's return of control of the mission to the Company. Bentinck now possessed a constitutional responsibility which he declined to exercise on political grounds. The influential secretary at India House, Peter Auber, recommended that Bentinck should bring this anomaly into the open and state clearly that he thought the Iranian mission should be European and that 'it has little or nothing to do with India'.[52] It was true that Bentinck would not have appointed Campbell, whose dispatches he found unimpressive, but he took the view he could not go against the strong expression of opinion by the Secret Committee in the July 1831 dispatch in favour of Campbell. As far as he was concerned, London controlled the mission and issued the instructions. The Indian Government gave no instructions to the Envoy in Iran.[53] In this way the episode may have paved the way for the resumption of control by the Crown. Secondly, the controversy shows into how sad a state British representation in Iran had fallen. Even before the long controversy, Bentinck had remarked that 'in no part of the world has party work and clan work run higher than in Persia', plainly seeing little merit in the co-operation of a Macdonald and a Campbell.[54] Malcolm's successor at Bombay, Lord Clare, denounced Campbell's appointment as 'a scandalous and flagrant job'. Campbell, he said, was unfit and the consequence of his appointment would be the eventual subjection of Iran to Russia.[55]

It was at this nadir of British influence in Iran that British interest in the Iranian alliance began to revive. The return of the control of the mission to India had forced the Indian Governments to give some consideration to the problem of Iran. This rethinking was carried forward by the return of Malcolm to Bombay in 1827 as Governor. Apart from his exchange over Iran with Canning in 1824, Malcolm had been out of the mainstream of the discussion, licking his resentment at being passed over for Bombay in favour of Elphinstone and for Madras in favour of first Munro and then Stephen Lushington. So bitter was he at the last rejection of his claims that he campaigned against Lushington, trying to exploit the hostility that existed between the Company and ministers. At last, however, he had gained the cherished Governor-

ship and Bombay was a good platform from which to comment on Iran.
His contribution to the discussion of strategy will be considered elsewhere; here it is sufficient to note that he took advantage of the interest
in Iran created by the Russo–Iranian war to promulgate his views,
notably through his old friend, Wellington, and to give support to those
of his friend, Macdonald, in Iran. The war had brought out very clearly
the question of Russia. Malcolm discussed this in detail in a minute on
British relations with Iran written in the autumn of 1828, which was
discussed at the highest level and prompted an interesting minute in
reply from Metcalfe. Metcalfe opposed Malcolm's advocacy of a
stronger British policy in Iran. He did not contend that Russian gains
in Iran were of no consequence to Britain, merely that they could not be
prevented by a defensive alliance with Iran which was more likely to
drag Britain into an unwanted war with Russia. An independent Iran
was valuable to Britain but Britain should do no more than maintain
friendly relations and try to collaborate with Russia in that country.
'Our true policy . . . is to devote our attention to the improvement of
our Indian Empire,' he wrote, in words which might well have summed
up the views of Bentinck.[56]

The growing worries about Russian policy in Iran and its implications for India, as well as the Russo–Ottoman war of 1828 to 1829 also
caused concern in London, where it was strongly voiced by Lord
Ellenborough, who was appointed President of the Board of Control in
September 1828, greatly regretting that he had not been given the
Foreign Office. Ellenborough was a strange man. His odd appearance,
dominated by what Emily Eden called 'his horrid grey locks', made
him seem so absurd and contemptible that George IV is reputed to
have said that the very sight of Ellenborough made him sick.[57] Ellenborough's unattractive combination of extreme arrogance and grovel-
ling humility caused him to be widely disliked. His enemies were
alleged to comprise the whole of London society.[58] It was inevitable
that whereas the antics of Melbourne's wife won sympathy for the
husband, the scandalous infidelity and departure of Ellenborough's
second wife in 1829 should only excite further ridicule. Melbourne
possessed the ease and gentle cynicism which enabled him to survive;
Ellenborough was crushed by the humiliation. Perhaps in self-defence
he retreated further into his cocoon of pride and nourished his ambition
to demonstrate the greatness which he felt lay within him. His models
were Richard Wellesley and the great Duke himself. Only from the
latter would he accept guidance. But with all this psychological lumber
Ellenborough possessed considerable energy, and an imaginative
political sense.

Ellenborough was the first English statesman to become obsessed by dislike of Russia. Britain should resist Russian encroachment in the Ottoman Empire and in Iran. His first impulse was to call for a *jihad* to expel Russia from the latter country. He was persuaded to abandon this idea by Wellington, who had adopted the views of his old friend Malcolm. Iran, he believed, could never resist Russia successfully but could survive only by not providing her neighbour with excuses for intervention. British aid should be limited to help in constructing an army which would provide only internal security and not defence against an external foe. Wellington's advice provided the basis for Ellenborough's instructions both to Robert Taylor, the East India Company's representative in Iraq, who had put forward proposals for a more active British policy of support for the Mamluk Pashas of Baghdad, and to Macdonald in Iran.

Ellenborough instructed Macdonald: 'to inculcate on the Court of Tehran a spirit of peace and good neighbourhood, to recommend a strict and cheerful performance of Treaties, and the manifestation of a strong desire to remain on good terms both with Russia and the Ottoman state'. He was to encourage Iran to form a small disciplined force for internal security only.[59] With this in mind, Ellenborough, following Macdonald's advice, intervened to prevent the East India Company from recalling the British detachment, declaring that if the Shah would not pay for them Britain would.[60] He even offered to lend Abbas Mirza money to buy small arms.[61] He explained to Bentinck that the real danger to be feared was not that Russia would conquer Iran but that Russia would establish such a permanent influence in that country as to place its resources at Russia's disposal.[62] One way or another, he informed Wellington, Russia intended to use Iran as a stepping-stone to India.[63] In the end, however, the only way in which her advance could be prevented was by British action in Europe. Britain should declare to Russia that Britain, in her capacity 'as an Asiatick Power', would regard any encroachment on Iran as an unfriendly act.[64]

Ellenborough was thus the first Cabinet Minister to reverse the relative weight to be attached to Europe and India. Hitherto European interests had always prevailed over Indian; now Ellenborough was asserting that Britain should use her European influence in defence of India. The claim had been made before from India, but this was the first echo in London. But it was an isolated and short-lived response. Wellington promptly refused to make any such declaration and Ellenborough had to accept defeat. In the latter part of his tenure of office it is possible to discern a much less ambitious policy in the East. This is revealed both by his rejection of the proposal to make Hart paymaster to the Iranian army and in his attitude to the reform of the 1814 Treaty.

In March 1830 Abbas Mirza revived his 1828 suggestion to insert a new article into the treaty to replace the abrogated subsidy clauses. As before, Macdonald supported the proposal officially, but wrote privately to say that a refusal would do little harm.[65] After Macdonald's death Abbas Mirza tried again. This time Ellenborough refused, adding some characteristic gratuitous advice that 'the true defence of states is to be found in the love of the People for their National Sovereign and in the prudent provision of disciplined Troops and military Stores.'[66] He explained to Bentinck that while Britain favoured an independent Iran, the Government 'will not directly pledge itself for that purpose'.[67] There was an additional factor in his decision. The Iranian ministers had coupled the request for the revision of the treaty with certain financial claims and Campbell claimed that the treaty suggestion was merely a device to extract money.[68]

Ellenborough was the only Cabinet Minister to support an active policy against Russia. Wellington had some sympathy, but a much more realistic assessment of British priorities. Of the others, Peel was neutral and Aberdeen supported the policy which had become traditional since 1815, of following the lead of Austria in the Near East. He, however, was too weak to have much influence. Most of the others adhered to the Canning policy of seeking co-operation with Russia in Europe. India formed no significant part of their thinking.

The further lapse of interest in Iran which characterized the latter part of Ellenborough's period of office was continued under his Whig successor, Charles Grant. By conviction Grant was inclined to concentrate on internal developments within India and by disposition was incapable of decisive action. Nor did Campbell urge any more active policy. In his early days Campbell had veered round to the belief that no danger from Russia existed; the whole question was raised by Iran in the hope of obtaining money and the best policy for Britain was 'to affect a proper degree of indifference to our alliance with it'.[69] He blocked a fresh attempt to send an Iranian mission to London.

British complacency about the situation in Iran was rudely shaken by the expedition of Abbas Mirza to Khurasan in 1831. There was nothing new about Iranian ambitions in this direction. Large parts of Afghanistan and Turkestan had formed elements in the Safavid and Afshar Empires. During the civil wars of the later eighteenth century Iranian claims had not been pressed and during the first part of the nineteenth century the attention of the Qajars had been focused on the threat from Russia in the north-west and upon relations with the

Ottomans. The Iranian claims in the east had never been abandoned, however; according to the *Qa'im maqam*, Afghanistan, up to a point to the east of Kabul, belonged to Iran, although Ghazni was the point more usually mentioned.[70] With the settlement of the north-western frontier in 1828 it was therefore natural that Iran should revive her eastward ambitions in the hope of finding some compensation for her losses. It was not surprising that Russia should encourage this. Russia was content with the Aras frontier and was anxious to divert Iranian attention from the area. Also Russian relations with the Uzbek Khanate of Khiva were not good and it seemed possible that she might eventually be able to exercise indirect pressure on that state through a friendly Iran. In fact Russian relations with Iran had improved dramatically since 1828. Following the conclusion of the Turkomanchai Treaty a Russian embassy led by the well-known writer A. S. Griboedov, was sent to Tehran to re-establish peaceful relations. Religious feelings had led to a tumult in the Iranian capital in which the Russian Ambassador was murdered. A hasty embassy of apology was sent to St. Petersburg and the incident resulted in a politic display of necessary Russian benevolence in which Nicholas I remitted half of the outstanding balance of the indemnity and gave Iran five years to pay the rest.

Abbas Mirza was first drawn to the east in 1830. In that year his brother, Hasan Ali Mirza, the Governor of Kirman, revolted and seized the neighbouring town of Yezd. Fath Ali promised to make Abbas Mirza Governor if he would suppress the rising. Hoping to redeem his own blemished military reputation, Abbas Mirza accepted. Campbell agreed to allow the British detachment to accompany him, although this was technically an infringement of the 1814 Treaty.[71] After restoring order in Kirman in 1831 Abbas Mirza looked further east towards Khurasan. Quite apart from Iranian claims there was evident justification in the raids of the Turkoman slavers, who preyed especially on pilgrims to Mashhad. Campbell, however, discovered a much more sinister motive. Putting various scraps of information together he concluded that the Khurasan expedition was undertaken at the instigation of Russia and was aimed at Khiva and Afghanistan.

Campbell did not see in the Khurasan expedition a danger to India. He did not think that Abbas Mirza had either the ability or the desire to go beyond Khurasan. His fears were for Abbas Mirza himself. If he were defeated his claim to the Iranian throne and therefore the future stability of Iran would be threatened.[72] On this point Campbell's views never changed, even after Abbas Mirza established control over Khurasan and went on to attack Herat. He did not think Abbas Mirza had the strength to take Herat and certainly not the power to retain it. Campbell always denied that British opposition to Abbas Mirza's eastward ambitions arose from fears for India.[73]

Nevertheless, the British handling of the affair left the impression of fear for India. It was natural that Campbell should attempt to persuade Abbas Mirza to abandon his ambitions. At the end of 1831 he tried and failed. The real blow to British interests was delivered by the Commander of the British detachment, Captain Benjamin Shee. The detachment had not distinguished itself in Khurasan, where the Iranian hero had been a Polish adventurer named Borowski, who had recently joined Abbas Mirza. Shee, whom Campbell thought incompetent, was perhaps anxious to redeem himself by some diplomatic *coup*. At all events he took it upon himself to go to Abbas Mirza at Mashhad to protest about rumoured Russian aid and a projected embassy to Khiva. He was like clay in the hands of Abbas Mirza and the *Qa'im maqam*. They worked on his fears with fantasies of Russian armies, embassies, and aid and persuaded him to sign an unauthorized agreement by which Britain was to pay Iran 100,000 tomans in return for the abandonment of the Khivan embassy, the rejection of the alleged Russian aid, and the expulsion of two so-called Russian observers from the Iranian camp. In this way they hoped to win some of the concessions which had been refused in 1828 and 1830. Like the victims of the best confidence tricks, Shee retired feeling he had made a good bargain.[74] Although Campbell promptly repudiated the agreement and Shee enjoyed the distinction of being dismissed simultaneously by Bentinck and by Abbas Mirza, the damage was done. Far and wide went the impression that Britain feared a Russian attack on India and that she connected this menace with the Iranian threat to Afghanistan. In the following months Abbas Mirza's example was followed by the rulers of Herat and Bukhara and by Shah Shuja, the exiled monarch of Afghanistan. All tried to extract money or aid from Britain by the same means.

Abbas renewed his eastward progress in the summer of 1832 when he turned against Herat, and Campbell renewed his efforts to persuade him to desist. This time he sent his assistant, John McNeill (1795–1883), to Khurasan. McNeill, who did not believe the stories of Russian instigation, based his arguments on the same ground as Campbell, namely the danger to Abbas Mirza's own position in Iran.[75] But McNeill did believe that a threat to India existed. He thought it probable that Herat would soon fall and that Iranian influence could then be extended to Qandahar. In this way Iranian and Russian influence could become established in Afghanistan. It was impossible to prevent this by representations to Iran because article 9 of the 1814 Treaty forbade interference between Iran and Afghanistan. Therefore he recommended that the Indian Government should make arrangements with the rulers of Afghanistan to provide for the defence of India.[76] Campbell, who had already recommended, at the end of 1831, that the Indian Government should use its influence in Lahore, Sind, and Afghanistan to counteract Iranian designs, now supported McNeill. He added a further suggestion that Britain should seek to consolidate Afghanistan into a single buffer state.[77]

The Khurasan expedition therefore constitutes a landmark in the formation of ideas about the defence of India. The previously ill-defined fears that Russia could threaten India, either through the conquest of Iran or through the control of that country's resources, had now focused on a specific threat; namely that Iran would become the vehicle for the expansion of Russian influence into Afghanistan. In this context Herat emerged as a vital strategic position in the defence of India, a position it was to retain for many years. During his attempt to find a basis for agreement between Abbas Mirza and Kamran Shah, the ruler of Herat, McNeill had employed as an intermediary a British officer who happened to be in Herat at the time. This was Dr. Gerard, who had accompanied Alexander Burnes on his journey to Afghanistan. Gerard, who firmly believed that Russia had instigated the eastern campaign and that Iran had become a Russian tool, wrote to his friend, Charles Trevelyan, in India, that Herat was 'the key to India and even Toorkistan'.[78] There had been many keys to India, but this was to be one of the most durable. To meet this threat two possible counters were suggested. One was the familiar remedy of strengthening British influence in Iran; the other was a reversion to the old Minto strategy of the creation of an alternative buffer in Afghanistan. The pattern of 1808 was beginning to re-form, although the situation of Russia was very different from that of France.

The significance of 1832 is largely one achieved by hindsight; at the time the repercussions were very limited. Abbas Mirza failed to take Herat and, after his death in October 1833, his son, Muhammad Mirza, withdrew to Tehran; the Herat question dropped from the forefront of speculation. Some interest in the problem was shown in India, where Campbell's reports and recommendations fitted into the new ideas which were developing there; Campbell was ordered to collect more information about Iranian designs in the area.[79] There was also some reaction in London. On the grounds of the ninth article Grant ordered the withdrawal of the detachment, and Palmerston, as Foreign Secretary, took his first steps in the problem. He questioned the

Russian Envoy, Count Orlov, who denied any Russian interest, and later asked Durham, as new Ambassador to St. Petersburg, to approach Nesselrode. Palmerston's words, however, only serve to show his lack of understanding. He wrote:

Although Great Britain may appear at first sight to have no particular interest in what may happen in so remote a quarter as Khiva, yet when it is considered that the possession of that country would place Russia nearly in command of the navigation of rivers which lead to the very frontier of our Indian Empire, the matter assumes a different aspect and becomes the subject of proper concern to H. M.'s Government.[80]

The most important immediate consequence of the Khurasan expedition was its contribution to the general review of British policy in Iran which was instigated by Charles Grant. Grant's own responsibility is difficult to assess. He is usually described as lazy, and certainly suffered from ill-health, whether real or imagined. His outstanding quality was indecision, and it was this which led Russell and Howick to force him out of the Cabinet (in which he was Colonial Secretary) in January 1839. Macaulay wrote that 'Grant's is a mind that cannot stand alone. It is . . . a feminine mind. It turns, like ivy, to some support.'[81] C. H. Philips considers that Grant's policy was formed by Macaulay and Benjamin Jones. Jones certainly had been closely connected with Indian political affairs for many years, but by now was on the verge of retirement. Another secretary, William Cabell, also played some part. But it seems most likely that the driving force was Henry Ellis, whose long experience was refuelled by his friend Willock. William IV, who was also particularly concerned about the Russian threat to India, prodded Grant as well. Palmerston does not seem to have taken a leading part in the review.

The review took the form of the collection of memoranda from men who knew Iran. These included Willock, Ouseley, Ellis, and David Wilson, a former Resident in the Gulf. Together with Campbell's dispatches the memoranda provided a basis for the development of future policy.[82] The writers agreed on the decline of British influence in Iran as a consequence of neglect, Iranian resentment over broken promises, and the unsatisfactory state of the treaty. There was also general fear of Russia. Ouseley wrote of the dangers of an invasion of India via the Caspian; Willock, more subtly, foresaw the gradual extension of Russian influence into Turkestan and Afghanistan and a threat to India, not from direct invasion, but from unrest fomented inside India. There was less agreement on how the danger should be met. Ouseley and Willock (both of them former Crown representatives in Iran) advocated a new effort to recover British influence there, beginning with the resumption of control of the mission by the Crown. 'The experiment of transferring Persian politics back to Asia and the attempt of putting an end to the relations of Europe has been tried and failed', wrote Ouseley. Ellis and Campbell on the other hand opposed the return to Crown control. Ellis alone suggested the restoration of the abrogated clauses; Campbell suggested support for the succession of Abbas Mirza, remonstrances at St. Petersburg, and, if all else failed, the adoption of the Gulf strategy of neutralizing Iran by inciting disturbances in the south. Ellis and Campbell, in fact, were both inclined to write off Iran as a buffer state and to look to the creation of new buffers, particularly in Afghanistan. With a political catholicism which ignored realities, Ellis would have tried anything. 'Our course is to meet Russian agents, Russian commerce and Russian influence on all the routes approaching India', he wrote.

One of the most interesting of the memoranda was one dated 8 February 1833 and written by a Captain John Macan. Macan argued that it was worth retaining the Iranian buffer if this could be done cheaply. Of the alternatives, Turkestan was impossible—an Uzbek league against Russia was doomed to failure because the Uzbeks disliked one another more than they did Russia. But Russia could be stopped only by action in Europe. If necessary Britain must be prepared to go to war for India. In fact Macan did not think there was any danger of a Russian invasion of India because of the physical difficulties. The real danger was that Russia might cause unrest among the Muslims of Afghanistan and northern India and in the Indian army. The best defence against this threat was a close alliance with the Sikhs, who formed a Hindu buffer against Muslim unrest; to open the navigation of the Indus; but above all to maintain the fidelity of the Indian army and the goodwill of the Indian people in general by investing in internal development. Macan's memorandum picks up several ideas which go back to Manesty, Malcolm, and Metcalfe, but it also anticipates many arguments which became more prominent subsequently. Arthur Conolly's 1840 Uzbek league is considered and rightly rejected; George Clerk's 1841 idea of the Hindu buffer on the Indus is sketched out; and the arguments of Henry Lawrence in the 1840s on the central importance of the fidelity of the Indian army and those of John Lawrence as Governor-General in the 1860s, which expanded the earlier views of Charles Metcalfe on the value of good government as the basis of security in India, are also foreshadowed. But the memorandum attracted no attention at the time.

Following these discussions a new effort was made to recover British influence in Iran. The shape of the new initiative was sketched by Ellis in a memorandum probably written in August 1833 in which he followed in part Campbell's recommendations. These were to strengthen the detachment, in order to ensure the succession of Abbas Mirza; to revise the political treaty by inserting a new article promising general protection; and to return control of the mission to the Crown. While still contending that British interest in Iran derived from her position in India, Ellis now conceded the argument of the Indian Government that the connection with Europe made London control essential. Finally, Ellis recommended the sending of a confidential agent to the area. All these measures were tried during the following two years.

To aid Abbas Mirza, Campbell was given permission to advance up to 100,000 tomans to facilitate his succession to the throne when Fath Ali died. The small arms promised earlier were now to be sent to Iran and also a fresh detachment of British officers and sergeants to discipline his army. The new detachment arrived at Bushir in November 1833 and reached Tehran the following March. It consisted of eight officers and fourteen non-commissioned officers and included many men who were later to distinguish themselves as agents of British policy in Iran and Afghanistan. Among these were Justin Shiel, Francis Farrant, Henry Rawlinson, Edward Lynch, and D'Arcy Todd. At the same time another officer was sent from England. This was Sir Henry Lindsay Bethune, who, as Lieutenant Lindsay, had served with Abbas Mirza in 1812. Bethune had offered his services to the British Government and was paid by the Foreign Office, not the Company. It was intended that he should act as Chief of Staff and not possess any authority over the detachment, but inevitably there were disputes with Colonel Passmore, the new commander of the detachment, and Campbell became involved. These disputes did not help either the detachment or the mission. Until the death of Fath Ali in November 1834 the detachment was employed at Tabriz, drilling the troops of Muhammad Mirza, who had succeeded his father as Governor of Azerbaijan. In the succession campaign the detachment played a useful part in the operations of Muhammad Mirza's army, which was commanded by Bethune. Thereafter the officers were dispersed to different provinces; Rawlinson raised three Kurdish regiments in Kirmanshah. But divided, the detachment was less effective and in 1836 to 1837 was again withdrawn from service after Muhammad Shah attacked Herat.

Britain began also a new political initiative. In December 1833 it was decided to offer a revision of the 1814 Treaty by the insertion of a general declaration to the effect that Britain was interested in the integrity of Iran and would mediate in the event of any dispute between Iran and a European power. In return for this concession Iran was to agree to abrogate the eighth and ninth articles, the limiting effects of which on British actions had been demonstrated in 1832.[83] Contrary to Ellis's advice, it was also decided to take the opportunity to negotiate a commercial treaty. This was because of a change in the pattern of trade between Britain and Iran. Until the late 1820s such trade had normally passed through Bombay and Bushir. But for many years British merchants and envoys, supported by Abbas Mirza, had urged that a northern route through the Black Sea should be opened. In 1830 James Brant was appointed as Consul at Trebizond, partly to facilitate this development, which Campbell did much to promote in the face of the Indian Government's lack of interest. After 1831, when the Russian Government imposed duties on goods passing through Georgia, the trade through Trebizond and Tabriz began to expand rapidly, until in 1837 its value was estimated at nearly £1 million. Some better framework was needed for this trade since Malcolm's 1801 Treaty was useless. Campbell had been given permission to open discussions on the subject in 1831, but he had had no success. It was now decided to try for a regular commercial treaty which would both provide legal protection and permit the appointment of Consuls in Iran.[84] For the purposes of this negotiation it was necessary to provide Campbell with Crown credentials. This marked the first step towards the resumption of Crown control. Campbell had already been given a knighthood in January 1833 to increase his prestige in Iran.

The third aspect of the new initiative was the dispatch of a special agent, James Baillie Fraser, on a fact-finding mission to Iran and Iraq. Fraser had previously travelled extensively in the Himalaya area and in Iran and had written several books. His instructions were very wide ranging, but the main emphasis was placed on the collection of information about Iran, Iraq, and the extent of Russian influence in all the countries between the Caspian and the Indus.[85] Although he was sent on behalf of the Foreign Office, his instructions were the product of careful consultations within the Company and the India Board and the basis of them appears to have been an unsigned memorandum, possibly written by William Cabell, one of the Board's secretaries, in about November 1833.[86]

The new initiative was essentially the work of the India Board, in which the driving influence was Henry Ellis. The Foreign Office was brought in because of the Board's view that Canning's attempt to separate Asian and European politics had failed. The Board was not yet willing to concede that the failure was complete and still hesitated to press for the return of the control of the mission to the Crown. Neverthe-less, it was recognized that the Foreign Office must be brought in, in some degree and, particularly through Fraser's mission, the way was opened for a further, larger step if it were found to be appropriate. But at this time the initiative was still clearly with the Board and Palmerston still seems to have had very little grasp of the problem.[87]

Before the fresh political instructions were dispatched to Campbell a new urgent problem had appeared in Iran which caused the initiative to be postponed. On 22 October Abbas Mirza died at Mashhad of dropsy. A remarkable man, alternately praised and abused by British officers as pro-British or pro-Russian, he was consistently pro-Iranian. In different circumstances he might have been the Muhammad Ali of Iran. His death left a vacuum, both in the long term and in the immediate political situation. It had always been accepted that he would succeed his father, but the succession was now wide open and a dispute might allow Russian intervention. There were four candidates. Campbell favoured the fat Muhammad Mirza, the son of Abbas Mirza. Willock described him as dull and bigoted, a view endorsed by Henry Rawlinson. Muhammad Mirza was a great admirer of Napoleon and had had some of his letters translated into Persian. Possibly through the influence of his tutor, he believed himself destined as Shah to revive the glories of Nadir Shah. The second candidate was Ali Khan Shahzadeh, better known as the Zil al-Sultan, who was full brother to Abbas Mirza, and strategically placed as Governor of Tehran citadel and therefore in control of the treasury. The remaining two were sons of Fath Ali by another wife. They were Husayn Ali Mirza, Farman Farma, who had governed Fars for thirty years and was very powerful in southern Iran where he enjoyed the support of the Bakhtiyari tribe; and Hasan Ali Mirza, the former rebellious Governor of Kirman. Fath Ali wavered between these candidates and contemplated sending a mission to Europe to seek British and Russian advice.

Before Britain could decide which candidate to support, it was necessary to ensure that the same candidate was supported by Russia. Accordingly, in February 1834 Campbell was authorized to advance to another candidate the 100,000 tomans previously promised to Abbas Mirza, providing that candidate was nominated by the Shah and supported by Russia.[88] As it happened, Nesselrode had already approached the British minister, the Hon. John Bligh, with a suggestion that both states should support Muhammad Mirza.[89] Grant urged prompt acceptance, but Palmerston did not take up the question until June 1834 and when he did he sought assurances concerning a rumour, reported by Campbell, that Russia was threatening to occupy the northern Iranian province of Gilan if the remainder of the indemnity was not paid. Once satisfactory assurances were given on this point co-operation was arranged.

Fath Ali had also nominated Muhammad Mirza to be his successor in June 1834. Campbell said that this was because Muhammad Mirza had offered to make himself personally responsible for the payment of the last crore (£25,000) of the indemnity. Campbell became obsessed with this sum during 1834. He saw it as the major lever of Russian influence and even suggested that Britain should advance the necessary money to pay off the debt. In this way Britain would gain the same influence that Russia possessed.[90] The faulty logic of this is apparent, but Campbell became so convinced by his analysis that he sent his assistant, McNeill, to London to plead the case in person. Almost certainly, Campbell had been bluffed by the Iranian ministers. There is no evidence that Russia used the balance of the indemnity in that way. Palmerston and Grant turned the suggestion down.

The news of the Anglo–Russian agreement on the succession reached Iran just in time. Fath Ali died at Isfahan on 20 October 1834 and the struggle for the throne followed immediately. At Isfahan the army commander, Allah Yar Khan, Asef al-Dawlah, supported the oldest Prince who was present, Ali Taqi Mirza, the former Governor of Qazvin. In fact it seems likely that the Asef al-Dawlah knew that Ali Taqi Mirza could not hold the position, but that this was the only way in which he could keep the Zil al-Sultan from power until the arrival of Muhammad Mirza. The Zil al-Sultan took advantage of the departure of Ali Taqi Mirza and the funeral party for Qum to seize power in Isfahan and to begin to collect an army. In the meantime Muhammad Mirza had been proclaimed Shah at Tabriz, where he was supported by Campbell and the new Russian Ambassador, Count Simonich. Simonich, a rather coarse-looking fat man, who limped from a wound received at Ganja, had been born in Dalmatia and had joined Napoleon's army. Captured on the Moscow campaign he had entered Russian service and had arrived in Tehran as Russian minister in February 1833. With the aid of Campbell's £30,000, Muhammad Mirza advanced to Tehran almost without opposition, having blinded two rivals at Ardebil. As he advanced, the Asef al-Dawlah at Qum declared for him and the Zil al-Sultan's army also deserted. The only real opposition came from the Farman Farma in the south. He had had the support of Fath Ali's Chief Minister, Abdullah Khan, Amin al-Dawlah, but Abdullah had been out of Isfahan when Fath Ali died and he had missed his chance. Now Bethune's force scattered Husayn Ali's army. Husayn was imprisoned at Tabriz where he later died and

Hasan was blinded. Husayn's three sons escaped to England and the Zil al-Sultan to Russia. Muhammad Shah then confirmed his position by a general purge of his rivals, who were dismissed from their governorships.

Campbell now believed that Muhammad Shah would show his gratitude for British help by co-operation in the postponed treaty negotiations. He was sorely disappointed. Campbell concentrated his attention on the commercial treaty; in the revisions of the political treaty he had little faith. He wrote to his father: 'The proposed treaty is evidently considered as a panacea for all existing evils while unfortunately its discussion, which will clearly show that England does not contemplate giving any immediate assistance to Persia, will rather augment than remedy them.'[91] Campbell's judgement was apparently vindicated when the Shah rejected the proposals on the grounds that they failed to specify what aid Britain would give.[92] His hopes of the commercial treaty, however, were also shattered. Negotiations broke down over the question of Consuls. The Iranian ministers would not grant Britain the right to Consuls in case Russia insisted on exercising the right to appoint Consuls which she had won at Turkomanchai.[93] This was in accord with their previous position.

Campbell declined to see any merit in the Iranian arguments. Instead he assumed that this 'singular and ungrateful conduct' was part of a plot against him. To the same alleged plot he attributed his own obvious unpopularity. Behind the conspiracy against him was, he thought, the Shah's chief advisor, the same *Qa'im maqam* who had served Abbas Mirza. Earlier he had described the *Qa'im maqam* as the only able and honest Iranian minister;[94] now he denounced him as an incompetent in the pay of Russia.[95] This was nonsense. Far from his being a Russian puppet, Simonich tried to get rid of the *Qa'im maqam*, as he was also to do in the case of the next chief advisor, Haji Mirza Aghasi, whom Campbell's successor, Henry Ellis, also denounced as a tool of Russia. Whatever the *Qa'im maqam's* failings as a minister—he would not delegate authority—there is no reason to suppose that he was other than a dedicated Iranian public servant. It was Iran's loss when the Shah ordered the *Qa'im maqam* and his family to be strangled on 26 June 1835. In the light of Campbell's hostility to the minister it is just possible that the Envoy may have played a part in the minister's fall by encouraging his rivals. The murder was hailed as a triumph for Campbell. But there is no evidence to connect him directly with the grim event.

The Shah's new chief advisor was his former tutor, Haji Mirza Aghasi, although the wily Asef al-Dawlah, now Governor of Khurasan, retained considerable influence. Haji Mirza Aghasi was a Sufi ascetic with a predilection for astrology and prophecy. He had been born at Erivan, which had been annexed by Russia in 1828, was a member of the old Turkoman Bayat tribe, and his early life had been devoted to religious activities, including the pilgrimage to Mecca. He had come under the patronage of Abbas Mirza's former minister, Mirza Bozorg, who had made him tutor to his master's son. Layard described him as small, and shabbily dressed with forbidding features and a loud, shrill voice. At the time he came to power he had no previous experience of administration and appears to have relied extensively upon intuition, and a strong religio–national feeling which led him to advocate a return to the frontiers of Nadir Shah. He was certainly not a partisan of Russia, as most British representatives asserted. They found him very difficult to deal with, but so did the Russian diplomats and there is every reason to believe that the regular Persian bureaucrats found him just as uncertain.[96]

With the *Qa'im maqam* out of the way, Campbell hoped for success in his negotiations. Once more he was disappointed. Now he blamed past British policy for his failure. We have spoiled them, he complained, or they would have been glad to accept anything.[97] It was a dismal excuse for failure and ran counter to much of his previous advice. Campbell had been consistently wrong over a long period and the suspicion grows that he misrepresented the situation in Iran to obscure his own inadequacies. The Government in London, however, were now fully aware of his deficiencies and had decided to replace him. The new minister was to represent the Crown not the Company. Canning's experiment had at last run its course.

The Anglo–Iranian alliance was like many a marriage. After a breathless courtship and a whirlwind ceremony the groom had begun to examine his situation. First he had complained about the bride-price and soon after had sickened of the union. For long the bride had sought to make the marriage work in the way she had understood it was intended, but after many a rebuff she had counted her bruises and begun to look elsewhere. But within the husband there was a calculating jealousy that was alarmed by the appearance of the new suitor and in middle age he began to discover attractions in his wife that he had previously despised, but the habits of a lifetime could not so easily be overcome and his renewed advances were grudging. It was a question whether the future held a second honeymoon or a divorce.

The Collapse of the Iranian Buffer,
1835–1838

> If the Shah should take *Herat* we shall not have a moment
> to lose, and the stake will in my opinion be the highest we
> have yet played for. We *must* be secure in Affghanistan—
> able to check and to punish intrigues carried on there
> against our peace in India—able to exclude foreign agents
> and emissaries from all that country—or our security in
> India will be greatly diminished, and our expenses there
> very largely increased.
>
> John McNeill to Justin Sheil, March 1838.

In 1835 control of relations with Iran was returned to the Crown. The absurdity of Canning's logic was thus formally recognized: Britain could not have two foreign policies. In practice, of course, she had never attempted to do so; control by India had been only nominal. Throughout, instructions had been drawn up and even appointments made in London. But in London there had been no real co-ordination of policy because of the division of influence between the Board of Control and the Foreign Office. The situation had indeed borne some resemblance to that which had obtained before 1782 when the conduct of British foreign policy was divided between two secretaries on a rough, geographical basis. Then co-ordination had been achieved only by the Cabinet or by a dominant Prime Minister. In the case of Iran, first Canning's dominance over Wynn and then Wellington's influence over his colleagues had produced some uniformity. But under the Whig Ministry, although no apparent differences of opinion between Grant and Palmerston emerged, this was because of inattention rather than design. Palmerston's lack of interest in or understanding of what was involved in policy in Iran before 1835 left a greater influence to the members of the India Board who were able to influence Grant, and to the men in Iran. Their vested interests prolonged the period of nominal Indian control. Nevertheless, there was a steady drift towards Foreign Office control.

The eventual decision to resume Crown control over the mission in Iran was taken by the short-lived Conservative Ministry under Peel. The men chiefly responsible were Ellenborough, restored to the Board of Control, and Wellington, but a significant influence was exerted by Henry St. George Tucker (1771–1851), then Chairman of the Court of Directors. Tucker, who was in effect the chief advisor to the Conservatives on Indian affairs during these years, was a man of parts. By his conspicuous abilities he had hoisted himself from obscurity to the position of Accountant-General of Bengal at the age of thirty. Disaster then struck him down. Undeterred by his own surpassing ugliness, he had such unbounded confidence in his own personal attractions as to be induced to press his attentions on one lady to the point when he was given six months for attempted rape. Unabashed, he thanked his gaoler politely for his care and set about rebuilding his career with such determination that he was appointed Accountant-General again in 1805 and rose to be Chief Secretary in 1814 before leaving India. His skill in finding financial economies had secured his reputation and this same quality ensured his rapid rise to power after he became a Director in 1826. The Iranian mission was one obvious economy, but he based his arguments on strategic grounds. In the first place, Iran could be defended only from Europe, not from India; in the second, the Ottoman Empire (including Syria and Iraq) and Iran must be considered as an indivisible whole from the point of view of British policy and relations with them ought therefore to be directed by the Foreign Office.[1] This, of course, had been implicit in the thinking behind the mission of James Fraser, who also played a part in the building of the new policy.

Fraser had sent in regular reports on the situation in the Middle East throughout 1834. In the early part of 1835 he returned to England where he held discussions with Henry Ellis and submitted a lengthy report.[2] Fraser took the idea of a Russian threat to India seriously. According to him, Russia planned to occupy all those territories which intervened between the present borders of Russia and British India in order to be able to influence affairs within India. Several easy lines of approach existed. The safety of India could be secured only by keeping Russia at a distance through an elaborate system of buffer states, including Iraq, Iran, Afghanistan, and Turkestan. In Iran British influence could be established by a combination of several measures. Britain should send a Crown mission; pay off the Russian indemnity; remodel the Iranian army by assuming responsibility for its pay and administration in return for assignments of revenue; raise a new army in Khurasan; and promote internal reform. This last was of vital importance. It is obvious, wrote Fraser,

that the general object must be to transfuse by degrees as much of British feeling and moral influence as possible into the councils of the State, and to extend it if possible to the executive departments, so as to discourage and diminish corruption and venality and to increase public confidence by affording protection of property and person to all orders of the people.'[3]

In Turkestan Britain should sign treaties of alliance with the Uzbek states. Afghanistan should be consolidated into a single state to form an 'ulterior bulwark' or 'an inner wall of defence'. (Fraser thought that this would be accomplished by Shah Shuja in 1834). Iraq should be detached from the Ottoman Empire and either annexed or made into a protectorate in order to provide a defence against both Russia and Muhammad Ali.

All the points in Fraser's recommendations have been encountered before in the recommendations of various agents. The novel feature of Fraser's policy was that he conceived of all of them not as separate and often conflicting possibilities but as constituting one single defensive system for British India. It must be all or nothing:

All are links of one chain, part of one whole, and the omission of one renders the whole imperfect and unsafe. . . . Dress up the truth in whatever terms we may, it must come at last to this, that in order to protect our most important national interests, every Asiatic state, from the Indus to the Bosphorous must be subsidised in greater or lesser degree by British means and be under the influence of British councils.

Later, under the influence of Urquhart and Bell, Fraser was to become yet more ambitious. In December 1836 he recommended that Britain should check Russia in the Caucasus and Circassia. The alternative, he wrote, was to subsidize every country between the Danube and the Indus.[4]

Fraser's ambitious system illustrates a significant feature of British strategic thinking. The great majority of the strategic discussions of the time were initiated by local agents. Consistently, these agents advocated more active policies in the areas for which they were responsible. But inevitably, as they were occupationally bound to do, they took a restricted view of strategy. For them a more active policy in their own area was an alternative to a more active policy elsewhere and was often incompatible with such a policy. Of course in many cases they were right in their views; local interests made certain combinations difficult or impossible. But to an extent their advocacy was influenced by their awareness that British resources were limited and that strategic initiatives had to be restricted by money. In this case their prospects of advancement were linked with their ability to demonstrate that better prospects existed in their area than in others. There is nothing very remarkable in this situation which is one familiar at all levels of government and in large corporations. It is assumed that the various recommendations will be weighed at the top and a decision made on a view of the whole. The problem with British policy-making through the greater part of this period was that there was no real top. Authority was too divided between various bodies in India and in Britain. The Cabinet, which in the last analysis was the only body which could make the decision, almost never had time for the defence of India. Therefore the men who did take a general view of the strategy of Indian defence were very rare indeed. What made Fraser almost unique was that he was occupationally obliged to take a general view; he had been given the whole of the Middle East as his field. The result was that he put together the various recommendations of Campbell, Taylor, and others, picking up in the process ideas which went back to the beginning of the century, and produced a completely artificial construct. No such policy as he advocated was ever advocated by anyone else. Only by agglomerating the recommedations of individual officers could the illusion of such a policy be created. Fraser had in fact fallen into the same trap which yawns before the historian. His strategy was that of the defence of Olympus, not of British India.

Fraser's comprehensive strategy had little effect upon British policy. Nor indeed had many of his detailed recommendations. His Iranian proposals would have converted that state into a country under closer British control than even the average Indian state in subsidiary alliance. His humanitarian ideas of the coincidence of moral duty and political expediency obtained short shrift from Palmerston, who wrote 'Stuff' in the margin against the first of the two longer passages quoted above. But his ideas of domestic reform did have some effect on Ellis and the army proposals were to remain prominent for some years. At least he helped to circulate ideas about the defence of India.

The man chosen to lead the new Crown mission was Henry Ellis. Ellis was well qualified by ability and experience. He spoke good Persian and had long acquaintance with the problems of British relations with that country. His diplomatic talents had been enlarged by missions to Sind and China. In the event he proved to possess a major disqualification. He was too ambitious. He had sought the post because of the money and because it offered the chance of honours. His personal situation was uncertain. His sinecure post of Clerk of the Pells had disappeared in 1834 and he had failed to obtain the post which he had thought was promised to him—that of Comptroller-General of the Exchequer. His patron, Lord Ripon (formerly John Robinson), still looked after him, but now had little influence. The Iranian embassy, therefore, offered the hope of salvation in the form of a knighthood and a pension. But Ellis wanted quick and spectacular results. Once he virtually refused to go unless he was given the rank of Ambassador and Wellington appears to have regretted that Ellis had been chosen for the post.[5]

The instructions given to Ellis were the product of long discussions with Fraser and others. Their evolution may be traced in the various drafts and memoranda written by Ellis.[6] They embody that same assumption which was made by Macdonald and which has been designated as the rational fallacy, namely, that because Russia threatened Iran and Britain did not, British influence must always prevail. 'It should be assumed' wrote Ellis, 'as a fundamental principle of diplomatic conduct in Persia that every Shah of Persia is disposed to prefer British connection and British advice to Russian and that all his subjects not positively bought by Russian gold have a natural dislike to the Russian name and people.'[7] It followed from this assumption that British influence must prevail if the Shah could be persuaded of its truth. Large offers to Iran were therefore unnecessary. Instead Ellis could concentrate on strengthening Iran by urging domestic reform. He should also encourage co-operation between Iran and the Ottoman Empire (an idea which thus in the 1830s resumed the place which it had briefly held in British thinking in 1809) and work as closely as possible with the Iranian ministers. Ellis was to negotiate a commercial treaty, but not reopen the question of the revision of the political treaty.

It is clear that in the later stages of the discussion Ellis came to have some doubts about the validity of his basic assumption concerning the identity of British and Iranian interests. Following his discussions with Fraser a gloomier note appeared in the drafts. More emphasis was given to the dangers which would ensue if Iran attacked Herat. Ellis suggested that an effort should be made to remove the ninth article of the 1814 Treaty and also that Afghanistan should be consolidated as 'an inner outwork to the Indian Empire'.[8] But Palmerston, now back at the Foreign Office, would not give him permission to reopen the treaty negotiations and his final instruction of 25 July 1835 stated only that 'you will especially warn the Persian Government against being made the tools of Russian policy by allowing themselves to be pushed or to make war against the Afghans.' Ellis, however, had begun to foresee the possibility of failure; Russian influence might prove too strong. Reason might not persuade the Shah and threats might be required to induce the Shah to agree to the British demands. These suggested threats were of that variety, familiar since the eighteenth century, which Ellis now colourfully described as producing 'the rule of the tribes' in southern Iran.

Some of Ellis's difficulties had arisen from the return to power of the Whigs. It is clear that his proposed instructions from Wellington and Ellenborough were a good deal more cautious than Ellis would have liked, but Palmerston reduced the scope of the mission much more drastically. While making little change in the instructions themselves, he reduced Ellis's mission to a mere complimentary affair of only two months' duration. Palmerston did not want the mission at all. 'The strong bias of my own mind is against the Embassy', he wrote to Hobhouse.[9] A special embassy was unnecessary and would only excite Russian jealousy and create unrealizable hopes of commercial advantage in England. Of Ellis's objectives the complimentary ones could be undertaken by a new permanent minister (McNeill), the political treaty was not to be attempted, and the commercial treaty had been tried and failed. A second failure could produce a breach with Iran 'which would be highly disadvantageous to the permanent interests of England' and increase Russian influence. There was a refreshing realism about Palmerston's attitude towards Iran which is shown in his comments on a letter from Campbell, which he said would make him laugh if the matter were not so grave. 'An Envoy who fancies that he can persuade an ambitious, self conceited and powerful Minister to mend his ways, by writing such a lecture as this, may as well rest upon the laurels he has gained; and endeavour to acquire in some other company a little practical knowledge of human nature.'[10] Palmerston plainly had no more confidence in Ellis's judgement, but evidently did not think this of sufficient importance to insist on stopping the mission or drastically revising it. In the end he gave way to Ellis's repeated pleas to be allowed to try the commercial negotiation on condition that the first approach came from Iran and that Ellis was sure of success. 'Ellis is very anxious to appear to have some Business to do while at Teheran', he wrote sarcastically, 'and if he *should* find the Persians disposed to give us our Treaty, it would be a pity to lose the opportunity.'[11] In the end the main effect of Palmerston's intervention was to delay Ellis's departure from April until August. Ellis did not arrive in Teheran until 3 November 1835, a whole year after the decision to send a Crown mission had first been taken. The prospects of success represented by the important new initiative involved in the return to Crown control were thus diminished by the delays and by the very limited instructions which Ellis possessed. They were also reduced by the tight financial restrictions on the mission.

The financial restrictions were the consequence of a dispute between the Foreign Office and the East India Company. The enthusiasm of the Directors for the transfer was partly owing to their hopes of ridding themselves of the expense. They were soon disillusioned. When Ellenborough originally proposed that the Crown should resume control of the mission he foresaw that Parliament would object on the score that 'the mission to Persia arises solely out of our interests as an Asiatic Power.'[12] Wellington agreed, commenting 'I am convinced that Parlt. would not vote such expense; nay more, that Sir Robert Peel would not consent that the Proposition be made.'[13] Consequently, although the Company was to surrender nominal control, the Directors were asked to continue to pay the charges of the mission. Very reluctantly they consented, specifying a limit of twelve thousand pounds a year. After considerable pressure Ellenborough succeeded in extracting a further concession; that the Company would also continue to pay the costs of the detachment for a further year, during which time the Shah would be asked to take over the burden. In fact, the Shah was never asked and the Company continued to pay for the detachment until it was withdrawn in 1838. But the mission was still reduced to a meagre level. Ellis was given only eight hundred pounds for presents. 'Screwing economy, public and private, is the creed of the mission', wrote one observer.[14]

A final limitation on the hopes for the mission was imposed by the dissensions within it. It was the familiar story of British representation in Iran all over again. This time the supporters of Campbell resented the appointment of Ellis. Ellis did little to help the situation. Worried and insecure he quarrelled with several men of importance including the Shah's chief advisor, Haji Mirza Aghasi, with the result that they did not speak to one another for a month.[15]

Ellis was undeterred by all the difficulties which surrounded him. He was determined to achieve a notable success and to do so did not hesitate to evade both the spirit and even the letter of his instructions. The commercial treaty, which he believed Campbell had bungled, seemed to offer the best prospects. His instructions forbade him to broach the subject so he suggested privately to the Shah that Iran should take the initiative, adding a hint that he was prepared to compromise over the question of Consuls. But Ellis failed. The Iranians took a strong protectionist line and the commercial treaty was also opposed by the Russian Ambassador, Simonich, because of the possible threat which it represented to Russian interests in the Caspian. Simonich commented that Ellis was wrong to attribute to intrigue what was in fact merely the will of the Shah.[16] It was indeed one of the enduring weaknesses of British diplomatists in Iran that they could never concede that there could be a genuine conflict between the interests of Iran and those of Britain; all opposition had to be attributed to fanaticism, corruption, irrationality, or some nefarious intrigue, commonly inspired by Russia. Ellis had no more success with other matters. His advice on internal and external policy was received without enthusiasm and the Shah flatly objected to his warnings about Herat. 'The Shah and the Hajee are *all* and *only* for war and the preparations for it', wrote the knowledgeable surgeon, Dr. Riach.[17] Ellis's hopes of an understanding between Iran and the Ottomans were rudely shattered when he failed to prevent the departure of a mission to Muhammad Ali of Egypt which was sent to discuss a joint attack on the Ottomans.[18]

As a result of his failure Ellis quickly abandoned the rational fallacy. The scapegoat was Russia. Russian influence, he declared, was unshakeable. It rested not only on fear but on the fact that the Shah's ministers, predominantly from Azerbaijan, wished to stand well with the power which they believed was destined to rule their native province. Britain's answer should be first, to take a strong line and to make satisfaction over Herat and the commercial treaty touchstones of Iranian good intentions. If this were unsuccessful Britain should reverse her policy in Iran, seek an alternative buffer, and neutralize Iran by creating anarchy in the southern and central parts of that country. To this drastic conclusion, foreshadowed in his last writings before his departure from London, Ellis came, within a week of his arrival.[19] Less than two weeks after this he was already threatening the Shah, in what he conceived to be his capacity as a private individual.[20] Finally, just over two months from his arrival he abandoned hope of Iran: 'Our policy should be to consider her no longer as an outwork for the defence of India but as the first parallel from which the attack may be conceived or launched.'[21] In place of Iran Britain should create a new buffer in Afghanistan. As it was, Iran was threatening to destroy that new buffer even before it was built. Ellis attributed the Iranian ambitions against Afghanistan to the influence of Russia; it was Simonich who was encouraging the Shah to attack Herat. Going far beyond his instructions, he took it upon himself to warn the Iranian Government that Britain would view any attack on Herat with grave displeasure.[22]

Ellis's fears for the security of Afghanistan were enhanced by the arrival in Tehran of two Afghan envoys. One, named Haji Husayn Ali Khan (?), was an adventurer who claimed falsely to be an emissary of Dost Muhammad Khan in Kabul, sent to negotiate an agreement for the partition of Herat. Ellis, completely deceived, dispatched him to India to discuss an alliance between Britain and Kabul.[23] The other, Aziz Muhammad Khan, was a genuine envoy from Qandahar, who reported that the Barakzay rulers of Qandahar, fearing both the menace of the Sikhs and of the Sadozays of Herat, sought an alliance with Iran, directed against Herat. The terms, he stated, were agreed, and added that all Afghanistan was ready to submit to Iran and to join in a Muslim march on Delhi.[24] Alarmed by these dark perils, Ellis raised his tone still further. He warned the Shah and even Simonich that they should leave Herat alone. In addition, he offered to mediate between Herat and Iran. Such words went far beyond his instructions, but Ellis compounded his deception of the Iranian ministers by informing them that all his communications on political and commercial matters had been in accordance with his instructions.[25]

Ellis's mission was now over. In May 1836 he left Tehran to meet his successor, John McNeill, at Tabriz. With some effrontery he claimed to have succeeded in the two major problems of his mission—the commercial treaty and Herat. For the first he had obtained a firman from the Shah which, he submitted, granted all that could have been hoped for from a commercial treaty; and for the second he claimed to have shaken the Shah's resolve to attack Afghanistan.[26] It is scarcely necessary to comment that both contentions were unfounded. The firman was worthless and the Shah's determination to attack Herat as strong as ever. Muhammad Shah promptly departed on a preliminary expedition to Turkestan.

Ellis's mission had been a disaster. He had achieved nothing. His threats, especially when contrasted with the subsequent attitude of McNeill, weakened the force of later remonstrations. No action was taken to enforce Ellis's threats and Simonich apparently informed the Shah that Ellis did not have the support of his own Government.[27] Worse, Ellis had repeated on a larger scale the errors of Shee in 1832 and suggested both an obsession with fears of a Russian attack on India and impotence when it came to taking action against it. The truth was that Ellis had, knowingly or innocently, drawn the wrong conclusions. The Herat expedition was perfectly comprehensible in terms of the ambitions of Muhammad Shah. The alarming and fictitious bogey of Russian instigation was an unnecessary creation by Ellis.

The responsibility for the failure of the mission is shared by Ellis and Palmerston. Ellis's ambition had driven him to try to give his mission a far greater importance than had been intended; his hasty misreading of the situation had compounded his original error. Palmerston's responsibility is perhaps a heavier one. He had sent a man he did not trust on a mission he did not want. He had allowed Ellis to stay ten months instead of two. He had tried to limit Ellis's powers, but when Ellis exceeded his instructions he neither reproved nor supported him. No guidance was ever given to Ellis. In truth Palmerston had little time for Iran.

Ellis, after an abortive attempt to negotiate a commercial treaty with Brazil in a further search for elusive honours, in 1848 was gratified at last by the knighthood for which he had craved so long, and was succeeded by John McNeill. 'McNeill', wrote Palmerston, 'is far the ablest man we have ever had in Persia'[28] and for once he was right. There was a breadth and a quality to McNeill's mind which only Malcolm surpassed, and McNeill had qualities as a diplomatist which Malcolm did not possess. A passage from a later dispatch to Aberdeen may be quoted for its flavour of warming humility and for a careful and philosophical precision in the use of language which would have done credit to McNeill's fellow countryman David Hume:

Englishmen, even those best acquainted with Asiatics, continually fail to divine their intentions or accurately to estimate their views; for though we may arrive at a general knowledge of their motives, we are rarely able to assign to each its due influence, or to judge accurately of the value attached by them to the different objects they may have in contemplation.[29]

The son of a landowner on the small Hebridean island of Colonsay, McNeill had trained as a surgeon and first entered Iran in the service of the Company in that capacity. From the beginning he had found himself also employed on political work by Willock, Macdonald, and Campbell. For eighteen months, while Campbell's eyesight was seriously impaired, McNeill had conducted most of the work of the mission. Sent to London by Campbell in the autumn of 1834, his ability was quickly recognized. Ellenborough selected him for the post of First Secretary with Ellis and in the summer of 1835 Palmerston withdrew him, intending to send him to Iran as Resident Minister after the conclusion of Ellis's brief congratulatory mission.

Palmerston's habitually dilatory attitude towards the affairs of Iran delayed McNeill for almost a year. McNeill repeatedly urged the need for a rapid decision, but it was not until 21 May 1836 that he received permission to draw up his instructions. These were the product of long discussions involving Palmerston, his Under-Secretary John Backhouse, Grant (now Lord Glenelg), and the new President of the Board of Control, Sir John Hobhouse. But the principal influence was that of McNeill himself. The instructions, however, fell far short of what McNeill wanted and from the beginning he had little confidence of success.[30]

McNeill's instructions embodied the same general view which inspired Macdonald and Ellis.[31] Iran was a natural ally. All that was required was to make the basic facts of the situation clear and British influence must predominate. The only question at issue was how much in the way of assurances should be offered to Iran and on this subject there was considerable disagreement between Palmerston and McNeill.

The question of the assurances hinged upon what should be inserted into the 1814 Treaty to replace the abrogated clauses. As long ago as February 1833 McNeill had argued that the treaty was worthless in its existing form because it threw all the obligations upon Iran alone. He criticized as contradictory the arguments which were advanced against offering Iran assistance; on the one hand men contended that it was dangerous to offer support to Iran in case she was encouraged to attack Russia and on the other that it was wrong to do so because Iran was subservient to Russia.[32] McNeill's conversations with Iranian ministers had led him to believe that a new offer would be acceptable. The 1833 offer, which had amounted to one of moral support only, was clearly inadequate. Palmerston's attitude to this was ambivalent. On the one hand he conceded that the absence of a British guarantee had compelled Iran to acquiesce in Russian policies. But on the other, he was, like Canning, opposed to guarantees on principle, and well aware that Parliamentary approval was both necessary and unlikely. In addition he did not wish to offend Russia by apparently encouraging Iran to make war upon her. Accordingly, Palmerston designed a clause which bristled with qualifications. The treaty was stated to be strictly defensive. If any European nation invaded Iran, Britain would send (from India) either arms and troops or an annual subsidy of 200,000 tomans subject to the following conditions: the subsidy would not be paid if the war was the result of Iranian aggression; nor if Britain had not previously had the opportunity to investigate and to mediate; and it would be forfeited if Britain decided that Iran was not justified in taking up arms. The clause had more escape holes than a colander, and McNeill pressed for at least an additional guarantee to meet the event of a sudden, unprovoked assault. Palmerston, however, would allow only verbal assurances on this point.[33] In the end McNeill inclined to the view that it would be better to restore the abrogated articles. He wrote about the final draft of the new article: 'these engagements, it appears to me contain the minimum of concession to the wants and wishes of Persia with which it can be hoped that government will be satisfied or from which it can acquire confidence in England.'[34] The remainder of McNeill's instructions followed a pattern similar to those of Ellis, but with some significant differences. He was to negotiate a commercial treaty of which he was supplied with a detailed draft, but he was given permission to settle only for the substance. McNeill believed that it was possible to secure a commercial agreement, providing that the demand for British Consuls was limited to Tabriz and Tehran and that Iranian agents were accepted elsewhere. Like Ellis, McNeill was also instructed to urge the Shah to concentrate upon internal reform. For this purpose McNeill could assist in building a strong Iranian army for internal security, but not for foreign conquest. The assistance was not to be financial and this limitation represented a further defeat for McNeill.

McNeill believed that the keys to domestic reform and the construction of a strong Iran were a strong army and the reform of the taxation system. A people alienated from their own government by oppressive taxation would be useless as allies. The twin questions of the army and taxation were obviously linked. The only way in which the two institutions could be reformed was through the acceptance of direct responsibility by Britain. McNeill recalled Abbas Mirza's earlier offer to make Hart the paymaster of the Iranian army by assigning revenues for that purpose and put it forward as a proposal. So far-reaching an arrangement would have involved Britain deeply in the internal affairs of Iran, anticipating the twentieth-century system which obtained under the Americans, Shuster and Millspaugh, and was intended to operate under the abortive Agreement of 1919. There are also obvious associations with earlier developments within Indian states and later developments in China. The rejection of this proposal in 1835 was apparently not because of fears of the involvement, but because the money was not available to prime the pump. For this purpose a British subsidy was needed and Palmerston said that H. M. Government could not provide the money 'however important the objects to be obtained' without Parliamentary assent. He would not ask for this, he went on, because it would involve giving publicity to the fears of Russia which had inspired the request.[35] Instead he suggested that Hobhouse should ask the East India Company to find the £30,000 a year which would be needed, but Hobhouse refused. The episode exposes, like the earlier argument about the expenses of Ellis's mission, some of the limitations on the use of India as a bank for political purposes. Without financial assistance the project was abandoned.

With regard to foreign policy, McNeill was instructed to advise the Shah to practice conciliation towards Russia, to pay off the remainder of the indemnity, and to settle his differences with Herat by negotiation. Subject to various qualifications, McNeill was authorized to offer to mediate between Iran and Herat but was warned: 'you should act with great caution in this matter and refrain from offering to interfere unless you should have good reason to expect that your mediation will be accepted by the Persian government.' McNeill was told always to remember the ninth article. If possible, he was to persuade Iran to drop the article, but he was instructed not to press the matter if the Iranians seemed unwilling. There was little disagreement between Palmerston and McNeill on this matter; both treated the questions of Russia and Afghanistan with great caution and rejected the strident tones of Ellis's advice. McNeill, in particular, disputed all of Ellis's pessimistic conclusions about foreign affairs. He did not believe either that Russian influence was so strong or Iranian indifference to the British alliance so great as Ellis claimed. It was a mistake to threaten Iran and premature to talk of abandoning the Iranian alliance. While he doubted whether Iran could be maintained as a buffer indefinitely, he yet thought that it was possible to maintain British influence long enough to create a substantial buffer in Afghanistan before the Iranian buffer collapsed.[36] McNeill thought that Ellis had allowed himself to be bluffed over Afghanistan and led to give too much prominence to the ninth article. He did not share Ellis's fears of the consequences of Iran's eastern ambitions. Providing Iran could be made a sure ally and diverted from Herat, her eastern interests could become a source of advantage to Britain. If she could forestall a Russian occupation of Khiva and establish her influence at Bukhara, Iran could become the agent by which British influence could be spread in Turkestan.

This last argument advanced by McNeill illustrates most clearly the difference between his approach and that of Palmerston to Iran. Palmerston saw Iran's role in British strategy as a purely passive one; she fulfilled her purpose merely by existing. Like Ellis, he opposed an Iranian expedition to Khiva.[37] McNeill on the other hand, more concerned with the defence of India and with a vested interest in a more active part for Iran, cast that country as a dynamic character. Later events tended to bear out his view that the extension of Iranian power eastwards could benefit Britain more than Russia, and, in 1879, following the fresh collapse of the Afghan buffer, the project was to be briefly revived.

There is one curious exception to the generally sceptical reception which Ellis's gloomy prognostications were accorded in London. This is a dispatch sent by Hobhouse through the Secret Committee to the Governor-General, Lord Auckland, on 25 June 1836. It is a famous dispatch because it was later held by Auckland Colvin and by many other subsequent writers to be the basis of Auckland's whole Afghan policy.[38] As will be shown in chapter 6, that view is mistaken, but some mystery still surrounds the circumstances in which the dispatch was sent. In it Auckland was recommended to establish British influence in

Afghanistan either by sending a confidential agent to observe events in Kabul, or by opening political and commercial relations with the Amir Dost Muhammad. He was also given discretion to use any other measures to counteract Russian influence.[39] The dispatch was written after consultation with Palmerston and with the approval of the King, following the receipt of reports from Ellis of alleged approaches to the Shah by Afghan emissaries. Although the dispatch was permissive and reflected a genuine doubt in the mind of Hobhouse concerning the choice of Iran or Afghanistan as a buffer. it yet implies some measure of belief in Ellis's contention that the Iranian buffer was rapidly crumbling, if it had not already disappeared, and that it was necessary to start immediately to build a new defensive barrier in Afghanistan.[40] Such a rapid new initiative ran counter to the long-term policy of building political influence in Afghanistan by means of commercial contacts, and it was to this latter policy that Hobhouse promptly reverted. Indeed, after Ellis returned to England, Hobhouse discussed the situation with him and wrote to Auckland that he was opposed to Ellis's suggestion of an offensive and defensive alliance with Dost Muhammad. He favoured only the strengthening of relations and more frequent intercourse with Afghanistan.[41] As late as the end of 1837 Hobhouse still looked to a continuation of the 1830 policy of the gradual extension of British influence beyond the Indus through commerce.[42] The strange shift of attitude in June 1836 therefore is more apparent than real and was not followed up. The instructions to McNeill, which carried an implied rejection of Ellis's conclusions, were not amended in any way as a result. Once again one is left to think that the true explanation of the inconsistency is that neither Hobhouse nor Palmerston took the matter sufficiently seriously to be aware of it.[43]

McNeill left London for Iran on 5 June 1836. He bore the title Minister Plenipotentiary and Envoy Extraordinary. His subordinates were already in Iran. They included Captain Justin Sheil (1803–71), Secretary; Captain Charles Stoddart, (1806–42), Military Secretary; Captain R. D. H. Macdonald (d. 1850, Macdonald's nephew), commanding the escort; Dr. Charles W. Bell, Surgeon. Dr. James P. Riach, who bore the title First Medical Officer, was used primarily on political duties. In addition McNeill could draw upon the officers of the detachment if necessary. As was customary, the Resident in the Persian Gulf at Bushir was under his control for matters relating to Iran, but remained directly under the Bombay Government for matters relating to other areas of the Gulf.

McNeill met Ellis on the Ottoman–Iranian frontier in September 1836. Ellis brought the news that the Shah had departed on a new campaign against Herat. In fact, Ellis was in error; the expedition involving twenty-eight thousand men and forty-four guns was directed not against Herat, but against the Turkoman tribes of the area to the north of the Afghan state. After a reverse at Suknak, it was abandoned for a year. McNeill, however, was led by Ellis to believe that Russia had instigated the expedition, and complained to Palmerston, who took up the matter with the Russian Government. While denying that Simonich had encouraged the Shah, Nesselrode agreed to recall him.

The extent of Russian involvement in the expedition is obscure. Simonich himself favoured the extension of Iranian control in the east, providing that arrangements were made which would open access for Russian trade. But he saw Iranian control as only a short-term measure; in the long-term he believed that the whole area to the south-east of the Caspian including Khiva and Shahrud should become Russian. He shared the general Russian view that this area would provide an important outlet for Russian manufactures. 'La Turcomania et l'Asie Centrale doivent devenir le marché exclusif de la Russie.'[44] In his memoirs, however, Simonich reveals that there was a party within the Government in St. Petersburg which was opposed to the use of Iran as an agent through which the area could be opened to Russian commerce. This party wanted the area to become a separate state with a view to its ultimate conquest by Russia. If this is true then it suggests both a reason for Simonich's support of the Turkoman expedition and also a reason for his proposed recall.

Inevitably, McNeill's action in complaining of Simonich did not help relations between the two men. Matters were made worse by quarrels over precedence. So, personal dislike came to accentuate the political divisions which already existed, by reason of McNeill's notorious hostility towards Russia and his tendency always to see the policy of that state in Machiavellian terms. Simonich, who oddly enough had enjoyed excellent personal relations with Ellis, developed an intense dislike for his new colleague, even affecting to find his character far inferior to that of Campbell.[45] There seems little doubt that the absence of free communication between the diplomatic representatives of the two states was an important contributory factor in what was to follow. In retrospect it is clear that the political gulf between Britain and Russia was far narrower than was imagined at the time and might have been bridged by better relations between Simonich and McNeill, rather than widened by the bad relations which prevailed.

McNeill drew a second, unfortunate conclusion from the news of the failure of the Turkestan expedition. This was that he need not worry about Herat for some time to come. Ever since 1832 he had believed

Iran unequal to conquering Herat and the 1836 reverse confirmed his judgement. Muhammad Shah, he thought, was not likely to try again in the near future and therefore it was unnecessary to raise the question. Consequently he made no use of the permission which he had been given by Auckland to make representations to the Shah so as to prevent a renewal of the expedition. McNeill's silence on the subject, when contrasted with Ellis's strident protests, must have confirmed the Shah and his advisors in their belief that Ellis had had no authority for his threats and that the British Government would not oppose a further expedition.

McNeill settled down to the long, slow haul of rebuilding good Anglo–Iranian relations. He assisted in removing the Foreign Minister, Mirza Masud, whom he declared was a Russian pensioner. The Russians denied that he was, but admitted giving him a large sum of money when he visited St. Petersburg. Britain's own pensioner, the former Foreign Minister, Mirza Abu'l Hasan Khan, was still out of favour after his implication in the Zil al-Sultan's attempt to seize power in 1834. McNeill weakened Masud by supporting Haji Mirza Aghasi against him and in June 1837 the Foreign Minister left for Mecca. McNeill's own personal influence steadily increased. He was consulted on frontier questions; he reported that the Iranians appeared well aware of the danger from Russia and the value of the British alliance; and on 28 February 1837 he announced that British influence was second to none.[46] Having advanced to this point he decided to put his influence to the test.

In February 1837 McNeill opened negotiations on the revision of the political treaty and on the proposed commercial treaty. Ignoring Mirza Masud, he went directly to the Shah and Haji Mirza Aghasi. No immediate success came his way. As he had feared, the replacement article was insufficiently attractive to the Iranians; they would not pay for its inclusion by agreeing to the removal of the ninth article. If the treaty was to be amended, they wanted an offensive and defensive alliance. McNeill made little greater progress with the commercial treaty. He found the Iranians very hostile to the establishment of Consuls anywhere. They considered that the firman granted to Ellis had ended the matter and were unwilling to reopen it. It seemed clear to McNeill that Britain would have to increase her offers to Iran, preferably with money.[47] It was apparent that the problems were more stubborn than he had realized.

McNeill's hopes were finally destroyed by the recrudescence of the Herat question. He had tried hard to avoid becoming involved in this. In December 1836 when the renewal of the expedition was mooted he had studiously avoided any action which might have been construed as British intervention. He evaded an attempt by Haji Mirza Aghasi to elicit his views and even assisted the minister in making catapults for the siege of Herat.[48] McNeill's discretion was the outcome of his desire not to jeopardize the influence so painfully acquired by his conciliatory policy; of his consciousness of the limitations imposed by the ninth article; of his sympathy with the Iranian claim that by her encouragement of the slave-trade Herat was really the aggressor; and of his belief that the Iranians were bluffing—that they had no intention of undertaking an expedition in which they could not succeed and were merely trying to extract further concessions from Britain.[49]

McNeill made his first cautious move towards involvement in the Herat dispute in February 1837. He then proposed a general mediation by Britain between Iran on the one hand and Khiva, Bukhara, and Herat on the other, with the object of abolishing the slave-trade. By this formula he avoided breaching the ninth article.[50] Nothing came of this offer, however, and McNeill did not press the matter. In May 1837 he made a new attempt to mediate, this time between Iran and Herat alone. The occasion was provided by the arrival in Tehran of an Herati envoy, a young and able man named Fath Muhammad Khan. McNeill claimed that he had been asked to mediate by both Iran and Herat and, therefore, was within the ninth article. Simonich, whose information came from Iranian sources, denied that Iran had asked McNeill to mediate.[51] McNeill advised Fath Muhammad not to meet Simonich. The terms which Fath Muhammad offered were probably suggested by McNeill. They amounted to a renewal of the 1833 Agreement between Iran and Herat, which had been signed when the death of Abbas Mirza had forced the abandonment of the earlier expedition against Herat. This agreement involved the payment of tribute; the striking of money in the name of the Shah; the protection of Shiites who formed the majority of the population of Herat; the ending of raids on Iranian territory; the reduction of the fortifications of Ghuriyan, the Herati fortress to the west of the capital; and an offer of hostages.

These terms McNeill believed ought to have satisfied all the legitimate demands of Iran. The Shah rejected them on the grounds, according to McNeill, that they did not amount to a recognition of Iranian sovereignty over Herat.[52] Whether this was the real reason for rejection is unclear. Certainly the reported concessions on coinage and tribute went a long way towards recognition of sovereignty, even though they did not include the customary formula of the reading of the Shah's name first in the *khutba* or Friday prayer. The Herati attitude was ambiguous. Herat had earlier given tokens of recognition of Iranian

suzerainty and Fath Muhammad did so again in 1837, although he
informed McNeill that Herat had no intention of acknowledging Iranian sovereignty. Of the letters which he brought with him, that of Yar
Muhammad Khan, the Chief Minister of Herat, appeared to acknowledge Iranian suzerainty, while that of Kamran Shah preserved the
style of an independent sovereign. On balance it seems probable that
the real reason for rejection was scepticism. There was no good reason
to suppose that Herat would carry out in 1837 what she had not
accomplished in 1833. The Shah wanted security that Herat would
implement the agreement. The evidence of Simonich bears this out. He
stated that the negotiations broke down on the Shah's demand that the
Heratis should give hostages and reduce the Ghuriyan fortifications
before he would sign the treaty.

   Simonich was not responsible for the breakdown. Like McNeill, he
sympathized with the Iranian complaints against Herati brigandage.
In 1836 he had thought that an expedition to Herat was justified.
However, he had adopted an attitude of complete neutrality and in
May 1837 he did his best to persuade the Shah to accept the Herati offer
and not to attack that state. Like McNeill again, he thought that the
agreement was favourable to Iran. There was an additional reason for
his opposition to the Herat expedition in 1837. He had recently
received news of a new departure in Russian policy towards Afghanistan. The details of this policy are discussed in chapter 7; here it is
sufficient to note that the Russians wanted an Afghan confederation
established under Iranian protection. The Herati offer could be seen as
a step towards the achievement of that end. Finally, Simonich, once
more like McNeill, believed that an expedition against Herat could not
succeed and that failure might have disastrous results for Iran.[53]
Simonich's account of his attitude to the negotiations of May 1837 is
confirmed by two other pieces of evidence. In a dispatch to Nesselrode
of 28 May 1837 he reported that he had urged the Shah to accept the
Herati offer, but that the Shah had refused partly because of pressure
from the ulema of Mashhad.[54] And in an interview with McNeill on 28
June 1837 he admitted that he had favoured an expedition in 1836, but
maintained that he had opposed it in 1837, both because of his own
views and because of instructions from St. Petersburg.[55]

   After the failure of the negotiations McNeill wanted to take a much
firmer line over Herat. He had always anticipated that this might
become necessary and in December 1836 had asked for authority to use
'language of a very firm and decided character'.[56] In February he
hinted that words alone might not be enough and that action might
become necessary.[57] Receiving no response from England, in July he

asked Auckland to write the Shah a threatening letter on the subject of Herat.[58] Auckland, however, would not support McNeill. In November 1836 he had authorized McNeill to try to dissuade the Shah from attacking Herat, to offer mediation, and if necessary to withdraw the British detachment from eastern Iran.[59] In April he had allowed McNeill to inform the Shah that the Governor-General 'views with umbrage and displeasure schemes of interference and conquest on our western frontier'.[60] But he would not himself write directly to the Shah, and in September 1837 merely repeated his permission for McNeill to use the 'strongest language of remonstrance'.[61]

Because of the lack of support from London and Calcutta McNeill's position was very weak. He believed Herat was the key issue, but did not dare to do anything about it. Partly his hesitation arose from doubts about whether Herat was indeed an independent sovereign power and partly from worries about the ninth article. But the main factor in his reluctance to commit himself was the failure of Palmerston and Auckland to give him full backing. His subsequent actions are only intelligible in the light of this assessment of his position. He foresaw that Britain would probably need to break the treaty in order to be free to take whatever action was necessary in the matter of Herat, but he also saw that the Herat issue would not be an adequate ground for a breach. His aim, therefore, was to build plausible legal grounds for breaking off relations if it became necessary.

The question of the commercial treaty offered one opportunity to strengthen Britain's case. McNeill reopened negotiations and the Shah first agreed to accept a draft and then withdrew his consent. Now the 1814 Treaty had specified that a commercial treaty should be arranged. With some distant echo of plausibility, McNeill could argue that the Shah's refusal to conclude the commercial treaty placed upon Iran the onus of breaking the treaty. Accordingly, he informed the Shah that his departure for Khurasan without first signing the commercial treaty would be evidence that Iran was determined not to abide by the 1814 Treaty and Britain would then have to consider if the treaty were not thereby annulled. It was feeble stuff and it did not succeed in preventing the Shah from departing for the east in July 1837. Although Muhammad Shah apparently agreed to sign, McNeill found himself unable to complete the treaty after the Shah had gone.[62]

McNeill was not especially worried by the Shah's departure. It is important to understand that in the summer and early autumn of 1837 McNeill still clung to his belief that Herat was in no danger. The Shah's army would not even reach Herat, let alone capture it. He saw no likelihood that the Shah would receive help from Afghanistan. The greatest danger arising from the expedition he still thought to be that of revolution inside Iran in the event that the Shah's failure was a disastrous one.[63] So little was he concerned, that as late as November he was still planning to take sick-leave the following summer. It was not until the end of November that McNeill began to revise his views, as a result of the Shah's early successes. Muhammad Shah had collected a force of thirty-six thousand men with sixty-six guns, brought them to Herat, captured Ghuriyan, and now menaced the capital itself. McNeill still believed that the Shah could only succeed by an accident, but the accident was now a real possibility.[64]

Just as McNeill was beginning to show concern, he was presented with new grounds for a break with Iran, far superior to the affair of the commercial treaty. This new opportunity arose from two apparently serious breaches of diplomatic etiquette by Iran. In the first, Haji Mirza Aghasi was reported to have threatened the personal safety of McNeill and in the second, a messenger, sent by McNeill to accompany Fath Muhammad on his return to Herat, was stopped (seemingly by mistake) on his way back, by Iranian soldiers, who searched and ill-treated him. McNeill decided to use these two incidents to force the issue.[65] He demanded redress from the Iranian Government and immediately sent his secretary, Justin Sheil, to put the facts before Palmerston in London. As it happened, the first complaint collapsed when Haji Mirza Aghasi denied having issued the reported threats, but the episode of the messenger survived to become the original and one of the major causes of the dispute between Britain and Iran, according to the subsequent official British presentation of the question.[66] Henry Rawlinson described it as a symbol of the struggle between Britain and Iran for supremacy within their alliance. It was indeed a skilful choice of battle ground by McNeill. The Iranian Government played into his hands in the matter. Instead of apologizing, the Iranians first argued that as an Iranian subject the messenger was not entitled to diplomatic immunity and secondly, that even if he had ever possessed any diplomatic immunity he had forfeited it when he visited Herat. These were poor arguments. With regard to the second, McNeill could argue plausibly that the messenger's visit to Herat was in connection with the mediation which he had undertaken with Iranian agreement. The first argument was one which neither Britain nor Russia could accept and Simonich was obliged to join McNeill in protesting against it. Simonich commented that McNeill was delighted with the outcome of the affair because it gave him an excellent position from which to argue.[67]

While the affair of the messenger dragged on through the winter McNeill became steadily more anxious about Herat. He had never expected that the Shah would be able to maintain his forces before the city during the months of scarcity. His worries were increased by his growing conviction that Russia was behind the expedition. Reports reached him of the passage through Iran of a Russian agent, Paul Vitkevich, and of an offer by Simonich to forgo the demand for the outstanding crore if the Shah captured Herat.[68] In February 1838 McNeill announced that if the Shah conquered Herat, Russia and Iran would become dominant in Central Asia. He recommended that Britain should disregard the ninth article and that he should be given permission to go to Herat to inform the Shah that, if Iran persisted in assaulting the city, Britain would give aid to Herat and in any case would not permit the Shah to retain the city, even if Iran should succeed in taking it.[69]

Without waiting for instructions McNeill set out for Herat on 8 March 1838. He justified his action partly by reference to a message received from the British agent at Qandahar, Captain Leech, to the effect that instructions from Auckland ordering him to persuade the Shah to withdraw from Herat, were on the way to McNeill. Other reasons given for his action were the refusal of redress in the messenger affair and new evidence of what he believed was the Russo–Iranian plan to dominate Afghanistan and threaten India. This evidence consisted of copies of letters written by the Kabuli envoy to Iran, Haji Ibrahim, and by Simonich to Dost Muhammad Khan in Kabul. The letters contained, McNeill claimed, 'an unequivocal intimation of an intention to attack the English in India.'[70] McNeill was not optimistic about his chances of inducing the Shah to withdraw from Herat and he took the further important step of urging Auckland to send an expedition to the Gulf to support British representations.[71]

Upon his arrival at Herat McNeill suspended his bellicose determination and reverted to his former conciliatory policy. This tactical switch was the consequence of the situation which he discovered at Herat. First, there seemed to be no immediate prospect that Herat would fall to Iran. Properly directed the Iranian army could easily have overcome the resistance of Herat's five thousand defenders, but disunion among the Iranian commanders prevented a concerted assault. Individual generals made desultory attacks, but for the most part the Shah relied upon an inaccurate artillery bombardment. Second, British remonstrance had already been tried and failed. McNeill's Military Secretary, Colonel Stoddart, who had accompanied the Iranian army, had in February informed Haji Mirza Aghasi that Britain would take steps to ensure the continued independence of Herat.[72] Stoddart claimed that such language was authorized in a dispatch sent by

Auckland to Wade, the British agent at Ludhiana, but Auckland denied that he had ever authorized such a threat.[73] In any case Stoddart's effort had been unsuccessful and McNeill did not wish to repeat the failure. Instead he avoided all reference to Herat and began again to try to restore the Shah's confidence in himself. What the Shah understood by these curious fluctuations in British policy can only be the subject of speculation; the difficulty for him was to know when the cycle was to end.

McNeill's conciliatory policy had some success, and the Shah gave him permission to try to mediate Iran's differences with Herat. The negotiations took place on 19 and 20 April, but they broke down. McNeill blamed the Shah for insisting on the recognition of Iranian suzerainty and complained that his obduracy on this point was the consequence of the arrival of Simonich. Simonich had followed McNeill to Herat with the announced purpose of seeking the return of a battalion of Russian deserters who were serving with the Iranian army. This may well have been the real reason because there is evidence to show that Russia attached great importance to this point.[74] McNeill saw a more sinister purpose behind his visit and refused to discuss his negotiations with Simonich, apart from suggesting that their failure was the outcome of Kamran's insistence that the Shah must first of all evacuate Ghuriyan.[75] If Simonich's account of his conversation is true there is a curious discrepancy between McNeill's remark and his version of the failure in his official dispatch. More importantly, the deep distrust which existed between the two men prevented possible co-operation. It is an odd but significant fact that when Simonich himself tried unsuccessfully to mediate between Iran and Herat after the failure of the Iranian assault in July 1838, the agreement which he offered was almost identical with that of McNeill. Had the two Envoys worked together, Simonich might have avoided the error which he was to make and which apparently confirmed all McNeill's analysis of Russian policy.

At the end of April the Shah decided to try again for peace. He then accepted McNeill's draft agreement but shortly afterwards killed the hopes of settlement by introducing a new demand for a large indemnity from Herat.[76] McNeill attributed this second failure to achieve a negotiated settlement to the arrival in the Shah's camp of an envoy from Qandahar, Allah Dad Khan, accompanied by the Iranian envoy to that state, Qumber Ali. Allah Dad brought a proposal for an alliance against Herat. Hitherto, the Qandaharis had declined to commit themselves, because of hopes of better offers from Britain, but, as will be described later, these had not been forthcoming. McNeill was disgusted at Auckland's failure to hold the Afghans together against Iran. 'This was laying me flat on my back', he wrote.[77]

It was the Qandahari–Iranian Treaty which led Simonich to err. He was asked to guarantee the treaty and he did so. He had no instructions to take such a step, but his general instructions urged him to promote the formation of an Afghan confederation under Iranian leadership. He argued that if Russia gave such a guarantee Dost Muhammad would also join the alliance and the confederation would thus be accomplished. Besides, he wrote later, how could he refuse an opportunity to make Russia, at a stroke of the pen, 'l'arbitre de l'orient'?[78]

Simonich's action was repudiated by his Government. Nesselrode did not object to the treaty as such. He claimed that it was essentially a defensive alliance designed to secure the eastern frontier of Iran against brigandage, by placing Herat under the control of Qandahar. But Russia would not guarantee the treaty because the area was outside Russia's chosen political sphere.[79] Unfortunately, the orders to Simonich to refuse his guarantee arrived too late. As it transpired, Simonich's guarantee was the cause of tension between Britain and Russia and Simonich was accused by his colleagues of wishing to plunge Russia into war with Britain. Simonich argued that there was no danger of war in 1838; Britain was too frightened for India. He wrote: 'La postion de la Russie en Perse, était tellement imposante, en commencement de 1838, que pour mettre la combustion dans les Indes elle n'avait qu'à le vouloir.'[80] This, of course, was precisely the danger which alarmed the more sophisticated British strategists and Simonich's arguments must restore the possibility that McNeill and others were justified in their suspicions of Russian policy. For, although he was repudiated by his Government, the chance must exist that these views were shared by others, and that under different circumstances they might well have become official Russian policy. The question, however, is one which cannot be decided. It is not certain that Simonich himself held these views at the time; his memoirs were written some years later to justify his own conduct and may well not indicate his own feelings in 1838. His actions are another matter and the copies of his dispatches which were shown to the British representative at St. Petersburg, John Milbanke, bear out the version in his memoirs. There were reports that Simonich and Vitkevich had been given unauthorized instructions by K. K. Rhodofiniken, a bandy-legged Greek, then head of the Asiatic Department of the Russian Foreign Ministry. Rhodofiniken, it was alleged, had private financial and commercial interests in the East.[81] This story seems unlikely: had such instructions existed they would have tended to exculpate

Simonich and he would surely have referred to them in his memoirs. Rhodofiniken, who died in 1838, was just a convenient scapegoat. On balance I incline to believe that those who held views similar to those expressed by Simonich in his memoirs were very few; official Russian policy was opposed to such commitments and preferred co-operation with Britain; and that Simonich's ambition, isolation, and the absence of consultation with McNeill led him to overreach himself.

Once committed to the Iranian cause Simonich compounded his errors. He asked one of his officers, Captain I. F. Blarenburg, to submit a plan for the better conduct of the siege, although he observed ruefully that the Shah did not like it and would have been better pleased with Russian approval of his own plans.[82] He gave the Shah money to enable him to continue at Herat. The last major Iranian assault of 24 July was largely planned and directed by Russian officers. When news arrived of projected British operations in Afghanistan, Simonich repeated his recommendations for a more active Russian policy. Russia should gurantee the Qandahari–Iran Treaty so as to put Qandahar in possession of Herat before the British expedition arrived there. This would at least delay the establishment of British control over that city. British predominance in Afghanistan would be most injurious to Russian interests, he claimed. All hopes of forming, in Central Asia, a secure market for Russian manufactures would be at an end and even the security of Russian territory would be in jeopardy.[83]

McNeill broke off relations with Iran in June 1838. A last effort to persuade the Shah to withdraw had failed in May. The Shah had offered to abandon the seige if McNeill would give him a reasonable pretext for so doing. He wanted a threat of war.[84] Such words were far beyond McNeill's instructions, so, with his habitual caution, he decided to phrase his note to the Shah in such a way as to avoid making Herat the sole issue and not to make any direct reference to war. Instead, he merely included Herat as one of a number of issues in dispute between Britain and Iran. The list also included the commercial treaty, the messenger affair, an incident at Bushir, and an insult which had been offered by an Iranian officer named Haji Khan. Simonich advised the Shah to accept all the British demands, except that relating to Herat, but the Shah played into McNeill's hands by insisting upon rejecting them all.[85] By this time McNeill had received instructions from Palmerston which authorized him to break off diplomatic relations if he received no satisfaction over the messenger. On 3 June he announced that this was his intention, and after the failure of one final effort at agreement, he left the Shah's camp on 7 June.[86]

McNeill blamed Russia for his failure in part, but the principal responsibility he attached to Auckland and Palmerston. They had neither given him adequate instructions nor taken positive action. Auckland's failure to support Alexander Burnes in Afghanistan, which had pushed Kabul and Qandahar into the Iranian camp, was the last straw. If the Afghan states had supported Herat, or even remained neutral, the Shah, McNeill declared, would never have been able to take Herat.[87] In a bitter, private letter to James Fraser, which he sent open to Backhouse, presumably with the intention that it should be read by Palmerston, he complained:

the fact that Russia having had the courage to come forward, we, as usual *slink* away and leave the field to her, having done just enough to prove to the whole world that we would have done more if we dared. It is vain to suppose that we can possess or retain or obtain influence anywhere on these terms.[88]

Some of the responsibility for the failure belongs to McNeill himself. His conciliatory policy, in contrast with Ellis's premature aggressiveness, misled the Shah about Britain's attitude towards Herat. Right until the end it must have been difficult for the Shah to decide what were the views of the British Government and what were those of the British Envoys. McNeill also misled Palmerston. Particularly in his private letters he was too optimistic for too long and continually underestimated the capabilities of the Iranian Army. Finally, he was handicapped by his intense suspicion of Russia. There is evidence that there was sufficient common ground between Russia and Britain to have provided the basis for joint action, as had been the case in 1834. Whatever their personal beliefs, McNeill and Simonich could have worked together within a common framework. Instead McNeill's hostility, if it did not drive Simonich to extremes, at least provided him with an opportunity to exceed his instructions and to try to reshape Russian policy. It could be said that the main problem for Britain and Russia in Iran was not to control the Shah but to control their own agents.

There is a paradoxical element in the story of the decline and fall of British influence in Iran. British influence had been allowed to decline after 1814 because there was no fear of Russia and it had fallen in 1838 because there was such fear. The warnings of Willock, Malcolm, and Macdonald concerning the Russian threat to India through Iran had been disregarded. When the warnings were repeated in the 1830s by Campbell, Ellis, and McNeill the British response was too slow, too little, and too great. There is no doubt that the true inspiration behind the Herat campaign was Iran, not Russia. Vitkevich admitted as much in Qandahar when he declared that Muhammad Shah was 'neither assisted nor induced by the Russians, and is come himself to try his fortunes'.[89] Accordingly, it could well be argued that no danger to India existed. The belief that such a danger did exist hinges on the assumption that Iran was under Russian influence and there is no good evidence that this was so. Why then, one might ask, did British representatives in Iran so often (although not very consistently) complain that Russian influence was predominant? It has been suggested in these chapters that for many this was both a way of explaining their failures and of giving greater importance to their own position. With McNeill the explanation is more complex.

McNeill's attitude to Iran was really the mirror image of that of the new Russian school of policy-makers. Just as the Russians hoped to make Iran the agent of Russian policies in Central Asia, so McNeill hoped to make Iran the agent of British influence. Not until a very late stage did he see the Herat expedition as a real danger to British India; until then it was a nuisance because it created friction between the two countries, and a menace because it endangered the stability of Iran. His advocacy of the extension of British influence in Afghanistan was only partly influenced by the need to find a new buffer to replace Iran; partly it was also because he hoped that a strong, united Afghanistan would deter Iran from attacking her, remove the source of friction with Britain, and so allow Britain to recover her influence in Iran. Iran and Afghanistan would then be able to act together against Russia.[90] For McNeill the Afghan and Iranian buffers were not so much alternatives as complementary.

Both in Iran and in India the creation of an Afghan buffer had long been contemplated. Fraser and Ellis had recommended it. In March 1837, McNeill had constantly urged upon the Afghan envoys to Iran the need to unite Afghanistan. In India, ever since 1830, Britain had been moving slowly and unsteadily towards a similar view. By the time the breach with Iran came in 1838 the decision to seek an alternative in Afghanistan was almost inevitable. What had yet to be decided was the form of the Afghan buffer. The story of the development of British policy towards Afghanistan will be the subject of Part II.

PART II

THE ROAD TO CENTRAL ASIA

The Frontier of
British India, 1765–1830

The one universal principle never to be departed from, either in the present condition of the Native Powers, or in any future revolutions amongst them, is that we are completely satisfied with the possessions we already have, and will engage in no wars for the purpose of future acquisitions.

Secret Committee to Governor-General in Council,
21 July 1786.

The problem of the defence of British India arose when that institution was born in Bengal in 1765. It was no longer a matter of defending trading bases but one of protecting valuable territories and the revenues which they produced. The central task was to preserve Bengal itself.

Bengal could not be made secure by a system of static defence. The armies of the Indian states which menaced the province were composed principally of light cavalry; the Bengal Army on the other hand was predominantly a force built out of disciplined infantry and artillery and its cavalry arm was weak. Although the inability of armies of light cavalry to defeat the British Indian armies in battle was amply demonstrated, it was also evident that the Bengal forces could not intercept and destroy bodies of Indian cavalry except under especially favourable circumstances. Allowed to range unchecked, lightly-encumbered horsemen could quickly lay waste entire districts and thus undermine the whole basis of the British position in India as it existed after 1765. For only the revenues of Bengal could finance the heavy overhead costs of defence and administration throughout the Presidencies of British India, support the Company's operations in Britain, and also provide funds for the purchase of trade-goods for sale in Europe. If those revenues were substantially reduced for a considerable period by the devastation which accompanied the raids, then the Company's credit would evaporate and India become unprofitable to hold. It followed from this situation that wars must take place beyond the Company's frontier; other states must pay the price of the ruin inflicted by the passage of armies. Ultimately it was this logic which underlay the long search for a suitable defensive position on the north-western frontier of Bengal; appropriately enough it was the accountant rather than the general who determined the strategy of British India.

The solution chosen by Robert Clive was to make Oudh into a buffer which would preserve Bengal inviolate. Oudh, he thought, should be strong enough to stand without the Company's assistance, but should not be strong enough to threaten the security of Bengal. This delicate balance proved too difficult to achieve and Clive's successors were obliged to commit troops to the defence of Oudh, which gradually exchanged its appearance of a passive buffer for that of a base for the operation of British influence in northern India. Under Warren Hastings the Oudh strategy underwent a further evolution when the Indian state was strengthened and extended and the British forces stationed in it were increased. Hastings was induced to make these changes by his perception of the enhanced power of the Marathas as the major threat to the British position in India and it was in the light of this analysis that, in 1777, he went to the support of the Bombay Presidency when the independent action of its Government against the Marathas had rebounded to the detriment of its fortunes.

In pursuit of his Maratha policy Hastings outlined a unified defensive system for British India. His policy in Oudh had already given Bengal an undeclared defensive frontier on the Ganges. Now the Governor-General moved rapidly beyond that river and beyond the Jamna as well through an alliance with Gohad (1779), a state lying to the west of the Jamna, by gaining control of the great fortress of Gwalior (1780), and by a project for treaties with various Rajput states, including Jaipur, Udaipur, and Jodhpur. 'These countries', he wrote, 'form a continuous chain from the Jumna to Guzerat.'[1] Under British control the Rajput states would furnish a safe line of communications across India, linking the Bengal and Bombay Presidencies; they would threaten the Marathas; and they would form a band across India which would confine the Marathas to central India, exclude them from the north-west, and keep them away from the Company's territories. Hastings's scheme implied the abandonment of what had been a basic assumption of British Indian defence, namely that British security depended upon the existence of a balance of power among the Indian states, and the replacement of that assumption by the presumption that in the long run nothing but paramountcy could guarantee British safety.

Hastings's grandiose scheme became a major element in British strategic thinking until it was achieved forty years later. It was not carried out in the time of Hastings himself chiefly because of the weakness of the third component of British India, the Madras Presidency. From 1765 until 1799 Madras was the Achilles Heel of British India. The long, thin territory of Arcot was a quite inadequate shield for the defence of Madras against attacks from Mysore and Haidarabad. It was the menace from Mysore which obliged Hastings to abandon almost all his gains in the north and make peace with the Marathas at Salbai in 1782 in order to concentrate his resources against Mysore. The lesson taught by Hastings's wars was that a satisfactory solution to the problems of the defence of Madras was an essential precondition of a more active British policy in northern India.

The achievement of permanent security in southern India was the work of Richard Wellesley, Earl of Mornington and subsequently Marquess Wellesley, who was Governor-General from 1798 to 1805. The threat from Mysore itself had already been largely dissipated by the actions of one of his predecessors, the Marquess of Cornwallis. In 1790 Cornwallis allied with Haidarabad and the Marathas against Tipu Sultan of Mysore, defeated the Mysore ruler, and, by the Treaty of Seringapatam (1792) made important gains: the loss of the Malabar coast cut Mysore off from the sea; the acquisition of the valley of the Baramahal gave Britain control of the main route from Madras to the capital of Mysore at Seringapatam; and the loss of valuable territories reduced Mysore's ability to sustain a future contest. But the Company's position in southern India was still not wholly secure: there was no land connection between the Malabar and Coromandel coasts; and the powerful presence of Haidarabad and the Marathas posed a continuing threat which was magnified by the defeat of Haidarabad by the Marathas in 1794. It was Wellesley's victory over Tipu in 1799 which gave Britain final and complete domination in southern India. Britain gained new territories, absolute control over what was left of Mysore, and a firm alliance with Haidarabad. From a source of weakness and a drain on British resources Madras was turned into an element of strength to British India; the resources of Madras could now be employed in the extension of British power in northern and central India.

Wellesley's second great achievement was the transformation of the situation of the Bengal Presidency which, despite the diversion of attention to Madras, remained, for the reasons given above, the heart of the problem of British Indian defence. The successors of Hastings had achieved little in northern India, preferring to concentrate on strengthening the British position in Oudh and being willing to abandon Hindustan to the Marathas and more especially to the great Maratha chief, Sindhia.

In 1802 when Wellesley turned his attention principally to them, the

Marathas occupied a broad area roughly nine hundred miles square, stretching at its extreme limits from Delhi in the north to the Tungabhadra river in the south and from the Bay of Bengal in the east to the Indian Ocean in the west. There were five principal Maratha states, although the term is misleading, for their territories were only partly consolidated, their possessions frequently intermingled, their rulers prone to wander, and their degrees of independence ill defined. The *de facto* head of the confederacy was Baji Rao II who had become Peshwa in 1796. Baji Rao's capital was at Poona and the bulk of his territories in western India. Also in the west was the Gaekwad of Baroda, whose territories included parts of Guzerat and Kathiawar. The death of the Gaekwad Govind Rao in 1800 led to a succession dispute which temporarily paralysed Baroda's ability to act decisively. The territories of the Bhonsla, Raghuji, Raja of Berar, were spread through central and eastern India from Nagpur to Cuttack and from the frontiers of Haidarabad to those of Bengal. West and north of the Bhonsla's territories in central India were those of Holkar, which were centred on Indore. The famous Tukoji Holkar had died in 1797 and his once prosperous territories had fallen upon evil days. Most notable among Tukoji's descendants was his illegitimate son, Jeswant Rao Holkar, whose determination to carve out an inheritance for himself provided Wellesley with his opportunity to act against the Marathas. The dominant figure in the Maratha confederacy, however, appeared to be Daulat Rao Sindhia, who had inherited from his father, Madaji, in 1794 extensive lands in Malwa, Kandeish, and in the Ganges–Jamna Doab in northern India.

All the Marathas possessed disciplined forces under European or Eurasian officers, but those of Sindhia were by far the most powerful. Under the command of the French adventurer, Pierre-François Cuillier, better known as Perron, these forces were based on the Middle Doab in the area of Aligarh. Wellesley claimed that these forces were the equivalent of a French army sitting on the Company's frontier and he set himself to destroy the power of Sindhia.[2] But first it was necessary that he should deal with Oudh.

Shortly after his arrival in India Wellesley came to the conclusion that Oudh was useless as a buffer for the protection of Bengal and he determined to set it aside. After long negotiations he achieved this end with the Treaty of 10 November 1801 by which the Nawab of Oudh ceded to the Company all his territorial possessions lying between the Ganges and the Jamna. The Bengal territories now extended in an unbroken wedge from the Bay of Bengal up the Ganges–Jamna plain into the lower Doab, where they abutted that part of Sindhia's territories which was hypothecated to the support of the troops under the command of Perron. This was a situation not to be tolerated by Wellesley and the Oudh Settlement therefore made a settlement with the Marathas both more possible and more necessary.

Wellesley's opportunity arrived in October 1802 when Jeswant Rao Holkar attacked Poona and defeated the combined forces of the Peshwa and Sindhia. Baji Rao turned to the British for help and on 31 December 1802 signed the Treaty of Bassein by which he accepted British control over his foreign relations and agreed to allow a force of Company's troops to be stationed within his lands and to be paid for by the cession of territory. Wellesley claimed that all the Marathas (including Sindhia) were bound by this treaty. To many observers, however, it was plain that the other Maratha leaders would not accept so great a reduction of their power and such indeed proved to be the case.

War broke out in August 1803 and the Marathas were defeated in western and central India, in Cuttack, and in Hindustan. Had Wellesley had his way, British paramountcy would have been established forthwith by means of annexations of territory, the formation of alliances which would have subordinated other states to Britain, and the creation of a belt of British-protected territory right across India linking the territories of Bengal, Madras, and Bombay. In this way Wellesley would have fulfilled the dream of Warren Hastings and anticipated the success of the Marquess of Hastings. Wellesley failed to achieve his end, partly because his orders were misunderstood–wilfully or accidentally—by his own officials, partly because of his inability to bring his wars to a final close, and partly because of hostility to his policies in England. Wellesley eventually fell a sacrifice to his own ambition and the settlement made under his successors fell short of his aims in several important respects, most notably in the British abandonment of central India and with it the opportunity of linking the Bombay and Bengal Presidencies.

Although incomplete, Wellesley's work had transformed the position of the British in India. In the west the Bombay Presidency had seized the opportunity to acquire substantial territorial possessions in western India; in the east the annexation of Cuttack had linked the Bengal and Madras territories by land; and, most important of all, in northern India Sindhia and Perron had been swept aside and the new British defensive frontier was formed by the Jamna which was itself screened by a belt of British-controlled territory beyond the river.

In this brief survey of the process of British Indian expansion between 1765 and 1807 it has been suggested that the motives for expansion are to be found within British India and principally in the strategic situation of the British possessions. It is not pretended that this is a complete explanation; the important commercial and official interests of the Company's servants have not been described, although such factors were particularly important in the growth of Bombay.[3] Several other factors have been omitted, among them one, the absence of which may occasion particular surprise, namely that of defence against the external enemy. It is necessary here to comment briefly upon that factor because it forms an essential element in the connection between British expansion within India and the creation of that system of strategic defence to the north-west of British India which is the subject of this book.

At various times three external enemies were held to imperil the security of British India. One, Russia, may be disregarded here, for the Russian threat appeared only briefly and insignificantly at the end of the period with which we have been concerned in this chapter, and it played no part in the formulation of higher policy. The second, Afghanistan, appeared twice—once during the 1760s when the activities of Ahmed Shah Abdali aroused fears for the safety of Bengal and were exhibited as reasons for a more active British policy in the north-west; and once during the 1790s when the renewed threat from Afghanistan under Zaman Shah was employed first by Sir John Shore and subsequently by Richard Wellesley to justify their policies in Oudh. Most important of the external enemies during this period, however, was France.

It was in the course of the struggle with France for supremacy in the Carnatic that the political ambitions and the military capability of the East India Company were forged, and although the French position in India was reduced to insignificance by the British victories during the Seven Years War, the prospect of a revival of French influence among the Indian states was never far from British minds during the following years. It was French intrigue which Warren Hastings employed to justify his Maratha policy in the 1770s; French intervention which made it the more necessary for him to concentrate his forces against Mysore in 1782; and it was the threat of France which was displayed pre-eminently by Wellesley in order to justify his attacks upon Mysore and upon the Marathas. If, as has been argued, British Indian policies are perfectly explicable without reference to the French (or, for that matter, Afghan threats) what importance should be attached to the prominance given by British Indian statesmen to the dangers allegedly presented by the external enemy?

Two explanations may be discounted. These are first, that the various French threats were real (that is, that the French seriously intended at any time to do more than create a minor diversion in the direction of India)—they were not; second, that the British authorities in India believed that the French (or Afghan) activities constituted a real threat to British power in India—they did not so believe. To rehearse the evidence on these points would consume too much space and to the understandable annoyance of readers I must present these negatives as assumptions rather than conclusions and move on to what seems the real reason why the threats were displayed in so eminent a position.

Only a forward policy, it has been argued, could provide security for the British possessions in India, yet a forward policy was expressly and explicitly forbidden by the East India Company Directors, by the British Government, and by Act of Parliament. Precautionary measures of defence would not be tolerated; British India was allowed to go to war only if it were attacked or in imminent danger of attack. These rigid prohibitions, however, could be dissolved by the solvent of the external enemy. Operations designed to frustrate the designs of France were the only ones which could reconcile the authorities in England (and particularly the President of the Board of Control, Henry Dundas) to the necessity of war against the Indian states. Until Dundas left office in 1801 the French threat served as the most acceptable excuse for expansion within India. Subsequently the matter proved more difficult; Castlereagh was less receptive to the argument of the French threat, although Wellesley continued to display it with great force in 1803. Without the benefit of the French threat in 1804 Wellesley found it exceedingly difficult to gain acceptance for his policy.

If this argument has any merit it may lead us to adapt from Walter Bagehot a distinction between the dignified and the efficient aspects of British Indian foreign policy. The dignified aspect—that which was intended for public consumption in England—stressed the danger to British India from the external enemy, in this period chiefly from France; the efficient aspect—the real mainspring of British expansion in India—was the overriding need to find a more secure defensive system for British India which would protect it against the internal enemy represented in this period by the Indian states. As has been suggested in chapter 1, Wellesley's Iranian policy belongs to the dignified aspect; it was intended to heighten the impression that a real danger from France existed and it was not designed to protect British India from non-existent French designs.

Under Lord Minto, who replaced the Acting Governor-General, George Barlow, in 1807, the dignified and efficient elements in British

Indian foreign policy became confused. For Minto, like Henry Dundas, really believed in a French threat to India and his extensive plans in the north-west were intended to combat what he saw as a major threat to British Indian security. Minto believed that the approach of a French army, possibly accompanied by assorted Russian, Ottoman, Iranian, or tribal forces, would be the signal for insurrection within the British territories and the formation of hostile coalitions among the Indian states. To Wellesley such a prospect would have been an ideal justification for completing the destruction of Maratha power, but Minto rejected the opportunity so presented to him because he thought the French danger too serious. It was essential, thought Minto, to create a system of alliances which would impede or prevent the approach of the French. It was this reasoning which persuaded Minto to send Malcolm to Iran and Iraq and to embark upon similar initiatives in Afghanistan, Sind, and the Panjab. As relations with these countries are important to the argument of this book, these latter episodes will be examined in some detail. Minto's initiative in Sind, which had little immediate consequence will be considered later in this chapter, and at this point the examination will be confined to Minto's policies in connection with Afghanistan and the Panjab.

The idea of an alliance between British India and Afghanistan was not wholly new. Something like it had been suggested by Harford Jones in 1799 and had found favour with Henry Dundas. Wellesley, however, had rejected an approach to Afghanistan because his strategy in northern India depended so heavily upon depicting Afghanistan as an irreconcilable foe. By 1807 this motive for hostility to Afghanistan had disappeared and powerful arguments began to suggest to Minto that the idea was worth pursuing. In a broad sense the French threat made it desirable to cultivate good relations with all the countries which lay to the north-west of British India, and in this sense Minto's approach to Afghanistan fits into the general pattern of the contemporary missions to Iran, Sind, and the Lahore state. More specifically, from the middle of 1808 onwards, the apparent impossibility of breaking French influence in Iran led him to think much more seriously about the possibility of an Afghan alliance: an Afghan buffer was also compatible with the Gulf strategy.

Early in 1807 a mission had been sent to Bombay from Shah Shuja al-Mulk, the ruler of Kabul. Barlow had rejected this overture, but, possibly in response to evidence that Minto was interested in the area, Jonathan Duncan suggested in February 1808 that he should send a return mission.[4] Minto sought advice from other quarters, notably from Archibald Seton who, as Resident in Delhi, was chiefly responsible for the collection of information about Afghanistan. Seton's report of civil war in Afghanistan led Minto to postpone action for the time being, while he concentrated on recovering the British position in Iran, but on 18 June 1808 his increasing worries about the danger from France, combined with disquieting reports of Malcolm's lack of progress in Iran, decided him in favour of sending missions both to Lahore and to Kabul.

The post of Envoy to Kabul was given to Mountstuart Elphinstone (1779–1859), who had previously solicited it.[5] Elphinstone's linguistic aptitudes and diplomatic skills had already attracted considerable attention, when he deputized for Josiah Webbe in the negotiations with the Bhonsla in 1803 to 1804. His mission was similar in purpose to that of Charles Metcalfe to Lahore, which is considered below. The two Envoys were to encourage Kabul and Lahore to oppose any French invading force. Elphinstone's mission, however, was regarded as the more important of the two and to mark the difference the Kabul mission was given a deliberate superiority of equipment, although, in fact, Elphinstone was disappointed with the appearance of his embassy. Nevertheless, it appeared impressive enough to the Afghans. Elphinstone acquired a reputation for munificence comparable to that won by Malcolm in Iran and was known as Hatum Tai after the legendary Arab philanthropist.

From the very beginning the fortunes of the Kabul mission were indissolubly linked to the misfortunes of that which went to Iran. British policy-makers assumed that Iran and Afghanistan were permanently hostile to one another and that an alliance with one was wellnigh incompatible with a close alliance with the other. Thus, if Iran allied with Britain, there was no place for an Afghan alliance; indeed Malcolm's 1801 Treaty with Iran, which formed the basis of his and Jones's negotiations in 1808 to 1809, was in effect a defensive alliance against Afghanistan. Equally, it could be supposed that if the Franco–Iranian alliance held it was unlikely that France would be able to negotiate an alliance with Afghanistan, except possibly on the basis of French aid for the recovery of the Panjab. Minto's dilemma was that he did not know whether first Malcolm and later Jones would succeed in Iran or not. If they did a close Afghan alliance might be a grave embarrassment.

Elphinstone's instructions demonstrate Minto's uncertainty both in their content and in their timing. When they were finally prepared on 19 August the instructions were couched in very cautious terms. Elphinstone was told that although the Company was in principle willing to send troops to help to defend Afghanistan, he could not make any specific agreement on the subject without further authority; it was for the Afghans first to submit detailed proposals. Just as what Malcolm could offer Iran was limited by Minto's doubts about European politics, so Elphinstone's offers to Kabul were limited by the Governor-General's doubts about Iran, and to a lesser extent about the situation in Sind. Minto's doubts were eased, but by no means removed, by the return of Malcolm to Calcutta and by the adoption of the Gulf strategy; quite apart from the question of Jones, Malcolm's new instructions still gave Iran one last chance before Britain adopted the new policy. So, on 29 August, Elphinstone was informed that, although Iran's actions could be held to have released Britain from any remaining obligations under the 1801 Treaty, for the time being Britain would still act as though that treaty were still in force. In order to leave Elphinstone some slight room for manœuvre the ingenious argument was put forward that the Iranian treaty could be made compatible with an Afghan treaty providing that the Kabul ruler had no designs upon India.[6] Not until December 1808 did Minto finally decide that Iran was irredeemably hostile and that Elphinstone could be allowed to discuss proposals for a full offensive and defensive alliance against Iran.[7] This was the centre-piece of the mission. Apart from that, Elphinstone was instructed to investigate Seton's suggestion that the Uzbeks of Bukhara might be persuaded to oppose France and, especially, to collect information. Information alone was of great importance: 'If no other object shall be obtained by your mission it will not be considered to have been unprofitable.'[8]

Elphinstone, who left Delhi on 12 October and travelled via Bikanir and Multan, reached Peshawar on 25 February 1809, just eleven days after Jones's entry into Tehran had, unknown to Elphinstone, made his entire mission redundant. Oddly enough, Peshawar, which was then still part of the Kabul state, was all he saw of Afghanistan; the justly celebrated account of Kabul, which he later published, was based largely upon Afghan informants.[9] Like Arthur Waley, Elphinstone was one of that very select body of men who have had an enormous influence in interpreting a country which they have never visited. This omission may partly account for the curious impression which he fostered. For Elphinstone found an Afghanistan very different from that state whose fearsome image had spread such recent alarm in northern India. The Afghan state which had been created by Ahmad Shah Durrani out of the ruins of the eastern part of the Empire of Nadir Shah Afshar had fragmented. Ahmad Shah's Empire had depended upon a tribal unity which in turn was founded upon a common interest in plunder. While loot had flowed in and new revenues became available for division the Empire had flourished. By the time of Zaman Shah, however, the cracks in the edifice had already become apparent. Rebellions in outlying provinces reinforced the destructive potential of dissension among the tribal chiefs and within the ruling Sadozay family itself. When Elphinstone arrived in Peshawar Afghan authority to the east of the Indus had virtually disappeared and Afghanistan itself was divided between Mahmud, who held the west and south, and Shuja, who clung to the north and east, including Peshawar and Kabul itself. Essentially it was the common story of a tribal empire, but to Elphinstone, perhaps conditioned by his upbringing to think in such terms, it became transmuted into the deceptive story of the struggle between the monarchical and republican spirits.

The negotiations which began on 4 March did not proceed in the manner which had been anticipated. Partly this was because of a further change in the British attitude, which was occasioned not by news from Iran but from Europe. The Spanish rising made it clear that there would be no French invasion of India and therefore no need for a defensive alliance against Iran. On 6 March new instructions imposed much more severe limits on what Elphinstone could offer in any alliance.[10] Elphinstone himself was not displeased. Like the Commander-in-Chief, he had never liked Minto's proposal to send troops to Afghanistan. Elphinstone considered that from the strategic point of view the Panjab constituted a much stronger natural frontier and he believed that the main British effort should be made there.[11] Partly the reason was the attitude of Shuja. Far from harbouring any designs against Iran, Shuja's main concern was to acquire aid against Mahmud, who captured Qandahar and then on 17 April, Kabul itself. Shuja demanded a subsidy of £150,000; Elphinstone offered £20,000, and Minto agreed to £30,000.[12] But none of this was ever paid, for the treaty was worded in such a way as to avoid the necessity.

The Anglo–Afghan Treaty of 1809 was a very simple document which consisted of a mere three clauses. By the first two articles, which were to last only so long as the Franco–Iranian alliance (which had of course already come to an end), Britain agreed to give financial assistance to Afghanistan in the event that she was attacked by France and Iran and in return Afghanistan promised not to allow French and Iranian forces to penetrate into British India. Elphinstone interpreted this to mean that Britain would give assistance if Afghanistan were attacked by Iranian forces alone, providing that the Franco–Iranian alliance was in existence at the time, but Minto disagreed and ordered the insertion into the preamble of a clause which was designed to exclude this contingency. The third article, which of course soon

became the only one of any significance, provided for perpetual friendship, non-interference in each others' affairs, and for the exclusion of
the French from Afghanistan. In Elphinstone's draft the final obligation had been mutual, but Minto clearly could not agree to exclude
Frenchmen from British India for ever and he amended this clause to
put the obligation upon Afghanistan alone. With these changes, which
were accepted by Shuja, Minto ratified the treaty on 17 June 1809.

The treaty was a dead letter. Partly this was because of the progress
of events in Iran, but partly also because of the rapid eclipse of Shuja's
fortunes in Afghanistan. His forces were defeated by those of Mahmud
in June 1809 and again in November when Shuja made an unsuccessful
attempt upon Qandahar. Finally, he was completely routed near
Peshawar on 12 September 1810 and was compelled to flee from
Afghanistan, leaving Mahmud in apparent control. Although the British alliance had failed to preserve his power, it was of some value in
protecting his person, for he was given a pension and allowed to take up
residence at Ludhiana, where he kept alive his hopes of new triumphs
and where he and his retinue formed a valuable, if scarcely impartial,
channel of information for the British Political Agents who were
charged with their care. For some time after the withdrawal of the
mission Minto had kept it in being at Delhi in the hope that the civil war
in Afghanistan might be quickly resolved and that it might be possible
to form a similar agreement with Mahmud, who did invite the mission
to return.[13] But the prolonged conflict led Minto, on 14 March 1810, to
order the mission to be broken up and the return of the conduct of
relations with Afghanistan to Seton at Delhi.

Minto's novel and ambitious plans for making Afghanistan into a
crucial element in a new strategy for the defence of India had foundered
and in the event, there appeared to have been little substance to the
Afghan alliance at any time. The appearance however was deceptive,
for Minto had been hamstrung by circumstances outside his control.
Initially he had been prevented from making a decisive offer by the
problems of relations with Sind, Lahore, and above all, with Iran.
Latterly, the termination of the French threat had made the alliance
redundant even before it was built. In the end, the anarchy in Afghanistan had drawn the final curtain on the affair. But it is clear that the
tenuous relationship of 1809 did hold possibilities of developing into a
stronger, more permanent arrangement. Jones and others in Iran
foresaw this and Elphinstone recommended ambitious Afghan proposals to carry the idea along. He proposed that Britain should buy
Sind from Shuja for £200,000 a year. The money would enable Shuja to
build a strong friendly power in Afghanistan; the possession of Sind

would greatly strengthen the British frontier in India, by enabling her to block the southern invasion route and to attack the flanks of any enemy force attempting to use the northern route across the Panjab; the continuing payments would give Britain a permanent influence in Kabul; and the revenues of Sind would ensure a handsome profit for the Company.[14] Minto, however, was unready for so ambitious a project and refused: it was unnecessary because Afghan authority over Sind had virtually disappeared; too dangerous because Kabul could not be converted into a protected Indian state; and too expensive—subsidies were bad in principle. It was also immoral.[15] In the changed situation in Europe Minto presumably knew how the proposal would be received in London; after the end of January 1809 his own enthusiasm for the Afghan alliance evidently waned. Nevertheless, the fact that for some time he kept open the possibility of maintaining the alliance is indicative that he believed that it had possibilities of future use.

It is clear that the Government in England had no sympathy with the major change in Indian defensive strategy which was implied by Minto's support of the Gulf strategy and of the Afghan alliance during the latter part of 1808. In Iran they had opposed the Gulf proposals, preferring an agreement with Tehran. Accordingly, although Robert Dundas had, during the urgency of the moment, encouraged Minto to seek arrangements with all the countries to the north-west in September 1807, London was not interested in an Afghan alliance which might jeopardize the conclusion of an Iranian alliance and the exclusion of the French from Iran. Certainly there was no idea that the Afghan connection might have any permanency. When the dust had settled Minto was informed in March 1812: 'In truth we do not, under present circumstances, consider an intimate connexion with the Court of Caubul as an object worthy of much anxiety or expense.'[16]

There was no further British political interest in Afghanistan before 1830. The rule of the Sadozays over a united Afghanistan was eventually replaced by that of the Barakzays. Mahmud's authority was confined to the western city of Herat and the cities of Qandahar, Ghazni, Kabul, Jalalabad, and Peshawar became the seats of various Barakzay rulers.

More significant in its immediate effects was Minto's initiative in the Panjab. The Panjab, the land of the five rivers, was formed by those rivers which, issuing from the hills which formed the north-easterly boundary of the region, flowed southwards across the Panjab plains, eventually to unite their waters in the Indus and empty them into the Arabian Sea. These five rivers, meandering across the plains and frequently changing their courses, divided the Panjab into a series of compartments, called Doabs. Between the Indus and the Jhelum was the Sind–Sagar Doab; between the Jhelum and the Chenab was the Jech (Chej) Doab; between the Chenab and the Ravi lay the Rechna Doab; between the Ravi and the Beas was the Bari Doab; and between the Beas and the Satlej lay the Bist Jalandhar Doab. The area to the south-east of the Satlej, intervening between that river and the Jamna, can be called the Satlej–Jamna Doab, but here will normally be denoted by the contemporary British term of the Cis–Satlej territory, because to Britons, contemplating the area from the south-east, it bore that aspect. Another important geographical feature was the hills which lay to the north-east of the Panjab. These Panjab Hills were part of the main Himalaya structure which formed the northern frontier of British India. Control of the Hill States (including Jammu and Kashmir) had always been sought by rulers of the Panjab and of northern India for commercial, recreational, and strategical reasons.

In the mid-eighteenth century Mughal power in the Panjab had been replaced by that of the Afghans, whose power was in turn challenged by the militant, heterodox Hindu sect of the Sikhs. Politically the Sikhs were loosely organized in confederacies (*misls*) of which the largest in the late eighteenth century was that of the Bhangis who controlled most of the northern and central Panjab, including the cities of Amritsar and Lahore. Possession of the large, wealthy city of Lahore, located on the river Ravi on the borders of the more fertile eastern Panjab and well placed to serve as a base for operations against the Hindu states of the north and the Muslim states of the south-west, was essential to the control of the region.

At the end of the eighteenth century the Panjab was unified by the efforts of a man of exceptional ability, Ranjit Singh. In 1792 he became chief of the obscure Sukarchakia confederacy, centred on Sialkot in the northern part of the Rechna Doab and extending into the Jech Doab to the east. By judicious alliances and careful conflicts he defeated the other confederacies and in 1799 inherited full power in the wake of the retreating Afghans. Subsequently he consolidated his power over the other confederacies and began to expand north-eastwards into the hills beyond the Indus and southwards down the Indus towards Sind.

The East India Company knew little of events in the Panjab during these early years and completely missed the importance of the rise of Ranjit Singh. For long it was believed that he had received Lahore by agreement with Zaman Shah. In May 1800 Wellesley sent a Muslim agent to Lahore, but the instructions given to the agent showed that Wellesley knew little and cared less about the area.[17] It was the British advance to the Jamna in 1803 which transformed the Sikhs from an object of mystery and strategic speculation into a border problem, focused upon the Cis–Satlej area. The power of Ranjit Singh had not yet been extended into this area which was dominated by four Sikh confederacies of which the Phulkian (controlling the principalities of Nabha, Patiala, and Jind) was the most important. Under the weight of attacks from the Irish adventurer, George Thomas (based at Hansi), the Cis–Satlej Sikhs had been obliged to seek the aid of Sindhia's lieutenant, Perron, who had exacted a heavy price for his services in the form of tribute and had extended Maratha influence into the area. Wellesley's victory over Perron in 1803 therefore offered the Governor-General the possibility of assuming the mantle of Maratha power in the Cis–Satlej area.

Wellesley wanted no influence in the Satlej–Jamna Doab as he hoped to make the Jamna the firm boundary of British influence in that region. Raids from the west, however, forced him to modify this wish and to advance beyond the Jamna and to occupy Jinjanna and Karnal. Karnal was a significant British acquisition. It became the main British advanced base in the north-west and served both to protect the upper Jamna frontier and to facilitate operations beyond the river.

The first clear suggestion that the Company should adopt the Satlej and not the Jamna as its frontier in the extreme north-west was made in December 1804 by David Ochterlony (1758–1825), who was then serving as Resident at Delhi. Ochterlony proposed that the Jamna–Satlej Doab should be annexed or that the local chiefs should be placed under British protection. His suggestion was rejected, however, and the Chief Secretary, John Lumsden, proposed instead that Britain should avoid any dealings with the Sikhs who, he argued, were not to be trusted.[18]

Wellesley's wish to avoid entanglements with the Sikhs was frustrated by the renewal of the Maratha war in 1804. The following year the Company's forces under Lord Lake advanced to the Satlej and beyond in pursuit of Holkar. A treaty was then signed with Ranjit Singh by which the Sikhs agreed not to aid Holkar and the British not to enter the territory of Ranjit Singh. Subsequently Holkar left the area and the British forces were withdrawn to the Jamna.

The rejection of all connection with the trans–Jamna region by Cornwallis and Barlow left Ranjit Singh a free hand to extend his authority over the Cis–Satlej Sikhs. In a series of campaigns in 1806 to 1807 Ranjit began to draw the independent Sikh rulers under his control. The Cis–Satlej Sikhs turned for help to the British Resident at Delhi, Archibald Seton, who recommended that Britain should try to construct a neutral zone in the Cis–Satlej territory, in which neither

Ranjit nor Britain would interfere. This appeal from the Sikhs coincided with the renewal of the French threat and with the arrival in India of Minto.

The principles of Minto's external policies have been considered already. But the Panjab was not wholly an external, but partook also of the character of an internal problem for British India. Minto's policy towards Indian states was generally one of non-interference, a course of action which he believed to be equally recommended by his own uncertain personal position, by financial pressures, by the injunctions of London, and by the political situation within India as he understood it. The greatest danger that Minto feared was that of a general Muslim conspiracy manifesting itself in an internal insurrection of which the Vellore mutiny of 1807 seemed to have provided a foretaste. The fear that such a rising might be triggered off by the approach of a French army led Minto to adopt a conciliatory policy towards the Indian states and he rejected the opportunity which was presented to him to settle accounts with the Marathas and to establish British paramountcy.

Minto was caught in two minds about the best policy to pursue towards the Panjab. He believed that sooner or later Ranjit Singh's ambitions would force Britain to extend her protection to the Cis–Satlej Sikhs in order to safeguard her frontier; at the same time he did not wish to alienate the Sikh leader in case his help was needed to repel a French attack. Accordingly, Minto tried to compromise. Seton was reproved for encouraging the Cis–Satlej Sikhs to hope for British protection by forwarding their request for help. Minto would not give help. Instead he decided to send a mission to Ranjit Singh.[19] The mission therefore fell into place as part of his diplomatic strategy against France.

To lead the mission to Lahore Minto chose Charles Metcalfe (1785–1846), Seton's first assistant at Delhi and one of the rising men in the Political Department. Metcalfe had been hoping for the job, for he needed the money to repay his debts, having recently been forced to accept a reduction in income on his transfer from the Secretariat to Delhi. He made a favourable impression on Minto, who described him as 'the ugliest and most agreeable clever person—except Lady Glenbervie—in Europe or Asia'.[20] Minto intended originally to send Metcalfe to Kabul as well as to Lahore, but dropped this proposal when he reflected that Shah Shuja in Kabul might be affronted if he did not receive a mission superior to that sent to Lahore.[21] Accordingly, Metcalfe was sent only to Ranjit Singh and instructed to obtain the exclusion of French and Iranian influence from Lahore and permission for a British army to march through the Panjab if it were found necessary to meet an invasion upon the Indus. Metcalfe was to try to avoid discussion of the future of the Cis–Satlej Sikhs, but if it became absolutely necessary, that is, if a French attack was imminent, Minto was prepared to give Ranjit Singh a free hand in the area.[22]

Metcalfe, who had already been set in motion by Seton, left Delhi on 28 July and met Ranjit Singh on 12 September 1808 at Kasur, west of the Satlej. Metcalfe already had visions of himself as Resident in Lahore, the nerve-centre of an intelligence network stretching far beyond the Indus.[23] His hopes were rudely and abruptly shattered. Ranjit Singh proved suspicious and even hostile. He saw no danger from France and wanted no alliance with Afghanistan which would restrict his own plans for expansion beyond the Indus and into the territory of the Muslim states to the south-east of the Panjab. Most immediately the Sikh leader feared that Britain might try to obstruct his plans to extend his influence in the Jamna–Satlej Doab. He was already preparing his third expedition into the area. Metcalfe's presence was an embarrassment and Ranjit asked him to deliver his message and depart. He would ally with Britain only if he were given a guarantee that there would be no interference either with his relations with Afghanistan or with the Cis–Satlej Sikhs.[24] After some discussion, during which Metcalfe, following his instructions, avoided any reference to the Cis–Satlej Sikhs, Ranjit Singh announced on 25 September that he agreed to everything and would deliver his final answer the next day. Instead of which, to Metcalfe's fury and consternation, the Sikh leader broke up his camp on 26 September, crossed the Satlej, and embarked upon a campaign in which he established his authority over all the Cis–Satlej chiefs except those of Patiala, Thanesar, and Kunjpura. Metcalfe could do nothing but recommend that the Company should capitulate to Ranjit Singh and agree to his demand for a free hand in relation to the Cis–Satlej Sikhs and to Afghanistan.[25]

Minto had changed his policy. The French threat was still uppermost in his mind, but Ranjit Singh's scepticism concerning that danger and the Sikh leader's generally uncooperative attitude convinced Minto that he would be an unreliable ally against France. To allow Ranjit Singh to extend his power on British India's north-western frontier, possibly to the detriment of states allied to the Company, or even to inspire the disaffected within British territories to revolt, would make the problems of British India worse.[26] In this ingenious logic, which turned the French threat into its Wellesley form, one seems to discern a subtler brain than that of Minto; the outcome at least was pure Wellesley. Minto decided to extend British protection to the Cis–Satlej Sikhs, whether they liked it or not. New instructions were sent to Metcalfe, and David Ochterlony was instructed to lead a force up to the Satlej. Minto contemplated the replacement of the power of Ranjit Singh in the Panjab with several small states in alliance with Britain.[27] This would have carried the British defensive frontier up to the Indus and have established a direct link with Afghanistan, the centre-piece of Minto's system of alliances against France, and thereby anticipated the policy of Alexander Burnes.

Metcalfe's position was transformed by Minto's new policy. After Ranjit Singh's departure from Kasur he had wandered, like Mary's lamb, unhappily in the wake of the Sikh chief, until he had settled at Gongrana at the end of October. On 20 November he received Minto's new instructions and immediately exchanged the role of the lamb for that of the Hound of Heaven. 'I shall have a selfish gratification in paying him for all the uneasiness he has caused me', he wrote to Edmonstone.[28] Metcalfe hastened to Amritsar where he delivered Minto's demands on 12 December. When Ranjit Singh moved to Lahore Metcalfe pursued him thither and thence back to Amritsar again. Ranjit Singh became thoroughly alarmed and asked for a treaty to safeguard his own position. Metcalfe was inexorable, and recommended that the Sikh leader should be offered nothing, apparently hoping to drive him into resistance. In that event, wrote Metcalfe, he would be overthrown by internal enemies. Even the excuse for war was provided by an unsuccessful attack by Sikh zealots on Metcalfe's camp in February. The extension of British power to the Indus seemed to be on the verge of accomplishment.

Minto was not the man for such enterprises and was now ready to compromise. The news of the Spanish rising had terminated his fears of French invasion and he was ready to accept the continuation of Ranjit Singh's power west of the Satlej. In February Ochterlony's force advanced to the Satlej and Ochterlony issued a proclamation announcing that the Cis–Satlej Sikhs had been taken under British protection. In March Metcalfe was authorized to form a treaty of friendship with Ranjit Singh. By the Treaty of Amritsar (25 April 1809) Ranjit Singh agreed to abandon his claims on the Cis–Satlej Sikhs and to maintain only limited forces in his own possessions south of the Satlej.

The 1809 Settlement carried the British frontier up to the Satlej. During the course of the operations the state of Haryana had come under British administration. George Thomas's old fief beyond the Jamna had been given to Abd al-Samad Khan in 1806, both to get rid of it and to compensate the chief for his military services in 1803. Unable to hold it, Abd al-Samad had sold it back to the Company in 1807 and since then the British authorities had sought a new chief in vain. In 1809 Haryana was seen as a useful barrier against Sikh expansion and was taken under British control.[29] The most important part of the settlement, however, was that with the Sikhs east of the Satlej. The Cis–Satlej chiefs were offered favourable terms. By the proclamation of 3 May 1809 they were called upon to co-operate fully with the Company in matters of defence and to admit British troops to the area. By the proclamation of 22 August 1809 British control was extended by adding the right to intervene to prevent disputes between the chiefs.[30] But in general the chiefs were left to manage their own internal affairs and were not called upon to contribute to a subsidiary force. Ochterlony was not happy with this modest influence and from the beginning pressed for increased British intervention within the states. He wrote: 'if policy suggests the protection of the Sikhs south of the Sutlej from external violence, humanity and the honour of the British name no less imperiously call upon us to shield them from the more disastrous consequences of their own base passions, their universal rapacity and their internal discord.'[31] Although Minto would not accept the principle which underlay this view, he was obliged to concede some intervention in practice. Nevertheless, the position of the Cis–Satlej Sikh chiefs remained a privileged one among the Indian states associated with the Company.

The settlement involved the establishment of a new advanced British position on the Satlej at Ludhiana. In October 1808 Minto had wanted Ludhiana, partly with the French threat in mind. By the middle of 1809, however, this motive had finally disappeared and he did not want this post as a permanent feature of the new arrangements. He gave Ochterlony permission to hold it only until the return of Mountstuart Elphinstone's mission from Afghanistan.[32] He was later persuaded to change his mind and to agree to the indefinite retention of the post at Ludhiana, which was converted into a Political Agency in 1810. The case for the retention of Ludhiana had been argued by Ochterlony, Metcalfe, and Seton on the basis that it was essential in order to give the Protected Sikh Chiefs confidence in the willingness of the Company to support them and also in order to maintain some check upon the activities of Ranjit Singh. The Satlej–Jamna Doab, north of Mathura, therefore, was now protected by a quadrilateral of British forts. In the south was Delhi itself, which remained both a military centre and the centre for political relations in the north-west; in the north-west was George Thomas's old post at Hansi near the border with the Rajput state of Bikaner; in the north was Ludhiana which formed the main post towards the Lahore frontier; and in the north-east was Karnal which remained an important military base for the support of the advanced post at Ludhiana.

A third feature of the 1809 Settlement was that Lahore became the main buffer state for the protection of the extreme north-westerly frontier of British India. The full significance of this development had not been foreseen in 1809. At that time the power of Ranjit Singh was still seen as relatively insignificant. It was to grow considerably in the years which followed. While leaving him his existing possessions on the east of the Satlej the treaty had prevented further expansion in that direction, but it had left him free to extend his influence elsewhere. He took advantage of this to expand his authority northwards over the Hill States, westwards across the Indus, and southwards to Multan. Even more importantly, he changed the whole basis of his military system. His former light cavalry and irregular infantry were supplemented and partially replaced by new troops, disciplined on the European style, with the aid of a large number of European adventurers. His artillery and disciplined infantry became the most formidable of any possessed by Indian states.[33] His state took on a further aspect as a result of the settlement. By dividing the Sikhs between the British and Lahore territories and directing his expansion into Muslim and other non-Sikh areas, the new arrangement aided the transformation of the state of Lahore from a basically Sikh state into one in which the Sikhs, although still continuing to play a major role through old Sikh families such as those of the Sindhanwalas, the Majithias, and the Attariwallas and through the lasting predominance of Sikhs in the army, played a much smaller part than previously. There rose to power and influence Rajputs from the hills such as the family of Dhian Singh, Brahmins from Kashmir and northern India, Muslims like Fakir Aziz al-Din, and the European adventurers. There emerged a very different, much more formidable Government which came to form a Hindu buffer between the territories of the Company and those of the Muslim peoples to the west. As such, Britons came to regard it as a valuable component of the British defensive system.

The favourable view of the strategic value of the Panjab took some time to achieve acceptance. Robert Dundas had welcomed Minto's vigorous stand against Ranjit Singh and, despite the fact that it contradicted established Company policy, had welcomed the extension of the British defensive frontier to the Satlej.[34] The thought of Ranjit Singh as a permanent neighbour was, however, not so attractive to Dundas, who was very sceptical about his willingness to assist in the defence of India. In India, however, the merits of the new arrangements were quickly appreciated. In 1815, when Ochterlony proposed a closer defensive alliance with Ranjit Singh, he was informed that British relations with Lahore could not be improved.[35] Throughout the 1820s, despite occasional strains on the relationship of the two powers, the Company's Government remained well satisfied with the 1809 system, refused all proposals for alliances against the Sikhs, and vigorously upheld the policy of non-interference in trans–Satlej affairs. The settlement appeared to have weakened Lahore as a rival to Britain but strengthened it as a buffer state which seemed to provide the strong north-western frontier shield which it had once been vainly hoped would be provided by Oudh. At the same time the Protected Sikh States of the Cis–Satlej region acted both as a cushion to soften any abrasive contacts betwen Ranjit and the Company and as a shield to protect the vital and exposed positions at Delhi and Karnal.

The dignified and the efficient elements in British policy, initially confused by Minto had thus been restored to their former situation. Minto's initiatives in Iran, Iraq, the Gulf, Afghanistan, and Sind had come to nothing. In the Panjab his original plan had been discarded and the only tangible result of all his activities in the north-west was the carrying forward of the British frontier from the Jamna to the Satlej, an achievement in direct line with the policies of his predecessors, which had always given priority to expansion and the achievement of security within India.

The completion of the system of paramountcy adumbrated by Warren Hastings and carried forward by Wellesley was the work of Minto's successor, the Earl of Moira, better known by his later title of Marquess of Hastings (1754–1826). Hastings has been as much underrated by historians as Minto has been overrated. He came to India surrounded by a cloud of political intrigue and royal patronage and he departed enmeshed in accusations of corruption and inefficiency. He was not remarkable for his intelligence and he certainly lacked the vision of his namesake and of Wellesley. In the circumstances historians have tended to blame him for the things that went wrong and to give the credit for the undoubted achievements of his Governor-Generalship to his subordinates. Such judgements do not do him justice, for Hastings had one supreme quality—complete confidence in the rightness of his own judgement. Not for him the self-doubt of his more brilliant predecessors—the struggles for recognition of Warren Hastings or the passion for praise which inspired the antics of Wellesley; Hastings had the confidence born of effortless aristocracy and once persuaded that a course was right, he moved forward along it without a backward glance. The plans were those of others but the directing force was Hastings.

When Hastings assumed office in 1813 the territories of British India roughly resembled a horseshoe. Inside the horseshoe it had been hoped that settled states would emerge with which the Company could live in peace. In certain Maratha states some development in that direction had indeed taken place. But inside the horseshoe there was also a new element of instability—the Pindaris.[36] Pindaris is a generic term given to numbers of soldiers grouped in formidable bands; they acted under their own leaders, sometimes in the employment of a ruler, sometimes independently. Unable to support themselves from the plunder of Central India alone the Pindaris began to raid the territories of the Company and its allies. The long, virtually defenceless, land frontier of the British territories was extremely vulnerable to their attacks.[37]

In his search for a solution to the problem of the Pindaris Hastings was guided by officials who had learned their trade under Wellesley and who had now attained important positions in the Secretariat or in Residencies in Indian states.[38] One of them, Charles Metcalfe, in 1814 propounded the solution which was eventually adopted—the destruction of the Pindaris in their own strongholds after first securing the co-operation of the Marathas and the other powers whose territories would be required for the necessary operations.[39] This mode of action, however, involved a repudiation of the principles of the 1805 Settlement and was contrary to the strict instructions of the authorities in London. For some time therefore Hastings investigated other plans which could more readily be accommodated within the 1805 Settlement and it was only when these appeared to have no success that he adopted Metcalfe's plan of general action.

It is evident that for Hastings and his officials the attractions of the general plan did not end with the prospect of bringing the depredations of the Pindaris to a conclusion. The scheme of general co-operation would also have the effect of forming the Marathas into an alliance with the Company and of making Britain paramount within India. It would also solve the problem of the frontier; by extending British control over central India the Bengal and Bombay Presidencies would be linked and the land frontier greatly shortened—in effect the frontiers of British India would become the sea and a continuous land line from the Arabian Sea to the Bay of Bengal. The link between the Indian states and the independent states of the north-west would be broken and the army could in the future be concentrated at the most vulnerable positions along the land line. Hastings believed that the resources of British India were too small to provide for its internal and external defence under the prevailing arrangements; only through paramountcy and the radical simplification of the problem of defence, which would be the consequence of the establishment of British supremacy, could the problem of British Indian security be met.[40]

It was the destructive Pindari raids into British territory in 1816 which broke the opposition to Hastings's general scheme. His own Council and the authorities in London agreed that the 1805 system would have to be discarded and alliances formed with the Indian states in order to prevent the Pindari raids. From that concession it was but a short step to Hastings's general alliance system. In the course of 1816 to 1817 his alliances were formed and in the operations of 1817 to 1818 the Pindaris were crushed, with them falling the Peshwa, Baji Rao II, and the ruler of Nagpur. In the new settlement the power of the Marathas was broken, their territories annexed, redistributed, or held on terms which put them under ultimate British control. The small states of Rajputana were also brought into the system of alliances. By 1818 the political map of India was completely changed: in the west the Presidency of Bombay had completed its evolution into a great territorial power; central India and Rajputana were divided into a number of small states under British control; a ring-fence had been created; and British paramountcy was established.[41] The whole problem of British Indian defence, as it had existed since 1765, had been altered. No further danger was apparently to be feared from any Indian state or combination of states unless such a threat was combined with one posed by an enemy outside the ring-fence or with a mutiny of the Company's army. From 1818 onwards therefore, British Indian stategic thinking was directed much more to the situation outside India and especially to that which obtained in the north-west.

The frontier created in 1818, with the addition the following year of Cutch (Kachch), lasted theoretically until 1843 and substantially until 1838. Thus twenty years of hectic activity were succeeded by twenty years of comparative peace, when the conquests were digested. During the latter period Hastings's ring-fence underwent a subtle evolution. It was created not so much as a frontier as a prison wall, from which the inmates might be overawed and by which they could be insulated from contact with the outside. In the course of the twenty years which followed its creation Hastings's boundary gradually assumed first the aspect of a true frontier and then that of a springboard for expansion into the territories beyond, towards the Indus and central Asia.

The new north-western frontier consisted of an inner belt of directly administered territory shielded by a string of states over whose foreign relations the Company possessed complete control, whose military forces were substantially at its disposal, and over whose internal affairs it possessed a varying influence. The frontier formed by the north-western boundaries of these Protected States and subsidiary allies was a trip-wire rather than a Maginot Line; their territories provided insulation against sporadic raids and the protection of strategic depth against the incursions of more formidable foes.

In the west the defensive frontier was formed by Cutch which had been brought under British control in 1819, an event which marked the culmination of a series of efforts by the Bombay Government to dominate the state.[42] By the Treaty of 13 October 1819 Britain controlled, through the Resident and a military force stationed in the capital, Bhuj, the foreign relations of Cutch. Its importance, remarked the Governor of Bombay, Mountstuart Elphinstone, was to insulate the Company's possessions from Sind and to provide Britain with a way of striking against Sind if war with that state ever came.[43]

The British defensive frontier therefore was formed by the northern boundary of Cutch from where it met the sea at Kori Creek, and ran north-eastwards along the most southerly of the mouths of the Indus, the East Nara. Subsequently the line followed the Rann of Cutch, an area which was desert in the dry season and a great flooded plain in the rains. Near the eastern end of the Rann of Cutch the Parkar Oasis formed a salient driven into the frontier from the north, so facilitating the entry of raiders. The Bombay frontier turned northwards around the eastern flank of the Parkar Oasis and ran northwards and then eastwards to join the Bengal frontier at Mount Abu on the western frontier of the small Rajput state of Sirohi. In fact until the Sirohi Treaty was formed in 1823 the junction was imperfect. From Mount Abu the Bengal frontier followed the western frontiers of the large Rajput states of Jodhpur and Jaisalmer as these ran through the waterless Thar desert. Throughout this southern stretch of the frontiers of Bombay and Bengal, from the sea to a point near Kishangarh, the Company's frontier bordered that of Sind. From Kishangarh the frontier continued in a north-easterly direction through the desert, following the western frontiers of Jaisalmer and Bikaner. In this sector the frontier was coterminous with that of the Muslim state of Bahawalpur. The Bahawalpur frontier met that of the Protected Sikh States on the river Satlej at a point about sixty miles south-west of the town of Firuzpur. From that point the defensive line was formed by the western frontier of the Protected Sikh States which was the Satlej itself, as far as the hills which formed the northern frontier. Along this stretch of the frontier the British-protected territories faced those of the state of Lahore. As a result of the war with Nepal a belt of British-protected states extended deep into the hills, obstructing, although not entirely preventing, any possible land connection between Lahore and Nepal.

In the whole vast area from the sea to the Himalayas only three states bordered the Company's defensive frontier. Of these, relations with Lahore have already been considered. Relations with Bahawalpur need not detain us because it was a state of minor importance and relations with it were minimal. It was a narrow, fertile strip carved out of the desert by the Satlej and the Indus which formed its western boundary. The bulk of the partly agricultural, partly nomadic, population were Jats; the ruling tribe was that of the Daudputras. Grain and cotton goods were exported to Rajputana. Its comparative wealth and its evident weakness made it an attractive object of the ambitions of its neighbours on the Indus. There remains the British position with relation to Sind, which must now be described.

The extensive land of Sind stretched along the Lower Indus. Richard Burton described it as 'a sloping surface of silt and sand'.[44] It was bounded on the south-west by the sea; on the south-east by the Rann of Cutch; on the east by the Thar desert frontiers of Rajputana; on the north by Bahawalpur, and on the west by the mountains of Baluchistan. Economically it was the product of the Indus. The spring and summer floods provided the basis for the rice which grew in the south and the *jowari* of the north. The bulk of the population were Jats or Sindians, the indigenous peoples who had adopted Islam in the eighth century. The dominant minority was that of the Baluchi tribes who had entered Sind from the western mountains and established themselves as landlords, while preserving often their former nomadic way of life. The trade of the area was controlled by Hindus, who from their centre at Shikarpur in northern Sind controlled a commercial and financial network which linked northern India to Central Asia.

Following the breakdown of Mughal authority in the early eighteenth century, power in Sind had been seized by the Baluchi family of the Kalhoras, By judiciously alternating submission and resistance to the rulers of Iran and Afghanistan they had contrived to maintain a substantial degree of independence during the troubled years which followed. In the late eighteenth century they were overthrown by another Baluchi family, that of the Talpurs. Eventually the Talpurs contrived a rough separation of their inextricably interwoven family interests in Sind, as a result of which arrangement three governments emerged in Sind by the early nineteenth century. The largest and most important division was that of Lower Sind or Haidarabad, which lay in the south. This was ruled, until his death in 1801, by Mir Fath Ali Khan, who had led the original successful rising of the Talpurs. He left Haidarabad to his three sons—Mir Ghulam Ali Khan (d. 1811), who was the nominal chief; Mir Karim (d.c. 1829), and Mir Murad Ali (d.

1834). The second most important division, that of Upper Sind or Khairpur, was ruled by Mir Sohrab Khan (d. 1830); and the third was that of Mirpur, which lay to the east of Haidarabad, on the direct road to Cutch. Mirpur had been given by Fath Ali to Mir Tara and Mir Baga, two of his associates in the original rising.

Throughout the eighteenth century British relations with Sind were purely commercial. In 1758 a factory was established at Tatta, a town on the Lower Indus half-way between Haidarabad and the sea. In 1761 Ghulam Khan Kalhora agreed to accept a British Resident and to grant the Company a monopoly of trade in Sind. Political unrest, however, made profitable trade impossible and in 1775 the last British factory was closed. After the establishment of the Talpur Amirs, British commercial interest revived and during the 1790s the question of reopening a factory was again considered. Strategic arguments now appeared side by side with those derived from trade. A factory, it was thought, could supply information about the activities of Zaman Shah of Afghanistan. In 1797 Sir Charles Malet suggested that the Amirs might be persuaded to allow themselves to be used to divert Zaman from northern India.[45]

Malet's suggestion for the use of Sind against Afghanistan was brought to Wellesley's notice by Sir James Craig. Wellesley saw limited possibilities in this manœuvre. He was prepared to offer the Amirs arms and equipment for use against Afghanistan, but he would not become further involved.[46] Accordingly, an Indian Muslim, Agha Abu'l Hasan, was sent to Sind to investigate the situation. Following his favourable report a British agent, George Nathan Crow, was dispatched to Sind in 1799 to make an agreement to reopen the factory. Wellesley commented that this mission was 'not so much with a view to commercial as to political advantage'.[47]

Crow's mission was a failure. Initially the Amirs were accommodating and agreed to British factories at Tatta and Karachi. Later the attitude changed, and Crow was forced to leave Sind in October 1800. The cause of the trouble was unclear to Crow who suspected the influence of the Marathas and of Zaman Shah. It may simply have been suspicion of Britain and the opposition of local merchants. Crow's failure which involved some financial loss on the new factory, combined with the ending of the threat from Afghanistan, resulted in a loss of interest in Sind on the part of the Company. Duncan, in Bombay, still advocated British action there, but Wellesley, who had now almost completed his arrangements with Oudh, and no longer needed to excite alarm about Afghanistan, wanted no further involvement.

British interest in Sind revived under Minto.[48] In 1803 and 1806 the

Amirs of Sind made overtures for British assistance against Afghanistan. Duncan at first paid little attention to these approaches, but when news of the possible revival of the French threat to India was received from Europe he began to show more interest. Two obstacles to a closer agreement immediately presented themselves. In the first place, the envoys from Sind had no authority to negotiate and in the second, the Supreme Government under Barlow was not interested. Minto's arrival changed the attitude of the latter Government. The new Governor-General was particularly apprehensive of the dangers of a French landing on the Sind coast, and was worried by reports of the growth of French and Iranian influence in Sind. Accordingly, he decided to send a new mission to Sind with the objectives of reopening the factory and introducing a Political Agent. Instructions to this effect were sent to Duncan and arrived at the same time as did a new Sindian envoy. Duncan decided to send Captain David Seton, now Resident at Muscat, back with the envoy to Sind to establish good relations with the Amirs and win their co-operation against France, and to obtain permission to reopen the factory, which could serve as a cover for the gathering of political intelligence.

Seton's mission was a minor disaster. He left Bombay on 28 March 1808, did not hurry, and when he arrived in Haidarabad on 15 July discovered an Iranian envoy already there and the Amirs in possession of a letter from Jean-Baptiste Rousseau, French consul at Basra and son of Jean-François. Encouraged by the Amirs, Seton fell into a panic and was induced to sign a treaty of alliance (18 July 1808) which granted the Company the desired factory at Tatta and an agency at Haidarabad, but which gave Sind in return the unlimited right to British help. Ghulam Ali proposed to employ this against Afghanistan. He may have been alarmed by reports of the simultaneous mission of Mountstuart Elphinstone to Afghanistan and feared that British help could be given to Shah Shuja for use against Sind. He also wished to restrain Britain in Cutch.

Minto disavowed the treaty and recalled Seton. He had no wish to find himself defending Sind against Afghanistan. In his system of calculation Afghanistan was a much more prized ally than Sind and he had, indeed foreseen the possibility that Britain might be called upon to support Afghan claims on Sind.[49] Seton had, in fact, already brought his unhappy mission to a close. He had been caught in correspondence with the Afghans and obliged to leave on 13 October 1808.

A new mission to Sind was led by Nicholas Hankey Smith, the Resident at Bushir. Unlike Seton, who had been under the orders of Duncan at Bombay, Smith was placed under the direct authority of the

Supreme Government and ordered to assume a superior, patronizing demeanour which would put the Amirs in their place. He was instructed to inform the Amirs that Seton's treaty had not been ratified and to negotiate in its stead a new agreement, providing for a British agent to be established permanently in Sind. Minto was after influence in Sind, not an alliance, and, in early 1809, the news of the Spanish uprising made Sind of still less significance in his plans. Smith's mission was reduced in scale and his instructions modified.

The mission achieved only partial success. The Amirs did not want it. Although their envoy in Bombay said that it would be quite acceptable, they placed continual obstructions in its path in the hope that Smith would give up in exasperation.[50] The Hindu merchants, who feared British competition in Sind, did not want it either. The Governor of Karachi tried to persuade Smith to go back to Bombay and when he eventually gained permission to proceed to Haidarabad there was a long wrangle about diplomatic ceremonies; Smith strove to assert his prestige and the Amirs to reduce his status. When it came to negotiations the Amirs refused to admit a permanent British agent unless they received an adequate return, either in the form of assistance against Afghanistan or permission to attack Cutch. They were fearful of British designs on Cutch and wished to prevent that land falling under British control. Smith, of course, could agree to neither. In the end, on 22 August 1809, he secured a treaty which provided for the residence at Haidarabad of an Indian agent only and for the meaningless exclusion of the French from Sind.[51]

Minto's initiative in Sind had produced meagre results. It had, of course, been conceived as the least important of his diplomatic missions in connection with the French threat to India and it had at least the merit of being the cheapest of his failures. Its political value had been nil and the political connection this time had handicapped rather than advanced the Bombay Government's commercial interests. Its one useful by-product was the collection of information about Sind, although the Amir's suspicions limited the amount gained and this information, as it turned out, was a mixed blessing. Among Smith's companions on his mission had been the young Lieutenant Henry Pottinger (1789–1856), who had joined the Bombay Army two years earlier. Pottinger's experiences were incorporated in his subsequent *Travels* and his exaggerated account of the merits of the river Indus contributed considerably to the inflated notions of its potential which persisted for many years in Bombay.[52] More useful information was contributed by the two surveyors, Lieutenants Maxfield and Christie.

Minto had lost interest in Sind by this time and rejected other proposals that Britain should take direct action against the Amir. One such proposal was put forward by Mountstuart Elphinstone who had derived the false impression that Smith's failure had been the consequence of strong Iranian or French influence at Haidarabad. Elphinstone suggested that Britain should annex Sind, but Minto refused.[53] Another proposal came from Archibald Seton at Delhi. In June 1809 the Rajput ruler of Jaisalmer wrote to Seton reporting that France and Iran proposed to invade India with the help of Sind. He offered to co-operate in resisting this attack by assisting Britain in displacing the Talpur Amirs in favour of the deposed Kalhoras. If Britain did not take such action, he went on, Amir Khan and Ranjit Singh of Lahore might join together to conquer Sind. The motives of the Jaisalmer Raja were, no doubt, not wholly altruistic in this matter. Minto, however, in reply merely stated that Britain's relations with Sind were friendly and that, since the renewal of the British alliance with Iran, he had no fear of a French or Iranian invasion.[54]

Between 1809 and 1830 British interest in Sind sank to insignificance. Such interest as there was derived from the attacks upon Cutch and other British-protected territories made by the Khosa bandits from the Parkar Oasis, which have already been mentioned. In 1820 joint action against the bandits was proposed and a Bombay force was actually sent to co-operate with a force from Sind. Unfortunately, co-operation proved impossible and the British and Sindian forces clashed among themselves. The Bombay Government, which always took a stronger line over border disturbances than the Supreme Government, suggested that Britain should threaten the Amirs with war if they would not co-operate. Hastings refused, commenting: 'Few things ... can be conceived more impolitic than war with Sindh, and its successful prosecution would not only be unprofitable, but an evil.'[55] Hastings wanted no entanglements with Sind. The occupation of that country would be an embarrassment. It was true that in the future, Britain might be forced to move forward in self-defence, but for the present, there was to be no war. When the Bombay Government protested against this decision he overruled them. A new treaty with Sind was signed in November 1820 which restored friendly relations, settled frontier disputes, repeated the condition concerning the exclusion of the French, and added the Americans to the list of prohibited immigrants. A new mission, under Captain G. F. Sadlier, was sent to Sind by the Bombay Government to obtain ratification of the treaty in 1821 and revealed the continued suspicion of the Amirs concerning British intentions. The frontier problem continued to bubble and after 1819 was made worse by the assumption of control over Cutch. In 1825

the Supreme Government had to intervene to prevent a further collision when five thousand Company troops were assembled in Cutch to
stop the incursions from Parkar.

The general policy of avoiding any involvement in Sind received
confirmation in 1828. In 1827 Dr James Burnes, a surgeon in the
employment of the Company at Bombay and the elder brother of the
soon to be famous Alexander, was sent to Haidarabad, following a
request from the Amirs, to treat Murad Ali. He liked neither the
Government of Sind nor his patient, whom he described as a cruel and
gloomy hypochondriac. Sind itself, however, seemed to him to possess
considerable economic potential, as well as offering, through the Indus,
the possibility of communication with Central Asia. Accordingly, he
urged that a British Resident should be introduced into Sind and that
the country should eventually be annexed.[56] His views were brought to
the notice of Malcolm, who was Governor of Bombay, by Henry
Pottinger, now Resident in Cutch. Malcolm rejected them: 'I find' he
wrote: 'it has been our policy here and I believe on good grounds to
discourage every advance to a more intimate connection with Sind.'[57]
But the policy of non-intervention in Sind was then coming to the end of
its span. Within two years Ellenborough had launched a scheme which
incorporated Burnes's vision of the Indus as the high road to Central
Asia.

After 1809 there was a lack of interest on the part of policy-makers in
London and Calcutta in the countries which lay beyond the frontier
which came to be formed in 1818 to 1819. The development of British
policy in Cutch and Sind, however, confirms the impression already
gleaned from previous consideration of the agents in Delhi: namely,
that interest was much stronger the nearer one approached to the
frontier itself; thus the Government of Bombay was more ready for
intervention than was that of Calcutta, and it was the frontier agents
themselves who produced the recommendations for strong action. The
development of a frontier agency system, accordingly, is of crucial
importance in the development of frontier policy for its effect was to
institutionalize expansion.

The frontier agents had a threefold role. They were responsible for
the conduct of day to day affairs in the states within whose limits they
were placed; they carried on such ordinary diplomatic relations with
states beyond the frontier as seemed requisite; and they collected
information, directly or through newswriters, concerning the affairs of
all the countries which lay to the north-west of British India. Their
experience and their monopoly of information gave the frontier agents a
peculiar importance in the shaping of British policy on the north-west

frontier. Situated as they were, they had a vested interest in inducing their Governments to look outwards beyond the frontier. It was the men who came up through the newly-created frontier posts who became the motive force behind the new policies of the 1830s and 1840s.

Although a few of the new frontier agents were military officers with considerable regimental experience behind them, and a few were Civil Servants, the great majority were Company officers who had served only briefly with their regiments. Within five years of joining the army they had passed an interpreter's examination, usually in Persian, transferred to the staff, and then secured an assistantship in the Political Department. Unless death or disaster (in the form of a blunder which caused them to be returned to regimental duties) supervened, the remainder of their careers was normally passed in the Political Department. They could hope to rise to the position of Resident or its equivalent, a post more coveted than any other below the Supreme Council. Political work, by virtue of its interest, its financial rewards, and the power and responsibility which it offered to young men, attracted some of the ablest and most ambitious men in the Company's service. In the Political Department seniority mattered less than the capacity to seize the right opportunity at the right time; hence Political Agents tended to be men of considerable initiative, or to put it more crudely, men with an eye to the main chance. One of the most notable among them, Henry Rawlinson, once compiled his own rules of conduct, which might serve as a creed for all the Politicals. 'Create business for yourself. Lose no opportunity of making yourself useful . . . Grasp at everything and never yield an inch . . . Above all, never stand upon trifles.'[58] Some may have taken this advice too literally and fallen before the many temptations which were set before the Politicals. Of the agents on the Panjab frontier, Edward Colebrooke was definitely corrupt and Ochterlony and Claude Wade probably so. George Clerk's hands were apparently clean, as were those of George Broadfoot, although the latter was often offered bribes. Even the much praised Henry Lawrence was not above accepting an indirect bribe in the form of a donation of £10,000 from Ghulab Singh towards the expenses of his beloved Lawrence Asylum.[59] But direct corruption was probably much less important than the indirect corruption of ambition, the temptation to represent a situation in a manner which could advance the agent himself, commonly through the extension of British authority, but occasionally through the maintenance of a situation already favourable to the agent concerned. The vital importance of the role of the agents makes it worth examining, in some detail, the structure and personnel of the system which developed in the years after 1818 to 1819.

In the south the important role which had been played in previous years by the Residents in Baroda—men like Alexander Walker and James Carnac—was inherited, after 1819, by the Resident in Cutch. It was he whom Malcolm described as the warden of the southern border.[60] From 1820 this post was occupied by Henry Pottinger, who had earlier visited Sind, Baluchistan, and Iran. Pottinger became the main source of information on Sind and, during the 1830s the obvious man to conduct negotiations with that state. The work of the Cutch Residency grew and Pottinger had an assistant assigned to him. In 1830 Lieutenant Alexander Burnes was appointed to this post and began the apprenticeship to his famous and fatal frontier career. The Cutch Residency, under the authority of the Government of Bombay, remained the main centre of British activity in this section of the frontier until June 1838, when Pottinger was appointed as Resident in Sind under the orders of the Supreme Government. This decision was in response to the sudden awakening of interest in Sind in the summer of 1838. Up to that time it had been envisaged that the Residency in Sind would be only a minor post, subordinate to the Resident in Cutch and it had been offered to Pottinger's then assistant, Captain Melville, who, apparently through the influence of his wife, had turned it down.[61]

In the northern sector of the frontier the situation was complicated. From 1785 to 1803 the principal British agent in northern India had been the Resident with Sindhia who gradually came to displace the Resident at Lucknow as the main source of political information. The Resident with Sindhia normally resided at Ujjain. Warren Hastings had sent an agent, Major James Brown, to the Mughal court at Delhi in 1783, but he had been obliged to remove him after Sindhia took control there. From 1803 until 1821 the Resident in Delhi became the major British agent in the north-west. This post was held by David Ochterlony from 1803 until 1806. Ochterlony was regarded as a soldier who lacked the necessary qualities for so responsible a position and it was proposed to replace him in 1804. His replacement, Colonel William Scott, died *en route* to his post and Ochterlony was confirmed for the time being, although Lake kept direct charge of most political relations during this period. Ochterlony remained until 1806 when Archibald Seton of the Bengal Civil Service took over the post, having been transferred from Bareilly. Seton served until 1810 and was succeeded the following year, by his former assistant, Charles Metcalfe, who remained in charge until 1818, playing an important part in the Hastings Settlement. In January 1819 Metcalfe was recalled to the Secretariat and was replaced by Ochterlony, under whom the system continued until 1821. From that time the unified control of the affairs of the northern frontier by the Delhi Residency began to break up, although, in one form or another, the unity was broadly maintained until it was finally dissolved in 1832.

The problem was that since the 1818 Settlement the work of the Residency had greatly increased. The Resident was responsible for relations with the Mughal Emperor; the superintendence of relations with the states of Malwa or Rajputana; the oversight of relations with the Protected Sikh and Hill States; and the control of relations with the states beyond the frontier, notably with Lahore. Each of these constituted, in effect, a different job, but it was long before this was fully recognized and the relative importance of the jobs identified. A complicating factor in sorting out these duties was the ambitions of the various officials. The influential Ochterlony was a particular difficulty. He had long been underrated, but after his success in Nepal his claims could not be denied. In March 1818 he had been appointed as agent in Rajputana and was delighted to be transferred to Delhi, while retaining control of Rajputana. Ochterlony ruled like an Indian Emperor in Delhi, and his name transposed into Persian appropriately and euphoniously as Loony Akhtar. In the evenings he was reputed to parade with his thirteen wives mounted on thirteen elephants.[62] He was reluctant to give up any part of his political empire. In 1821 he was given the title of Resident and Agent in Rajputana and Malwa, but retained broadly the same powers. Under him was a battery of assistant agents who undertook the detailed supervision of parts of the work. In Delhi H. J. Middleton took responsibility for relations with Bikaner, the Cis–Satlej Sikhs, and Lahore. Within the Protected Sikh States there were agents at Ambala (Lieutenant R. Ross) and Ludhiana (Lieutenant William Murray) and another agent at the new Hill station of Sabathu. In Delhi itself, William Fraser looked after local affairs. In Rajputana Ochterlony had James Tod at Udaipur with responsibility for Harauti. In Jaipur, until 1821, was Captain J. Short, but, because of continual troubles in that state, the former Acting Resident with Sindhia, Captain Josiah Stewart, who was later to have great influence with Bentinck, was moved into Jaipur in 1821, to be succeeded by Lieutenant-Colonel F. N. Raper in 1824. Most of the other Rajput states came under Captain F. Wilder, the Superintendent at Ajmer, who was also subordinated to Ochterlony. Broadly speaking, this situation persisted until 1831 to 1832 under Ochterlony, who eventually resigned in 1825, and under his successors, Metcalfe again (1825–7), Sir Edward Colebrooke (1827–9), and then a succession of officers until the abolition of the Residency. However, the process which gradually developed during the years and culminated in 1831 to

1832 was the devolution of real power over Rajputana to the Superintendent at Ajmer and over the Protected Sikh States and relations with Lahore to the agents in Ambala and Ludhiana. It will therefore be more convenient to follow the fortunes of these two areas separately.

Under Ochterlony there was a strong movement to closer control over the Rajput and Jat states. Finance provided both an incentive and an excuse; it was necessary to ensure that the tribute was paid. The maintenance of peace was another justification and questions of succession often provided further opportunities. A letter to Stewart, his newly-appointed deputy at Jaipur, in 1821, makes Ochterlony's attitude clear:

It is only imperious necessity which perhaps will warrant or induce the authorities to exercise a more positive and direct interference. When that necessity is proved and the happiness of the people, the welfare of the state and the interests of the infant Raja are shown to be involved or benignant the government will no longer hesitate.[63]

Essentially this was a clear invitation to Stewart to demonstrate the 'imperious necessity' for intervention. Stewart did so and Government intervened. Ochterlony had more trouble, however, with another subordinate, James Tod. Tod, of course, had been one of the architects of the 1817 to 1818 Settlement and his favourable attitude towards Zalim Singh of Kotah had been one of the factors which contrived to mould the moderate character of the Hastings arrangements in Rajputana. Tod had subsequently been appointed as Political Agent for Marwar (Udaipur) and Harauti (Kotah and Bundi). Later his designation was changed to Political Agent to the Western Rajput States and he was given additional authority over Marwar (Jodhpur) and Jaisalmer. Ochterlony thought he was too favourable to the Rajputs. He wrote of him that he was 'too much of a Rajpoot himself to deal with Rajpoots'.[64] Differences between them in 1821 over policy towards Tod's beloved Kotah resulted in Tod's sphere of influence being limited to Udaipur. Tod resigned in 1822 and went home to write his classic work on Rajputana. He was succeeded by Captain Cobbe, at Udaipur and Captain J. Caulfield at Harauti. The phenomenon of expatriate patriotism continued to bedevil British relations with Rajputana: in 1824 Raper in Jaipur found himself at loggerheads with Caulfield in Harauti. On this occasion Ochterlony was obliged to reprove Raper for excessive intervention in internal affairs and in 1825 Raper was replaced by Captain John Low (1788–1880).[65] Ochterlony however, overreached himself a few years later over Bharatpur. In 1823 Raja

Randhir Singh (reg. 1805–23) died without issue. The succession went to his younger brother, Baldeo Singh, who was reported to have bribed Ochterlony to agree to this. Ochterlony also later agreed to recognize Baldeo's infant son, Balwant Singh, as heir. Balwant's succession in 1825 was opposed by other groups within Bharatpur and the crown was usurped by a cousin of Balwant. Ochterlony advocated intervention, not, he stated, merely in defence of Balwant's claims but because: 'the interference in Bharatpur was necessary to have a control over the state and the control of Bharatpur is essential for the peace and tranquility of the British dominions in northern India'.[66] Ochterlony collected a force and announced his intention to support Balwant with force. The usurper, Durjansal, offered to negotiate and Amherst ordered Ochterlony's advance to be stopped. Furious at this intervention Ochterlony resigned and died soon after. He was succeeded by Metcalfe, who, although in general opposed to Ochterlony's interventionist policy, in this case rejected Durjansal's profferred terms and recommended force. Amherst agreed. Two factors seemed to have weighed in this decision. The first was the desire to administer a sharp lesson to Bharatpur in order to impress other states who were contemplating intervention in support of Durjansal. 'The existing disturbances at Bhartpur, if not speedily quieted, will produce general commotion in Upper India', declared a Court Resolution of 16 September 1825. Bharatpur, wrote Lady Amherst, the wife of the Governor-General, 'formed a kind of *point d'appui* for the hopes of all who were hostile to British rule'.[67] The second, almost certainly, was to avenge the defeat suffered by Lake before Bharatpur in 1805. In December 1825 a large force of twenty-one thousand men under the Commander-in-Chief, Lord Comber-mere, an old Peninsular War veteran, besieged Bharatpur, which fell in January 1826. Balwant was installed as Raja with Major Lockett as Political Agent.[68] Bharatpur had achieved the dual purpose of removing Ochterlony and demonstrating the power and determination of Britain in northern India. The affair was a classic demonstration of the power of the internal enemy to compel intervention, through the need to maintain British prestige and the opinion of invincibility.

The centre of British relations with Rajputana was now moving to Ajmer. Ajmer had been in the possession of Jodhpur until it had been ceded to Sindhia in 1791 and it had been made over to Britain in 1818. It was in a commanding position at the north-eastern end of a range of hills called the Aravali range. These hills, which ran in a north-easterly direction, formed the boundary between Udaipur and Jodhpur, and offered a good position for the control of central and western Rajputana. Under Captain F. Wilder, who was Superintendent from 1818 to 1824, Ajmer steadily increased in prosperity. His success and the obvious utility of the Ajmer position, in British possession, led to control over other states being attached to the Ajmer office. In 1822 Wilder was given charge of relations with Kishengarh and Jaisalmer. Over the next years the influence of Ajmer increased until in 1832, on the advice of Metcalfe, control over all relations with Rajputana was removed from the hands of the Delhi Residents and placed in those of the Superintendent, now Resident at Ajmer. This change coincided with the reorganization of the Government of the North-Western Provinces and, ultimately, the Resident at Ajmer was removed from the direct authority of the Supreme Government and placed under that of the Lieutenant-Governor of the North-Western Provinces at Agra. This circumstance allowed Metcalfe, who held the office of Lieutenant-Governor from 1834 to 1835 and 1836 to 1838, to retain a footing in the affairs which, from one office and another, he had guided for so many years, and gave him a platform from which to launch his increasingly unfashionable views on frontier affairs. The change also represents the end of a long-term decline in the importance of Rajputana in British eyes. From 1803 to 1818 the region had been the centre of British interest in the north-west, and for some years after 1818 the habit thus formed persisted and Rajputana continued to be regarded as the most important of British frontier interests. Its subsequent decline in importance is a symptom of the process of frontier inversion remarked above; the spotlight had shifted from Ajmer to the station which looked outwards beyond the Satlej—Ludhiana. When Arthur Conolly was sent as assistant Political Agent to Rajputana in the 1830s he felt that he was in a backwater.[69]

The Resident at Ajmer continued to be a man of political significance. From 1834 to 1839 the post was held by Major N. Alves, who pursued a policy of interference in the internal affairs of Rajputana in opposition to the instructions he received from the Supreme Government and contrived to blame the resulting troubles on the interference of Iran, a characteristic device of the Political Agent.[70] From 1839 until 1847 the post was held by a man of real ability, Colonel James Sutherland, although he became increasingly wayward in his last years. Auckland consulted him regularly about political matters during the 1830s and when he came to select the new Envoy to Kabul in 1838 hesitated over Sutherland's name before choosing William Macnaghten. Later he regretted that he had not selected the Ajmer Resident for the post. But the true importance of the Ajmer Resident was in relation to the internal frontier; of all areas within the British defence frontier, Rajputana was regarded as the most delicate and potentially the most turbulent. It was this circumstance which seems to have prompted Auckland to restore the Ajmer Resident to direct official subordination to the Supreme Government in 1840; in 1839 dangerous disturbances in Jodhpur had forced an armed British intervention at a time when all the frontiers of British India were combustible. Auckland transformed the role of the Agra Government, in relation to Rajputana, into that of a mere post office, transmitting, with comments, the dispatches of the Resident. Powers of decision, except in an emergency, were reserved to the Supreme Government. The then Lieutenant-Governor, Thomas Campbell Robertson (1789–1863), protested at this reduction in his authority, but the Court of Directors upheld Auckland's views. The change also formed part of Auckland's general policy of bringing all relations with Indian states under the direct control of Calcutta. The continuing importance of Rajputana in relation to the internal frontier ensured that the Ajmer Residency remained one of the key political appointments in India and under Hardinge and Dalhousie was held by men of the calibre of John Low (1847–52) and Henry Lawrence (1853–7).

The story of the years 1818 to 1830 is really that of the rise of Ludhiana to a position of dominance in the frontier system. After the establishment of the 1809 Protectorate over the Cis–Satlej states, Ochterlony had been left as Resident at Ludhiana (1810–15) under the control of the Delhi Resident. From 1814 to 1816 Ochterlony was away from his post in connection with the Gurkha war. During that period his assistant (since June 1810), Captain G. Birch, deputized for him. As a result of the war several Hill States passed under British protection and Ochterlony, whose own reputation had also been much enhanced by the war, was appointed to take charge of the affairs of the Hill States and of the Protected Sikh States and for this purpose was placed under the direct authority of the Governor-General. Ochterlony's empire was still centred within the British frontier and, to enable him to control it more effectively, in October 1815 he moved his headquarters further south-east from Ludhiana to Karnal. Birch was moved to Nahan where he could deal with the Hill States and another assistant, Lieutenant R. Ross, was also located in the Hills at Sabathu. In November 1816 a third assistant to Ochterlony, Lieutenant William Murray (1st Bengal N. I.), who had been placed under Ochterlony in July 1815, was sent from Karnal to take charge at Ludhiana. Murray's duties included responsibility for the family of the exiled Shah of Afghanistan, Shah Shuja al-Mulk. From this date onwards there was always an agency at Ludhiana, subordinated first to the Political Agent at Karnal, subsequently to the agent at Ambala, and then to the Resident at Delhi, before the Ludhiana agent established the coveted direct contact with the Supreme Government.

In March 1818 Ochterlony was given charge of Rajputana; Ross, now Captain, was left in charge of the Karnal agency. General control over the Cis–Satlej Sikhs reverted to the Delhi Residency to which Ross was subordinated. In March 1822 the headquarters of the Karnal agency were moved to Ambala, some fifty miles further up the Jamna than Karnal and nearer to the Sikh, and especially the Hill States. In 1825 Ross was replaced by Murray as Agent for the Protected Sikh States and Murray retained this post until his death in 1830. Murray's place at Ludhiana was taken by Lieutenant Claude Martine Wade (1794–1861), who served on the Panjab frontier from 1823 to 1840 and during that time became a man of great influence and power in the shaping of British policy. It was Wade and frontier logic which made the Ludhiana agency.

Wade soon found himself in dispute with Murray about the division of their responsibilities and particularly about who should conduct relations with Lahore. In 1827 the Supreme Government intervened. Murray, with the new title of Political Agent, Ambala, was given control of relations with the Protected Sikh States, and Wade was made independent of Murray's authority and, with the title of Political Assistant, Ludhiana, and under the general control of the Delhi Resident, was given charge of relations with Lahore. In May 1827, before these changes had taken place Wade, accompanied by Captain Pearson and Dr. Gerard, the latter better known subsequently as the companion of Burnes, had already led a complimentary mission to Lahore. Also in the new arrangements the new agent at Sabathu, Captain C. P. Kennedy, was given charge of relations with the Hill States.

Wade won virtual independence of the Delhi Resident in 1831, when he was instructed to correspond directly with the Governor-General and not to send his dispatches through the Resident in Delhi. His victory was confirmed the following year when the Delhi Residency was at last broken up and Wade was given the title of Political Agent, Ludhiana. His own empire quickly began to grow. In October 1832 he was given an assistant, Lieutenant Frederick Mackeson (1807–53) of the 14th B. N. I. Mackeson was also to have a distinguished career on the frontier. When Mackeson was deputed, still under the supervision of Wade, to a post on the Indus in 1835, Wade acquired a new assistant, Lieutenant Joseph Davey Cunningham (1812–51) of the Bengal Engineers. Cunningham also became a dominant figure in frontier policy in the early 1840s, although he became best known for his opposition to British policy towards the Sikhs.

During his career at Ludhiana Wade steadily increased his authority in matters relating to the affairs of the states beyond the Indus. He built up a system of unofficial correspondents in Tibet, Peshawar, Kabul, Qandahar, Herat, and Bahawalpur. An official newswriter had been maintained at Lahore since 1809. After 1830 the unofficial correspondents were gradually replaced by official newswriters, paid by the Government of India; such appointments were made at Bahawalpur in 1831 and in Qandahar and Kabul in 1832. Through his monopoly of information, his close contacts with Lahore (Ranjit Singh maintained a permanent agent at Ludhiana), his long experience, and his undoubted intelligence, Wade made himself a dominant figure in the formation of British policy in the north-west. In 1835 his position in these affairs was officially recognized when he was put in charge of all political relations with Lahore and the states beyond the Indus. Wade's ascendancy led to jealousy on the part of Pottinger. Charles Masson, who became official newswriter at Kabul under Wade in 1835, had formerly been an unofficial correspondent working for Pottinger. In the context of this struggle for the control of British north-west frontier policy, waged by the agencies at Bhuj and Ludhiana, the choice of Alexander Burnes, the assistant at Bhuj, to conduct a mission to Lahore in 1831, posed a significant threat to Wade's authority.[71]

With the rise of the Ludhiana agency that at Ambala, concerned with the Protected Sikh States, became of lesser significance. During the 1820s the superintendence of relations with the Protected Sikh States had been considered to be of greater importance than the conduct of relations with Lahore and the reversal of the positions illustrates once more the phenomenon of frontier inversion. Like the Rajputs, the Cis–Satlej Sikhs, once so large an item in British calculations, had acquired a recognized position within the British Indian system while the trans–frontier peoples now loomed large as the crucial unknown factor. From 1834 the demotion of the Ambala agency was recognized when the agent was made responsible to the Agra Government for the Cis–Satlej Sikhs, and not, as formerly, to the Supreme Government. Nevertheless, the Ambala agency retained some significance as a potential, alternative source of expertise on Sikh affairs and in the absence of Wade it was the Ambala agent who took over the duties of the Ludhiana agency. This fact was to become important in 1839 to 1840. In August 1831 one of the rare civilian officials to be appointed to frontier posts was given charge of the Ambala agency. This was George Russell Clerk (1800–89). Clerk was a man of real ability, seemingly marked out for a career in the Secretariat, and in 1822 he served as first assistant to the Secretary in charge of the Secret and Political

Department, the post of a high-flyer like Metcalfe or Adam. But Clerk became involved in a scandal and found a frontier appointment advisable, since his wife could not be received in Calcutta society. In 1829 he was first assistant to the Resident in Delhi, from which post he found his way to Ambala. Clerk substituted for Wade in 1836 to 1837 and again in 1838 to 1839, and eventually replaced him in May 1840 when Clerk was given the title of Agent to the Governor-General for the Affairs of the Panjab and North-West Frontier and placed directly under the control of the Supreme Government. Until 1842 Clerk's frontier influence was circumscribed by his continued subordination to the Agra Government in respect of the Protected Sikh and Hill States and by the existence of the completely new system of frontier agencies which had been constructed in dependence on the new centre at Kabul. The collapse of the Afghan position in 1842 brought Clerk into his own as the dominant figure on the north-west frontier. In October 1842 his empire was reconstructed. He then took general control over all affairs in the Protected Sikh States, the Hill States, and all relations beyond the frontier. Under his control were subordinate agencies at Ludhiana, Ambala, Firuzpur, and Sabathu. In June 1843 Clerk was appointed Lieutenant-Governor of the North-Western Provinces, from which position he could retain some oversight over his successor. His two successors in Ludhiana, Lieutenant-Colonel A. F. Richmond (1843–4) and Major George Broadfoot (1844–5), both played important parts in shaping frontier policy in a critical period.

Ludhiana thus became the main centre for British political relations with the north-west. It was not until quite late a significant military base. The position at Ludhiana itself was not quite as free as was desired. The British base there was sited, until 1834, on land rented from the Raja of Jind. Only in that year was full possession acquired through use of the doctrine of lapse. Ambala, Nahan and, Sabathu were also minor military posts, although the Hill stations were used increasingly for European troops in the later period and it was during the 1830s that Simla itself began to come into use as a great summer civil station in Upper India. But during the 1820s and 1830s the main military bases for the support of the northern frontier continued to be at Karnal and at Meerut, situated some forty miles north-west of Delhi in the middle of the Jamna–Ganges plain. When an important military base did develop on the Satlej it was not at Ludhiana but at Firuzpur, seventy miles west of Ludhiana, about twenty-five miles below the confluence with the Beas. Firuzpur had been singled out as a likely site for a base as early as 1823, when William Murray described it as 'the key to India'.[72] Too much importance should not, of course, be attributed to this description. According to Political and Military Agents, the keys of India were as plentiful as fallen leaves in autumn; the door they were intended to unlock was not that of India but of promotion. Murray thought Firuzpur a better point than Ludhiana from which to strike at Lahore if that proved to be necessary. It was indeed nearer and only one river-crossing was involved. His recommendation also provided another indication of the shifting attitude to the frontier. Interest in Firuzpur was aroused and, although nothing was done to obtain possession of the district at the time, it was resolved that Ranjit Singh should not be allowed to gain possession. In 1827 the decision was taken that it should be taken by lapse when the existing ruler died. The opportunity came in September 1835 and thereafter a base was constructed. In 1838 Firuzpur, rather than Ludhiana, became the assembly point for the army of the Indus. In the years before the first Sikh war Firuzpur became the principal military base upon the frontier.

As remarked above, between 1818 and 1838 the north-western frontier was formed as a military and political frontier in the true sense. It changed from being a ring-fence, turned inwards as an element in the policing of the Hastings Settlement, and became instead a complex, organized position looking outwards to the states beyond. Strategists came to see it in this light and to analyze its strengths and weaknesses. On balance the military judgement was very favourable and this is borne out by a detailed examination by the Commander-in-Chief, Sir Henry Fane (1778–1840), in 1837.

Fane considered all the Indian frontiers. In the east he regarded the Brahmaputra river as the basic line of defence and the provinces which lay to the east of that river (Arakan, Chittagong, Sylhet, and Assam) as advanced posts. The nature of the land on the east bank of the Brahmaputra and the frequency of floods made the river line very suitable for defence against attacks by any likely enemies from the east. He had in mind, of course, the Burmese, who were not considered potentially formidable enemies, especially when removed from their own jungles, swamps, and mountains. In the south he saw no real problems of defence. The frontier was formed by the sea and Britain commanded that element. On the exposed eastern coast of India there were no harbours which were accessible to an enemy. The western coast did offer possible landing-points for an enemy, but a landing on this side was made unlikely because of the British control of Ceylon, and especially the port of Trinkomali from which sea-borne attacks on landing parties could be made, and because of the problems presented to an invader by the western Ghats. The key frontier, therefore, he concluded, was the north-western frontier.

At first sight, remarked Fane, the north-western frontier appeared most vulnerable, but this was a misleading impression and it actually possessed great strength. The whole of the southern section of the frontier was protected by the Thar or Great Indian Desert. Only the northern section needed attention. This area Fane defined as the line of the 'Gharra' (that is, the Garrah, the name formerly given to the Satlej below its confluence with the Beas) from Uch (a town in Bahawalpur near the confluence of the Satlej and the Chenab) to Rupar, where the Satlej flowed out of the mountains. The lower part of this section, represented by the Garrah did not present any problem since any invading force which crossed the Garrah would also have to cross the desert area of Bahawalpur. Accordingly, by elimination, the only area of frontier which needed to be defended was one hundred and twenty miles of the Satlej from Firuzpur to Rupar. Any force attempting to invade British India from the north-west would be funnelled into this narrow gate into the Company's territories. 'In my opinion', wrote Fane, 'no force capable of seriously assailing our Empire from the west, can approach us at any other point.' Fane made some suggestions about how this stretch of frontier might be strengthened, including closer control over the Hill States, the fortification of Firuzpur, which he considered superior to Ludhiana as a military base, the development of strong depots in the rear near the Jamna and at Delhi and Agra, and the strengthening of Allahabad. He also stressed the importance of good relations with Lahore, the vital buffer for this stretch of the frontier. But, in general, Fane was well satisfied with the north-western frontier which he described as 'the most perfect a great empire can possess'.[73]

Fane never changed his view on the excellence of the British frontier as it had been formed in 1818 to 1819 and this was one of his objections to the policy of the first Afghan war. A tour of the frontier in 1839 only served to convince him of the correctness of his earlier appreciation. After his later tour he definitely ruled out an invasion across the Garrah; only the Satlej frontier needed protection. He recommended that this should be strengthened, when an opportunity was provided by the death of Ranjit Singh, by establishing three main forward defensive posts at Firuzpur, Ludhiana, and in the hills above Rupar, and the creation of a reserve post at Raikot, about twenty miles south-south-west of Ludhiana, which would be centrally positioned to reinforce any of the three advanced posts. With these improvements, he remarked, 'it is difficult to conceive a more advantageous frontier'. He was strongly critical of those in London and in the Indian Government who advocated the occupation of the Panjab and an advance to an Indus frontier.

He wrote decidedly: 'I beg to record my opinion, that whoever per-suades the Government of India to accept such a view and to act on it, will be an enemy to his country.' The Indus line was too vast and too dangerous and would place all the Panjab rivers behind the defending force and across their line of communications. The Panjab, under Sikh rule, made the best possible buffer for India against invasion from the west.[74] This later opinion of Fane's, of course, in the context of the developments which were taking place in connection with the first Afghan war, constituted a direct criticism of the strategic basis of that war and his strong warning was directed especially against Auckland himself.

No frontier, however, is to be judged upon purely military considera-tions and it was on wider, political factors that criticism of the 1818 to 1819 frontier came to be based. This dissatisfaction with the 1818 frontier will be examined in detail in subsequent chapters. Here it will be sufficient to note the Governor-General, Lord Auckland's own reply to Fane's analysis, in 1837, which shows how the strategic attitudes which shaped the first Afghan war were already formed before the events which produced that singular event in the history of the defence of India.

Auckland accepted Fane's views on the frontier of southern India. With regard to the eastern frontier he entered a significant dissent. He pointed out that Fane's support of the Brahmaputra line in effect treated the provinces to the east of that river as expendable. They were, he argued, far too valuable to be regarded in that light and would have to be fully defended. But his main criticisms were concentrated upon Fane's remarks on the north-western frontier.

It was improbable that India would be invaded by a formidable force, but if this happened, Auckland argued, Britain would be obliged to advance to the Indus and even beyond in order to meet the threat and this would have to be done whether the Sikhs co-operated or not. The Satlej was not defensible and the Panjab was too fertile a land to be abandoned to an invader. 'Our main strength would probably be on the Indus, our advanced posts beyond it', he wrote. In any case, he continued, eventually the dissolution of the Lahore state could force Britain to advance into the Panjab, even if it were not desired to do so. Auckland also questioned Fane's confidence in the impenetrability of the southern sector of the frontier. The desert and the Rann of Cutch were obstacles, but not impassable. If an enemy established himself in Sind, he could, in conjunction with the Amirs, operate against Guzerat and Bombay. To prevent this a British force would have to advance to the Lower Indus. Further, if Britain obtained control over the Lower

Indus she would be enabled to threaten the flank of any enemy force which was attacking through the Panjab in the northern sector. On these grounds alone, and quite apart from the question of facilitating political and commercial relations with Afghanistan, Auckland believed that a closer connection with Sind was necessary.[75]

The clear inference from Auckland's remarks was that the Indus was the main defensive frontier of British India and that British policy should now be directed towards the achievement of that frontier. In this view he reflected what had, by the 1830s, come to be the orthodoxy of the Political Department. Fane's views reflected only the military view of the frontier and he underrated the strength of the views which were ranged against him. The frontier expertise which had been built up between 1818 and 1837 had changed British views on the defence of India completely and attention was now firmly focused upon the countries which lay beyond the existing frontier, and along the Indus.

The first interest in the Indus frontier dates back to the late 1790s. At that time men in Bombay began to talk about the possibility of a French landing on the coast of Sind among other points on the west coast. It was also suggested, as noted earlier, that Sind could have some value in relation to defence against a possible move by Zaman Shah. Dundas seized upon these points and in October 1799 suggested that Wellesley should consider taking control of the Portuguese settlement at Diu and of the Guzerat coast so that if Zaman did attack from Afghanistan, Britain would be prepared to advance to the lower Indus and to operate against the flanks of his army in the Panjab.[76] Dundas clearly viewed the Indus as an advanced position and not as the main frontier and in fact he regarded it as unsuitable for the latter purpose; it was believed at the time that the Jamna was a much stronger barrier. Dundas, however, became frightened by the expense of such operations and, with the diminishing fears of France and Afghanistan, dropped the idea.

The interest in the Indus frontier was revived in 1802 by Henry Wellesley when he picked up the idea of a French landing on the Lower Indus and connected it with the presence of Perron in the Doab. It was then put forward, however, not with any idea of adopting the Indus frontier for the Company, but principally to provide an additional argument to justify Wellesley's Maratha policy. After the destruction of Perron's power the idea of a French landing on the Lower Indus and a connection with a French position in northern India disappeared until, forty years later, it was improbably resurrected by the Duke of Wellington. Wellington then recast the French officers in the service of Lahore, in the role of Perron and foresaw a similar link, somewhat to the suppressed amusement of his colleagues.

The revival of the French threat in 1807 and the possibility of an overland invasion of India led to new interest in the Indus. In December 1807 the first clear statement that the Indus frontier was that most desirable for British India appears in a letter written by Captain Archibald Blair, formerly of the Indian Navy. Blair considered how Britain might best defeat a combined attack by France and Russia. In the areas beyond the Indus he advocated a scorched earth policy. The real stand should be made upon the Indus itself. 'The Indus ought to be considered as the grand frontier for the preservation of India', he wrote. Every crossing-point should be occupied and all boats controlled. The Indus, he claimed optimistically, offered particular advantages because it was navigable as far north as Attock and therefore would provide a useful route through which reinforcements from Bombay could be brought into the action.[77]

Blair's opinion of the advantages of the Indus frontier was confirmed a month later in a memorandum written by General Charles Reynolds, the former Surveyor-General in Bombay, who made a major contribution to Wellesley's frontier plans. Reynolds postulated an overland invasion by France, possibly assisted by Russia and Iran, and probably joined by the Marathas. He predicted that such an attack would follow the route through Qandahar and Kabul and would reach the Indus at Attock. Because of the Baluchistan mountains and the Thar Desert the invasion would inevitably be funnelled into this route; only a small force could penetrate the Mekran and this threat could be countered by a force from Bombay supported by a fleet at the mouth of the Indus. In this analysis the origins of the military axioms enunciated by Fane thirty years later may be clearly discerned. Indeed Reynold's postulated route remained at the heart of British strategic thinking on this subject for half a century or more.[78] The British plan of defence, argued Reynolds, should hinge on preventing an enemy crossing of the Indus. A flotilla would be useful for this purpose, but the main reliance would have to be on a force of Company's troops. The advanced force on the Indus would require to be supported by reserve armies in the Panjab, and near Karnal and Patiala in the Jamna–Satlej Doab, in order to prevent a junction between the invaders and the Marathas. It was pointless to seek the co-operation of the Sikhs since they were too weak and too divided, but an exploratory embassy to investigate the possibility of an alliance with Afghanistan would be well worth while. In his information, in his analysis of possible invasion routes, and in his suggestion of the dangers of links between internal and external enemies, Reynolds was remarkably acute and prophetic. Robert Dundas was sufficiently impressed with the memorandum to show it to

Arthur Wellesley. Wellesley agreed with the general drift of the analysis and with the recommended defensive strategy, although, more realistically than Reynolds, doubted whether it would be possible to prevent the invader crossing the Indus. 'I have no great reliance on that river as the barrier to India', he wrote. Wellesley recommended that Attock should be seized and made into the base of operations. The most important preparatory steps were to assemble an adequately equipped British army in the north-western provinces and to make ready a field force beyond Delhi.[79] Dundas took up some of these suggestions and, in a dispatch dated 2 March 1808, recommended tentatively the establishment of a British post at Attock.[80]

Minto in India was already thinking on similar lines. Apart from his forward diplomatic preparations, he also had in mind the possible advance of a British force through the Panjab to the Indus. Metcalfe was instructed to obtain permission for this on his mission to Lahore in 1808 to 1809. Minto had originally proposed to send a large force much further—to Iran, but abandoned this plan, apparently on military advice. The Commander-in-Chief, Lieutenant-General George Hewett (1750–1840), who had taken up his post in October 1807, decided that defence should concentrate on the land frontier. Hewett calculated that an invading force would probably enter Afghanistan via Mashhad and then penetrate into India either through the Bolan Pass, from Quetta to Shikarpur, or, more probably, via the Khaibar pass from Kabul to Peshawar and thence to Attock. He, however, cautiously rejected the idea of advancing to the Indus to meet the enemy. 'Beyond the Jumna', he commented, 'all is conjecture', and he decided to wait for the invader on that frontier. He planned to assemble a force of twenty-seven thousand men at Delhi in six weeks. Minto, however, thought this plan too defensive and considered that the British forces should advance to the Indus, if not beyond into Afghanistan.[81] Others were still more ambitious. Mountstuart Elphinstone suggested that Britain should obtain full control over all states east of the Indus, annexing the states of Lahore and Sind in the process, and carry the frontier forward beyond the Indus to the line of the Sulaiman range, extending forward into the Mekran in the south. The system would be completed by a subsidiary alliance with Kabul.[82] Elphinstone, however, was eighty years before his time, and the system he envisaged did not come into existence until the forward policy of the 1890s. Elphinstone's memorandum, however, may have been the source of a very similar proposal which was put forward in 1812 by Benjamin Jones, the influential private secretary of Robert Dundas.[83] Jones remained at the India Board for many years and he was used extensively by Ellenborough in preparing his momentous revival of the concept of the trans–Indus frontier in 1830. It seems possible that Jones may have constituted one important bridge between the two periods of concern about the north-west.

After 1809 discussion of the Indus frontier lapsed. There was no thought of danger from the north-west and the frontiers of India which mattered were those with central India. In 1816 Canning declared his dislike for the idea of an Indus frontier,[84] while, with characteristic mental polarity, Ellenborough, in 1829, rejected it in favour either of the existing frontier on the Satlej or a new one on the Hindu Kush, indicating a firm preference for the latter.[85] It was during this period, however, that the persistent work of the frontier agents began to adjust men to the familiarity of the Indus frontier and its ultimate inevitability came to be accepted in Government circles and even found its way into discussions in the periodical Press.[86]

During the 1830s the reviews contain several references to the desirability of the attainment of the Indus frontier. A writer in the *United Services Journal* in 1831 advocated an advance to the Indus.[87] In 1835 a writer in the *Quarterly Review* argued that the proper frontiers of British India were the Irrawady in the east and the Indus in the west. 'If we cannot defend India, thus defined, out of her own resources, we must abandon her', he wrote.[88] In this case accountancy as much as strategy apparently dictated the desirable frontiers, which measured extent as much as defensibility. In another review in 1838 the writer urged the annexation of the Indus as far north as Attock and indeed of Afghanistan beyond, as far as Kabul, arguing that without such a measure there could be no security against foreign invasion.[89] For an *Edinburgh Review* writer in 1840 the Indus had become 'our natural boundary'.[90]

By 1840, of course, British India was in the middle of a new reconstruction of frontier policy, and the advance to the Indus was beginning, for many reasons, to seem more desirable and more inevitable. There was also another aspect. No one, reading the works of the frontier travellers, can avoid remarking upon the way in which the scenes they observed recalled their Classical education. In this context the Indus acquired a romantic attraction which added to the force of its appeal. The emotional attraction of the Indus is brought out clearly in the words of one of the last opponents of the Indus frontier, Lord Hardinge, whose comments afford a suitable conclusion to this chapter:

The very name of the Indus is associated with ancient recollections, which render it difficult to suppress the desire to make that magnificent river the boundary of the British Empire. Young civilians and gallant soldiers ardently desire annexation—and even sexagenarians might forget what is prudent in the patriotic pride of giving England's greatest conquest a frontier worthy of British India.[91]

6

The Indus and Beyond,
1830–1838

As long as our manufactures are conveyed to the North
Western Provinces of India by the long and tedious navigation of the Ganges and then through the Punjab and
Cabul to Buchara, we may doubt whether manufactures
of a similar description, and even our own may not be
conveyed at a less cost by the Caravans which pass from
Orenburg to Bochara; but if the produce of England and
of India could be sent at once up the Indus to such points
as might be convenient for their transport to Cabul we
cannot but entertain the hope that we might succeed in
underselling the Russians and in obtaining for ourselves a
large portion at least of the internal Trade of Central
Asia.   This is a subject to which we wish you to direct
your attention with a view to the Political effects which
would be the result of success.

Secret Committee to Governor-General in Council,
12 January 1830.

1830 was a momentous year in the history of British relations with the
countries on and beyond the Indus. Since the end of Minto's heady
ambitions in 1810 there had been no interest in the defence of India
against invasion from the north-west. The Indian Government was
indifferent to Iran, Afghanistan, and Turkestan; Sind and Lahore were
essentially border problems. Attention was concentrated first upon the
achievement of internal security within India and subsequently, apart
from the interruptions of the Gurkha and Burmese wars, upon internal
development, or good government on the cheap. Only a few agents in
Iraq, Iran, and in the Gulf, and a very few men like Malcolm in India
argued differently and drew attention to the potential threat of Russia.
But they were disregarded. The great majority of British officials in
India were united in their belief that there was no enemy to be feared
and no preparations to be made. Into this generation of innocent
isolationists, Ellenborough's dispatch of 12 January 1830 fell like the
biological warhead of a missile.

Ellenborough's dispatch began a revolution in British policy.[1] His
basic assumption was that a danger to British India existed as a
consequence of the alleged designs of Russia upon the Turkestan

Khanates of Khiva and Bukhara. There were three aspects to this
danger: a direct invasion of British India; a threat of invasion which
could cause unrest in India and so compel Britain to adopt expensive
military postures in order to preserve internal security and to provide
for external defence; and a threat of invasion of India which 'would
operate in a material degree as a check upon the free course of our
Policy in Europe'. The danger could be avoided only by preventing the
Russian advance into Turkestan. Two possible means of prevention
were suggested. In the short run, Britain could offer subsidies to
Central Asian states and make representations at St. Petersburg. In the
long term, British influence could supplant that of Russia through
trade. Russian influence in Central Asia was held to hinge upon her
dominance of trade with Bukhara. British goods could replace Russian
if the Indus were opened to navigation. (In a private letter Ellenborough expanded upon additional advantages to be obtained from the
Indus navigation; linked to that of the Ganges it could provide one vast
inland waterway system.[2]) The first essential was information, a com-
modity for which Ellenborough had an enduring passion. 'There is
nothing comparatively so cheap and at the same time so valuable as
information', he once wrote.[3] Information about the Indus area could
be obtained by sending an Indian merchant to try the trade and by
sending a present via the Indus to Ranjit Singh in Lahore.

Ellenborough's Russophobia and his earlier initiatives in Iraq and
Iran have been considered already. His interest in Turkestan had been
awakened by a new book by Colonel G. de Lacy Evans, entitled *On the
Practicability of a Russian Invasion of India*. Its main argument was that an
invading Russian army could easily reach the Indus, via the Caspian,
Khiva, and the Oxus, in two campaigns. The book had a deservedly
mixed reception from the Press, but Ellenborough was very much
impressed with it for it coincided with his own ideas. He wrote in his
diary on 3 September 1829: 'I feel confident we shall have to fight the
Russians on the Indus, and I have long had a presentiment that I
should meet them there and gain a great battle. All dreams but I have
had them a long time.'[4] With his customary energy Ellenborough
began, with the assistance of his secretary, Benjamin Jones, to collect
what information on Central Asia was available. He also formulated
ideas about how Russian influence might be counteracted through the
Indus trade. On 16 December he put his thoughts to Wellington. The
Duke, however, who had also read Evans's book, took a more sophisticated view of the Russian threat than Ellenborough's simple vision of a
Russian invasion. Just as he had done in reply to Ellenborough's
proposed Iranian initiative in 1828, he countered with the more subtle

arguments of his old friend, Malcolm. The real dangers to be feared from Russia were unrest and consequent expense in India and embarrassment in Europe. Ellenborough then suggested the idea of subsidies and, rather uncharacteristically, in view of his attitude over Iran, the Duke contributed the possibility of approaches to St. Petersburg.[5] The dispatch had taken shape, and Ellenborough could put his proposal to the Directors. In the Court he encountered the usual objections upon the score of expense. The Directors wanted the Crown to pay for the commercial experiment and the Lahore mission. Ellenborough overruled them. Despite its commercial guise the purpose was purely political; the Indian Government, Ellenborough argued, must be prepared to accept a trading loss for the sake of political advantage.[6]

Ellenborough sought information from three other sources: Heytesbury in Russia; Macdonald in Iran; and Malcolm in Bombay. From Lord Heytesbury, the British Ambassador in Russia, he received little encouragement. Heytesbury agreed that Russia had shown considerable interest in Central Asia in recent years, but ridiculed the possibility of a Russian invasion of India; Russia was too poor and the physical obstacles too great. Nevertheless, Heytesbury suggested that British observers at Bukhara and Kabul could be useful.[7] Heytesbury also passed on the request for information to Consul Yeames at Odessa, who was to be for many years an important source of information about Russian activities in the area. Ellenborough was not, however, discouraged by Heytesbury's scepticism; the Ambassador was 'a mere Russian', he wrote.[8]

In his reply John Macdonald, the Envoy in Iran, shifted the emphasis back to Iran again. He too thought the physical difficulties decisive against a Russian invasion via Turkestan. The real danger was that Russia would gain control of Iran and, by encouraging that state to attack Khurasan and Afghanistan, would make her the agent through which Russian influence would be extended to the borders of India.[9] This was the same argument which Macdonald had caused to be drawn up three years earlier by his assistant, John McNeill, and published in *Blackwoods Magazine*.[10] In fact it was much older still and originated with Malcolm.

Not surprisingly, in his own reply Malcolm confirmed Macdonald's views. There was no danger of direct invasion. The Indus was of secondary importance because the real threat was that Russia would gain control over Iran. This threat could be met only by an active policy in Iran and by making it clear to Russia that Britain was prepared, if it became necessary, to take action in Europe. Malcolm took the opportunity to set out his views on the nature of the Russian danger more fully: The principal object of a Russian threat to India, he argued, would be to embarrass Britain in Europe by inciting Asian states to disturb Britain's possessions in India.

The object of approximating her power to our Indian possessions for the purpose of encouraging her influence and strength in the councils and cabinets of Europe by the means she possesses of herself, and through combination with Asiatic states, of threatening and disturbing our Indian Empire in a degree that will have the immediate effect of injuring our resources and may ultimately endanger our Power.

Russia had additional, subsidiary objectives; to provide subsistence for her army and to maintain the security of her Asian provinces. Also, Malcolm pointed out, Russian expansion was often the product of the unauthorized action of Russian frontier forces.[11] Once again the prophetic preception and the formidable skill of Malcolm's arguments command admiration. The weakest element in his prescription was his recommendation that Britain should take action in Europe; long experience had taught him the unlikelihood that British statesmen would be prepared to sacrifice the peace of Europe for the sake of Asia. What was most ingenious was the way in which he sought to out-manœuvre the Canningites by his argument that a threat to India was really a threat to Europe. Of course Malcolm had to assume that British statesmen would not simply reply by abandoning India as a dangerous embarrassment, but by 1830 inertia and the growing sense of the value of India enabled him to discount that possibility.

The Governor-General, Lord William Bentinck, was much less enthusiastic about Ellenborough's proposals. He was doubtful both about the navigational possibilities of the Indus and about the reaction of the Indus states.[12] He referred the dispatch to Major Josiah Stewart, now Resident at Gwalior, for whose opinions he had considerable respect. Stewart did not take the Russian danger very seriously. It was true that Russia could, if she chose, overcome the very great physical obstacles, and take up a threatening posture in Central Asia; and it was true that this would cause disaffection and costly defensive measures in India. If Russia did make such a move Britain would be obliged to advance to the Indus. But the danger was so remote that it would be better to wait rather than to send agents and pay subsidies into Central Asia.[13] Bentinck agreed. The danger, and it was a very distant one, was that Russia would advance to Herat, and link with the wild tribes of Central Asia. In that event Britain might have to meet twenty thousand Russians and a hundred thousand irregular Horse on the Indus.[14] But for Bentinck, like so many others, the greatest danger was that of internal disturbances. As Hastings had written: 'If the efficiency of British rule in India does not degenerate, it appears to me more from insurrections in our own rear (when our army is advanced to the frontier to repel invasion) that we have to dread, than from invasion itself.'[15] This conviction that the British in India were sitting on a parcel of deliquescent gelignite was one which was characteristic of the older generation of Company's servants. It is this which makes the internal frontier the key to the understanding of British policy towards the external frontier. The differences between British Indian strategists were not so much differences about the identification and containment of the external threat as about the treatment of the internal sickness. Was it better to try to assuage it by good government in what became the John Lawrence tradition; or to control it through European military colonies as Stewart, Bentinck, and Henry Lawrence suggested; or to isolate it by keeping secondary infection at a distance in the manner proposed by Malcolm? On the view taken of this depended the frontier response.

Bentinck left it to Malcolm to recommend what action the Indian Government should take on Ellenborough's dispatch. This was most appropriate since, as has been shown, Malcolm was the inspiration of a substantial part of the dispatch and in his reply to Ellenborough's request for information had demonstrated that his ideas on external policy were still more profound, and more far-reaching than those of any of his contemporaries. It is scarcely too much to say that it was Malcolm who formulated the whole problem of the defence of India and that for the remainder of the nineteenth century others merely rehearsed his lines. Malcolm had in fact already taken action. He had collected additional information and despite the opposition of the Supreme Government, he had contrived to have large sections of the frontier surveyed.[16] He now gave his acting aide-de-camp, Captain Bonamy, the task of drawing up a comprehensive report on the north-western frontier of India and on the states beyond. Bonamy's report represents a digest of the state of knowledge in 1830 and its conclusions set out the future course of policy.

Like Hastings and Malcolm himself, Bonamy argued that the north-western frontier was the only possible region from which an external enemy could menace British India. The sea routes were commanded by the navy; no enemy existed on the north-east; and the northern frontier of the Himalayas and Kashmir was impassable. Along the line of the Indus were three possible invasion routes. In the south was the Mekran, investigated previously by David Seton, Grant, and Pottinger. Bonamy dismissed this route on the ground that any enemy force would be obliged to depend on the sea for supplies and would thus fall into the grasp of British sea power. Bonamy also ruled out the second route through the Bolan Pass because of the physical difficulties represented by the deserts and mountains of Baluchistan and the Indian desert itself. The only feasible route was the third, via the Khaibar Pass, and even this presented great physical obstacles. He concluded therefore that the main danger to British power in India came not from an invasion from without, but from the enemy within. Insurrection would be most dangerous if it were combined with an external threat. British external policy therefore should aim to keep the enemy at a safe distance. This could be done in three ways: by the establishment of British influence at Tehran, Kabul, and Lahore; by the collection of information about possible invasion routes; and by the collection of information about the Indus: 'a correct knowledge of this noble river is perhaps the greatest desideratum connected with the N. W. Frontier.' Bonamy saw the Indus as the key to the defence of British India. Control of it would enable Britain to cut the communications of an invading army and would also open a direct route between Britain and the North-Western Provinces of British India. From the point of view of commerce its exploitation could siphon off the trade of Central Asia which at present found its way to the Caspian.[17]

Attention was now clearly focused upon the Indus. The collection of information about the river was the first priority of British policy. Malcolm decided to implement Ellenborough's proposal of sending a present to Ranjit Singh via the river. At the suggestion of Henry Ellis at the India Board the present consisted of English dray horses to which was added, on the advice of Henry Pottinger, a heavy carriage. The latter item provided a plausible excuse for demanding a river passage.[18] Metcalfe denounced this device as a dangerous and unworthy trick.[19] To take charge of the present and to collect the desired information Malcolm selected Alexander Burnes (1805–41), the assistant to Pottinger in Cutch.

Of all the British political agents who were employed on and beyond the Indus during the hectic Central Asian years of British policy, Alexander Burnes is the best known. He was a Scot from Montrose and a distant relative of the Ayrshire poet. In 1821 Burnes had arrived in India as a cadet in the Bombay infantry. His energy and his talent for languages brought him to the notice of Malcolm. In 1829 Burnes had attempted to survey the north-western frontier, but had been recalled by Bentinck. From his effort, however, came his appointment in 1830 to the assistantship in Cutch, and the beginnings of his political career.

Kaye once wrote of him that it was Burnes's sad fate to be overrated at the beginning of his life and underrated at the end. His rise was certainly rapid. He had great talents and a marvellous facility of expression; especially he could communicate a sense of adventure, romance, and high drama. With Burnes the reader feels always that he stands near the hinges of history. It was a gift which he exploited to the full: there was nothing of the strong, silent frontiersman in Burnes. In his early years the praise that he won quite overcame him; particularly the adulation and the attentive respect of the mighty which he received in England in 1834 after his return from Bukhara. Thereafter it was difficult for him to accept junior positions in India and his boastfulness did not win him friends among those who thought his work over-rewarded already. Frustration sharpened his ambition and fed some of the less admirable features of his character. Ellenborough thought him intensely vain and self-sufficient.[20] Burnes's vanity, however, received a severe blow when his mission to Afghanistan failed in 1838. After that he became more sparing with the truth and more ready for intrigue. As Macnaghten's deputy in 1840 he did not scruple to carry on a private correspondence with Ellenborough, the Opposition spokesman on Indian affairs, and to criticize the policy of the Government of India. But in 1841 he kept his criticisms from his own Government lest his hopes of succeeding Macnaghten were impaired. Compromise was a fatal flaw in a man like Burnes. But for all the weaknesses of his character, weaknesses which were to have an important effect on the development of British policy, there was about Burnes that same redeeming largeness of mind found in Malcolm. Burnes might have been the true successor of Malcolm, whom in many ways he so much resembled. The flexibility of governmental organization and the mobility of the Indian political scene which had given such scope for Malcolm's ubiquitous talents had gone; routine restricted opportunity for distinction east of the Indus. But beyond the Indus there was another world to be moulded; Burnes hoped to make it his. To the student of Indian defence there is therefore a singular appropriateness that Burnes's Odyssey began just as Malcolm at last retired to England to begin a sadly short political career.

Burnes encountered difficulties with the Amirs of Sind right at the outset of his mission. He sailed from Cutch on 21 January 1831. Twice he was obliged to return when the Amirs refused him passage. Their attitude was unsurprising. They had not been informed of his coming lest they should deny him entrance and they regarded him as the harbinger of a British invasion. Why they eventually gave way is unclear. The Indian agent at Haidarabad suggested fear of Britain;

Burnes guessed divisions, intrigues, and hopes of British support in the matter of the succession; the most likely explanation is that the Amirs feared the Sikhs. Ranjit Singh had moved a force to threaten Shikarpur and uttered menaces to the Sindian envoys at Lahore.

Burnes accomplished the remainder of his mission without incident. He entered the Indus on 4 March, reached Haidarabad on 18 April, and continued up the Indus to Lahore where he arrived on 18 July. Ranjit Singh accepted his present without enthusiasm; he would have preferred, wrote Bentinck, thoroughbreds with long tails.[21] What the dray horses thought of the Panjab might have been a fascinating subject for Anna Sewell. By 1843 they were all dead, leaving one surviving foal. But the main object was accomplished and Burnes was able to make a detailed report on the Indus.

In his report Burnes made three points. First, he affirmed that the Indus and its tributaries were highly suitable for navigation, especially steam navigation. This, as it later transpired, was wrong and the Indus proved a most recalcitrant river. But at the time the most optimistic views of its capabilities prevailed. On the basis of reports from local agents Pottinger decided that there were fifteen fathoms of water at the mouth, no sand-bar, and that ships of the line could sail as far north as Tatta. Burnes did correct such wild hopes. Second, Burnes argued that the main obstacle to the opening of the Indus navigation was political: the attitude of the Amirs of Haidarabad—the Amirs of Khairpur were friendly and the Amir of Mirpur unimportant. Sind, suggested Burnes, was an oppressed land whose inhabitants longed for the blessings of British rule. Third, Burnes revised Bonamy's view of the Bolan, which Burnes thought could become a possible invasion route. In order to command the Bolan and to ensure control of the Indus, Burnes recommended that Britain should acquire the island fortress of Bhakhar, which was situated in the river not far from Shikarpur.[22]

Burnes's report went to swell the growing collection of information in the Secretariat, where Bentinck had set to work the young Charles Trevelyan (1807–86), later to win fame as the father of the modern English Civil Service. Trevelyan had the temporary assistance of a young Bengal Cavalry officer, Arthur Conolly (1807–42), who had recently returned from England to India by an overland route through Russia, Iran, part of Turkestan and Afghanistan, and who published an account of his travels in 1834. Trevelyan and Conolly together wrote a number of important reports.

The reports of Trevelyan and Conolly mark a significant stage in the development of thinking about Indian defence. Hitherto the dominant influence had been that of the Malcolm school which saw Iran as the locus of the only danger from Russia. In a report dated 15 March 1831 Trevelyan rejected Malcolm's argument that Russia was too poor to attack India directly through Turkestan. Russia, he claimed, was a vast armed camp and India her natural prey. Unless stopped (and this could not be through action in the Baltic or in the Black Sea) Russia would take Khiva and Herat and endanger India. Conolly was less positive, and also reaffirmed the argument that Russian would operate through Iran, pushing that state on to attack Herat. Together, they distinguished two possible invasion routes; one via Iran and Herat; the other via Khiva and the Oxus. The key positions were therefore Khiva and Herat—Britain's policy must be to deny both to Russia. This could be done only by building up powerful, independent buffer states between the Caspian and the Indus. Hitherto, Conolly and Trevelyan pointed out, Britain had relied upon Iran as her main buffer; now British influence in Iran had gone and an alternative was necessary. They proposed a strong, united Afghanistan. 'We have, let us fairly own it, been driven from our first position, we must retire upon our second.' But Afghanistan was to be not merely a buffer, but a springboard as well. Trevelyan discussed in detail the commercial possibilities of a united Afghanistan and of the access it would give to the markets of Turkestan. Thus the recommendations of Trevelyan and Conolly, linked with those of Ellenborough, Bonamy and Burnes: the Indus should be opened to navigation and Bakhar taken. British commerce would then become dominant, British political influence in Central Asia increase, prosperity and stability spread, and the region improve its ability to resist Russian pressure.

Trevelyan and Conolly were thus the first since the time of Minto to propound the concept of the Afghan buffer, not as a supplement to Iran, but as a replacement. Their knowledge of the area was slight and their forecasts poor. Conolly anticipated the early reunification of Afghanistan under Kamran Shah of Herat. 'All we have to do', he wrote, 'is to make the most of the opportunity and to obtain the gratitude and respect of all parties by following and assisting the course of events.' Conolly's religious humanitarianism and Trevelyan's Benthamite perfectionism contrived a singularly lofty, and dismally and naïvely unprophetic conclusion to their joint report:

It is gratifying to reflect that while we shall consolidate the Afghan empire for our own interests we shall at the same time establish a lasting claim upon the gratitude of that people and our name will become associated with all the blessings which will flow from the restoration of security and good order. The Afghans were formerly averse to the name of King but they are now a changed people.

Conolly's inadequate experience of the area proved a poor foundation for judgement, and the young strategists went badly astray in their estimate of the political balance in Afghanistan and in their premature reinstatement of the possibility of a direct Russian invasion through Turkestan. But in directing attention to the desirability of establishing a buffer state in Afghanistan they had given a significant twist to British thought.[23] In the summary of their reports which was prepared for Bentinck by the deputy secretary, E. C. Ravenshaw, their recommendation for a united Afghanistan was endorsed. This, wrote Ravenshaw, would block the only feasible invasion route, namely that via Qandahar and Kabul: 'with the co-operation of the Affghans and Beloochees the western frontier of India would be completely guarded and might oppose the invasion of all Europe united.'[24]

Bentinck rejected all proposals for an active policy in Afghanistan or anywhere else beyond the Indus. He admitted that such an alliance system would become necessary if India were threatened and conceded also that there were loopholes in Sind. Nevertheless, he concluded: 'it would be premature to enter at present upon any measures directed to events of such remote possibility, as the necessity of providing for the military and political defence of Hindostan on this side.'[25] He would not follow up Ellenborough's suggestions of agents and subsidies in Central Asia, but limited himself to seeking further information and opening the Indus navigation.

Bentinck's search for information led him to two expedients. First he took up Ellenborough's idea of employing an Indian merchant to try out the commercial possibilities. Twelve thousand rupees were lent to an acquaintance of Conolly named Mohan Shah, with which he traded in Kabul and Bukhara, repaying the advance in 1835. Second, and more importantly, Bentinck sent Burnes on an extended journey in Central Asia. Burnes went in the guise of a private traveller, ostensibly poor, but sustained by umbilical wealth. From the Panjab he made his way to Kabul and Bukhara returning to Calcutta by way of Iran in May 1833. This was the journey that established Burnes's fame. Apart from his published account, he submitted four reports, a lengthy narrative, and a memorandum. Of these reports those on politics, commerce, and military affairs are in the Consultations, but the geographical report is missing. The narrative is similar to his published *Travels* but contains accounts of lengthy political conversations which are omitted from the published version.[26]

Like Conolly and Trevelyan, Burnes repeated Evans's contention that a Russian army could advance through Central Asia to the Indus in two campaigns. Inevitably, he was led to the same conclusion that an

Afghan buffer was essential. In the longer term he recommended the annexation of the left bank of the Indus (including Sind and the Panjab) and alliances with powers on the right bank, notably with Dost Muhammad Khan of Kabul, thus predicting the defensive system which emerged in the 1850s. More immediately pertinent was his second recommendation which related to commerce. To open the large potential market for British goods which he believed existed in Central Asia, Burnes suggested the establishment of a great trade fair on the frontier and of a Commercial (not a Political) Agent at Kabul.

The Commercial Agency at Kabul was the crucial question around which debate focused in 1833 and it is worth quoting at length supporting arguments which Burnes brought forward in his memorandum.

The advantages of establishing some connexion with Cabool may be briefly stated as follows:– It will materially promote our commercial interests both in Affghanistan and Bokhara and lay open the navigation of the Indus to a more extended Commerce. Without seeking political ends, objects of the greatest importance will follow even on a commercial connexion. It will complete our line of relation between India and Persia and fix us in a position far more valuable and happily much less expensive than that Country. It is questionable indeed if our relations in Persia have any real value without an intermediate connexion with Cabool. It will bring us into direct contact with a patriotic people already well disposed towards us who may avail us on a future occasion. It will enable us to guide the chain of events in the Punjab while Runjeet Singh is alive and give us a paramount influence over them on his death. It will give us an influence in Sinde and bring the Ameers into a cordial co-operation with all our commercial views. It will strengthen our position Eastwards of the Indus, since it will overawe the chiefs lying between that river and India. Beyond the Indus it will check intrigues and satisfy both Afghans and Uzbeks that the vaunts of Russia are unmeaning and empty. All this shall we secure without having formed any embarrassing alliance. And lastly I express a hope that with such an agency we might improve our letter communication with Europe by means of our agents in Persia and Cabool. Certain it is that we should no longer be kept in ignorance of the true state of affairs in Central and Western Asia.

Apart from their interest as evidence of Burnes's sanguine outlook and conspicuous ambition (for he doubtless saw himself as the Commercial Agent), these arguments have several points of importance. They show the ultimate political intent of the Commercial Agency. They reveal Burnes's own view of the Afghan buffer as essentially supplementary to the Iranian, in the manner of McNeill, not in that of Conolly and Trevelyan. They show how the Afghan alliance could be seen in the context of what many, including Burnes, thought to be the inevitable ultimate annexation of the Panjab; thus, in the manner of Richard

Wellesley, Burnes used strategic defence to aid in solving the internal and border problems of British India. Finally, and perhaps most significantly, they posed a new possibility for Britain in Afghanistan; for the first time Burnes advocated a change of horses. Hitherto Britain had always backed the Sadozay family: Elphinstone had dealt with Shah Shuja, and Conolly and Trevelyan advocated support for Kamran Shah. But, as a result of the Afghan civil war, power in Qandahar, Kabul, Ghazni, and Peshawar had passed to various members of the rival Barakzay clan. By advocating an agency in Kabul, Burnes was asserting that Britain should recognize that Dost Muhammad represented the strongest and most stable power in Afghanistan.

There was a sharp division of opinion within Government upon whether to adopt Burnes's proposal. Despite his scepticism about some of Burnes's arguments, Bentinck supported the agency proposal. It would benefit commerce, facilitate the collection of information, and, by its implied threat of an Anglo–Afghan alliance, assist negotiations with the Amirs of Sind. But he did not anticipate other political benefits and opposed the idea of making Afghanistan a buffer state, or, as he put it, an expensively subsidized and worthless ally like Iran.[27] Bentinck met opposition from members of his Council, an opposition headed by Charles Metcalfe. Metcalfe had never liked any part of the Indus policy. He had no fear of Russia: the only way in which Russia 'could be formidable to our power in India', he remarked in October 1831, 'was by shortening the distance between us'[28] By advancing, Britain was precipitating the danger she sought to avoid. A Commercial Agent would inevitably become a Political Agent and Britain would become entangled in useless and embarrassing political disputes.[29]

Bentinck insisted that the policy be tried and a dispatch was sent to London recommending the formation of a Commercial Agency at Kabul. In London nothing happened for some time. The inconsistent Charles Grant, despite his activity over Iraq and Iran, was doubtful about moves on the Indus. He did not reject the recommendation, however; he just did nothing at all. There is no evidence of any activity in the Board of Control until William Cabell wrote a memorandum dated 4 August 1834.[30] This provides some guide to the drift of thought in London.

Cabell's basic assumption that Britain had to choose between the Iranian and the Afghan buffers was wrong and misleading. Although many men in India, including Bentinck, were quite opposed to the Iranian alliance, this did not make them supporters of an Afghan buffer; they did not want either. Equally there were man like Campbell, McNeill, Burnes, and to some extent Ellis, who saw the two alliances as complementary. McNeill, indeed, would have gone beyond Burnes and appointed a Political Agent in Kabul at once.[31] The differences between those who supported primarily an Iranian alliance and those who supported principally an Afghan alliance were differences of emphasis. Considering the main threat from Russia to lie through Iran, the Malcolm school advocated the Iranian alliance: believing that the Turkestan avenue was at least as likely, the Burnes school looked to an alliance with Afghanistan. But neither wholly excluded the other. The real difference was not between the Iranianists and the Afghanists, but between those who favoured a policy of forward defence and those, like Metcalfe and Henry Tucker, who wanted no advance and no preparations at all. Cabell missed this fundamental point and he also missed one of the most significant contributions Burnes had injected into the discussion. What, Burnes had asked, would happen when Ranjit Singh died? The solid-looking Panjab buffer, which had come into being almost by accident in 1809, might well collapse. In that case the opponents of a forward policy would be drawn forward, willy-nilly into a system of politics which would make their existing posture impossible. But the point was not debated. It is fair to conclude from the evidence that the level of understanding at the India Board was not high and that misunderstandings became the excuse for an inaction which favoured the position of the opponents of forward defence.

Grant's failure to make his mind up about Kabul left Ellenborough, as President of the Board of Control under Peel, to decide the question. Since it was so much in line with his 1830 recommendations he might well have been expected to welcome a Commercial Agency in Kabul. Possibly under the influence of Tucker, or possibly thinking that Afghanistan was an alternative to his contemporaneous initiative in Iran, he did not do so.[32] After enunciating some general principles Ellenborough left the decision to the Governor-General on the grounds, surprising in the light of his previous record, that he could not hamper the discretion of the Government of India in its diplomatic relations. Since he knew what were the views of the Acting Governor-General, Metcalfe, he must have known that this decision would kill the project. His general principles, which he actually took from a memorandum by Henry Ellis, do have some interest as illustrating the evolution of British thinking. Ellenborough evidently liked the idea of an Afghan buffer. But he took the argument further, declaring that British interests were best served by a balance of power in the north-west of India.

It is our political interest that the Indus and its tributary streams should not belong to one state. The division of power on the Indus between the Scindians,

the Affghans and the Sikhs is probably the arrangement most calculated to
secure us against a hostile use of that river, while it will not probably oppose
any real obstacles to the navigation of the River for commercial purposes,
which should be secured by Treaty.[33]

Apart from its interesting echoes of Clive and Cornwallis, the balance
of power argument is also interesting for its implications. For the
balance could not be expected to create itself and if a balance were
desired, effective British paramountcy would ultimately be necessary
in order to promote and preserve it. Ellenborough referred specifically
to the dangers that Afghanistan would control Sind, or that the Sikhs
would control Afghanistan. The first, which had seemed a real possibility in 1834 when Shah Shuja defeated the Amirs on his way to a fresh
disaster in Afghanistan, soon faded, but the problem of checking Sikh
power was to become a factor of great importance. It was to preserve an
artificial balance that Auckland first intervened on the Indus and
placed in jeopardy the Panjab buffer policy.

   The last possibility that Britain would acquire political influence in
Afghanistan during the early 1830s derived from the renewed ambitions of Shah Shuja and the question whether he should be given British
support. Shuja had originally been given asylum at Ludhiana in 1816,
after the failure of another attempt to recover his throne. At that time
the Ludhiana agent, David Ochterlony, had been instructed to inform
Ranjit Singh that the Afghan's admission 'far from being desired, or
encouraged, can only be a source of regret and inconvenience to the
British Govt.'[34] When Shuja returned again in 1821 he was granted
permission to remain only if he made no further attempt to regain his
throne without prior British consent.[35] When he sought such permission in 1827, 1829, and 1831 he refused, on the advice of Metcalfe. In
May 1832 he received the same answer, but in December of the same
year his request was granted. He was given an advance of £1,600 on his
pension, permission to purchase arms at Delhi free of duty, and permission to raise troops in British-controlled territory.[36] There is still some
uncertainty whether he might not have been promised still more. In a
subsequent letter to Bentinck, Shuja referred to certain promises of
help in retaining his throne if he should recover it. These were alleged to
have been made by Bentinck to Shuja's agent, the Khan al-Makhan. In
return Shuja promised 'all the countries from Meshed and Tusht to
Ludhiana will be made the property of the British Govt.'[37] The story
may well be false or exaggerated, but in the context of British interest in
a united Afghanistan and of the help which was given to Shuja, it seems
quite possible that some conversation about future Anglo–Afghan
relations did take place.

It is very difficult to reconcile this assistance with the statement that British policy was one of 'perfect neutrality'. This claim was set out in a dispatch to the new Ludhiana agent, Claude Wade, in March 1833.

As far as this Government is concerned it is a matter of indifference whether the Barakzye or Suddozye families hold paramount sway in Afghanistan but under any circumstances it is of real importance to us that our national character should stand with the peoples of the countries beyond the Indus, and that we should maintain such a cordial and friendly intercourse with the leading men as will predispose them to espouse our interests in case of the future occurrence of a state of affairs which may demand a more decided course of policy.[38]

The contradiction between the profession and the appearance was underlined by the use of Shuja made of the British name. He used forged letters purporting to be from Wade at Ludhiana and he enjoyed the unofficial assistance of the Company's newswriter at Qandahar, the former companion of Conolly, Karamat Ali, who had been appointed in 1832. Henry Pottinger, who witnessed some of Shuja's activities in Sind, commented that he had 'succeeded in instilling an impression into the minds of all classes that he is really supported by the British Govt. of India'.[39] Inevitably Britain became identified with the fortunes of Shuja. This would have mattered less had he been successful, but, contrary to British expectation, he was defeated. He marched from Ludhiana to Sind, where he spent nine months in raising money and troops at the expense of the Amirs whom he defeated at Rori in January 1834. Advancing into Afghanistan he was then defeated by Dost Muhammad at Qandahar. The effects on British interests were unfortunate. Shuja's supporters complained that British support had been inadequate, while Dost Muhammad was induced to look elsewhere for help—to Iran and Russia. The contrast between Burnes's support for Dost Muhammad and this kindliness towards Shuja is a striking one and there must be a question whether, when Bentinck recommended the establishment of a Commercial Agent in Kabul, he did not expect that the city would not once more be the capital of a united Afghanistan under Shah Shuja.

Between 1831 and 1834 Bentinck had undoubtedly toyed with the idea of establishing British influence in a united Afghanistan, the first step towards the Afghan buffer which he ostensibly rejected. He had sought to accomplish this by commercial means and by what could be called, at the very least, benevolent neutrality towards Shuja's project. The timing of his change of attitude towards Afghanistan strongly suggests that he was influenced by the Khurasan expedition of Abbas

Mirza. No doubt the waning of that threat contributed to his failure to press home the change. In the end Bentinck was defeated by his own doubts about whether the situation warranted any major effort, the tentativeness which this reflection induced in him, Shuja's incapacity, and the opposition which the Governor-General encountered in Calcutta and in London. As a result of his failure to do anything in Afghanistan the matter was left to his eventual successor, Lord Auckland.

Bentinck's main effort to establish British political influence beyond the frontier was limited to following up the original suggestion for the opening of the Indus navigation. There is no doubt that political, not commercial considerations dominated Bentinck's Indus policy and he considered carefully whether he should not make these political interests explicit in his negotiations with the Amirs of Sind. Bentinck accepted that the Indus would be the rendezvous for an invading army and that Britain must meet such an army on or beyond the Indus. He also accepted the consequential assumption that 'we must know beforehand our friends and our foes.' Ranjit Singh was clearly in the former category and at his meeting with Bentinck at Rupar in 1831 had put out a feeler for a defensive treaty against Russia. Although tempted to accept this offer Bentinck had in the end refused, saying that no such danger existed. But the Amirs were an unknown quantity and he was uncertain of their likely response to an offer of a political treaty. So he decided to base his Indus policy upon commercial arguments alone. But he realized that the Amirs would be no more impressed by commercial arguments than by grand strategy. Their interest was in local politics and Bentinck was determined to avoid involvement in these. For this reason he accepted the advice of Clare, Malcolm's successor at Bombay, to reject Pottinger's proposal to support the ambitions of one Amir alone, Nasir Khan. For the same reason he rejected Ellenborough's suggestion that he should use Ranjit Singh to coerce the Amirs into co-operation; at first Bentinck opposed the idea because he thought Ranjit too weak and finally, because he thought the Sikh leader was too strong and might establish his own control over Sind. In the end Bentinck decided to use only the implied threat of Ranjit Singh as the stick and the implied offer of British protection as the carrot, while avoiding any reference to either in the treaty which he hoped to negotiate.[40]

The mission to Sind was led by Henry Pottinger, accompanied by his brother William (H. M. 6th Foot) and Mr L. Scott (Bombay Civil Service) as assistants. The party left Bombay on 4 December 1831 and arrived at Haidarabad on 26 January 1832. Pottinger was instructed to negotiate a purely commercial treaty, refusing British help either against external enemies or in the matter of the succession. Bluff and the divisions among the Amirs were to carry him through. Both had their effect. The meeting of Bentinck and Ranjit Singh at Rupar in October 1831 and then of Bentinck and Clare alarmed the Amirs. The divisions between the Amirs of Haidarabad and those of Khairpur played into Pottinger's hands. Thoby Prinsep, who was Political Secretary at the time, stated that Murad Ali, the leading Haidarabad Amir, would probably not have signed but for fear that Rustam Khan of Khairpur might sign a separate treaty.[41] Nevertheless, before the Amirs signed on 16 April 1832 there were some tough negotiations which made Pottinger quite ill. The Amirs wanted a political treaty, offering assistance against Russia and Iran in return for protection against the Sikhs. At one point Pottinger wanted to give way and offer a guarantee against the Sikhs, but Bentinck refused. In the end the Amirs gave way and accepted a purely commercial treaty by which 'the rivers and roads' of Sind were opened to Indian merchants subject to certain conditions. These conditions forbade the use of the Indus for military purposes, and the settlement of English merchants in Sind, and provided for fair duties on goods.[42]

Agreements with the small state of Bahawalpur and with Ranjit Singh, by which the Indus navigation was opened on similar terms, completed Bentinck's first round of Indus negotiations. These latter agreements were not finally signed until August 1833. The main reasons for the delay were that Wade mishandled the negotiations and Ranjit Singh was intensely suspicious. The Sikh leader was worried about British intentions in general and about the effect of the indiscriminate entry of Europeans into Lahore in particular. At Rupar he had desperately but vainly sought to draw Bentinck on the subjects of Russia, Iran, and Sind and even proposed a joint attack on the last. He rightly foresaw that the affair would end in the restriction of his own ambitions towards Sind. Probably he realized that the common British view was that the Panjab would fall intact into their hands after his own death.[43] In the end Ranjit too had to give way.

Bentinck's decision to base his policy entirely upon commercial considerations had been amply justified by events; he had opened the Indus navigation without incurring any commitments. True, there were disadvantages: the treaties forbade the military use of the Indus; and the negotiations had aroused suspicion of Britain rather than laid a base for political influence. Prinsep criticized the treaties because they failed to give the control which was essential for the exploitation of the strategic value of the Indus and rightly thought their commercial value was nil.[44] But the one overriding vindication of Bentinck's policy lay in the changed attitude of London. There, only commerce could warrant an Indus policy; politics were no longer acceptable.

With the replacement of Ellenborough by Grant the policy of the India Board had changed radically. Ellenborough would have supported a strong line in the negotiations. As Clare put it: he always contemplated the necessity if they [the Amirs] proved refractory of tumbling them into the river.[45] Whether under the influence of the Directors, as Clare thought, or under that of Henry Ellis, Grant took a different line and supported Metcalfe's objections to Bentinck's policy. In a dispatch which Bentinck received on 14 December 1831, when Pottinger was already on his way to Sind, Grant informed the Governor-General that, while he could attempt a purely commercial agreement, he must abandon the project if the negotiations failed. Grant had stood Ellenborough's policy on its head. For Ellenborough commerce had been a means to an end; for Grant commerce was the only end. 'Let it be at once explained that our motive is to extend our commerce, and *only* our commerce along the waters of the Indus.'[46] Had Bentinck gone for the political connection the rug would have been pulled from under him. Perhaps he had an inkling of what might happen when he framed Pottinger's instructions. At all events he could claim, quite falsely, of course, that commercial interests predominated in his own views. To the Chairman of the Court, Sir Robert Campbell, he wrote:

I do not apprehend a Russian invasion more than [Metcalfe] does, and I am confident, if the authorities here and at home make a proper use of the resources which both countries afford, the British power is invulnerable against every attack. But of the means of promoting the commercial prosperity of India, I consider the establishment of our power, as protectors and mediators upon the Indus, to be of paramount importance.[47]

Bentinck's commercial treaties were soon found to be useless. In October 1833 he decided that it would be necessary to replace the system of duties by a single toll of 570 rupees per boat and to establish a British agent at the mouth of the Indus.[48] This change involved a further weary round of negotiations which was not completed until the end of 1834. The discussions with Sind were protracted by the succession problems which followed the death of Morad Ali (20 October 1833); by Shah Shuja's invasions; and by the Amirs' suspicions. The Sind Treaty, signed in July 1834, provided only for the occasional visit of a British agent to the mouth of the Indus and not for his permanent residence, as Bentinck had hoped. No time-limit for the visits was specified, however, and Bentinck, who would have accepted such a limitation, was glad to agree.[49] Some compensation was found in the new treaty with Bahawalpur which allowed for a British agent to be stationed at Mithenkot to superintend the navigation. Frederick Mackeson was appointed to this post. The round was concluded by the treaty with Lahore on 29 November 1834.[50]

Bentinck had successfully bluffed his way through again. He had avoided adopting Pottinger's recommendation to use coercion against Sind and also escaped involvement in the internal affairs of that country. His forbearance, as he pointed out, was required equally by justice and by the Government in England.

Fear, induced by a happy concurrence of circumstances existing at the moment, produced an unwilling assent to a treaty, which it was never intended to execute. The same fear will always obtain an adherence to the Treaty—and I have always contemplated the employment of military force and eventually perhaps the occupation of the [illeg.?country] to establish the free and uninterrupted navigation of the Indus. The use of this river is the natural right of all the states bordering upon the River itself and of its tributary streams.[51]

Bentinck's success nevertheless had severe limitations. The Indus navigation was still commercially unsuccessful. The physical difficulties of the river had been underestimated and continued to be so. As late as 1836 Trevelyan could still describe it as 'the beau ideal of inland navigation'.[52] In fact it was too shallow, too shifting, and too rapid for contemporary steamers. The potential market had been overestimated. Trade was discouraged both by political unrest and by the tolls, which had been set too high. Not until 1839, when the Sind tolls were abolished and 1840 when the Lahore and Bahawalpur tolls were reduced, did this latter problem disappear. To set against this commercial failure, Bentinck had secured many of the disadvantages of a political connection without the advantages. For all the skill which he had shown in evading formal political commitments, he had in effect accepted the view which was now enunciated in London, namely that Britain must maintain the balance of power along the Indus, particularly by restraining Lahore from attacking Sind. If Britain did not accept this obligation the work of four years would be thrown away. Most important of all, Bentinck had paid the precious price of time. He had spent four years on opening the Indus and done nothing in Afghanistan. In the light of the continued deterioration of the British position in Iran, his successors had little time left in which they could develop his foundations into a full alternative defensive buffer system.

Bentinck had seen no exigency that required speed; his successors would require stronger nerves to maintain the same composure.

The questions which Bentinck had left unsolved devolved upon his successor, Auckland. Bentinck left India in March 1835; his successor arrived in March 1836. In between, the Acting Governor-General, Metcalfe, eschewed all political initiative. The contrast between Bentinck and Auckland is an interesting one. Bentinck was the ideologue whom experience made a pragmatist. His previous appointments in Madras and in Sicily had both been marked by a sharp mistrust of common report and a strong predilection for theoretical systems; both had ended disastrously. As Governor-General he had tempered his intellectual enthusiasms with a sense of the possible, and the result had been one of the most successful of all the periods of British rule in India. Auckland, by contrast, was a pragmatists who became a Whig for political convenience, and because he had Whig political connections. But fundamentally he was a first-rate administrator—the *Edinburgh Review* described him as the best that Britain had ever sent to India. He had sought and accepted the post of Governor-General because it was the best-paid administrative job which was available. In 1834 he had hoped to be chosen as a possible successor to Bentinck. The short Conservative interlude had apparently ended his hopes when Ellenborough made the surprising choice of Heytesbury in preference to the Court's candidate, Metcalfe, but the return of the Whigs gave Auckland a second chance.

A correct appreciation of Auckland's personality is essential to the proper understanding of the events of his period of office. He had all the talents of the good administrator: the ability quickly to master the evidence; to present lucidly the essential issues; and to arrive at a sensible conclusion. He had honesty and integrity, and, although naturally reserved, was well liked by his colleagues and subordinates. Greville's remarkable tribute to him may have about it something of the *de mortuis nil nisi bonum*, but it is supported by the testimony of others and is in marked contrast to Grenville's rough treatment of Bentinck.[53] An unusual quality was that Auckland actually liked India; he was one of the few who did not regard it as an exile. Possibly this circumstance may have some connection with the fact that he never married, although his sisters, who acted as hostesses for him, complained all the time about the country. But Auckland had defects. His ability to see all round a problem was often a handicap to decisive action, The Marquess of Hastings, a man of smaller intellectual gifts, made up his mind unhesitatingly and usually got it right. Auckland, on the other hand, faced with a situation which required a snap judgement on inadequate evidence shrank from the decision. He disliked being forced to see black and white where, his reason told him, were only greys. All this would have mattered less if he had had the courage of his intellectual lack of conviction. But he had not; in a crisis Auckland became increasingly distressed and susceptible to pressure from those around him. Pragmatism failed him when experience was wanting.

Initially Auckland's frontier policy was a continuation of that of Bentinck. Before his departure from London he had discussed Central Asia with those concerned. Soon after the new Governor-General's arrival in India Charles Trevelyan drew up a comprehensive memorandum which surveyed all developments since Ellenborough's dispatch of 12 January 1830. Auckland's own ideas at this time were close to those of Bentinck. He feared neither a direct Russian attack nor any threat arising from Iranian projects against Herat. He set little store by the opinions of Ellis who was now on his embassy in Iran. T. C. Robertson, a member of his Council, and later Metcalfe's successor in the Lieutenant-Governorship of the North-Western Provinces, did believe that Ellis's warnings required action and supported a loose alliance with Dost Muhammad, but Auckland, supported by the Commander-in-Chief, Sir Henry Fane, did not think the situation enjoined any action which might jeopardize relations with Lahore. Fane believed that any Russian threat should be met in the Baltic or the Black Sea. Auckland preferred to continue the policy of gradual commercial penetration. On Afghanistan he wrote:

I would abstain from interference. I would not be forward even in intercourse. I would endeavour to preserve peace. I would cultivate commerce and if, at any time agencies, half commercial and half political could find admission, I should be glad to encourage them. But farther than this, in the present posture of affairs and unless new emergencies should arise, I would not go.[54]

To accept Henry Ellis's views would oblige Auckland to recall the detachment from Iran and to form an immediate alliance with Afghanistan. This would entail a premature breach with Iran. Holding these views Auckland, therefore, refused to form any military alliances with states lying between India and Iran.[55]

As we have seen, however, Bentinck's commercial policy carried the seeds of political involvement, through its implicit guarantee of the balance of power on the Indus. Very early Auckland was called upon to defend this balance. Although he had refused to make political approaches to Afghanistan, partly because it would annoy Ranjit Singh, he now found himself obliged to stand up to the Sikh ruler in defence of the Amirs of Sind.

Ranjit Singh had long coveted Shikarpur. He had failed to take it in 1825 and found his path blocked by Bentinck in 1831. Bentinck, however, had never formally opposed Sikh ambitions against Sind, partly because the success of his own negotiations depended on the credibility of the Sikh threat. Nor had Bentinck accepted any obligation to defend the Amirs. Metcalfe, who had never liked Bentinck's Indus policy, went much further in non-interference and in 1835 refused an offer by the Amirs of an alliance which would have laid the foundations of a British protectorate over Sind.[56] Sensing a change in British policy, the Sikhs probed further. Although they failed to obtain Metcalfe's sanction for an attack on Sind, they were left with the correct impression that the Acting Governor-General was indifferent. Possibly Sikh ambitions may even have been encouraged by Wade at Ludhiana.[57] Accordingly, Ranjit Singh prepared to move against Sind in the summer of 1836. In the course of operations against the plundering Mazari tribe he occupied a Sindian fort in October, declared the Amirs to be his tributaries, and demanded the cession of Shikarpur, which he also threatened to attack.

Auckland had to decide whether to oppose the Sikhs or risk all the gains of the Indus policy. Metcalfe advised him to let the Sikhs take Sind. The whole Indus policy was a mistake, he claimed. Strategically, an advance to the Indus to meet Russia across hostile territory could only weaken Britain: the Sikh Panjab formed the best possible buffer on a Muslim frontier. Commercially the policy was not worth saving. To oppose the Sikhs was to risk financial ruin and the loss of British power in India for 'an object so trivial and contemptible'.[58] Auckland rejected this advice. Two reasons for rejection appear in his correspondence. First, it seems that he was unhappy to abandon the Indus position just when it seemed that action to cope with the consequences of the Iranian threat to Herat might be necessary: his earlier expressed views on Herat make it seem unlikely that this was the decisive reason. Second, it seems that he wanted to make a demonstration of British power to impress Lahore. Recent Sikh actions, including contacts with Nepal and the Cis–Satlej Sikhs, the increased employment of foreign mercenaries, the purchase of arms, and aggressive behaviour along their frontier, all suggested that a lesson was needed.[59] Here again, however, there are doubts, inspired by Auckland's subsequent policy towards the Panjab, whether this was the main object. A third possible explanation, suggested by future events, is that he thought it was an opportunity to secure a firmer grip on Sind. But most likely of all, however, is that Auckland was simply carried along by the logic of Bentinck's policy and by the advice of Bentinck's men, now firmly established in his own Secretariat.[60]

Auckland's conduct during the crisis is marked by a curious change of gear. On 22 August he sent Wade to inform Ranjit Singh that Britain would not permit him to take Shikarpur and at the same time he began preparations for war. At the beginning of November, Ranjit Singh at last gave way and decided to make peace with the Amirs. Auckland then promptly sent Wade back to Lahore to stop the peace. The explanation of his change of front lies in his policy towards Sind. When Wade was sent first to Lahore, Pottinger was sent to the Amirs of Sind to take advantage of 'circumstances which must now doubtless induce them to seek cordially the friendship of the British Government'.[61] Initially it seems that Auckland sought only some improved system for the Indus trade. But by the end of September his demands on the Amirs had greatly increased. He then wanted a full-scale protectorate over Sind, including control of foreign relations, a British Resident, and a British subsidiary force stationed on the Lower Indus.[62] For this he had to be prepared not only to risk war with the Sikhs but also needed to keep alive the Sikh threat in order that the Amirs should remain pliant. Auckland had made his first major change of policy and he recognized the fact.

It is fair to say that I have departed from the extremely forbearing policy of my predecessor. We are henceforth, I conceive, irretrievably involved in the politics of the countries of the Indus. We are virtually the protectors of one state and the opponents of another. I grudge this enormous boon to Sind[63]

Sind would have to pay in full for the danger Auckland had run in his relations with the Sikhs.

The negotiations with Sind were long and hard. Fortunately for Pottinger's chances, the Amirs had already committed themselves to acceptance of a draft treaty when the news that the Sikh advance had been halted reached Haidarabad. But the difficulties were still considerable, and the atmosphere, between the Amirs' fears and divisions and the presence of large numbers of Baluchi troops, was tense. Pottinger did not handle the negotiations well. Auckland's tactics depended upon keeping the Sikh threat alive and his long-term strategy upon preserving the Sikh alliance. Wade was ordered to halt the Sikh advance, but not to require them to withdraw.[64] But Pottinger, although in possession of a copy of Wade's instructions, nevertheless promised British assistance to force the Sikhs to withdraw.[65] Auckland, of course, refused. Auckland would offer the Amirs very little in return for their alliance. In fact, over the next few months, even that little declined. In September 1836 he spoke of protection, in December of mediation, and in May 1837 only of good offices. Over the same period he steadily reduced his own demands. By the early part of 1837 he had abandoned his hopes of a protectorate and a subsidiary force and wanted only a British Resident at Haidarabad. Between these and other misunderstandings and the divisions among the Amirs, negotiations dragged on and on. Not until March 1838 was the treaty eventually signed.[66]

There is a strange pattern in Auckland's Indus policy in 1836 to 1838. His first decision for prompt but limited action to preserve the *status quo* was succeeded by a sudden, heady determination to establish a new order on the Indus, even at the cost of what would have been the greatest war since Hastings's time. But then, having taken so firm a posture, Auckland allowed his ambition to suffer gradual erosion and finally accepted a settlement which represented only a very modest advance in British influence in Sind. Then, as will be shown, before the ink was dry on this treaty, he suddenly reverted to a still more aggressive forward policy. I find it difficult to explain this behaviour in terms of the information which was available to him (although possibly Hobhouse's dispatch of 25 June 1836 may have had some effect in temporarily stiffening his determination) and I am inclined to see in his sudden September passion a foretaste of his similar somersault in May 1838 and to attribute it in part to an uncertainty of judgement at moments of crisis.

Sikh expansion presented Auckland with a second problem in relation to Afghanistan. The problem arose from a dispute between Dost Muhammad and Ranjit Singh over the possession of Peshawar. Until 1834 Peshawar had been ruled by a Barakzay family, whose leader was Sultan Muhammad Khan. Before his 1833 expedition Shuja had signed a treaty with Ranjit Singh by which he sold Peshawar to the Sikhs. In 1834 the preoccupation of Dost Muhammad with repelling the Sadozay attack had given Ranjit Singh the opportunity to seize Peshawar. Subsequently, Dost Muhammad tried to obtain control over Peshawar. After an appeal for British mediation had been refused he had launched an abortive attack. In 1835 the Kabul ruler had again sought British assistance. Charles Masson, the British newswriter in Kabul, and Claude Wade in Ludhiana had at that time both supported the idea of a political and commercial treaty with Kabul, and, of course, these events had also coincided with the consideration of Bentinck's proposal for a purely commercial treaty. But the decision came to Metcalfe who, of course, wanted no engagements of any kind with Kabul.[67] It was after this rebuff that Dost Muhammad had made his approaches to Iran and Russia. In the meantime Afghan–Sikh rivalry over Peshawar continued to pose a major threat to the peace of the Indus.

In 1836 Auckland was not conscious of any immediate danger arising from the Peshawar question any more than from that of Herat. He saw no reason to interrupt his intended continuation of Bentinck's commercial policy. In this area he decided the next step should be to expand Burnes's old suggestion of a trade fair and in fact to try to set up a series of such fairs along the Indus. For this purpose he decided, in August 1836, to send Alexander Burnes to Sind and Kabul. Burnes was to make arrangements for trade and to collect information. Auckland described his mission in these words. 'His public instructions are entirely from [sic] commercial objects, but, as he may be able, he will see everything and learn everything and make friends with everybody and give pledges for nothing.'[68] These instructions are entirely consistent with Auckland's professed desire to avoid political entanglements. The evidence is conclusive that Auckland did not attach any great importance to forward defensive strategy at this time. Writing about the mission of Burnes to Kabul and of a similar mission to Bhutan and Tibet he announced: 'These objects are more attractive but they are small in importance and difficulty compared with the questions of revenue, police and administration of justice upon which the strength of the government, and the real prosperity of the country depends.'[69] It has often been claimed that Auckland's Afghan policy was dictated by Hobhouse in his dispatch of 25 June 1836 in which he suggested the possibility of a political or commercial alliance with Afghanistan. This claim is clearly mistaken. Auckland received this dispatch after he had framed Burnes's instructions and he made no subsequent changes in them in consequence. The modifications which were made later were a response to events within India and Auckland's own changing views. Auckland had no interest in a political alliance and a commercial alliance had been under discussion for years. Auckland had already rejected the acceptance of Ellis's arguments which was implied in Hobhouse's dispatch. Far from feeling guided by these instructions, he hardly ever referred to them.

In the course of the latter part of 1836 and the early part of 1837 Auckland's attitude to the Sikhs and Afghans underwent a considerable change. In September 1836 he had been prepared for war with Lahore. Thereafter, whether partly through the influence of Metcalfe is uncertain, he began to change. Ranjit Singh was allowed to retain most of his acquisitions from Sind. An undertaking was given to the Sikhs that while further expansion down the Indus was prohibited, no impediment would be offered to expansion towards Afghanistan. By March 1837 it was clear that Auckland had come to set a high value indeed on the Sikh alliance. At the same time he modified his attitude towards

Afghanistan. In the summer of 1836 he accepted the conventional wisdom that a unified Afghanistan was theoretically desirable. By January 1837 he had concluded that union was unobtainable in prac- tive. This view was derived from Claude Wade, who argued that Barakzay divisions were so great that it was impossible that Afghanis- tan could be united under their rule. Wade recommended that Afghanistan should be controlled by means of commercial penetration and through fear of the Sikhs and of the revived claims of Shah Shuja.[70] In other words, Wade proposed to apply to Afghanistan the system which had proved successful in controlling Sind. This system, which made Lahore the fulcrum of British policy in the north-west, was an obvious one for Wade to advocate, since he was in effect the non- resident Envoy to Lahore. His bias can be seen by comparing his reports with those of Charles Masson, who supplied from Kabul most of the information on which Wade's arguments were based. Masson personally favoured an alliance with Dost Muhammad and his reports scarcely bore the weight of interpretation which Wade put upon them. Whether Auckland read Masson's reports, or only those of Wade, is uncertain, but it is clear that Auckland's acceptance of Wade's reason- ing completely pre-judged British policy in the dispute between Sikhs and Afghans. He wrote to Hobhouse: 'It would be madness in us . . . to quarrel with the Sikhs for him [Dost Muhammad].'[71]

The dispute between the Sikhs and the Afghans came to a head at the battle of Jamrud on 30 April 1837. Sikh power beyond the Indus had expanded steadily after the suppression of the frontier tribal and religi- ous disturbances associated with Sayyid Ahmad Khan Brelvi. This expansion had taken the form of the replacement of the system of indirect control through Muslim feudatories by a system of direct administra- tion, supported by military posts and the control of communications.[72] This process was part of an attempt to pacify the frontier, not a pre- paration for an invasion of Afghanistan, although the Sikh policy was often presented in this way. The decision of the Sikh General, Hari Singh Nalwa, to build a fort at Jamrud, near the mouth of the Khaibar Pass, was an enlargement of this frontier policy. The resentful Khaibar tribes appealed to Kabul for help. Under pressure from religious groups Dost Muhammad was obliged to order a military demonstration in the area. His commanders construed this as permission to give battle and a bloody but indecisive encounter took place at Jamrud in which Hari Singh fell.

Jamrud, therefore, was not, in its origins, a conflict between a Sikh desire to conquer Kabul and an Afghan wish to recover Peshawar. It was the inevitable outcome of a border situation into which the Sikhs were drawn in order to provide security for their own possessions and into which Dost Muhammad was drawn because, like other Kabul rulers, before and after, he found it politically impossible to refuse appeals for assistance which were based upon Islamic and Pakhtun tribal affinities. Nevertheless, the clash underlined the Sikh–Afghan confrontation and both in Lahore and Kabul it came to be regarded in this light. Sikh security appeared to demand a weak Kabul while for Dost Muhammad the Sikh presence in Peshawar was a continual threat that he would be drawn again into a similar situation.

The Afghan–Sikh confrontation menaced Auckland's policy of commercial penetration. Directly, war hampered trade. Indirectly, the conflict incited the Afghans to seek assistance elsewhere and threatened to open the door to Iranian or Russian intervention. During the latter part of 1837 and the early part of 1838 the major question which faced Auckland was whether he was prepared to throw in the weight of British influence in order to procure a settlement between Kabul and Lahore. The dilemma was a familiar one for great and super-powers alike. For Auckland the problem took the form of a choice between the recommendations of two men—Claude Wade and Alexander Burnes.

Wade's rise to dominance on the north-west frontier has already been described. In his Ludhiana base he was the acknowledged expert on Lahore and Kabul. He was a short, fat man fond of eating and sleeping. But this genial appearance was deceptive; Wade was acute, knowledgeable, and prickly. The crisis was his great opportunity to transform Ludhiana from a remote frontier outpost into the nerve-centre of British diplomacy in the north-west and its agent into a man of power and distinction. Wade's views had undergone a change. As noted above, in 1835 he had supported an alliance with Afghanistan and recommended that Britain should try to persuade Ranjit Singh to return Peshawar to Afghan rule. Metcalfe had rejected the first suggestion and Wade was told that the second was premature. Britain was to stay neutral. Wade had steadfastly followed this policy until 1837; when Dost Muhammad requested British help he had merely given a general recommendation for peace.[73] After Jamrud Wade made a rather more determined effort to restore peace, even advising the Sikhs to make concessions to the Afghans. Negotiations broke down over the refusal of Dost Muhammad to send a son to Lahore with presents and peace overtures.[74] After this Wade's views turned sharply against Dost Muhammad and against British intervention. Mediation, which would have been possible in 1835, was now much more difficult, he argued, because since then new vested Sikh interests had been formed beyond the Indus. Also, rather in contradiction, he argued that the Sikhs were the pacific party and that it was Dost Muhammad who had refused peace because he was inflated by hopes of British and Iranian aid. The best contribution which Britain could make to a settlement was to tell Dost Muhammad that they would give him no help and he would be obliged to accept the Sikh terms.[75] These, Wade suggested in August 1837, might take the form of returning Peshawar to its former ruler, Sultan Muhammad.[76] Thus, despite his now marked support for the Sikhs, he still advocated some Sikh concession over Peshawar. But in September he changed his views on this point too. He had been led to think the Sikhs contemplated such a solution to the Peshawar question by a conversation with the Sikh agent at Ludhiana and had approached Ranjit Singh for confirmation. Receiving no reply Wade reaffirmed his former view that it would be unwise for Britain to impose this or any other solution on the Sikhs.[77]

The change in Wade's views on the relative value to be attached to the Sikh and Afghan alliances requires some explanation. It could be a genuine conversion in the light of fresh evidence about the question. It was certainly true that since direct rule began in 1834 individual Sikhs had acquired new interests in the trans–Indus districts; nevertheless Wade gave up very quickly his efforts to follow up what was evidently an attempt by the Sikhs to sound out British views on the restoration of Sultan Muhammad. Doubts have already been expressed concerning Wade's assessment of the situation in Afghanistan and of the extent of the power of Dost Muhammad. There is another possible explanation of a more personal nature. Until 1836 Wade had dominated relations with Lahore and with Afghanistan, both through contacts with those states and because of the residence of Shah Shuja at Ludhiana. Now his monopolistic position in relation to Afghanistan was threatened by the mission of Burnes. If British relations with Dost Muhammad developed, Wade might be squeezed out in favour of Burnes. If Afghanistan became the main buffer state he would cease to be the dominant figure on the frontier and would meet instead the same fate which had befallen the Resident at Ajmer and before him the Resident at Delhi, the Resident with Sindhia, and the Resident at Lucknow. Wade would become merely the channel of communication with an Indian state. His position depended upon the primacy of the Lahore alliance.

During this period Alexander Burnes was slowly making his way up the Indus. His functions in Sind had been transferred to Pottinger as a result of the flare-up between Sind and Lahore, but Burnes hoped to do better out of the clash between Sikhs and Afghans. He had been given a minor role in this dispute by amended instructions which were sent to him in May 1837. If war broke out and the situation appeared that neither party wanted war Burnes was to carry on with his mission and to make some contribution to peace. This contribution was merely to transmit to the Indian Government, through Wade, any proposals Dost Muhammad might make; to encourage the Kabul ruler to make peace; and to dissuade him from insisting upon 'pretensions which he cannot maintain'.[78] These instructions, which were written before the news of Jamrud reached Calcutta, clearly reflect the general assessment of the situation which Auckland had already formed. They show the Governor-General's predilection for the Sikh alliance, his low valuation of Dost Muhammad's strength, and his desire not to become too involved in the dispute. What Auckland could not foresee, however, was the use that Burnes would make of this very limited discretion.

Burnes took a radically different view of his mission. Despite the clear evidences of Auckland's views which were in his possession, he persisted in thinking that the Indian Government really intended something quite different and altogether more ambitious. Before he received his new instructions he had written to Masson that from 'various kinds of hints and letters together with the chain of events now in progress' he had decided that 'a strong line of political action has arrived and I shall have to show what my Government is made of as well as myself.'[79] Burnes believed that his Government intended to break up the negotiations proceeding between Qandahar and Iran and to arbitrate between the Sikhs and Afghans. He had even worked out in his mind the basis of a settlement between the latter: this was no less than a secret agreement which would give Dost Muhammad the whole of the right bank of the Indus after the death of Ranjit Singh.[80] Thus Burnes had answered his own earlier question: after Ranjit what? It was to be the end of the Panjab buffer and the construction of a new buffer in Afghanistan.

Holding these expansive views Burnes was anxious to press on towards Afghanistan, and did not intend that anything should stand in his way. Receiving a letter from Dost Muhammad in which the Kabul ruler stated that he hoped, with British help, to expel the Sikhs from Peshawar, he said nothing in reply to discourage this hope, but merely stressed his own anxiety to reach Kabul.[81] When, on 22 June, he received his new instructions of 15 May, he realized that he had erred and wrote again to Dost Muhammad, claiming falsely that he had not previously observed the phrase or he would have urged the Amir to make peace.[82] The episode shows that Burnes found that his revised instructions fell far short of his anticipations. Nevertheless, he did not draw the obvious conclusion that he was mistaken, but adopted the contrary hypothesis that the Indian Government did not know its own mind. To Masson he denounced the Government's 'sleepy policy' and complained that he did not know why they had sent him, the same time claiming that he did not know what the Government's policy was.[83] Masson and Wade both warned him that his so-evident eagerness to reach Kabul could only swell Dost Muhammad's hopes, but he paid them no heed.

Wade and Burnes offered Auckland a choice of policies: to stand by the Sikh alliance or to turn to Afghanistan. Auckland decided for the Sikhs. He set out his views in a minute dated 9 September 1837. An Afghan buffer was impossible: a strong, united Afghanistan was neither practical nor desirable; and a weak, divided Afghanistan would always be driven by fear of the Sikhs to seek the support of Iran. To try to avoid this last danger Britain could make some small effort to secure peace between Sikhs and Afghans, but this effort was hedged with reservations. In the first place if Ranjit Singh preferred to go his own way and conquer Qandahar and Kabul Britain would not interfere. Ranjit was to be told that there would be no treaty between Britain and Kabul. Secondly, Dost Muhammad was to be told that Britain put her alliance with Lahore first and that she would not assist him unless he first abandoned any projects for war with Lahore and any contacts with Iran.[84] It was little indeed with which Burnes could work, although in the new instructions which Auckland now sent to him one small chink of light appeared. Following Wade's August suggestion (having not yet heard that its author had abandoned it) Auckland proposed as a possible basis for a settlement that Peshawar might be transferred to Sultan Muhammad, although he made it clear that he would not force this upon the Sikhs if they objected.[85]

Auckland's decision in favour of the Sikhs requires some comment. He had misread the situation in several important respects. First, he had got the balance of power in Afghanistan wrong; he thought Kabul the weakest and Herat the strongest power.[86] Second, he had got the balance of power between Sikhs and Afghans wrong. He had convinced himself that Dost Muhammad was on the defensive: 'it may reasonably be anticipated', wrote his private secretary, 'that whatever pretensions he may think it proper to advance in the first instance, Dost Muhammad Khan will really be extremely well satisfied if he can succeed in preserving his authority from further diminution.'[87] But the fact was that Dost Muhammad did not fear a Sikh invasion and it is most doubtful whether Ranjit Singh possessed the strength necessary for a successful invasion: he certainly lacked the desire. Third, Auckland had got the question of Iran wrong. McNeill's reports from Tehran suggested no danger to Herat from the Iranian attack and in Calcutta men were more concerned with the possibility that Herat might conquer Qandahar.[88] As a result Auckland saw no need to worry unduly that Dost Muhammad might turn to Iran, because of his disappointment with British offers; in fact, Auckland rather thought that Dost Muhammad would refuse the offer of British assistance. The Governor-General had no sense of urgency; there were still much more important problems in India, especially the famine that threatened northern India. The truth was that Auckland did not want to take any action. Wade's arguments suited him because the logic of them was that he did not need to do anything. He saw no reason to depart from the policy of long-term commercial penetration.

Knowing nothing of this latest formulation of Auckland's views and still replete with self-deception, Burnes arrived in Kabul on 20 September 1837. Whatever Auckland might think, Burnes had long since lost interest in the commercial aspect of his mission. After going through the motions of attempting to open discussions on commerce, he closed them for ever on 24 September and turned instead to the more congenial questions of politics. Burnes's closure terminated the policy of commercial penetration, which had been launched by Ellenborough in 1830 and which had provided the consistent theme of British policy on and beyond the Indus ever since. Willy-nilly, British policy now entered a new, political phase.

The first problem before Burnes was that of the Afghan–Sikh dispute. Burnes's instructions on this question have been described. Essentially he was to persuade Dost Muhammad to moderate his proposals and to send them to Wade. Burnes had nothing to guide him concerning what proposals might be appropriate; he had not yet received Auckland's September instructions with their suggestion that Peshawar might be given back to Sultan Muhammad. But between the general drift of his instructions and his own personal belief, founded on a conversation at Peshawar with Kharak Singh, Ranjit's son and heir, that the restoration of Sultan Muhammad would be an acceptable compromise, it might have been expected that Burnes would guide Dost Muhammad towards this solution.[89] And there is evidence to suggest that Dost Muhammad could have been persuaded to adopt this suggestion. In June 1837, after Jamrud, his principal advisor, Mirza Sami Khan, had proposed this solution to the Sikhs.[90] Masson's evidence confirms that at that time Dost Muhammad had no firm views on Peshawar.[91] Although Burnes's eagerness may have raised his hopes, there is good reason to suppose that when he began talking to Burnes in September 1837 Dost Muhammad still did not hope to secure Peshawar, a city he had never possessed, for himself. Mirza Sami Khan did not expect it, and Nawab Jabar Khan, the Amir's brother, urged Burnes to reject any such proposal.[92] Shortly afterwards Dost Muhammad wrote to his brothers at Qandahar: 'some hopes arise regarding Peshawar', suggesting that he had not previously expected much.[93] The Peshawar problem was created by Burnes's faulty judgement.

Burnes not only shared Malcolm's intellectual abilities but he also shared the master's poor judgement in diplomacy. Perhaps both of them had too much imagination to be successful in their chosen sphere; their vision leaped beyond the immediate points at issue towards some capacious future. A stubborn, less imaginative man like Harford Jones could accomplish much more. Burnes's powers of perception were too strong and original to make him a suitable instrument of British policy in Afghanistan. In nothing is this so well displayed as in the events of the autumn of 1837.

To Burnes the Peshawar question was only a minor, irritating obstacle in the path of his greater schemes. His haste to get to Kabul; his eagerness to turn to politics; his supplicating manner, which earned him the nickname of *gharib nawāz* ('your humble petitioner'); and his unwillingness to say things that would be unpopular with Dost Muhammad: all these sprang from his political hopes and all conspired to induce Dost Muhammad to put his demands high. Firmly rejecting a hint from Burnes that Peshawar should go to Sultan Muhammad, the Amir proposed that it should be given to himself, on payment of tribute to Ranjit Singh.[94] Burnes should have known that it was useless to send on such a proposal. Nevertheless, he did so. He made no comment officially, but his private correspondence suggests that he actually thought the proposal reasonable. 'How delightful it is', he wrote complacently, 'to be the humble instrument of calming a nation's fury.'[95] With Peshawar temporarily out of the way he could turn to the subject which most interested him.

Burnes saw his task as the establishment of British political influence in Central Asia. Kabul was to become the nerve-centre of a new political system. He sent two of his assistants (Dr. John Lord and John Wood) to the Uzbek state of Kunduz, immediately north of the Hindu Kush. He opened correspondence with Lieutenant Eldred Pottinger, who had earlier gone on a private visit to Herat and who was shortly to play a prominent part in assisting in its defence. And he opened relations with Qandahar.

Qandahar was the scene of Burnes's major effort. He proposed to replace Iranian and Russian influence in that city with British. Qandahar was the weakest of the Afghan states. Its rulers, feeling themselves menaced both by Dost Muhammad from Kabul and by Kamran Shah from Herat, looked outside Afghanistan for help. Believing Britain to be committed to Dost Muhammad they turned to Iran and received an Iranian envoy named Qumber Ali. Burnes decided to disrupt this connection. Auckland's instructions of 11 September, which Burnes received on 21 October, left him some discretion about the means of breaking intercourse between Afghanistan and the west. With some well-founded misgivings he convinced himself that these instructions could bear a very wide discretion. ('I like difficulties, they are my brandy', he wrote to a friend).[96] Accordingly, he sought the help of Dost Muhammad, who, although he had just himself failed to persuade Qumber Ali to visit Kabul, now formally renounced all connection with Iran. The Amir also hinted very plainly that Britain should give him help to annex Qandahar.[97] Burnes did not take up this suggestion immediately, but contented himself with sending warning letters to Qandahar. Reports of the strength of Iranian influence there continued and in November Burnes was very worried to hear that a treaty between Iran and Qandahar had been negotiated. While he believed that Iran could not take Herat if Qandahar were hostile, the matter would be very different if Qandahar allied with Iran. If Herat fell and the Shah then marched on Qandahar the whole British position in the East would be in danger. Consequently, after a month's hesitation, Burnes decided to take action on his own responsibility. He offered, in the event of the fall of Herat, to come to the aid of Qandahar with troops and money. To Auckland he admitted that this went far beyond his instructions, but he argued that his offer was only a dead letter, for if Qandahar were hostile to Iran, the Shah could not capture Herat quickly.[98] Whether Burnes really calculated in this manner is uncertain; it is true that his assistant, Lieutenant Robert Leech, whom he now sent to Qandahar, had no instructions to pay any money. But there is evidence from Burnes's private letters and from the testimony of Masson, that Burnes was actually preparing to march with Dost Muhammad to Qandahar.[99] There is a curious resemblance between Dost Muhammad's October plan to march to coerce Qandahar and Burnes's December plan to march to its assistance. There is at least a suspicion, voiced by Masson, that Burnes's information from Qandahar was inaccurate and that the British agent was being used by the Amir for his own purposes; in short that the project might well have ended in what both Burnes and Dost Muhammad desired, namely the annexation of Qandahar to Kabul.

The decision to support Qandahar was precipitated by two factors. The first was the unexpected success of the Shah in capturing Ghuriyan and in laying siege to Herat: the second was the arrival in Kabul of the Russian agent, Paul Vitkevich, whom we last observed briefly as he passed through Iran.

The origins of Vitkevich's mission to Afghanistan can be traced back to Dost Muhammad's appeal to Russia in 1835 or 1836 for help against Shah Shuja and the Sikhs. His appeal had come first to General Perovsky, the Russian Governor-General of Orenburg, who had recommended support for Dost Muhammad for what were essentially defensive reasons. He wrote to Nicholas I arguing that if the Sikhs became established in Kabul:

> our hopes for trade relations with this country will vanish. If Shuja al-Mulk captures Afghanistan with the support of the English, then Afghanistan will submit fully to the East India Company and the English . . . [will be] only a step from Bukhara. Central Asia must surrender to their influence; our Asiatic commerce will collapse: they might instigate against us the neighbours of our Asiatic people at an appropriate opportunity, and provide them with powder, arms and money.[100]

His Government was sympathetic, but rejected the notion of direct Russian aid to Dost Muhammad on the grounds that Afghanistan was too distant. Instead it was decided to try for influence in Afghanistan at second hand, through Iran. Dost Muhammad was to be advised to join with Qandahar in a confederation under Iranian suzerainty. Iran was the natural protector of Afghanistan.[101] Russia hoped too that Herat might also be persuaded to abandon her claims upon Qandahar and Kabul and to join with the others under Iranian protection. But Russia would contribute no more to this plan than advice; she would offer no assistance and play no direct part in the arrangements between Iran and Afghanistan. All that Russia would offer Dost Muhammad was a commercial agreement.[102]

To transmit Russian advice and to negotiate the commercial agreement, Paul Vitkevich was selected. A Lithuanian from Vilna, Vitkevich had first become involved in Central Asian affairs when he had been exiled to Orenburg after participating in student disturbances. Perovsky had been impressed by his talent, made him an aide-de-camp, and had employed him on secret missions in Turkestan. Instructions were given to Vitkevich in St. Petersburg, where he had conversations with Rhodofiniken, Head of the Asiatic Department. It has been suggested that he was then given additional verbal instructions, going far beyond the scope of the written instructions summarized above; these new instructions were said to authorize him to offer a loan of two million roubles to Dost Muhammad and to promise Russian help to the

Amir for the recovery of Peshawar.[103] Duhamel, Simonich's successor in Tehran, partly confirms this story. He stated that Rhodofiniken had given Vitkevich to understand that Russia would make a substantial loan to Dost Muhammad.[104] Duhamel always believed that Vitkevich's instructions indicated a Russian intention to play an active part in Afghan affairs. A further point in support of the theory of the additional instructions is that both Simonich and Vitkevich went beyond their written instructions and neither felt that he had been supported as he deserved. Finally, Senyavin, Rhodofiniken's successor as Head of the Asian Department, wrote to Duhamel that Vitkevich had merely carried out the orders of Simonich.[105] However, all this amounts to no more than a collection of hints, and the question of whether more lay beneath the surface of Vitkevich's mission than appeared, must be considered undecided. What is clear is that Russian policy was no more monolithic than that of Britain. Simonich, Vitkevich, Perovsky, and Rhodofiniken were all ready for a more active policy under the screen of commerce. What is unclear is how far they were supported at the highest levels. The similarity, however, with the British pattern is distinctive. In both cases local agents seek to radicalize the policy of their government with varying success.

Vitkevich travelled to Afghanistan in the autumn of 1837 via Tiflis, Tehran, Nishapur, and Mashhad, Near Herat he was observed by Henry Rawlinson. From the Shah's camp at Herat Vitkevich passed on through Qandahar to Kabul. At Qandahar he advised the ruling Sirdars to co-operate with Iran and promised them financial aid from Russia. He arrived at Kabul at the end of November or beginning of December and presented his letters and gifts. One letter from Simonich urged Dost Muhammad to tell Vitkevich all his secrets.[106] Vitkevich advised the Amir to place himself under Iranian suzerainty and offered him Russian protection.[107] Dost Muhammad also claimed that Vitkevich offered him money.[108] But the Amir was not, for the moment, interested in Vitkevich's offers. Britain could clearly be of more use to him than Russia or Iran. Accordingly, he tucked Vitkevich away in obscurity for the next three months. The Russian was both a reserve in the event that Britain failed him and a spur to Burnes to increase his offers, or, as the Qandahari agent put it, 'to be sharp and to put off delay in promoting our objects'.[109]

Burnes was strongly moved by the progress of events. Masson describes him binding his head with towels and calling for smelling-salts. His action over Qandahar has been described. Burnes wrote an impassioned letter to Auckland in which he urged the adoption of a more active policy in Central Asia. Britain should establish her influence in Kabul, form a chain of agents throughout Central Asia to neutralize Russian influence, and even bring into being a Sunni Muslim League to oppose Shi'i Iran. The one essential precondition was to settle the Peshawar problem, preferably by giving it to Dost Muhammad, but alternatively by making the city over to another Barakzay. Auckland, suggested Burnes, had misconceived the relative situations of Kabul and Lahore and placed too low a value upon the first and too high a value on the second.[110]

Auckland was unmoved. Dost Muhammad's original proposals had not been transmitted to Ranjit Singh. Wade had withheld them, ostensibly because Dost Muhammad had not yet fulfilled one condition of British good offices by renouncing all connection with Iran, but in reality because he thought them unacceptable not only to the Sikhs but also to Britain. For Wade still held to his view that a weak, divided Afghanistan was best for Britain; the possession of Peshawar would upset the balance by making Kabul too powerful.[111] Auckland agreed. Dost Muhammad was to be told to be content with what he had—'the immediate recovery of Peshawar would seem to be hopeless.'[112] Auckland offered no alternative: his earlier suggestion that Peshawar might be given to Sultan Muhammad, which he had repeated in October, was now, in December, withdrawn. On 20 January 1838 Auckland's negative was still firmer. The Amir, now held guilty of restless ambition, was to be told that the matter of Peshawar was one 'wholly to be decided by the Maharajah himself'.[113] All hope would seem to have been ended by this letter, but it is an interesting insight into governmental indecision that two weeks later Auckland's private secretary still held out hopes that Ranjit Singh might be persuaded to make over the administration of Peshawar to Sultan Muhammad.[114]

Auckland also repudiated Burnes's plans for the defence of western Afghanistan. Burnes had based his policy towards Qandahar on the assumptions that Herat was weak and likely to fall to Iran and that Russian policy represented a real menace to the interests of Britain. Wade attacked the first assumption; Herat would prove too strong and the Iran-Qandahar Treaty was non-existent—it had been forged by Dost Muhammad in order to win British support for his ambitious designs on Qandahar and Peshawar.[115] Auckland himself rejected the second assumption; Vitkevich's mission need not be taken seriously. Also Qandahar was too distant to allow effective aid to be given and in any case the ninth article of the treaty with Iran forbade interference between Iran and Afghanistan. Accordingly, by the same dispatch of 20 January 1838, Auckland informed Burnes that the envoy's promises to the Sirdars of Qandahar were disavowed.[116]

Burnes was completely downcast when he received this dispatch on 21 February. At one stroke Auckland had destroyed his policy. At every point Burnes's views had been rejected: there was, Auckland had said, no danger from Iran, or from Russia, and little or no value in an alliance with Kabul. But with that incurable optimism which was his most engaging feature, Burnes pulled himself together and began to try to rebuild something from the ruins.

First, he dealt with Qandahar. Unwittingly, the Sirdars had provided him with a way of escape. In vainglorious style they had written that they required no British assistance against Iran. That was fortunate, replied Burnes, for he had not been authorized to offer any.[117] This too-literal interpretation of a bargaining-phrase took the Sirdars aback. They had hoped, by keeping Russia, Iran, and Britain all bidding against each other, to obtain both protection, and, perhaps, Shikarpur as well. Burnes's sudden apparent withdrawal from the auction arrived just after Qumber Ali returned to Qandahar bearing the offer of a Russian guarantee of the Iran–Qandahar Treaty. Accordingly, the Sirdars decided to send a representative to Kabul to persuade Burnes to better this offer or, if that failed, to persuade Dost Muhammad to accede to their Iranian alliance. Clearly they would be in a dangerous position if they committed themselves to Iran and Dost Muhammad, after all, secured British help.

No such literary loophole enabled Burnes to escape his embarrassing encounter with Dost Muhammad. It should have been clear to Burnes from the latter part of January, when he had received Auckland's first reply to Dost Muhammad's proposals, that the Governor-General would do nothing about Peshawar. But, possibly hoping for a miraculous change of mind or, more probably, lacking the courage to tell the truth, he presented Auckland's views to the Amir in such a way as to give the impression that Britain was offering to induce the Sikhs to restore Sultan Muhammad and retire behind the Indus. In fact Auckland had specifically excluded this possibility. But the Amir was not yet prepared to accept even this non-existent compromise. He chose to argue that Sultan Muhammad in Peshawar would be even more dangerous to him than the Sikhs and persuaded Burnes to recommend a new arrangement by which Dost Muhammad and Sultan Muhammad would divide Peshawar and pay an annual tribute to Lahore.[118] Burnes must have known that this proposal was totally at variance with his instructions and one can only guess that his object in putting it forward was to gain time in the hope that new events and further information would bring about a change in Auckland's views. But when he received the dispatch of 20 January he realized that he had to tell the truth. On 22 February he gave Dost Muhammad the unwelcome news that Auckland would offer nothing. According to Masson, he made matters worse by blaming the Amir for making the proposals.[119]

Auckland's verdict produced a strong reaction in Kabul, where the Amir held nightly consultation with his advisors. Piecing together the available information it would appear that few men wished to persevere with the British connection. The strong Qizilbash faction, from which the Amir drew his principal counsellors, advised him to listen to what the Sirdars had to say. The Amir himself, however, despite the cruel blow to his prestige, was still unwilling to cut himself loose from Britain. He wanted some face-saving offer from Burnes. When Burnes asked what the Afghans wanted the reply was 'dignity and respect' (*izzut wa ikram*)—in concrete terms, some assurance of help over Peshawar and protection from the west. But Burnes could offer neither.

The Amir's reluctance to commit himself prolonged the last discussions for six weeks. Then, after the arrival of the Qandahari envoy, the Afghans presented their last formal proposal. They would agree to almost all Britain asked on two conditions: that Britain would promise protection against Iran; and that Britain would agree to use her good offices over Peshawar and to obtain some amelioration of the condition of Sultan Muhammad Khan. Burnes was forced to refuse even these modest requests. After a final hesitation therefore, the Amir at last committed himself. On 21 April he sent publicly for Vitkevich, whom he had been seeing privately since the middle of February. Four days later, Burnes withdrew from Kabul.[120]

The Afghans had been compelled to make a choice they never wanted. The Qandahari Sirdars each separately assured Leech, and also Lieutenant D'Arcy Todd, who passed through Afghanistan shortly afterwards on his way from Herat to India, that they had accepted the Russo–Iranian offers only because Britain would offer no assistance whatsoever.[121] The course of the last negotiations in Kabul also shows that Dost Muhammad did not want to break with Britain. The common belief, fostered by Auckland, that the negotiations foundered on the Amir's demand that Peshawar should be given to him, is quite inaccurate. Peshawar was important to the Amir: he had in Kabul many refugees from Peshawar, who constituted a potentially dangerous pressure group; he wanted a settlement which would allow them to return unmolested to Peshawar. But all he wanted from Britain was a gesture. He told Todd that he would be content if Sultan Muhammad had been allowed to hold the district. It was Burnes's misguided attempts at conciliation which had led the Amir to take up a position over Peshawar from which he had later found it difficult to recede with honour. When finally he did relinquish his demands he found that the British attitude, far from softening towards him, had apparently become less accommodating, even antagonistic. If the test of a skilled negotiator is that he makes it easy for his opponent to accept his views, Burnes was a wretchedly poor one.

There is good reason to suppose that agreement over Peshawar was possible. Certainly Ranjit Singh would have been unwilling to hand over Peshawar to Dost Muhammad. But he was never asked if he would re-establish Sultan Muhammad there. There are indications that he would have preferred not to have done so: Peshawar was a rich district; the destroyed Jamrud fort was replaced by another at Fathgarh; his minister stated that the Maharajah was working for peace on the basis of the *status quo*; and twice Ranjit Singh remarked pointedly that Sultan Muhammad and his brothers were content with their present position. But the second time there is also an implication (picked up by Masson) that if he had to decide he would prefer Sultan Muhammad to the Amir. The manner of these hints suggests that they were really reservations of the Maharajah's position; in the light of his previous experience over Sind in 1836 and his expectation that he would meet Auckland in 1838 for a general bargaining session, he was not going to surrender points in advance. But on the frontier he still used the Barakzays as managers and there was scope for further concessions.[122]

It is customary to say that Burnes's mission failed. But this is to assume that its object was that which Burnes sought—a political alliance between Britain and Kabul. Auckland himself never thought that this was its purpose; for him the mission was a continuation of Ellenborough's policy of long-term penetration. It was commerce which directed it towards Kabul, a state which Auckland considered to be politically and militarily the weakest of the Afghan states. Had he believed defence against the threat from the west to be the main problem he would surely have sent it to Qandahar, which he imagined to be more powerful than Kabul, or even to Herat itself.[123] It was only later that Auckland confused the issue, after politics had become the most important issue and when he had decided to intervene in Afghanistan in support of a rival candidate. Then he sought to throw the blame for failure on Dost Muhammad. Although as late as 14 March 1838, Auckland was still, thanks to Burnes, in genuine doubt as to whether the Amir was really demanding Peshawar or not, it is unbelievable that he could not have known in May that Dost Muhammad would have accepted Sultan Muhammad. Nevertheless, in his minute of 12 May he still argued that the Amir had demanded

Peshawar. Also he contended that there was 'infinite evidence' to show that Dost Muhammad had made up his mind, as early as November 1837, to throw in his lot with Russia and Iran in the hope of acquiring Peshawar and Kashmir.[124] This last statement is still more absurd in the light of the evidence. Like others, it was designed to show that Auckland had been right in a choice which he had actually never made, for he had had no interest in a political alliance at the time.

Auckland was unready for a political initiative in Afghanistan in the winter of 1837 to 1838. Partly he was fearful of further offending Ranjit Singh, who might be provoked into heading a hostile coalition of independent Indian powers, together with Ava and Nepal.[12t] Partly, he was afraid of embarrassing his own Government in England if he infringed the Tehran Treaty; indeed he seems to have thought that Afghanistan was itself a matter for London: 'it is in Europe and Persia that the Battle of Afghanistan must probably be fought', wrote Colvin.[126] Partly Auckland did not think the danger a serious one. But the principal reason for his abstinence was probably his preference for a weak, divided Afghanistan; he wrote frequently of the menace of a strong Muslim state placed on the borders of British India and of the value of Lahore as a Hindu buffer state. These were the old strategic assumptions of Bentinck, now sharpened by the arguments of Wade; everything was to be secondary to the old Panjab alliance; all beyond the Indus could wait. So Auckland thought in the spring of 1838: within a few weeks his policy was completely altered.

Hamlet at Simla

> I feel yet more strongly than ever what I have felt for
> months the obligation imposed upon us of playing a game
> requiring a clear sight, vigor and decision, in the dark and
> with our hands tied of [*sic*] counter interests and counter
> engagements.
>
> Auckland to Macnaghten, 29 May 1838.

Throughout the summer of 1838 Lord Auckland was at Simla, where
he had arrived at the beginning of April, to escape the heat of the plains.
Simla was then little more than a camp and bore no resemblance to the
gracious summer capital of later years. Amid the fresh hills and the cool
woods Auckland could reflect upon his policy in an atmosphere of
seeming detachment. His Councillors had been left in Calcutta when
he began his northern tour in the autumn of 1837 and with him were
only a small group of advisors. But a situation so eminently suitable to
others proved an unhappy environment for Auckland. For him Simla
became a place of tortured indecision as he struggled to find an answer
to problems which seemed suddenly to rush in upon him and as he
fought to keep control over the development of the policy he unleashed.

Some time during Auckland's first month at Simla his views of policy
in the north-west underwent a crucial change. The reasons for this
change cannot be established with precision for the vital volume of his
private correspondence which covers this month is missing and the
development of his thought can be traced only in those of his letters
which appear in other collections and in his less revealing official
correspondence. The change came in his view of the danger from the
west.

Auckland had rejected Burnes's policy because he did not believe in
the danger from the west and because he did place a high value on the
Sikh alliance. It was the first postulate which he abandoned in April.
Undoubtedly, one new factor was the deteriorating news from Iran. At
the beginning of March McNeill had decided to go to Herat in order to
withdraw the Shah and had asked Auckland to support his remonstrances with an expedition to the Gulf. Auckland, who had rejected the
idea of a formal protest to Iran in January, because of the 1814 Treaty,
now felt himself uneasily released from the limitations of article 9.

Secondly, Auckland changed his views on Russian activities and came to see the activities of Vitkevich and Simonich as endangering the security of India.[1] The third and possibly most important new factor was the evidence of internal unrest in India. In 1838 Auckland was confronted by the threat of war with Ava and Nepal, the intrigues of Nepalese envoys in various Indian states, and disturbances in a number of states including Baroda, Sattara, Indore, Jaipur, and Jodhpur. This connection of an external and internal threat was precisely that which had formed the core of all the most sophisticated arguments in support of a forward policy. One possible course of action existed which might scotch both dangers at once. This was a reaffirmation of the alliance with the Sikhs. At once it would confirm the great northwestern buffer and remove the most dangerous potential leader of an anti-British coalition within the subcontinent.

In the changed circumstances Auckland had two possible lines of action—intervention in Iran or in Afghanistan. The first he did not like. Although, in response to McNeill's plea, he sent a small expedition to occupy Kharag, he never felt happy about the affair, and he refused to adopt McNeill's further suggestion of a larger expedition of five thousand men to occupy Bushir.[2] Any further action would have to be in Afghanistan.

Auckland had a number of different options available in Afghanistan. The most obvious was to act at Herat itself since it was this state which was directly threatened by Iran. The Heratis had asked for financial help and the Commander-in-Chief, Sir Henry Fane, favoured action there. But Auckland refused to aid Herat on the grounds of time and distance.[3] That left only Kabul and Qandahar and it was the problem of what action to take in those states that Auckland pondered during the early part of May. His decisions to send the Kharag expedition and not to help Herat had been taken on 1 May; his proposals for Kabul and Qandahar were sent out in a long minute on 12 May.

In his minute Auckland finally buried the long-term policy of gaining influence through commercial penetration. It had failed and a new, more active policy was required. To work with the existing Afghan states was impossible because Herat was too far and the Barakzays of Kabul and Qandahar would merely employ British aid against the Sikhs. Accordingly, whether or not Herat should fall, the Barakzays must be replaced by a more reliable ruler, namely Shah Shuja al-Mulk, who should be placed in power by a coalition of Britain, the Sikhs, and the Amirs of Sind. Britain would contribute money, an agent, and officers; the Sikhs would supply troops; and the Amirs would give money and the use of Shikarpur as a base of operations.[4]

In thus supporting the idea of a coalition, Auckland, by implication, held to be less desirable the possible alternative that the Sikhs should act on their own. In a letter of 3 May, written before he had made up his mind, he commented unfavourably on this proposal, which had been put to him. The Governor-General rejected it on two grounds: first (and surprisingly) because 'Runjeet Singh could ill afford to leave his turbulent provinces behind him', and secondly, because a Sikh invasion was likely to unite Sunni Afghanistan and Shi'i Iran in a Muslim coalition against such an intrusion.[5] Nevertheless, the possibility of independent Sikh action was not entirely excluded at this time, although it was regarded as less eligible than the establishment of Shah Shuja.

The replacement of the Barakzays by Shuja was the plan which had been considered and rejected in 1833 to 1834. It must always have remained as a possibility in the minds of those who had been connected with the former episode, notably Wade, and Auckland's Chief Political Secretary, W. H. Macnaghten. The first reference made by Auckland to Shuja occurred in March 1837 in a reply to a letter from McNeill. McNeill had written supporting the unification of Afghanistan but doubting the reliability of Dost Muhammad and suggesting a Sadozay as an alternative. McNeill appears to have had in mind a Sadozay of Herat, but Auckland took it as a reference to Shuja and replied: 'We have long since determined upon keeping Shah Soojah quiet, so long as he remains under our protection, and this may, possibly become an useful instrument of influence in our favour with them against whom he has pretensions.'[6]

The possible uses of Shuja were rehearsed by Wade in July 1837. As Shuja's keeper at Ludhiana, he was always most alive to the Sadozay's advantages and had already drawn attention to them in June 1836. In 1837 he reported that the Kabul Qizilbash had approached Shuja and he recommended that British support for Dost Muhammad should not be pledged in writing because this would not only alienate some Afghans but throw away a means of controlling Afghanistan.[7] These, however, were only straws in the wind; a more important action was the working out by Macnaghten, in December 1837, of a contingency plan based upon Shuja's 1833 to 1834 expedition.

Macnaghten's plan was a comprehensive scheme for the reorganization of India's strategic defence. Based on Minto's buffer state system, it envisaged a complete reconstruction of political relations in the north-west. In addition to the re-making of Afghanistan, the dispute between Lahore and Sind was to be settled and the complete freedom of the Indus secured. Macnaghten looked ahead to the future of the

Lahore state after the death of Ranjit Singh and in this connection contemplated the formation of a powerful, united Afghanistan as a counterpoise to the Sikh army. Essentially, the plan was a revolutionary system based upon the creation of a British-controlled balance of power to replace the single Sikh buffer system. As such it bears some resemblances both to the system adumbrated in the discussions of 1830 to 1832, but never adopted by Bentinck, and to the suggestions of Burnes. Unfortunately, no copy of the scheme exists and the evidence concerning it comes only from the deputy-secretary, Henry Torrens, who was present at the time and played some part in its drafting.[8] Torrens states that it was prepared 'rather to propose something to the Governor-General in his uncertainty rather than to suggest a plan for absolute adoption'. In fact Auckland had flatly rejected it saying 'such a thing was not to be thought of.' Torrens goes on to say, however, that about a month later, after receiving instructions from England to adopt a very similar plan, Auckland had taken up the scheme again. This latter statement is evidently untrue since no such instructions were received from England and Auckland had clearly not made up his mind to consider such a scheme in January 1838. This is made clear by Auckland's comments on another plan submitted by Wade.

On 1 January 1838 Wade put forward an elaborate argument for replacing the Barakzays with Shuja in the event of a decision to consolidate Afghanistan and the fall of Herat.[9] This argument was in essence a defensive move by Wade designed to avert any change in British policy in favour of Dost Muhammad; he himself favoured a divided Afghanistan and did not believe Herat would fall. Auckland refused to comment on Wade's plan. 'No such scheme is in his Lordship's contemplation', wrote Macnaghten.[10] Burnes, who seems to have caught some rumour of these ideas, also took up the same point in a letter written apparently both in an attempt to fish for further information and to indicate his own views on the subject. To set up Shuja, he wrote, was the one genuine alternative to aiding the Barakzays. But he declared himself opposed to such a plan 'which has happily never been contemplated'.[11]

The rather meagre evidence suggests therefore that the plan to replace the Barakzays with Shuja was first worked out in December 1837 as part of a new system of forward strategy which had been familiar to Macnaghten in its broad outlines since his association with Bentinck's political schemes in 1832. Auckland, it seems, would not then accept it because he thought it quite unnecessary to take any action in Afghanistan. When, in April 1838, he did become persuaded that some plan of action there was necessary he inevitably turned back to this plan because, believing that he had burned his boats with the Barakzays, it seemed the only one available which would fit his situation.

There was still one important feature of the new plan which had not been resolved. This was the part to be played by the Sikhs. Throughout 1837 and the early part of 1838 Auckland had based his trans–Indus policy on the Sikh alliance. But the Macnaghten plan envisaged the development of a powerful Afghanistan as a counterpoise to the Sikhs. In short there was a fundamental difference between the policy of Wade, which Auckland had followed hitherto, and that of Macnaghten. The difference had been hidden while the two were united in opposing Burnes's policy of support for Dost Muhammad, but the divisions between them were soon to become clear. For Wade the elevation of Shuja meant the replacement of a weak, hostile ruler in Afghanistan by a weak and friendly one; Afghanistan had to be weak if the Lahore alliance was to remain the lynchpin of the strategic system. For Macnaghten the consolidation of Afghanistan under Shuja meant the eventual replacement of Lahore by Afghanistan as the centre-piece of forward defence. It is apparent from what ensued that Auckland did not appreciate this crucial distinction.

Auckland had built everything on the Sikh alliance since the end of 1836. To it he had sacrificed all prospect of agreement with the Barakzays. He had no intention of throwing it over in May 1838. The Sikhs were to have a prominent part in the new scheme. And yet it is clear that Auckland had misunderstood the nature of the Sikh position in the north-west. Always Auckland thought that Ranjit Singh was anxious to push further west and that if Britain sought to restrain him, the Sikhs might turn hostile. In his minute of 12 May Auckland wrote of permitting or encouraging the Sikhs to advance on Kabul. But he was wrong about Sikh enthusiasm for war with Afghanistan; only the Jammu faction had any interest in that and even their interest was turning increasingly towards Kashmir. The Sikh troops regarded the Khaibar with the greatest aversion and their leaders wanted no further acquisitions of expensive Afghan territory unless such territory was acquired and maintained by agreement with Britain. Burnes even argued that the Sikhs would have been glad of a chance to pull back behind the Indus and, although this was probably too extreme a view, there is some justification for it in the history of the Sikh efforts to maintain their position beyond the Indus.[12] Equally extreme was Auckland's dismissal of Burnes's argument with the words: 'The whole tenor of the Maharajah's conduct and indeed his own direct assertion leaves no room for doubt.'[13] Although Auckland would have liked to have believed that Peshawar was the stumbling-block, the truth was that Ranjit Singh's views had never been ascertained; Auckland had played him too gently for that. Now the validity of Auckland's assumptions about the Sikhs was to be tested in negotiations with Ranjit Singh.

The conduct of the negotiations with the Sikhs on the plan to reconstruct Afghanistan was entrusted to the Chief Secretary, William Hay Macnaghten. Macnaghten was instructed to propose two plans to Ranjit Singh: the first, a plan for joint Anglo–Sikh action in support of Shah Shuja; the second, a plan for independent Sikh action. According to the first, which Auckland claimed to prefer, a Sikh army, accompanied by British officers, would advance on Kabul via the Khaibar; Britain's role would be a minor one, confined to the occupation of Shikarpur by a division and to the supply of money and arms to Shuja; no British troops would enter Afghanistan. Auckland believed, however, in line with his assumptions about Sikh ambitions, that Ranjit Singh would prefer to adopt the second plan of entirely independent action.[14]

Macnaghten did not like his instructions and his criticisms of them provide important confirmation of Torrens's version of the 1837 plan. Macnaghten wanted the roles reversed. The expedition should be essentially a British one; the Sikhs were to be limited to a minor supporting part in the enterprise. He wanted the Sikhs to be told from the outset that Britain would support Shuja and that they could join if they liked, but that Britain would prevent them from taking independent action.[15]

Auckland declined to alter his instructions beyond giving Macnaghten permission to inform Ranjit Singh that the advance of Iran might force Britain to take independent action. Partly his refusal derived from his view of the Sikhs, but it is evident that it also emanated in no small degree from his defects of temperament. Lack of confidence in his own judgement made Auckland shrink from committing himself to action. He found innumerable reasons for refusing a decision: the Sikhs might decline to co-operate and attempt to thwart a British expedition; he had inadequate information about the situation at Herat; there were European complications; and there was danger in any action. Auckland wanted, he wrote, 'to stand still as nearly as circumstances will allow me to do so', and in a still more revealing passage he declared: 'It may be well by opposing our troubles to end them but it may be well to consider whether we are not flying to others that we know not of.'[16] Elsinore had come to Simla. But, as in the case of Hamlet, the dénouement was not entirely within his control.

It was Macnaghten who was in control of the negotiations and in a position to influence the direction which they took. Macnaghten was, with Malcolm, one of the two most influential men in the formation of British policy in Central Asia during the first half of the nineteenth century. Just as Malcolm was the principal architect of the system of strategic thought hinged on Iran, so Macnaghten was the dominant figure in the development of the system based upon Afghanistan. The two men, however, present a complete contrast. Malcolm was by training a soldier; Macnaghten was the archetypal Civil Servant, who had come to politics via the Judiciary and the Secretariat. 'A man of the desk', Henry Lawrence called him[17] and this appears to have been the universal view of his contemporaries. All unite in praising his intellectual powers and in doubting his executive ability and especially his capacity to understand and manipulate men. Many found him cold and reserved, although he was always scrupulously polite. Burnes, who saw much of him in Kabul, wrote: 'He is a man of good judgement but of no experience and quite unskilled with natives. He is also very hasty in taking up and throwing off plans and altogether the torch of ambition has been lighted too late in him.'[18] George Broadfoot took a still more unfavourable view. He believed Macnaghten's lack of understanding of other men was so great as to disqualify him for work in the Secretariat, let alone in diplomacy, and thought he should have remained an appeals judge, considering written evidence alone.[19] It is indeed apparent that Macnaghten lacked that humility which could admit error or accept criticism. Within the anonymity of the Secretariat this defect could escape notice; in Kabul it could not. Macnaghten was also a much more limited man than Malcolm. It was Malcolm's great breadth of knowledge of European and Asian affairs which enabled him to synthesize ideas and information into great, comprehensive schemes. Macnaghten, on the other hand, while he possessed a fine intellect, lacked that passion for knowledge and delight in concepts which mark the true intellectual; his comprehension was bounded by the papers which were before him.

In the light of this analysis it may seem strange that Macnaghten should have played so crucial a role in British policy in Central Asia between 1838 and 1841. Partly it was involuntary; in 1838 Auckland thought him the best man for the post of Envoy in Kabul, although, after the 1841 disaster, the Governor-General wished he had chosen George Clerk or James Sutherland instead.[20] In 1839 Macnaghten asked to be allowed to return to India, but Auckland persuaded him to stay in Afghanistan.[21] But partly it was Macnaghten's own ambition which drove him forward. He craved public recognition and thought that he should have been given a baronetcy long before the award was made. Kabul for him was a passport to future honours and a seat on Council, or even to the coveted Governorship which came his way too late.[22] Burnes's penetrating remark concerning his ambition suggests another influence. No one reading the private correspondence of the period, and especially the letters and journals of Auckland's sisters could but be struck by the character of Mrs. Macnaghten. It may best be described as a cross between Rosamond Vincy and Lady Catherine de Bourgh; a rare combination of snobbery and selfishness. Macnaghten, however, was evidently devoted to her. The contrast with Malcolm is again striking. In 1808 Malcolm's recent marriage served as a romantic spur to achievement; when later he tired of his wife he simply left her in England. Macnaghten, however, lacked either romance or indifference; he was nagged into ambition.

Macnaghten's only advisor of note on his mission was Claude Wade. His other companions included George Macgregor, a young man of ability who was serving as Auckland's aide-de-camp and who took advantage of his opportunity to lay the foundations of an enterprising political career; and William Osborne, Auckland's relative and Military Secretary, who left a journal of the mission. Burnes did not join the party until the main policy had been decided and Masson remained at Peshawar and was consulted only by letter. The first meetings were at the Maharajah's favourite summer residence at Adinagar, where Macnaghten arrived on 20 May 1838.

It was immediately decided that the first plan should be adopted. Auckland's assumptions about Sikh ambitions were soon proved wrong; Ranjit Singh resolutely repudiated any intention of taking independent action in Afghanistan. As Hasrat remarks, 'he had refused to act alone, for the reason that he had neither any intention nor the means to conquer Kabul.'[23] Some opposition to the co-operative plan came from the Jammus and from certain other Sikh leaders, but the Maharajah was determined to hazard no lone action and, according to Macnaghten, did not even wish to hear the second plan. A draft treaty was promptly drawn up on the basis of Britain's adhesion to the treaty formed between Ranjit Singh and Shuja on 12 March 1833.

Differences between Britons and Sikhs appeared when the details of the plan were discussed. Auckland had presented the scheme as one by which Britain would assist the Sikhs to realize their north-western ambitions: Ranjit, who had no such ambitions, saw it as one by which Lahore was asked to aid Britain against Russia and Iran and he wanted payment—money, certain lands (including Shikarpur) from Sind, and Jalalabad from Afghanistan, although the last demand was possibly simply a bargaining counter.[24] Macnaghten refused and the negotiations became deadlocked. From the Sikh court chronicle it is apparent that Ranjit Singh became intensely suspicious of the British intentions and convinced that the British intended to take Shikarpur for themselves. He desperately wished that Macnaghten would be content to leave empty-handed.[25] On 9 June he suddenly broke up his camp at Adinagar and moved to Lahore. Although it is clear that the British had been warned of the impending move and were not sorry to get away from the heat and cholera at Adinagar, there is, nevertheless, a curious similarity between Ranjit's action in 1838 and his similar attempts to evade Metcalfe in 1809. If he did hope to shake off Macnaghten Ranjit was disappointed. Negotiations were resumed at Lahore on 18 June. Ranjit then tried to drive a wedge between the British negotiators by playing off Burnes and Mackeson against Macnaghten. But this tactic failed and indeed Ranjit Singh derived the impression that Macnaghten, in some ways, was actually superior to Auckland himself. On 22 June Macnaghten brought matters to a head by stating that both parties should resume their freedom of action.[26] Ranjit promptly gave way, for he had neither stomach for independent action nor wish to see Britain alone and untrammelled in Afghanistan. A bargain was struck on 23 June by which Ranjit reduced his demands to an annual tribute of £20,000 from Afghanistan. Macnaghten agreed, providing that the sum was made to appear not as tribute but as payment for the right to call upon the services of five thousand Lahore soldiers.[27] Ranjit accepted this offer and the Jammus were pacified by being given a free hand in the area north of the Kabul river.[28]

The final version of the treaty was based, as contemplated, on the existing treaty between Shuja and Ranjit Singh. Articles 1 to 13 of the old treaty were unchanged. Article 14 was modified to become a general defensive alliance between Britain, Lahore, and Shuja. The size of the Sindian contribution was left open. Ranjit wanted £150,000 of the £200,000 which had previously been thought appropriate, so Macnaghten left the sum undecided in the hope that the Amirs might be induced to pay more. Article 15 provided for the £20,000 tribute, disguised as subsidy, payable by Shuja to the Sikhs.

It now remained to gain the assent of Shah Shuja. Macnaghten took his leave of Ranjit Singh on 13 July. In his last conversation with Ranjit he remarked 'that falsehood, which did some good, was always better than the truth which created trouble'.[29] It was an epigram which carried the full flavour of the Persian conversation in which Macnaghten excelled, but it also provided an apt illustration of an attitude towards his new career which was to carry him far but ultimately bring him to disaster. Full of his triumph at Lahore Macnaghten went to

Ludhiana, where he did not propose to allow Shuja to spoil his hopes. Although Shuja had hoped to be restored to an Afghanistan which extended to its former limits, he was in no position to argue at length. After obtaining some assurances relating to British financial assistance and promises concerning British abstention from interference in Afghanistan's internal affairs, he signed.[30] Macnaghten now returned to confront Auckland with what he had achieved.

Auckland's own agreement to his own plan was the most difficult to obtain. One suspects that, like Ranjit, he wished that Macnaghten would just go away. The Governor-General's letters written during this period are painful to read, as he desperately sought to avoid a decision and to resist the promptings of Macnaghten. Even after the Sikhs accepted the co-operative plan he had proposed to them, he insisted that he was not committed. He pleaded that his information was inadequate—he had no news from McNeill later than 7 March, nor from Herat later than 21 March and from England, he complained, he had no instructions at all.[31] The April mail which arrived at Simla on 22 June brought him no guidance. He had grave reservations about parts of the plan, notably about Shuja's popularity in Afghanistan, and the Sikh attitude, so surprising to him, caused him much disquiet. His obdurate refusal to make concessions to the Sikhs almost suggests that he hoped the negotiations would break down and leave him free again; he refused to give Ranjit any part of Sind or Afghanistan; he was ready to break off negotiations because of the Sikh delays; and he opposed any payment of tribute by Shuja. His private secretary, Colvin, on the other hand, would have given the Sikhs Jalalabad.[32]

Despite his reluctance to commit himself, Auckland was obliged to make minor decisions which propelled him insensibly towards acceptance. He allowed Shuja to approach his supporters in Afghanistan; and he authorized an increase in the armies of Bombay and Bengal in order to provide a disposable force for use in the west. So, when Ranjit finally accepted all his terms, Auckland reluctantly concluded that he would probably accept. 'I shall hardly be able to decline it', he wrote unenthusiastically.[33] About 12 July his provisional decision was confirmed by news from Herat, that McNeill's mission had failed, that Russians were assisting in the siege and twelve thousand Russian troops were marching on Khiva, that Palmerston had authorized McNeill to break off relations with Herat over the messenger affair, and that instructions were on their way giving Auckland discretion to do whatever was needful if the breach with Iran occurred.[34] Auckland had at last made up his mind.

Nothing in the history of the first Anglo-Afghan war has caused more controversy than the responsibility for the decision which began it. In his classic history of the war John Kaye claimed that the chief responsibility rested with Auckland's sisters, Fanny and Emily Eden, and with his secretaries, Macnaghten, Torrens, and Colvin.[35] This was the view most common in India at the time and rested heavily on stories which originated with Charles Masson, who obtained them from Burnes and Lord. Neither of these last were the most reliable of informants. Burnes told some fantastic stories.[36] According to one of Masson's stories, retold by Kaye, Burnes was accosted by Colvin and Torrens when he arrived at Simla and begged not to talk Auckland out of a plan which they had taken so much trouble to talk him into. This story may well have some element of truth in it; Torrens admitted that he had asked Burnes (who wanted modifications in the plan) not to confuse Auckland with other projects when all energies were required to carry out the existing plan. In fact, Torrens's evidence consistently reinforces the general impression of Auckland's indecision. But, while approving the policy, Torrens denied responsibility for it in a letter to the *Friend of India*.[37] The value of his denial, however, is put in doubt by his absurd contention that Hobhouse was responsible. Torrens's evidence, taken with that of the origins of the Shuja plan and the conflict between Auckland and Macnaghten, all strengthen the likelihood that so irresolute a man as Auckland was vulnerable to the advice which Macnaghten, Colvin, and Torrens were so well placed to give him. The overwhelming evidence of his painful indecision between May and July 1838 leads one to suppose that he entered the alliance under pressure.

The influence of the secretaries upon the decision therefore may be conceded. It is difficult to say which of them predominated. Torrens can probably be dismissed; he was an entertaining companion, but a light-weight. John Colvin, whom Kaye singled out as the most powerful influence, was certainly a formidable man, but his talents and interests were in the greyer fields of administration; he specialized in the influencing of appointments. In the light of the evidence now available it would seem most likely that Macnaghten himself was the dominant figure. But in accepting that Auckland's Secretariat played a substantial role, just as Hastings's secretaries had done before, it is not necessary to accept the discreditable motives which were held to govern their advice. Macnaghten certainly did not seek the post of Envoy to Kabul; Masson's story that he only volunteered to take it to prevent it going to Burnes is a clear fabrication by Burnes, who was never in the running. Nor is there any reason to accept Masson's story that Colvin and Torrens encouraged Macnaghten to take the post in order to get rid of him—Colvin so that he might have greater freedom for intrigue and

Torrens in the hope of replacing Macnaghten in the Secretariat.[38] On balance Torrens's implied explanation seems the most likely: Auckland could not make up his mind so his staff felt obliged to help him and simply refurbished the only plan they knew—that of 1832.

The other influences may rapidly be dismissed. Fanny's journals are now available and reveal her to have been uninformed about Central Asian politics and mildly hostile to the prospect of war with Dost Muhammad.[39] Emily, whose wit and intelligence led observers to think she must have had more influence than was the case, took a keen but patronizing interest in the subject. Her letters suggest she had neither real knowledge, nor understanding, nor influence in the affair. She claimed that the policy was Auckland's own and that the decision, made in the absence of his own Councillors, troubled him deeply.[40] Masson's story of the influence of Mrs. Torrens on the two sisters seems irrelevant. Kaye suggests that Auckland's absence from his Council was a major factor. No one knows whether his decision might not have been different had he remained in Calcutta, but it should be said that his Council apart from Fane supported his policy, individually and collectively, although Thoby Prinsep had some doubts about certain details.[41]

The second major theory about the responsibility for the war is that it was the work of the Board of Control. This proposition was first argued at length by Auckland Colvin in his life of his father. Auckland Colvin published Hobhouse's dispatch of 25 June 1836 and claimed that Auckland acted in accordance with this throughout.[42] This claim is evidently untrue; Auckland never referred to this dispatch throughout the crisis until he did so as an apparent afterthought in a dispatch of 13 August 1838.[43] On the contrary, all the evidence suggests that he felt himself to be without any guidance from England. The theory of Hobhouse's responsibility received some additional apparent support from a later statement by Hobhouse in Parliament to the effect that he was responsible. This has misled some naïve writers who confused a statement about the constitutional position of the President of the Board of Control with an admission of directing influence. It need not be considered here.

The evidence suggests that the plan was basically that of Macnaghten and the decision to adopt it was that of Auckland. Auckland disliked action. He preferred to cling to the old policy of commercial penetration as long as possible. He was driven to abandon it in the early summer of 1838 by the sudden emergence of external and internal threats. It was the reports of internal disaffection, reaching him at Simla, which were probably the decisive influence.[44] Emily Eden later argued that the success of the Afghan expedition was more important in defeating internal enemies than in combating enemies abroad.[45] In the last analysis Auckland went to war to safeguard the internal rather than the external frontier.

In retrospect one can see that Auckland was wrong both about the internal and the external dangers. He underestimated the danger from the west before May 1838 and overestimated it afterwards; The Shah could not take Herat and neither the Russians nor the Barakzays were really committed to him. The great conspiracy inside India melted away. Auckland claimed this was because of his decisive policy, but the evidence suggests the conspiracy never existed. Later investigations failed to substantiate the rumours that had poured in and there is evidence that in some cases, as in Jaipur, Political Agents found it convenient to invent a conspiracy to justify their own policies.[46] Auckland was also wrong about two other important points. He misjudged the attitude of the Sikhs and he misjudged the popularity of Shuja in Afghanistan. On the last point he took great pains to collect information and refused to give final agreement to the project until he was reasonably satisfied.[47] But most of those who testified in favour of Shuja knew little of Kabul: only Burnes and Masson were really able to give an informed opinion and both supported Dost Muhammad.

The key factor in the decision to go to war for the sake of a new defensive system was the character of Auckland. He was intelligent enough to perceive the weaknesses of those who pressed for drastic action, but not strong enough to stand indefinitely by his own judgement. A less intelligent man might have saved himself from war by adopting the policy of Burnes; a more determined man might have preserved himself by doing nothing. But being Auckland, because he did too little at the beginning he had to do too much at the end. Such was Hobhouse's verdict. Emily Eden captured more neatly the dilemma of the weak and rational man. 'Poor dear peaceful George has gone to war', she wrote, '—rather an inconsistency in his character.'[48]

The plan which Auckland put into operation was not at all the plan which he had originally envisaged. Had he known to what he would become committed by October 1838 he would have hesitated still longer in July. As noted, his original scheme had assigned the major role to the Sikhs. They were to advance with Shuja from Peshawar through the Khaibar to Kabul. Beyond stipulating the return of the Sikh army Auckland proposed to exercise no control over the Sikhs. None of his advisors liked this plan, however; they distrusted the Sikhs and believed their presence would threaten Shuja's popularity.[49] All wanted Shuja to make his way into Afghanistan through the Bolan Pass, avoiding Sikh territory. Auckland resisted this advice until it became apparent that the Sikhs themselves disliked the original role assigned to them. So it was decided that Shuja should go through the Bolan, with his own forces, officered and financed by Britain. But this rapidly raised a second doubt—would his own troops suffice? Would it not be safer and cheaper to use Company troops?[50] Certainly, if a Russian or Iranian force appeared in the area a British force would be essential.[51] Palmerston's permission to McNeill to break off relations with Iran relieved Auckland of his earlier fears of the diplomatic consequences of the employment of British troops. By about July 12 it had been decided to send a force of five thousand Company troops with Shuja. Thereafter the number grew week by week until, by September, a force of fourteen thousand was under discussion.[52] This figure was only slightly reduced after news was received of the Iranian withdrawal from Herat, although that event could have been held to have made the whole venture unnecessary. But by that time Auckland had decided that Company troops were indispensable.[53] And as the British share in the enterprise was augmented, so that of the Sikhs diminished until their final role was merely to make a demonstration in the Khaibar to divide the defences of Dost Muhammad. In fact, by the autumn of 1838 their contribution was a source of embarrassment.

Between May and September 1838 the whole character of the enterprise had changed. From a basically Sikh expedition it had been transformed into an essentially British venture, which bore a close resemblance to that outlined by Macnaghten in December 1837. From a temporary expedient designed to meet the immediate threat of menace from the west and allay discontent within India it had been transposed into a search for a new, permanent system of defence, through the creation of a buffer state in Afghanistan. In November 1838 Auckland described his object as 'to raise up an insurmountable and, I hope, lasting barrier to all encroachments from the Westward, and to establish a base for the extension and maintenance of British influence throughout Central Asia'.[54] Auckland had been reluctant to abandon the policy of commercial penetration, but when he had done so it was for a completely new strategy. In May Auckland had begun by questioning one of Wade's assumptions—that relating to the western threat: by September he had begun to question Wade's still more fundamental second assumption—that of the pre-eminence of the Sikh alliance. So, by a curious irony, within a few months the Governor-General had come to accept the main postulates of the rejected policy of Burnes; the only difference was that he proposed to carry it out under a different label. Auckland had revolutionized British policy in Central Asia. It remained only to carry out the revolution.

The plan of the expedition envisaged not only control of Afghanistan but also control of those countries which lay along the new lines of communication created by the British advance beyond the frontier. By taking the decision to send British troops through the Bolan and not the Khaibar, the lowering problem of establishing a route through the Panjab could be avoided and a suspicious, temporary arrangement with the Sikhs could be held to suffice for British needs. But the case was different with those countries which lay directly along the march of the Company armies. 'These were Bahawalpur, Sind, and Kalat.

The Company forces for the expedition were drawn from Bombay and Bengal. The assembly point was Shikarpur, the base for the march through the Bolan. The Bombay force went by sea to Sind and the Bengal force marched overland from Firuzpur, where Auckland met Ranjit Singh for the first time. They reviewed the troops together. As the Bengal force set off for Shikarpur, the old military adventurer, Colonel James Skinner, a veteran of Wellesley's wars, turned and remarked prophetically to Torrens: 'It will be a second Monson's retreat.'[55]

The first state along the route of the Bengal force was Bahawalpur. Supplies, and recruits for Shuja's hastily formed levies were required from the Nawab, who was also expected to use his influence to win over neighbouring Baluchi chiefs. A treaty of protection was offered him. While retaining internal autonomy, the Nawab was to accept British control over his foreign relations and supply troops when needed. In addition he was to supply provisions and three thousand men for the expedition. If he declined to co-operate he was to be told that the general welfare required that the resources of his country should be used anyway.[56] Auckland would tolerate no obstruction of the plan which had cost him so much pain. 'It must be a word and a blow with the first traitor who raises his head and it may be hoped that the others will be kept quiet', he wrote.[57]

Frederick Mackeson, who was given charge of the negotiations, was completely outmanœuvred by the Nawab. Auckland had intended that the protectorate treaty should be represented to the Nawab as a reward for co-operation. But Mackeson allowed himself to be drawn into haggling over the substance of the treaty itself as well as the Nawab's contribution to the expedition, and agreed to substantial concessions on both. He agreed to reduce the number of men required to assist the expedition, give them special rates of pay, and meet the cost of replacements employed during their absence. With regard to the treaty, he agreed to a limitation on the number of troops which could be demanded from Bahawalpur.[58]

Auckland was furious and promptly rejected the treaty. Mackeson was sent back to Bahawalpur with an ultimatum. The Nawab could accept the original draft or make his own arrangements with Shuja; if he interfered with the expedition it would be disastrous for him. The Nawab took the hint and signed the treaty immediately. At the outset of the negotiations he had declared: 'no-one in these times who understood his own interests would think of opposing himself to the views and wishes of the British Government,'[59] and while he had been too clever for Mackeson he did not intend to be too clever for himself. Auckland ratified the treaty on 22 October 1838, but even then the Nawab was not quite out of the wood. The supplies and levies offered to Shuja were reported to be inadequate and in January 1839 Auckland threatened to occupy Bahawalpur.[60] Mackeson, however, pleaded the Nawab's case; Bahawalpur was a poor country and could scarcely supply so large a force.[61] General Sir Willoughby Cotton, who was in charge of the Bengal force, reported that he was quite satisfied with support from Bahawalpur.[62] So Auckland, who had by now more important matters to occupy his mind, let the matter drop.

Attention had now switched to Sind, complete command over which was essential to the success of the plan. Sind was the main base of operations, with Shikarpur as the assembly point and nearby Bhakar as the site of the proposed boat-bridge over the Indus. In addition, Sind was to be a major investor in the expedition. The most extravagant ideas of the wealth of the Amirs prevailed in British India. They had originally been set down for a contribution of £200,000, but it had later been decided to increase the sum. The justification for this financial demand was that Sind would obtain a release from all claims by Shuja for suzerainty and tribute. The Amirs, who had never been consulted, in fact possessed a document given them by Shuja which released them from all claims to tribute on account of Shikarpur.[63] They were also seemingly protected from British demands by the treaty which had been completed as recently as March 1838. But none of this was to be any protection. Auckland proposed to present them with a brutal ultimatum: either they co-operated in full or Shikarpur would be occupied and Shuja permitted to press his claims on Sind. The clause in the newly-ratified treaty which forbade the transport of military supplies on the Indus was coolly and unilaterally abrogated. Pottinger was to advise on how much the Amirs could pay.[64]

Although the rough treatment of the Amirs could be justified by reference to the timetable of the expedition, there is more than a suspicion that other motives also lay behind the manner in which they were approached. Past experience of the Amirs' suspicions must have indicated that they would react unfavourably to the ultimatum, and the logic of Auckland's new defensive strategy demanded that British control over Sind should be established more firmly. This theory derives support from a letter written to Pottinger by Colvin.

If out of the events and feelings which may be the consequences of so important a movement you can obtain the means of fixing a subsidiary force in Sind, I need not repeat that you will add materially to the benefits which your connection with that country has already caused to the British Government.[65]

What Colvin called 'a golden opportunity' was found immediately.[66] Pottinger had been instructed to treat any hostile agreement between Iran and Sind as a *casus belli* and in that event to order the Bombay force to occupy Haidarabad. These instructions crossed a report from Pottinger to the effect that the Amirs had written a submissive letter to Muhammad Shah of Iran. Pottinger himself attached little importance to the letter because such contacts, although contrary to the 1838 Treaty, had been a common and innocuous feature of Sindian foreign relations.[67] Auckland, however, pounced on the incident. 'His Lordship must have it felt that those who are not our friends on the day of trial will be considered as our enemies and unhappily it is amongst these that Noor Mahomed has apparently chosen to rank himself.'[68] Pottinger was instructed 'to take the most energetic measures for placing our relations with Sind upon a more satisfactory and secure footing'. Precise measures were left to him: Auckland wanted to fix a subsidiary force upon Sind, but the needs of the expedition came first and Pottinger was given permission to reduce this demand if necessary.

The Amirs' reaction was such as might have been foreseen. As soon as he received his original instructions Pottinger realized that the Amirs would never willingly co-operate and he asked for military support.[69] In reply Auckland, who had by this time received the report of the Amirs' 'treachery', ordered the occupation of Shikarpur.[70] In October 1838 Pottinger went up to Haidarabad ahead of the troops to negotiate. He found the Amirs very frightened and undecided. They had refused admission to Shuja's levies and were busily discussing the situation with their cousins at Khairpur and with the Sirdars of Qandahar. Pottinger felt himself to be in some danger and was annoyed to find both his life and negotiations further jeopardized by the activities of Alexander Burnes at Khairpur.

The relations between Khairpur, Mirpur, and Haidarabad had

always been something of a mystery to Britons—were they independent states, equal partners in a federation, or were the Amirs of Haidarabad, the largest unit, superior to the others? The British answer varied both according to information and convenience. In 1831 Burnes had recommended that separate negotiations should be held with Haidarabad and with Khairpur. Pottinger had subsequently discovered that Rustam Khan of Khairpur was unwilling to act independently of the Haidarabad Amirs at that time. Since then British policy had been to treat all the Amirs of Sind as a single unit represented by the Amirs of Haidarabad. No separate negotiations with Khairpur had been held since 1831 and no negotiations had ever taken place with Mirpur, a state which indeed was known only by report to Britons. Nevertheless, the Amirs of Khairpur and Mirpur were held to be bound by all the agreements made with the Amirs of Haidarabad.

In 1838 Auckland, after hearing of the Haidarabad contacts with Iran, decided to reverse this unitary policy and deal separately with Khairpur, which controlled the vital river-crossing at Bakhar. If the Khairpur Amirs were willing to allow Bakhar to be occupied and to make supplies available to the forces of the Company and Shuja, then Auckland would recognize their independence of Haidarabad in a separate treaty.[71] Alexander Burnes was sent to carry out the negotiations, subject to Pottinger's approval. After brief discussions with the Khairpur Amirs, Burnes drew up a draft protectorate treaty providing for a British Resident and internal autonomy, and sent it to Pottinger for approval.[72]

Pottinger was wholly opposed to the new policy of splitting Haidarabad and Khairpur. The time was not ripe and what was worse, it was extremely dangerous to himself, since if the Haidarabad Amirs learned of the separate negotiations with Khairpur, they might well wreak vengeance on Pottinger. Further, Burnes's treaty was unnecessary since, unbeknown to themselves, the Khairpur Amirs were already bound by the protectorate treaty which Pottinger had concluded with the Haidarabad Amirs in March 1838. Finally, remarked Pottinger, Rustam Khan of Khairpur was untrustworthy.[73] Important as these considerations were, it is apparent that Pottinger was also influenced by more personal motives. This was his fourth series of negotiations with Sind. Each of the previous rounds had been wearying, frustrating, and subject to developments elsewhere. There is evidence that he saw the fourth round as the final settlement. To Masson he complained of previous restrictions on threats to the Amirs; this time they could be taught a lesson. 'We have spoiled them', he announced in grimly familiar style.[74] But it seemed now that success was once more to be snatched from him and by none other than his former assistant, Alexander Burnes, with whom he had quarrelled in 1834 and never been reconciled. He therefore disapproved of Burnes's conduct, accused him of disobeying orders, and, for good measure, added some gratuitious comparisons between Burnes's conduct at Kabul and at Khairpur.[75] But he was overruled by Auckland, who had already sent orders to Burnes to conclude a treaty with Khairpur. After some delay, due partly to events in lower Sind and partly to Rustam's reluctance to part with Bakhar, the treaty was signed on 24 December. The article relating to the temporary cession of Bakhar to Britain was kept secret.[76]

Meanwhile, in lower Sind the Amirs had accepted Pottinger's original demands and agreed to pay the contribution towards Shuja's expedition. But Pottinger would not now settle for this because the British demands had been increased. On 4 December Pottinger left Haidarabad and joined the Bombay troops under General Keane at Vikkur. Foreseeing resistance by the Amirs he ordered up the reserve force from Bombay to Karachi. The reserves, under General Thomas Valiant, occupied Karachi in February 1839. The official account of this episode gave a conventional picture of sturdy opposition judiciously overcome. Pottinger later unearthed a more bizarre and entertaining version, likely to be much more acceptable to a *Catch 22* generation. According to this second account, the fort at Karachi had neither garrison nor effective guns. Observing the approach of the British vessels the inhabitants decided to fire a signal gun in welcome. They were dismayed to discover this amicable greeting was interpreted as a hostile act. Broadsides promptly flattened the fort and the unresisting port was gallantly stormed.[77] Even if untrue, the anecdote captures the elemental quality of macabre comedy which sighs so mournfully through the history of British relations with Sind. Sometimes there are artistic truths which no feeling historian can resist.

Pottinger had not waited for this curious drama to unfold at Karachi. On 15 January 1839 he had sent his assistant, Lieutenant W. J. Eastwick (1808–89), back to Haidarabad with a draft treaty containing all the latest British demands, as set out in new instructions from Auckland dated 19 November 1838, and with a demand for the use of Karachi.[78] The Amirs refused to sign, Eastwick left Haidarabad, and armed conflict seemed inevitable. Keane, who was now only thirty miles south of Haidarabad, was seriously alarmed for the safety of his troops and decided that a settlement with Sind must take priority even over the expedition to Afghanistan. Accordingly, he instructed a brigade of the Bengal force, which had already reached Upper Sind, to march down river to join him. In fact it was already on its way. For a few days the fate of Sind and that of the Afghan expedition hung in the balance. Then, on 1 February, the Haidarabad Amirs gave way and on 5 February signed a treaty almost identical with that which they had rejected from Eastwick on 22 January.[79]

An ambivalence governed Auckland's policy in Sind during the autumn and winter of 1838 to 1839. On the one hand he wanted a speedy agreement, even if concessions were required. For if the Afghan expedition were to proceed it had to move quickly. Partly he feared that the Shah might yet renew the siege of Herat,[80] but more importantly he knew that the Army of the Indus, as it was called, had to pass through the Bolan into Afghanistan before the onset of the hot weather. On the other hand he had to have a satisfactory settlement with Sind, partly because he dared not leave a hostile force across his lines of communication and also because Sind had a permanent role in his new strategy of defence. If necessary, therefore, in the end he was prepared to postpone the expedition and settle with Sind first.[81] His various instructions to Pottinger reflect the conflict between these opposing arguments in his mind. On 19 November he set out his demands: the collective government of Sind was to be broken up and each Amir was to be made independent of the others; the Amirs were to accept a subsidiary alliance—the force to be stationed in their territory; the Indus was to be freed from tolls and all restrictions on its military use abolished.[82] But it is clear he would have settled for much less if he could have obtained a quick settlement. When it seemed that a settlement was impossible, and war and the postponement of the Afghan expedition inevitable, he wanted much more; the annexation of Lower Sind, no less. As Colvin pointed out: 'The revenues would be a most welcome compensation for the expense of our Kabul arrangements.'[83] One suspects that Colvin spoke for many who thought that Sind would be in any case a much better bargain than Afghanistan. Such is the singular nature of ambition, however, that when Auckland obtained the settlement he wanted, at a lower price than he was prepared to pay, he was still dissatisfied. First, he wanted Karachi retained as a base and ordered that all mention of it should be omitted from the treaty. Second, he refused to allow any limitations either on the size of the British force which could be stationed in Sind or on the number of troops which could be demanded from the Amirs. Third, he would not accept a clause which required Britain to consult the Amirs before making any treaty which might affect them. Last, he would make no pledges to any subjects of the Amirs.[84] To negotiate these changes necessitated further delay before final agreement was reached in Sind.

Auckland was fairly satisfied with his work in Sind. Effective British military and political control was established. He had still a small list of desiderata, such as bringing Mirpur into the treaty fold and acquiring Shikarpur, but he had no ambition for more. In August 1839 he wrote to Pottinger:

I have no appetite for territorial acquisition in Sind, but I want such a position there as shall disarm for ever the hostility and presumption which has prevailed against us in that state, which gives us a political influence beyond it, which shall secure its harbours and its rivers to our commerce and give us some control over the uses to which these avenues may be applied.[85]

The domination of Sind, achieved in 1839, was both a necessary element in the new strategy evolved by Auckland and a logical outcome of the older policy of commercial penetration which had been conceived by Ellenborough and Bentinck. It was the exigencies of external defence which had caused Auckland to forsake the caution which had hampered Bentinck and which had restricted his own policy in 1836 to 1837. Indeed, it had been admitted even by the opponents of the policy of commercial penetration that, if a threat from the west developed, it would be necessary for Britain to secure control of Sind in order to command the Lower Indus. A plausible threat had now appeared and, amid applause from Hobhouse, British predominance could be established. Although final annexation was postponed, this too was foreshadowed in the demands of Auckland during the crisis and in Colvin's prophetic utterance concerning compensation for Afghanistan. In the meantime the coveted Indus defensive frontier was now partly secured.

Throughout the whole period the main executive agent of British policy in Sind had been Henry Pottinger. Ever since 1809, when he had first set foot in Sind, he had played a continuously significant role as the provider of information and as the shaper of policy in that region. The 1839 Treaty, however, was his last contribution. Ill-health was the reason given for his retirement, but there is little doubt that Pottinger felt out of sympathy with recent changes. He disliked the new plan of forward defence[86] and he disliked the new British attitude towards the Amirs of Sind. In the past he had been a strong advocate of a firm policy, but now he wanted more conciliation. He felt the Amirs had been unjustly treated and in his later dispatches exposed some of the wilder fabrications concerning their behaviour. It is now clear that many of the reports of their hostility were untrue and that complaints against them, both in 1838 and afterwards, were deliberately manufactured by British officials in order to excuse their own mistakes. Finally, Pottinger felt that events had passed him by in Sind; the preference

given to the opinions of Burnes over his own was especially humiliating.[87] So Pottinger left India, to achieve greater fame as the negotiator
of the Treaty of Hong Kong in 1842, as Governor of Hong Kong, and
later of the Cape, and eventually to return to India as Governor of
Madras.

Pottinger's departure from the frontier scene was a significant symptom of the times. Before 1838 the frontier duumvirate of Pottinger in
Cutch, and Wade at Ludhiana had wielded great authority through
their knowledge and their command of information. Pottinger now left
and was replaced in Lower Sind, by James Outram (1803–63), a
Bombay army officer who had acquired political experience and reputation first among the wild Bhil tribe and later in Guzerat. In Upper
Sind Pottinger was replaced by Ross Bell (d. 1841), a Bengal Civil
Servant who was friendly with Colvin and who had previously served
as magistrate in Delhi. Wade also departed at the end of 1839. Even in
1838 he was relegated to the minor task of accompanying Shahzada
Timur, the eldest son of Shuja, through the Khaibar to Kabul. Not long
after his return to his duties he was removed at the request of the Sikhs
and replaced by George Clerk, who had deputized for him during his
absence. These were new men in posts which had lost much of their
former importance. Like Lucknow, Ujjain, and Delhi they had seemingly been left stranded by the advancing frontier. It was now to Herat,
Qandahar, and Kabul that fresh men looked to find the as yet unused
observatories of the frontier. Auckland had new men to carry out his
new policy.

The Afghan expedition now rolled on into Baluchistan, into the
territories of the Khan of Kalat. Kalat was a large, barren, mountainous area bounded on the south by the sea, on the east by Sind, on the
north by Afghan lands, and on the west by Iran. Until the eighteenth
century it had formed part of the Mughal Empire. In the latter half of
that century a notable ruler, Nasir Khan (*reg*. 1751–94), first asserted
his independence and then expanded his boundaries, subject only to
the nominal suzerainty of the Durrani state in Afghanistan. After his
death the authority of the Khans was considerably reduced until, by
the reign of Mihrab Khan (1817–39), it had sunk effectively to the plain
of Kacchi and the two main centres of the Brahui tribes—the provinces
of Jhalawan and Sarawan. Mihrab possessed little authority either in
the southern parts of his territory or in those north-eastern areas which
were inhabited by the fierce Baluchi tribes of the Maris and the Bugtis.
Although during the period 1837 to 1839 Mihrab was engaged in
actively extending his power over the tribes, his was still only a tenuous
authority.

The British route through Kalat ran through the flat plain of Kacchi and thence ascended the Bolan Pass (through the Kalati province of Mastang) to Quetta (in the Kalati province of Shal). Mihrab Khan's co-operation was required both for permission to pass through his territories and for supplies and transport. Alexander Burnes had been supposed to arrange matters in advance with the Khan, but he had been fully occupied with Khairpur and his deputy, Robert Leech, to whom he had delegated the task, had fallen ill. As a result very little had been done by the time the Army of the Indus was ready to continue its march westwards. This situation led to some confusion and a significant change of plan.

Under the original plan the forces from Bengal were to march in two sections from Firuzpur. First went the levies raised by Shuja, accompanied by D'Arcy Todd as Acting Political Agent with Shuja until Macnaghten could assume his new post. Shuja's forces were to continue recruiting as they marched. Behind the levies came the Company's own Bengal forces under General Willoughby Cotton (1783–1860). At Shikarpur these two forces were to wait to be joined by the Bombay contingent under the command of General Sir John Keane (1781–1844), the Commander-in-Chief at Bombay. Keane was then to assume over-all command of all the military forces. The Commander-in-Chief of Bengal, Sir Henry Fane, had decided not to lead the force after it became plain that it would not encounter a foreign invading force. Political control of the expedition was vested in Macnaghten. It was impressed upon Keane and Macnaghten that the Company forces were present in an essentially supporting role only and that it was of the greatest political importance that Shah Shuja, together with his own forces, should occupy a prominent position in the van of the expedition.

The original plan was disrupted by the shortage of supplies, and by military particularism. Cotton, who was not anxious to wait to come under Keane's orders and lose his own independent command, ignored Shuja's troops, took whatever supplies and carriage were available at Shikarpur, and pushed on westwards without waiting for Keane, who, not surprisingly, protested violently when he arrived at Shikarpur. Some time elapsed before Keane was able to assemble sufficient supplies and carriage for his own troops and even so he was obliged to advance over territory swept clean by the hungry Bengal troops and their still more famished camp-followers. For Shuja's levies Keane cared no more than did Cotton. Dismissing them as a rabble, he left them behind at Shikarpur.

Against this background of supply problems, negotiations with

Kalat were conducted in an atmosphere of strain. The British were anxious about provisions and the plundering raids by tribes: Mihrab Khan feared for his own position, trapped as he was between the menace of the British and of Shuja if he did not co-operate with them, and the possible vengeance of the Sirdars of Qandahar if he did. In return for his assistance he wanted substantial payment and guarantees.

Macnaghten first tried a mixture of conciliation and threats. In 1834 Mihrab Khan had assisted Shuja and it was assumed that he would be willing to do so again. But in case he was reluctant to do so Macnaghten had a second string to his bow. In Shuja's camp was a claimant to the throne of Kalat, one Shah Nawaz Khan. In the hope of inducing a favourable attitude in Mihrab Macnaghten mentioned this fact in a letter to the Khan, adding, 'a hint to the wise is sufficient.'[88] But it seemed it was not, for supplies did not appear and the plundering continued. Lacking troops with which to coerce the Khan, Macnaghten offered an annual subsidy of £10,000, in return for supplies, transport, and Mihrab's recognition of Shuja's suzerainty. Although Burnes, who was sent to negotiate the treaty, raised the offer to £15,000, he had no success. Mihrab wanted to remain independent and was not satisfied with Burnes's assurance that he would remain independent in practice. So, although he agreed to come to do homage to Shuja, he never appeared and matters went on as before.[89]

Macnaghten now proposed a drastic solution to the problem of Kalat. During Burnes's absence at Kalat in March 1839 Macnaghten had decided that Mihrab was deliberately opposing the expedition. The plundering, the absence of supplies, and the production of certain letters purporting to be written by Mihrab Khan to his local agent, and giving instructions to oppose the British, all combined to leave no doubt in the Envoy's mind. Accordingly, both for revenge and to ensure safe communications in the future, Macnaghten proposed that the three Kalati provinces which lay along the line of communications, namely Kacchi, Shal, and Mastang, should be annexed to Afghanistan.[90] Until this deed could be carried out he established *de facto* control over the line through three British agents appointed in April 1839. These were Lieutenant Eastwick in Shikarpur, Lieutenant Loveday in the Bolan, and Lieutenant Bean in Quetta. All were instructed to act without reference to Mihrab Khan.

The final settlement with Kalat was postponed until the Afghan expedition had been completed. But it is clear that the plan carried out at the end of 1839 was one which had been evolved earlier in the year.[91] In the meantime Bean and Loveday won over certain Kalati chiefs with bribes. The actual reduction of Kalat was carried out by the Bombay contingent on its return from Afghanistan under the command of General Thomas Willshire (1789–1862). Kalat was taken by storm on 13 November and Mihrab Khan, like Tipu Sultan of Mysore, was killed in defence of his capital. In his place Shah Nawaz Khan was installed as ruler. A treaty was formed with him which gave Britain control over his foreign relations, and over communications and certain commercial concessions. In return Nawaz was given £5,000 and the promise of 'political support' to assert his authority over his diminished possessions. Loveday was assigned to Kalat as Political Agent.[92] The coveted provinces on the line of communications were nominally annexed to Afghanistan, although in practice they remained under British control, exercised through Bell at Shikarpur and Bean at Quetta.

British interest in Kalat derived only from communication needs. Macnaghten did add, as an extra argument for his policy, that the revenues from the annexed provinces would greatly benefit Shuja, but in fact the Afghan ruler never saw a penny of them.[93] Once control over the line of communications between Shikarpur and Quetta had been secured it apparently mattered little who ruled in Kalat itself. British indifference to the future of the state was well illustrated by the sight which greeted Nawaz when he entered his new palace. Since it had been taken by storm, its former contents had become the legitimate spoils of war and were sold and the proceeds distributed among the troops. In consequence the palace was completely empty, except for a little furniture and 'a vast number of large cooking utensils' which Bean had thoughtfully purchased from the prize agent for five thousand rupees so as the disguise the bareness of the walls. Shah Nawaz, reported Bean, 'seems to appreciate this attention and seems full of gratitude to our Government'.[94] Apparently he later melted the pots down to provide a new copper coinage.[95]

Kalat had been disposed of too hastily. There was no good evidence against Mihrab. As far as the absence of supplies was concerned, it was impossible that a poor country like Kalat, made poorer by the blight which had destroyed the last year's harvest, could have fed almost a hundred thousand men and their animals.[96] Nor could Mihrab really be blamed for the activities of the plundering tribes over whom he had little or no control, as Macnaghten admitted.[97] Mihrab's agent reported: 'I particularly enjoined the Belochie tribes to refrain from thieving and plundering the Feringhees, but it was just like telling a mad man "take care and do not burn the Place" and he replies "thank you, you have well reminded me" and fires at once.'[98] Certainly the

British had no more luck with the Baluchis after they won control of the province. The most damning evidence against Mihrab was the incriminating letters given to Macnaghten by Mihrab's agent, Muhammad Husayn, who professed to be wholly pro-British and made his own private agreement with Macnaghten.[99] But in fact Muhammad Husayn completely mistrusted the British and, after the fall of Kalat, letters were discovered which proved that he had throughout been writing to Mihrab feeding him with reports of British hostility.[100] Therefore even if the Mihrab letters were genuine they were written under exculpatory circumstances.

The speed with which Macnaghten reached his decision on Mihrab's guilt, his failure to investigate further, and the rapidity with which he proclaimed his solution to the problem of Kalat suggests three possibilities. The first, by no means impossible, is that worry and inexperience relaxed his judgement in April 1839. The second is suggested by Colvin, who described the whole affair as a striking moral lesson to all;[101] Macnaghten may have wished to demonstrate the long arm of British vengeance so as to intimidate other would-be laggards. The first possibility, however, is weakened by the confirmation of the decision in November 1839 and the second by the long delay between contemplation and execution. I incline to believe that Macnaghten was mainly influenced by a third possible motive; the desire to take the opportunity to achieve a permanent settlement of a strategic problem by assuming control over one of the two main entry routes into India. This would be consistent with his original defensive system and the Kalat policy was certainly entirely of his devising. Auckland did not want to annex the three provinces to Afghanistan but, having no information apart from that sent to him, felt obliged to leave discretion to Macnaghten.[102]

In retrospect it is clear that Macnaghten acted too hastily. Unlike the situation in relation to Sind and Bahawalpur, Britain had had no previous dealings with Kalat and little information concerning the country had been assembled. In particular, Macnaghten did not know how vital Kacchi was to the balance of the Kalati state. Without it Kalat was not viable and so inevitably Britain was committed to its maintenance. Ross Bell discovered the truth too late to prevent Willshire's assault.[103]

Macnaghten's error over Kalat was an important factor in modifying Auckland's new system of strategic defence. Auckland had intended that the new system, based upon Afghanistan, should provide permanent security for India: he had certainly not intended that a permanent British military presence beyond the Indus should be required to maintain it. It had always been envisaged that direct involvement of British forces would be confined to establishing Shuja in a consolidated Afghan state under British influence. Thereafter the troops were to be withdrawn. Hobhouse also adhered to this view and warned Auckland specifically about the dangers of involvement in Kalat. 'We would wish to leave no causes of future irritation behind us at the time our troops shall have evacuated Afghanistan', he stated.[104] But the reorganization of Kalat was the first step towards permanent British intervention beyond the Indus.

The institution of British influence in Afghanistan itself was the central feature of the new system. The mechanics of the operation were simple. The Army of the Indus, finally united in the early part of April 1839 at Quetta, and immediately set out for Qandahar, which was taken without resistance on 25 April. After remaining two months at Qandahar the final march on Kabul was resumed on 27 June. Ghazni was taken by storm on 23 July and Shuja restored to Kabul on 7 August. Except at Ghazni there was little resistance. The Barakzays were not liked; several prominent chiefs deserted them. Dost Muhammad's forces were divided by a threat from Kunduz in the north and from Wade and the Sikhs in the east. The Amir fled to Turkestan to evade capture.

Shuja made Kabul his capital and Jalalabad his winter capital. The choice seemed an obvious one: Kabul had become the capital in the latter part of the reign of Timur Shah and remained so under his successors. But from Shuja's point of view there might have been much to recommend Qandahar. It had been the original capital of the Durrani Empire and Shuja's main support was still thought to lie among the Durrani chiefs of western Afghanistan. From the British viewpoint too Qandahar made much more sense since it offered good communications with British-controlled territory through the Bolan Pass and avoided that dependence upon the Khaibar–Panjab route which the choice of Kabul made inevitable. Qandahar was also nearer to Herat and therefore better placed for defence against the attack from the west which had been the main British preoccupation. In 1842, and again in 1880, Qandahar was to be regarded as the most important strategic position for Britain in Afghanistan and Kabul was then considered to be of much less importance. But in 1839 the experience which led to this assessment still had to be bought and the consequences of the hasty choice of Kabul were not understood.

Having enthroned Shah Shuja, Auckland had to construct a framework for future British relations with that country. The Tripartite Treaty of 1838 had been intended only to provide a basis for Shuja's restoration and it was always contemplated that a fresh treaty would govern the subsequent intercourse of Britain and Afghanistan. Although Auckland intended to withdraw Company troops immediately, he wished first to implant the seeds of permanent control. His original plan was outlined in his first instructions to Macnaghten dated 8 December 1838. At that time Macnaghten was advised to obtain from Shuja, before his formal installation as ruler in Kabul, an agreement which would provide for: a British Resident; the maintenance of a disciplined force in the service of the Shah; the exclusion from the Shah's service (without British permission) of all Europeans other than Britons; and a system of moderate commercial duties. Of these provisions the most significant was that which related to the disciplined force, known as the Contingent. It was to be formed originally from the Hindustani levies recruited in India in 1838. As soon as they became available Afghans were to replace the Hindustanis. The officers, however, would remain British. The force was to be cantoned separately from the Shah's other troops and would be used primarily for external defence and not for internal constabulary duties. It was to be entirely under the control of the British Resident, who, by virtue of his control of the only really effective military force, would become the dominant figure in Afghanistan. Although the Resident would not interfere directly in the internal administration of Afghanistan, he should persuade the Shah to reform any institution which was not conducive to the proper execution of British policy, that is, which did not contribute to the maintenance of peace and the freedom and independence of commerce.[105] The sweeping possibilities of this last instruction can be grasped immediately.

In London, ministers who paid little attention to the progress of events in India, were yet quick to grasp the far-reaching control which was adumbrated in Auckland's instructions. Several of them pencilled comments on it. Hobhouse remarked justly 'This is perpetual interference and control.' Palmerston, characteristically, thought it 'highly necessary and proper'. Just as characteristically, Howick announced his violent opposition. He rightly believed that the instructions implied that Afghanistan would become a British dependency and stated: 'I can only express my entire disapprobation of this policy.' Melbourne put it most succinctly of all: 'Mr Macnaghten is King of Affghanistan.' The concern expressed had its effect upon British policy. Hobhouse warned Auckland to be cautious over the question of the Resident's control of the Contingent and not to conclude a Definitive Treaty without approval from England. 'People at home', he wrote, would look upon such an engagement as indicating an intention to extend our actual military control over parts of Central Asia, and would be alarmed lest some scheme of indefinite aggrandizement should result from your present enterprise. I happen to know that these fears have already arisen in quarters where you would least expect to find them and that even Lord Wellesley and the Duke [of Wellington] himself are not altogether free from them.[106]

In the official dispatch which accompanied this private letter Auckland was told bluntly 'we would never sanction any arrangement having for its object territorial acquisitions in Central Asia.'[107] This caution was partly inspired by the Parliamentary vulnerability of ministers during the first part of 1839 and evidently did not truly represent Hobhouse's own views, both as expressed before and after these months. Yet the warning from England was in time to have some effect upon Auckland's formal arrangements for control over Afghanistan.

Macnaghten negotiated a treaty with Shuja on the lines of his original instructions and the Shah signed it at Qandahar on 7 May. The only minor change was that while accepting British control over the Contingent, the Shah asked that its pay should appear to come from him. Even at this early date it was becoming clear that it would be some time before he would be able to meet the cost of the force out of his own revenues.[108] After some correspondence between Macnaghten and the Indian Government concerning particular clauses, namely those concerned with the exclusion of foreigners and the Sind contribution, an agreed revised version was sent to Macnaghten on 12 September 1839.[109] This version was ratified by Shuja and returned by Macnaghten on 1 October and finally ratified by Auckland on 24 October.[110] Comparing the final treaty with Macnaghten's original draft, the influence of the Cabinet's intervention is immediately apparent. The final treaty was short and simple and went into very few details of the arrangements between the two states. It seems clear that, after receiving Hobhouse's warning, Auckland had decided to eliminate the formal statement of the bases of British influence in Afghanistan. But the fact that that influence was no longer set out in a formal diplomatic document made it no less real and profound.

In the event Auckland was not obliged to rely upon the Contingent for influence, because he was forced to retain Company troops in Afghanistan, at least during the winter of 1839 to 1840. Three new pieces of evidence brought him to this unwelcome decision. First, it was clear that Shuja lacked the money to stand on his own and that Britain would have to subsidize him in any case. The revenues of Kabul and Qandahar had been grossly overestimated and it was apparent that Shuja was unable to pay even his own administrative expenses let alone meet the charges of the Contingent. Second, it was now obvious that Shuja possessed no reliable military forces. The Contingent was undisciplined and he could scarcely rely on the Barakzay forces, although most of these troops now entered his service. Third, it was undeniable that Shuja himself lacked popular support in Afghanistan.

The revelation of Shuja's unpopularity was a major blow to Auckland. Had he not been satisfied on this point he would not have agreed to the expedition, and throughout he had urged that Shuja should not be allowed to appear as a British puppet: 'It is not only his (Shuja's) own success *but the character of our whole policy* which is involved in his finding a willing reception from the Afghans.'[111] Now evidence was steadily accumulating that Shuja was received, if not unwillingly, at all events without any enthusiasm. The hearty reception which he had won in Qandahar was not repeated in Kabul. Macnaghten was virtually alone in his steadfast claim that Shuja was popular. Despite Auckland's admonitions, Keane and the other British commanders treated Shuja with contempt. The Afghan chiefs held themselves aloof: the Ghilzays were rebuffed and the Durranis of western Afghanistan, whose support had been expected, were alienated by the decision to retain the Barakzay bureaucrats at Qandahar. The powerful adventurer, Haji Khan Kakar, was bought over, then promptly alienated, arrested, and sent to imprisonment in India. This last act inspired considerable fear among other chiefs. The ordinary tribesmen, cultivators, and artisans were alienated by the casual plundering committed by the troops and camp-followers and by the inflated prices caused by the demands of the army. In Turkestan and Iran the refugee Barakzay rulers constituted a potential rallying-point for the disaffected. In the light of all this Auckland dared not withdraw his forces and in June he agreed to the recommendation which Macnaghten had made as early as May.[112]

Despite this significant modification of his plans, Auckland was well content with the results of his revolution in strategic policy. When he had reluctantly abandoned the policy of commercial penetration he had taken a leap in the dark. It appeared to have succeeded. British influence was paramount in Bahawalpur, Sind, Kalat, and Afghanistan, while the Sikhs were chained in a new alliance. The danger from the west had disappeared, Russia had repudiated her agents, and the mysterious internal menaces had dispersed. Although the prosecution of his plans had involved a greater commitment than he had intended and although the financial burden would clearly continue for longer than he had hoped, he yet thought that he could see his way ahead towards a stable security system. The Afghan people would be won over to Shuja; the Contingent would replace the Company's troops and eventually would emerge as a national Afghan force; British influence would become confirmed through the activities of the Resident and his assistants, and would work to direct Afghanistan along the path of internal reconstruction and away from that of foreign conquest; and, in the process, beneficent conditions would be created in which commerce could flourish.[113]

Auckland had not forgotten the old policy of political influence through commercial penetration of the Indus. He had simply stood it on its head. He now hoped for commercial benefits to compensate for the losses incurred through political penetration. But as before, the object was political influence. Commerce, which had formerly been the oil to lubricate the political track, had now become the sugar to coat the expensive political pill. A letter from Colvin makes this point clear. The Indian Government sent out a circular to all Political Agents along the Indus asking for information about the siting of commercial fairs so as to promote trade with Central Asia. In a letter to Bell, Colvin revealed that the object was to win wider support in England for the new policy by demonstrating its supposed commercial advantages.[114] In subsequent years Auckland was to produce statistics to drive home his argument that trade was increasing as a consequence of his policy. A closer scrutiny of the evidence suggests that his claims were exaggerated. But it matters little. The new system of Indian defence was to be judged by its political and strategic merits and not by its commercial by-products.

London and Central Asia,
1838–1839

The question is 'who is to be the master of Central Asia?'
Melbourne to Spring Rice, 29 Oct. 1838.

The advantage of a direct operation in Afghanistan is,
that there we go at once to our point; every blow there
struck, tells; Every advantage gained, is one which we
mean permanently to keep; There *we* are strong and Russia and Persia are weak; we commit no body to arms with
the intention of afterwards abandoning them; and in short
we are throwing up works not to serve as a Diversion but
to become the permanent Defences of our frontier.

Palmerston, Memorandum, 29 Aug. 1838.

All the vital decisions regarding the shape of the new British strategy in
Central Asia were taken in India. This was because they were *not* taken
in London. Throughout 1838 Auckland and McNeill sought urgently
for instructions from the Cabinet. But by the time instructions came the
die was cast and Auckland was already committed to intervention in
Afghanistan. In the event ministers in London came to a similar
decision—that is in favour of action in Afghanistan rather than in Iran,
the Baltic, or the Black Sea, or in support of no action at all. Nevertheless, the delay had had an important effect on the formation of policy,
just as the circumstances of the ultimate decision influenced its subsequent development. The subject of this chapter, therefore, is the reasons
for the delay and for the decision, their implications and consequences.

The main initiative in London came from Palmerston. Apart from
the factors of his personality and position, others had to wait upon him
because, as Foreign Secretary, he controlled policy towards Iran and it
was through Iran that the threat to Indian security had emerged. For a
long time Palmerston saw no reason for precipitate action in Iran. He
was not so fearful of Russia as has sometimes been supposed; Russia
could always be stopped by exposing her aims and by strengthening the
national will to do whatever was necessary to oppose her. Too aggressive a policy in Iran might be dangerous because it might bring on a
needless confrontation with Russia before British opinion was ready to
support Palmerston. This caution helps to account for the modest offers

which Palmerston permitted McNeill to bear to Iran in 1836. Palmerston's confidence that he had chosen the right path was reinforced by the optimism of McNeill's early reports from Iran and by the news of the Shah's withdrawal from Khurasan in 1836.[1]

The position began to change at the end of 1837. McNeill then became convinced that stronger action was necessary and sent his assistant Justin Sheil, to London to explain the position. But even then there was no great feeling of urgency. McNeill gave as an additional reason for sending Sheil to London that he was himself proposing to take sick-leave the following summer and he wished first to ensure that Sheil had Palmerston's confidence.[2] McNeill also was still not concerned so much for Herat as for Iran itself in the likely event of the Shah's failure. Nevertheless, in the early part of 1838 the question was fairly posed to Palmerston—what should he do to withdraw the Shah from Herat?

Sheil, supported by Hobhouse, wanted an expedition to the Gulf.[3] Palmerston refused and gave a number of reasons. First, he wanted to see what happened at Herat before he decided what to do. In view of McNeill's advice that Herat was unlikely to fall this was not unreasonable, although it is apparent that ministers had accepted that the fall of Herat was quite possible and that the Shah would then march on into Afghanistan. Palmerston's other reasons, however, are more interesting. One was financial; action in the Gulf would be expensive. Another was political; such an expedition might provoke Russian intervention, leading either to a partition of Iran in which Russia would take the north and Britain the south (for which region Palmerston said Britain had no use) or to the establishment of a Russian protectorate over the whole of Iran. The last reason was plainly strategic; to oppose Russia in Iran was bad policy 'since the weak part of our blade would be pressed by the strong part of hers'.[4]

The implication of Palmerston's refusal to take action in Iran was that Auckland might have to do something in India. Hobhouse, who throughout 1838 was much more disposed towards vigorous action than Palmerston, made this clear to Auckland. Britain had done either too much or too little in Iran, he wrote, and British prestige was now involved. If Herat should fall Iran could not be permitted to take Qandahar. Auckland would have to take action to prevent this happening and Hobhouse suggested, apart from an expedition to the Gulf, a system of alliances (similar to that of Minto in 1808 to 1809) to contain Iran.[5]

Discussions in London continued for three months before a decision was reached. During this time the pressure for action mounted. The tone of McNeill's dispatches on Herat changed and he now declared the town to be of great strategic and symbolic importance and its protection to be essential.[6] Sheil and Hobhouse continued to entreat Palmerston to authorize an expedition to the Gulf; if Palmerston would not accept this advice Hobhouse suggested that action should be taken in Afghanistan.[7] Still Palmerston would not be moved. Partly he had other problems, partly the Cabinet was not interested in India, and partly he did not know what to do and wanted more information. In the end he thought it would be necessary to order the Shah to withdraw from Herat, but 'I cannot as yet authorise you to hold so decided a language', he informed McNeill, aggravatingly.[8] The ninth article of the 1814 Treaty was an obvious obstacle to action. Although Palmerston informed McNeill on 14 April that he did not feel bound by the treaty, Hobhouse wrote to Auckland the same day that the ninth article did make it difficult to interfere.[9] As late as 10 May Hobhouse, on Palmerston's instructions, still took the view that, although, if the Shah continued his attack on Afghanistan, Britain would have to reconsider whether to abide by the treaty, it was yet desirable to obtain the Shah's consent to any modifications.[10] In fact only at this time did Palmerston seem to have understood the problems raised by the ninth article.

In the early part of May the pressure on Palmerston momentarily slackened. This was because of a mistaken deduction by Palmerston himself. Hearing from Istanbul a report that McNeill had left Tehran for Herat he wrongly inferred that this must be because the Shah had given way to the minister's demands and that the urgency was thereby removed from the situation.[11] Hobhouse transmitted this pleasing fantasy to Auckland and in so doing executed a quick and disconcerting retreat from his previous, belligerent gloom. In his official dispatch he approved all of Auckland's proceedings in Afghanistan, including the Governor-General's reproof to Burnes for that agent's promises to Qandahar. He advised Auckland to take no action in Afghanistan until he had heard from McNeill and agreed with the Governor-General in attaching little importance to the mission of Vitkevich. In an accompanying private letter Hobhouse remarked that he would have worried about Vitkevich more if Herat had fallen, but that the latest news 'makes it very doubtful whether that event will take place at all'. He went on:

That Russia has some sinister views it is impossible to doubt, but it does not become our great position to shew a premature jealousy or alarm at any of her misdemeanours. Our politicians at home are attempting to frighten us as to these designs—and the same may be said of most of our diplomatists and agents abroad; with one splendid exception—namely yourself. I conclude however that you are not quite comfortable; nor, to say the truth, are we on this head.[12]

Only the last sentence of this letter would seem to reflect something of Hobhouse's real views. The official dispatch, which was substantially modified at Palmerston' request, and most of the private letter follow exactly the views of Palmerston which were expressed in his letters to Hobhouse.[13]

Ministerial euphoria was rudely dispelled on 20 May when news was received that the Shah had not given way and that McNeill had actually asked Auckland to send an expedition to the Gulf. In fact Palmerston had been shaken shortly before by information sent by Consul Yeames at Odessa confirming reports that Russia was planning an expedition to Khiva and Bukhara. Following this news from Yeames, on 18 May, Palmerston had sent McNeill new instructions permitting him to use slightly stronger language towards the Shah, allowing him to send an agent to Bukhara, and ordering him, for the first time, to insist upon the deletion of the ninth article when he discussed the revision of the Tehran Treaty, and to refuse to continue discussions on the subject if the Shah refused.[14] The latest information also increased the pressure from Sheil and Hobhouse for action. Palmerston himself made vigorous noises: 'I certainly think that we ought to take our stand on this matter and tell the Shah that we shall consider him as in Hostility against us, unless he evacuates Affghanistan whether Herat be taken or not', he wrote to Hobhouse, after receiving the news on 20 May.[15] At that time he seems to have thought that he had the support of Melbourne for the action he proposed, but this belief may have been erroneous, for the following day he wrote to Hobhouse again, enclosing a letter from Melbourne and contemplating that it would be necessary to hold a Cabinet meeting to discuss the matter.[16] It seems reasonable to suppose that Melbourne foresaw disagreement among ministers over Palmerston's prospective declaration of war on Iran and it is clear from what ensued that Palmerston was persuaded to moderate his language to Iran, rather than try to force the Cabinet to reach a decision. At 8.0 p.m. on the evening of 21 May Palmerston wrote again to Hobhouse enclosing a draft dispatch to McNeill and asking for Hobhouse's agreement, before the dispatch was sent to Melbourne for final approval. Hobhouse grudgingly accepted the draft with the proviso that it must be followed by an order to Auckland to act on it.[17] The upshot was that Palmerston refused to threaten the Shah with war until McNeill's official dispatches had been received. In his dispatch of the 21 May he went no further than to allow McNeill to inform the Shah that, whether Herat had fallen or not, if he persisted in attacking Afghanistan Britain would declare the alliance at an end and take whatever steps were appropriate. If the Shah refused to withdraw from Herat, McNeill should retire from the Shah's camp.[18]

In the event Palmerston's dispatch of 21 May did produce a breach with Iran. As shown in chapter 4, McNeill had been stretching and anticipating instructions ever since March 1838 and retired from the Shah's camp on 3 June. When he received Palmerston's dispatch of 21 May McNeill sent his Military Secretary, Lieutenant-Colonel Stoddart, back to the Shah's camp with a note demanding the Shah's withdrawal. The Shah asked if this meant war if he refused and Stoddart, a simple soldier with little regard for those fine distinctions of diplomatic language which had so troubled both Palmerston and McNeill, immediately went beyond his careful instructions and answered, yes.[19]

But this is looking ahead, and in the meantime Palmerston continued to shrink from the decisive action which he had unwittingly unleashed. He speculated about war with Iran and about action in the Gulf, but did nothing.[20] It had been his intention, following Hobhouse's demand, to send Auckland, within two weeks of his new instructions to McNeill, guidance about what action he should take if the Shah did not withdraw from Herat, but all that was sent was a general injunction to support McNeill and to protect Afghanistan from Iranian encroachment.[21] An attack of gout which incapacitated him for ten days at this time may have contributed to his inaction. Lack of time, lack of understanding, lack of confidence in the support of his colleagues, and lack of information all contributed to a problem now made more complex by developments within the Ottoman Empire.

It is impossible to understand Palmerston's policy in Iran during 1838 without referring to the important changes in the Near Eastern situation at the same time. The reports of Muhammad Ali's intention to declare his independence of the Porte, which arrived in London at the end of May and the beginning of June seemed to presage the onset of the dissolution of the Ottoman Empire. With its repercussions on the European balance of power and its threat of a European war, this was an event of infinitely greater consequence to British interests than the simultaneous happenings in Iran. It is plain that apprehension of the possible consequences of the inter-relationship of action in Iran and action in the Ottoman Empire was a factor in determining British policy in Iran. Action in Iran might lead to difficulties with Russia, which in turn would make more difficult successful combined action against Egypt. Also it seemed possible that moves against the Shah could be linked with those against Muhammad Ali.

The significance of this line of thought can be seen in Hobhouse's attitude towards an expedition to the Gulf. In a letter to Auckland dated 9 June 1838 Hobhouse suggested that to counteract Muhammad Ali's ambitions for independence, expeditions should be sent to seize Kharag and Aden. The occupation of the island of Kharag was seen as essentially connected with the prospect of operations against Muhammad Ali in Iraq. Only as an afterthought did Hobhouse add that it might also assist McNeill in his negotiations at Herat.[22] This is not to argue that Hobhouse was primarily interested in combating Muhammad Ali in this manner; only that it is significant that he chose to present the occupation of Kharag in this light. In fact there is little doubt that much older ambitions were also mixed with the decisions of 1838, which antedated both the Iranian and Muhammad Ali crises. Before the eastern crisis blew up, and on the same day on which he had written optimistically to Auckland about the prospects of a settlement with Iran, Hobhouse wrote a revealing letter to Sir Robert Grant, the Governor of Bombay. In accordance with the traditional Gulf policy of the Bombay Government, Grant had suggested taking Kharag. Hobhouse complained that Grant offered no facts to justify occupation of the island, but continued 'I can only say that I shall be very glad to hear of any circumstances which could justify such a measure.'[23] The two letters indicate that Hobhouse's advocacy of an expedition to the Gulf as a means of putting pressure on Iran cannot be taken at face value. He saw Kharag, the obvious goal of such an expedition, first of all in Indian terms, as a possible base in the Gulf, and only incidentally as a means of pressure either on Egypt or on Iran. When this evidence is placed with his simultaneous powerful support of the Euphrates expedition in Iraq and his desire for a stronger frontier in India, it is clear that, for Hobhouse, the early summer of 1838 was a time when international events created opportunities which, judiciously exploited, might enable him to achieve several separate and more ancient objectives.

For Palmerston, on the other hand, the international climate was a restrictive factor, which made him stand back from decisive action in Iran. He was undoubtedly increasingly disturbed by McNeill's reports. According to these, Herat would fall if it were not supported (preferably by a British force) and this event would be followed by the collapse of British influence in Afghanistan. The news of the Russian guarantee of the Iranian–Qandahar Treaty also alarmed him. He wrote to Hobhouse on 18 June: 'it seems to me that we ought now to strike.'[24] But where and when he did not say. All he did was to express his confidence in McNeill and trust that Auckland and McNeill had made joint arrangements for future policy.[25] No official instructions were sent to Auckland about what he should do, although Hobhouse wrote privately, urging the Governor-General to save Herat. Hobhouse suggested either an expedition to the Gulf or that Auckland should encourage the Afghans to attack the Iranian army at Herat. He wrote 'I think I can promise you that you will be supported to the utmost in what decisive measures you may think fit to adopt for this object.'[26] But this was no real substitute for clear instructions approved by the Foreign Secretary.

Not until July 1838 did Palmerston finally decide to break the Treaty of Tehran. Even then, although he announced his intention to Hobhouse on 18 July, official instructions were not sent to McNeill until 27 July. In the intervening period the direct reference to declaring the treaty at an end was removed; instead McNeill was to inform the Shah that, since Iran was subverting the spirit of the treaty, Britain would act without reference to it.[27] Hobhouse wrote to Auckland about this decision on 4 August, pointing out that, assuming McNeill did make such a declaration, Auckland would now be free to offer the Afghan states whatever aid he chose. Combined with the expedition to Kharag, which Hobhouse approved, Hobhouse hoped that such aid would put an end to the threat from Iran. If it failed to do so and the Shah took Herat and continued his advance into India, direct British military operations would be necessary. Hobhouse continued: 'The war once lighted up in Central Asia, both you and ourselves must be in readiness for a conflict with that mighty Power which has in effect set Persia in motion and with which, I presume, we must one day or the other contend for domination on the banks of the Indus.'[28]

It was this possibility of war with Russia which was the ultimate fear which had held Palmerston back from decisive action. Now it seemed that control of events was slipping from him as it became clear that McNeill and Auckland were beginning to take their own initiatives. The Kharag expedition, which pleased Hobhouse, Palmerston found especially worrying. On 10 August he set out the issues in an illuminating letter to McNeill. The Kharag expedition he thought would probably be insufficient to persuade the Shah to abandon the siege of Herat:

and we shall probably be obliged to make war against Persia in Affghanistan by marching an army in conjunction with Runjeet Singh to re-establish the Affghan Monarchy, and to drive the Persians out of Herat and Ghourian. This would I think be the best policy; and Runjeet Singh might be rewarded by Peshawar and Cashmeer. But we must not let the Russians wound us deeply by using the Persian Hand and weapon to strike the blow. Russia will go as far as she can without war with England; but her system of aggrandisement is founded on the principle of encroachment and not of war with equal or superior Powers and whenever she finds such a war likely to be the result of further encroachment, she will stop for the moment, and wait for a more favourable opportunity. On the other hand the English Govt. cannot make war without the support of Parliament, and therefore must not run even the risk of war without having a case which could be stated to the conviction of the House of Commons, because the only chance of Russia pushing matters to extremity would arise in the event of her thinking that on the Point at issue between her and us, we were so palpably in the wrong as not to be able to obtain the sanction of Parliament to our Proceedings. The article abt. the Affghans in the Treaty with Persia is a difficulty at first sight, but I think we should be justified in declaring the Treaty at an end, and we have certainly a right to defend ourselves agst. Parties who pervert the Treaty from its original intention of being a Protection for us, and convert it into an instrument of attack[29]

The inevitability of some action and the fear of the consequences for British relations with Russia of action against Iran was steadily driving Palmerston towards support for action in Afghanistan. The movement of his thought was perceptibly strengthened by the receipt of further news from McNeill on 24 August. From this Palmerston learned that McNeill had broken off relations with Iran on what appeared to the Foreign Secretary to be good grounds, namely that McNeill had mixed up the doubtful ground of Herat with the more solid grievances of the affair of the messenger, etc. But with this news came less pleasing tidings — McNeill's scathing criticisms of British policy and more especially his recommendation to Auckland to send a second, larger expedition against Bushir itself. This last move could drive Iran into the arms of Russia and produce the Iranian Unkiar Skelessi which Palmerston feared, but which McNeill was now ready to accept if it were the price to be paid for maintaining British prestige. Dreading the confrontation with Russia which might ensue, Palmerston now came down firmly in favour of action in Afghanistan. He wrote to Hobhouse on 25 August:

the true measure to take would be to make a great operation in Affghanistan, to push on Runjeet Singh, sending an English Corps to act with his army; to drive the Persians out of Affghanistan and to reorganize that country under one chief, and to pay Runjeet by giving him Peshawar and Cashmere. A good Affghan state in connection with British India would make a better barrier than Persia has been because it would be worth more under our control. We should have the same kind of geographical pull on such a state that Russia has upon Persia.[30]

Thus, apparently independently, Palmerston had in August arrived at a plan very similar to that which Auckland had selected in May. Although the possibility that he had received some private advice from India cannot be excluded—the repeated suggestion that Ranjit Singh should be paid with Peshawar and Kashmir is obviously something picked up from some not too well-informed advisor—Palmerston does not seem to have received any direct news of Auckland's plans at this juncture. The last letter received from Auckland had arrived in London at the beginning of August and had been written on 3 May. Auckland had at that time authorized the Kharag expedition, and, although considering the possibility of allowing Ranjit Singh to advance, had nevertheless opposed the idea and had refused action at Herat without further information. Auckland's minute of 12 May, his instructions to Macnaghten of 15 May, and the account of the subsequent negotiations did not reach London until much later. Communications between England and India were particularly disturbed during the summer of 1838. The Red Sea route was closed by the south-west monsoon until September and the June mail, sent via the Gulf, was lost in the Syrian desert. Fairly conclusive evidence of the absence of any detailed information on Auckland's plans is the absence of any reference to the key figure of Shah Shuja. So there was a seemingly remarkable coincidence of strategic appreciation in London and Simla. But on maturer reflection the coincidence does not seem so remarkable after all. Palmerston's long hesitancy throughout 1838 proves that he had never wanted to take action in Iran. That an Afghan buffer was the alternative was a point which had been argued ever since 1830 and even before. The correspondence relating to Burnes's mission showed that the Sikh connection was ineluctable. Palmerston had simply made a virtue out of a necessity and moulded it into a plan. Equally, it was Palmerston's reluctance to take action in Iran that eventually obliged an unwilling Auckland also to turn to the only obvious alternative line of action within his control. Inaction is often the most revolutionary course.

By a more conventional coincidence Hobhouse received Palmerston's letter on the same day that he received the first details of Auckland's plans. These were contained in a letter from Grant in Bombay, dated 4 June, in which Grant included a summary of a private letter dated 19 May which he had just received from Auckland.[31] Hobhouse, although he knew that it was too late to do anything about the project, had grave reservations about parts of it. He preferred Burnes's plan and wished Auckland had acted earlier in support of the Barakzays. He had never quite rid himself of the impulses of his radical past and to Melbourne he wrote sarcastically, that it was comforting to learn that

Auckland thought the Barakzays had no right to their possessions, 'but it is better not to regard the question with reference to right; or at least, not to that sort of right which enters into the consideration of European politics.'[32] If a Sadozay had to be chosen, Kamran Shah of Herat would have been better; he was the legitimate king and Britain was bound to him in justice and good faith.[33] Nor did he like the involvement of the Sikhs. In fact he thought Auckland had been far too slow in the past; if he had only written to the Shah and warned him to leave Herat alone, all this new great plan would have been unnecessary.[34] But some of these criticisms were scarcely fair. Auckland could hardly have taken the action in Iran which Palmerston had dared not essay and which Hobhouse had feared to recommend. In a sense, by asserting that Auckland should have done just this on his own responsibility, Hobhouse was reasserting the exploded and always bogus Canning theory of the distinction between Britain as a European and as an Asiatic power. The history of relations with Iran had shown the fraudulent pretensions of that argument.

In contrast to the reaction of Hobhouse, Palmerston was delighted at this confirmation of his own line of thought. He liked the suggestion of a permanent defensive system which was implicit in Auckland's plan, and he liked the emphasis on Afghanistan: 'The advantage of operations in Affghanistan is, that there we aim directly at the object we mean to attain; and, whatever we accomplish there, we can afterwards maintain it; and we are not striking a blow in one place in order to produce an effect in another.'[35] He had no regrets for the Barakzays or concern about Kamran Shah. The only part of Auckland's plan about which he had doubts was that which related to the Gulf. He did not object to the Kharag expedition, but he was worried by a misleading reference in Grant's letter to an intention to occupy Shiraz. Such an action, he thought, would be likely to force Iran to seek Russian protection.

By the end of August 1838 the broad outlines of Auckland's strategy were known and approved in London. True, Palmerston was its only ardent supporter. Hobhouse had strong reservations, but felt there was no alternative to supporting the Indian Government, while Melbourne, who read Grant's letters, understood little of the matter. Melbourne merely commented that it was childish of Grant to suggest further increases in the military forces at Bombay since the resources were not available.[36]

Between the end of August and the Cabinet meeting of October 6 to 7, opinion in London hardened in favour of Auckland's scheme. Palmerston continued to argue vigorously in favour of action in Afghanistan. There Britain was strong and Russia and Iran weak and there could be erected the permanent defences of the frontier. Action in southern Iran, on the other hand, was increasingly deplored. Local chiefs who were induced to rise in support of Britain must afterwards be abandoned to Iran; southern Iran could not be held because, if it were, Russia would seize the north and thus threaten both Britain and the Ottoman Empire. As before, Palmerston stressed the interconnections of Middle Eastern strategy: 'Persia in the hands of Russia is a double edged weapon; it has one cut for India, and another for Turkey; and if Persia were completely subservient to Russian policy; Persia would be pushed on to attack Turkey, whenever Russia may choose to make war upon the Sultan.'[37] British control of Afghanistan would frustrate this possibility because Iran could be held in check by the threat of an attack from the east. Action in Iran could be justified only if Britain could find and maintain in power a suitable Shah. But for this Britain lacked the means and might be defeated by Russia—'tho' it would be a grand thing to succeed in, it would be a hard thing to fail in.'[38] Thus, for Palmerston, the creation of a permanent defensive system for British India was only one motive; at least as important were the avoidance of European complications and even the positive use of British India as an indirect influence on the European balance of power. For his colleagues, Melbourne and Lord John Russell, European considerations were clearly paramount in the choice of strategy. Both deplored the larger Iranian expedition because it might lead to war with Russia, Russell adding that the consequence of a defeat in Iran might endanger British supremacy in India.[39]

Much of this September discussion was based upon a misunderstanding. From Grant's letter ministers believed that Auckland had taken up McNeill's second suggestion for a large expedition to Bushir. In fact, Auckland had adopted only the first proposal of a small expedition to Kharag and had rejected the larger expedition to the mainland, correctly divining what the Cabinet's view would be. Not knowing the truth, however, ministers were concerned about the possible outcome and in the light of this, Hobhouse suggested that Auckland should be informed of the opposition to further action in Iran. Curiously enough, in view of the gravity of the consequences which were generally supposed to rest upon the decision, Palmerston and Russell were opposed to sending Auckland instructions on the ground that it might fetter his discretion. Palmerston would have informed him of the Government's views, while leaving him full discretion to take his own course.[40] As with the discretion once vested in Ponsonby at Istanbul to summon up the fleet, effectively it implied resigning to one man, not a member of the Cabinet, the power to involve Britain in war, and sheds an interesting light on the constitutional implications of inadequate communications. Hobhouse, at least, found this omission quite anachronistic and waxed indignant at what he saw as an abdication of responsibility. Only Palmerston, as Foreign Secretary, he argued, was competent to judge the European implications of Auckland's Gulf policy, and if he thought it might lead to war he should say so. Otherwise Auckland should be told that the Cabinet supported him in everything. Hobhouse himself did not fear war with Russia which, like Grey, he thought inevitable. He wrote firmly:

Had the decision been left entirely to myself, I should have instructed the Indian Govt long ago, in a few words, amounting to this."At *all risks, save Herat*". The more I reflect on this subject the more I am convinced that if our influence is not predominant in the Affghan state that of Russia must be. The Affghans themselves, and Persia are not worth a thought. We have but one formidable rival in Central Asia—that is, Russia . . . and unless we are prepared for that great struggle, we had better quit the field, and wait for the attack, which will assuredly not long be delayed, upon our Indian frontier.[41]

Thus the pattern of Dundas and Grenville, Wynn and Canning was repeated with Hobhouse and Palmerston, once more reflecting the opposing tugs of Europe and India in Britain's policy.

Hobhouse's shafts went home and a Cabinet was called at Windsor during the week-end of 6 to 7 October. The increasing alarm about the prospect of war with Russia made agreement essential. Seven ministers were present at Windsor: Melbourne, Palmerston, Lansdowne (Lord President of the Council), Cottenham (Lord Chancellor), Glenelg (formerly Charles Grant and now Colonial Secretary), Russell (Home Secretary), and Hobhouse. Spring Rice, the Chancellor of the Exchequer, was unable to be present, as were Minto (First Lord of the Admiralty), who would certainly have supported Palmerston and Auckland, and Howick (Secretary for War), who would have firmly opposed them and later, in correspondence, did so. The main discussions were held late on Saturday night or early on Sunday morning. Queen Victoria recorded the account of them given to her by Melbourne on the Sunday:

'We've had a long sit of it,' Lord Melbourne said to me. And he said that they had agreed that Sir J. Hobhouse should write to Lord Auckland, that *no* expedition should be sent into Persia (which they hope and are almost certain Lord Auckland has *not* done), but to strengthen and protect our Indian Possessions on the side of Affghanistan and Cabul; and that Lord Palmerston should write a Despatch to Pozzo [di Borgo, the Russian Ambassador] strongly remonstrating with Russia; Lord M. said these were the principal points of the conversation; and that they were 'all for strong measures'. Asked him if Lord John or *he* (Ld. M.) should sit next to me at dinner; and he said, 'Oh! Lord John!' 'which I was very sorry for, though Lord John is an agreeable man.[42]

As anticipated, the decision had thus gone in favour of action in Afghanistan rather than in Iran. Hobhouse confirmed this; the casual cynicism of his final phrase rivalling the delightful comment on the importance of the defence of India which is implied in the young Queen's last sentence:

The general inference from both our instructions being that the first and best mode of contending with Persian armies and Russian intrigues must be to consolidate an opposition to both among the Afghan Chieftains; using the Sikhs and the Ameers of Sinde, perhaps, in the way most advantageous for our purposes.[43]

Melbourne's interesting comment that all were for strong measures is confirmed by Palmerston, who wrote to Minto: 'I was much pleased & surprised to find them all strongly impressed with the necessity of making a stand against Russian Encroachments. John Russell and the Chancellor [Cottenham] were particularly strong upon this subject.'[44] There was a general feeling, he reported, that it was better to stop Russia now rather than later, and this feeling was very good 'because our difficulties hitherto have been to persuade our Colleagues to think that there is any danger from Russia'.

Palmerston was too hasty in his assumption that he had at last won over his colleagues to his view of policy towards Russia. Opposition to the firm line which had been agreed now rapidly developed. Russell, who appears to have had something of an aberration at Windsor, soon resumed his previous advocacy of a more pacific approach, and blamed the troubles in Iran on McNeill's hot temper.[45] Melbourne himself was by no means as confident as he had sounded. He gloomily predicted an immense crisis and a crash in Central Asia and was especially worried about the small expedition to Kharag. 'How to get out of it with credit, or rather with the least discredit, is now the question.'[46] But the most serious attack came from Howick, who would have resigned over the issue, but for the fact that he regarded the policy as that of Auckland and not of the Cabinet. His arguments were contained in two letters to Russell, written in what Palmerston contemptuously described as the 'Parson Adams style of politics'.[47] Howick contended that Russia was too weak to attack India and that Britain had therefore nothing to gain from intervention in Central Asia; the only importance that Herat possessed was what had been given to it by British actions. Britain should instead concentrate on providing good government within India, thereby winning the loyal support of Indians. British power, which was already dangerously over-extended in Asia, should be stretched no further. McNeill had led Britain into a false position from which she should pull back before she was drawn into war with Russia. In a fascinating combination of Whiggish principle and imperial self-interest Howick thus linked the attitudes of Burke with those of Metcalfe and of John Lawrence and set out the elements of a continuing, minority view of Empire. The argument which tipped the balance against him is no less interesting, for essentially it was the argument of the internal frontier, which had been expounded most clearly by Malcolm. Neither Russell nor Spring Rice, Howick's most likely supporters, feared a direct invasion of India by Russia. They agreed that Russia was probably too weak for that course. What they feared was that Russian influence, established on the frontiers of India, would produce disaffection within the subcontinent.[48] Melbourne agreed: 'the danger, Lord M. said, is that it may convulse the Mahrattas behind.'[49] If Afghanistan became hostile, the Sikhs and eventually all the states within the British frontier would follow suit. Like Russell, it was on this ground that Melbourne rejected the arguments of Howick.[50] In this way the arguments of Metcalfe and of Malcolm, which had clashed in India, thus also met in the Cabinet and with the same result. In the end, for the Cabinet, as for Auckland, it was the internal enemy which tipped the balance in favour of a forward external policy.

Palmerston quickly informed McNeill of the Cabinet's decision. He approved the Kharag expedition as a defensive measure only and not as one intended to raise insurrection in southern Iran. British policy towards Iran had not changed; it was still wished to strengthen Iran so that she might form an independent buffer against Russia. All that was required of her was redress in the affair of the messenger and to leave Afghanistan alone. There was no intention of deposing the Shah, partitioning the country, or of weakening Iran by fomenting disturbances in the south. In so far as it tended to produce such results the proposed Bushir expedition was bad policy. It was also dangerous because of logistical problems and because it made possible Russian intervention. If it were not too late, it should be stopped.[51]

Hobhouse's advice to Auckland was delayed, mainly by criticisms by Russell, until the Malta packet of 27 October. In it Hobhouse condemned the Bushir expedition more frankly, because it might lead to war with Russia in Europe. Auckland should instead act to secure in

Afghanistan 'the complete predominance of British influence' by advancing the candidature of Shuja. The Sikhs were to be employed as auxiliaries only; they were to be confirmed in the possession of Peshawar, Kashmir, and Multan alone and these only if it proved impossible to restore the old boundaries of Afghanistan. In this mistrust of the Sikhs reappeared Hobhouse's former sympathy for the policy of Burnes and it broke out again in the permission given to Auckland to make a final effort for agreement with the Barakzays, if the Governor-General saw fit to do so.[52]

The dispatch to Auckland had scarcely left his hands when Hobhouse was delighted to receive, at last, news from India which set his fears at rest; Auckland had rejected further action in Iran. 'You have relieved me from a load of anxiety', Hobhouse wrote.[53] Now Hobhouse looked forward with pleasure to British domination of the Indus and to predominance in Afghanistan. His only reservations concerned the declaration of intent which Auckland had issued on 1 October (Hobhouse was always a man for silence) and the two moral issues of the treatment of the Barakzaya and the demands made on the Amirs of Sind, which touched his Radical conscience.[54]

One final decision remained to be taken by the Cabinet in October 1838 although, like the others, it had already been taken by Auckland in India. Should the expedition to Afghanistan proceed now that the original reason for it—the threat to Herat—had disappeared? News that the Shah had raised the siege in September 1838 was first received in London on 13 October and confirmed four days later. In the circumstances the Cabinet felt they could scarcely order Auckland to go on.[55] At the same time Palmerston and Hobhouse were looking for a permanent solution. Accordingly, it was decided officially to leave the question open, with a vague hint to Auckland that he should continue.[56] Privately, Auckland was urged to go on and even to establish a garrison at Herat.[57] Palmerston already foresaw a possible estrangement between Shuja and Kamran and the latter's turning to Iran and Russia for support. 'This seems to me the moment to strike', he wrote, 'and to make the whole of Afghanistan practically and for military purposes, ours.'[58]

The discussions and decisions of the British Government in 1838 present three features of interest. The first is that their chief practical importance was negative. Had Palmerston done what was urged at the end of 1837 and authorized strong language to the Shah and an expedition to the Gulf, the Shah might then have withdrawn from Herat and the need for further action could have disappeared. Because Palmerston would say neither yes, nor a definite no, to any prospect of action in Iran McNeill received no support and Hobhouse was unable to frame instructions for Auckland. McNeill and Auckland were, therefore, left to devise their own solutions. McNeill, who lacked instructions from Auckland as well, drove on with a more vigorous policy in Iran, anticipated his instructions in the language he used, and recommended extensive action in the Gulf and support for Herat. Auckland, however, refused to be drawn into relatively modest arrangements in Afghanistan, declined to authorize strong remonstrance in Tehran, and consented to only minor and belated action in the Gulf. Because he was so cautious over Iran and Lahore the Governor-General missed the chance of agreement with the Barakzays and eventually found himself committed to an extensive plan for the remodelling of Afghanistan, from which he could not recede, when eventually the modest efforts made in Iran, combined with his own lack of success, persuaded the Shah to withdraw from Herat. Auckland's sensitivity concerning the reactions of Ranjit Singh is a complex factor which has already been discussed. His scruples about Iran, however, were more simple; he was waiting for Palmerston to tell him what he could do there. Thus Palmerston's indecision was a major factor in the eventual strategy which was chosen. Hobhouse would gladly have sanctioned more vigorous action either in Iran or in Afghanistan, but throughout he played only a supporting role. Palmerston was the dominant figure. This was not simply because, as Foreign Secretary, he was responsible for the conduct of relations with Iran, but because his personality and experience gave him an authority which Hobhouse never disputed. Palmerston and Hobhouse discussed all important dispatches but, while Hobhouse often disagreed, he always gave way. This was true even in matters relating to Hobhouse's own departmental responsibilities. One Freudian slip illustrates their relationship perfectly. In 1841 a dispatch relating to Afghanistan was received at the India Board. The clerk asked if it be shown to Palmerston. Hobhouse replied: 'yes, ask him if he has any direction to give', and then crossed out 'direction' and wrote 'opinion' instead.[59] Hobhouse, the former friend of Byron, was, as Melbourne remarked, a man 'of immense knowledge and acquirements; there's nothing he don't know.'[60] As a Radical he carried weight in a Government dependent upon Radical support. But his furtive moral scruples, unlike the self-confident arrogance of Palmerston, served as a weakness. He was a man too much accustomed to playing second fiddle ever to lead an orchestra. His advice, good as it was, never commanded followers. It was Palmerston who played the key role in the Cabinet. Partly the reason for Palmerston's delay may be sought in his preoccupation with affairs in Europe and the Near East; partly in the lack of information and in the misleading inferences which he drew from McNeill's communications; and partly in the limitations of the Treaty of Tehran. But more and more as time went on, the principal cause of indecision was the fear of provoking a clash with Russia. The Foreign Secretary feared such an eventuality both because of his need for Russian co-operation elsewhere, but still more because he feared that he would not be supported either by public opinion, Parliament, or by his own colleagues if he provoked a quarrel with Russia over Iran. To stand forth and then retreat on such an issue would have led to a loss of British influence not only in Iran but throughout the Near East and in Europe as well.

The second notable feature of the discussions concerns the decision to intervene in Afghanistan and not in Iran. Slow as he was to evolve it, Palmerston's analysis of the likely consequences of action in Iran had much to commend it. It is true that McNeill's proposals for firm words and an expedition to Karag might well have succeeded, but what if they had failed? McNeill's answer was a still larger expedition to Bushir, which was the strategy chosen in 1856. At that later date, in the aftermath of the Crimean War there was no fear of Russian intervention, but yet the expedition failed to defeat Iran and Britain launched a further landing and began a march into the interior. What should be the strategic object of such a march was unclear. The occupation of Shiraz, Isfahan, or Tehran would increase the hazards without promising any definite result. With its minimal government and its strong compartmentalized tradition Iran was like an amoeba, which could sacrifice cells without impairing its fundamental vitality. This feature of Iranian political geography was also a weighty argument against the now antique notion of provoking anarchy in southern Iran. The assumption that such action would necessarily weaken and neutralize Iran was based upon an essentially Eurocentred view of political organization and scarcely applied to Iran with the same force that made such proposals the strategic small change of discussions of similar action in Ireland or La Vendée. Also, as Palmerston pointed out, the strategy of anarchy was self-defeating, for it was Britain's object to strengthen Iran against Russia and not to pave the way for Russian control. And thus the question returned to the problem of Russia. The great objection to action in Iran was that it made a clash with Russia more likely and that such a clash could not be localized in Iran but must inevitably have its repercussions in Europe. It was this feature which so worried members of the Cabinet.

The Cabinet's rejection of action in Iran in 1838 had important implications for the development of strategic thinking about the problems of Indian defence. Ever since the early nineteenth century, when it had been officially enshrined in Jones's instructions, the policy of creating anarchy in southern Iran had existed as a possible fall-back policy; an alternative which could be adopted with reasonable prospects of guaranteeing the security of India if the buffer strategy was seen to have decayed beyond redemption. Now, on Palmerston's analysis, it had to be excluded from further serious consideration; it was a mere chimera, more—a dangerous trap. But logically the rejection of the anarchy strategy also dealt a heavy blow at Malcolm's strategy of an independent British power base in the Gulf, for the prospective success of that scheme depended upon the creation of a beneficent, neutralizing anarchy in the states which bordered the Gulf. The war of 1856 apparently demonstrated that Malcolm's Gulf strategy could win modest success, although it also exposed some of its weaknesses. It was not, however, a fair trial, because of the temporary eclipse of Russia. In truth it was only at such times, when Russia was preoccupied elsewhere, that Britain could gain strategic freedom in the Gulf, and the situation did not recur until 1917. At other times, far from British supremacy in the Gulf affording an effective defence against Russia, it was the fear of Russia which prevented the achievement of full British control of the Gulf. On such constricted terms the Gulf strategy could be no real answer to the problems of defending India. If that were true, control of Afghanistan was the only alternative to dependence upon European diplomacy for the defence of India.

Although the major factor in the rejection of action in Iran was the belief that such action could lead nowhere but to an unwanted war with Russia, there were also subsidiary motives. Among these was the question of finance. Action in Iran, unlike action in Afghanistan, would have to be paid for, at least in part, by the British Government. If a parsimonious Parliament were presented with the bill, it would scrutinize the policy behind it most carefully. A bill to the East India Company, on the other hand, for action in Afghanistan, would attract little Parliamentary attention. The complaints of the Court of Directors could be muzzled and those of the Proprietors ignored. Since there were many features of British policy in Iran, including sharp financial practice, the disregard of the ninth article, and the embarrassing fears and suspicions of Russian conduct, which would not bear close investigation, it was desirable to keep these matters as close as possible.

There is a strong negative aspect to the choice of action in Afghanistan. Afghanistan was chosen because it was the only obvious alternative to Iran once it was decided to rule out the notion of doing nothing at all. Palmerston first decided that he did not want to act in Iran and then began to look for merits in action in Afghanistan in order to justify his decision. In this way he discovered the virtues of permanence and of Afghanistan's possible use as a check on Iran and the problematic ramifications through the Ottoman lands into Europe. What had been a *pis aller* became a cornucopia. But the positive attractions of Afghanistan were always much less compelling than the negative reasons for the preference he gave to it; its main attraction was that Herat could be preserved without a clash with Russia.

The third feature of the 1838 decision worthy of notice is the ambivalent motives of those who were party to it. Although the nominal problem was to counter a threat to Indian security, all members of the Cabinet were strongly affected by other motives in reaching their eventual decisions. This applies even to Hobhouse, of all ministers the man most concerned with Indian defence. Hobhouse had long advocated the annexation of Sind and the Panjab and his letters to Auckland make it clear with what pleasure he greeted the opportunity which the crisis offered to assure these older goals. In one revealing letter, dated 5 December, but never sent possibly owing to objections from other ministers, he urged Auckland to secure permanent garrisons on the Indus, especially at Bakhar and Atak:

with garrisons in these two positions and with the armed steamers which will, ere long, I trust, navigate the river, I should regard the Indus as a barrier, almost impassable—and this proceeding will pave the way for that which, I trust, will be accomplished in my life time, namely the peaceful annexation of the Punjab and Sinde to our dominions.[61]

Hobhouse was, in fact, already beginning to look beyond these goals to the further expansion of British power in Asia, as a preparation for the war with Russia which he saw as inevitable and which his Radical sympathies welcomed. In a letter to McNeill he repeated his Indus plans and went on:

Add to this that I shall expect to see a Resident with a strong escort of British soldiers at Caubul and Candahar—and, above all, at Herat and that to these results I would also subjoin the establishment of friendly and intimate relations at Khiva and Bokhara, and perhaps the navigation of the Oxus by two or three steam boats hoisting the British flag.

I hope you do not think me crazy in conceiving and silly in confessing that I entertain such magnificent projects. The more I think on the subject, the more I am convinced that our Russian battle will be fought in Central Asia, and that conviction makes me more rejoiced than most men at the triumph of your policy in Persia.[62]

Plainly, for Hobhouse, it was not merely a question of the defence of

India nor even of the greater expansion of British dominion in Asia but of the defeat of the major threat to the liberties of Europe.

For Palmerston the canvas was still wider. Inaction in Iran and action in Afghanistan were both closely related to the state of Britain's international relations. In the summer of 1838 there was tension with Russia, arising not only from Iran but also from Russian naval and commercial policies and from the Near East, where Russia's threat of unilateral action against Muhammad Ali ran counter to Palmerston's plan for the concerted action by the powers which he carried out in 1840. On October 9, immediately after the Windsor Cabinet, Palmerston made verbal threats of war to Pozzo arising from the Near Eastern situation.[63] In this context vigorous action by Auckland in Afghanistan lent strength to Britain everywhere. To Hobhouse he wrote, at the end of October, that it

will do us the utmost good in India, in Europe and at home. We shall utterly defeat the Russian schemes in the East and that will tell upon Persia; and probably re-establish our influence there and that again will tell on Turkey, and give us a good footing there. That will tell again upon all other European questions now pending, and upon American ones too.[64]

Action in Afghanistan therefore promised to help to solve a problem which had vexed Palmerston ever since 1832, when he had failed to carry his colleagues with him in support of action against Muhammad Ali. Since then he had stimulated a fear of Russia which could serve to strengthen British resolve and to justify a build-up of British strength, especially of naval power. There is some reason to suppose that he used the 1838 crisis as he used other crises, to force his colleagues into a position in which they would be obliged to consent to an increase of naval strength. This was accomplished in November 1838.[65] It was not that Palmerston himself thought that Russia would fight, but that, as Foreign Secretary, he worked best from a position of strength.

The decisions made, it remained to carry them out. This involved dealings with Iran, Russia, and with Parliament, where the decisions had eventually to be defended.

In Iran McNeill had seemingly triumphed. After withdrawing from the Shah's camp at Herat in June 1838 he had begun to make his slow way towards the Ottoman frontier. At Shahrud on 10 July he had received news of the landing at Kharag and Palmerston's instructions of 21 May. As described above, Stoddart was sent back to Herat, where he arrived on 11 August and resolutely cut the Gordian knot. The Shah now had the threat of war which he had demanded and he had to decide whether to withdraw. His appetite for the siege had previously received a severe set-back on 24 June, when a massive assault had been launched and repulsed at a cost of 279 killed, including a large number of senior officers, and 1,196 wounded. Simonich, who put Herati losses at 700 killed and wounded out of a garrison of 4,000, believed, possibly correctly, that the Herati resolve had been still more badly shaken and that a renewal of the attack would be successful. But Haji Mirza Aghasi had had enough.[66] Thereafter the siege became no more than a block-ade and Simonich made his own unsuccessful attempt at mediation. Stoddart's threat therefore fell on fertile ground and on 10 September the Shah raised the siege. McNeill believed he had won and that relations with Iran could now return to their former footing.

McNeill was exquisitely hoist with his own petard. He had been too clever. To avoid appearing to infringe the ninth article, he had deftly buried the Herat question among a host of minor problems. Now the minor problems became the major stumbling-block in the way of the resumption of relations with Iran. Bitterly hurt by defeat and deeply resentful of the treatment he had received, Muhammad Shah refused to make any further concessions, retained Ghuriyan at the eastern end of the Herat valley, and appealed to Russia for help. McNeill was bewil-dered:

It hardly appeared to be possible that after having yielded in the matter of Herat he would have so obstinately resisted compliance in a matter of so such smaller importance [the apology for the ill-treatment of the messenger]. I even calculated on its being the goal of Russia to yield on a point on which he was so clearly wrong for the purpose of enabling him with more effect to urge whatever arguments he might have to adduce in support or defence of his measures in Afghanistan and in depreciation of ours.[67]

Still seeking an explanation comprehensible in terms of his own values, McNeill had already concluded that the Shah must intend to renew his attempt on Herat.[68] Ill and dispirited, and the object of the personal dislike of the Shah and his ministers, McNeill decided to return to England. Sheil, who had recently returned from England, was left in charge of the mission which was now established outside the Iranian frontier, at Erzerum in eastern Anatolia. The detachment had already been withdrawn. After an attack upon Admiral Maitland at Bushir on 25 March 1839, the Resident in the Gulf withdrew to Kharag. Just when victory had seemed at hand the breach was thus made complete. Sheil abandoned hope that Iran could ever become an effective buffer and instead advocated weakening its capacity to injure Britain.[69]

The withdrawal of the mission left Palmerston in direct charge of relations with Iran. The Shah now looked to direct negotiations in London and to the aid of Russia. For these negotiations he chose as envoy Husayn Khan, who had previously been appointed to lead a congratulatory mission to Queen Victoria in 1837. Husayn had risen to prominence through the patronage of Hart, which had enabled him to make a fortune as an army contractor, and had later found favour with the Amir-i Nizam. NcNeill had spurned Husayn's effects to attach himself to the British mission and he had later accepted Russian patronage, although Sheil believed him to be neutral[70] Palmerston wanted nothing to do with Husayn until Iran had first met the British demands, and instructed British Ambassadors along the route to inform Husayn of this. Under the impression that the Shah had given way, the Istanbul Embassy allowed the Iranian envoy to proceed in November 1838, but he was warned in Vienna that he would not be received in England. Despite this Husayn went on to Paris and was eventually admitted to England as a private citizen. In conversations with Palmerston at Stanhope Street on 19 June 1839 he was given brusque treatment. As on previous occasions, the Iranian Government had hoped that the Foreign Office would repudiate their minister when the Iranian case was explained. Palmerston speedily disillusioned Husayn, whom he termed 'an arrant knave'.[71] Husayn was given a lecture and a now very lengthy list of British demands which ranged from the evacuation of Ghuriyan and the conclusion of a commercial agreement down to apologies and compensation for insults and mal-treatment of British subjects and employees.

Husayn sought compensation in Paris for his failure in London. Apparently on his own initiative he endeavoured to persuade France to supplant Britain in Iran. 'Il avait fait les offres les plus séduisantes, avait représenté son souverain comme porté ardemment à une alliance intime avec la France.'[72] But Soult was uninterested in a political alliance and sought only a commercial agreement and information. Husayn did extract something more from his French visit, however, and returned to Iran accompanied by a latter-day Gardane, in the person of General Damas, at the head of an unofficial military mission equipped with arms purchased in France on credit. He was followed shortly afterwards by a French commercial mission under the Comte de Sercey. But the results were disappointing to both sides. The French soldiers received neither pay nor rations, and acquired a memorable reputation for drunkenness and riotous behaviour: the commercial mission returned empty-handed. Sercey found the Iranians barbarous, especially when Haji Mirza Aghasi threatened to send his army to Calcutta, seize Queen Victoria, and hand her over to the brutalities of his soldiers in a public place.[73] Husayn himself received the bastinado, although whether this was for his failings in diplomacy or in financial honesty is unclear. After the flogging the Shah repented and ordered that Husayn should be given a robe of honour. Unfortunately none was available and the unhappy envoy had to supply it himself.[74] The note of farce on which British political relations with Iran faded away is an appropriate one in view of the history of their beginnings. Palmerston was undisturbed by their passing and was in no hurry to reopen contacts. The Afghan position now appeared much more desirable.

Palmerston had also to readjust relations with Russia. There was clear evidence, which could not be overlooked, that Simonich, and his assistant, Goutte, had encouraged Muhammad Shah to attack Herat and that Vitkevich had made offers to Kabul. The Windsor Cabinet decided to demand an explanation and on 25 October Palmerston delivered a lengthy note on the subject to Pozzo. In it he reviewed the course of Anglo-Russian relations concerning Iran. Both European states had avowed an intention to encourage the Shah to maintain internal order and eschew foreign conquest: Simonich's actions were palpably at variance with Russian professions. What was the explanation?[75]

As it happened, a Russian explanation was already on its way, because Pozzo had previously reported Palmerston's verbal remonstrances. Nesselrode's dispatch clearly showed that Russia would not go to war over British actions in the Gulf. The Russian Chancellor disavowed any designs upon India, claimed that Russia had attempted to persuade the Shah not to attack Herat, and defended the Qandahar Treaty as merely intended to promote the independence of Afghanistan. He blamed Britain for disturbing the peace of Iran and of Central Asia. He reaffirmed the view that British and Russian interests in Central Asia were identical; the two states should limit themselves to commercial rivary and avoid political disputes. 'Enfin, plus que tout le reste, respecter l'indépendance des pays intermédiaires qui nous séparent'.[76] On the margin of this dispatch Nicholas II wrote 'excellent'.[77] This comment, however, was perhaps a tribute to drafting skill rather than honesty, for it is clear that Simonich and Vitkevich were held by their own Government to have exceeded their instructions. It had been decided to replace Simonich in 1837 and after his guarantee of the Qandahar Treaty he was recalled, although he did not leave until his successor, Duhamel, arrived in the late summer of 1838. Duhamel promptly recalled Vitkevich who returned to St. Petersburg on 15 May 1839, to be told that his Afghan activities were disowned and he was to return to Orenburg. On the night of 20 May Vitkevich shot himself.[78]

Despite its deficiencies, Palmerston was content to accept Nessel-rode's explanation. The main point was that Russia was not going to intervene. As he wrote to Hobhouse, 'what we want is to carry our posts without a rupture; and as the Russians are disposed to back out it is not for us to criticise their gait in so doing.'[79] After Nesselrode's official reply to his note of 25 October had arrived in December 1838, Palmerston informed Pozzo that it was highly satisfactory and that he would consider the matter closed.[80]

Nesselrode assumed from Palmerston's acceptance of his explana-tion that Britain would now be willing to return to the previous situa-tion, withdraw from Afghanistan, and settle with Iran.[81] He was soon disillusioned. Palmerston was only diplomatically satisfied with Rus-sia. He had no intention of settling with Iran except on his own terms and every intention of establishing a permanent position in Afghanis-tan. So the Afghan expedition and the occupation of Kharag continued. Palmerston and Hobhouse were now in a mood of exultant expansion-ism which communicated itself to Pozzo, whose judgement was weak-nened by ill-health and great personal problems. Pozzo gave the mood more weight and permanence than it deserved in his reports to Nessel-rode. He announced that Britain intended to occupy the entire area between the Indus and the Caspian and that McNeill was planning the conquest of Iran.[82]

These much-exaggerated reports took Nesselrode aback. Russian prestige was involved in achieving a settlement of the difference bet-ween Britain and Iran, and, to a lesser extent, between Britain and the Barakzays. Although Simonich and Vitkevich had been disowned, a residue of moral commitment remained. Nesselrode had himself prom-ised Iran his good offices, later advanced to mediation, in achieving agreement with Britain. Now he was in the position of Castlereagh and Canning after 1813. Force was ruled out. Serious consideration had been given to the occupation of northern Iran as a counter to the British occupation of Kharag, but, apart from the inherent dangers of the operation, Russia lacked the necessary forces, which could be made available only by weakening her position in relation to the Ottomans.[83] Also, it was difficult to see where such an operation could lead, since annexation was excluded. Russia faced the same dilemma in the north that Britain faced in contemplating action in the south.

There was no immediate alternative open to Nesselrode but to try conciliation. He offered Britain mediation, a return to the 1834 policy of co-operation in Iran, and an agreement to maintain the independence of the states which intervened between the Russian and British zones of influence. The mission of Baron Brunnow to London was part of this

policy, which, as Palmerston had anticipated, also extended to other
problems in Anglo–Russian relations. But Palmerston was unyielding.
No more than Nesselrode in the past was he prepared to accept the
mediation of another European power. So, like Castlereagh and Canning earlier, Nesselrode was reduced to urging Iran to meet the
demands of his rival. He had understood from McNeill that British
demands were limited to the evacuation of Ghuriyan and a written
apology for the treatment of the messenger.[84] Duhamel persuaded a
reluctant Haji Mirza Aghasi to write a grudging letter of apology in the
matter of the messenger; no mention was made of Ghuriyan.[85] Nesselrode sent the letter to Palmerston, claiming that it constituted an
adequate apology and that if Britain rejected it she would place herself
in the wrong. Palmerston did reject it. He would not accept it at the
hands of Russia; it was inadequate as an apology; and it failed to cover
all the other numerous British demands.[86]

Palmerston's inflexible attitude towards Russia had yielded much
success. He had bought time for the new British position beyond the
Indus to be secured. Russia had been obliged to acquiesce in the
establishment of British control over Afghanistan and in the continued
occupation of Kharag and had had to suffer a serious blow to her
prestige. At the same time Palmerston had not jeopardized co-
operation with Russia in other areas of the world. But he had achieved
all this at a price. He had rejected an opportunity to define the limits of
power in Central Asia and to secure the defence of India by agreement.
Confident in the strength and permanence of the Afghan position he had
spurned Nesselrode's offer. In doing so he committed both countries to
a policy of competition, not co-operation, in Central Asia. The first
result was the Russian expedition against Khiva.

The British Government had also to persuade Parliament to accept
the new policy in Iran and Afghanistan. This was by no means a
formality. The divided Whig Government was desperately weak
throughout 1838 to 1839: Radical support was alienated by the split
with Durham over Canada; in March and April 1839 the Ministry was
shaken by disputes over Ireland, the Corn Laws, and reform; in May it
was defeated over Jamaica and Melbourne resigned, only to be fortuit-
ously restored by the Bedchamber question. At the least a policy of
caution was indicated. The defence of the British policy was also made
more difficult by two new factors. First, the Iranian withdrawal from
Herat removed the ostensible justification for the Afghan expedition.
Wellington, who had been consulted earlier, now declared that he
thought the expedition should not go.[87] Second, the acceptance of
Nesselrode's explanation had made it diplomatically impossible to

express the doubts about Russian intentions which constituted the true motive for the expedition. As Hobhouse pointed out, the expedition was meaningless, unless it was seen as a defence against Russian encroachments.[88]

The presentation of the Government's defence was skilfully handled. The tactical details were apparently worked out by William Cabell, the clerk in charge of the Secret Department at the India Board.[89] After a brief reference in the Queen's Speech at the beginning of the session two documents were laid before the House on 8 March 1839. These were the Tripartite Treaty of July 1839 and Auckland's declaration of 1 October. The treaty was only a crude modification of a former agreement between two Asian monarchs and Auckland's declaration was a limping, awkward apologia for the expedition. Unsurprisingly, opposition speedily developed. In the Lords Aberdeen cautiously moved for the presentation of more papers; Brougham attacked the declaration as illogical since it began by denouncing Iran and concluded by announcing an intention of invading Afghanistan: Ellenborough denounced the expedition in his most majestic style; it was folly which might yet turn out to be crime. In the Commons Sir James Graham gave notice of a motion.

In response to this gathering attack ministers gradually produced more papers; no less than seven sets relating to Iran and Afghanistan were produced during the session. The papers were cleverly chosen so as to demonstrate the nature of the activities of Russian agents while carefully dissociating them from those of the Russian Government. They were also edited with a view to strengthening the case against Dost Muhammad by making him seem more obdurate than was the case; favourable references to him in the letters of Burnes were excised.

The treatment of Burnes's correspondence achieved considerable notoriety, particularly after some of his original letters were privately published by Dr. Buist, the editor of the *Bombay Times*. The revelation of the garbling led to demands in Parliament for the publication of all the originals. The Whigs and later Peel too refused and not until 1859 was the original correspondence presented to Parliament. Much controversy took place over the question of responsibility for the deception. The evidence suggests a number of hands were at work, including those of Palmerston, Hobhouse, McNeill, and Cabell. According to Hobhouse and Disraeli, however, the main responsibility was Palmerston's When Hobhouse raised the question much later Palmerston told him that the reports of confidential agents were never given to the Commons as they stood.[90] Although Palmerston's general policy on the editing of

Parliamentary Papers has been discussed extensively,[91] it may be appropriate at this point to quote a general statement of his policy which has been overlooked.

The practice of this office in selecting papers for publication is to make results public and to abstain from unnecessarily communicating details, and it is especially objectionable to publish without necessity Papers tending to shew a constant and unceasing interference on the part of an Agent of His Majesty in the internal affairs of a foreign government.[92]

Palmerston was therefore at least consistent, if not especially admirable in his presentation of the new policy to Parliament. In fact, whatever the importance of the principle involved in deceiving Parliament, the actual changes made in the dispatches were of less significance than has sometimes been argued. Principally they frustrated some moral objections to the treatment of Dost Muhammad.

One revelation which greatly assisted the Government's case was that of the identity of independent strategic thought in London and Simla. As Hobhouse wrote to Auckland, the papers were 'to shew that your policy and our policy by a marvellous co-incidence had been the same'.[93] Hobhouse's satisfaction was sadly impaired, however, by Auckland's failure even to acknowledge the dispatch in which the President had set out Cabinet policy at the cost of so much trouble and argument. It has already been shown that the coincidence was not so marvellous as Hobhouse claimed; the Cabinet had been aware of the main outlines of Auckland's policy at the time the October decisions were taken. The omission of Hobhouse's earlier 1836 dispatch need not be assumed to be deceptive; the choice of papers was confined to a shorter period, and the June 1836 dispatch was probably not considered.

Ministers themselves said little, preferring to leave the papers to speak for themselves. Emily Eden complained of ministers' silence in the face of the early Opposition attacks and attributed this to ignorance. But while this accusation might fairly have been directed against Melbourne, ignorance was not the reason for the abstinence of Palmerston and Hobhouse. It seems more likely that their silence was tactical—to encourage the Opposition attack to develop and eventually to overreach itself and to deploy the full defence only if the Opposition chose to press a formal debate.

In the event the Tories dropped their opposition. The motions by Aberdeen and Graham were not pressed. Graham's motion in the Commons was the vital one. It was first put down for 2 April, then postponed until after Easter, and finally abandoned altogether. For ministers this was a fortunate outcome for, as Hobhouse informed Auckland, if it had come to a vote the Government would have been defeated.[94] Public debate would also have weakened the Government by exposing the opposition to their policy in the Court of Directors. Although the Chairman, J. L. Lushington, had approved the Secret Committee dispatch of 24 October, his Deputy, the Tory Richard Jenkins, never saw it, being at Brighton at the time. Lushington assured Hobhouse that Jenkins would have approved, but other evidence suggests that this was not so and that Jenkins shared the widespread feeling in the Court that the money would be better spent on improving India. William Butterworth Bayley, the third member of the Secret Committee in 1839, was also an influential critic of any tendency towards permanent occupation.[95] In the light of this the Opposition's failure to press the motion needs more explanation.

The Conservative leaders were advised by two men with direct knowledge of the problems involved. These were Henry Willock and Henry Tucker. Willock's opposition was based upon a straightforward preference for Iran over Afghanistan as a buffer; Afghanistan would be unstable, unreliable, and the British presence there would push Iran into Russian hands; subsidizing Iran would be better and, if necessary, Iran could be used to disturb the Russian frontier.[96] This of course echoed Ellenborough's 1828 *jihad* policy. Tucker's criticism was more fundamental. In the first place he denied the existence of any danger to India from either Russia, Iran, or Afghanistan. The expedition was therefore unnecessary and, furthermore, it was dangerous because, by concentrating British forces in the north-west, it exposed India to attack by other enemies. The policy involved an undue reliance on the Sikhs and involved the immoral treatment of the Amirs of Sind. It was also too expensive; further, if the expense had to be borne it should fall upon Britain, not on India, because the war was for national objectives and arose out of what was essentially a European question. This last was a point argued by Tucker ever since he had opposed the 1835 decision to spend Indian money on the Iranian alliance. The war in Afghanistan was launched, he argued: 'Because it is not convenient for the home government to enter the lists with that Power (Russia) in Europe and because it is more convenient to throw the whole burden of a perilous war and the charge of onerous treaties and alliances *upon the resources of India*.'[97]

Tucker urged Ellenborough, Peel, and Wellington to oppose the Afghan expedition in Parliament. In the Ellenborough papers is a long memorandum dated 23 April 1839 which reproduces many of Tucker's

arguments, supplemented by material apparently obtained from correspondents in India, including Burnes and General Cotton. The
grandiloquent phrasing suggests that it was a speech rather than a
memorandum, intended to be delivered in the debate that never was.
Ellenborough argued against the new policy on the grounds that Russia
had as much right in Afghanistan as Britain had; and that the expedition would be too expensive and dangerous because of the diversion of
troops; he supported, in its place, a policy very similar to that of Burnes;
to check Sikh expansion; to uphold Dost Muhammad; and to withdraw
the army from Afghanistan.[98] The striking divergence from the position
Ellenborough had adopted in 1830 and 1835 is very evident and
strongly suggests that he had merely seized upon whatever arguments
against the expedition lay to hand. It was perhaps a speech that he was
not sorry not to have delivered. Wellington also was not in a good
position to oppose the expedition. He himself saw it as a national, not a
party question and, unlike the Cabinet, actually believed in the existence of a great Russian plan to attack India. At the end of 1838 he had
been consulted privately by ministers and shown some of the papers. In
a memorandum dated 21 November he had argued that firm control of
the Indus was necessary and had revived the 1830 plan of economic
penetration.[99] If circumstances made it necessary he would approve the
expedition, although, especially after the lifting of the siege of Herat, he
hoped it would not go. Somewhat inconsistently he argued later that
the existing frontier was best, and compounded the confusion by representing the Indus to be the actual dividing line between Sikhs and
Afghans. He then condemned the new policy as likely to aggrandize the
Sikhs and involve Britain in continual interference in Afghanistan.[100]
Between the ambiguity of his position and his soldierly reluctance to
criticize a policy while troops were actually involved in carrying it out,
it was not easy for him to come out in public opposition and indeed, in
November 1838, he announced that he would not oppose it in the
Lords.[101] Peel was wary of Afghanistan and preferred the safer tactical
grounds of Canada and the Corn Laws.[102] Graham himself seems to
have come to the same conclusion that the Central Asian question was
poor tactical territory for an attack on the Government. Although he
claimed that he had dropped his motion rather than embarrass an
already-committed Indian Government, there is evidence that he was
worried that he might run into trouble on the subject.[103] Finally, the
Tories may well have thought it too early in the session for an outright
attack on the Government. Even in May Peel had reservations about
forming a Ministry; earlier he was still more doubtful about the necessity of dependence on unwanted Radical support.

Probably the Tories were wise to avoid a debate on Central Asia; the later military successes in Afghanistan, although greeted by Melbourne with contemptuous derision, were treated as triumphs. The question was not raised in Parliament again until after the disasters of 1842, apart from a brief mention by Lord Stanley during a no-confidence debate in 1840. As a result the Parliamentary analysis of the great changes in Central Asian policy never took place. The silent Hobhouse did not regret this; there had been altogether too much interest in India for his peace of mind.[104] Tucker, who did regret the omission, attributed it to the traditional British apathy towards the possession of India; the British public did not appreciate the value of a possession without which Britain 'would be as melancholy an object as Palmyra in the desert'.[105] Metcalfe and Emily Eden would have agreed with Tucker and there may, after all, be much justice in their view. Although one can explain the Parliamentary silence in terms of tactics, the lack of interest even by independent members suggests an indifference to a subject alien to the British heart because it was believed to be remote from the British purse.

In the Press the Afghan expedition received a mixed reception. The *Edinburgh Review* which supported the policy, conceded that there was probably a majority against it.[106] But there was influential support from some papers. The *Quarterly Review*, which might have been expected to oppose the Government, came out with an article in support of a buffer state in Afghanistan, a wonder explained by the fact that the reviewer was McNeill.[107] The *Times*, always strongly anti-Russian, supported the Government in a manner, almost surpassing its customary style:

From the frontiers of Hungary to the heart of Burmah and Nepaul, from the eastward of the Ganges to the Nile and Danube, the Russian fiend has been haunting and troubling the human race, and diligently perpetrating his malignant frauds and perfidies to the vexation and disturbance of this industrious and essentially pacific empire.
England . . . has at length apparently shaken off her death-like sleep. She detected seasonably the treacherous conspiracy, framed and encouraged by the known agents of Russia, along the whole northern frontier of British India embracing Burmah on the one extremity, on the other Cabul.[108]

It is a question whether such support was not more alarming than the words of the Government's critics.

The difficulties which the Ministry encountered in Parliament, in the Court of Directors, and to a lesser extent in the country at large explain some of the vacillations observable in its policy during 1839.

The vaulting enthusiasm shown by Palmerston during the autumn of 1838 soon disappeared as the winter wore on, and a strong note of caution was sounded. Thus Hobhouse, ignoring the fact that Auckland's demands on Sind fell far short of his own previous suggestions, admonished the Governor-General for contravening his own declaration in that state.[109] Auckland was also criticized for sanctioning arrangements for Kalat which tended towards permanent involvement and warned not to take any action tending to result in the permanent occupation of any position in Afghanistan. Oddly enough, in view of what had been said earlier, he was advised not to advance on Herat.

The caution was purely tactical. Although Hobhouse may have had some genuine fears lest Auckland should over-extend himself, his main concern was to placate his critics. In a letter to Palmerston he explained that criticism of Auckland's actions in Sind and Afghanistan was to satisfy the Directors who made up the Secret Committee and Melbourne himself.[110] To Auckland he explained. 'It is of the utmost importance, not only so far as India but as Europe is concerned that there should be no appearance of any intention on your part to acquire any permanent possessions beyond the frontier.'[111] As late as September 1839 he found it necessary to repeat the same point: 'above all remember, that not only the Home Authorities but their Parlimentary critics look with the utmost apprehension, not to say jealousy, at any extension of British Power beyond the Indus.'[112] Palmerston was much less affected by criticism than was Hobhouse, and never thought it necessary to temper his early conviction that the permanent occupation of Afghanistan would, in the long run, prove to be the best and cheapest policy. Although he stated that he would prefer control without military occupation, he plainly never believed this to be possible.[113] The news of the victory at Ghazni which arrived in October delighted him. 'This glorious success of Auckland's in Affghanistan will cow all Asia and make everything more easy for us', he wrote.[114] Hobhouse too was vastly relieved and at last began to drop his caution. By December he was back in his familiar role of the advocate of more vigorous action in Afghanistan.[115]

At the beginning of this chapter it was claimed that the new Central Asian policy was made in India. The history of procrastination and inconstancy in Whitehall would seem to confirm this. But those same characteristics illustrate a vital feature of the strategy of Indian defence. London left the defence of British India to the Indian Government, but in a negative way it defined the limits of strategy. The limits were set by the general needs of British foreign policy, in which Europe had priority, and by the circumstances of the domestic political situation. The Indian Government had to make its choice within the framework imposed by these considerations. In this light Palmerston played an important role in the making of the new Afghan policy. By his delays in 1838 he forced Auckland into Afghanistan and by his refusal of agreement with Russia in 1839 he made it impossible for Auckland to withdraw. Palmerston's failure to appreciate the limitations of British Indian resources led him to continue to press for further expansion and greater permanence and contributed in no small measure to the eventual débâcle. Palmerston imagined that India could carry part of the burden of British foreign policy and that it might serve as a powerful support to the Foreign Secretary: he was to discover that India too imposed its own limitations on British foreign policy.

PART III

THE AFGHAN SYSTEM

Afghanistan, 1839–1841

> We found India easy to govern because she was like the
> pack horse, well accustomed to carry a burden, and the
> one we have imposed may be light in comparison with
> others she has borne, but Affghanistan with its unsubdued
> mountain tribes is a horse which has never known bit or
> bridle and never been mounted, that will plunge and fret
> as she feels the curb, and none but a skilful rider should
> mount him, and he will best manage him by keeping a
> tight rein and alternatively caressing him and punishing
> him with the cold iron.
>
> Mackeson to Maddock, 9 November 1841.

A strong Afghanistan under firm British control was to be the centre-piece of the new British policy in Central Asia. Afghanistan was not to be either another Iran, subsidized but uncontrolled, or an Assam, garrisoned and controlled; it was to be a new type of buffer state. Shah Shuja was to have full internal independence; although continually prompted to introduce reforms which would make his government popular, his army efficient, his revenues productive, and his commerce free and abundant. Auckland anticipated some opposition to reform from the old nobility and the wilder tribes, but believed that this would be outweighed by the appreciative support of the trading, artisan, and agricultural classes, all of whom would feel the benefits of the British connection. British control would be limited to foreign affairs: Russian and Iranian influence would be excluded; and the Shah persuaded to renounce any ambitions to expand beyond the established borders of Kabul and Qandahar.[1] It was a dream which was not to be realized; and this chapter is the story of the reasons for the failure of the Afghan buffer to develop as planned, of the attempts to construct an alternative system, and of the eventual complete and tragic failure.

In theory Shuja controlled the Government of Afghanistan. He had his own Government. At its centre, in Kabul, was a Council and a bureaucracy. The Council was composed primarily of Durrani tribal chiefs, particularly members of the Sadozay clan to which Shuja belonged. Many had shared his exile in Ludhianna and now lusted for the recompense of their fidelity; others had rallied to his support after his return to Afghanistan and now looked for the reward of their treachery. The bureaucracy on the other hand was that which had formerly served Dost Muhammad; its members were recruited mainly from the Persian-speakers of Kabul. In almost every province Shuja appointed a Governor, who was often chosen from among the loyal, local chiefs, but was occasionally a man sent from Kabul. An exception was the situation in Qandahar where there was a second royal government, subordinate to that of Shuja in Kabul, but superior to the Governors of the provinces which lay within the old Qandahar state limits. This government was headed successively by three sons of Shuja; first, until October 1840 by Fath Jang; then until May 1841 by Safdar Jang; and finally, by Shuja's eldest son, Muhammad Timur. These princes each maintained in Qandahar their own Council, formed from the great Durrani chiefs of western Afghanistan, and their own bureaucracy. As in Kabul, the latter was initially that inherited from the former Barakzay Sirdars and was recruited from the Parsiwan community in Qandahar: under the supervision of a minister the bureaucracies in both capitals were responsible for the collection of revenue and the maintenance of accounts. In Kabul the supervisory minister was chosen by Shuja himself. He selected a man named Mulla Shakar Ishaqzay, who had served him as Chief Minister in Ludhiana: according to Burnes, the Mulla was old, deaf, and had no memory. At the end of 1840 a new Chief Minister was chosen: this was Usman Khan Sadozay, who was given the title *Nizam al-Dawla*. Usman was a strong, capable man and much more acceptable to the British, but he had many enemies among the great chiefs. Nevertheless, with British support he became, in 1841, the most powerful man within the Afghan Government.

Judged by British standards the personnel of Shuja's Government were entirely inefficient. The Persian-speaking bureaucrats appear to have been reasonably competent, although they were continually accused of fraud, embezzlement, and the pursuit of private feuds. But the chiefs had no interest in or capacity for carrying on an orderly government: to them, administration was an opportunity to fill their pockets. Shuja's own example was not calculated to persuade them of the virtues of abstinence. In contrast with the frugal Dost Muhammad he lived luxuriously, spent lavishly, and by 1842 had put by a fortune of £200,000. All this was achieved while he complained bitterly of poverty. As a Sadozay Shah, he felt impelled to present a more splendid front than his predecessor, and insisted on the recognition of his dignity, referring to himself as 'our Blessed Self'. The British dismissed him as arrogant and haughty, but there was more to him than this. Despite his dismal record of political failures, Shuja was intelligent and perceptive and much of his irritating punctiliousness sprang, like that of Charles de Gaulle, from a feeling of impotence. For long Macnaghten was the only British official who sought to defend him, but at length the Envoy himself succumbed to the common view of Shuja. He is 'an old woman, not fit to rule this people', Macnaghten wrote in September 1841.[2] Macnaghten never had much opinion of the Afghan chiefs who surrounded Shuja. 'The character of this class of people is, I regret to say, very much alike and very indifferent', he remarked at an early stage.[3]

A more important factor in the failure of Shuja's government than the want of able men was the want of adequate resources. The revenues of Kabul and Qandahar were puny. Qandahar yielded only 600,000 rupees, all of which were consumed in its government. The gross revenue of Kabul was 3,200,000 *kham* rupees; 2,300,000 net. The sum did not cover the cost of Shuja's personal military forces, let alone his personal expenses which amounted to 1,000,000 rupees.[4] From the outset of his reign Shuja could survive only with the aid of British subsidies.

Shuja's army was quite inadequate. His military forces may be divided into three groups: his regular units, his feudal cavalry; and the Contingent. The regular units may be subdivided into two elements. First, directly under his own control, were certain semi-disciplined infantry forces, which he had inherited from Dost Muhammad. These were recruited from Hindustanis and Arabs and were housed within the Shah's own fortress in Kabul, the Bala Hissar. Second, nominally under Shuja's command, were a number of specialized units which were scattered throughout the country. Most prominent amongst these was the artillery, formed out of that of the Barakzays and comprising twenty guns and over four hundred men, under the command of a British officer, Lieutenant Robert Warburton (1812–63). The cost of the artillery—65,000 rupees a year—was paid directly from the British treasury. The artillery was employed extensively in small units in minor campaigns, usually associated with the collection of revenue; in the period up to August 1841 there were no less than fifteen such campaigns.[5] Next was a corps of six hundred Sappers and Miners, developed from a unit formed originally by its commander, Lieutenant William Broadfoot, in 1840 and later enlarged and renamed. Essentially it was a pioneer corps, employed in the construction of forts, bridges, and roads. Like the artillery, it was paid by the British and effectively under full British control. Last was the largest group of all, consisting of a number of specialized local forces, all raised, paid and commanded by British officers. In western Afghanistan, at Quetta, were the delightfully named Bolan Rangers, nominally eight hundred but in practice about five hundred Kakars from the Shal valley, under the command of Captain J. D. D. Bean. Between Quetta and Qandahar, nominally employed in safeguarding communications through the Khojak Pass, was a small force of one hundred and fifty cavalry named the Achakzay Horse and commanded by Lieutenant J. B. Bosanquet. In the most easterly part of Afghanistan two groups protected communications between Peshawar and Kabul. These were the Khaibar Rangers, a force of a nominal strength of eight hundred mainly Afridi tribesmen, who were employed in the Jalalabad region. Their headquarters were at Gandamak and their commander Captain H. P. Burn. Immediately to the east of this unit and primarily responsible for the security of the formidable Khaibar Pass, as well as assisting in the area further west, was a mixed force of Yusufzays, Laghmanis, and Bajauris, known as the Jezailchees, from the traditional long rifles with which they were equipped. They numbered a thousand; their headquarters were at Beshbulaq; and their commander was Lieutenant Ferris. The various elements in the corps had originally been raised separately for particular duties and were amalgamated into one unit within Shuja's army only in 1841.[6] In the mountainous area immediately to the north of Kabul was the Kohistan Corps. Originally this unit had numbered nine hundred men, but by April 1840 it had declined to only half this number and by November was still little more than five hundred. It was composed of Sunni Tajiks (Persian-speakers) from the Kohistan valley and had been founded in an attempt to enlist support in a wild and, because of its proximity to Kabul, a dangerous area. To conciliate the local chiefs concessions had been made to tribal feeling and recruitment of companies on a clan basis allowed. But service remained unpopular and requests for discharge were frequent; when ordered on service in Zarmat in the summer of 1841 one hundred and fifty men deserted. The strength of the corps was then only three hundred and fifty men and Macnaghten considered disbanding it altogether. The unit was commanded by Lieutenant Maule and its headquarters were at Charikar.[7] Finally, a regiment of Afghan infantry was raised soon after the restoration of Shuja by Captain P. Hopkins, but it deserted to Dost Muhammad during the former Amir's effort to recover his power in September 1840. Including the Artillery and the Sappers and Miners there were some four thousand men, nominally owing allegiance to Shuja, but in reality under British control. Their military value was slight: essentially, the local corps represented a device for employing the local population in the hope of winning their loyalty, or at least of inducing them to refrain from outright hostility;

they were thus fundamentally political units and as such represented an important potential agency of British influence and a considerable challenge to the traditional local power structure.

The second part of the Shah's forces consisted of what may loosely be termed 'feudal' forces. It comprised the cavalry which was provided by chiefs in return for grants of land revenue. At the musters of 1839, 5,662 horsemen were recorded at Kabul and 1,218 at Qandahar. In 1840 Kabul produced 5,797. But these figures greatly exaggerate the real strength of the feudal cavalry. Originally the horsemen were the tribal followers of the chiefs; more recently it had become the practice of the chiefs to hire Kabuli artisans and shopkeepers for the occasion of the muster, mount them on hired horses, and dismiss them immediately after they had been enumerated. The money for their maintenance was pocketed by the chiefs. For military purposes the feudal cavalry was unusable; they occasionally performed military parades for purposes of political prestige, as in the Kohistan in 1840 and at Girishk in 1841, but on these occasions it was necessary to pay them additionally for each campaign. But their importance was not military but political. It was described in the following words by Captain R. S. Trevor who was given charge of the feudal Horse:

We must not look on the Irregular Cavalry merely as a military body, in that light 3 Regiments might annihilate it tomorrow, but as an instrument which enables H. M.'s principal subjects to appropriate the greater part of his revenues without making any return, and which has continued so long that its destruction would certainly be considered an invasion of private property.[8]

The charge of providing a body of horsemen was in fact the equivalent of a payment to the chief concerned, for with the charge he received an assignment of revenue. This assignment might be on his own lands, in which case he lived tax-free, or it might be on the lands of others, in which event he collected the money with the aid of his own men. His profit came from the difference between what he collected and what he actually paid his horsemen. The feudal cavalry therefore provided a major source of income for the chiefs. 'All H. M.'s Ministers, I might say every Affghan who has access to him, are interested in the increase of the Irregulars', wrote Trevor. As will be described, it became an object of British policy to reduce and eventually to eliminate the feudal cavalry and to replace it with new, disciplined cavalry corps, namely the Janbaz and the Hazirbash. A head-on conflict over the future of the feudal Horse thus became inevitable.

The third part of the Shah's force was the Contingent. The origins of this force have been described in chapter 7. Its intended role was

central to Auckland's thinking on Afghanistan. The Shah was expected
to maintain internal security by the use of his ordinary regular forces
and with the aid of the feudal cavalry. The Contingent was to be
reserved for defence against external foes and to be entirely under the
authority of the Resident. The officers were British and the men were
Hindustanis. It had been intended that the Hindustanis should be
gradually replaced by Afghans as these were trained. Shuja would
never be safe, wrote Auckland, until he could rely upon Afghan troops.[9]
It was accepted that Britain would pay for the Contingent until Shuja
established himself, but it was intended that he should then take
responsibility for its support. To all intents and purposes it was the
equivalent of the Contingents which were being established within
Indian states under British control.

The planned establishment of the Contingent comprised the following: a small unit of artillery under the command of Captain Anderson;
two regiments of irregular cavalry, numbering two thousand men; and
five regiments of disciplined infantry, each containing eight hundred
men. Each of the cavalry and infantry regiments had two British
officers. Command of the whole Contingent was originally given to
Major-General Simpson, who received his orders, nominally from
Shuja, but actually from Macnaghten. Three Staff Officers assisted
him: Captains J. Griffin (ADC), T. McSherry (Brigade Major) and H.
Johnson (Pay and Commissariat).[10]

The Contingent never became an effective force. Hastily recruited,
many soldiers were of poor quality and it was left behind on the
advance. Nor was it ever brought together in Afghanistan for proper
training but was committed piecemeal in small actions throughout the
country and scattered in garrison posts. Unsurprisingly, service was
unpopular; in March 1840 it was almost two thousand men below
strength.[11] The cavalry was particularly inefficient, for the pay was too
low to enable the men to maintain their horses properly. The British
officers disliked their duties: Afghanistan was too expensive; Shuja too
proud; and the work unsatisfactory. Many of them looked upon the
Contingent merely as a stepping-stone to more lucrative political
duties. Simpson soon left and was replaced by Colonel Abraham
Roberts (d. 1873), who in his turn quarrelled with Macnaghten and
was replaced by Brigadier T. J. Anquetil (1781–1842), 'a very odd
worthy little Jerseyman' as his General, Keith Elphinstone, described
him.[12] Elphinstone added that Anquetil had been thirty-four years in
India and knew no one, so perhaps Anquetil was well suited to the command. So little control did the Shah have over his own Contingent that
Macnaghten even forgot to inform him of the change in command.[13]

Several attempts were made to improve the Contingent. The number of European officers was increased to five in each regiment of infantry, three in each of the cavalry regiments, and from two to four officers in the artillery. A sixth infantry regiment was added. Also the pattern of recruitment was changed. The Hindustani recruits were unsatisfactory and after the disastrous episode when Hopkins's Afghan infantry deserted to Dost Muhammad and the unencouraging example of the local corps, the original idea of replacing the Hindustanis with Afghans was allowed to slip away. Instead the British began to recruit Gurkhas, or more correctly those men from the hill-country of eastern Nepal and Bhutan who later came to be known inaccurately, but gloriously, as Gurkhas. Half of one of the original regiments had been recruited from the Gurkhas and they were found so suitable in Afghanistan that the number was steadily increased and replacements were sought. Anquetil did not like them and complained, in terms that were to be all too familiar in the future, that they were spendthrift, too fond of drinking and gambling, and overburdened with women and children.[14] Their training, however, was not adequate to develop fully their undoubted fighting qualities in Afghanistan. The employment of these redoubtable Hindu mercenaries, however, was a symptom of the changing British attitude towards Afghanistan; if control would not be conceded willingly it would be enforced by alien arms.

Neither the Shah's forces nor his revenues were therefore able to meet the expectations which had been held for them. Even with the addition of three thousand local troops the Shah's own regular and feudal forces were unable to maintain internal security. The Contingent, which was to have been reserved for foreign defence, was accordingly called upon to perform continual constabulary duties. But it too was quite unequal to the task of preserving internal quiet. Consequently the forces of the Company and the Crown, which were to have been withdrawn altogether from Afghanistan, had to be retained in the country and were constantly employed in the suppression of disturbances. Shuja's revenues too were quite inadequate to meet the costs of maintaining his rule. He could not even pay his own administrative and personal military expenses, let alone the costs of the various local corps and of the Contingent. The burden of maintaining these fell entirely upon the Company, which also paid a subvention towards the regular budget. By 1841 the cost of subsidizing the Shah's military forces had risen to £454,000.[15]

The failure of the Sadozay Government to meet out of its own resources the demands made upon it was partly because its means were fewer than anticipated, but mainly because the demands were so much higher than had been foreseen. In short, the Government of Shah Shuja was quite unacceptable to large numbers of Afghans and they demonstrated their disapproval in continued disturbances which upset the peace of Afghanistan throughout the years from 1839 to 1841. Elsewhere I have considered in detail the causes and character of these disturbances.[16] For our purposes it will be sufficient merely to repeat the results of that analysis.

The disturbances took place in many areas of Afghanistan. In the area of Jalalabad in eastern Afghanistan there were disturbances in Bajaur, Kunar, and among the Khugiani tribe. In the north there were major uprisings in the region of Bamian and in the Kohistan. In western Afghanistan there was widespread unrest among the Ghilzays and among the Alizay section of the Durrani confederation in Zamindawar. A common pattern covered all these disturbances. They originated in local disputes and factional rivalries, which were often exacerbated by changes in local authority and in the balance of local power which followed the Sadozay restoration. They were further inflamed by economic discontent. Afghanistan was a poor country with poor communications. The demands of the occupation forces pushed up prices, according to some estimates, by as much as five hundred per cent. At the same time the incomes of many chiefs and members of the ulema were static, or increasing less rapidly than prices. Often there was an increase in the effective demands of tax-collectors, who could now call upon the support of superior military force. The consequences of such demands were frequently armed resistance, attacks on Government forces, and the closing of roads. The Government would retaliate by punitive expeditions, which increased in size as they failed to achieve their purpose until finally Company troops were employed. But the risings remained essentially local in character and there was little contact between one and the other. Charges were often made that they were inspired by Sikh or Herati intrigue, but, as will be shown, these charges were unfounded. They were not part of any nationalist movement for no such movement existed. In so far as they had any common element, it was religion. As might be expected, most opposition was justified in religious terms; Shuja was accused of introducing an infidel government into Afghanistan and of making it impossible for Muslims to live according to the Sharia.

From the point of view of Britain the principal significance of the risings was that they demonstrated that Shuja could not survive without continued British support. This meant that men and money must be poured into Afghanistan indefinitely. Afghanistan thus became a far greater commitment than had been anticipated; its relationship with

British India must therefore be something other than that which had been planned. In practice the modification took the form of the steady growth of British interference in the internal government of Afghanistan. By the latter part of 1841 this interference had reached the point where the real government of Afghanistan had been taken into British hands and British agents were proposing a total revolution in the social and political structure of the country.

The media of British control over Afghanistan were the Army and the Political Agency system. The nature of British command of the Contingent and of the local forces which were raised in the name of Shah Shuja has already been considered. In effect all these forces came under the ultimate power of Macnaghten. In addition to these forces the British could also call upon the Crown and Company forces which were retained in Afghanistan in 1839 and reinforced in 1841. By the summer of 1941 these forces numbered ten thousand men. All in all, the British disposed of over twenty thousand troops in Afghanistan by that time.

The Political Agency system grew to form a shadow government alongside the Afghan Government, both at the centre and in the provinces. At its head was Macnaghten as Envoy and Minister. His character has already been discussed. It may simply be remarked that he was as proud and vain as ever, resenting with almost childish passion any reflection upon his honour or judgement. After the departure of General Keane at the end of 1839 he had no rival. Keane was a rough, brutal soldier, but he stood up to Macnaghten. His manners, however, made his leaving a happy moment not only for Macnaghten. His successor as military commander, Sir Willoughby Cotton, by contrast got on well with Macnaghten, although Cotton said this was only because he always gave way to the Envoy, even against his own better judgement.[17] In 1841 Cotton was succeeded by General Sir Keith Elphinstone. Elphinstone was an old, sick man and knew nothing of Afghanistan. With him Macnaghten usually got his own way, although Elphinstone never had much opinion of Macnaghten. He believed that the Envoy, like other Political Agents (with the exception of Burnes), was too fond of military expeditions, 'although, between ourselves,' he confided, 'I never saw anyone less conversant with the necessity of means and measures for carrying them on.'[18] But the effect of Macnaghten's dominance over his military counterparts was that his political schemes were never subjected to a scrutiny of their military implications. It was the Political Agents who directed military operations.

Under Macnaghten was a chain of agents. His chief assistant and prospective successor was Alexander Burnes. Burnes never knew whether he wanted to be an original man or a wise man; an *enfant terrible* or an *éminence grise*. In his last years he adopted the public appearance of the latter. He had learned the apparent value of reticence and was now content to sit and wait for his turn. He described himself as a highly-paid idler. 'I give paper opinions but never work them out', he wrote.[19] Although he was once employed on political work in the Kohistan in 1840, for the most part he concentrated his efforts on the reform of the Afghan customs system and upon collecting intelligence from Central Asia. Apart from Burnes and his other assistants in Kabul, Macnaghten controlled a chain of agents located in all the principal provincial centres. At Jalalabad was Captain George Macgregor; at Qandahar, first, Major Robert Leech, and, from May 1840, Major Henry Rawlinson; at Quetta was Captain J. D. D. Bean; in northern Afghanistan was first, Dr P. B. Lord and subsequently, Major Eldred Pottinger; in Ghazni, until March 1841, Lieutenant Charles Burnes (a brother of Alexander) acted as Political Agent and was then replaced by the military commander, Lieutenant-Colonel J. MacLaren, who in his turn was replaced by the new military commander, Lieutenant-Colonel Palmer in June of the same year. These were the principal agents: each had assistants either serving with them or on detached duties at posts or with troops on campaign. Their numbers grew steadily throughout the period. By their access to Macnaghten they were able to control the disposition of troops and to intervene in the Afghan Government.

In every area of Afghanistan there was a steady tendency towards the domination of the local Government by the Political Agents. They commonly advocated 'unlimited interference'.[20] They mistrusted Afghans and advocated the extended use of British agency in the government of Afghanistan. Their motives were mixed. Partly their actions and recommendations were pragmatic; they were drawn into treating the consequences of a disease which they thought could have been prevented. Partly their interventions were ideological; Utilitarian and Evangelical impulses thrust them forward to the creation of a better society. Interference was equally justified by a humanitarian sympathy with the oppressed; a philosophical predisposition to favour the greatest good of the greatest number; and a Eurocentred contempt for Asian institutions. Older officials like Wade, brought up in the softer tradition of Malcolm, deplored this tendency among the younger men:

There is nothing more to be dreaded or guarded against, I think, in our endeavours to re-establish the Affghan Monarchy than the overweening confidence with which Europeans are too often accustomed to regard the excellence of their own institutions and the anxiety that they display to introduce them in their new and untried soils.

Such interference will always lead to acrimonious disputes if not to a violent reaction. The peoples of these countries are far from ripe for the introduction of our highly refined system of Government or of Society and we are liable to meet with more opposition in the attempt to disturb what we find existing than from the exercise of our physical force.[21]

But Wade's own day of power was nearly done and the tendency which he deplored was in the ascendant. In Afghanistan British officials found it impossible to stand back from what they regarded as abuses. Commonly, their interpositions were against the chiefs and in support of the cultivators. Humanitarianism was here supported by the political assumption that British rule could find a firm foundation in the hearts of the Afghan masses. Partly, however, the simple motive of ambition cannot be passed over. Military pay was low and promotion slow. The Political Service offered high pay and allowances; responsibility and power—even over senior army officers; and the prospects of rapid fame, distinction, and reward. The political officers thus had a ready incentive to enlarge their sphere of action and all arguments which they advanced must be read with this condition in mind.

In Kabul Macnaghten long sought to resist the pressure from his subordinates and to implement the non-interventionist policy which Auckland had expounded. But his agents did not follow his advice. At Bamiyan Lord had full control over the local Government. The Afghan Governor was ignored and recalled to Kabul before the end of 1839 at the insistence of Lord, to whom everyone came with their grievances.[22] Thereafter Lord ruled on his own in the north, although he once remarked that had an Afghan Governor existed he might have been able to avoid the use of force to control the local tribes.[23] But Shuja would not appoint a new Governor. No suitable man was available, he declared, adding, in a significant revelation of his own attitude to the functions of government, in any case the revenue was not due.[24] In Quetta, Bean acted in virtual independence.[26] At Qal'a Abdullah, Lieutenant J. B. Bosanquet was 'by his own account Governor of the district—the chief. . . can do nothing without his sanction'. Rawlinson reported that Bosanquet intended to introduce British supervision of the collection of revenue.[26] In Jalalabad, Macgregor moved cautiously but in the same direction. He secured control of the administration by bribing an Afghan official in the revenue department to supply him with a list of revenue items. With the aid of this information he was able to intervene to secure the changes he desired.[27] But the best evidence of the progress of intervention comes from Qandahar.

Qandahar had not been integrated within the Kabul Government, but had retained its own administrative system. The first Prince-Governor, Fath Jang, took little part in affairs of state, preferring to amuse himself with occasional homosexual assaults on members of the garrison. Neither did his deputy, the prominent Durrani notable, Ata Muhammad Khan Popalzay, possess much power. The actual work of administration was in the hands of two Parsiwan officials, Taqi Muhammad and his brother, Wali Muhammad. They received little pay but, by their control of all income and expenditure, had ample opportunity to supplement it. Taqi was the lessee or farmer of all the land revenue and of the miscellaneous taxes levied in the town and district. The brothers were employed despite all accusations of oppression and fraud, because they were the only men who understood the system.[28] Inevitably they looked for support in office not to the Sadozay Government, which was thought to represent the interests of their Durrani enemies, but to the British agents.

The first British Political Agent in Qandahar was Major Robert Leech, who had previously served there as assistant to Burnes in 1837 to 1838. Leech was an odd and amiable character. A fat, jolly man, he was popular with other Britons who went to surprising lengths to protect him from the consequences of his errors. For, as an administrator, he was completely miscast. He had few literary skills; his reports were illiterate and brief to the point of enigma. Accountancy was a complete mystery to him; he submitted no accounts, and although, after his dismissal from Qandahar, he was given six months leave in Kabul to complete his accounts, there is no evidence that he ever did so. But worst of all was his inability to prepare the ground for any proposal.

Leech found the instructions which he was given neither acceptable nor workable. Macnaghten had laid down two broad rules for his guidance. He was neither to appear to interfere in the government nor was he to employ Company forces except in an emergency. In general he was to stay in the background and to leave administration to the Afghan Government. Leech could not contemplate leaving anything important to the Qandahar Government 'if the assemblage of the few inefficient and dishonest individuals collected here deserve that name'.[29] The Parsiwan revenue-managers, he declared, were corrupt; Ata Muhammad was evil, and Fath Jang wholly dependent upon Leech. Leech claimed that he advised on everything except the Sharia and even drew up the instructions for the *Kotwal* (Chief of Police), the *Kalantar* (Mayor), and the *Mirab* (Superintendent of canals) in Qandahar, instructions which Fath Jang issued as though they were his own. In May 1840 Leech suggested the replacement of the revenue-managers by a new man, Mirza Ahmad, although this substitution was not carried out until much later. At the same time Leech submitted a list of nominations for the Governorships in fourteen Qandahar districts, having selected his candidates 'for their quiet unpretending dispositions, and for their attachment to his Majesty's interests and not for their abilities or influence in their respective clans'.[30] The only real limitations on Leech's ability to control the administration were his lack of information and his dependence upon Afghan executive agency. He therefore produced a series of proposals designed to remove these limitations.

Leech fired his first salvo in January 1840. At that time there was a disturbance near the River Helmand in western Qandahar. A revenue-collecting expedition led by Muhammad Alam Khan, son of Muhammad Taqi, had encountered resistance and a British officer accompanying the force, Captain J. Macan, had reported evidence of misrule. Leech promptly proposed to establish a British agent in the Helmand area, who would reform the administration and promote agricultural development.[31] Before he had received Macnaghten's rejection of the suggestion, Leech followed this with a more formidable barrage of proposals for the entire reform of the Government of Qandahar. Fath Jang, he declared, was incompetent. Leech, himself, should be given the title *Na'ib Shahzada*, i.e. deputy to the Prince, and authority to interfere in all affairs, whether political, military, or financial. With this authority Leech intended to reconstruct the Qandahar Government. Afghan government was bad and fostered discontent. In its place should be established full British control. British officers should be placed in each district to superintend the collection of the revenue. The inefficient feudal army should be abolished; and the chiefs responsible for supplying horsemen should be given pensions instead. Afghan regular troops should replace the feudal army. All this, of course, would be expensive and Leech proposed to pay for his reforms by taxing the Durranis, many of whom enjoyed rent-free land-grants (*tiyul*).[32]

Macnaghten refused to accept these far-reaching proposals. Leech, he announced, had failed to provide adequate information by which the merits of his proposals could be judged: the proposals themselves involved sudden and undesirable changes in Afghan customs: but above all, the proposals involved 'nothing more or less than the assumption of the Government of the country by European officers'.[33] Such interference was forbidden by treaty, disavowed by declaration, and impossible if all Company troops were to be withdrawn, as intended, in the summer of 1840. To implement Leech's proposals 'would be proclaiming to the world what it is desirous to avoid, that we are exercising a direct control in the Government of this country'.[34]

Leech had gone too far too quickly. His unhelpful dispatches, his failure to produce adequate financial statements, certain of his actions, and now these extensive proposals which betrayed, according to Auckland, 'the dangerous eccentricity of his judgement'[35] made it imperative to remove him from Qandahar. Auckland insisted on his dismissal. But before he left Leech delivered one final, comprehensive broadside affecting not merely Qandahar but the entire Government of Afghanistan. He now proposed not just European superintendance of Afghan agents but European superintendence of Indian agents. No chiefs, *mullas*, or any Afghans at all should be employed in administration. Afghanistan should be divided into twelve districts and the method of accounting and the system of payment of the bureaucracy revised. The power of the Afghan nobility should be broken and the existing chiefs replaced by new men. The independence of the two great tribal confederations of the Ghilzays and the Durranis should be broken; both should be taxed and the Durrani chiefs obliged to live near the capitals where they would be under close Government control. *Waqf* lands (the main financial support of the ulema) should be taken under state control and the revenue surplus from them appropriated by Government. Lastly, Afghanistan should be disarmed; only Government servants should be permitted to bear arms.[36]

Leech's Shogunate proposals misfired because they were premature and because they were put forward by Leech. He had given too many hostages to fortune to champion any cause, especially one so radical. Moreover, he lacked that skill in presenting his arguments which his successor, Henry Rawlinson, possessed in such abundance. But Leech had fairly anticipated the inevitable direction of British policy in Afghanistan. Rawlinson was to carry on the same policy and it was already being put piecemeal into practice.

One of the earliest examples of the use of British agency in Afghanistan was in the district of Gurmsel in north-western Qandahar. There the new Governor, appointed because of his loyalty to Shuja, was very unpopular. He was able to maintain himself, reported Leech, only because of the assistance of a British officer, Lieutenant Duncan.[37] But Duncan had no official position. The first formal breach of the policy of non-intervention occurred when Lieutenant E. P. Lynch (16th Bombay N.I.) was appointed Political Agent in the Ghilzay area in the summer of 1840.

The large Ghilzay confederation was spread all through eastern

Afghanistan as far west as Kalat-i Ghilzay, where the hills begin to give way to the plains of Qandahar. In this western section of the Ghilzay country, across the main road from Kalat-i Ghilzay to Mukur, lived the Tokhi and Hotaki tribal divisions of the Ghilzays. In August and September 1839 their existing chiefs had been displaced in favour of chiefs who were thought to be more loyal to Shuja. But the new chiefs had little power and preferred to live in Qandahar. Leech advised that to achieve effective power they would require the support of regular troops, a garrison at Kalat-i Ghilzay, and the supervision of a British Political Agent.[38] In April 1840 disturbances took place in the area and eventually regular troops were committed. Accompanying them as Political Agent was Lieutenant Peter Nicholson.

Nicholson argued that the Ghilzay problem was a special case which required, for its solution, European intervention. Ghilzay chiefs were not reliable and Durrani chiefs were unacceptable to their ancient enemies. Nevertheless, reforms were necessary in order to prevent anarchy: smaller tribes should be merged with larger; nomads encouraged to settle; the power of chiefs increased; and the interests of the cultivators protected. Nicholson proposed to accomplish this through the appointment of a British Political Agent to supervise the Afghan revenue-collectors.[39] It was a proposal very similar to that which Leech had made in relation to the Helmand, but now Nicholson presented it as an exception to the rule, and it was on this basis that the proposal was accepted.

Macnaghten's acceptance of Nicholson's Ghilzay proposal marks the first breach in the policy of restricting interference to the giving of confidential advice and the avoidance of formal, ostentatious intervention in the government of Afghanistan. He wrote to Calcutta:

Averse as I am in principle to interference on the part of British officers with the internal administration of this country, yet I feel convinced from the degeneracy and corruption which a long course of misrule has brought about, that a modified and limited degree of interference on our part exerted with as little ostentation as possible will be absolutely necessary for the establishment of tranquillity and the security of His Majesty's interests.[40]

Auckland accepted the change in his policy with still more reluctance. He urged Macnaghten to keep interference to the minimum and to make it as unobtrusive as possible so that 'all arrangements should be shown to the world as guided by an Afghan leader'.[41] In a private letter accompanying the official dispatch Colvin emphasized the Indian Government's strong wish to avoid interference, but went on:

it is a wish, our hope of realising which, is gradually becoming much diminished. If we are forced to come forward more generally to bring the entire country into order we must at least strive to make our interference as little obtrusive and offensive as possible.[42]

The principle of formal intervention was thus accepted and its future extension contemplated. Nicholson's recommendations were put into force after he had suppressed, with considerable severity, a Ghilzay rising in June 1840. Nicholson executed some rebels, replaced one chief, settled new allowances, redistributed land, and imposed on the chiefs a nominal obligation to supply horsemen. To maintain control in the future a military force was retained in the area, a fort planned, and Lieutenant E. P. Lynch appointed as Political Agent. Lynch was a member of an Irish family and one of several brothers in the service of the East India Company, one of whom was prominent in Iraq. Like Henry Rawlinson, Lynch had served with the British detachment in Iran. He was instructed to hold 'unreserved intercourse with the ryots [cultivators] and give prompt attention to their complaints'.[43]

The Ghilzay country became quiet for a time. The fort was not built and in October 1840 Lynch withdrew the military force and retired to Qandahar for the winter. Trouble soon recommenced and in January 1841 Henry Rawlinson recommended drastic action. A fresh military expedition should be sent against the Ghilzays in the spring, to teach them a firm lesson with 'no concession whatever to expediency or importunity'.[44] Macnaghten agreed and it was decided to proceed to establish a fort on the great mound at Kalat-i Ghilzay, even now a forbidding and commanding position, alongside the main road from Qandahar to Kabul. Macnaghten also suggested a new measure of control over the Ghilzay chiefs: the formation of two regiments of Ghilzay Janbaz, that is, disciplined cavalry under Afghan officers and European inspectors. Apart from their military use, the Janbaz also embodied the notion of providing employment for tribesmen and so reducing the power over them which was possessed by their chiefs.[45]

Until troops were available Lynch was sent back to the Ghilzay lands to try conciliation. Although the policy had considerable success, it is clear that Lynch did not intend it as more than a temporary expedient. As soon as a small force arrived from Qandahar on 21 April, Lynch adopted a much more aggressive policy. He occupied the mound, hoisted Shuja's flag, and fired a salute. He then laid out plans for a fort including accommodation for hostages, an alarming feature which became known to the Ghilzay chiefs. On 30 April Lynch attacked a fort seven miles from Kalat and killed almost all its inhabitants. Lynch later produced stories of extensive conspiracies to justify this act, but they appear to have been without foundation. The evidence suggests that Lynch was deliberately trying to cow the Ghilzays by a demonstration of ruthless force and determination.

Lynch did not report one other fact which none the less caused great anger amongst the Ghilzays. One of the chiefs who had been involved in the May 1840 uprising was named Walu Khan Shamalzay, and was connected with the powerful Shah-al-Din family from which the rebel Ghilzay leaders of 1839 had come. Walu had been given a free pardon by one British officer, Captain W. Anderson, but was arrested and nearly executed by Nicholson in June 1840. Nicholson did not carry out his intention, but his haste is suspicious and one possible reason for it is suggested by the fact that immediately afterwards Lynch took Walu's sister as his mistress.[46] Leech even suggested that some Ghilzays, who were executed by Nicholson, might have been silenced to prevent them from disclosing information which was dangerous to other Afghans.[47] But no reliance should be placed on this last story, for Leech and Nicholson had quarrelled bitterly over the suppression of the 1840 Ghilzay rising and Leech's story is not supported by other evidence. But what is known is that when Lynch performed his ostentatious ceremony Walu's sister stood next to him and the Ghilzay chiefs bitterly resented this visible demonstration of their humiliation.

As a consequence of Lynch's actions, reported and unreported, the Tokhi chiefs deserted him, a fact that he did not choose to reveal either then or later, and shortly afterwards he found himself at the centre of a widespread rising and besieged amid the foundations of his fort at Kalat. Lynch reported that the situation was hopeless and decided to resign. Earlier, in an effort to stave off impending disaster he had persuaded a number of Ghilzay chiefs to go to Macnaghten and plead his cause and had induced Muhammad Timur also to write on his behalf.[48] But Lynch was too late. Macnaghten had already ordered Rawlinson to replace him. 'I regret to have observed Indications that he would prefer his private Interests to those of the public service', he wrote.[49] When he later discovered more of the true facts he wrote that Lynch was not only imprudent 'but a very dangerous character'.[50] Lynch was replaced as Political Agent by Rawlinson's assistant, Lieutenant E. K. Elliott, but shortly afterwards Elliott was transferred to western Qandahar and none other than our old friend Robert Leech, who had been sent back to the area as interpreter with a punitive force, took his place. For personal reasons Leech remained directly responsible to Macnaghten and not under the orders of Rawlinson.

Order was now restored in the Ghilzay country. Two Company

regiments were sent to destroy the crops of the rebels and to keep open communication. Macnaghten, however, did not continue with the policy of increasing interference in the Ghilzay area. The cost was too great. The puppet chiefs were restored and left to pacify the Ghilzays. 'Our policy', he wrote, 'should be to content ourselves for the present with keeping the roads safe and refrain from attempting to pursue the insurgents into their strongholds.'[51] In August 1841 the Company regiments, having completed their task, were withdrawn and Leech was left in the now completed fort at Kalat with a small garrison and a few hostages.

The most interesting feature of the Ghilzay disturbances is the way in which they demonstrate the power of the Political Agents. Once in the field they possessed almost a monopoly of information and it was virtually impossible for Rawlinson and Macnaghten to dispute their conclusions. They were able, therefore, to enjoy a free hand in pursuing their own policies so long as they could avoid disaster. In the case of Lynch it seems clear that he ceased to be an independent arbiter, standing above tribal politics, but became deeply involved in them. The evidence indicates that he hoped to become all-powerful in the Ghilzay country; as early as December 1840 Macnaghten revealed that Lynch was trying to free himself from Rawlinson's control.[52] It was Lynch who persuaded Rawlinson to adopt a severe policy and to reject a policy of conciliation by which the chiefs who had been expelled in 1839 would have been restored to favour. Lynch had no authorization for the provocative policy which he adopted in April 1841 and which may well have been inspired by private objects. His own statements about the causes of the uprising cannot be accepted. Lynch pushed too hard, his flagrant disobedience became too noticeable, and with his removal his policy was reversed. Even so, Macnaghten's reluctance to dismiss him was evident. Macnaghten was always loyal, perhaps too loyal to his subordinates, and worried about the effect of dismissal on their prospects. His own unwillingness to enforce ruthlessly his policy of non-intervention thus served to weaken it. In the right hands Macnaghten was malleable and this is nowhere better demonstrated than in his relations with Henry Rawlinson.

Rawlinson took over as Political Agent at Qandahar at the end of June 1840. His later career in Iraq, Iran and as an influential member of the India Council in London, testify to the range and quality of his intellect. After the withdrawal of the detachment from Iran at the end of 1838 he had returned to India. His knowledge of Persian made him an obvious candidate for employment in Afghanistan and his political talents won him the respect of Macnaghten and employment at Qandahar. The instructions given to Rawlinson regarding non-interference were similar to those which had been given to Leech. He was told to confine himself to 'judicious council without assuming an ostensible part in the Civil Administration of the Country'.[53] But Rawlinson immediately encountered the same problems as his predecessor and reached similar conclusions about their solution.

Rawlinson soon decided that the Afghan Government of Qandahar was bad. Fath Jang was impossible and Rawlinson recommended his replacement by Muhammad Timur. Since Timur was not available Rawlinson suggested that he should be allowed himself to intervene directly to prevent misgovernment. Macnaghten opposed this last suggestion, but agreed that Fath Jang should be deprived of real power in favour of his deputy, Ata Muhammad Khan, although everything should be done in the name of Fath Jang.[54] But Rawlinson persisted and, in October 1840, Fath Jang was packed off to Kabul where, significantly, he was given a very favourable reception by his father. In his place was put his brother, Safdar Jang, who quickly proved to be even more troublesome; he quarrelled with the *vaqil*, Muhammad Taqi, and accused him of fraud. Rawlinson complained and Macnaghten empowered him to threaten Safdar Jang with recall to Kabul if he did not behave himself.[55] In May 1841 Safdar was replaced by Muhammad Timur. Rawlinson also had trouble with Ata Muhammad, of whom he endeavoured to make use in his relations with the Durranis. Eventually, Rawlinson unearthed a mysterious plot, involving several prominent Durrani notables including Ata Muhammad, and in consequence Ata was dismissed and sent to Kabul with other chiefs in June 1841. Most important of all, Rawlinson began to intervene in the bureaucracy.

Rawlinson had at first supported the Parsiwan revenue-managers against the Qandahar court nobles and used them to supply the evidence to remove the opposition in the Court. But the same mysterious plot that felled Ata Muhammad also placed the activities of the Parsiwans in a curious light. As a result they were dismissed and Taqi imprisoned in Kabul. In his place was put the very able Mirza Ahmad, already proposed by Leech. Mirza Ahmad worked closely with Rawlinson. Apart from this hold on the revenue system, Rawlinson also intervened directly in the administration of Qandahar. British officers in the Qandahar garrison refused to admit the jurisdiction of the *Kotwal* over their sepoys. This led to much resentment in Qandahar and Rawlinson was forced to intervene 'to protect the Townspeople from the violence of the Hindoostanees'. He proposed that a British officer, Lieutenant Jackson, should be appointed as *Kotwal*.[56] Rawlinson also proposed to dismiss as corrupt the *qadi* of Qandahar, who had been appointed by Shuja, and reinstate his Barakzay predecessor. In March 1841 Rawlinson wrote to a friend 'I have practically the whole local Government in my hands.'[57]

Side by side with his gradual extension of *de facto* control Rawlinson produced a series of extensive proposals for social and political reorganization. These hinged on the destruction of the power of the Durrani confederation, the tribal group which surrounded Qandahar and extended westwards. It was the Durranis who both provided the rulers of Afghanistan and were also the greatest menace to the security of the state. In the heyday of the Durrani Empire, in the late eighteenth century, the Durranis had been conciliated by a share in the profits of expansion; when the Empire began to shrink they turned on their own Government. Recognizing the danger of dependence upon the Durranis, the Barakzays had adopted a different policy from that of the Sadozays and had endeavoured to exclude the great confederation from political power. The Qandahar Sirdars had recruited their bureaucracy from the Parsiwans, and their meagre forces from the Parsiwans, Ghilzays, and other minority groups in Qandahar. Within the compass of their limited means they had sought to remove the economic basis of Durrani power, namely to resume, where possible, grants of rent-free land; and to employ the resources thus gained in strengthening their own Government. This system, recorded Rawlinson, 'continues to be a favourite project with all the financiers of Qandahar unconnected with the Dooranees'.[58] The most notable of these 'financiers', of course, were the Parsiwan revenue-managers, who had been employed by the Barakzays and continued in office by Shuja.

The restoration of Shuja had rekindled Durrani hopes of renewed pre-eminence. In Kabul they found that they had returned only to the appearance, but not the reality of power. In their homeland of Qandahar the position is complex. Broadly speaking what had happened was that Shuja had resumed some of the rent-free tenures granted by the Sirdars to their own supporters and given them to his own supporters. But, in general, he left the Durrani land-holding system substantially unaltered. Even as early as June 1839 Macnaghten anticipated that it might be necessary to exact real, and not merely token, military service in return for the grants.[59]

The Durrani hopes of quick financial benefits from Shuja's restoration were largely frustrated. The old Barakzay assessments continued to be applied by the old Barakzay revenue-managers, abetted by Leech. The Parsiwans continued the same, apparently deliberately brutal method of tax-collection by which free subsistence for the revenue troops were demanded. Elliott, and to some extent Rawlinson, thought that the revenue-assessments and collections were a significant cause of the disturbances which were later to disrupt the district of Zamindawar in the far west. Rawlinson considered the assessments too severe.[60] From this evidence and from the evidence of his recommendations for the resumption of rent-free tenures, Leech was obviously strongly influenced during his stay at Qandahar by the philosophy of the Parsiwans. The Durranis derived little benefit from his control of the Government.

Following the dismissal of Leech a new attempt to conciliate the Durranis was made. In August 1840 Shuja announced fresh concessions. He reduced the nominal obligation to supply one horseman for every ploughland (*qulba*) to one horseman for every two ploughlands. But in so far as the obligation had been largely nominal, the concession had little practical importance. Nor had another concession, involving the offer of increased opportunities for paid military service, since this depended upon the willingness of British political officers to employ Durranis. The third concession was the most important. This involved the restoration of certain rent-free tenures, formerly resumed by the Barakzays. However, it would appear that the concession was not widely applied; some important chiefs were excluded and few gained any real benefit.[61] In the short run no one enjoyed any advantage. The Durranis complained that they had not received any concessions and Shuja sent a Durrani notable to investigate the situation at Qandahar. When questioned, Taqi Muhammad admitted that he had not given the concessions and claimed that he could not afford to do so. He owed Shuja money and, in any case, since the current year's revenue had already been spent in advance it would have to be collected on the old basis.[62]

Widespread discontent now existed amongst the Durranis, who were encouraged in their opposition to the Parsiwan tax-farmers by Safdar Jang, Ata Muhammad, the Durrani court nobles in Qandahar and Kabul, and probably even by Shuja himself. So much is clear from Rawlinson's vast, obscure, and ramifying plot, the details of which are unimportant, but which had the effect of clearing away both the Durrani leaders and the Parsiwans and leaving Rawlinson a free hand in Qandahar. The plot also demonstrated a link between the Durranis of Qandahar and the single major Durrani uprising in the area to the west of the Helmand, centred on Zamindawar.

Zamindawar was one of the main centres of the Alizay section of the Durrani confederation. The leader of the rebellion in Zamindawar was one Akhtar Khan Alizay, who had once been governor of the province, but who was dismissed by Rawlinson. Akhtar's strong influence in the province made him a man to reckon with and by the end of 1840 his defiance of government had reached the point when Rawlinson decided that military action was necessary to secure control of an area which was strategically situated between Herat and Qandahar.

The familiar pattern of escalation soon revealed itself. First Rawlinson sent an Afghan force to the area. This was defeated and succeeded by a regular force which won a brief victory in January 1841. But Akhtar promptly recovered his strength and Rawlinson felt obliged to send a larger regular force. In March 1841 a compromise was reached through the mediation of a number of Durrani notables led by Ata Muhammad. Although he did not believe the peace would last, Rawlinson accepted the agreement, for he had come to fear a general Durrani rising and hoped that a settlement with Akhtar would avert it.[63] The regular troops were withdrawn from Zamindawar. Rawlinson, supported by Macnaghten, would have liked to retain them on the Helmand, but for once the Political Agents were defeated by military resistance. The Commander at Qandahar, General William Nott, was as stubborn and ruthless as Keane and he was able to induce Elphinstone to support his demand for their return to Qandahar.[64] In consequence, the Helmand was left undefended when Akhtar resumed his defiance in May 1841 with an attack on the fort of Girishk, where the main road to Herat crossed the Helmand. Girishk was successfully defended by its small garrison of Afghan and Hindustani troops. Regular troops had to be sent back to the area and once more Akhtar was driven off. But this time Rawlinson was determined to enforce a more drastic solution. He obtained permission to use regular troops throughout the area and by August 1841 had forced the rebels to submit. In September and October 1841 a much larger force, comprising two sepoy regiments was sent to pacify the area more permanently. To obtain this result the Political Agent with the force, Elliot, was instructed that 'such a degree of stringency must therefore be observed in carrying out your measures as shall produce a strong and lasting impression.'[65] The expedition had some success, but this was not to be permanent.

The chief importance of the Zamindawar rebellion was that it confirmed Rawlinson in the view which he had derived from his other experiences that a drastic solution of the Durrani problem was necessary. Earlier he had sympathized with many of the Durrani complaints of revenue oppression and in February 1841 had consented to the removal of Taqi and Wali Muhammad. But in March he concluded that he had been mistaken, that the complaints of oppression were bogus, and that the root cause of the troubles was 'the hatred in which we are held by the Dooranees as Infidels and Conquerors'.[66] It is possible to trace from the end of January 1841 the gradual evolution of Rawlinson's views until he came to the conclusion that Durrani power would have to be broken if British control of Afghanistan were to be secured. Fifty or sixty of the most powerful chiefs should be seized and sent to India; the privileges of the rest should be reduced. If Britain was not prepared for such action she should evacuate Afghanistan.

Of the necessity for such drastic action Rawlinson found it difficult to persuade Macnaghten. On reason was Macnaghten's slow under-standing of the nature of the troubles. 'What made this Akhtar Khan Yaghee [i.e. rebellious]?', he asked Rawlinson. 'I know that he is sulky and impudent but the cause I was never able exactly to trace.'[67] Another reason was Macnaghten's reluctance to concede a proposition that struck at the basic assumptions of all his policy in Afghanistan. He argued that Rawlinson was wrong about the nature of Durrani hostil-ity; it was based not upon inveterate enmity but upon local abuses in revenue-collection; and when these were remedied all would be well. 'I do not apprehend the slightest danger from Dooranee ascendancy', he wrote in February 1841.[68] In truth the Envoy was caught in a dilemma. To admit Rawlinson's postulates would undermine the plans to with-draw British troops and commit Britain to a course of interference which would amount to a revolution in Afghanistan. Apart from the injustice to Shuja and the damage to Britain's reputation for faithful-ness, such a policy would require ten times the number of British and Company troops which were at present stationed in Afghanistan.[69] Even so, he claimed, if he did admit the existence of inveterate hostility this would still not require a choice of either the extreme of taking over the government or that of withdrawal.[70] At the same time Macnaghten could not entirely ignore the evidence of Durrani hostility or the advice of his key subordinate. So he dithered. In 1840 he had briefly supported wholesale confiscations and a greater enforcement of obligations in order to weaken Durrani power. In February he refused to consider such ideas. But gradually Rawlinson won him over. As late as July 1841 Macnaghten still tried to play down the Zamindawar disturbances. The rebels were merely 'perfect children' and the troubles no worse than those encountered around Calcutta.[71] But a month later his patience ran out and the 'perfect children' became 'without exception the most worthless and faithless set of wretches I ever knew'. It was then that he consented to send two Company regiments into Zamin-dawar.[72]

At the same time that Macnaghten came to accept the necessity of military coercion he gave his assent to a reform programme aimed at the basis of Durrani power in Qandahar. Under this programme the whole system of rent-free military tenures was to be reduced and eventually eliminated. Although its final form is not clear, the evolution of this programme can be traced. It originated with the notion of the Janbaz.

Both for military and political reasons it was thought desirable to form a force of paid and disciplined Afghan cavalry, under British control. Such a force would be more useful than the worthless feudal array and would also serve as a safety-valve while the feudal cavalry was being eliminated, for it would give alternative employment. Disciplined cavalry of this type was introduced in Kabul in April 1841 and Shuja was persuaded to give his reluctant consent to the formation of two similar regiments of Janbaz at Qandahar. Shuja had long resisted pressure for such action and as long ago as August 1840 had refused to agree to the establishment of disciplined cavalry and had advocated the strengthening of the feudal system.[73]

Macnaghten hoped to recruit Durranis into the Janbaz. They would be released from the obligation to perform military service in return for their agreement to pay rent on their rent-free grants. To persuade the Durrani chiefs to agree to such a manifestly poor bargain he was prepared to employ pressure. He wrote to Rawlinson in July 1841:

The moment we feel strong enough I think we should take a number of all the Dooranee Horse claiming exemption under the Koolba system and absolutely reject all that are unserviceable and assess their Koolbas, requiring the remainder to attend at Candahar for eight months of the year. By this means we shall gradually get them into the category of tax payers.[74]

The disturbances in Zamindawar, he wrote, offered a good excuse for 'retrieving the error into which His Majesty fell when he granted these indulgences to the good for nothing Dooranees'.[75] Loyal chiefs should be given pensions and the best of their followers recruited into the Janbaz.

The weakness of Macnaghten's proposal was that Rawlinson did not want Durranis in the Janbaz. He wanted a non-tribal force.[76] In any case the Durranis were neither prepared to serve outside Qandahar nor to fight other Durranis. It was necessary to recruit the Janbaz from Ghilzays and Parsiwans instead. Consequently the Janbaz could not be used as the engine for the destruction of the *tiyul* system. Macnaghten was nonplussed and could only suggest the gradual reduction of the *tiyul* system by 'expedients to curb the influence of the Dooranees and render their Koolba privileges rather a nuisance to them than other-wise'.[77] The fertile Rawlinson did offer a temporary compromise, by which the number of Durrani Horse should be reduced to seven hundred and fifty, at which size they could easily be annihilated if they proved dangerous.[78]

What was the final decision and how far it was implemented is impossible to say, for the matter was not discussed in official letters but in private correspondence between Rawlinson and Macnaghten and no letters dealing with the subject later than July 1841 have come to light. It seems probable, however, that the extended policy of coercion adopted in Qandahar in the autumn of 1841 was accompanied by further inroads into the former system. After the removal of the Par-siwan revenue-managers, Rawlinson found in Mirza Ahmad a willing and more able instrument in his financial campaign against the Dur-ranis. But the general point which can certainly be made with confidence is that British policy at Qandahar resulted in effective British control of the internal government of the province and that this control was employed to carry out a social and political revolution. The inevitable inference to be drawn from this development was that the 1839 policy had failed and that Britain was in Afghanistan to stay.

The tendency of British policy observed at Qandahar can also be discerned in Kabul itself. There Macnaghten was in direct control of policy and in immediate contact with Shah Shuja. He was not depen-dent upon the information supplied by subordinate agents and upon the loose system of control over local authorities which characterized Shuja's governmental system. In Kabul, if anywhere, he could carry out the policy of non-interference which had been enjoined upon him and of which he was the foremost advocate. It is therefore of especial significance that, even in the capital, Macnaghten was forced to give way to the various pressures for greater British control and the eventual reformation of Afghanistan.

From the earliest days it is apparent that Macnaghten's unofficial advice amounted to considerable interference. Shuja himself always felt powerless. In July 1840 he complained to Burnes that his subjects regarded him as a mere puppet (*masli*; lit. 'radish'). He explained that he was

assailed night and day by moolahs (priests) and others who represented the present state of things as anything but a Mohamadan kingdom and that if H. M. was of the same opinion a rebellion or insurrection (lulwa-i-am) was easily raised, but of course, said His Majesty, I have endeavoured to correct the erroneous opinion of these men by assuring them that the English and I were as two souls in one body but yet I cannot hope to get them to think so when in the Capital the Troops are not my own and in the provinces interference takes place without my knowledge on all occasions.[79]

When the court moved to the winter capital of Jalalabad the Shah's plight was yet more visible, for Macnaghten took the best house and Shuja was allotted a miserable residence.[80] The Shah both exaggerated his situation and hinted at rebellion in order to improve his lot but he was yet capable of resisting British pressure for change. Nevertheless, there was much justice in his complaints; British interference had already, even by the summer of 1840, advanced far beyond what had been contemplated in August 1839—possibly the inevitable consequence of the retention of British forces. But so far the interposition of British influence had remained informal; it was in the latter part of 1840 and throughout 1841 that the basic assumptions of British policy in Afghanistan were themselves called into question in a major debate which was conducted at all levels.

The great debate was initiated by Burnes in a long private letter which he sent to Macnaghten in August 1840. The Shah's Government, he claimed, was useless; it was inefficient, expensive, and unpopular and if it were not reformed Afghanistan would have no value to Britain as a strategic buffer. Although Burnes himself was theoretically opposed to the extension of British control, his proposals for reform inevitably involved much closer scrutiny of Afghan Government than had hitherto been the practice.[81]

Macnaghten disagreed entirely and took the opportunity to set out the philosophy of moderation which was implied in his policy of non-interference. It was an argument long made familiar in the course of the debate within India on the correct policy to be pursued towards the Indian states. Macnaghten's position was that of Malcolm earlier and of Henry Lawrence after. The Shah's Government, he argued was not useless; the disturbances which had taken place were not the result of any deep-seated hostility to the new system, but were only the product of the capricious nature of the people of Afghanistan. Drastic reform was unnecessary and greater British interference would be a serious error.

I am of opinion that it is the duty of the British representative here rather to watch carefully the opportunities of suggesting reform and to treat His Majesty with all possible consideration than to urge sweeping innovations or to assume towards His Majesty anything like a tone of dictation. Such proceedings would reduce His Majesty to the condition of a cypher and would afford to our enemies the means of successfully propagating reports to our prejudice and to the effect that our design was to seize the Government of the country . . . it is preferable to work at minor abuses which are inherent in every Eastern monarchy than to exercise frequent and authoritative interference, the good effects of which would be at least problematical.

His own interference, Macnaghten claimed, had been limited to bringing serious complaints privately to Shuja's notice, and to urging the Shah to select a good minister and to reduce his own expenditure.

These and other objects will be gradually obtained by kind and persevering counsel. This is not a country in which objects are to be obtained *per saltum*. His Majesty's wishes must meet with some little attention. The prejudices of the people must be respected. Minor abuses must be overlooked and our proceedings at every stage must be guided by caution, temper and forbearance[82]

Burnes and Macnaghten were agreed on one point. This was that the root cause of many of the troubles in Afghanistan was the activities of the Sikhs and of the rulers of Herat. For the future stability of Afghanistan it was important that Herat and Peshawar should be annexed to the domains of Shah Shuja. The fate of these proposals is reserved for later chapters and this chapter is confined to the development of British policy within Shuja's territories. Nevertheless, the issues cannot be entirely separated: Macnaghten's moderation within Afghanistan had its inevitable corollary in his aggressiveness outside; for if the Shah's Government was not to be blamed for the troubles then a scapegoat had to be found without. The prospective annexation of Herat and Peshawar would also justify the retention of Company forces in Afghanistan. For Burnes, of course, the annexation of Herat and Peshawar to the Kabul Government would represent the achievement of the grand new strategy which he had outlined in 1838. Afghanistan would become the single north-western buffer, replacing both Iran and the Panjab. The Panjab would inevitably become totally subordinated, if not actually annexed to British India. Although Burnes would not himself have gone on to annex Afghanistan, there was, he reported in February 1841, a strong current of feeling among British officials in Afghanistan in favour of such a move.[83] The logic of the annexation of Afghanistan, of course, would have been to place the frontier of British India on or beyond the Hindu Kush and to imply the creation of a new strategic buffer beyond in Turkestan, or possibly in Iran.

Burnes did not abandon his opinions in favour of reform, but continued to press them intermittently. A suitable opportunity was presented in the autumn of 1840 when the return of Dost Muhammad led to the most serious threat to the Anglo–Sadozay monarchy which had yet been encountered. At that time, with the support of a frightened Macnaghten, Burnes was able to persuade Shuja to dismiss the incompetent Mulla Shakar and to appoint Muhammad Usman Khan in his place. But Burnes muted his public criticisms of British policy lest they should endanger his hopes of succeeding Macnaghten. In private his comments were more caustic. 'There is nothing here but downright imbecility', he wrote to a friend in September 1840.[84]

Burnes may have been worried by Macnaghten's action in making Burnes's private letter public and in sending it to Auckland. Auckland's general views in favour of non-interference were still unchanged, although he recommended rather stronger pressure on the Shah in favour of certain specific objects of reform. Auckland disagreed completely with both Burnes and Macnaghten in their diagnosis of the cause of the troubles and their recommendation of the annexation of Herat and Peshawar.[85] Auckland, in fact, was unwilling to abandon any part of the new system which he had so reluctantly adopted in 1838 to 1839.

The attitude of the authorities in London was quite different from that of Macnaghten and Auckland. Apart from the exchange of letters, etc., which had been initiated by Burnes, Hobhouse took other evidence into account. First, was the growing conviction that Shuja would be unable to dispense with the help of British troops for some time to come, and, if Macnaghten's views on the character of the Afghan nobility were correct, possibly for ever. This opinion was confirmed by the disturbances, particularly the great wave of unrest which accompanied the return of Dost Muhammad and an extensive uprising which took place in Kalat. Second, Hobhouse took into account the Russian expedition to Khiva in 1839 which had convinced him and Palmerston of the strategic value of the Afghan position.[86] Accordingly, although he was yet convinced that a prolonged occupation of Afghanistan would be undesirable, especially because of its adverse effect on relations with Russia, Hobhouse abandoned the strong opinions in favour of non-interference which, under Parliamentary pressure, he had expressed in 1839, and came down in favour of a much more vigorous policy in Afghanistan.

Believing Auckland was not facing up to the realities of the Afghan situation, Hobhouse framed a dispatch which was intended to force Auckland to adopt a more determined policy. First he consulted his Cabinet colleagues, among whom Palmerston was as buoyantly confident as ever: he had no fears for Afghanistan, except for the expense, and roundly asserted that Indian defence would have cost much more if Afghanistan had fallen to Iran or to Russia.[87] Burnes's criticisms, the Foreign Secretary declared, were worthless and the position in Afghanistan was most promising; all that was needed to complete it was to annex Herat and advance into Turkestan.[88] Apart from strengthening Hobhouse's determination to retain the Afghan position, this extravagant optimism was unhelpful, and Hobhouse took a much less rosy view in his dispatch, which came near to endorsing the views of Burnes. The policy envisaged in 1838 to 1839 had failed, he proclaimed: Shuja's Government and army were not adequate to form a suitable buffer state; and the hope of withdrawing British forces must be abandoned. Afghanistan should either be relinquished or it should be held in strength. In the latter case much more expenditure, much larger British forces, and much greater control over the Afghan Government were required. No Afghan should be given any position of trust and Shuja should be made to obey absolutely. The basic fact that 'the British are masters of the country' must be recognized.[89] The apparent alternative of withdrawal, of course, was not intended seriously; Hobhouse believed that retreat from Afghanistan was out of the question.[90]

Auckland refused to accept Hobhouse's analysis. The dispatch was considered by his Council in Calcutta in March 1841 and Auckland set out his own position in a lengthy minute. He conceded that a large British force would be required for many years to come, but did not agree that large reinforcements or direct control over the Government of Afghanistan were necessary. He drew up a balance sheet of the advantages and disadvantages of the Afghan position. The advantages were strategic; control over Afghanistan had enabled Britain to preserve Khiva from conquest by Russia and produced peace within India. 'The repose of the public mind in India from our command of the avenues by which the approach of invasion has been so keenly apprehended', he wrote, 'is a benefit and a blessing of the greatest conceivable value.' The main disadvantage was financial. The Governor-General estimated the cost of the Afghan position at one million pounds a year and remarked that such a burden could not be sustained indefinitely. It could be tolerated only for some two or three years in which time something might turn up to alleviate the situation. The revenues of India were increasing and might be further enhanced by the annexation of the Panjab. Because of this uncertainty about the future an immediate decision was unnecessary. If, however, at some future time it was decided to withdraw from Afghanistan the event should be preceded by some compensatory advantage such as the annexation of the Panjab or a diplomatic agreement with Iran and Russia, providing for the neutralization of Central Asia. Until a decision became necessary Britain should mount a mere holding operation in Afghanistan. Only the main cities and lines of communication should be held in strength; Shuja should concentrate on ruling in the open, cultivated areas only and leave the wilder tribes alone. Certainly there should be no advance beyond the existing frontiers of Shuja's kingdom, whether to Herat or Turkestan. For these limited purposes the existing forces and political influence should be adequate; political officers should confine themselves to advice—'I would not allow them to put themselves forward as managers of the country.'[91]

Two reasons for Auckland's rejection of Hobhouse's analysis call for immediate comment. The first was his view that Hobhouse had written his gloomy dispatch under the influence of the uncertainty induced by the Dost Muhammad uprising. Auckland wrongly assumed that Hobhouse would modify his views when he learned of the surrender of the former Amir and of the restoration of peace. The second was much more fundamental. Auckland, in bringing in the financial burden of the Afghan position, had introduced a factor the importance of which Hobhouse, despite promptings from the Court of Directors, had completely underrated. In India the cost of controlling Afghanistan had been a subject of discussion since it was raised in November 1840 by the Commander-in-Chief, Sir Jasper Nicolls (d. 1849). Nicolls had argued that since Shuja appeared unable to stand alone a permanent British occupation of Afghanistan would be necessary and consequently also a permanent increase in the size of the Indian army.[92] Indeed the shortage of available troops in 1840 and the need to reinforce Afghanistan and Kalat had forced Auckland to postpone a settlement with Nepal. As it happened, the surrender of Dost Muhammad seemed to change the prospects in Afghanistan and when the Council considered Nicolls's proposal in January 1841, all (including the Commander-in-Chief) agreed that an increase was now unnecessary. In the discussion, however, it was accepted that if it were to be decided to make the occupation permanent a further increase in the Indian army with additional financial commitments would be inevitable. Hobhouse certainly failed to appreciate this point for in April 1841 he wrote to Auckland disapproving of further defence expenditure. Auckland already had sufficient troops for his needs and 'We are not at all inclined to encourage more expenditure than is absolutely necessary for the security of your Empire.'[93]

In the policies of both Auckland and Hobhouse there were therefore elements of contradiction. Hobhouse was recommending on the one hand, a policy which would tie down most of the disposable forces in India and so endanger Indian security and on the other, he was bowing to pressure from the Directors to hold down military expenditure and prevent the creation of a force which could replace that committed to Afghanistan. Auckland also had accepted in January 1841 the implied proposition that a decision to retain troops in Afghanistan would require an increase in the Indian Army, but in March had both agreed to the indefinite stay of British forces in Afghanistan while making no provision for any increase in the Indian army. On his own logic he was accepting for the duration of the stay of British troops in Afghanistan some considerable restriction on his strategic freedom of manœuvre elsewhere.

The explanation of the ambivalence in the attitudes of both men arises partly from their differing attitudes to the problem of Indian defence. For Hobhouse the defence of India was primarily a matter of defence against external aggression. India's vulnerability to attack from outside weakened the general freedom of British foreign policy; India's ability to strike far beyond her frontiers gave extra power to the position of Britain in European affairs. The position in Afghanistan therefore seemed a matter almost independent of the ordinary concerns of Indian government and one not to be thrown into the same scale of advantage. To Auckland, on the other hand, the main problem of Indian defence was the internal frontier; the threat of external attack was merely an aggravating factor in that situation. The position in Afghanistan was therefore beneficial, but only upon an equation of costs and benefits. If Afghanistan tied down too large a proportion of British Indian resources it could become a liability, for it would make it impossible to provide adequate defence elsewhere. It is quite clear that by March 1841 Auckland was beginning to view Afghanistan as a potential liability. The whole logic of his holding operation in Afghanistan pointed to the eventual withdrawal which he began to contemplate in his minute. Hobhouse had included the alternative of abandoning Afghanistan merely to spur Auckland on to greater efforts; Auckland, however, saw evacuation as the wiser policy.

Auckland was working towards the rejection of the Afghan buffer policy. Despite his claims for its advantages, he believed that it was a system of defence India could not afford. In its place he looked to a strengthening of the north-west frontier and of India's financial resources by the annexation of the Panjab and possibly of Sind as well. Forward defence beyond the Indus was to become the responsibility of the Government in England and was to be achieved through diplomatic agreement. In short Auckland was coming back to a modified version of the policy which he had advocated before May 1838.

The implications of Auckland's attitude were not explicit in his minute. Like those of Nicolls, his arguments could be interpreted as a contention that Afghanistan could be held if the Panjab were annexed, both because of the financial gain and the easier communications, which would allow fewer troops to be held in Afghanistan itself. But on closer examination and in the light of their future views it is plain that this was not their true position; for them the Panjab was a substitute for Afghanistan, not an auxiliary position. But Auckland dared not be too explicit for to so would be to admit that his whole Afghan policy had been mistaken and so precipitate a major clash with London. Since he was himself due to leave India within a year he believed the matter could safely be left to his successor. As Burnes wrote, with the customary perception of his mature years, 'après moi le deluge is his motto—he wishes to get home but is afraid of what he has already done.'[94] Possibly it was because he wished to postpone an admission that he believed to be inevitable that Auckland deliberately understated the gravity of the financial position in his March minute. Only two days after that minute Colvin painted a much darker picture in a private letter to Macnaghten. 'Money—money—money is our first, and second and our last word. How long we can continue to feed you at your present rate of expenditure I cannot tell. To add to the weight would break us utterly.'[95]

Auckland's fellow Councillors were unable to share Auckland's very short-term view of the situation. In particular Nicolls was critical of Auckland's postponement of a decision, because of his responsibility as Commander-in-Chief for ensuring that sufficient troops to meet any emergency were always available. Of course this was ultimately a financial question and Nicolls attacked Auckland especially for understating the financial problem. But this was an area where Nicolls could claim no expertise and he was forced to give way to the opinions of the civilian Councillors. But these too disagreed with Auckland. William Wilberforce Bird supported Hobhouse: retreat from Afghanistan was unthinkable; British prestige would suffer; Russia would become established on the banks of the Indus; a Muslim coalition to invade India might be formed; and there would be unrest in India. The only effective and economical policy, argued Bird, was to hold Afghanistan in strength.[96]

The most striking opposition to Auckland on his Council came from Henry Thoby Prinsep (1792–1878). Prinsep had served Hastings as Assistant Secretary and Bentinck as Chief Secretary and had long been involved in the formation of strategy. Emily Eden dismissed him as 'the greatest bore Providence ever created and so contradictory that he will not let anybody agree or differ with him.'[97] There was nothing boring, however, about the solution which he now expounded with fearsome logic. Afghanistan should be held, he argued. This could only be accomplished by the destruction of all feudal and tribal independence and by the centralization of government; under these conditions Afghanistan would become as peaceful and industrious as Hindustan. Such a programme would require time, troops, and money—Prinsep estimated one and a quarter million pounds a year. This could not be found from existing Indian resources so Prinsep coolly proposed the annexation of the third of India which yet remained independent. At present, he complained, Britain bore the cost of defending all of India with the revenues of only two-thirds. Annexation could be accomplished through the wholesale application of the doctrine of lapse, that is, the theory that an Indian state should pass under British rule if the ruler died without an heir of his body or an adopted successor duly recognized by Britain. In his minute Auckland had mentioned the possibility of additions to the revenue through the lapse of rent-free grants and pensions, but Prinsep argued that this was not enough; lapse must be enforced with regard to Indian states.[98]

Prinsep's argument was not entirely novel. The annexation of Indian states had frequently been discussed and, as recently as July 1840, a writer in the *Edinburgh Review* had argued in favour of the annexation of Indian states on the twin grounds of providing good government and of defence, namely that Britain was defending India with the revenues of less than two-thirds.[99] The author may well have been close to Prinsep himself, because the reference to good government was one which might well have come from the Councillor. Although in his minute Prinsep based his annexationist arguments wholly on the defence position, there is good reason to suppose that he would have been equally content to have supported it on humanitarian grounds. Like his Benthamite brother, James Prinsep (1799–1840), he shared the belief (increasingly common among Bengal Civil Servants during the 1830s) that the Indian states were anachronisms; they should be swept aside and replaced by direct, efficient, British rule. This belief, already common under Auckland, was to gather strength until it reached full flowering in the time of Dalhousie, before the cold wind of the Mutiny led to a reversion to the older Malcolm policy which conserved Indian states as a useful political safety-valve. What is here of the greatest interest is the way in which an argument about the defence of India could be skilfully manipulated so as to justify a policy which was advocated, but was found entirely unacceptable, on quite different grounds.

There was clear division within the Council over Afghanistan.

Nicolls, and possibly the military member, Sir William Casement, favoured withdrawal; Bird and Prinsep wished to hold the position at whatever cost. The situation was ideal for Auckland. There seems little doubt that in the long run he thought withdrawal inevitable, but wished to postpone it until he had gone from India. His suggestion of a holding operation could apparently bridge the gap between the rival groups on his Council. He got his way and Hobhouse was obliged to accepted the verdict for the time being.

In the months which followed, the equivocal nature of Auckland's Afghan policy became more and more apparent. One factor inducing greater uncertainty was the political situation in England. The defeat of the Whigs began to seem inevitable; a Conservative Government might order a withdrawal from Afghanistan. But the principal factor which influenced Auckland was the financial problems.

From the beginning Auckland had persistently underestimated the financial burden, arising principally from military costs, of his new policy. In 1838 he had hoped to have his troops back in twelve months. In 1839 he had expected their return in the summer of 1840. As late as January 1840 Macnaghten was still talking of withdrawing regular troops by the autumn, but in May he abandoned this hope and demanded reinforcements both to provide for internal security and to meet the possibility of a Russian attack via Khiva. Auckland then consented to allow the existing troops to remain until the summer of 1841, but refused to send reinforcements.[100] In September 1840, however, Auckland had to bow to pressure and send more troops. Still Auckland continued to talk optimistically of an early evacuation and to use this hope to refuse to contemplate consequential rearrangements. But the financial burden of keeping the regular troops in Afghanistan was considerable and to this must be added the other items of British financial assistance, including payment for those elements in Shuja's forces which came under British control and a budget subsidy to the Government of the Shah.

The financial pressures began to make themselves felt early in 1840. The financial years 1835 to 1836, 1836 to 1837, and 1837 to 1838 had been good years with surpluses ranging from £1·5 million to £0·75 million. But bad harvests and the cost of the Afghan war changed this happy situation into a deficit of £2·4 million in 1839 to 1840. The first effect was felt upon the cash flow position of the Indian Government.[101] In March 1840 Auckland considered and rejected the suggestion of a new loan to replenish his depleted cash balances.[102] In his minute of 19 March 1841 he seriously understated the rate of the run-down of cash balances. He calculated that between the end of 1838 and March 1840 they had been reduced by only £1 million, whereas the Accountant-General's figures showed that by 30 April the total amounted to £3·75 million. Already, on 31 March, Auckland found himself compelled to open a new loan at 5 per cent compared with the normal rate of 4 per cent. Before the rate of interest was again reduced to 4 per cent at the beginning of 1843, £5 million had been borrowed and the total of Indian debt raised from under £30 million, the figure to which it had been reduced in 1836 by the sale of some of the Company's commercial assets, to £36 million. Even so the response to the 5 per cent loan was too slow for comfort and Auckland was forced to resort to other measures to safeguard his liquidity position. He raised the rate of interest charged to merchants in order to cut down their demands on his reserves, an act which, in the interlocking system of Asian trade, was bound to have a wider, restrictive effect. Also, he was reluctantly obliged, at the beginning of 1842, to adopt his Accountant-General's advice to stop remittances of money to England, a drastic move which had before brought down the wrath of the Court of Directors upon the heads of his predecessors.

What was the real cost of the Afghan war is difficult to say. In March 1841 Auckland estimated it at £1 million and Prinsep at £1·25 million per year. According to calculations made for Ellenborough in September 1841, the average cost for each of the years 1839–1840 and 1840–1841 was £1·9 million.[103] The author of these calculations was probably Henry Tucker, who produced new figures early in 1842 which showed the cost of the Afghan position to be £2·5 million. Tucker then estimated 'that ere six months elapse, the treasures of India will be completely exhausted'.[104] The discrepancies are largely the result of decisions to allocate sums to military costs. Auckland argued that the costs of the troops stationed in Afghanistan would have to be met even if they were retained in India. But apart from the fact that this ignored the additional costs of moving and supplying troops in Afghanistan, this took no account of increases in the Army in India. Although in 1841 Auckland had rejected Nicolls's plea for a permanent increase in the establishment, he had already allowed expansion in 1838, which, with other increases, led to a total enlargement of the Indian Army between 1838 and 1841 by over 50,000 and an increase in military charges from just over £7 million to nearly £9 million a year. Of course part of this increase could be attributed to other factors, notably the demands of the first China war, but it was the virtually permanent military commitment beyond the Indus which had swallowed up the strategic reserve and made the other increases necessary.[105]

Another way of estimating the cost of the Afghan war is to consider

the total deterioration in Indian finances during the period 1838 to
1842. If one adds together the decline in cash reserves and the amount
of new debt the result is a figure of £8·2 million. This is roughly the
same as that given by Tucker in a calculation covering the period down
to 30 April 1842. But of course this figure again cannot be accepted as it
stands. On the one hand there is the cost of extraordinary operations
other than those beyond the Indus. The cost of the China war, for
example, was estimated in 1840 to 1841 at £0·5 million, although the
British Government promised to repay this eventually to the Indian
Government. On the other hand the figure takes no account of the
increase of revenue during the period; an allowance for this would
inflate total cost. Indeed Tucker later increased his total estimate of the
cost of the Afghan wars to £15 million, but by that time he was less
concerned with exact calculations of their cost, than with persuading
the British Government to accept part of the financial burden of
policies which, he argued, served British and not Indian interests.
Tucker proposed that the Crown should pay an annual subsidy of
£266,000 to the Company, corresponding to interest at $3\frac{1}{2}$ per cent on
the sum of £8 million for which he held the Cabinet directly responsible.[106]

Probably one would not be far wrong in estimating the direct annual
cost of the Afghan strategy during the years 1838 to 1842 at £2 million,
or £8 million in all. This was a large sum in relation to British Indian
resources, but not an unbearable burden. Wellesley's wars had added
about £20 million to the Indian debt, and their average annual cost
must have exceeded £3 million. At £4 million Hastings's Pindari wars
were comparatively cheap, but Amherst's Burma War had cost a
prodigious sum, estimated as high as £15 million although this figure
was challenged. Going beyond the Afghan war, the period 1846 to
1851, which included the two Sikh wars, led to an addition of a further
£8·5 million to the debt, to which should be added a further sum to
allow for surplus revenue, bringing the total cost of these wars to nearly
£12 million, or an annual cost approximately the same as that of the
Afghan position. All in all, the cost of the wars fought between 1838 and
1850 was £30 million, of which about £13 million was met from current
revenue and the remainder by adding to the Indian debt, which in 1850
reached £47 million. The increase in debt charges since 1839 was
almost £1 million a year. In the light of these figures the Afghan war
does not appear to be the financial incubus it is sometimes supposed to
have been. Nicolls was wrong in arguing that Britain would be forced to
withdraw from Afghanistan on financial grounds alone, even though he
underestimated the cost; and Auckland was right in believing that on

financial grounds alone he could temporize for some time. The true cost of the Afghan war must be sought in a different perspective.

Unlike almost all other Indian wars, the Afghan war was a dead loss. Although Wellesley spent over £3 million a year on war, he added a total of £7 million a year to the receipts of British India. Hastings's wars were extremely profitable and the Sikh wars added a large revenue. The nearest equivalent to the Afghan war was the first Burmese war and even that added potentially valuable territories in Assam, Arakan, and Tenasserim. Nevertheless, the Burma war left great burdens on the finances of British India from which they took years to recover. The effect was felt in the restriction of credit for trade and the limitation on investment in public works. This, of course, meant a general limitation on economic expansion, on the capacity of India to consume British goods, and on the growth of revenue. In other words, India became less profitable to Britain. The situation was duplicated in the case of the Afghan war. Increased expenditure on defence had another aspect of great significance in the context of strategic argument. From the early nineteenth century the more sophisticated argument which had been advanced in support of a policy of forward defence had stressed that such a policy enabled British India to avoid the burden of increased defence expenditure which would be forced upon her by the presence of a European enemy on her borders, able to promote disaffection within British India. But the evidence of Afghanistan indicated that forward defence had produced precisely that same financial burden which it was intended to avoid and which it was anticipated would make India unprofitable to Britain. The experience of the first Afghan war, therefore, greatly strengthened the arguments of those who contended that the best defence for India lay in reducing military expenditure and in investing in good government in India so as to attach the people to British rule and make them impervious to foreign incitement. Equally, in subsequent years it strengthened the determination of those who still supported a forward strategy to find some profitable compensation for the expenditure in Afghanistan. The cost of the Afghan strategy therefore made the Sind and Panjab wars more likely.

In 1841 financial pressures forced Auckland to look for quick economies and new sources of revenue. Since military expenditure could not be reduced he cut items of civil expenditure, notably the experiments in cotton cultivation and steam navigation. Perhaps with an eye to the reaction in London, he rejected the time-honoured expedient, now suggested by T. C. Robertson, of a forced loan from Oudh,[107] but despite the opposition in the Court, he began to move hesitantly towards Prinsep's policy of enforcing the doctrine of lapse. In

a minute, dated 30 September 1841, he showed plainly how this departure was the consequence of the defence burden. Although he would not
act with injustice, he stated,

I regard concession beyond this point as error and weakness in respect of our
position and in regard to the majority of cases as a great injustice to the mass of
the population affected by the continuance or the lapse of an extinct native
chiefship.[108]

In December 1841, after hearing of the Kabul rising, Auckland set out a
policy according to which, when expedient, Indian states should be
annexed wherever there was no clearly valid claim to the succession.[109]
Where lapse was not applicable Auckland proposed another change in
policy towards Indian states which was also designed to shift part of the
burden of military costs on to them. Wherever possible he proposed to
commute a general obligation to render military assistance to Britain
(as in Rajputana and the Protected Sikh States) into a specific obligation to support a military contingent, disciplined and commanded by
British officers.[110] In this way the policy of forward defence was exercising a powerful influence on the political structure of India and forcing
changes in the situation on the internal frontier.

Afghanistan itself was also called upon to contribute to the economy
drive. Auckland rejected proposals for new military works, including a
new citadel at Kabul and a fort at Qandahar, commenting 'I would see
more clearly than I do at present what is to be the ultimate form of
Afghanistan before I would incur any very great expense in buildings
even for this purpose.'[111] Another casualty was the proposed Mission
House at Qandahar about which Colvin wrote in a still more revealing
passage:

The truth, however, is that while the question of our continuing in Afghanistan
remains one of grave debate in England every expense of a permanent kind not
required for protection is regarded as premature. This thought should colour
all your recommendations.[112]

Colvin scarcely told the whole truth. As Auckland's letter shows,
fortifications were also included in the prohibition and there was no
move by Hobhouse to evacuate Afghanistan. The truth was that it was
Auckland himself who believed that abandonment was ultimately
necessary.

The principal target for economy in Afghanistan was Shuja's own
budget, of which the major part was attributable to the cost of his own
military forces, which contributed virtually nothing to internal

security. Auckland pressed for a reduction of these forces and from December 1840 onwards Macnaghten was regularly instructed to persuade the Shah to do so. Macnaghten fought a delaying action. First he submitted a copy of the Afghan budget which showed a deficit of 900,000 *kham* rupees. Macnaghten proposed to meet the deficit partly by reducing the Shah's military forces and partly by an increased British subsidy.[113] Auckland asked for more information, but this he found most difficult to obtain. Throughout the course of 1841 Macnaghten dribbled out further details of Afghan finances in a series of reports which Auckland found incomprehensible. Auckland came down to the basic question of how it was that, with a larger revenue than that of Dost Muhammad and with Britain paying for his regular army, the Shah found it impossible to make ends meet. In June 1841 Auckland warned Macnaghten that if he did not economize the British position in Afghanistan was likely to break down for want of money to pay for it.[114] Eventually Auckland concluded in October 1841 that there was 'obviously room for retrenchment' and set out a string of proposals.[115]

Auckland's new policy involved the complete abandonment of the policy to which he had clung so tenaciously since 1838. Shuja should meet his own expenses; British assistance would be limited to payment for forces under British officers. If this meant more British interference in Afghan government then Auckland welcomed it; Britain had acquired obligations towards Afghanistan and had a duty to establish a satisfactory form of government. There should be reforms by which Britain would acquire effective control of Afghan finances, revenue-collection, the administration of justice, and payment of the bureaucracy; and alter the system of internal transit-duties. In some respects Auckland's changes bore a curious resemblance to the proposals of Leech, which he had rejected so indignantly in the early part of 1840, and to those of Hobhouse, which he had declined to accept in the spring of 1841. From outright opposition to interference he had moved round to justifying British control, partly on humanitarian, but mainly on financial grounds. It might be concluded from this that Auckland had after all come down in favour of staying in Afghanistan and of accepting the implications of that decision. But such a conclusion would be wrong. Auckland knew that he would shortly leave India, before any of this policy could be implemented. His proposals stand, therefore, rather as evidence of a desire to be seen to be actively concerned about the policy with which he had become identified rather than as a sign that he intended actively to uphold it. In the event, of course, the recommendations had no effect because long before they reached

Afghanistan the fate of the Afghan position was sealed by the Kabul rising.

In the course of his protracted struggle against change Macnaghten ran through the whole gamut of reasons for doing nothing. The financial cost was not so great as was supposed; the real expense arose from Kalat and China. Peace and retrenchment in Afghanistan was always just around the corner; and he railed at his subordinates for their failure to look on the bright side. All could be made right by a lucrative war with the Panjab; this would provide revenue and remove what Macnaghten unconvincingly argued was the major source of his Afghan troubles. Pressure for economy could alienate Shuja and his nobles and cause more problems than it was worth; 'every man from whom a rupee is taken and they are almost all the men of influence here make about it as great a wail as stout Hercules for the loss of Hylas', he wrote.[116] Greater economies could be secured only by the dangerous policy of virtually taking over the government.[117] All, however, was ultimately in vain and Macnaghten was forced to give ground, and accept both retrenchment and intervention.

The main area where economy and interference coincided was the question of the reduction of the feudal army. The first inroads into the old system were made in June 1840 when, as mentioned earlier, Shuja reluctantly consented to the formation of a body of disciplined cavalry with British officers known as Janbaz. Three such corps were raised at Kabul, totalling twelve hundred men, as well as the units raised at Qandahar. It was intended that the formation of the Janbaz would prepare the way for the ultimate disbandment of the feudal cavalry by providing suitable alternative employment for the chiefs and their followers, without having the disadvantage of the feudal cavalry, inasmuch as the Janbaz did not reinforce the tribal system. In Afghanistan, as elsewhere, one of the main features of the traditional army was that it enabled a chief to maintain a patron–client relationship with his tribesmen and so strengthen other links between them. As Eric Hobsbawm has pointed out, in such societies wealth in money terms is of less importance than the ability to maintain followers.[118] The Janbaz did away with this socio–political function of the old system; prominent chiefs were not wanted, especially when they served as officers in control of their own tribesmen. 'Our system' wrote Macnaghten, 'requires that we take no man as a Janbaz whom we cannot conveniently turn out at a moment's notice.[119] It was the British who were to replace the tribal chief as patron and thereby destroy an important cement of the tribal system.

In 1841 the Janbaz system was extended. A quicker method to

reduce the feudal cavalry was required and the answer found in the formation of a sort of second-class Janbaz, known as the Hazirbash, (lit. the Ever-readies, or militia). The Hazirbash had Afghan officers and European inspectors and their duties were limited to an area near Kabul. Their pay was only two-thirds of that of the Janbaz. Eight hundred men were quickly recruited. Captain R. S. Trevor, the officer in charge of the irregular cavalry, reported that service was especially popular among minor chiefs and their followers. He anticipated that after the best of the chiefs had been enlisted in either the Janbaz or the Hazirbash, and pensions given to some of the great chiefs, the remainder of the feudal cavalry could be disbanded. In 1840 the feudal cavalry had been estimated at nearly six thousand; by September 1841 this number had been reduced to fourteen hundred and final disbandment at the end of the year was intended.

This rapid elimination of the feudal cavalry struck at the heart of traditional Afghan society and politics, by destroying the whole foundation of the patron–client system. Cash compensation, during a time of rapid inflation, was of much less value. The consequence was a reaction similar to that experienced by Selim III when he had attempted to carry out a similar operation in the Ottoman Empire thirty years earlier; Shuja and his chiefs became sharply hostile to British interference. With the support of the ulema the chiefs fought against the Hazirbash. Would-be recruits were told that the dress and discipline were contrary to the teachings of Islam. In June 1841 Macnaghten was compelled to intervene to prevent the execution of the father of a recruit for blasphemy. In reply Macnaghten, supported by Muhammed Usman Khan, pressed Shuja to enforce submission by his chiefs, who were obliged to sign a bond of loyalty. The hostility of the chiefs, however, was undiminished and they were among the leaders in the attack on Burnes's house in Kabul on 2 November 1841, which marked the beginning of the Kabul rising.

Macnaghten himself had drifted reluctantly with this tide of innovation. It was Trevor, a man who disliked the chiefs and wished to sweep them aside, who led the attack on the feudal cavalry; Macnaghten's sympathies were with Shuja, whom the new policy would doom to the station of a mere pensioner, and the Envoy regarded the feudal cavalry as 'a safety valve for our reforming operations'.[120] Macnaghten never thought the money saved was worth the political risks. His long-sustained opposition to interference was partly the outcome of political conviction; but partly also the consequence of his own lack of ruthlessness. The same characteristic which made him unwilling to remove incapable subordinates, such as Leech and Lynch, is reflected in his generosity to Dost Muhammad after the former Amir submitted, and in his unwillingness to press Shuja too hard. Macnaghten could be tough with a pen, but he could not bear hostility when he encountered it in the flesh.

In the end Macnaghten had to give way against his own judgement. Partly the great pressures brought to bear upon him gave him no alternative, but partly his surrender was due to his knowledge that he would not be in Afghanistan to work with the consequences of British intervention. He had, indeed, never wanted to stay, but Auckland had persuaded him to continue in office. As Burnes remarked, Auckland seemed 'literally to believe that the whole of Affghan politics would stand still if Macnaghten left the country'.[121] As soon as Macnaghten received news of his appointment as Governor of Bombay he could not wait to be off; even Auckland was surprised at his haste.[122] Even so, Macnaghten was not quick enough to leave before the rising burst over his head. The economies in the feudal cavalry combined with reductions in tribal allowances led to disturbances in eastern Afghanistan in October 1841 and the rising in Kabul in November.

The experience of 1840 to 1841 had shown that the policy of 1838 to 1839 was unviable. Auckland's preconditions could not make Afghanistan into an effective buffer. The choice, as Hobhouse said, was to take over Afghanistan or to get out. It was a view shared by almost everyone concerned, with the exception of Auckland and Macnaghten. Most men supposed that control and eventual annexation were inevitable. It was not, as the debate showed, a matter to be decided purely on the abstract merits of the best policy for the defence of India. For Hobhouse and Palmerston the retention of Afghanistan benefited Britain in Europe; for many Political Agents retention and control meant promotion and rewards; to some men, both in Afghanistan and outside, humanitarianism justified increased intervention; to Prinsep and those who thought like him, the true merit of Afghanistan was that its possession provided an excuse for completing the extension of British control over the resources of India. Curiously enough, the strongest opposition to the Afghan policy came from the military: Fane had opposed it at the outset; Nicolls and Casement supported withdrawal; the military commanders in Afghanistan were far less enthusiastic for British intervention than were the Politicals—Elphinstone had grave doubts about the policies pursued, while Nott's reluctance to hazard the safety of his troops in political adventures became so marked as to lead to threats of dismissal. The military attitude can be explained by reference to several factors. Service in Afghanistan was expensive, uncomfortable, and unpopular; Macnaghten reported, the day after a brigade of reinforcements arrived at Jalalabad, that 'the officers are all sick of the country already.'[123] Neither glory nor promotion was to be won in remote clashes with barbarous tribes; such rewards that were obtained went to the detested political officers. Beyond this petty, but not unimportant level, there were larger misgivings about the security of the Afghan position, and, at the highest levels, about the security of India itself, while the Afghan haemorrhage of troops continued. No more striking testimony exists concerning the relative unimportance of strategy in the question of the retention of Afghanistan than the uniform hostility of the army to maintaining the position there.

Nevertheless, it was Auckland and Macnaghten who still possessed the decisive voices and both men refused to adopt either of the alternatives which were recommended. The objective reasons for their attitudes have been considered, but they are less than satisfying. In the end the factor of personality cannot be ignored. They were the main architects of a policy which was evidently unworkable and neither wished to admit to misjudgement. Macnaghten hoped that the system would outlast him and meantime maintained a facile, ostrich-like optimism. Auckland too thought to get away from India before the moment of truth. His opposition to further involvement was not the outcome of conviction but of lack of conviction; he had ceased to believe in the value of the Afghan buffer policy. In 1838 he had adopted a policy of a low-cost buffer after agonizing indecision; in 1841, faced with escalating costs, he found himself in the same dilemma. He believed that Afghanistan was not worth the price, but he lacked the strength to admit it and to confront the arguments of all those who believed that a more active policy was necessary. So he chose not so much to drift with the tide as to coast downhill with his brakes on. The responsibility, therefore, for the Afghan disaster rests squarely upon Auckland and Macnaghten. It is true that the Kabul rising might have been contained had the military officers shown more enterprise. But it was Auckland and Macnaghten who, by pursuing a policy of greater intervention in which they did not believe and without the resources to make it work, created the situation in which decisive superiority in Afghanistan was lost.

Auckland and Macnaghten were both wrong and right. They were wrong to put in hazard men's lives for want of moral courage; they were right to doubt if Afghanistan was worth the price that was asked. The experience of the years 1839 to 1841 showed that Afghanistan could only be retained at a price which, if not beyond the resources of British India, imposed so great and continuing a strain on those resources as to make the possession of India markedly less profitable to Britain. Defence on that basis was no defence at all; Afghanistan was a strategic loss. Even when the British base was on the Indus and communications much shorter, Afghanistan proved, in the second Anglo–Afghan war, too great a burden to sustain; still more was it impossible while the British base remained upon the Satlej. Above all else it was clear that the Afghan strategy was premature; military and financial considerations argued first for the domination of the Indus by the annexation of Sind and the Panjab. In 1841, whatever the views of the majority, withdrawal from Afghanistan was inevitable. Burnes and Ellenborough, the nominated successors of Macnaghten and Auckland, had come to the same conclusion.

The Boundaries of Afghanistan

> Jutting out like a bold promontory into the Ocean of
> Central Asia it commands everything around it, and the
> power which may possess Herat if it be not greatly
> deficient in military means must be the dominant power
> in all the Countries intervening between Russia, Khiva
> and Bokhara.
>
> McNeill, Memorandum, 30 November 1841.

Between 1838 and 1841 Afghanistan had a dual significance in British
Central Asian policy. Primarily it was a buffer for the defence of India,
but it was also a springboard for the penetration of Turkestan.
Whichever concept was chosen the boundaries of Afghanistan were
important; in the case of the first for defence and in that of the second for
offence. In 1839 the boundaries of Aghanistan were not determined
with any precision; indeed, the state created for Shah Shuja was a novel
construct in Afghan history. Where those boundaries should lie therefore became a subject of important debate in which major issues of
strategy were discussed. With regard to northern Afghanistan the
debate focused on two crucial areas—Balkh at the eastern extremity
and Herat at the western—and these two areas form the subject of this
chapter.

THE HINDU KUSH

The northern frontier of Afghanistan was dominated by the mountains
of the Hindu Kush and their westerly continuation, the Paropamisus
range. The eastern part of this great massif, including the areas of
Badakhshan and Wakhan, was of no concern to Britain during the
period under discussion. Dost Muhammad had possessed no authority
in that area and no danger from it was anticipated. Although several
passes through the mountains existed in the eastern area, these were
unknown to the British who were therefore untroubled by them. British
interest began further west and concentrated on the string of passes
which extended from Bamiyan to Balkh. The problem was to decide
where, between those two points, to fix the frontier of Shuja's domains.

For the Hindu Kush was not the well-defined rampart, Nature's Great Wall of China, which it had appeared to be in Calcutta, but a belt of mountains ninety miles thick.

The attention of Macnaghten was drawn immediately to Turkestan when Dost Muhammad took flight in August 1839, evaded the pursuit, and settled in Balkh, where he apparently constituted a danger to the newly-constituted Empire of Shuja. Macnaghten resolved to dislodge the former Amir, by sending into Turkestan an agent, Dr. P. B. Lord, to persuade the local chiefs to expel their unexpected guest. Lord was also instructed 'to place on a solid footing the relations between His Majesty [Shah Shuja] and the Turkestan states south of the Oxus'.[1] Macnaghten hoped to achieve this second objective through an alliance with Mir Murad Beg, ruler of the Uzbek state of Kunduz.

Macnaghten's information about Murad was out of date. It was true that for many years past Murad had been the dominant figure in the area. He sprang from a prominent local family and had begun his own rise to power as a lieutenant of one Qilij Ali, Atalik of Khulm, who had in turn seized control of the area when Sadozay authority disappeared at the beginning of the nineteenth century. Qilij Ali had remained content with nominal allegiance to Kabul but *de facto* independence. After his death, which took place about 1815, Murad had succeeded to the greater part of his domain, although Balkh itself was seized by the Uzbek rulers of Bukhara. Murad had then flourished as a glorified bandit-chieftain, supplementing his revenues by levies on passing caravans and selling to the Chinese slaves captured in Badakhshan and Afghanistan. He had acquired an unsavoury name in British India because he was thought to have had a hand in the death of William Moorcroft in 1825.[2]

In 1832 Burnes had traversed Kunduz and recorded a more favourable impression, which was developed by Lord when he visited the area in 1838. They depicted Murad as a powerful ruler, who could be malevolent, but was not to be despised. Both, however, exaggerated the extent of his power which was already in decline. In the winter of 1838 to 1839 Murad was forced by Dost Muhammad to surrender the valleys of Saighan and Kamard, stop slaving, and relinquish customs-dues levied on caravans passing between Turkestan and India. At the same time his power was menaced by his vassal, a son of Qilij Ali named Mir Muhammad Amin Beg Khan, better known as Mir Wali, the Governor of Khulm, who had allied with Dost Muhammad during the Amir's winter campaign. From Lord, Macnaghten knew that Murad's authority was under challenge, but he thought that this circumstance would only induce the Uzbek chief to welcome British support. Macnaghten hoped, through Kunduz, to control the vassal states of Khulm and Haibak.

The agent chosen, Dr. Lord, was a recent recruit to political work. He had been employed as a surgeon on the Bombay establishment and in this capacity had been selected to accompany Alexander Burnes on his mission to Kabul in 1836 to 1838. He had then been employed on semi-political duties, because there was no one else, but, like Graeme Mercer, John McNeill, and other physicians before him, he was delighted to make the change. In 1838 he had been given further political duties in connection with the advance of Shahzada Timur through the Khaibar, where his efforts won him the contempt of Masson. Having accompanied Wade and Timur to Kabul he was both available and possessed some knowledge of Turkestan and so was an obvious choice for the projected mission. He was also, as it turned out, an unfortunate choice, for while he did not lack intelligence, there was an errant impulsiveness about his judgement which was to cost Britain dear.

Lord had proceeded only a few miles on his road to Turkestan when he recommended a totally new policy for the northern frontier. Macnaghten's policy was based on misinformation; the power of Murad Beg was too far decayed for British moral support to save him. Instead he should be given military aid in return for his allegiance to Shah Shuja. In this way Afghanistan could annex the whole area between the Hindu Kush and the Oxus.[3] This rapid change was rejected by Macnaghten who told Lord to proceed with his original mission. Lord, who seems to have had a not unnatural aversion to adventuring his unprotected person in Turkestan, then tried a new tack. He reported that a hostile coalition had been formed, comprising Murad Beg, Mir Wali, and Dost Muhammad. This brought a different response from Macnaghten. Whether it was the mention of Dost Muhammad or because Macnaghten required a justification for his decision to retain Company troops in Afghanistan or some other reason is uncertain. But Macnaghten decided to change his policy and, although it was too late to do anything before the winter snows blocked the passes, he announced that a brigade would be sent beyond the Hindu Kush in the spring of 1840. In the meantime he told Lord to proceed with a modified form of his mission. Lord was now to go to Khulm and Haibak to conciliate the local rulers; try to procure the expulsion of Dost Muhammad from the area; and keep alive the prospect of a military expedition.[4]

Lord did not go to Khulm, but instead did what he had always wanted to do and what Macnaghten had originally forbidden. He settled down amid the great Buddhist monuments of Bamiyan for the winter. His interest was not antiquarian but political. Bamiyan was to be the base from which he ruled the surrounding area and conducted a vigorous forward policy with the object of extending the authority of Shah Shuja northwards into and eventually beyond the Hindu Kush.

Lord's first success was in Saighan, a small valley some thirty-five miles north of Bamiyan with a population of between 1,500 and 2,000. A dispute between two chiefs gave him his chance. One of the chiefs had appealed for the mediation of Mir Wali of Khulm who had sent his son to adjust the quarrel. Lord promptly claimed that Saighan was under Afghan jurisdiction and gave Mir Wali's son twenty-four hours to leave. A rapid march enabled him to fall upon the Uzbeks as soon as the time-limit expired and to drive them from the valley, which Lord immediately annexed and in which he planted an Afghan garrison.[5] But Saighan was only a beginning. Lord's aims still extended to Balkh. In January 1840 he reported that all the chiefs between Bamiyan and Kunduz were friendly and would welcome Afghan rule; 'Can you reject a province which thus offers itself to be taken?', he demanded rhetorically.[6] Macnaghten could not; several arguments now seemed to support an advance to Balkh.

The arguments in favour of an advance to Balkh were strategic, political, humanitarian, and financial. The strategic argument was first put forward by Eldred Pottinger who passed through part of the area in 1839 on his return from Herat to Kabul. Pottinger decided that the true northern frontier of Afghanistan was that which ran from Herat to Balkh, passing north of the mountains; it was shorter; easier for movement; its possession would deny the fertile northern foothills of the mountains to an invader, who would still have to cross the Turkoman desert; and it would give Britain command of the Oxus.[7] Macnaghten, however, was less influenced by this argument than by immediate political problems. Apart from the threat to the peace of Afghanistan represented by Dost Muhammad, he was concerned by the attitude of certain Turkestan states, notably Bukhara, whose ruler had recently imprisoned a British agent, Colonel Stoddart, who had been sent to his court. But most of all Macnaghten was worried about a possible Russian attack. Exaggerated reports of the Russian expedition to Khiva, which was launched at the end of 1839, led to something approaching panic among the British authorities in Kabul.[8] The humanitarian argument was put forward by Lord, who argued that an advance to Balkh would end the Uzbek slave-trade. This was an argument likely to receive sympathetic attention in England, but Lord's benevolence was not unmixed with calculation. He had already declared the slave-trade abolished in districts which paid tribute to

Shuja, the object being not only to reduce slavery but to induce the chief victims of the Uzbek slave-traders, namely the Hazara tribes, to accept Afghan rule, something which they had not done willingly in the past.[9] Finally, Lord chose an argument dear to Macnaghten's heart. Shuja's revenues, he pointed out, were inadequate and those of Kabul and Qandahar incapable of substantial improvement. The Cis–Oxus territories, on the other hand, developed on European lines, could yield a much greater revenue.

Auckland refused to permit the annexation of Balkh. From the beginning he had insisted that Shuja should eschew expansion and concentrate on the consolidation of his rule within his own territories. He ordered Shuja to refuse to accept the allegiance of any chiefs in the area even if it were offered.[10] But Auckland found it easier to oppose the principle of a forward policy than its practice. He had already felt obliged to agree to the retention of a brigade to be used in the projected expedition across the Hindu Kush and, although he was unhappy about Lord's unauthorized advance to Saighan, he accepted this as an accomplished fact. Now he was faced with a proposal for a further limited advance. To the north of Saighan lay the twenty-two mile long, larger, and more populous valley of Kamard. In the middle of the valley, at a particularly narrow point, was a place called Bajgah. Bajgah, claimed Lord, with Macnaghten's support, was the ideal frontier position.[11] While he could stand out against Balkh, Auckland felt that he could not oppose the occupation of Bajgah, on the importance of which he felt that he must trust the judgement of the man on the spot.[12]

From Bajgah Lord continued his pressure for an advance to Balkh and beyond. A yet more advanced position, he argued, would be essential in the long run, both to meet an attack from Russia and to be able to control Bukhara.[13] But in the meantime he seemed content, like Wilfrid Rhodes, to get them in singles. In this campaign his next step was to secure an agreement with Mir Wali by which a British Resident would be established in Khulm with control over the foreign affairs of that state. As an immediate by-product of this approach, Lord hoped to persuade Mir Wali to surrender the family of Dost Muhammad, who, since the former Amir had gone to Bukhara, now lived at Khulm supporting themselves by caravan-dues which, Lord claimed, belonged to Shuja. To induce Mir Wali to accept his demands Lord mixed threats with his softer words. He wrote menacing letters, hinted at a forthcoming expedition, and sent out a series of survey parties, partly to collect information about routes through the mountains but partly to convince Mir Wali that the expedition was coming.

The surveys provided a diverting and influential consequence quite apart from their effect upon Mir Wali. There were at least three surveys. The first two in April and in June and July 1840 were conducted by Captain Hubert Garbett and produced much valuable information. The third, which was carried out by Lieutenant John Sturt (Bengal Engineers), accompanied by Captain Rollo Burslem (H. M. 13th L. I.), would scarcely be worth noticing but for its distant repercussions. Burslem left an account of his journey, coyly entitled *A Peep into Toorkisthan*, which was published in 1846. He and Sturt visited Khulm in July 1840. There they found themselves embarrassed by want of credentials, Macnaghten having declined to supply any on the odd ground that to give them an official character might alarm the people of the area. During their travels they met a man who claimed to be a British agent and who had secured for himself some local advantage from this misrepresentation. Observing his condition and style, Burslem, evidently a devotee of Sir Walter Scott, observed sarcastically, that he must have been trained in the school of Captain Dugald Dalgetty.[14] Unfortunately, his sarcasm and his reference to *Montrose* were equally lost on N. A. Khalfin, the Soviet historian who had made a special study of this period. Khalfin interpreted Burslem's remark as an admission that such a spy-school did exist and he proceeded to locate it in Calcutta.[15] Other Soviet historians took their cue from Khalfin and the famous Dalgetty spy-school was quickly established in the Soviet mythology of British imperialism. Like the false image of Father Brown, it proved impossible to remove. Perhaps Soviet historians should be forgiven—a country which prides itself that its foreign policy is based upon self-interest must expect a Machiavellian reputation—and, indeed, British writers, from Rudyard Kipling to John Masters, have themselves revelled in the thought of frontier spies. But the assumptions are wrong: a foreign policy based on self-interest may be no less foolish and incompetent than one based upon idealism; Alexander Jacob, the original of Kipling's cunning Lurgan Sahib, was no more than a con man.

Lord's own confidence trick had some success. In June 1840 envoys from Khulm and Kunduz came to Kabul to negotiate. In the discussions Macnaghten maintained the bluff, for such it had now become, that an expedition was intended. Macnaghten had been wavering over the desirability of the planned expedition for some time. In April he wanted to abandon it; in May he supported it again; and in June he decided he lacked sufficient troops and asked Auckland to send a further brigade to Afghanistan so that an advance could be made to Balkh, matters north of the Hindu Kush settled, and Bukhara threatened and forced to release Stoddart.[16] But it is doubtful if Mac-naghten were really serious, for on 14 May he had informed Lord that 'our policy should still be to make it appear as if an advance at least as far as Khoolm were intended though that such an advance should ever take place is now more than ever improbable.'[17] Quite possibly Mac-naghten was using the Khulm expedition as an excuse for requesting the reinforcements which he really wanted for Afghanistan and Herat. At all events he could not have received them in time for an advance to the north before 1841 and in any case Auckland would not give him more troops for that purpose.

By now Auckland was under considerable pressure not only from Afghanistan but also from London, where Hobhouse, who had origi-nally opposed an advance to Khulm, had been induced by the news of the Russian expedition to Khiva to change his mind. In December 1839 the President announced that an advance would be necessary if a threat from Russia developed.[18] In face of this Auckland gave some ground and at the end of May 1840 agreed to an advance under certain conditions. These were that only Afghan troops should be used; that the purpose should be limited to the capture of Dost Muhammad; and that all other disputes with Khulm should be settled by negotiation. While it was desirable on general grounds that Shuja should control all the passes into Afghanistan, this end should be accomplished, if at all, by diplomacy.[19] Hobhouse subsequently criticized Auckland both for his limited aims and for his refusal to permit the use of Company troops. In August 1840 Hobhouse ruled that any expedition should be a strong one and that its aims should not be limited to the capture of Dost Muhammad, but should include permanent occupation.[20] This dis-patch, however, arrived too late to affect the issue.

Lacking sufficient resources to mount an expedition, even if he had wished to do so, Macnaghten was obliged to continue to rely upon bluff. With the aid of Lord he continued to keep alive the threat of an armed advance; troops occupied Bajgah and reinforcements were sent to Bamiyan. In his negotiations in Kabul he threatened the emissaries of Khulm and dangled before the Kunduz minister the renewed prospect of British help for Murad Beg against Mir Wali. By August 1840 Macnaghten seemed to have succeeded. In June or July the family of Dost Muhammad surrendered themselves and it became known that the ex-Amir was a fugitive, fleeing from Bukhara. Defensive alliances were concluded with both Khulm and Kunduz; Mir Wali agreed to accept Afghan suzerainty, and an Afghan garrison; to pay a small tribute; and to hand over to Shah Shuja the caravan-dues which he collected. In return Mir Wali was given Saighan and Kamard. Apart from the two larger states, friendly relations appeared to be well established with the other petty states between Bajgah and Khulm, including Haibak.[21] Lord appeared to have completed another stage in his drive into Turkestan.

At the very moment of his seeming triumph Lord's little empire fell into pieces. Dost Muhammad returned to Khulm from Bukhara, allied with Mir Wali, and fell upon the British position at Bajgah on 30 August. The British evacuated Bajgah and withdrew to Bamiyan, where, with the aid of reinforcements from Kabul, they were able to repel the Uzbek attack and save the British position in northern Afghanistan from total destruction. It is unnecessary here to examine in detail the reasons for revolt: it will be sufficient to remark that Dost Muhammad took the initiative and that Mir Wali threw in his lot with the former Amir partly because of fear of British intentions and partly because he hoped for plunder from the smaller chiefs.[22] From the viewpoint of British policy, with which we are concerned, the real importance of the revolt, was that it brought to a sudden end the policy of extending Afghan frontiers and British influence in the direction of Balkh.

The forward policy in the north was wound up by an agreement with Mir Wali on 28 September. The Uzbek leader had already separated his forces from those of Dost Muhammad, who later made his way to the Kohistan where he led a fresh rising against Shuja. By the agreement with Khulm Britain abandoned the position acquired in the north. The valley of Kamard and the possessions of the lesser chiefs of Haibak, etc., were made over to Mir Wali. Saighan was to remain nominally attached to Afghanistan, but Mir Wali was informed that he could have this area also if he behaved well; indeed Macnaghten was prepared to give it up during the negotiations. The garrison was withdrawn from Saighan and the British fort demolished. All the other elements of control in the north—suzerainty, garrisons, and control of the foreign relations of Khulm—were abandoned and Mir Wali left to go his own way. The British forces at Bamiyan were withdrawn immediately. Lord had wanted to reinforce them, but Macnaghten, frightened by the prospect of a general rising under the leadership of Dost Muhammad, would spare no troops for the north. In fact, without a major effort troops could not have been retained at Bamiyan through the winter because the barracks had been destroyed by fire and no food was left in the valley.[23] Finally, the British agency at Bamiyan was withdrawn and relocated at Charikar, only forty miles north of Kabul, in the area of the Kohistan. An Afghan Governor was installed at Bamiyan. Appropriately enough, the main exponent of the forward policy in the north, Dr. Lord, died with his policy. He was killed in November 1840 during the course of the campaign against Dost Muhammad in the Kohistan.

To some extent the abandonment of the forward policy in the north could be explained by contending that it had achieved most of its aims. Dost Muhammad's family was already in British hands and the Amir himself surrendered and was sent into captivity in India at the end of the year. The only notable member of his family still at large was his son, Muhammad Akbar, who remained at Khulm, causing Macnaghten some concern, although the Envoy never pressed Mir Wali concerning Akbar's surrender. The Russian threat could be discounted after the failure of the Khiva expedition. It is doubtful if the idea of meeting Russia had ever been very influential in shaping the views of Lord and Macnaghten, but the removal of the Russian factor was the most important consideration in causing Hobhouse to abandon his pressure for an advance to Khulm. The only major argument which remained to indicate an active northern policy was that which held that an advance could induce the ruler of Bakhara to release Stoddart. But here too an apparent improvement in Stoddart's position could be regarded as reducing the need for strong action. When Mir Wali invoked the British name to justify his own ambitions in the direction of Bukhara, Macnaghten not only refused to assist him but wrote to Bukhara denying any thought of countenancing Mir Wali's attack.[24]

Some of the arguments in favour of the forward policy had clearly been disproved by events. The revenue benefits were evidently mythical; the expenses had always outweighed the returns. Lord's claims of enthusiasm for the British connection had been shown by the rising to be without foundation; his friendly chiefs had disappeared. 'I never supposed we had a single friend', wrote Garbett.[25] Further, Lord's strategic analysis had been revealed to be mistaken. The invaluable Bajgah was seemingly indefensible, and there was evidently nothing to be gained from control of the line of passes which led from Khulm to Bamiyan. Garbett's first survey in April had established that the route was impassable to regular forces without elaborate road-works, while the discovery of a network of alternative passes, bypassing sections of the line, proved that it was impossible to devise any system of defence which would exclude irregular forces. In short, a forward policy was military madness; Britain could move forward only by making roads for an enemy and was continually exposed to outflanking movements.[26]

The main reason for the abandonment of the forward policy in Afghanistan, however, was the abandonment of the forward Political Agency. It was Lord's monopoly of information which had enabled him to manufacture arguments in favour of an advance and, as some arguments were abandoned, a resourceful Political Agent could always find more. Forward policies were manufactured by the simple process of placing an agent in a forward position and they could be reversed by the equally simple act of removing him. With his removal the arguments which had seemed so objective, so compelling, and so unanswerable fell to the ground. Macnaghten had never been anxious for a forward policy in the north, but had found himself drawn along inexorably by Lord and indeed had found the espousal of an advance to Khulm an attractive device in relation to other policies. But now the Dost Muhammad crisis had forced Auckland to give him the reinforcements he needed and the excuse of an expedition to Khulm was no longer required. Auckland had been positively opposed to any forward movement in the north, but had found that he too was unable to stand against the combined pressures of the men on the spot and the men in London. Now, with both pressures gone, the Governor-General could get his way.

The debate about the advance to the Oxus provides a model demonstration of one of the main themes of this book. That theme is the relationship between individual ambition on the frontier and grand strategy. The forward movement in the north was the sole creation of Lord, who skilfully deployed his information and thoughtfully phrased his arguments in order to lure his superiors into supporting a policy which was designed to place him at the head of an unnecessary empire in Turkestan. He had slotted Turkestan into a theoretical structure of strategic defence and in the process had modified that structure substantially. It was almost by accident that the casual reverses of September 1840 had exposed the system for the fantasy that it was. Lord's death had completed the collapse of the Hindu Kush strategy. It was now clear that the best defence for Afghanistan was to leave the area unguarded. Nevertheless, Macnaghten was occupationally incapable of appreciating the lesson of events. Although he withdrew the northern agent from Bamiyan, he installed him in the Kohistan where, on a minor scale, the same pattern began to unfold once more. In May 1841, Major Eldred Pottinger, who had returned from Kabul, was appointed as Political Agent for the Turkestan frontier. At Charikar, however, his main concern was not with the Uzbek frontier but with the Tajik tribes of the Kohistan and surrounding valleys. Macnaghten advised him to interfere with them as little as possible. 'You will take conciliation as your guide', he wrote.[27] But, inevitably, Pottinger found himself following a similar policy of escalation and before he had been there a month, had produced convincing arguments why it was necessary that expeditions should be sent to bring the area under control. Macnaghten fought hard to resist the pressure, but it was in the Kohistan that some of the earliest outbreaks leading to the final collapse in Afghanistan took place. Like Lord, Pottinger was an infection, not a poultice on the frontier.

HERAT

The debate about an advance to Herat—the western gateway to Afghanistan, as it was regarded—bears some resemblance to that which concerned Khulm, but in the case of Herat the arguments for a forward policy were stronger and more ardently supported, and caused Auckland much greater trouble than those which related to the northern frontier. That Herat was a key strategic position was a belief firmly held long before the expedition to Afghanistan was launched. The importance of Herat had been discussed intermittently for many years and more regularly in the 1830s. The conviction of its strategic significance was most strongly held among British diplomats based in Iran and through them had been transmitted to London. In Calcutta, however, the Government had been slower to accept that control of Herat was vital; not until he was subjected to the various submissions of McNeill and Burnes during the course of the Iranian attack on the city in 1837 to 1838 did Auckland concede that its fate was a matter of importance to British India. Even then he refused direct aid to the town and concentrated his efforts at Qandahar and Kabul.

The assistance that Herat did receive during the long agony of its siege was purely fortuitous and arose out of the accidental presence in the city of Lieutenant Eldred Pottinger (1811–43), nephew of Henry Pottinger, the Resident in Sind. Eldred Pottinger had no official status in Herat; he was engaged in an unofficial tour of Afghanistan, partly at the instigation of his uncle, partly out of interest and with a view to bringing himself to the notice of his Government. When the siege began Pottinger assisted in the defence of the city with advances of money and by advice and example. Many British writers have followed Sir John Kaye in making Pottinger's efforts the decisive factor in the defeat of Iran, although this claim seems to exaggerate his influence. The point, however, is not one which concerns us here, for our interest is in the situation of Herat after the termination of the siege.

In September 1838 Herat seemed ruined. The city had been smashed by bombardment and the valley pillaged by Iranian soldiers and their estimated ninety thousand camp-followers. Crops and irrigation systems had been destroyed and trade was at a standstill.

Shortages caused a steep rise in the price of grain during the following winter; the population was starving, and the Government, its treasury empty, could do nothing to help even if it had so wished. In this situation Pottinger could wield great influence. By issuing bills on the Indian Treasury he alone could supply what was needed to prevent famine, revive the economy, and re-invigorate the Government. But Pottinger would help only if certain conditions were met. He wanted reforms in the Herat Government, whose system he detested on humanitarian grounds. The nominal ruler, Kamran Shah, was by now little more than a shadow monarch and real power was in the hands of the *wazir*, Yar Muhammad Khan Alikozay, whose habit was to raise money by torturing his rivals and selling his Shiite subjects to the Turkoman slave-dealers.[28] Pottinger therefore demanded, as the price of assistance, control of Herati foreign relations and changes in the administration. His method was to become a tax-farmer himself. He advanced to Yar Muhammad a sum equal to the estimated yield of the taxes of Herat and then tried to collect the taxes himself. Although he collected no more than a tenth of their estimated value, he effectively acquired control of a major part of the administrative system. Pottinger made other advances of money as allowances to the Afghan chiefs, financed an agricultural recovery, and set up a system of public works to provide employment, and public kitchens to provide food.[29] During the ten months which followed the lifting of the siege he spent over £30,000. To Auckland it seemed as if Pottinger had taken over the running of the state.[30]

Pottinger's apparent power was an illusion. He could not supervise everything and political expediency forced him to turn a blind eye to certain abuses; he was obliged to ignore the slave-trade lest he should jeopardize British interests in Turkestan.[31] Nor could he enforce his control of Herati foreign relations. The Iranians were still in occupation of Ghuriyan at the eastern end of the Herat valley and Yar Muhammad was busily exploring with them the possibility of a deal by which he would dismiss Pottinger in return for their evacuation of Ghuriyan.[32] Pottinger's attempts to interfere in internal affairs led to frequent clashes and continual friction with Yar Muhammad. After one series of bitter quarrels Pottinger's colleague, Colonel Charles Stoddart, who had entered Herat after the Iranian withdrawal in September 1838, was ordered by Yar Muhammad to leave Herat. Stoddart then departed on his ill-fated mission to Bukhara. Pottinger was allowed to remain only because he supplied money and formed a useful bargaining counter for the *wazir* in his dealings with the Iranians. But the dispute endured. On one occasion Pottinger quarrelled so violently with the *wazir*'s brother, Sher Muhammad, that the British officer ordered his servants to remove the Afghan from his house. Not surprisingly, his servants hesitated to lay hands on so influential a chief and Sher Muhammad turned to Pottinger and asked who would dare to turn him out. Pottinger's account continues: 'I immediately arose and collared him, interpreting it as a challenge to myself.'[33]

Enshrined within this delightful mixture of Henty and Greyfriars is one of the leading features of the British experience in Central Asia. The relationship was one between two uncomprehending value-systems and it could not be cemented merely by assigning the players complementary parts in the great strategic drama of Indian defence. It was a relationship which could be resolved only by violent conflict, or by complete divorce. The reaction took place where the agents of each system encountered one another in the flesh; far away in Calcutta and in London the conflicts were incomprehensible, unless they could be seen as part of the strategic fantasy which had been created. So Auckland looked at Pottinger's troubles from the viewpoint of politics and found them quite unnecessary; Pottinger's acts might drive Yar Muhammad to look to Iran. Accordingly, Auckland wrote to Kamran apologizing for the conduct of Pottinger and Stoddart and asking him not to blame the British Government for its agents' unauthorized interference.[34] Auckland's private secretary, Colvin, deprecated Pottinger's attempt to create 'a Utopia of Justice and forebearance' at Herat. 'Why is it', he inquired of Burnes, 'that Englishmen everywhere are rough, overbearing, without tact and address and more disliked by foreigners than any other people?'[35] The Indian Government decided that Pottinger must be replaced at Herat.

This decision arose not only from Pottinger's actions but from his alarming recommendations. As early as February 1839 Pottinger had decided that it was vain to hope for improvements in Herat under its present rulers and had recommended that it should be annexed to the prospective domains of Shah Shuja. Auckland was quite opposed to this proposal. It was possible, though doubtful, that Kamran and Yar Muhammad might eventually agree to accept pensions and retire in favour of Shuja, but in no case could any part of the Army of the Indus be diverted to Herat.[36] Macnaghten also thought the suggestion premature, warned Pottinger to be careful, and asked Kamran to send an envoy to negotiate with himself at Qandahar. But these negotiations were most unsatisfactory since the Herati agent wished only to discuss the cession of Kabul and Qandahar to Kamran. It was plain that further negotiations would have to be conducted by a new British agent at Herat.

The agent chosen to lead the mission to Herat was Major D'Arcy Todd (1808–45). Macnaghten first offered the job to Burnes, but Burnes refused unless it was to carry out a policy of annexation. Todd, inexperienced as he was, was one of the few men available. Todd's rise had indeed been rapid. From service with the detachment in Iran he had become McNeill's Military Secretary, in which post he had acquired some diplomatic experience and had been fortunate enough to be sent to India with dispatches, via Herat. He had thus been available to deputize for Macnaghten with Shah Shuja. He was now not needed in this post and, as the only man available who had any knowledge of Herat, was an obvious choice. And, on the surface, despite his inexperience, Todd seemed a good choice, for he spoke Persian and was likeable, solid, practical, and reliable. He also had deep religious convictions and, as with Arthur Conolly later, this was to prove Todd's greatest problem. A more cynical, less scrupulous, unambitious man might have been a better Envoy at Herat.

Todd was given detailed instructions by Macnaghten for the conduct of his mission.[37] His main task was to negotiate a treaty which would give Britain, through her Resident in Herat, effective control over the foreign affairs of that state. Herat should also agree to abolish slavery and promote trade. In return Britain would recognize Kamran as ruler and promise not to interfere in the internal affairs of Herat. In apparent contradiction to this promise, Yar Muhammad's personal position was safeguarded by a private, written agreement recognizing him as hereditary *wazir* and the sole channel of communication between Britain and Herat; he was to receive all monies to be spent in Herat.[38] In Todd's instructions it was recognized that Britain would have to be prepared to spend a lot of money on Herat to rebuild the defences, and to train and re-equip the army. Todd was also instructed to settle the boundary between the domains of Shah Shuja and Kamran. Lastly, it is clear from the instructions that Herat was regarded not merely in a negative sense as a buffer to be supported but in a positive sense as a base for the penetration of British influence into Turkestan: Todd was ordered to make British policy known to the rulers of Khiva, Bukhara, and other states in the area.

Todd replace Pottinger at Herat at the end of July 1839 and was horrified at what he saw. 'Everything about the place denoted devastation, desolation and ruin', he reported.[39] He quickly negotiated the treaty, which was signed on 13 August,[40] and immediately began paying out large sums of money: £10,000 in immediate compensation and a regular subsidy at the rate of £30,000 a year. But he rapidly came to the conclusion that this was the wrong policy for Herat.

Todd set out his analysis of the situation at Herat in a long dispatch of 2 October 1839. Herat was, he argued, the strategic key to India. Like Pottinger, he believed that the true first line of defence for British India was that which ran from Herat to Balkh; control of this line would enable Britain to meet an attack either from the Oxus or Mashhad. Herat was the vital western bastion of this line and had to be made safe. Of the three possible ways of controlling Herat, Todd, with his experience of Iran, dismissed the existing method of subsidies. Best would be annexation, but the recent treaty made this impossible, although, if it were decided that Herat should be taken, a plausible excuse for setting the treaty aside could be found. Accordingly, Todd recommended the third possibility: to place a British garrison in Herat.[41]

Although Todd based his arguments entirely upon strategic considerations, it is doubtful whether these were the only, or even the principal factors which weighed with him. His strategic arguments were almost identical with those of Pottinger, with whom humanitarian considerations had clearly predominated in his relations with Herat. Pottinger's clashes with Yar Muhammad had occurred not over the *wazir*'s negotiations with Iran, although Pottinger had mistrusted these, but over the internal condition of Herat, and particularly over the slave-trade. Indeed, one reason why Pottinger had originally advocated taking control of the Herat–Balkh line was that it would enable Britain to stop the slave-trade. As will be seen, Todd's own views were very similar: he could tolerate neither the slave-trade nor the cruelties of Herati government. Annexation or military control were measures which would also prevent these abuses.

Todd had scarcely sent off his dispatch of 2 October when he found the plausible excuse which he had sought for setting aside the treaty and clearing the way for annexation. In defiance of the treaty Yar Muhammad had negotiated with Iran and even offered to recognize Iranian suzerainty over Herat in return for help against Shuja; 'I swear to God', he had written to the Governor of Mashhad, 'that I prefer the fury of the Kings of Kings [the Shah of Iran] to the kindliness of a million of English.'[42] Todd sent Macnaghten a copy of this letter and recommended that Herat should be annexed.

Macnaghten had come round to support annexation. He had supported Todd's garrison recommendation and he now supported annexation. The argument on which he laid greatest stress was that of the threat from Russia, following the reports of the Khiva expedition, and, no doubt, that was an influential factor in the alteration which had taken place in Macnaghten's views since May. But, once more, subsequent events lead us to question whether this was the major factor in his decision. With Shuja established in Kabul, Kamran's power had begun to appear an anomaly in the policy of a strong buffer state in Afghanistan. The annexation of Herat, wrote Macnaghten, 'was the one step necessary to consolidate the power of our ally Shah Shuja ool Moolk, to establish British influence on a solid footing in Central Asia, and to promote the interests of humanity'.[43]

Auckland had not changed his mind about Herat and was as opposed to annexation as ever. All that Britain required from Herat was that it should have adequate defences, good government, and no slavery, and all this could be accomplished through the existing Government of Herat, if the confidence of Yar Muhammad could be gained and the independence of Herat guaranteed. Although he had sanctioned the August Treaty, he disliked it because it contemplated too great a degree of British control. Interference, he wrote to Hobhouse in December, should be kept to a minimum and withdrawn completely as soon as possible.[44] Close control would be self-defeating. Nothing, Auckland observed realistically, could prevent the Heratis corresponding with Iran and to try to prevent such exchanges would lead only to embarrassment. The strategic arguments for annexation, he dismissed: he feared neither a Russian nor an Iranian invasion of India. He concluded that there was no other feasible policy but that Todd should try and gain Yar Muhammad's confidence. If he could not win the *wazir*'s trust any other way he should buy it; if that method also failed Todd should withdraw to Qandahar, although Auckland believed that the threat of such an action would induce the Heratis to give way. But, in the last analysis, withdrawal, not annexation, was the final solution to the problem of Herat: 'Even if a contrary course were warranted by the proceedings of the authorities at Herat, it would require from this Government further exertions and sacrifices of such magnitude as cannot at present be contemplated.'[45] Concluding his rejection of Todd and Macnaghten's recommendations, Auckland renewed his appeal for the avoidance of expansion and for concentration on peace and the consolidation of Shuja's existing possessions.[46]

Long before Auckland's negative reached Herat in early February 1840, Todd changed his own mind about annexation. If Britain pressed Herat too hard Yar Muhammad might ally with Iran and lead a Muslim coalition against Shah Shuja. With this in mind Todd dropped his recommendation for annexation on 22 October and reverted to support of his earlier proposal for a garrison. In the meantime he continued the expensive subsidy policy.[47] This policy, however, was becoming more and more costly, as Yar Muhammad revealed a remarkable talent for persuading Todd to disgorge. On one occasion he induced him to advance £1,000 as expenses to send Sher Muhammad on a visit to India; the money was used to finance a plundering expedition in the eastern Herati province of Farah.[48] Another device was to pretend to a sore conscience about his dealings with Iran and to demand money as a proof that Todd was not angry. Even so, by the time Auckland's verdict arrived, Todd had decided that he would soon be forced out of Herat because of the *wazir*'s growing suspicions of British intentions.

Auckland's decision, therefore, apparently had the effect of saving Todd's position at Herat because Todd was able to inform the *wazir* that his past sins were forgiven and the British would uphold the treaty. This led, however, to still more ingenious schemes for extracting money from Todd. For Yar Muhammad, while grateful for his absolution, yet complained that he could not feel entirely easy in his mind until he could prove both the gratitude and the utility of Herat by the performance of some signal service for Britain.[49] Upon examination his proposal proved to be merely another scheme to enrich Herat.

Yar Muhammad tendered the services of Herati troops. In return for this useless offer he wanted fresh guarantees for himself and an additional subsidy to enable Herat to extend her power throughout her former territory. The boundaries of this former empire, according to the *wazir*, extended from the Hari Rud in the west to the Helmand in the east and from Sistan in the south to Panjdah in the north.[50] This was a proposal which possessed some merits in British eyes, representing as it did a way of extending British influence into Central Asia by using the agency of Herat. Although the claim to the Helmand in the east had disturbing implications in relation to Shuja, it was not an immediate problem, and could be ignored. The proposals relating to the western and northern frontiers on the other hand offered possibilities. To extend Herati control to the Hari Rud would involve driving the Iranian garrison from Ghuriyan and this would have useful repercussions on relations with Iran. The extension of Herati rule to Maymana offered yet another mode of establishing indirect British control over the Herat–Balkh line.

The Herat–Balkh line could be divided into two sections. In the west, between Herat and the Murghab river, were a number of nomadic tribes who struggled fairly effectively to maintain *de facto* independence of the Government in Herat. In the east, between the Murghab and Kunduz, were a group of four small Uzbek-dominated states known as the Char Vilayats: Maymana, Ankhui, Shibargan, and Sir-i Pol. These small states both fought among each other and simultaneously strove to resist outside encroachment, whether from Kabul,

Herat, Khiva, Iran, or Bukhara. Their position was graphically described to a British traveller by the ruler of Maymana in November 1840. 'No doubt', he said, 'you know the saying that it is difficult for a man to sail with his legs in two boats, but how can a man escape drowning who is obliged to shift them among five, according as the wind changes?'[51]

Pottinger's policy had been to control the area by annexing it to Afghanistan: Lord had wanted to achieve the same end from a position of dominance in Balkh. But Auckland had ruled out annexation to Afghanistan and by the spring of 1840 it had begun to seem as if it might not be possible to obtain sufficient influence at Balkh, even if an agreement with Khulm were formed. So Macnaghten was inclined to look favourably upon a proposal which offered the prospect of achieving British control by a movement from the other side. When, after the breakdown of the British position on the Hindu Kush in September 1840, Macnaghten abandoned any hope that Shuja would be able to annex Maymana and dominate the Char Vilayats, he became quite willing that Herat should take them, although, believing them to be nominally dependent upon Bukhara, he thought it best that they should be left alone.[52] As it happened, in October 1840 Yar Muhammad did persuade the ruler of Maymana to sign an agreement by which he recognized a species of Herati sovereignty over his tiny state. But, in fact, neither Kabul nor Herat really possessed the power to establish control over the area and, in the end, the rulers remained independent.

Apart from the strategic possibilities, Macnaghten was persuaded to recommend the proposal on other considerations. It would both strengthen the Government of Herat and thereby make that state into a more effective and independent buffer and it would also provide some justification for the present subsidy payments, which Macnaghten claimed, unconvincingly, were not intended to be exceeded as a consequence. Somewhat more surprisingly, after first regarding the proposal with disapproval, Auckland also accepted the suggested policy. In the light of his previous attitude and in view of the obvious possible complications, this change in his opinions is good evidence of the strong pressures to conduct a more active policy at Herat which were now being brought to bear upon him.

Once more the weight of the Government in London had been thrown behind the forward policy. Palmerston had never wavered in his belief that it was necessary to make sure of Herat and, after his Parliamentary worries of the early part of 1839 had been put behind him, Hobhouse once more took up the cudgels by his side. At the beginning of December 1839, prompted by Palmerston and McNeill, who were then under the impression that Iran was on the point of yielding to Britain's demands, Hobhouse urged Auckland to take the chance to break the August Treaty with Herat and to consolidate Afghanistan.[53] Palmerston feared that once Iran had given way it would be impossible to justify a subsequent annexation. Ironically enough, when Hobhouse had opposed the suggestion of garrisoning Herat in the summer of 1839, the President had said that only Iranian aggression would justify such an act: now it appeared that the greatest stimulus to action was Iranian submissiveness. As it happened, it had become clear before the end of December that Iran would not give way and Hobhouse then changed his position again; now he opposed completely any attempt to annex Herat to Afghanistan. The only development, he stated, which could justify such a move, was a Russian advance in Central Asia.[54] Before another month was out this very eventuality had arisen and Hobhouse switched once more to support for action at Herat. It was at this point that he received the papers relating to Todd's October 2 proposal for annexation and learned that Auckland had rejected a fine opportunity to secure control over Herat.

It was the Russian factor which weighed most heavily with the Cabinet and a general discussion of the issue took place between the ministers most concerned, namely Palmerston, Hobhouse, Melbourne, and Russell. As usual, it was Palmerston, with the support of Hobhouse, who was the principal advocate of a forward policy. He set out his views in a letter dated 20 February 1840. For the safety of British India it was necessary to control the military and political resources of Herat. If Britain did not control Herat, Russia would, and would thus control the two great gates of India: Khiva and Herat. He continued:

These dangers may appear remote to those who have not turned their serious attention to these matters—but those who have watched the rapid progress and gigantic strides made by Russia towards the East during the last twenty years, cannot consider the distance which yet separates their advanced posts from the Indus as any permanent security for our possessions nor those countries which still intervene as points which the British Government can, with any safety neglect.

The policy and intentions of Russia in this direction are as clear as day, and require counteracting precautions on the part of Great Britain.[55]

He and Hobhouse believed that a successful outcome to the Khiva expedition would result in direct Russian control over Khiva and indirect control over Herat through Iran. In such a situation it would become impossible to consolidate Afghanistan under Shuja. To avoid that situation it was necessary to pre-empt Russia at Herat and secure that city against any Asian enemy. How Herat should be secured

Palmerston did not specify; annexation would be the simplest solution, but Hobhouse, as an alternative, suggested the occupation of Sistan and control over Herat from that position,[56]

Melbourne and Russell took a quite different view. Melbourne, believing that no danger existed from Russia and that, having defeated Khiva, Russia would retire within her own frontiers again, opposed provoking Russia by annexing Herat.[57] In his characteristically irritating fashion Russell tried to argue both ways. Peering mournfully into the future he remarked that 'Russia makes great advances, and, if England dies of decay and decrepitude, Russia will be her heir in the East—as the United States will be in the West.' Nevertheless, discerning no immediate danger, he sided with Melbourne.[58] As a result of their opposition the strong advice to annex Herat, which Palmerston and Hobhouse would like to have given Auckland, was toned down. Instead, Auckland was merely told that he must somehow consolidate British influence at Herat, but the means were left to him.[59]

As a result of this pressure from London, even diluted as it was, Auckland was virtually compelled to take some action over Herat. Hitherto he had fended off Macnaghten and Todd by talking vaguely of future possibilities. But, if he had to do something at Herat, there was one proposal which appeared to have some attractions; this was to retake Ghuriyan by force. For Auckland the attraction of Ghuriyan lay in its possible connection with Kharag. It seemed likely that in a future settlement Britain would evacuate Kharag in return for the restoration of Ghuriyan to Herat. But Auckland wished to retain Kharag as a useful base in the Gulf and as a vital weapon to be used in any future contest with Iran.[60] If he could win back Ghuriyan before a settlement he might avoid the exchange. The proposal was also acceptable in London where Ghuriyan was seen as the principal obstacle to a settlement with Iran.[61]

The possibility that Herat might recover Ghuriyan by force had been first mentioned by Todd in August 1839. At that time he had discouraged the idea in the hope that a peaceful settlement might make it unnecessary. By October, however, he had come to support an expedition, not only as a means of re-establishing Herat's western frontier, but also because its determined prosecution would demonstrate the sincerity of Yar Muhammad's professions that he had forsworn his flirtations with Iran.[62] In February 1840 Auckland gave unofficial permission to make the attempt.[63] So delicate a matter was kept out of the official correspondence throughout 1840.

The Ghuriyan expedition was a complete fiasco. In June 1840 Todd advanced £20,000 to Yar Muhammad to finance the movement of troops. But no attack upon Ghuriyan was ever made. For several days Todd camped in the desert with the Herati force until it eventually dawned upon him that Yar Muhammad had no intention of attacking the Iranian garrison.[64] Todd was the victim of yet another of the *wazir*'s ingenious confidence tricks. For Todd it was the crowning blow and all his pent up distaste for the Government of Herat now burst out in passionate letters and in entries in his journal.

Although hurt pride no doubt played some part in Todd's revulsion against Herat and his now renewed call for annexation, there is no doubt that it was his Evangelical conscience which finally overcame his political discretion. The Government of Herat was irremediably bad; its revenues were inadequate for the support of so expensive a court and in consequence the Government could only support itself by oppression. Todd's fascinated disgust is evident in his description of the practices by which money was raised:

The person was generally a Khan who had enjoyed favour and was therefore supposed to possess wealth, or an executioner convicted of amassing wealth in the non-performance of his *duties*. The culprit was then put to the torture, the commonest method being by boiling or roasting or baking over a slow fire. The horrible ingenuities practised on these occasions are too disgusting to be more than alluded to. The wretch, writhing in agony, gradually disgorged his wealth and learned before he died that his wives and daughters had been sold to the Turkomans, or divided amongst the sweepers and (illeg.) of his murderers. Of two recent victims one was half roasted and then cut into very small pieces, the other parboiled and afterwards baked.[65]

The opposition between the outlook of Todd and that of Yar Muhammad was total. Todd later recalled one remark by the *wazir* which illustrated the difference between them. 'One toman', said the minister, 'wrung from a rich man by the aid of red hot pincers, or gained during a successful chappao (raid) was sweeter than ten acquired by the tame and tardy process of realizing revenue, or furnished by the generosity of a friendly government.'[66] Even allowing for the probability that Yar Muhammad was not wholly serious in this unabashed sadism and simply could not resist the temptation to shock his English watch-dog, the mere fact of the statement suffices to illustrate the unbridgeable gulf between Todd's idea of government for the good of the governed and Yar Muhammad's view of government for the entertainment of the governors. Simple humanitarianism thus made Auckland's policy of cautious restraint at Herat unworkable. It was neither ambition nor strategy which led Todd to revolt against it, but instinctive Christian abhorrence of evil. His fundamental lack of interest in the political and strategic importance of Herat and, indeed, in the ostensible purpose for his presence there is shown in his suggestion that an agreement might be made with Iran by which Britain allowed Iran to retain Ghuriyan in return for Britain being given a free hand at Herat.[67]

Although once more loyally supported by Macnaghten, Todd's proposal for a British expedition to annex Herat was predictably rejected by Auckland. Todd was forced to continue under the old policy. His position at Herat now steadily weakened; the unrest in Afghanistan and Kalat made the *wazir* bolder; he renewed his negotiations with Iran, demanded more money, threatened the mission, and talked of an expedition against Qandahar. Todd held on only by paying up and through the distraction of fortuitous disputes within the Herat Government. But his patience was certainly not inexhaustible and in January 1841 it gave way at last.

The final breach was provoked by Todd, who appears to have misunderstood instructions given him privately by Macnaghten. Anxious to overcome Auckland's opposition to annexation, Macnaghten had asked Todd to collect evidence against Yar Muhammad so as to build up an unanswerable case to present to the Governor-General. Macnaghten later claimed that he had warned Todd not to provoke a breach.[68] Todd, however, understood his unofficial instructions to mean that he should look for a satisfactory pretext for a rupture.[69] This he did, and accused Yar Muhammad of treacherous negotiations with Iran. The accusation was perfectly just, but the crime was scarcely new and Auckland had made it no more than a misdemeanour. In reply Yar Muhammad asked for forgiveness and, according to Todd, actually offered to admit a British brigade into Herat as evidence of his good intentions. It seems likely, however, that if Yar Muhammad made such an offer it was at Todd's prompting and was certainly not meant seriously. But Todd, to whom it represented the achievement of his long-sought garrison solution, did take the proposal seriously and recommended that if Yar Muhammad defaulted on his promise Herat should be attacked. Not daring to put such an ultimatum to the minister he contented himself with stopping the monthly allowances given to Kamran and his chiefs.[70] Todd's actions were clearly provocative and produced the expected result. Yar Muhammad demanded more money; Todd countered with an offer of a smaller sum in return for the admission of a British brigade into the citadel; and on 9 February Yar Muhammad expelled Todd from Herat.[71]

Todd had chosen a bad time to provoke a crisis; his expulsion coincided with a crucial stage in the achievement of the long-awaited settlement with Iran. Ghuriyan had always been the vital issue and even as Todd left Herat for Qandahar, a British agent approached Ghuriyan from the west with the object of superintending the Iranian evacuation. After the failure of Husayn Khan's mission, Iran had made several attempts, with Russian support, to persuade Palmerston to accept a compromise. Palmerston had held firm, fearing that unless there was a clear Iranian withdrawal from Ghuriyan, the Iranian attack on Herat might yet be renewed or even that Herat might negotiate a separate settlement with Iran. Hopes of such an agreement may indeed have lain behind the Iranian offer to evacuate Ghuriyan in April 1840. Palmerston certainly did not think that Iranian aims had changed and did not take up the offer immediately, preferring to await the result of the Herati expedition against Ghuriyan in August 1840. It was only after this had failed that he began, at the end of November, to take firm steps towards a negotiated settlement. The main precondition was the evacuation of Ghuriyan and a British agent was detached from the British mission, still in refuge at Erzerum on Ottoman soil, to go to Ghuriyan to superintend the evacuation of that fort and its return to Herat. The agent was Dr. James Riach, another of the surgeon-diplomatists who abounded in Central Asia. Riach had much experience in Iran and his tiny figure and prodigious moustaches feature regularly in the memoirs of travellers.

Todd's breach with Herat almost ruined Riach's hopes of success. Todd had not known of Riach's approach or, as he confessed later, he would have stayed in Herat.[72] Macnaghten's warning reached Todd too late. In consequence of Todd's departure the Iranian authorities estimated that the Herat Government might be driven to settle directly with Iran. They delayed evacuation, but later appeared to allow themselves to be pursuaded by Riach to carry out the agreed surrender of Ghuriyan on 31 March.[73] Riach breathed a sigh of relief, but what he did not know and what was not discovered by Britain until the middle of November 1841 was that a treaty between Herat and Iran was actually signed in March 1841, before evacuation was carried out.[74] The Shah thus hoped to snatch some consolatory prize from the jaws of defeat, but ironically it was Russia who would not support him. The Russian Ambassador, Duhamel, remained faithful to his instructions to support British policy and refused repeated attempts by the Iranian Government to persuade him to support their Herat ambitions. An appeal directly to Nesselrode achieved no better result.[75] Thus it was that, by one of those deathless ironies which so confound strategists and delight historians, Britain came to owe her success at Herat to the good offices of the very power whose alleged evil designs her presence there was intended to frustrate.

Auckland was furious with Todd for provoking a break with Herat and rejected Macnaghten's unhopeful suggestion of annexation. Even though his first impression was dispelled—that Todd had walked out of Herat when the Envoy's request for a British garrison that Auckland had never wanted was refused—Auckland nevertheless dismissed Todd from the Political Department and ordered him to return to the comparative poverty of regimental employment. Todd, Auckland wrote, had damaged Britain's reputation and jeopardized the hopes of peace in Afghanistan. An expedition to Herat was out of the question; British India had neither the men, equipment, nor money. Auckland based his estimates of what would be required on the figures given by Captain Edward Sanders (d. 1844), an Engineer officer who had accompanied Todd's mission to Herat. Working on the extravagant assumption that the enemy might number twelve thousand, Sanders had asked for twelve thousand men, twelve eighteen-pounder siege guns, and twelve eight-inch mortars and howitzers. His commissariat requirements were in proportion; one hundred days' provisions, 41,537 camels, and at least 36,000 camp followers.[76] Probably no expedition would in any case have been possible in 1841, but Sanders's excessive prudence gave Auckland all the opportunity he needed to declare that nothing could be done. He was strongly supported by General Elphinstone, the Commander-in-Chief at Kabul. In the hope that an optimistic recommendation from his military commander would oblige Auckland to give way, Macnaghten had attempted to persuade Elphinstone to support the proposal for an expedition. He had chosen the wrong man. Elphinstone was too old and sick to contemplate such a venture. Like Auckland, he grasped eagerly at every difficulty; Herat was too far and the information was inadequate. In any case, wrote Elphinstone, the Helmand was a much better frontier for Afghanistan, because the fearsome territory which lay between that river and Herat would exhaust any invading army. Seemingly, Elphinstone had become so convinced by his own arguments about the difficulties of the terrain that, unusually for a General, he had come to see them not only as a handicap to himself but even to a potential enemy. His apparent strategic predilection for the Helmand frontier should not, however, be taken too seriously, for in April 1841 he supported Nott's wish to withdraw regular troops from the Helmand, against the advice of Rawlinson and Macnaghten, and thus opened the way for the revival of the ambitions of Akhtar Khan in Zamindawar.[77]

The unanimous military opinion gave Auckland all the excuse for inaction that he required. The siege guns were not available; the troops could not be spared; and the weather made an expedition impossible, for from June to March there was insufficient water or forage, and in April and May the rivers were impassable. Nothing could be done before June 1842 at the earliest. Accordingly, Auckland decided to take no action but simply to accept the fact of Todd's expulsion and to turn the whole problem over to London with a recommendation that a diplomatic settlement should be made with Iran.[78]

Auckland's decision over Herat caused considerable dissension. On his own Council only Prinsep supported annexation; Bird agreed that it was a matter for London; while the military members, Nicolls and Casement, wanted to be out of Afghanistan altogether. In Bombay, however, Carnac, and in the North-Western Provinces, Thomas Robertson, who described Herat as 'the portals of our Empire', both supported annexation.[79] In London a majority in the Court of Directors supported Auckland; many of the Directors disliked the whole Afghan strategy. But the crucial factor was the attitude of Hobhouse and Palmerston and both remained unrepentant advocates of annexation. Their views had only been strengthened since the ministerial discussions on Herat in February 1840. The failure of the Ghuriyan expedition had indeed led Palmerston to seek a settlement with Iran, but it had also increased his appetite for Herat. It was made clear to Auckland in November and December 1840 that he was expected to take Herat.[80] Even though Palmerston relaxed this injunction slightly in February 1841, when he gave Auckland permission to wait while no immediate danger from Russia or Iran existed, the Foreign Secretary's views remained unchanged.[81]

The Cabinet decided in favour of annexation when, at the end of May and the beginning of June 1841, they considered the papers relating to Todd's withdrawal. Although Russell, Lansdowne, and Normanby all had some misgivings, Hobhouse and Palmerston carried their point.[82] On 4 June 1841 Auckland was sent orders to take Herat before June 1842; no discretion was left to him.[83] Palmerston summed up the general view in almost the same terms that he had used in February 1840: Britain must control Herat and Russia could be allowed no influence there; the only way to achieve these ends was to annex Herat at once. 'The iron is hot, let us strike it', he wrote. 'If we let it grow cold, it will be too hard for our blows.'[84]

Even confronted by these clear and unambiguous orders Auckland was unmoved. When the dispatch of 4 June was considered by his Council the decision of March was reaffirmed. Still only Prinsep supported annexation: the others agreed that an expedition was neither possible nor desirable; the resources were lacking and the consolidation of Shuja's existing possessions must come first. If there were a danger that Iran might take Herat then the danger should be met by action in Iran.[85] Thus Auckland had at last come full circle in his efforts to escape from the expansionist logic of his Afghan strategy. In 1838, confronted by a threat to Herat from Iran, he had decided that action in Iran was too dangerous and had chosen to meet the threat by action in Afghanistan; in 1841, chastened by his experience of Afghanistan, he preferred action in Iran. Thus the way was open for the strategy of 1856.

Time and chance, as Auckland probably calculated, came to his aid and saved him from the consequences of his refusal to carry out his orders. At 3 a.m. on the very morning following the sending of Hobhouse's dispatch ordering Auckland to take Herat, the Whigs were defeated on a motion of no-confidence. Parliament was then dissolved and the Conservatives won a majority at the election and formed a Government at the beginning of September. One of the first actions of the incoming Conservative Cabinet was to consider the question of Herat at Claremont on the afternoon of Saturday 4 September. The Conservatives had not then formed their policy on Afghanistan, but evacuation was recognized to be a possibility and the annexation of Herat would obviously make that more difficult as well as adding to the alarming financial burdens. Nor did Aberdeen, as Foreign Secretary, wish to espouse an act which might jeopardize good relations with Russia. So, while it was not decided to abandon the Herat expedition, Auckland was instructed to disregard the dispatch of 4 June and to suspend any attack for the time being.[86]

Time and chance also made the annexation of Herat irrelevant. From November 1841 onwards the British were caught up in a life-and-death struggle in Afghanistan by the side of which possession of Herat was a trifle. In any case the expected ill consequences of the British withdrawal had not been experienced. Russia's refusal to help made it impossible for Iran to press her claims. Yar Muhammad had never seriously wished to surrender the independence of Herat. Indeed he had embarked upon an attempt to make himself sole master of Herat, during which contest both he and Kamran appealed to Britain for help against one another, before the struggle eventually terminated in the murder of Kamran in 1842. But Britain was now uninterested in the result.

It was the British Mission in Tehran which had been the major proponent of the theory of the importance of Herat and it was the same mission which survived as the residual custodian of the conviction of its strategic importance. McNeill and Sheil wrote important memoranda on the subject on 30 November 1841. They still contended that Herat's military, political, and strategic importance was such as to make a

British garrison essential. Its unique, fertile valley could not be bypassed by an invading army. Politically, it formed an essential counterpoise to the position of Russia at Khiva and it was essential for the control of Afghanistan. Both saw the Afghan buffer as strategically far more important than the Iranian. 'Afghanistan is our true and natural frontier . . . The value of Persia has perhaps been at times magnified, and this value, whatever it was, has been much diminished since a large portion of Afghanistan has fallen into our hands.' But the Afghan and Iranian buffers were now seen not as opposed but as complementary and it was suggested that Herat might also form a base from which Britain could co-operate with Iran in an attack upon Russia.[87] Despite the changed European situation, hostility to Russia was still the main concern of the British diplomats in Tehran. Although Aberdeen personally favoured collaboration with Russia to restrain Iran from attacking Herat, he supported McNeill in his rejection of Duhamel's offer to mediate between Britain and Iran over Herat.[88] In February 1842 Aberdeen instructed the British representative to inform the Shah that any attack upon Herat, taking advantage of the Afghan rising, would be regarded as an attack upon Britain and would be met by appropriate action.[89] Nevertheless, although Aberdeen acted thus firmly in the emergency, his policy remained to seek agreement with Russia in Asia as well as Europe. In London as in Calcutta, the postulates on which the forward strategy had been based were increasingly questioned. Only in the British Mission in Tehran and in a few minds in India did the doctrine of the strategic importance of Herat still survive but this was sufficient to bring the question to the fore once more in the late 1840s and 1850s.

The debate about Herat in the years 1838 to 1841 was partly a debate about strategy. All agreed on the strategic importance of Herat in the defence of India and on the need to deny control of it to Russia, which power, it was feared, might gain indirect supremacy through Iran. Taken in conjunction with the real possiblity that Russia might occupy Khiva, there was a visible threat to the security of India. The principal difference between the debaters was not about the existence of the threat, although there were differences about the weight to be attached to it, but about the manner in which it should be met. The policy of Auckland, of his Council, and of the military authorities was that it should be met primarily by support for the existing Government at Herat and, if this failed, by direct action by London against Iran, with or without Russian agreement. The policy of the Cabinet (primarily of Palmerston and Hobhouse), and of the Political Agents in Afghanistan and Iran on the other hand, was to meet the threat by action carried out from Afghanistan, namely annexation, or at least the establishment of a British garrison in Herat; satisfactory control, they argued, could not be established by Auckland's method.

Behind these two policies lay radically different assumptions about the defence of India. Until 1838 forward defence had been represented by the Iranian buffer. Although it is clear that the London Government had never been very much interested in the question of Indian defence, that the Indian Government had lost faith in the Iranian buffer as early as 1808, and that even the British representatives in Iran had despaired of the policy during the 1830s, the switch to the Afghan buffer policy was not made until 1838. After that date those who approached the question from the side of Iran and London, being aware of all the difficulties of the working of the Iranian buffer policy but yet being insulated from direct experience of the disadvantages of the Afghan buffer system, steadfastly upheld the latter and wished to see it consolidated by the annexation of Herat. Auckland and his supporters, on the other hand, dismayed by the resource cost of Afghanistan, had, by 1841, lost faith in the Afghan buffer policy; it was no answer to the problem of the defence of India because India could not afford it. Auckland did not advocate a return to the Iranian buffer policy and it is doubtful if he saw clearly what the alternative to Afghanistan should be, or, in view of his forthcoming departure, thought it necessary to formulate it in detail. But the evidence suggests that he was returning to an older Indian defensive strategy, in which the frontier should be strengthened by an advance to the Indus and a disruptive strategy, founded on Malcolm's old Kharag system, should be substituted for a forward buffer system. Beyond this limited effort the responsibility for defending India belonged to the Government in England.

Strategic considerations, however, were neither the only, nor probably the most important factors in the debate about Herat. For Auckland, temperament as much as strategy decided the issue. As Macnaghten said of him in 1840: 'he has had his belly full of glory.'[90] In Simla in 1838 Auckland had screwed up his nerve for adventure; in Calcutta in 1839 to 1841 he found support for his natural aversion to danger and fresh responsibility. His arguments against action lack conviction. His acceptance of the absurd military estimates has been mentioned; at other times the Governor-General argued that he lacked an excuse, or that annexation might cause complications in Iran for which he could not take the responsibility, despite his knowledge that the man whose concern such repercussions were was the foremost advocate of annexation. Behind Auckland's arguments lay a deep fear of possible disaster.

Nor was the defence of India the primary consideration in the mind of Palmerston. To throw the burden of Indian defence upon India itself would ease his difficulties with his Cabinet colleagues and free his hands in Europe; if Auckland took Herat that problem would be thereby removed from his relations with Iran and hence Russia. Dependence upon Russian goodwill in Central Asia limited Britain's freedom of action in Europe and in the Near East. On the other hand, a strong British position in Central Asia would provide Palmerston with a valuable lever against Russia which could be employed with beneficial effects in other places. These are attitudes which will be considered again in the next chapter, but they can be seen to place Palmerston's support for the annexation of Herat into the same Eurocentred strategy which had dictated his decision in 1838 to intervene in Afghanistan and not in Iran. His aim, at Herat, was not to defend India but to defend Britain.

At the lower levels of discussion a similar ambivalence can be detected. For McNeill and Sheil the annexation of Herat could ease their way in Iran; it would remove one of the most contentious issues which divided Britain and Iran and, by placing a British force on the Iranian frontier, give Britain a powerful purchase on Iranian policy, and one similar to that possessed by Russia through her position on the Aras; Herat could thus become a substitute for Kharag. If Afghanistan, and not Iran, were the main British buffer their problems in Iran would be much simplified. For them the annexation of Herat could be seen as important not so much because it was the key to the defence of India, but because it was the single act which could remove from British relations with Iran the intolerably complicating factor of Indian defence.

Macnaghten's support for annexation was essentially the product of his political difficulties in Afghanistan. For him the possession of Herat was a panacea for all his ills: it would, he claimed, strengthen the prestige, revenues, and authority of Shah Shuja; provide employment for the Afghan chiefs who were being squeezed by British policy in Kabul and Qandahar; eliminate one of the principal causes of the disturbances which had plagued him in his attempt to pacify Afghanistan; as well as giving Afghanistan a strong western frontier. 'Herat' he wrote, 'may be said to be the point of all operations affecting the safety of our possessions in the East.'[91] Of course all this was fantasy; the real value of Yar Muhammed was that he was an excellent scapegoat for British failure in Afghanistan and an expedition was a good excuse to obtain reinforcements to quell discontent within Shuja's existing domains.

Finally, at the grass roots, it is plain that, although Pottinger and Todd put great weight on their strategic arguments, their true motive was humanitarian. For them the Government of Herat was a barbarous tyranny, kept alive by British money. Britain, they believed, had acquired a moral responsibility to provide Herat with good government, but they saw their efforts to improve the lot of the ordinary Heratis frustrated by the actions of the Government they subsidized. Annexation for them was a moral question. No doubt some might argue that the reverse was true; that they used humanitarian arguments to disguise personal ambition or political and strategic conviction. My own reading of their arguments and those of their companions convinces me that such an interpretation would distort completely the historical reality. It is the contrary which is true; they sought to cloak humanitarianism with strategy. The indelible impression left by their letters and journals is of the primacy of morality.

Although the debate about Herat was more intense, more prolonged, and more dramatic than that which took place over Balkh, the pattern is remarkably similar. In both cases the original support for a forward policy proceeds from the local agent. In both he is supported by Macnaghten and opposed by Auckland. In both the influence of London is exerted in favour of a forward policy and compels Auckland to make concessions. But in both Auckland ultimately triumphs and refuses to follow an active policy. And in both not a dog barks thereafter. For the strategic problem can now be seen to be imaginary—a mirage created by the agent himself to further his own ends. The solution is to attack, not the dream, but the dreamer himself; the removal of the agents removed the strategic problem of the northern frontier of Afghanistan. Under British rule Afghanistan never had a northern frontier; it was unnecessary. The enemy lay within; only wishes placed him without.

The Limits of Forward Defence: Turkestan, 1839–1842

I feel very confident about all our policy in Central Asia for I think that the designs of our Government there are honest, and that they will work with a blessing from God, who seems now to be breaking up all the barriers of the long closed East, for the introduction of Christian knowledge and peace . . . If we treat the Toorkistan question liberally, we shall, I think, secure the great position which we have now gained, and make our jealousy of Russian advance in this direction the means of purifying and enriching to our future advantage the whole of Oosbeg Tartary.

Arthur Conolly to T. C. Robertson, May 1840.

The establishment of British control over Afghanistan in 1839 opened up Turkestan, for the first time, as an area of British action. During the years 1839 to 1842 Britain had her first and only real opportunity to frustrate the Russian advance into Central Asia. By the time the second opportunity for action in Turkestan presented itself, in 1878, Russia had already mastered the Uzbek states of Khiva, Bukhara, and Kokand, and Britain shrank from the dangerous expedient of challenging her authority. In 1918 the third and final opportunity presented itself when Russian authority in Central Asia was under attack and the British forward policy in the Middle East was at high tide. But once more the will to exploit the opportunity was lacking and the chance was allowed to slip away. In the decision not to support the Muslim independence movement in 1918 to 1919 may be seen something of the disillusionment which was the legacy of the first sad step into Turkestan.

The vast area which lay between the northern boundary of British control in Afghanistan and the southern boundary of Russian control in Siberia may be divided into two distinct parts, corresponding to modern Kazakhstan in the north and to the republics of Uzbekistan, Tajikistan, and Turkmenia in the south. It was the southern part to which the name Turkestan was usually given. It was a flat, dry country, bounded on the south by the Hindu Kush and the Parapomisus, on the east by the Pamirs and the Altai mountains, and on the west by the

Kopet Dagh which divides Turkestan from the Iranian plateau. Much of Turkestan was desert and the greater part of the remainder provided only sparse grazing; agricultural and urban life was largely confined to three ancient river valleys. In the east, where the River Sir, or Jaxartes, issued from the Altai mountains into the fertile Farghana valley, now the main centre of Soviet cotton production, was the core of the state of Kokand. In the south, along the waters of the beautifully named Zarafshahan, which also fed the famous old city of Samarkand, was Bukhara, the capital of a small state. In the north, standing, like Cairo, in the desert at the head of the delta of a great river, was Khiva, heir to the Khwarazmian state of the Middle Ages which had once dominated the lower Amu or Oxus river.

Some countries seem doomed to be always the countries of tomorrow; in the nineteenth century Turkestan seemed to have joined the company of those for whom it was always yesterday. The names of its cities and its rivers were like a roll-call of antiquity and the glories of the Muslim past, but its last great flowering lay as far back as the fifteenth century, when the mighty Empire of Timur had faded in the brilliant sunset of the Timurids. At the beginning of the sixteenth century Timur's descendants had been supplanted by a fresh group of northern Turkish nomads, the Uzbeks, who had subsequently both dominated the political life of the area and come to form the largest single element in its varied population. During the course of the eighteenth century the political structure of Turkestan underwent further evolution, as a result of which the three Uzbek khanates of Kokand, Khiva, and Bukhara took shape.[1]

Seemingly the most vigorous of these states in 1839 was Kokand. This state had been formed from the various principalities of the Farghana valley at the end of the eighteenth century under the inspiration of Chinese pressure and an energetic leader, Narbuta Beg (1774/5–98). Narbuta was succeeded by his two sons, Alam (1798–1810) and Omar (1810–1822), under whom Kokand grew to include Tashkent. The expansion was continued under Omar's successor, Muhammad Ali (Madali) (1822–42), and by 1839 Kokand had reached the peak of its fortunes. Authority was claimed and taxes collected from the nomadic Karakirghiz of the east and the Kazakhs of the north; the Chinese were forced to concede Muhammad Ali the right to collect taxes in certain cities in Sinkiang; and to the south-west Kokand supplanted Bukhara as the dominant power in Ura Tube.

Bukhara had fallen into the hands of a new dynasty in the eighteenth century. With its many colleges it remained, however, the main centre of Islamic study in Turkestan and, indeed, the new rulers were from a family of Sayyids and both Haidar (1802–26) and his successor, Nasrullah (1826–60), were noted for their great piety. Although the rulers of Bukhara occasionally employed the title of king (*padishah-i ghazi*), it was with a religious significance, and their preference was for the title *amir al-muminin*. Bukhara declined under Haidar, but rapidly revived under his determined successor. With the aid of his newly-created disciplined infantry and artillery corps Nasrullah was able to restore the boundaries of 1802. It is unnecessary to describe these activities in detail, and it may merely be observed that the claims of Bukhara conflicted with those of Kokand in the east over Ura Tube, with those of Khiva in the west over Merv, and with those of Khulm in the south over Balkh. Bukhara was certainly the leading Uzbek state in terms of cultural advancement, trade, and possibly wealth. Its population, variously estimated between one and two and a half million, was spread along the Zarafshahan river. The population of the city of Bukhara itself was in the region of a hundred thousand.

The state of Khiva was a model of ribbon development, being spread out in a narrow strip for three hundred miles along the Oxus. Outside these limits it had claims to authority which also conflicted with those of its neighbours. Khivan claims to rule the Karakalpaks of the right bank of the Sir formed the basis of a dispute with Kokand, and her shadowy claims to influence rather than authority over the Kazakhs to the north was a potential source of difficulty with Russia. In the reign of Muhammad Rahim Khan (1806–25) Khivan authority was extended westwards over the Turkomans and in 1822 a Governor was established at Merv, earlier in the possession of Bukhara. Under Rahim's successor, Allah Quli Khan (1825–42), the Khivan Khans enjoyed a further increase in their power. What the population of Khiva was is anyone's guess. Estimates range as high as seven million, but a more probable figure is one million, of which half lived in the cultivated areas and the other half as nomads or semi-nomads in the surrounding lands.

To nineteenth-century European observers the Uzbek Khanates of Turkestan presented a picture of desolate decay. Their governmental structures appeared primitive and their rulers cruel, ignorant, and tyrannical. History seemed to have left them behind. But this was a superficial impression, which did not take notice of the changes which were in progress in Turkestan. The irrigated river valleys which formed the hearts of the Uzbek states had always ensured a prosperous agricultural base on which ancient handicraft industries still flourished. In the nineteenth century their governments too were adapting themselves to new conditions with more sophisticated bureaucracies and more modern armies and were extending their authority at the expense of the power of previously independent groups within the community; chiefs, nomads, and ulema all found their independence reduced. The process was uneven and there were reverses, but the direction was unmistakable; the Khanates of Turkestan were taking the first, hesitant steps on the path of modernization. It was at this time of uncertain assertion that their new contacts with Britain and Russia took place.

In the northern area, corresponding to modern Kazakhstan, the situation was quite different from that in Turkestan. The great steppe lands which stretched from the Caspian to far beyond the Aral Sea were still the home of a nomadic people—the Kazakhs, or, as they were confusingly and inaccurately named by the Russians, the Kirghiz.[2] The Kazakhs lived primarily on the produce of their flocks and by hunting, although they supplemented their income by cultivating some grain in those areas where the rainfall made it possible and by acting as carriers in the caravan trade between Russia and the Uzbek states of Turkestan. Their political organization was primitive; they were divided into three hordes, but the authority of the nominal chiefs was slight and individual clans possessed substantial independence, although occasionally they rallied under a chief who, by his pre-eminence in war or the hunt, could command followers. On the basis of various alleged submissions from 1730 onwards Russia claimed suzerainty over the Kazakhs, but in practice possessed no authority south of a narrow strip of territory which immediately adjoined the fortified Russian lines.

Although they inhabited areas which, for the most part lay outside the area of Kazakhstan, it will be convenient here to mention certain other groups which in their tribal organization and their nomadic predilections were similar to the Kazakhs. Amongst these groups were the Tajiks of the Pamirs; the Karakirghiz of the eastern hills, which now form the basis of the state of Kirghizia; and the Turkomans of the western deserts and oases. Because of their position along the eastern shore of the Caspian and throughout a strip of territory on the slopes of the Kopet Dagh, from the Caspian south-eastwards to the Afghan border, the Turkomans were apparently well placed to form a vital bridge for Russian penetration into Turkestan.[3]

The Russian frontier towards Central Asia had been first created in the early eighteenth century. It had been built up to meet local needs and there was no unity of control. Authority was divided between three, and later four separate Governorates. From east to west these were those of western Siberia, Orenburg, Astrakhan, and the last addition of Georgia. Each Governor controlled the broad sphere of interest adjacent to his own frontier, but further afield this partition of authority could lead to confusion and at various times it is possible to find different Governors taking the initiative. Thus it was the Governor-General of western Siberia, General G. I. Glazenap (d. 1819), who sent Philip Nazarov on his mission to Kokand in 1813;[4] and it was General A. P. Yermolov of Georgia who sent Captain N. N. Murav'ev to Turkmenia and Khiva in 1819.[5] But during the period with which we are concerned the most important initiatives came from Orenburg, where the Governor was mainly responsible for dealings with the Kazakhs, and from Astrakhan, which was the base for Russian activities on the Caspian and hence among the Turkomans of its shores.

The Russian frontier towards Kazakhstan took the form of a line of forts and posts manned by regular troops and by Cossacks. The aspect of this frontier had originally been defensive; the Orenburg line, which was established in 1839, had been intended to sever communications between the troublesome Bashkirs to the north and their potential Kazakh allies to the south. But after the eradication of Bashkir opposition the frontier line began to assume a new aspect as a base for the further penetration of Kazakhstan. Until the early nineteenth century, despite her claims to suzerainty over the Kazakhs, Russia had made little impression on the steppe; administrative authority was exercised only in the far north; further south Russia possessed only a vicarious cultural influence. Concern about this situation, about the extent of Kazakh resistance to Russian rule, and about the raids on Russian caravans, led to discussions at the highest level. In 1825 these led to a recommendation by the Asiatic Committee that Russia should adopt a much more forceful policy in pushing forward military control over the Kazakhs. The Committee blamed Khiva for inciting disturbances among the Kazakhs and anticipated that there would never be peace until Russia had demonstrated her ability to coerce her enemies.[6]

Following on this recommendation it is possible to discern a new determination in Russian policy towards Central Asia. This was revealed in actions which emanated both from Orenburg and from Astrakhan. Under General V. A. Perovsky, Governor-General of Orenburg 1833 to 1842, the Orenburg line was extended southwards. After the reorganization of 1835 it ran from Gur'ev on the Caspian, at the mouth of the Ural river, up that river to Uralsk, and thence, mainly following the line of the river Ilek, eastwards to Orsk, and thence north-east to Troitsk, joining the Siberian line on the Tobol river. In all, the Orenburg line measured over fifteen hundred versts and the Siberian line continued the fortified frontier for a similar distance until it reached the Chinese frontier.[7] It was the beginning of that slow process which was to gather speed after the Crimean war and culminate in the giant pincer movement, launched from the Orenburg and

Siberian lines, which led to the envelopment of Central Asia in the 1860s.

The second initiative is linked with the Orenburg line extension but had as its main objective the securing of a new base on the eastern shore of the Caspian. In this movement the most notable figure was Grigory Salich Karelin (1801–72). Karelin had once been attached to the Chancellery under Arakcheev but had fallen into disfavour and was sent to Orenburg. There he developed scientific interests in the natural history and ethnography of the steppes and travelled widely among the Bashkirs, Kazakhs, and Turkomans, ranging during the course of his life from the Caspian coast to the Altai. His memoirs of his travels in Turkmenia, published in 1883, are a major source for the history of that area in the early part of the nineteenth century.[8] In 1832 Karelin led an expedition to the north-east coast of the Caspian to investigate suitable sites for forts. The Mangushlak peninsula had been claimed by Russia following a submission by the Turkomans of the area in 1803 and there had been a number of Russian expeditions including those of General Fel'kerzam in 1805, and General Berg in 1825 to 1826. Karelin now selected a position on the bay of Mertvyy Kultuk where the fort of Novo-Petrovsk was completed by 1834. Novo-Petrovsk remained the main Russian base in the area for some years, serving to protect fishermen on the Caspian and to allow for the exercise of some control over the Turkomans and Kazakhs. In 1846 the base was transferred to a new site, some miles further south at Tyub-Karagan on the tip of the Mangushlak peninsula, and renamed Novo-Alexandrovsk. The latter fort still survives under its present name of Fort Shevchenko.[9] Karelin was aware that the establishment of the fort would cause annoyance to Khiva and he sent a messenger, Turpaev, to Khiva to explain the reasons for Russian policy.[10] The Khivans were not satisfied and relations between Khiva and Russia deteriorated rapidly after the establishment of the fort. Hostility with the Kazakhs also grew and in 1837 a major Kazakh uprising against Russia took place under the leadership of Kenesari Kasim and lasted until 1846.

Further difficulties with Khiva were also caused by a second initiative with which Karelin was associated. This was the project of opening up trade across the Caspian and extending influence among the Turkomans to the south-east. This policy, although it was partly concerned with establishing control over the Turkomans, had a second aspect of developing trade with Turkestan.

Russia had maintained commercial relations with the Uzbek states of Turkestan since the sixteenth century, although the difficulties of transporting goods across the steppes had always conspired to keep the level of exchange low. Apart from a premature and disastrous attempt to seize control of Khiva by Peter the Great in the early eighteenth century, there had been little or no political interest in the area. At the end of the eighteenth and beginning of the nineteenth centuries there were signs of increased interest in Turkestan in the proliferation of Russian travellers in the area. The travels of Nazarov and Murav'ev have already been mentioned, but there were many others, including those of Blankennagel to Khiva in 1793 to 1794, Burnashov and Beznosikov to Bukhara in 1794 to 1795, and Negri, Meyendorff, and Eversmann to Bukhara in 1820.[11] Partly this quickening of interest was the product of simple curiosity on the part of ambitious officers, partly it was the consequence of changes on other Russian frontiers which had freed resources for action in Central Asia and increased the desirability of furthering interest in that area. The achievement of the Black Sea frontier had ended the major preoccupation of eighteenth-century Russian policy and the conquest of Transcaucasia had added a new dimension. Above all, the ending of the wars with the Ottomans, Iran, and France in the years 1813 to 1815 gave new scope for Russian activities. Partly there was a strategic factor, although as yet only vaguely developed. But from the eighteenth century onwards it had become clear that Russia would not be left alone to pursue her struggles with the Ottomans and Iran, and that she must contemplate the possibility that a European power—Austria, France, or Britain—might ally with these powers against her. It was therefore necessary for Russia to look to the security of her southern and eastern land frontiers. But there is little doubt that the main motive for expanding interest in Central Asia was economic.

Russian manufactures were scarcely competitive with those of western Europe in European and Mediterranean markets. For Russia it seemed that it would be best to concentrate on those markets in which her geographical position offered her the advantage of lower transport costs, namely those of northern Iran, northern China, and Turkestan. Of course this was no more than a development of older ideas, such as those which had inspired the British merchants, Antony Jenkinson in the sixteenth century, and John Elton and Jonas Hanway in the eighteenth century. In 1826 this view of Russian commercial strategy was given a broader theoretical foundation by the Chevalier Gamba in the introduction to his *Voyage dans la Russie Meridionale, 1820–4* (Paris, 1826). Gamba there formulated an early version of the theory later made famous by Sir Halford Mackinder and the geopoliticians. He contrasted British commercial predominance based upon the sea with the position of those Continental powers whose central position in the heartland could enable them to respond by developing land routes into Turkestan. It was ideas of this sort which shaped Russian policy in Turkestan.

During the first part of the nineteenth century there was a rapid growth in the value of Russian trade with Central Asia. Between 1804 to 1807 and 1824 to 1827 imports almost doubled and exports more than quadrupled, although the characteristic adverse balance of Russian trade with this area persisted.[12] The trade with Turkestan apparently increased more rapidly than that with Kazakhstan; the adverse balance was more pronounced in the case of the trade with the Kazakhs. The adverse balance of trade was one problem, for it was Russia's main aim to find markets for her manufactured goods. Other problems were raised by the conditions under which the trade was conducted. Goods were carried by caravans from Petropavlovsk to Tashkent in the east and from Orenburg to Bukhara in the west.[13] Control of the trade was in the hands of Asian merchants; the caravans were subject to levies and attacks by the Kazakhs and others; and to other duties, exacted by states, such as Khiva, through which the Orenburg caravan passed.[14] It was desirable to find some new means of conducting the trade which would increase its profitability and volume and which would particularly stimulate the growth of exports. One way was by collecting information and trying to improve relations with the parties involved; another was by coercion; but the main hope in the mid-1830s was to open a new route, via the Caspian.

In Russian thought, the Caspian played a role similar to that of the Persian Gulf and even more the Indus in British thinking. For the Caspian was to be the channel through which Russian commerce was to penetrate and to command Turkestan. In the wake of Russian commerce would come Russian political influence to anticipate and exclude that of Britain. Whether the political or the economic motive predominated it is difficult to say. In the British case the political argument, as we have seen, was always the more important, but the Russian commercial position was not the same as that of Britain; to Russia a closed market was important. Probably motives were mixed and different ideas influenced different groups. One of the most active proponents of the development of trade with the Turkomans was an Astrakhan merchant, Alexander Gerasimov, who in 1834 made an agreement with the Yomut Turkoman tribe on the south-east Caspian coast and followed this in 1836 by a more far-reaching agreement for the development of the natural resources of the area.[15] The merchants in Astrakhan and in Moscow certainly put commercial interests first, but they did not have the final word. The plan they envisaged was to open a route for goods from the great trading fair at Nizhni Novgorod (Gorki) on the Volga, down river to Astrakhan, and then across the Caspian to Astrabad on the south-east shore.[16] Russian command of the Caspian had been assured since 1813 and the Caspian flotilla played a role in exploration and development not dissimilar to that of the Bombay Marine. From Astrabad the journey to the trading centres of Turkestan was short and, it was thought, easy.

Once more a significant role in the evolution of the new plan was played by Karelin. In 1836 he led an expedition to the south-east Caspian to investigate the situation among the Turkomans. The plan that was worked out by the Russian Government in consultation with Moscow merchants on the basis of his recommendations was to establish a base on the south-east Caspian through which trade could be regulated. A large-scale trading company would be built up under the guise of a fisheries company.[17] How far the project then developed is unclear. It can be connected with the increased Russian activity on the Caspian at this time and the occupation of the islands of Cheleken and Ashurada. But it seems likely that the plan did not prosper during the 1830s. Among the reasons for the slow rate of progress may be mentioned the hostility of Iran to Russian control of the Caspian and influence among the Turkomans; the resentment of Khiva which was reflected in persistent Turkoman hostility; physical difficulties represented by navigational problems on the Caspian and the lack of fresh water on the islands and eastern shores; the grave doubts about the proposal harboured by Russian merchants, especially as the Russian Government stressed that the venture was more for public benefit than private profit; and the strength of British competition in the markets of Turkestan.

The policy of commercial penetration, both for its economic and still more its political benefits, dominated Russian policy towards Turkestan until 1839. The activities of Simonich and of Vitkevich show clearly that it was intended to extend this policy to Afghanistan. In many respects the Russian policy resembles the identical British policy pursued during the same period. But as with British policy, there was a potential conflict between the problem of the border and the problem of forward defence and there was also the question of the time-scale in which the policy had to operate. It was these two factors, together with the example of the British movement into Afghanistan, that led to the abandonment of the policy of commercial penetration and its replacement by the policy of military advance. This change was represented by the Khivan expedition of 1839.

Although the timing of the Khivan expedition was certainly affected by the British advance into Afghanistan, it would be wrong to regard it as a simple riposte to that move. Perovsky at Orenburg had long been dissatisfied with the results of the Astrakhan-based policy of commercial penetration and had for some time agitated to be given permission to take more violent measures against Khiva. The causes of dispute with Khiva were numerous: the conflicts of claims on the eastern shores of the Caspian have already been mentioned; so have the charges that Khiva was the major cause of the disturbances among the Kazakhs which disturbed the Russian frontier and obstructed the Russian caravans; finally there was the fact that Khiva was the principal market for Russian subjects, usually fishermen, who were captured by the Turkomans and sold as slaves. Attempts to settle these disputes by negotiation failed. Turpaev had no success, nor were economic sanctions effective against Khivan merchants. The policy of controlling Khiva through Iran, which can be seen behind Simonich's support for Muhammad Shah's eastern ambitions, also had no success. A military expedition seemed the only recourse which remained and was apparently agreed in 1838, although its execution was postponed until 1839.[18]

Nesselrode was not enthusiastic for the expedition, although he recommended it to the Tsar. In his arguments he stressed the importance of prestige; 'elle rétablira parmi les peuplades voisines cette crainte salutaire du nom russe, qui, en Asie surtout, est le meilleur garantie de nôtre repos.'[19] He also linked the expedition directly with the contemporaneous British action in Afghanistan and Iran: 'En effet, elle servira de contrepoids à l'expedition anglaise dans l'Afghanistan.' But there is good reason to suppose that he would have been happier if the Khivan expedition had never been dispatched, and that he offered it to Nicholas I as a salve to the injured pride of the Tsar, who felt the humiliation which Russia had suffered in Iran and in Afghanistan. Some action to uphold Russian prestige was inevitable and Nesselrode preferred that it should take place at Khiva, where it was not likely to produce dangerous international complications, than in Iran and Afghanistan where Russian intervention could lead to a head-on clash with Britain. The Khivan expedition in this aspect therefore can be seen, like the British expedition to Afghanistan, as the price of inaction in Iran and peace in Europe.

Perovsky, however, was no Auckland but an enthusiastic advocate of expansion. He had argued for the expedition ever since 1833 and in November 1839 he informed Nesselrode that if Russia did not act Britain would occupy Bukhara and Khiva and convert the Oxus into a British waterway.[20] Perovsky had all the ability of the true Political

Agent to confuse his local problems with grand strategy. Now he gained permission to make the attempt on Khiva. Like Auckland, Perovsky waited until the expedition started before he issued a proclamation, dated 2 December 1839. In this the objects of the expedition were stated to be the release of slaves held at Khiva and an end to repeated Khivan raids upon Russian caravans.[21] Because of problems of water the movement from Orenburg was made in the winter. An advance party of three hundred and fifty under Colonel Danilevsky left Orenburg on 2 November 1839 and advanced to the Emba river, five hundred versts from Orenburg. This group was followed, on 26 November, by the main body of four thousand, six hundred men marching in four columns; this second group reached the Emba on 19 December and the force then made a further advance of one hundred and seventy versts to Aq Bulaq, one hundred and sixty-five kilometres south-west of the Emba. But this was the limit of the advance and in the early part of February 1840 the expedition was forced to retreat to the Emba and returned to Orenburg on 25 to 26 April 1840. It was defeated not by the Kazakhs, but by the weather; the winter of 1839 to 1840 was one of the coldest on record, the temperature being continually 30 degrees below freezing point. Although the troops could stand it, the baggage camels could not and died in great numbers; more than two thousand perished on the advance from the Emba to Aq Bulaq. When added to the huge British losses in camels suffered in 1839, the Russian experience prompts the observation that camels were probably the principal sufferers from the forward policy in Central Asia during these years. Logistics are a vital factor in all strategies and it could be concluded that a strategy based upon camel transport was unviable in Central Asia; next time, with the aid of railways, the European powers did much better.

There is an apparent conflict of evidence about the Russian expedition to Khiva. According to the account given above, which is based upon that of I. N. Zakharin, who spoke to survivors and also had access to the papers of Perovsky, there was no movement from Orenburg until 2 November 1839. But reports of the expedition had reached Burnes at Kabul as early as July 1839 and were seemingly confirmed in news received on 29 October from a native agent in Bukhara. According to another report, received via Würtemburg and based upon the testimony of a survivor, there was an earlier advance from Orenburg to the Emba of two thousand men under a Colonel Heck (?Beck). The object of this movement, in June 1839, was to form a depot. In this account the total expedition is put at seven thousand men and all troops were reported to be back in Orenburg by March 1840. The major discrepancy, however, concerns the starting-date. It is possible that Perovsky did authorize an advance party to set up food depots and there is a story that these were ruined by a sudden thaw. There is also a letter by Perovsky, written in June 1839, in which he mentions a wish to send a large scientific expedition to the Aral Sea. But, unless one assumes that here was a massive deception by Perovsky, the Russian evidence indicates that there was no troop movement until November. In this case the British panic in Kabul in 1839 must have been the result of rumours based upon leakages concerning Russian preparations. This supposition raises the question of how far the British in Kabul believed the reports and how far they saw them simply as an opportunity to retain troops in Afghanistan.

The consternation among the British in Kabul was certainly very evident, but the reaction was muted. By December rumour had placed fifteen battalions of Russian troops at Khiva and others marching on Iran.[22] But it was Todd at Herat who was called upon to act. He received a letter from the Khan of Khiva reporting that a hundred thousand Russian troops were advancing on Khiva and asking for artillerymen to help him repel them. Todd had to act quickly on his own initiative and he was unsure how to respond. He had already sent a native agent, Mulla Husayn, to collect information, but now he was asked to take action which he well knew might lead to a clash between Britain and Russia. Todd decided in favour of caution. He refused to supply military assistance or even money and contented himself with sending a British agent, Lieutenant James Abbott (1807–96), to Khiva to establish friendly relations, explain the nature of British policy in Central Asia, and advise the Khan to remove the pretext for Russian intervention by releasing all the Russian slaves whom he held in captivity. If Abbott found, when he arrived at Khiva, that war between Russia and Khiva was actually in progress he was authorized to offer mediation. The basis of a settlement made under these conditions was to be the recognition of the independence of Khiva, the withdrawal of all foreign troops, and the restoration of all Russian slaves.[23]

Abbott was not a good choice to conduct a delicate diplomatic mission to Khiva. Todd's choice among the few British officers at Herat was very limited, but he could have done better. Perhaps Todd was attracted by Abbott's Evangelical enthusiasm. Although he later enjoyed a successful political career on the Panjab frontier and also acquired a reputation as poet, antiquarian, and man of letters, Abbott's future qualities were certainly not in evidence in 1840. On the basis of his actions and writings in 1840 one would conclude that he had little imagination and rejoiced in that peculiarly British sense of humour which finds foreigners funny in so far as their habits differ from those current in England. The balance of forces in Turkestan was a mystery to him and his feeling for diplomacy was non-existent. From the beginning he did not think it possible that he might succeed in his mission unless he was permitted to offer Khiva greater advantages. With this in mind he produced a stream of recommendations, all involving a far greater degree of British intervention in Turkestan. These included military assistance to Khiva; the conquest of Balkh and Bukhara; and a complex series of alliances between Britain and the states of Turkestan. Eventually he allowed himself to be persuaded by Allah Quli Khan, the ruler of Khiva, to agree to a treaty between Britain and Khiva for which Abbott had no authority whatsoever. This treaty provided for the establishment of a British agent at Khiva; British mediation between Russia and Khiva; and the exclusion by Khiva of all Russians from her territory. Abbott further agreed to go himself to Russia to carry out his mediation and, on 7 March 1840, left Khiva for the Russian fort of Novo-Petrovsk on the Caspian.

Abbott's unauthorized actions to some extent misled the Soviet historian of this episode, N. A. Khalfin. Khalfin inferred that Abbott's mission was designed as part of a British plan to form a coalition of all the Uzbek states against Russia and that Abbott got his way with Allah Quli Khan by threatening that if he did not accept the alleged British plan a British army would advance upon Khiva.[24] This interpretation is totally inaccurate: Britain had no intention of allying with Khiva; Todd had not authorized such an alliance; and far from cowing Allah Quli Khan, Abbott was undoubtedly gulled by the Khivan ruler. But whether Khalfin was really misled is another question, for his account is so mendacious as to lead to the supposition that any mis-understandings are quite intentional. He gives a completely inaccurate account of Abbott's arrival at the Russian frontier and argues that Abbott's principal object was to create dissension between Russia and Khiva, omitting to point out that the object of his mission was to end a warlike situation which already existed between Russia and Khiva.

Macnaghten supported Todd's policy towards Khiva. Worries about a possible Russian attack persisted in Kabul at least until the summer of 1840. Weeks after the Russians were back at Orenburg Macnaghten wrote that he had certain intelligence of the rapid advance of Russian troops towards Khiva and Herat, while Burnes apparently believed them to be already in Khiva.[25] Macnaghten asked for further reinforcements to meet the danger and proposed to send Burnes to the Russian camp.[26] Burnes, however, refused and the choice eventually fell upon Arthur Conolly. It was some time, however, before Conolly departed and in the meantime the initiative remained with Todd at Herat.

By contrast with the apparent situation in Kabul the Russian expedition produced no excitement in India. Both at the time and subsequently Auckland was completely unperturbed by the Russian threat. 'I have no great fear that the Cossack and the Sipahi will shortly meet on the Oxus', he wrote in June 1840, 'nor do I apprehend that overwhelming armies will be poured down the Volga from Russia into Turkestan.'[27] Even if the Russians should take Khiva he was confident they would not attack Afghanistan.[28] He refused to send reinforcements to Afghanistan and would do no more than agree to retain in Upper Sind the Bombay troops under General Willshire, which had retired from Afghanistan via Kalat in the autumn of 1839.[29] Although he gave Todd's intructions to Abbott his qualified approval, Auckland made it clear that he did not want a permanent agent at Khiva.[30] When news arrived of Abbott's unauthorized promises to the Khan, the Governor-General's disapproval was immediate. He would offer Khiva neither troops, nor guns, nor even mediation, but only advice to make amends to Russia and 'civil words and watches and telescopes'.[31] He refused to take any action to meet the alleged Russian threat other than to send an agent to the Russian camp to request an explanation if it should appear that the Russians seemed to contemplate the establishment of permanent control over Khiva, contrary to Perovsky's proclamation of 2 December 1839, which announced that Russia would withdraw as soon as she had obtained satisfaction. But even in such a case, Auckland preferred that any communication with the Russian commander should be by letter rather than by the dispatch of a British agent.[32] The only other move which he would contemplate in connection with the Russian expedition was that mentioned in the previous chapter, namely the sending of Afghan troops to expel Dost Muhammad from Khulm, and he justified this action primarily with reference to the security of Shuja in Afghanistan.

Throughout the whole Khiva crisis Auckland remained entirely consistent in his view of the situation. As far as he was concerned, the new British strategy stopped in Afghanistan; its object was to set up Shuja, create a friendly buffer state in Afghanistan and withdraw British troops. Particularly in view of the threatening situation developing in the Panjab, British India could not spare the resources to support operations beyond the Hindu Kush. Auckland conceded that the establishment of Russian political supremacy at Khiva would be very dangerous for the security of British India and that the danger would be still more serious if, as Macnaghten and Burnes anticipated, the Russian advance continued to Bukhara. Yet:

it would scarcely, under any circumstances be consistent with any prudent application of the means and resources of India that its Government should enter on a direct contest in arms within the States of Turkistan in order to arrest or counteract their submission to the authority of Russia.

If it were then asked whose responsibility it was to check the Russian advance in Central Asia Auckland had a clear and unequivocal answer: 'We must mainly look to the exertion of the power of our country in Europe for the purpose of checking, beyond the limits of Afghanistan, the unjustifiable advances of Russian aggression.'[33] Four months later, in August 1840, he spelled out more plainly what he meant: 'I would look to a tripartite Treaty of the West, [*sic* ? East] under which a limit shall be placed to the advance of England, Russia and Persia and under which all shall continue to repress slave dealing and plunder.'[34]

For his policy Auckland won general support in India and in Afghanistan. The general feeling was that too much of the burden of Indian defence was being left to India and that the Government in England should shoulder a greater share. Of his Councillors, Prinsep did support an advance to Balkh and Herat, but opposed any action in Turkestan beyond these points.[35] The others supported Auckland entirely. In Afghanistan, Burnes, although he regarded the Russian threat as a serious menace, agreed with Auckland that it could not and should not be met by action from Afghanistan in Turkestan.

The implication of Auckland's policy was that Turkestan should be abandoned to Russia. For, although he continued to insist that the Government in England must accept responsiblity for resisting the Russian advance in Turkestan, Auckland was very well aware that England would never go to war over Khiva.[36] Most of those who supported his policy accepted this view; only Bird among his Councillors thought that the Cabinet might be prepared to do so.[37] Thus, Auckland's proposal for a diplomatic settlement, similar to that advocated by Nesselrode in 1838, could have any meaning only if Russia were willing to withdraw. If she chose to persist British India would offer no opposition to Turkestan passing under Russian control. Auckland had sketched out the lines of John Lawrence's later policy towards the Russian advance into Central Asia in the 1860s. In the cost-accountancy of the defence of India Turkestan had to be expunged from the ledger.

Just as Auckland had placed the responsibility for opposing Russia

with the Cabinet, the ministers in England placed it firmly upon
Auckland. News of the expedition had reached England via St. Petersburg in January 1840. Palmerston read Perovsky's statement of his
aims, but did not believe that Russia would rest content with these
modest goals. The Foreign Secretary believed that Russia aimed at the
domination of Central Asia and, while he did not object to fair commercial competition, he had already protested about military movements
in 1835. Seeing the Russian expedition in this light, Palmerston con-
luded that Russia intended to establish permanent political control
over Khiva. Russia, he believed, would set up a puppet Khan, make an
offensive–defensive alliance with him, and then use Khiva as the
spearhead for an attack on Bukhara and so on to the Hindu Kush,
where a confrontation with Britain would take place.[38] Apparent
confirmation of this hypothesis was supplied by Nesselrode, who disclosed that it was intended to dethrone Allah Quli Khan and replace
him with his brother, although Nesselrode still denied any ulterior
political aims.[39] Supported in his interpretation of Russian policy by
Clanricarde, his Ambassador in Russia, and by Hobhouse, Palmerston
was able to dominate the reaction of British ministers, despite the
inclination of Melbourne and Russell to accept Russian reassurances.

Palmerston's first line of approach was to order Auckland to take
vigorous action to demonstrate his willingness to oppose Russian aims.
At the end of February 1840 instructions were sent to Auckland to
counteract the Russian advance by taking Herat and, if necessary, by
advancing to Balkh.[40] 'If Russia is to control one end of the Oxus it is
but fair that we should have the other', wrote Hobhouse, bravely.[41]
Auckland, of course, declined to act upon these instructions.

Palmerston's second line of approach was to threaten Russia with
what Auckland might do. This blackmailing technique was developed
during a series of discussions held with the special Russian Envoy in
London, Baron Brunnow. Brunnow protested Russian innocence of
any ulterior motives and restated the objectives contained in
Perovsky's proclamation; when the Khan had promised to behave
Russian troops would retire and no garrison would remain at Khiva.[42]
But Brunnow conceded that the timing of the Russian expedition was
unfortunate and might lead to problems between Britain and Russia;
he was especially concerned lest Auckland should advance to Balkh
and urged Palmerston to order Auckland not to do so. In place of
confrontation he offered conciliation and undertook to recommend that
a Russian mission should proceed to Bukhara and Kunduz to inform
the rulers of those states that Britain and Russia had reached an
understanding concerning Central Asia.[43]

Palmerston exploited Brunnow's total misreading of the situation. He himself, the Foreign Secretary replied untruthfully, was perfectly satisfied with Russian assurances, but he regretted that Lord Auckland might not be so. He added, falsely, that the Government in England could not fetter Auckland's discretion, and went on to present Brunnow with a complete travesty of the position of the Government of India, portraying it as virtually independent of control, active, and strongly anti-Russian.[44] He later explained the situation to Auckland as follows:

Our chief argument is that you look upon the Invasion of Khiva as a measure so hostile in its appearance and effects that you are determined to do all you can to thwart or counterbalance it, and that the only way by which our Indian Government can be kept quiet is that Russia should give up any further attack upon Khiva.'[45]

Readers of *David Copperfield* will recall the figure of Mr. Jorkins, who, it will be remembered, 'was a mild man of heavy temperament, whose place in the business was to keep himself in the background, and be constantly exhibited by name as the most obdurate and ruthless of men'. The part fitted Auckland exactly; his views were as pacific as those of Brunnow himself and indeed bore a strong resemblance to the latter's, but they were not to be heard; Palmerston had set him up for the role of ogre.

Absurdly enough, Brunnow was totally deceived by this transparent device, the most elementary technique in the interrogator's book. It was not that it suited him to appear to believe it, but Brunnow genuinely did accept Palmerston's picture of the Indian Government. When Duhamel in Iran complained of a lack of correspondence between British protestations and actions relating to Central Asia, Brunnow explained the situation to his colleague. The problem, wrote Brunnow, was that while the British Government in London was willing to work with Russia, the same was not true of the Indian Government: 'Au centre de ce Gouvernment il règne malheureusement une deplorable prévention contre nous.' All his own efforts, remarked Brunnow naïvely, had been directed towards reconciling the divergent views of London and Calcutta.[46]

No sudden improvement in Anglo–Russian relations concerning Central Asia followed the news of the failure of the Khivan expedition. The British feared its renewal; the Russians were sore at defeat and particularly resented British activities in Turkestan. On instructions Brunnow asked for a written statement that Abbott's mission to Khiva had not been authorized by the Government in London; that it was purely temporary; and that its sole object was to induce Khiva to abandon the enslavement of Russian subjects. Since this last objective had apparently not been fulfilled the Tsar asked that Abbott should be withdrawn from Khiva.[47]

In the circumstances Abbott himself received a cool welcome when he arrived at Novo-Petrovsk, minus a number of fingers which he had lost from a sword-cut sustained on his adventurous journey from Khiva, and a still more chilly reception in St. Petersburg. The letter which he brought with him, written by Allah Yar Khan to the Tsar, was scarcely worded in a style calculated to assuage the hurt suffered by Nicholas's dignity and the Khivan terms were promptly rejected.[48] Abbott himself did not help to ease Russian suspicions. He had forged his own documents in order to justify his journey to Russia, but when the Russian Government complained of this the British Government jumped to Abbott's defence. Only after Abbott's return to England was the truth discovered. He had been invited to Hobhouse's home at Erle Stoke and one morning he departed early leaving behind a confession. Hobhouse was shaken by the incident and there is little doubt that Abbott's deception, combined with his Government's support of him, did much to foster Russian suspicions that further British duplicity was still concealed. Of course the Russians were quite correct in supposing that there was more deception, but they could never have guessed that the deception was designed to conceal innocence of aggressive intent, not guilt.

Palmerston continued to maintain his bluff. He declined to accept the Russian demands presented by Brunnow: to agree to withdraw any British agent from Khiva would be to admit that Russia had some right to restrict the diplomatic intercourse of Khiva. Also Palmerston was anxious to prevent a second Khivan expedition. Accordingly, he requested Hobhouse to give him a written statement that the Government of India attached great importance to the independence of Khiva and would undoubtedly take all appropriate steps if that independence were placed in jeopardy.[49] Knowing Auckland, Hobhouse thought this was going too far, and in the end the ministers agreed merely to inform Russia that a renewal of the Khivan expedition would complicate the situation in Central Asia.[50] This moderate language, however, merely reflected a just appraisal of Auckland's pacific intent and in no way indicated that Palmerston and Hobhouse had relaxed their view that an active policy to oppose Russia in Turkestan was required. Auckland was again urged to occupy Balkh and informed that any agreement that he made with Khiva would be supported in London.[51] In his official dispatch Hobhouse declared:

that the permanent establishment of Russian power in Khiva would prove to be incompatible with the safety of the British Indian Empire, and that we have a full right to do whatever may appear expedient to ward off or counteract such a manifest danger.[52]

The question of who was to take the necessary action—whether it should be the Indian Government, as Palmerston and Hobhouse declared, or the London Government, as Auckland firmly asserted, was never answered because action became unnecessary when Russia abandoned the Khivan expedition. The great debate upon ultimate responsibility for British policy in the defence of India against Russia was about to be launched in August 1840. The arguments put forward by Auckland and his Council in June had been received in London and supported in the Court of Directors. It was suggested that London should play a larger part in resisting Russia, that the Cabinet should consider the matter, and that strong representations should be made to St. Petersburg.[53] Then, in the same month, Russia gave way and announced that she would not renew her expedition to Khiva if a suitable agreement could be made. She offered the following terms; no indemnity; Russian retention of the fort of Novo-Petrovsk; Khiva to release her Russian slaves and promise to enslave no more; Khiva to undertake not to molest Russian caravans. Another demand, which was later dropped, was that the Khivan Khan should send three hostages to St. Petersburg. After receiving this welcome news Palmerston informed Hobhouse that it was unnecessary to pursue the question of action any further.[54] The bluff had worked and what was the reality behind it was no longer of interest. To the regret of the historian, Palmerston's cards remained hidden.

The initiative was now with Khiva and also with a new British agent there, Lieutenant Richmond Shakespear (1812–61) who was, agreeably enough, a cousin of William Makepeace Thackeray. Shakespear had been sent to Khiva from Herat by Todd in May 1840 to replace Abbott. What had happened was that after receiving the expression of Palmerston's views on the Khivan expedition, Auckland had communicated them to Macnaghten, who had framed consequential instructions for Abbott, whom he believed still to be at Khiva. By the time Todd received these instructions in Herat he was aware that Abbott had left Khiva, so he selected Shakespear to replace him and gave the instructions to the new agent. According to these instructions, Shakespear was to persuade the Khan to accept any reasonable terms which the Russians offered him, including the release of Russian slaves. As an inducement to the Khan to surrender his slaves Shakespear was authorized to offer him £10,000. The objective was to try to secure Khivan independence without committing Britain to any act which might arouse Russian resentment.[55] These instructions were plainly very far from the sort of vigorous action contemplated by Palmerston.

Shakespear's mission to Khiva was the most successful British venture in Turkestan. The new agent set off in a frame of mind very different from that of the gloomy Abbott, correctly seeing in his mission an opportunity to win honours. 'The chances of distinction are so great and the hazards so slight', he wrote, 'that the head of even a wren would be gladdened by the prospect.'[56] He arrived at Khiva on 12 June 1840 to discover that the Khan's conciliatory demeanour had evaporated with the retreat of his enemy. Also, having imbibed the opinion that Britain was afraid of Russia, Allah Quli was correspondingly contemptuous of British advice. Like Abbott, Shakespear concluded that Britain would obtain no substantial influence at Khiva unless she was prepared to offer some material inducement. He suggested that Britain should supply officers and money and assert a right to interfere between Khiva and Russia. This was tantamount to declaring a protectorate over Khiva, but Shakespear defended his proposal on the grounds that this was the only way in which the independence of Khiva could be assured and war with Russia averted. Such an agreement, he argued wildly and optimistically, would enable Britain to withdraw from Afghanistan because she would have established a new buffer. He did not explain how Britain was to support her new buffer without a position in Afghanistan. Shakespear actually went as far as to promise the Khan, quite without authority, that Britain would conclude an alliance with him as soon as Russia had been satisfied. However, his promise at least gave him some influence over the Khan and Allah Quli agreed to cease enslaving Russians and Heratis, although he refused to extend the boon to Iranians. Whether this very general undertaking was worth any more, except for propaganda purposes, than the promises of Shakespear, is doubtful. But the Khan also agreed to release the Russian slaves whom he already possessed into Shakespear's care and with these and a Khivan envoy, Shakespear arrived triumphant at Orenburg on 1 October 1840. There is no evidence, whatsoever, to support Khalfin's absurd suggestion that Shakespear went to Orenburg under instructions to spy on Russia.[57]

The major obstacle in the way of the restoration of peace between Russia and Khiva was now removed. Khiva could be said to have fulfilled the conditions laid down by Nesselrode in August. Accordingly, in October 1840, a Russian proclamation announced the re-establishment of peaceful relations between the two countries.[58] Of course, apart from the release of the Russian slaves, nothing had really changed. The Russians attempted to induce the Khivan envoy to make additional concessions, but he declined, insisting that any treaty between Russia and Khiva must be negotiated at Khiva. There followed a series of missions between the two states. In 1841 a Russian envoy, Nikiforov, went to Khiva, but died on his way back.[59] Two Khivan envoys who were with him went on to St. Petersburg in April 1841. In 1842 a second Russian mission to Khiva, led by the same Danilevsky who had commanded the advance guard in 1839, was claimed to have obtained a commercial agreement, but the Khan later denied this. In fact the Khivans resumed their slave-raids and also their support for the Kazakh rebels.

Palmerston, having achieved his objective with the abandonment of the Russian expedition, was content to sit back and try to ensure that Russia did not achieve by negotiation what she had failed to achieve by force. Shakespear and the Hon. John Bloomfield, the British Minister at St. Petersburg, were instructed to keep watch on the negotiations at St. Petersburg to see that Russia did not obtain any political influence and Auckland was urged to plant a British agent at Khiva to observe any negotiations which took place there. But beyond this system of observation Palmerston was content to do nothing and he dropped his former proposals for an advance to Balkh and for an alliance with Khiva.[60]

Palmerston's proposal to retain an agent at Khiva came in time to clothe the remains of what had been the most wide-ranging British initiative in Turkestan: the mission of Arthur Conolly. The story of Conolly's mission begins in England in 1839. Conolly was then a disappointed man; the bright promise of his early career entirely withered. In 1829 to 1831 he had been among the first to travel to India by the overland route through Central Asia; with Trevelyan he had in 1831 to 1832 played a formative role in drafting recommendations for British policy there; and in 1834 he had entered the coveted Political Department. But since then he had been eclipsed: laurels which might have been his had been given to Burnes; his appointment in Rajputana had turned out to be an undistinguished backwater; and by going to England in January 1838 he had contrived to miss the prospect of new employment beyond the Indus. To cap it all, his hopes of marriage and settlement in England had been frustrated by a woman's whim. Like Lugard later, in similar circumstances, he turned his face back towards the East in the hope of finding some new great purpose in life.

As it happened, the purpose was already waiting for him. In England he had made contacts with members of the India Board and found himself caught up in discussions of how to exploit the new horizons which seemed to be opening up in Central Asia. At the end of 1838 Hobhouse was poised on a spring tide of imperial enthusiasm as he gazed already beyond Afghanistan into the challenging depths of Central Asia. He saw the new problem as the containment of Russia in Turkestan. Supported by Thomas Love Peacock, Conolly argued that Russia, baulked in Afghanistan, would try to control Khiva and Bukhara; and would find a legitimate excuse in the existence of the slave-trade. It should be British policy to remove this excuse by stopping the trade. Peacock's ideas on how this might be done were in line with Palmerston's general policy towards the African slave-trade, namely, that the incentive to engage in slaving would disappear as the opportunities for legitimate trade increased. Accordingly, Peacock proposed the extension to Turkestan of the policy which he had helped to shape for Ellenborough in 1830: the rivers Oxus and Jaxartes should be opened to steam navigation; there would follow a rapid growth in British trade in Turkestan; this would be succeeded by British political influence; and finally there would take place the spread of civilization.[61] Conolly's own solution was at once more simple and more fantastic. He proposed that a British agent should be sent to Turkestan to explain the nature of British policy and, with rational argument, to persuade the Uzbek rulers to abandon slavery. Splendid missions and the offer of alliances were unnecessary: 'All that an envoy would require, would be to make the appearance of a gentleman among them.'[62]

Despite the large measure of agreement between them, the objectives of Peacock and Conolly were radically different. For both the extension of civilization was the major goal and the frustration of the designs of Russia essentially secondary. But, for Peacock, civilization meant technical progress and was symbolized by steam-power; for Conolly, civilization was an attribute of morality or even of Christianity and it was to be manifested in a crusade against slavery. Like Todd, he was a passionately religious man; he had already felt the evils of the slave-trade when he visited Turkestan in 1830 and, even then, had seized upon the destruction of that institution as the most important issue; it would be better, he had written, that Russia should occupy Turkestan than that such barbarity should continue.[63]

Hobhouse was strongly attracted by the idea of combating the spread of Russian influence by establishing British influence on a basis of trade and civilization. For once he was not led forward by Palmerston, whose robust scepticism about the project indeed induced Hobhouse to modify substantially his plans. In fact Hobhouse found little support in England for the project and, faced with opposition within the Court of Directors, was obliged to leave the initiative to Auckland in India. Nevertheless, Hobhouse decided to advance the project to the extent of sending Conolly to India with a view to his employment in Turkestan. He set out the objectives of the mission in a dispatch dated 24 January 1839. These followed precisely the lines laid down by Peacock and Conolly. Conolly was to go to Turkestan and explain the nature of British policy in Afghanistan, persuade the rulers to release their Russian and Iranian slaves, and open up the Oxus as 'a grand channel of trade'. British commerce would enter, followed by British political influence, Turkestan would become civilized and strengthened and so form a buffer against Russian expansion.[64] In addition, Hobhouse began arrangements for the acquisition of steam vessels for use on the Oxus.

The staid Hobhouse's acceptance of this visionary project is surprising and must be attributed to the influence of Conolly. It is true that the stirring news and decisions of the autumn of 1838 had produced in the President an almost feverish excitement, and that he had always been attracted to the possibilities of steam navigation. But there seems to be something else and one would suggest that this was the personality of Conolly, who seems to have exerted on Hobhouse the same hypnotic effect which was once achieved by the very different figure of Byron. To read Conolly's naïve arguments today and to remember his futile career and unhappy end is to wonder how his contemporaries could have been so readily deceived. For it is apparent from the remarks which were made about him by his acquaintances that he possessed that same compelling spiritual ascendancy which radiated from Alesha Karamazov. The cautious and reserved Hobhouse described him as an 'intelligent, able, zealous, and, I think, very trustworthy person'.[65] Conolly contrived to leave the impression of a saint even on the cynical Eastwick, whose sardonic chronicle of the follies of British policy in Upper Sind is one of the most memorable literary deposits of the period.[66] Kaye, who was always ready to present the best features of the subjects of his biographies, yet discovers new superlatives for Conolly. Without conceding the existence of this personal magnetism it is difficult to explain how Conolly contrived to go so far as he did; the men who supported him supported a man, not a policy. The weakness of his dependence upon personality was that his persuasive influence disappeared once his physical presence was removed.

Things began to go badly for Conolly as soon as he left London in February 1839. In Istanbul he lingered so long as to attract censure from Hobhouse and a request to account for £500 of travel expenses. His response was revealing, for he at once became indignant and claimed that his character as a gentleman was being impugned; it was plainly the appearance of a very sensitive gentleman that he intended to make in Turkestan.[67] By the time Conolly arrived in India in November 1839 Hobhouse's early enthusiasm for expansion had withered under the blast of Parliamentary criticism. Auckland, who had never liked the concept behind Conolly's mission, was at a loss to decide what to do with him; the situation in Turkestan was unpromising, with Bukhara hostile, Kunduz and Khulm doubtful, and the question mark posed by the Russian expedition to Khiva. In the end Auckland sent him off to Macnaghten.[68]

In Afghanistan Conolly's prospects began to revive and new hopes of missions to Turkestan arose. Macnaghten was not only a kindly chief but he was also Conolly's cousin. The Envoy was persuaded to devise a new mission to Turkestan, focused this time on Kokand. The ruler of Kokand was accustomed to send occasional envoys to the Ottoman Sultan in Istanbul. In 1838 Henry Rawlinson had encountered one of these, Sayyid Muhammad Zahid, in Iran, and had been informed that the Uzbek states were ready to unite against Russia under British protection.[69] Conolly had met the same envoy in Istanbul and had there discussed with him his plans for combating Russia and slavery and had received an invitation to visit Kokand.[70] Upon this slender connection Macnaghten and Conolly now, in April 1840, constructed an imposing, but fragile edifice. Rawlinson and Conolly were to travel to Turkestan on a broad, and ill-defined mission. They were to collect information, explain British policy, and urge Kokand to promote trade by instituting a system of moderate duties. But the most striking part of their instructions was the direction to urge the Uzbek states to combine against Russia under the leadership of Kokand. It was not intended that this combination should take the form of armed resistance: quite the contrary; the Uzbeks should concentrate on internal reforms and upon the avoidance of such actions as slaving which would cause offence to Russia. There would be no British protection and Conolly and Rawlinson were particularly instructed not to offer any British support against either Russia or Iran:

It is obviously desirable for the future peace of Central Asia, and for the tranquillity of Hindostan especially, that neither of the powers in question should encroach upon Turkestan, and the Policy which lately prompted us to maintain the unity of the Affghan nation, leads us to desire the independence of all the other states lying between the British Indian frontier and the borders of Russia and Persia; but we can now take no steps to effect this extension of our Political security except such as friendly negotiation may induce, and you will declare in the most decided tone, that even if she were less confident than she has reason to be in her ability to resist every aggression upon her Eastern possessions, England would not consent to protect them by supporting continual rapine and desolation in any country through which they might be assaulted.[71]

The whole plan bears the unmistakable imprint of Conolly. The arguments are his and so is the clear priority given to humanitarianism over strategy. The political arguments are weak: the idea of the neutralization of Turkestan was certainly not so widely accepted as the statement assumes; and there is a vagueness about the statement that only friendly negotiation is 'now' appropriate—there appears to exist an implication that, in the future, if the Uzbeks behaved themselves and co-operated, there might be a prospect of more material British assistance. Indeed this implication was present in the original 1839 design of Conolly's mission and its reduction to an almost imperceptible presence in these instructions was presumably in deference to the existing situation in Turkestan and to Auckland's expected hostility to any involvement there. The weight placed upon Kokand was most sanguine in view of the lack of information about that state. Kokand was selected as the potential leader of what Conolly later called the 'pacific Oosbeg confederation for the independence of Turkestan'[72] mainly for the reason that Khiva was excluded, because it was under direct Russian threat, and Bukhara, because it was hostile to Britain. There is no evidence that any thought was given to the problems that would be raised by the conflicts among the Uzbek states. Burnes, who knew more about the political situation in Turkestan than anyone else in Kabul, was opposed to the mission: Britons, he thought, had no business in Turkestan and the containment of Russian expansion was best done from London.[73] But he was overruled.

Conolly's plan was not put into operation in this new form. Auckland refused to approve it and the constantly changing situation in Turkestan prompted frequent modifications. At the end of May, news from Khiva inclined Macnaghten to think that the mission should proceed first to that state; on 14 June Conolly suggested that he should go first to Bukhara, but Macnaghten refused. In the summer of 1840 the situation began to look more promising: Shakespear had established himself at Khiva and a Khivan envoy, Yakub Beg, arrived at Kabul with a proposal for a defensive alliance against Russia. Conolly received an encouraging letter from his Kokandian acquaintance and Auckland lifted his original ban on the mission. Still Macnaghten was unsure about the future and particularly about the possibility that the Russian attack on Khiva would be renewed. Nevertheless, in September,

1840, he hesitantly gave Conolly permission to proceed to Turkestan; fortunately for himself, Rawlinson had escaped to Qandahar.

Macnaghten's doubts were reflected in the uncertainty which appeared in Conolly's new instructions. These were designed to cover two contingencies. Conolly was to go first to Khiva. If he then found Khiva under Russian attack he was, if requested by the Khan, to undertake a mediation with the twin objectives of preserving the independence of Khiva and giving satisfaction to Russia. He was also to inform the Russian commander that Britain would resist any attempt to subvert Khivan independence. If Conolly discovered that the Russian commander was not acting in accordance with Russian professions (as communicated to Palmerston) he was to draw the commander's attention to those professions. This part of his instructions obviously operated only if the Russian attack were renewed. If it were not renewed then Conolly was to be guided by the second part of his instructions, which amounted to Conolly's original plan for an Uzbek confederation. Conolly was to inform the Khan that although Britain could not agree to his request for an alliance, he would be well advised to co-operate in an Uzbek confederation. From Khiva Conolly was to go on to Kokand, once more to advocate the formation of the Uzbek confederation in which 'Kokan would appear to be the State best fitted to take the lead' by virtue of its friendly connections with Russia, its allegedly intimate alliance with Khiva, and its unlikely, though presumed close, acquaintance with European politics through its mission in Istanbul. At that time there was no proposal for a visit to Bukhara, but it was hoped that together Khiva and Kokand would persuade Bukhara to enter the Uzbek alliance. The objects of the Uzbek alliance were spelled out once more: the intent was not to oppose Russia by force; the alliance was to be an organization for the conciliation of Russia, so depriving that power of any excuse for intervention; or, in other words, a league for the suppression of the slave-trade. Lastly, Conolly was to explain British policy and discuss commercial development.[74]

Once again we are confronted with the problem of how Conolly won support for a policy in which no one but he believed. Although Macnaghten backed him, it is clear that the Envoy never had any confidence in the project. Auckland always disliked the proposals: he wanted no relations with Turkestan. Perhaps, in the long run, when Afghanistan had been consolidated, commercial and then political influence in Turkestan might be acquired, but for the moment the Uzbeks were too barbarous, and, as the fate of Stoddart at Bukhara revealed, attempts to establish political influence by the employment of

European agents were too dangerous.[75] Besides, Britain lacked the resources to support an active policy in Turkestan. 'What is the use', asked Colvin, 'of our going to make what would prove only a personal display of our impotency in that region?'[76] Auckland criticized the instructions given to Conolly in September because they suggested a degree of support for the Uzbek states which Britain could not maintain. In particular, he singled out from the papers a hint which had been given to the Khivan envoy that Britain would join the projected Uzbek confederation. Auckland declared that he wanted no British involvement whatsoever; Conolly should promise only sympathy and a willingness to mediate.[77]

Holding the views that he did, it is surprising that Auckland consented to the mission at all. On 4 May 1840 he had rejected Conolly's original April project, but a week later, on 11 May, he had changed his mind. In his second letter he had repeated his own view that the possible advantages were outweighed by the dangers and his hope that in the end Conolly would not go to Turkestan, but he had given Macnaghten discretion to put the plan into operation if the Envoy believed that any 'grand and direct support to our position in Afghanistan' could be expected.[78] Even shrouded as it was, in these conditions so unlikely to be fulfilled, Auckland's shift of ground is surprising. Auckland hinted to Hobhouse that he had relented rather than disappoint Macnaghten and this is not wholly improbable.[79] But a more likely explanation is that Auckland felt it necessary to make some gesture as a concession to the pressure for action in Turkestan which was being put upon him. From England and Afghanistan he was urged to advance to Balkh and Herat and to make an alliance with Khiva. These he would not do, but he was reluctantly prepared to make an inexpensive gesture to abate the pressure and buy time. Conolly's meaningless mission was just such a gesture and it was in the same category as the permission, hedged by stringent conditions, given by Auckland in April 1840 for an agent to be sent to the Russian camp. In July 1840, however, Auckland imposed new restrictions upon Conolly's mission; he could go to Khiva, but not Kokand,[80] and Auckland maintained this prohibition for some time in the face of requests to lift it from Macnaghten. This firmer line was undoubtedly the result of Auckland's new hope that the failure of the Russian expedition to Khiva would signal the end of Anglo–Russian rivalry in Turkestan and would make it unnecessary to take any action in that inhospitable area. In consequence of this more restrictive attitude Conolly was forbidden, despite his instructions, to go to Kokand and when he left Kabul it was to go to Khiva alone.

Conolly's mission was a sad story of continual disillusionment, a
subject which would require the different pens of a Graham Greene or a
Somerset Maugham to do it justice. His unpleasant awakening began
on the way to Khiva. In Kabul his companion, Yakub Beg, had
enthusiastically supported Conolly's views on the need to extirpate the
slave-trade. Conolly was horrified therefore, when, inquiring about the
status of some children who had mysteriously become attached to his
party, he discovered that they were a speculative purchase by the
Khivan envoy and were intended for sale on Yakub's return to Khiva.[81]
Conolly's opinion of Yakub sank lower when the Khivan envoy
reported, quite accurately, to Allah Quli Khan that Shuja was a mere
puppet and the British position in Afghanistan precarious.[82] This
report, and the news of Todd's expulsion from Herat seriously
weakened Conolly's influence with Allah Quli Khan, who was presumably also annoyed that Shakespear's promises had not been fulfilled.
His attempts to reason with the Khan and to educate him in world
geography and politics bore little fruit, judged by the statement in an
official history of Khiva that the British were a section of the Russian
people whose land lay north of the Russian empire.[83] Conolly was
ignored by the Uzbeks and he found them disgusting; the slave-market
revolted him. His beloved Uzbek confederation made no progress at
all. When he arrived at Khiva he found the Khan preparing an expedition against Kokand. Conolly remonstrated, pointing out that union
was the only defence against Russia. The Khan agreed, but said he
must first retaliate on Kokand. Conolly commented bitterly: 'I question whether for his own part, he would not rather run the risk of all that
foreign enemies may do to Toorkestan than tie himself up in a confederation of justice and peace with both his Oosbeg neighbours.'[84] Khiva,
it seemed, was a lost cause, but on 5 March 1841 news arrived which
lightened his gloom: Auckland had lifted his veto on Conolly's visit to
Kokand.

Auckland's change of mind at the end of December 1840 was the
consequence of the receipt of the news that Russia had formally abandoned her designs upon Khiva. Although Auckland still did not want
Conolly to go to Kokand, he now thought there would be no danger
and, perhaps, he wished to soften the blow caused by his simultaneous
reduction of the scope of Conolly's duties at Khiva. He now prescribed
that Conolly should do no more than urge the Khan to make further
concessions to Russia, including the removal of restrictions upon Russian caravans to Bukhara and persuading tribesmen to cease their
attacks on Russians.[85] Auckland placed still more restrictions upon
Conolly's activities at Khiva when reports reached him, in April 1841,

of his doings at that place. He discovered that Conolly had gone far beyond even his September instructions in the course of his political discussions and the Governor-General was particularly incensed by Conolly's pressure on the Khan to introduce humanitarian reforms. Auckland sent instructions that Conolly should return to Khiva from Kokand and remain there as a mere collector of information until he could be replaced by Richmond Shakespear. Auckland did not want any agent at Khiva but, since London had told him he must have one, he would obey, but he would not have the unpredictable Conolly. As for Conolly's larger schemes, they were completely worthless: 'The Governor General in Council must regard as almost visionary the proposal of an effectual union amongst the Oosbeg states.'[86] But these reproofs never reached Conolly.

Conolly was still contriving yet further twists to his saga. Eagerly grasping the opportunity afforded him by Auckland's December instructions he had left Khiva at the beginning of May 1841. About his mission to Kokand I have been able to find only the meagrest information, since the letters which he wrote from there have gone astray. His journey took fifty-five days, he was well received, and he remained there for two and a half months.[87] What was the outcome of his conversations is quite unclear, although it is recorded that the war between Khiva and Kokand was concluded through his mediation.[88] But the next certain point in his story is his decision not to return to Khiva, but to make his way to Bukhara.

Bukhara presented a special problem for Britain, because of the problem of Colonel Charles Stoddart (1806–42). Stoddart was a British army officer who had given up his post as secretary of the United Services Institute in 1835, to accompany Henry Ellis as Military Secretary in Iran. He had continued to serve in the same post under McNeill, who had employed him to deliver Palmerston's decision on Herat to Muhammad Shah. McNeill had also given him another errand designed by Palmerston: to go to Bukhara to persuade the ruler to release his Russian slaves so as to avert the threat of Russian attack and to collect information. McNeill also allowed Stoddart to hold out the prospect of a treaty of friendship.[89] But Stoddart did not go straight to Bukhara: instead he first joined Eldred Pottinger in Herat and only went on to Bukhara after his expulsion from Herat in November 1838. He eventually reached his destination on 17 December. Stoddart was no diplomat. His close friend, Captain Grover, wrote of him that 'he was a man of impulse, with no more power of self-control than an infant . . . for a diplomatic mission, requiring coolness and self-control, a man less adapted to the purpose could not readily have been found.'[90] The accuracy of Grover's judgement has already been illustrated by Stoddart's behaviour in Iran and at Herat and it was now to receive further confirmation at Bukhara. Why McNeill chose him is a mystery; there were certainly better officers in the detachment.

Within four days of his arrival Stoddart was in prison. Apparently the Amir Nasrullah had already received unfavourable reports about his behaviour from Herat. Stoddart's majestic and unconciliatory bearing at their first interview did not dispel the impression inculcated by those reports. It was the custom in Bukhara for envoys to be hurried into the presence of the Amir, supported under each arm by a bearer. The impression given, intentionally, was an undignified one and Stoddart would not tolerate it. Flinging off his bearers, he strode forward alone towards the Amir. Unimpressed by such arrogance on the part of a mere infidel, the Amir put him in prison and there Stoddart remained, off and on, until October 1840.

The treatment of Stoddart dominated British relations with Bukhara for three years; the refuge given to Dost Muhammad in Bukhara was of less importance, particularly after the ex-Amir became prisoner rather than guest. British efforts were mainly directed towards obtaining Stoddart's release. The obvious possibility of an armed expedition, which Macnaghten advocated, was discussed but never adopted, because the forces were never available and Auckland was wholly opposed to the use of force beyond the Hindu Kush. The alternative was persuasion and the years 1839 to 1841 were decorated by a series of richly comical episodes as missions proceeded to Bukhara.

Auckland's first communication to Nasrullah was sent in January 1839, before the news of Stoddart's imprisonment had reached the Governor-General. Auckland's object was to stress the innocence of Britain's Afghan policy and to allay any fears that the Amir might have. His letter arrived at Bukhara on 18 May 1839 and the account of its reception, although long, is worth quoting for the insight it provides into the incomprehension which characterized relations between Britons and Uzbeks:

The King opened the letter with his own hand and after looking over a few lines of it, called for a Mirza who read it all deliberately. Upon this ensued a consultation between the King and the Mirza which ended in their saying that the letter appeared to have no *mutlub* (meaning) and that they could not conceive what kind of answer they were expected to send to it. They then both turned to the messenger and questioned him as to the purport of his verbal communication which they expected might explain more of the objects of the mission, but he of course had none to make. The King then said he would send the letter to the Feringe (Colonel Stoddart) but of the results of their reference the messenger heard nothing. However he was several times subsequently summoned to the King's presence and questioned both publicly and privately to try if anything could be elicited from him—the King always expressing his vexation that no Vakeel or man of responsibility had been sent with the letter, as, if so, he would in return have willingly sent one of his chief nobles. The interview always terminated in some expression of this sort or declaration of his incapacity to understand the meaning of the letter he had received, unless it was to tell him that we had come to take Cabool and Candahar with which he said he did not see that he had any business.[91]

Different approaches were tried to persuade the Amir to release Stoddart. At Herat, Todd favoured a strong line. He wrote a firm letter declaring that the British Government would not lower itself 'to sue for its rights with sweet words'.[92] At Kabul, Macnaghten preferred an indirect approach. He learned of the existence at Peshawar of a family of Sayyids who were reputed to have considerable influence in Turkestan. Their name is not given, but they were probably either of the family of Maulvi Muhammad Husayn or of Sayyid Fazl al-Haq. Macnaghten gave them money to travel to Bukhara to try to obtain Stoddart's freedom. The Sayyids did nothing for Stoddart but treated the affair as a trading venture and having lost money on it asked Britain to make good their losses.[93] An indirect approach was also attempted from London. Help was sought from Russia and letters written to the Ottoman Sultan Abdülmecid and Allah Quli Khan of Khiva requesting their assistance. A personal letter was sent by Queen Victoria to the latter in which she addressed that suspicious Muslim slave-dealer as 'our Good Friend' and concluded 'we pray God to have our Good Friend in his Holy Keeping.'[94] But all was in vain.

The improvement in Stoddart's position which took place in the autumn of 1840 was the consequence of the Russian failure at Khiva which produced an adventitious rise in British prestige. The Amir released Stoddart from prison and offered a treaty by which all territory north of the Hindu Kush should be given to Bukhara. The Amir gave the treaty to a messenger, Muhammad Husayn Khan, who contrived to lose it on his way to Kabul. Macnaghten wrote back offering a treaty dealing only with friendship, commerce, and the free return of agents and made no mention of any territorial deal.[95] In view of the recent settlement with Khulm, the Amir's territorial proposals were most embarrassing. Macnaghten's reply did not satisfy Nasrullah who pressed repeatedly for recognition of his territorial claims, but Macnaghten refused to introduce the subject, and Auckland would have offered no more than a commercial agreement.[96]

During the course of these negotiations Stoddart had come to feel in high favour at Bukhara. He now dropped the question of his own departure and, instead, his thoughts turned to the accomplishment of some notable feat similar to that of Shakespear at Khiva. He hoped to persuade the Amir to release all his Russian slaves.[97] In June 1841 Auckland agreed that Stoddart could remain if he wished. Nevertheless, there is evidence that Stoddart was still uneasy and, for all his bold amibitions, would have been happy to have left Bukhara if he could have done so. It is sometimes claimed that Stoddart could have left with a Russian mission under Buten'ev which visited Bukhara in the summer of 1841 and that he declined to do so rather than owe his freedom to Russia. This story seems unlikely. It is true that the Amir asked Stoddart if he wished to leave with Buten'ev in August and Stoddart replied that he would not wish to do so unless there was some special reason.[98] But the Amir never indicated that he would have let Stoddart go and the question may simply have been intended to discover his reaction. Buten'ev's mission was ill used by the Amir, had no influence, and Stoddart states that the Amir did not even bother to reply to the Russian requests for Stoddart's release.[99]

Stoddart was now joined at Bukhara by Conolly, whom he had invited thither at the request of the Amir. Nasrullah's initiative may have been caused by suspicions of Conolly's activities at Kokand. Stoddart's letter of invitation clearly reveals his own suspicions of the Amir and it is obvious that he would have left Bukhara without waiting for Conolly if he had had the opportunity.[100] But Conolly came willingly; for him it was a final opportunity to bring into existence his beloved Uzbek confederation. Once he had thought that Khiva and Kokand might together compel Bukhara to join; now he hoped to persuade Nasrullah to join with Madali of Kokand in the coercion of Khiva.

Conolly's unfortunate Odyssey ended at Bukhara in final disillusionment and death. He arrived in October 1841; the following month the Kabul rising broke the British hold on Afghanistan; in December the Amir thrust Conolly and Stoddart into prison. Nasrullah was suspicious of British policy; his treaty proposals had been rejected; Queen Victoria had not answered his letters; and he disliked Conolly's doings at Kokand. In fact he was even then planning war against that state and in May 1842 he attacked, killed Muhammad Ali, and recovered control of Ura Tube. Upon his return to Bukhara he had Conolly and Stoddart executed, probably in June 1842.

Some of the details of the last months of Conolly's life survive in a few letters, in his journal, and in a mass of conflicting evidence which lies in the Foreign Office and India Office Records. He retained his steadfast pride to the end: 'We are', he wrote to his brother, 'resolved to wear our English honesty and dignity to the last.'[101] But in those months the misleading veneer of political speculation which had always disguised his basic humanitarianism was at last removed. He now looked neither to the containment of Russia, nor to the neutralization of Turkestan, but to joint intervention by the European powers in the interests of civilization. In a memorandum written on 27 March 1842 he advocated an agreement between Britain and Russia to settle Turkestan and re-draw its frontiers. Nasrullah should be deposed; his territories divided between Khiva and Kokand; and the frontiers of Afghanistan extended to the Oxus.[102]

For all the contemporary speculations and the subsequent imaginings of Soviet historians, there was little substance to British policy in Turkestan during the years 1838 to 1842. The most ambitious project was Conolly's Uzbek confederation, which, if it had been vigorously supported, could have led to a British protectorate over Turkestan. But it had no support: Macnaghten gave only literary assistance; Auckland wanted no contact with Turkestan; and Hobhouse's early enthusiasm had evaporated before Conolly ever set foot in Turkestan. The Oxus steamboats of course never materialized. After the spring of 1839 Hobhouse's only interest was in checking the Russian drive on Khiva: in so far as Conolly's schemes chimed with this aim, well and good, but once the Khivan expedition was abandoned by Russia, Hobhouse lost all interest; he declined to use force in Turkestan,[103] supported Auckland's veto on the Kokand visit, and wrote disapprovingly of the September 1840 instructions to Conolly that they contemplated too much interference in Turkestan.[104] The refusal of the authorities in either London or Calcutta to give positive backing to the confederation meant that its success depended on voluntary agreement between the Uzbek states and it soon became obvious that their own disputes were too great to permit this.

Apart from Conolly's Uzbek confederation, four distinct possible policies can be discerned. The first was that of a bilateral alliance with Khiva alone—the alliance with Bukhara was never intended seriously. This Khivan alliance was advocated by Abbott and Shakespear both as a means of preserving the independence of Khiva against Russia and as a bait to help their own negotiations. At the height of the Khivan crisis the proposal was supported in London, but Auckland, with the aid of his Council, held out against it, and when the crisis subsided the proposal was dropped. It foundered primarily upon Auckland's conviction that he lacked the resources to support any military action in Turkestan.

The second policy, which also formed one element in Conolly's comprehensive plan, was to persuade the Uzbek rulers to preserve their independence by conciliating Russia, especially by abandoning the slave-trade. In essence this was the same policy that Britain had pursued towards the Ottoman Empire and towards Iran ever since 1812. It was applied to Turkestan generally from the time of Palmerston's approach to Bukhara in 1838 and it had its greatest success in 1840, when Shakespear's mission to Khiva procured the release of the Russian slaves and the abandonment of the second Khivan expedition. But despite the lip-service regularly paid to the policy, it was never pursued with any consistent vigour. When Conolly hinted that Britain might buy the freedom of Russian slaves the suggestion was not adopted. In any case, only Russian slaves would have been involved because Iranian slaves were so numerous as to constitute a vital part of the Khivan economy. Also, only existing slaves would have been affected. A regular subsidy would have been necessary to have induced the Uzbek Khans to forswear enslavement permanently and even this could not have stopped all slave-trading because of the degree of independence enjoyed by the Turkoman chiefs. But without some financial incentive there was nothing but fear to restrain the Uzbek rulers and this incentive was removed by the defeats suffered first by Russia and then by Britain.

A third policy was to try to control Turkestan by threats. This policy, which involved the extension of the frontiers of Afghanistan to the Oxus and to Herat, has already been considered in the previous chapter. It was strongly advocated from London in 1840 as a counter to Russia, and by Macnaghten and others in Afghanistan for a variety of reasons from 1839 onwards, although few of these reasons had much to do with obtaining influence in Turkestan. Such a policy might have been successful in so far as it would have provided an advanced base from which a credible threat of coercive action against Khiva and Bukhara could have been posed, although it may well be that a further advance would then have proved necessary. However the scheme failed through the unwillingness of Auckland to allow such a movement.

The fourth policy which emerged during the years under study was that of resolving the problem of Turkestan by agreement between Britain and Russia, with the possible admission of Iran to the concert. Conolly was the principal advocate of this course, but it appears frequently, in various forms, in the writings of several of the actors in the Central Asian drama. It rested on three assumptions which came to be quite widely held: namely, that Britain and Russia had no hostile designs on each other's Asian possessions; that both powers were likely to be drawn into involvement in the area by the common problem of civilized powers sharing a frontier with unsettled peoples; and that the present, essentially defensive battle for influence was likely, if unchecked, to escalate into a situation of what Auckland called 'open exertion and counter-action', which Auckland believed British India lacked the resources to sustain. Conolly and others would have added a fourth assumption; that Britain and Russia shared the common duty of a civilized power to promote civilization. Among those who came to share the main assumptions, there was broad agreement on the action that should be taken: agreed limits should be set to the advance of frontiers; the area still remaining should be divided into spheres of influence adjoining each frontier, and a neutral zone; conflicts between either European power and an Uzbek neighbour should be settled by the mediation of the other European power; and Britain and Russia should combine to put an end to warfare among the Uzbek states, stop the slave-trade, promote trade, and, in general, introduce the habits of civilization.

Elements of this fourth policy can be seen scattered through the history of the period. It was foreshadowed by Nesselrode in 1838 to 1839; in 1840 to 1841 Clanricarde felt sure something like it would be acceptable to Russia.[105] Despite his earlier advocacy of an alliance with Khiva, Shakespear came to favour an understanding with Russia and the limitation of the advance of the two powers and he made some impression on Hobhouse with his views. Auckland's letters and memoranda make it clear that as early as 1840 he was moving towards a solution of this type and in April 1841 he came to believe that the same feeling was about to prevail in London. He wrote to Macnaghten: 'My private letters give me the impression that there is a growing disposition on the part of the English and Russian cabinets to abstain from interference with the Oosbeg states.'[106] The policy remained a live issue in future years also: it was pursued by Peel and Aberdeen in their discussions with Russia in the 1840s; it reappeared in the Clarendon–Gorchakov discussions of 1869; and something like it formed the basis of the 1907 Anglo–Russian Agreement. But it failed to make any progress at the most critical period because of the opposition of Palmerston.

Palmerston declined to explore the possibilities of agreement with Russia. He would have been happy to see Khiva become a neutral 'non-conducting body interposed between Russia and British India and separated from both by a considerable width of space',[107] but he did not think this could be achieved by agreement with Russia. Russia might have no present intention of attacking India, but she certainly coveted Khiva and once in possession she would be in a position to produce disturbances in British India during any future dispute with Britain.[108] Therefore, particularly since the prospects for British expansion appeared so bright, Palmerston was not interested in agreement with Russia. During the latter part of 1840 and the early months of 1841, buoyed up by his successes in the Near East and untroubled by fears of European repercussions, he urged on Auckland a vigorous policy of expansion beyond the Hindu Kush: 'Now is the time for you to belay in Asia; make fast what you have gained in Afghanistan; secure the Kingdom of Cabul and make yourself sure of Herat.'[109]

In the same letter Palmerston entered into a general discussion of British policy in Asia and Africa, writing of opening new markets in those continents to replace those lost to European competitors in Europe. 'It is the Business of the Government to open and secure the Roads for the Merchant', he remarked, and expressed great hopes of commercial gains from the wars in Afghanistan and China. Such statements could be used to support the contention that Palmerston's aggressive expansionism and his refusal to seek agreement with Russia in Central Asia were dictated by motives of economic imperialism. This, I submit, would be mistaken; in an effort to stimulate Auckland's flagging enthusiasm for expansion, Palmerston simply transposed the justification and the motive. Certainly this was the meaning which Auckland took from it. He assumed that Palmerston meant what statesmen of the time usually meant when they discussed the relationship between trade and politics, and replied: 'I entirely agree with you in what you say upon the compensation which we should obtain for our risks and sacrifices, both in China and Afghanistan, in the openings of new avenues for commerce.'[110] In other words, wars were for politics and commercial profit was a bonus. Nor was it thought to be an unreasonable bonus. Just as seventeenth-century Puritans like Governor John Winthrop of Massachusetts and even Oliver Cromwell himself, saw financial gains as a proper reward for righteous living, so nineteenth-century men saw nothing odd in the expectation that a just war might show a judicious profit. The profit did not need to be and indeed should not be the motive, but it could well be the compensation.

In the last analysis Palmerston's expanionist policy in Asia was not for Asian objects at all. At the same time that Palmerston was making his vicarious threats of British action in Asia to Brunnow he was cheerfully seeking his co-operation in the Near East and in Europe; indeed, at that point, in January and February 1840, of his negotiations on the Near East with Russia, France, and his Cabinet colleagues, it may well have suited the Foreign Secretary's purpose to appear to take a strong line with Russia on another subject. It was always the problems of European diplomacy which exercised him most. From this view-point the danger of Turkestan was twofold. Asian rivalries might endanger European amity and limitations might be imposed upon European action by threats which appeared in Asia. For Palmerston, agreement in Asia was no solution to the problem because, although Asian differences might be capable of being composed in this way, much more vital European problems could not be so resolved. Therefore it was inevitable that a European power would be tempted to upset an Asian agreement in order to bring about a situation in Asia which could influence a European negotiation. Palmerston's view was that it was better that Britain, and not Russia, should be in a position to exercise such pressure in Asia; if Britain could take up a commanding position in Turkestan Russia would be unable to coerce Britain by threatening India; whereas Britain on the other hand would be in a position to influence Russia. In this view Palmerston's advocacy of expansion in Asia can be seen as a European–centred policy designed primarily to insulate Europe from the policies of Asia and secondarily to ensure that if the Asian balance were to affect the European balance it should be to the advantage of Britain. For all the striking differences between their policies, Palmerston and Canning were at one in their wider concept of a European–centred world.

In the end it was Auckland who had the last word in Central Asia. Palmerston's logic was good, but the resources to apply it were lacking. Auckland from Calcutta could control the application of British Indian resources and he would not commit them to Turkestan. He had set himself in 1838 one limited objective: the creation of a buffer state in Afghanistan; he certainly would not go beyond it and by 1841 he was coming to the conclusion he could not even afford Afghanistan. So the debate about Turkestan ended by exposing the limitations of the Afghan buffer strategy; far from being the stalwart bulwark of India, let alone the springboard to Turkestan, Afghanistan was simply another hostage to fortune. A Russian threat to Khiva threatened the British position in Afghanistan much more than it menaced the peace of British India. To protect Afghanistan it was necessary, wrote Auckland, for Her Majesty's Government to intervene in Turkestan, for the Indian Government certainly could not do so with the resources which it possessed. Far from insulating Europe from Asia, Palmerston's Afghan strategy had in fact involved Europe and Asia more closely.

The debates about Turkestan also underline a feature of the mechanics of imperial expansion which has been commented on before: the role of the frontier agent. For British and even British Indian statesmen,

Turkestan was *terra incognita*; those few men who knew something of it, and especially those employed in it, could exercise a strong influence on policy through their monopoly of information. As it happened, Abbott, Shakespear, Stoddart, and Conolly were all junior men, but even so they were able to affect the course of policy. In such a situation the factor of personality becomes of great importance and at various times the lack of judgement and the penchant for violent solutions which characterized Abbott and Stoddart and the moral fervour of Conolly, allied to his political understanding and his ties with Macnaghten, could produce new strategic vistas and threaten to involve Britain in far-reaching imperial manœuvres. The Political Agents came uncommonly close to starting a chain of action which might have rolled Britain like a snowball into Turkestan. They were frustrated partly by their own lack of skill, partly by the objective realities of the situation, but most of all by the stubborn refusal of Auckland, despite pressures from England and from the frontier, to become involved.

Thus the story of British involvement in Turkestan in this period closes with a double negative. The first negative is that of Auckland who refused to be pushed into Turkestan to resist Russia; the second negative is that of Palmerston who refused to be persuaded to make an agreement with Russia. Between the two, both possible policies failed: confrontation and conciliation. The result was that Britain came out of Turkestan with no policy, but with a number of experiences which would shape her future policies.

Afghanistan Abandoned, 1841–1842

Our great experiment of consolidating Afghanistan is, in short, a failure, except at a cost, which, even if we could, for any period, continue to bear it, would be wholly disproportionate to its objects.

Colvin to James Colvin, 22 Dec. 1841.

The events of 1841 to 1842 may be quickly summarized. In November 1841 a rising took place in Kabul; the rising was not suppressed and it flourished until, late in December, the British in Kabul agreed to evacuate Afghanistan. During the retreat to Jalalabad the entire Kabul force was wiped out, leaving only a handful of prisoners, hostages, women, and children in Afghan hands. At Ghazni, the garrison held out longer, but eventually surrendered and was destroyed. At the other main posts of Qandahar, Kalat-i Ghilzay and Jalalabad, the British forces endured throughout the winter and were reinforced during the spring. In the summer of 1842 two British armies—those of Nott from Qandahar and Pollock from Jalalabad—converged upon Kabul and re-took the city. At the close of the year British forces were withdrawn from Afghanistan, to which the former Barakzay rulers returned in 1843 to re-establish their power in Kabul and Qandahar as it had existed until 1839.

The bare outline of event conceals two questions which are of major interest to this study. The first concerns the reasons why Britain came to lose temporary control over Afghanistan during the winter of 1841 to 1842; and the second surrounds the decision to abandon Afghanistan and the forward strategy which had been inaugurated in 1838. This chapter will examine these two problems.

It is apparent that there were important differences between the November 1841 rising and the earlier disturbances which had been suppressed by military force. The previous disturbances had taken place in areas remote from the main centres of power and had had their origins in local disputes of a traditional character. The uprising of November 1841, on the other hand, took place in the capital and involved groups which had hitherto formed the main props of the

Anglo–Sadozay regime, namely the bureaucrats who had formerly served the Barakzays and who had continued to serve Shah Shuja, and the great Durrani nobles who formed the monarch's court. These men together with the populace of Kabul itself formed the new core of rebellion around which traditionally disaffected groups clustered. Among these traditional groups were the restless tribesmen of the Kohistan and the adjacent valleys to the north, and the Ghilzay tribes who controlled the passes which led eastwards from Kabul to Jalalabad. Quite rapidly, the movement spread to involve other groups, including the hitherto quiescent Ghilzay tribes who inhabited the area around Ghazni to the west of Kabul, and always turbulent Khaibar tribesmen, who controlled the communications between Peshawar and Jalalabad.

The outbreak in Qandahar province also involved new elements, notably the important Durrani nobles who were connected with the Sadozay court at Qandahar and the Durrani tribesmen who lived in the villages in the immediate vicinity of Qandahar. Curiously, it was not until some months after the first signs of unrest at Qandahar that the two groups which had previously been the principal sources of unrest in Qandahar took an important part. The Alizays of Zamindawar contented themselves with purely local action until May 1842 and the western Tokhi and Hotaki Ghilzays remained quiet until their attack upon Kalat also in May 1842. It is important to note that there was little connection between the risings at Qandahar and at Kabul. The Qandahar rising took place much later than that at Kabul, was slow to gather momentum, and its leaders took no steps to co-ordinate their actions with those of the rebels at Kabul.

The involvement of what might be called establishment groups in the struggle against the Anglo–Sadozay system indicates that hostility to that regime had entered a new dimension. The causes of this enlargement of the conflict have already been indicated in chapter 9. In essence the steady increase of British interference had first abridged and now threatened totally to destroy the economic basis of the social and political influence of the traditionally dominant groups; their reaction was partly anticipated, but seemingly underestimated. But, significant as this widening of the area of hostility was, it should not be supposed that the British were washed out of Afghanistan by an irresistable tide of national feeling. The grievances which their enemies felt were narrow, sectional injuries. Those who launched the rising of November 1841 had no idea that they might succeed; like the leaders of the Easter Rising of 1916, they believed they were making a hopeless demonstration, not a revolution. It was the British failure to strike quickly and drastically against them that enabled the rising to gain head, and the rebels to rally under the banner of Islam.

The first cause of the failure of the British to suppress the November 1841 rising was a purely military factor; the Kabul garrison was weak. One brigade, under General Sir Robert Sale (1782–1845), had been sent to clear the passes between Kabul and Jalalabad and had stayed at the latter city. The passes had been blocked in October 1841 by a rising of Ghilzay tribes who were protesting at the reduction of their allowances. Sale's brigade had encountered stiffer resistance than anticipated, had fired off most of its ammunition, and now found it difficult to return to Kabul. A second brigade, under Colonel James Maclaren, had earlier been sent back to India as part of the plan to reduce the British commitment in Afghanistan. Maclaren's brigade, however, was still at Qandahar at the time of the rising and was ordered to return to Kabul. Its failure to return may well have tipped the balance against the British in Kabul. Maclaren turned back to Qandahar at the first sight of snow, although it is clear that he could have forced his way through. It seems likely that Maclaren's decision may have been influenced by the attitude of General Nott, the Commander at Qandahar, who was conscious of the weaknesses of his own force, and who never wanted Maclaren to leave. Nott was a good general, but a very selfish one. It could be that the price of relieving Kabul would have been the loss of Qandahar, but it seems more likely that the suppressing of the Kabul rising would have freed Qandahar from the danger that later developed. The consequence of the failure of either Maclaren or Sale to relieve Kabul, added to the destruction of the small garrison in the Kohistan, meant that there were at Kabul only four thousand troops, of which only one quarter were British, principally the 44th Foot.

Despite the weaknesses of the Kabul garrison it should have been strong enough to suppress the rising. The original rebels were few in number, ill organized, and had no united leadership; those who made the first attack on Burnes's house in Kabul were reported to have had their horses saddled ready to flee. Even when they failed to suppress the rising immediately, it was still open to the British to retire into the great fortress of the Bala Hissar which still commands the city of Kabul. Once inside its walls and dominating the great hills which line the southern limits of the city, the British could, with the aid of Shuja's own troops, have organized an adequate defence and held out until reinforcements could reach Kabul from India when the snows melted in the spring. The failure to suppress or contain the rising was the result of bad military leadership.

Primary responsibility for the failure to organize an adequate military response belongs to the Commander, General Keith Elphinstone. Something has already been said of his caution. During the summer of 1841 he became seriously ill. From 7 June onwards he was confined to his room and knew that he was too helpless to continue in his post. On 26 July he was pronounced totally incapable of transacting business. 'In fact,' continued his doctor, 'in my humble opinion his constitution is shattered beyond redemption.'[1] But, despite his knowledge, Elphinstone did not ask Auckland to relieve him until 9 August. The Governor-General agreed on 6 September and Elphinstone arranged to accompany Macnaghten to Peshawar in October or November 1841. Auckland's comment on Elphinstone was a revealing one: 'he has been in this office everything that I could wish', he wrote to Macnaghten.[2] In fact, to Auckland's knowledge, Elphinstone had been ill and more or less incapable ever since his arrival in Afghanistan and his comment can only be interpreted as an endorsement of Elphinstone's stubborn refusal to supply troops to carry out some of the more ambitious schemes of the Political Agents; in particular Elphinstone had opposed the projected march on Herat. This negative attitude chimed in so well with Auckland's own views that one can only suppose that the Governor-General wanted an inactive commander, even if he was also incompetent.

Elphinstone was unable to leave Kabul and his condition deteriorated still further. When George Broadfoot saw him in October 1841 he was in pain and confined to bed, his joints swollen with gout, and his memory so poor that he appeared childish. Burnes remarked to Broadfoot that he doubted if the General was quite sane and one doctor described him as 'fatuous'.[3] As a consequence of his incapacity combined with his failure to relinquish command the power of military decision fell into the hands of his staff officers, especially the Adjutant-General, Captain Grant (27th N.I.). Broadfoot described them as violent, overbearing men and Grant treated Elphinstone with disdain and abused Macnaghten.[4] The Staff Officers came to exercise even greater control from the beginning of the rising because on 2 November Elphinstone suffered a bad fall.

There were two experienced senior officers who might have replaced Elphinstone and introduced more vigour into the British defence. Of these Brigadier W. Anquetil, who commanded the Shah's Contingent, was a quiet, sensible man, but, as noted earlier, he lacked either the influence or the self-confidence to permit him to take the initiative under such circumstances. Also for much of the time he was ill. The other, Brigadier J. Shelton, was the complete reverse. Shelton was

Colonel of H. M. 44th, and, with his British army background, was the obvious successor to Elphinstone. But during the early days of the rising he was placed in the Bala Hissar, away from the centre of the decision and was not summoned to return to the cantonments until 9 November. There the defects of his character and judgement made him more of a handicap than a help to the conduct of operations. No one had a good word for him and the universal obloquy heaped upon his head was seemingly well deserved. Although personally brave, he had no capacity for command; he was a rigid disciplinarian, a bitter, impossible colleague and, what was worse, he had no idea of what to do. Elphinstone and he disliked each other. Elphinstone complained that

his manner was most contumacious from the day of his arrival, he never gave me information or advice, but invariably found fault with all that was done and canvassed and condemned all orders before officers—frequently perverting and delaying carrying them into effect.

He appeared, Elphinstone remarked, 'to be actuated by an ill-feeling towards me'.[5]

Without purposeful leadership the defence floundered. Actions were mishandled and control of vital positions was lost. The supply position became increasingly difficult. The truth was that the soldiers had had enough of Afghanistan; service there was uncomfortable, expensive, and frustrating; without a determined plan morale slumped. The soldiers' plan was only to sit tight in their cantonments and wait for Macnaghten to arrange a political settlement by which they could go home to India. Unfortunately, the cantonments themselves were almost untenable without an active defence. Laid out on a plain to the north of the city and commanded by a hill, they were quite unsuited to resist a siege; the permanent works which had been planned had never been built because there had never been a decision that Britain was there to stay.

Under these circumstances Macnaghten had no alternative but to seek a political settlement. While he did so, his bargaining position was steadily eroded as the insurgents tightened their blockade of the cantonments. Even so, Macnaghten possessed the authority, had he chosen to exercise it, to invigorate the defence. But he himself lacked the will for stubborn resistance. He had long since obtained all that he wanted from Afghanistan—a baronetcy in 1839, a provisional seat on the Governor-General's Council in 1840, and the unexpected Governorship of Bombay in 1841. He had never liked the country or the work and he had particularly disliked the trend of events in 1841 which had forced him into more and more interference. His original concept of the

Afghan position had been entirely eroded and he was aware that under his successor drastic change was almost certain. His designated successor, Burnes, had wanted a rapid withdrawal of British forces from Afghanistan, leaving Shuja to stand or fall by himself, and the assumption of a strong position on the Indus.[6] Burnes was now dead, killed in the first action of the uprising, but it was inconceivable that another man would continue Macnaghten's policy. When he received the news of his appointment to Bombay on 29 September Macnaghten could not wait to be gone. On personal and political grounds he was already inclined to write off Afghanistan even before the outbreak of the rising. That event seemingly confirmed him in his view and shortly before his death he confided to Eldred Pottinger, who had escaped the massacre in the Kohistan, 'that he thought Government would be glad of what had occurred as forming a pretext to shake off its connection with the country'.[7]

Despite his fatalism, Macnaghten did not want to leave behind him a disaster. He made valiant efforts to persuade the military officers to shake off their paralysis and win him some room for manœuvre. But their fatal inaction continued and the insurgents tightened the blockade around the British position. When Macnaghten began negotiations with the rebels his bargaining position was already greatly weakened. He still made one last attempt to recover something of the British position. There had risen to prominence among the rebel leaders a son of Dost Muhammad Khan, named Muhammad Akbar. Akbar had returned to Kabul from Turkestan when he heard of the rising and there was jealousy and suspicion between him and the Durrani chiefs. Late in December Macnaghten thought he perceived an opportunity to make an agreement with Akbar by which he could divide and defeat the rebels. But he had never possessed much diplomatic skill. Given all the cards Macnaghten could play them gracefully enough, but he was never the man to fight for the odd trick; Akbar easily outwitted and killed him.

The death of Macnaghten, following that of Burnes, left the British with no effective political leadership. No Political Agent now possessed the authority and experience to stand up to the military pressure for virtual surrender. Eldred Pottinger, who took over the conduct of the negotiations, urged the soldiers to fight, but he carried no weight; only two years earlier he had been an unknown lieutenant. So Pottinger negotiated an agreement for withdrawal in which he had no faith. His judgement was soon proved correct; the Kabul force was completely destroyed, together with all its camp-followers, by snow, cold, and the Ghilzay tribes, before it reached Jalalabad.

Nothing Auckland, in Calcutta, could have done could have saved the Kabul force; from the death of Burnes until Dr. Brydon arrived exhausted at Jalalabad with the news of the disaster was a matter of only two months. But Auckland never seriously tried to do anything for the British in Afghanistan. From the moment when he learned of the rising on 24 November he seems to have decided that it was useless to send help and that Afghanistan must be abandoned.[8] His decision was partly the result of logistical and strategic factors: any help sent from the principal British bases in the Jamna–Satlej Doab could not reach Kabul before the snows blocked the passes; and he was worried by the problem of preserving security within India. Just as it had been the fear of a rising within India which had driven him to adopt the Afghan strategy, so the same fear now impelled him to abandon it; if troops were sent to Afghanistan the security of India might be jeopardized.[9] But most important of all, he was paralyzed by doubts about whether the Afghan position was worth saving.

The development of Auckland's scepticism about the value of the Afghan position has already been traced. During the course of 1841 he had come to believe that India could not afford the Afghan strategy, let alone assume the burdens of exploiting it beyond the borders of Afghanistan. He now looked for a settlement with Iran which would provide an excuse for withdrawal to a strong position on the Indus. Like Burnes, he hoped that a friendly Afghanistan might survive by its own devices.[10] On 4 December he gave his opinion to Macnaghten that Afghanistan could not be held except at a cost incommensurate with any likely benefits.[11] Convinced that the whole 1838 strategy was untenable and that his successor might well wish to abandon it entirely, Auckland was unprepared to throw good money after bad. Still, it was argued by some, that whatever the future of the Afghan strategy, Britain must avenge her defeat and rescue the survivors; she could not afford the damage to her prestige which would be wrought by an unavenged repulse. But Auckland was past caring even about prestige. Crises brought out the worst in him and the Kabul rising, coming at the end of an apparently successful career of Indian administration, broke his spirit. He could hardly bring himself to take any action at all. At the beginning of February 1842 his demoralization was completed by the news that the Kabul force had been destroyed utterly and that a scratch force, assembled at Peshawar under the command of Brigadier Wild, had been thrown back in ignominy when Wild attempted to force the Khaibar and relieve Jalalabad.

At this nadir of the British fortunes there was no hope of any quick resumption of the offensive. The Chief Secretary, Herbert Maddock, proposed to cling to an advanced position, presumably at Peshawar, and wait for better times. Different advice was put forward by the formerly hawkish Thoby Prinsep, who recommended a retreat to the Satlej; no further advance beyond the Indus should be made until firm control over Sind and the Panjab had been secured.[12] Thus, even in a crisis, Prinsep maintained the view which had always underlain his strategic thinking; the vital problem was the extension of British control within India. Fear drove Auckland to adopt Prinsep's suggestion; on 10 February he ordered a retreat to Firuzpur, on the left bank of the Satlej, safe within the British frontier; the remaining garrisons in Afghanistan must fend for themselves.[13] It was Auckland's last act; on 28 February 1842 he was replaced by Ellenborough as Governor-General.

Just as an understanding of Auckland's character is essential to an appreciation of the original concept and the development of the Afghan strategy, so a grasp of that of Ellenborough is indispensable to the comprehension of its demise. Some features of Ellenborough's personality have already been explored, notably the curious combination of powerful intelligence, energy, and alienation from his fellows that led him to base his policies on what may be termed rational intuitions; and his excessive vanity and sense of destiny that verged on megalomania. Within the sphere of English politics his qualities could be tempered, harnessed and usefully employed; in British India they had a freer rein.

Ellenborough had been appointed to the post of Governor-General with some misgivings by those concerned. The first choice of the Conservatives had been Lord Heytesbury, formerly Ambassador in Russia, who had missed his chance in 1835.[14] But Heytesbury refused and the choice lay between Ellenborough and Lord Wharncliffe, the Lord President of the Council. Despite his fears of Ellenborough's precipitancy, Peel gave him the preference because of his knowledge of India and the advice of Wellington.[15] Auckland's reaction is significant because, for all his weaknesses, he was a sensible and perceptive man. Before hearing that Ellenborough was the Conservative choice he had written strongly in his praise. There was a danger, he wrote, that Ellenborough might have too many fixed notions, but his energy and liberal sentiments made him the best choice.[16] But after he had had an opportunity to study the new Governor-General during the two weeks of enforced leisure which elapsed between the arrival of his successor and his own departure he changed his views completely. He informed Hobhouse later that Ellenborough had no capacity for business and that he wondered if he were sane.[17]

For, under an Indian sun, Ellenborough's fatal defects of character flourished like rank weeds. In London he had ruled the Board of Control and the Directors autocratically but efficiently; in India he became an inefficient despot, surrounded by slaves rather than counsellors, and refusing to delegate work. Criticism he regarded as treachery when it came from his Cabinet superiors and lese-majesty when it appeared in any other quarter. His intellect was still strong, but it was now clouded by the chemistry of unreason. While it is still possible to analyze British Indian strategy, after February 1842, on the assumption that it was the product of rational calculation, it becomes increasingly difficult to rely upon this assumption alone; into the analysis there must be built some elements of the irrational.

At the time of his arrival in India Ellenborough was uncommitted to any decided Afghan policy. In 1830 he had initiated the policy of commercial penetration and in 1839 he had opposed the switch to the new forward strategy. During the course of 1840 he had come to support the Afghan movement on the basis of Auckland's original 1838 concept, namely that after making Shuja secure and supplying him with British advice, officers, and non-commissioned officers, the British forces should be withdrawn to India, leaving a friendly Afghanistan behind. Like the bulk of military analysts, he preferred the line of the Satlej and the desert to the Indus or any other defensive position.[18] All this was unexceptionable, if impracticable, and it was not really until the Conservatives returned to power in the summer of 1841 that serious consideration was given to the question of Afghanistan.

The Conservatives received influential advice from Henry Tucker and Henry Willock. As mentioned in chapter 9, Tucker concentrated his attack upon the cost of the Afghan position; India could not afford it and in any case it served no useful purpose; whatever the earlier situation had been, no danger from Russia presently existed and if Russia ever should become a threat it was for the Crown to pay the costs of defending India against it.[19] In a very able memorandum which he submitted to Aberdeen in September 1841 and which was circulated within the Cabinet, Willock adopted a different approach.[20] He gave some weight to the financial argument and to the restrictive effect which defence expenditure had upon public works in India and he laid some emphasis also on the moral arguments against the 1838 strategy and upon the acquisition of Aden and Kharag by 'fraud and violence.' But the main thrust of his argument was more fundamental. The Afghan strategy was wrong, he claimed, because it tended to draw Britain and Russia into closer proximity. In an effort to stabilize the weak Government of Shuja in Afghanistan, Britain would push further into Turkestan, so precipitating a collision with Russia. Hobhouse's claim that retreat would be fatal to the Indian Empire was false; on the contrary, rapid withdrawal was all that could save it.

Willock's argument is important, both for its shrewd exposure of the character and tendencies of Macnaghten's frontier policies in Afghanistan and still more for its blunt confrontation of the arguments of Palmerston. The essence of Palmerston's argument was that a neutral zone was unattainable—Britain and Russia would go on expanding until the frontiers of their Empires touched, and it should be British policy to ensure that the meeting-point was as distant from the Indian frontier as possible. During the course of 1840 to 1841 Palmerston's arguments had been increasingly questioned by Auckland and others who had come to support the creation of a neutral zone. The weakness of this view, however, was that it assumed a British willingness to take action if necessary in Europe and much of the point of Palmerston's (and Canning's) arguments had been to ensure that British India was at least not a liability if it could not be an asset to British policies in Europe. Willock now took the debate one step further by proposing that the neutral zone should be created by unilateral British Indian action, simply by withdrawing to the Indus (rather than to the Satlej). In its effects this was basically the policy of Burnes, Auckland, and Prinsep and it was the one which came to be adopted during the next decade. If attainable, an agreement with Russia would be useful, but if such an agreement could not be negotiated then the defensive arrangements of British India should be decided solely with reference to British Indian wants and capabilities.

Ellenborough also sought advice from Sir George Murray, formerly Minister of War and the Colonies. While denying any expert knowledge of the area, Murray recommended that the area west of the Indus should be abandoned and the main defensive line of British India established upon the Indus itself, with bridgeheads on the right bank at Attock and Bakhar. The general framework of his ideas was that of the conventional military analysis: any attack on India from the north-west would be funnelled into the area between the desert and the Himalayas and the defenders would thus be able to concentrate their force against an enemy who was hampered by an extended line of communications. Although he had thus pushed the line forward from the Satlej to the Indus, Murray did not favour the annexation of Lahore—it would be sufficient to secure enough control to guarantee free military movement. Kashmir could become independent under British protection, while in Kabul and Sind, Murray hoped to see friendly independent regimes, but proposed to offer no political guarantees to them.[21]

Murray's arguments are interesting, partly because of the light they

shed on the drift of thought and partly because they show the continuing military hostility to the forward strategy of 1838. Military men saw
the problem in simple military terms as a prospective clash between
two armies. For them the question was simply on what line did they
wish to fight. But, of course, this type of analysis had been rejected as
inadequate in 1838 for it took no account of the complex interleaving of
political and military factors which ultimately involved the nature of
British rule in India and the connection of the internal and external
frontiers. If the military judgement had been found wanting in 1838 it
seemed doubtful if it could be decisive in 1842. For Murray had pushed
his logic almost to the limits of Fane's 1837 view. While he had
conceded an advance from the Satlej to the Indus, Murray proposed to
abandon all the hard-won political gains in Sind. Even on military
grounds this was now questioned: the ideas of using the Indus to act on
the flanks of an enemy, for communications, and in order to deny its use
to others were all established and both Wellington and Ellenborough
were to place considerable weight on such arguments.

The balance of advice received by the Conservatives supported the
abandonment of Afghanistan. 'I am afraid', wrote Palmerston, 'the
Tories will throw away the high Position which we have established for
British Interests in the East.'[22] During the course of the autumn of 1841
Ellenborough himself had come to favour evacuation. In September he
stressed the difficulties of holding Afghanistan in view of popular
disturbances there and the dependence on long land communications
through the Panjab.[23] In October he looked to withdrawal following an
agreement to be made with Russia. Like Auckland, he saw the recent
settlement with Iran as providing a good excuse and was quite content
to abandon Kharag to obtain the settlement.[24] In November, at the
traditional dinner given by the Court of Directors to each newly-
appointed Governor-General, he declared that his object was 'to
restore peace in Asia' and to use the money saved from war for public
works in India.[25] At this time financial arguments seemed to weigh
most heavily with him.

But, despite appearances, Ellenborough was not committed to any
definite policy. In a letter to Aberdeen in October 1841 he proposed a
phased withdrawal to be completed by 1843 to 1844, subject to two
conditions. Of these, the first, a settlement with Iran, had already been
accomplished. But the second put him right back where he started, for
it was that Shuja should be able to support himself with the aid of
British officers alone.[26] Of course this was just what Auckland had
been planning sinced 1838 and the condition had never yet been met.
Accordingly, despite his seeming inclination towards withdrawal,

Ellenborough's position was basically no different from that of Auckland; namely attachment to the strategy of 1838 in its original conception.

Ellenborough's ideas were all thrown back into the melting-pot by his discovery, on his arrival in India, of the extent of the Afghan disaster. In deciding what to do he faced the same dilemma as Auckland and was equally conscious of it. He had to weigh the dangers in Afghanistan against the perils of the internal frontier, the possible loss of prestige through withdrawal from Afghanistan against the possible loss of physical control in India if he sent more troops to the north-west, particularly if British arms should suffer another reverse. The apparent contrast with Auckland was in Ellenborough's approach to the problem; Auckland's self-doubt was replaced by Ellenborough's magnificent egotism. Writing to Ripon two years later he stated: 'for myself I never shrink from responsibility—*you know how others do*—I am ready to take any amount of responsibility upon my shoulders. I do not know what moral fear is.'[27] In 1842 the tone was not yet so strident, but the sentiment was already palpable. So too was his conspicuous failure to live up to his own claims for himself. As Lord Chief Justice, Ellenborough's father could afford a fierce, fearless, and uncompromising demeanour. Had his son not been blinded by the conviction of his own incorruptible abilities, he might have discovered that the posture was unsuitable for a politician and statesman. Political courage is a rarer quality than mere moral courage; had Ellenborough possessed the former he might have been another Wellesley; lacking it he was just ridiculous.

Ellenborough needed two policies: a short-term operation to salvage the British position and a long-term policy to decide the future pattern of British relations with Central Asia. Inevitably the two became confused, as decisions in relation to one affected the other, and from the beginning Ellenborough himself brought them together. This was plain in his first action on 15 March 1842 when he proclaimed that the buffer state policy was to be abandoned: British desiderata were limited to the relief of the beleaguered garrisons; the release of the prisoners and hostages; and the restoration of British military reputation 'by the infliction of some signal and decisive blow upon the Afghans'.[28] The gulf between principle and execution became apparent when Ellenborough began to spell out what his principles meant in actual military operations.

The military position in March 1842 was as follows. At Peshawar there had been assembled mainly through the efforts of local agents a relief force under the command of General George Pollock (1786–1872). Ellenborough ordered Pollock to advance to Jalalabad and bring off the garrison. At Qandahar, Nott's force was still intact and a reinforcement under General Richard England (1793–1883) was being prepared at Quetta to assist Nott. Ellenborough ordered Nott to relieve the garrison at Kalat-i Ghilzay and then retire. No mention was made of the garrison at Ghazni, although, so far as Ellenborough knew, it still held out; presumably it was to be abandoned. No action to obtain the release of the captives, other than negotiation, was contemplated; there was no consideration of what might be done if negotiation failed. Nor was there any indication of where and how the 'signal blow' was to be struck. The lion had been delivered of a mouse.

Even this incongruous caution proved too much for Ellenborough. In April, a month after the issue of the above orders, he learned that England's force had been repulsed at the Khojak Pass when advancing to the relief of Qandahar. Subsequently it became clear that England had been too easily deterred by insignificant resistance, but Ellenborough completely lost his nerve. New instructions were issued to Nott and Pollock on 19 April which, when their evasive language was peeled away, proved to have removed the relatively wide discretion left to his generals in March. They were now ordered to retire as soon as possible.[29]

Ellenborough's orders to withdraw were never carried out. At Qandahar Nott insisted that he could not retire before October because of the weather; instead he persuaded England to make a second, more successful advance from Quetta. When his orders reached him Pollock was already at Jalalabad. After waiting at Peshawar until the sickness which had ravaged his troops had subsided and reinforcements, including badly-needed European troops, had arrived, he advanced on 31 March, entered the Khaibar on 5 April, and relieved Sale at Jalalabad on 16 April. Pollock now declared himself unable to retire because of a lack of troops and transport and because his withdrawal would prejudice the safety of Nott at Qandahar. In truth, Pollock was anxious to advance beyond Jalalabad and grasped eagerly at any excuse for remaining. The most tenuous of such excuses was provided by the simultaneous arrival of Nicolls's orders transmitting Ellenborough's command to retire and a direct dispatch from Ellenborough which instructed Pollock to retire even if he had advanced to Kabul.[30] Ellenborough's dispatch was plainly not intended to change his original orders of 19 April in any way, but merely to cover the contingency of Pollock's advance beyond Jalalabad. But Pollock chose to interpret it as meaning that he could stay at Jalalabad![31] A few days later, however, he found a more plausible reason for remaining. He had been given permission to delay withdrawal if retreat would prejudice negotiations for the release of the prisoners. Although Pollock's negotiations were hardly in the position which Ellenborough had contemplated in allowing this element of discretion, they nevertheless could be presented so as to take advantage of this loophole.[32]

This comical situation persisted until July. By that time it had become glaringly obvious that the military situation, far from being so desperate as Ellenborough had imagined in April, was actually favourable for an advance to Kabul. The Governor-General seemingly either had to insist on withdrawal and risk the criticism that he had sacrificed a golden opportunity to recover the prisoners and Britain's military reputation or to admit that he had previously been mistaken and to order an advance on Kabul. With a display of verbal dexterity that, in a better cause, might have commanded admiration, Ellenborough evaded the choice. His orders to retire were unchanged, but Nott, if he chose, was now permitted to retire via Kabul and not Quetta! Ellenborough even expressed a preference for the Kabul route, but took care that all the responsibility should rest on Nott. Pollock too was to retire as arranged, but in the event of Nott electing to retreat via Kabul, Pollock was himself permitted to make a supporting move on Kabul![33] As Kaye remarked concerning this extraordinary convolution: 'no change had come over the views of Lord Ellenborough but a change had come over the meaning of certain words of the English language.'[34]

In the event Ellenborough was served better than he deserved. Nott did elect to 'retire' via Kabul and Pollock to move in support. They overcame Afghan resistance and on 15 to 16 September entered Kabul, where they remained until 12 October. During that time the prisoners were recovered before they could be transported into Turkestan; military operations against rebel forces were carried out, including an attack on the town of Istalif in the area of the Kohistan; and as an act of retribution the great bazaar of Kabul was destroyed. The entire force was then withdrawn to Jalalabad and thence, through the Khaibar, to Peshawar and so finally behind the Satlej once more.[35]

Throughout these operations Ellenborough's primary concern had not been with Afghanistan but with the internal frontier; his main object was to secure the safety of his armies. He had stressed that Pollock should be governed only by military considerations and his consent to the 'retreat' on Kabul had been given reluctantly in reponse to the clamour in India concerning the safety of the prisoners. The withdrawal of the armies to India, he informed Pollock on 1 June, would accomplish all the Government's political objects in Afghanistan.[36] In this he was quite consistent, for his actions flowed naturally from his abandonment of the buffer state policy and his insistence on the priority of ensuring the immediate security of British India. But in practice he had to compromise, not only in the matter of the prisoners but also in the matter of political relations within Afghanistan.

At least four factors made it necessary for Ellenborough to frame some sort of political policy in Afghanistan. He had to negotiate with someone for the release of the prisoners. Since his armies were in the country it was necessary to deal with some constituted authority in order to obtain supplies. In order to carry out his operations Ellenborough required the support of the Sikhs, both for communications and military assistance. Most of all, he was compelled to concede some discretion to his subordinate agents and many of these held views about strategy and the future of Afghanistan quite different from those which were held by the Governor-General.

During his stay at Jalalabad Pollock had opened contacts with several Afghan groups. With Muhammad Akbar he negotiated for the release of those prisoners who were in the hands of the Barakzay leader: in return Akbar wanted the release of his own family from captivity in India and certain guarantees to operate in the event of a British decision to retain control of Afghanistan. Pollock was also in correspondence with Fath Jang, who had become leader of the Sadozay group in Kabul after the murder of his father, Shah Shuja, an event which took place in March 1842. It was argued by some British officers that Britain had moral, if not legal obligations towards the surviving members of the Sadozay family. Ellenborough, of course, rejected this argument and took the position that he would deal with anyone who held actual power, but would support no claimant to power.[37] In the circumstances, however, his distinction between those who held and those who merely claimed power was too delicate to maintain and after his occupation of Kabul Pollock felt obliged to ignore Ellenborough's instructions and to grant recognition to the Government of Fath Jang in order that he might obtain supplies.[38] Pollock's action led to a dispute with Nott, who, possessing supplies adequate for his own force, would have been happy to have helped himself to anything else that he required, destroyed Kabul, and retired to India. Nott's troops became notorious for their uncontrolled looting during their stay at Kabul. Pollock's force, on the other hand, had insufficient supplies and carriage and was compelled to remain at Kabul for some time in order to collect whatever was necessary. Because of this need, Pollock proposed to establish some form of regular government under Fath Jang and to support it by preventing looting and destruction and by granting an amnesty to former rebels who were now willing to throw in their lot with Fath Jang. Pollock believed rightly that if a Sadozay Government were not established, the Barakzays, who between January and June 1842 had come to dominate the government of Kabul, would return and re-establish themselves in control; and he naturally assumed that they would be hostile to Britain. Although it was justified in a quite different manner, it is clear that the punitive expedition which he sent to Istalif was in part intended to aid the Sadozay cause by destroying their enemies: Pollock hoped to reduce the strength of the rebels in the Kohistan, the area from which much of the opposition to Fath Jang came.

It is therefore apparent that Pollock's plea of supply problems was not the only motive behind a policy which looked towards salvaging something from the Afghan buffer strategy. There can be little doubt that the main proponents of this political policy were the survivors of the old Political Agency system, notably George Macgregor, who had served Macnaghten loyally at Jalalabad, survived with Sale, and subsequently attached himself to Pollock; and Henry Rawlinson, who had accompanied Nott on his march from Qandahar to Kabul. They were supported by other officers, including George Broadfoot and Henry Havelock, who after distinguishing themselves during the siege of Jalalabad, had joined Pollock. Partly for motives of prestige and partly for strategic reasons they advocated the annexation of Afghanistan and its direct rule by the Company.[39] Although their independent political power had been removed from them by Ellenborough, the Politicals were still indispensable because of their knowledge and experience, and invaluable because of their abilities, and they were able to persuade Pollock of the need to preserve a base for the future restoration of British influence in Afghanistan. It was therefore strategy, as well as logistics, humanity, and military pride, which prompted Pollock first to remain at Jalalabad, then to advance to Kabul, and finally to try to set up a government under British influence. Ellenborough certainly believed this to be the case and complained bitterly that Pollock had fallen into the hands of the detested Political Agents.

The Politicals failed to repeat with Nott the success they had had with Pollock. Nott was a soldier's soldier: surly, savage, and selfish, he was contemptuously indifferent to anything but the welfare and safety of his troops. His uncooperative attitude had led to clashes with the Politicals in the days of their ascendancy and Nott was not the man to be more pliant after their downfall. Encouraged by Ellenborough's official injunction to disregard politics, Nott did so; he determined to leave Afghanistan as soon as possible and resolutely to disregard any temptation to swerve from that path. What would have happened if Nott had adopted the view of Pollock is pure speculation, but it seems probable that the course of events would have been very different. In July and August 1842 Ellenborough himself was weakening in his earlier resolve to abandon all political connection with Afghanistan and was beginning to think that Britain might preserve some political influence there; he hoped to see a stable, friendly government under Fath Jang.[40] In this situation, if Nott had joined with Pollock in recommending a concerted policy of support for Fath Jang, Ellenborough might have been induced to change his political views, as he had earlier changed his notions of military possibilities, and he might have agreed to go further in assisting Fath Jang. The plan, if so cloudy a prospect could be so described, foundered on the rock of Nott's obstinacy.

The possibility of Britain's retaining some political influence at Kabul rapidly evaporated. When Fath Jang learned that British troops would not remain at Kabul after October 1842 he resolved not to try his fortunes alone; he feared the friendship of the Durrani nobles even more than the hostility of the Barakzays. Efforts to persuade him to change his mind failed and he arranged to accompany the retiring British troops to India. Still there existed the possibility that another Sadozay would be willing to place himself at the head of the anti–Barakzay party, which included the Popalzay nobles and the Qizilbash. This party persuaded Fath Jang's younger brother, Shapar, to accept the throne and Pollock asked to be allowed to support Shapar with men, money, and guns. Ellenborough refused and all that Pollock was able to do to assist the new ruler was to plan the promised act of retribution so as to leave intact the great fortress of the Bala Hissar, in which, with the aid of some guns, Shapar might hope to survive, and to limit revengeful destruction to a non-military target, namely the great bazaar of Kabul. Pollock also asked Ellenborough to postpone the release of Dost Muhammad in order that Shapar might be able to establish his position before the former Barakzay ruler returned from his Indian captivity; prompted by Macgregor, Pollock still clung to the belief that a strong, united, friendly Afghanistan, comprising Kabul, Qandahar, and Herat, would be most advantageous to future British interests; and thought that this could be achieved only through a Sadozay ruler.[41] But Ellenborough would have none of it. He had toyed with the hope that he might obtain a friendly Afghanistan for virtually nothing, but he now abandoned that enticing notion; he would do nothing and be committed to no one. Pollock, he concluded, was bemused by the Politicals, and he promptly released Dost Muhammad. Ellenborough was content that Kabul should work out its own destiny.

There remained, in eastern Afghanistan, the question of what should be the fate of Jalalabad. By his decision on this matter Ellenborough had still the power to create a new political balance in Afghanistan, replete with new possibilities for British strategy in the north-west, for the problem of Jalalabad involved also that of the Sikhs. From the outbreak of the Kabul rising Britain had been heavily dependent upon Sikh support and co-operation. The Sikhs were needed to keep open communications between British bases in the North-Western Provinces and the forces in Peshawar and, later, in eastern Afghanistan; their supplies were needed for the relief force at Peshawar; and their assistance was required to force and to hold open the Khaibar Pass. George Clerk, who had succeeded Wade as Political Agent at Ludhiana in 1840, had been in charge of negotiations with the Sikhs and, with the help of Mackeson and Henry Lawrence at Peshawar and of Nicolls and Robertson in the North-Western Provinces, Clerk had been the architect of Pollock's army. To gain Sikh co-operation had not been easy: the Sikhs had their own political problems; they were suspicious of British intentions; and the Lahore Government's control over its own troops was precarious. Indeed the Sikh army was reluctant to hazard itself in the Khaibar again. Accordingly, Clerk and the other Political Agents decided that some substantial inducement was needed in order to procure Sikh compliance and they suggested that Jalalabad would be a suitable bait. During the period of panic which followed the defeat of Wild, Mackeson and Lawrence proposed to give Jalalabad directly to Gulab Singh, brother of Dhian Singh, the First Minister of the Lahore Government; they contended that Gulab's necessary assistance could be obtained only if Jalalabad was to be his personal property and not that of his Government.[42] Clerk, however, would not countenance a proposal which would inevitably promote discord between the Jammu faction to which Gulab belonged and the Sikhs. Clerk advocated the transfer of Jalalabad to the Lahore Government.

In his proposal to give Jalalabad to the Sikhs Clerk based himself on much more fundamental grounds than those of mere tactical expediency. To him the transfer was a vital ingredient in a new strategy for the defence of the north-western frontier of British India. Clerk's new strategy was essentially a development of the old strategy so eloquently defended by Wade and to which Auckland had committed himself in 1837. From 1838 until 1841 British strategic thinking had been based upon a strong Afghanistan and a weak Lahore; now Clerk returned to the older strategy of a weak, disunited Afghanistan held in check by a powerful Lahore. He had written in January 1842:

I have taken the liberty repeatedly to observe that it seems to me to be sound policy to endeavour to maintain an isolated sect, fostered in the direct persecution of it by the Mahommedans; and now forming a state replete in wealth and resources, endued with a military spirit, and fortunately so placed as to break the chain of Mahommedanism between Central Asia and Hindoostan.[43]

In February he now enlarged the concept of the Hindu buffer state; the addition of Jalalabad would both strengthen Lahore and weaken Afghanistan.[44] In April he went further still and sketched a broad plan involving the complete break-up of Afghanistan: Kabul and Ghazni should go to Dost Muhammad; Qandahar to Shah Shuja's eldest son, Muhammad Timur, with British control of his foreign relations; and Jalalabad, Swat, Buner, and the Yusufzay lands to the Sikhs. Clerk recognized that in practice the Jammus would be the principal beneficiaries from this transfer, for the possession of those Afghan lands would seemingly form an appropriate extension of their growing apanage in the hilly country to the north of the Panjab, from Jammu to Kashmir and beyond.[45] The position of the Jammus already foreshadowed the new system which would emerge in 1846. But in 1842 Clerk's plan formed a coherent whole; the independent Barakzay area would be severely limited in extent and held in check by the British-supported Sadozays on one flank and by the Sikhs on the other.

Ellenborough was strongly attracted towards Clerk's plan. Apart from its merits as a container of a resurgent Barakzay state in Afghanistan, the Governor-General foresaw that the possession of Jalalabad would also oblige the Sikhs to over-extend themselves, and thereby make themselves more vulnerable to a British attack, and consequently more susceptible to British pressure.[46] Accordingly, at the end of May 1842 he instructed Clerk to open negotiations for the transfer of Jalalabad, subject to certain conditions which were to be enshrined in a new Declaratory Treaty, to replace the old Tripartite Treaty of 1838, now held, since the murder of Shah Shuja, to be defunct. The original proposal to modify the 1838 Treaty had, in fact, come from the Sikhs who had proposed, in April 1842, that Britain and Lahore should replace Shuja by Sultan Muhammad Khan Barakzay, the former ruler of Peshawar and presently Sikh feudatory at Kohat. The Sikhs envisaged the establishment of an Anglo–Sikh condominium in Afghanistan through control over the appointment of Sultan Muhammad's Chief Minister.[47] Ellenborough disliked this proposal, which implied too great a British commitment for his taste, but on the other hand, he was unwilling to stand back and allow the Sikhs a free hand either in Afghanistan or in Sind. Through the device of the Declaratory Treaty he hoped to reaffirm the provisions of the Tripartite Treaty in so far as they related to Sind and the Panjab and at the same time to prevent the Sikhs from recognizing any Afghan ruler who was not acceptable to Britain.[48]

The negotiations between Britain and Lahore stalled on the question of the Declaratory Treaty. Before they would sign, the Sikhs wanted further assurances about future British policy. Seemingly, they perceived the danger of over-extending their resources and were unwilling to take on the task of holding Jalalabad if it were Ellenborough's intention to evacuate Afghanistan, particularly if he did so without first crushing the Afghans.[49] Ellenborough too began to have doubts about the strategy which he had welcomed in May for, by August, he had come to think that a friendly, united Afghanistan under Fath Jang might, after all, be attainable. Such a goal was clearly incompatible with the hostile but powerless state of Kabul which was a necessary constituent of Clerk's system. Ellenborough, therefore, ordered Clerk not to press the Sikhs to accept Jalalabad.[50] Not until October did Ellenborough finally abandon his hopes of a united Afghanistan and return to the Jalalabad plan. Just at this moment the Sikhs decided to accept Jalalabad with Ellenborough's conditions. But they were too late. On 27 October Pollock withdrew from Jalalabad leaving its fortifications a smoking mass of ruins.[51] No one could now hold it. Left to make their own arrangements for eastern Afghanistan the Sikhs tried to establish a satisfactory system by detaining Dost Muhammad, when he passed through Lahore, at the beginning of 1843, on his way back to Afghanistan and inducing him to sign a treaty with them. The treaty might have heralded a new order on the north-west of British India by establishing Afghan–Sikh co-operation against Britain but, in practice, both parties were too preoccupied with their own affairs. Clerk's more ambitious strategy had failed. Ellenborough had contrived, more by accident than by design, to choose neither Pollock's Afghan nor Clerk's Sikh buffer.

The rest of the story of eastern Afghanistan is soon told. Shapar's Government survived only briefly after the departure of the British forces; before the end of 1842 the Barakzays were back in power, Shapar in flight to Peshawar, and many of the Qizilbash to Laghman. The various Barakzay leaders decided, for the time being, to divide power among themselves. Muhammad Akbar's share was Jalalabad and it was appropriate that the man to whom the destruction of the Anglo–Sadozay system was, above all, due, should have been ready to greet his father as the Amir returned to Afghanistan in the early summer of 1843. Within a short time Dost Muhammad had re-established himself in Kabul and had set in motion the reconstruction of his political authority in eastern Afghanistan, so laying the foundations for his subsequent achievement, by the time of his death in 1863, of rule over a united Afghanistan.

The future of western Afghanistan was a question apart. Clerk had linked it with the problem of eastern Afghanistan, but essentially what he was doing was to build into his scheme a proposal for the retention of British control at Qandahar which had been advanced originally as a quite separate proposal. The main advocate of British domination in western Afghanistan was Henry Rawlinson, the Political Agent at Qandahar.

Rawlinson had not come immediately to his western Afghan strategy. His first reaction, on hearing of the Kabul rising, was to replace his earlier plans for strong British control with a system closer to that of 1838, although with one significant addition; namely, that after the suppression of the rising, British forces should withdraw gradually to the Indus and British influence should be maintained in a united Afghanistan by means of a British Resident at Kabul with a branch agency at Qandahar, and aid to Shah Shuja in the form of a few officers, and an annual subsidy of £500,000.[52] Rawlinson's suggestion of an annual subsidy was an important one. Subsidies had been discredited by the experience of Iran, but in 1857 the subsidy system was adopted in relations with Dost Muhammad and with intermissions it continued, down to 1919, to be the main instrument of British influence in Afghanistan. But as an immediate possiblity it was soon abandoned by Rawlinson himself. The news of the total collapse of the Anglo–Sadozay system in eastern Afghanistan and of the murder of Shah Shuja led him to abandon the hope that future British strategy could be constructed around a united Afghanistan and instead to concentrate on Qandahar alone.

At Qandahar the British had emerged from the rising with credit. Nott had defeated every assembly of rebels and it seemed clear that British control could be maintained, if it were so desired. Indeed the rising seemed to pave the way towards closer control in the future because it provided an excuse for crushing the power of the Durrani nobles which had previously provided the major obstacle to British domination; Rawlinson now advocated giving the Durrani lands to non-Pashtun Hazara colonists, remodelling the Durrani tribal structure, and establishing a new government at Qandahar, independent of that at Kabul, with Muhammad Timur as King.[53]

The idea of independent action at Qandahar received support from the British officials in Baluchistan. Earlier, such action had been contemplated by E. S. Eastwick[54] and it was now strongly urged by the new Political Agent for Sind and Kalat, James Outram. Outram argued that a strong position at Qandahar would enable Britain to exercise control over both Kabul to the east and Herat to the west. In addition, Qandahar could easily be supplied and reinforced through Quetta, a point which, no doubt, accounts in part for Outram's support of the project, since a decision to retain Qandahar would necessarily imply a decision to retain control of Sind and Kalat as well.[55]

Whatever the interested motives of its two protagonists, the Qandahar strategy was an attractive conception and was to be revived under very similar circumstances during the second Afghan war. In 1878 Lytton hoped to establish a predominant British influence within a united Afghanistan. When resistance in eastern Afghanistan made this strategy too expensive to sustain he turned instead to the idea of breaking up Afghanistan and of retaining a strong British influence only in Qandahar. Both in 1842 and in 1878 the Qandahar system was essentially a second-best strategy, only to be adopted when the preferred system appeared to have failed. But on purely military grounds it had much to recommend it. In 1837 to 1838 Burnes and McNeill had both argued that Iran could not succeed against Herat without Qandahar support; in this context the British position at Kabul was only useful as a lever on Qandahar. Indeed, on the basis of conventional military analysis Kabul was an irrelevancy, for all serious writers agreed that the route from Bukhara through Balkh and the Hindu Kush to Kabul was impracticable for an invading force and that the only likely route was that through Herat. Since the direct route from Herat to Kabul through the Hazarajat was also impracticable it followed that any would-be invader of India could be encountered by a force operating from Qandahar. British control over Kabul made sense only in the context of a strong Afghan buffer state, able to conduct its own defence. Once it was seen that a strong, friendly, united Afghanistan was a pipe-dream (and this was becoming increasingly apparent from the latter part of 1840 onwards) then the arguments for abandoning Kabul became very strong; if the defence of Afghanistan must necessarily be undertaken by British troops they could perform this function much more easily and cheaply from a base at Qandahar. So long as Britain was morally, legally, and habitually bound to the Sadozay buffer such a switch was impossible, but once death and disaster had ended the commitment to the Sadozays, the Qandahar alternative became a matter for serious consideration.

Ellenborough rejected the Qandahar strategy out of hand. There is no evidence that he ever considered the merits of the strategic arguments; it was sufficient for him that this was a political proposal submitted by Political Agents. 'I must tell you', he wrote to Wellington about this time:

that in not ordering on the army to Ghuznee and Cabool without the means of movement and supply, and in giving up the irrational schemes of extending our dominions to the westward, I stand alone, and have to contend especially against the whole monstrous body of political agents scattered everywhere and depending upon [sic? for their] continued existence upon perseverance in the folly which called them into life. I have acted altogether in all I have done upon my own Judgement.[56]

The momentary interest in political possibilities in eastern Afghanistan which events sparked in Ellenborough was not duplicated at Qandahar. Qandahar was evacuated completely and left to be repossessed by its former Barakzay rulers. One last suggestion of the ingenious Rawlinson received short shrift. The Political Agent had proposed that the pro-British Parsiwan colony in Qandahar should not be left to the mercy of the Barakzays, but should be transplanted bodily to a new home on the Indus; typically, Rawlinson gilded this essentially humanitarian proposal with a disquisition on its strategic advantages. Ellenborough was unimpressed and rejected the suggestion with magnificent sarcasm. He did 'not deem it necessary to protect the frontiers of the British Empire with colonies of Parseewans'.[57] He was even unwilling to offer asylum to those chiefs who had compromised themselves by their support for Britain. 'I wish to have nothing to do with any of them', he wrote.[58]

For Ellenborough had finally reaffirmed his original decision to cut all connection with Afghanistan. In the words of his proclamation of 1 October 1842: 'the Governor General will leave it to the Affghans themselves to create a Government amidst the anarchy which is the consequence of their actions.' Britain would recognize any government acceptable to the Afghans themselves and 'which should appear desirous and capable of maintaining friendly relations with neighbouring states'. But Britain herself would do nothing to shape such a government.

In his proclamation Ellenborough hinted at a strategic justification of his decision: 'The rivers of the Panjab and the Indus and the mountainous Passes and the barbarous tribes of Affghanistan will be placed between the British army and an enemy approaching from the West, if indeed such an enemy there can be, and no longer between the army and its supplies.'[59]

In this comment are enshrined the logistical worries which had impressed Ellenborough before his departure from England, and also a doubt that Afghanistan could ever be sufficiently stable to form a buffer state. There is, in addition, contained within the parenthesis, an implied doubt whether there was ever a serious danger from Russia. But in entering this doubt Ellenborough had ignored the whole basis of the 1838 strategy and reduced the argument once more to that of a direct invasion; in this way he had avoided entering into the major problem of the connection between outside influence, internal unrest, and military expenditure. As a strategic appreciation his comment was quite inadequate.

Like an iceberg, the greater part of Ellenborough's strategic appreciation was hidden from sight, perhaps even from his own consciousness. His actions between March and October 1842 cannot be explained by reference to the levels of strategic analysis with which we have hitherto been principally concerned. At one level the only explanation of his conflicting decisions is fear—fear of defeat in Afghanistan, fear of the ramifications of future involvement, fear of repercussions within his own frontiers, and simple fear of responsibility. He made no attempt to formulate a consistent strategic view with which he could refute the arguments of the Political Agents. His attitude to them, indeed, betrays an unreasoning hostility; their ideas were tainted at source; and one of the Governor-General's first actions was to place them in strict subordination to the appropriate military commanders. Politics, he thought must be submerged in, rather than be subordinated to military considerations, an argument which, superficially, was strategic nonsense. War, as Clausewitz remarked, is an extension of politics; and armies are political instruments. Yet there is another, older way of contemplating an army; it can be seen as a symbol of prestige and power to be cherished for its own sake and not lightly hazarded in war. This was the medieval and Renaissance view of armies and it was the view which Ellenborough found most appropriate to the situation of the Army of British India. To grasp the central role of this concept of the position of the British Indian Army is vital to the understanding of Ellenborough's Afghan policy and to his final settlement of the frontier.

Ellenborough saw India as a country where the British Government was totally alien to the people. To that Government the Indian people felt no natural loyalty and they would obey it only so long as they believed in its superior might. British power, therefore, ultimately rested upon continued military success and upon the sustained loyalty of the army. 'It seems to be forgotten', he wrote later,

that I found in India a defeated Army, and an Empire in danger. It was in danger because acquired only by Arms, by Arms alone could it be preserved, for in the heart of the People it has no foundation.

Ours has been a repulsive Government. It has established no sympathy with the Governed. . . . It rests only upon the continuance of Military success by which the fidelity of the Troops is mainly preserved and I found a defeated Army.[60]

This was no afterthought, for Ellenborough had made the same point immediately after his arrival in India. To Peel he wrote that 'to hold this country you must have a contented army', and to Nicolls, that 'our supremacy rests upon the opinion hitherto entertained of our invincibility.'[61]

To Ellenborough, to secure the well-being and reputation of the army was the overwhelming political and strategic problem; Afghanistan and the whole frontier were secondary to this quest. His conviction of this necessity accounts for his otherwise inexplicable actions and for the grandiloquent language in which he disguised his evasions. He wanted a victory, but he dared not risk a defeat. Like Jellicoe between 1914 and 1917, a good decision might win him a battle, but a bad decision could lose a war and an empire in a single day. The safety of the army was for Ellenborough the safety of the state.[62] What he wanted was a cheap and riskless triumph that would impress the people of India with a sense of undiminished British power. With his unerring instinct for bathos he selected the Somnath gates.

The Somnath gates were the gates on a Hindu temple, which had allegedly been taken to Afghanistan by the great Muslim conqueror, Mahmud of Ghazni (998–1030). Ellenborough wrongly believed that they still graced the tomb of Mahmud at Ghazni and instructed Nott to carry them away from there. In part at least Ellenborough hoped to strengthen British rule in India by deliberately dividing Hindus and Muslims. He explained that he made the order 'knowing very well that the Hindoos will value it as the guarantee of the future security of themselves and of their religion against Mussulmans';[63] and in the same letter made clear his conviction that great anti-British feeling existed among Indian Muslims at this time. He intended that the gates should be paraded and displayed around India and finally restored to the temple at Somnath. But the gesture turned out disastrously and it brought upon him nothing but ridicule, both in India and in England. The gates, as Rawlinson observed when he supervised their removal, were not from Somnath at all; they could not be restored because the temple was in ruins; and Hindus generally were totally indifferent to the whole proceeding. Nevertheless, Ellenborough went through with the solemn farce; accompanied by an imposing escort the gates were hawked around northern India and at every stopping-place earnestly and ceremonially exhibited to bewildered bystanders. Finally, the gates were quietly laid to rest in the old Muslim fort at Agra. By the most exquisite of ironies, the man who was placed in charge of the pilgrimage of the gates was none other than the jovial, cynical Major Robert Leech. Leech was the arch-survivor among the Afghan Politicals and during the uprising had actually acquired new merit by his tenacious resistance at Kalat-i Ghilzay. The gates were his reward. It is pleasing to reflect upon what must have been his feelings as he presided over this Evelyn Waugh-like ending to the bright hopes of 1838 and composed his glowing reports to Ellenborough. But the historian does not have the artistic freedom of the novelist: Leech should have died at a great age, surrounded by medals and in the odour of sanctity; instead he enjoyed his next appointment as Political Agent at Ambala in succession to Henry Lawrence for only two years. He died in September 1845, to be replaced by that most literate of civilians, R. N. Cust.

Ellenborough's visions seemed doomed to figure in such divine comedies. In connection with his desire to enhance the impression of military might he planned an imposing reception for his troops as they returned from Afghanistan to the soil of British India. At Firuzpur he assembled an awesome army of welcome and came himself to greet his soldiers as they crossed the bridge of boats which spanned the Satlej. As a final touch he had ordered a triumphal arch to be constructed over the bridge of boats. Both the boats and the arch were covered in yellow, blue, and red cloths to represent the gorgeous hues of the Eastern dawn. The arch resembled nothing so much as a gigantic gallows and one observer recalled:

Under this arch, as they called it, the whole army marched, and peals of merriment as they did so, burst from the soldiers, it was such an absolute caricature of anything triumphal. I have no doubt but that the natives fully expected it had been originally erected in order to hang Akbar Khan upon, should we be fortunate enough to catch him, but failing that an attempt was made to induce them to believe it had only been erected to do honour to the victorious army.[64]

Despite the shadow which lies between conception and execution, Ellenborough had seized upon a point of considerable importance. The history of British India had been punctuated by military discontent both among officers and men. Ever since Bentinck's army economies there had been a strong feeling among army officers that they had been neglected and that their importance was undervalued by comparison with that of the Civil Servants. If anything, the apparent safety-valve of the Political Department exacerbated resentment because to the feeling against civilians was added dislike of junior officers who had acquired the powers, status, and rewards of civilian work. The unhappy Afghan imbroglio completed a process of demoralization and led Eldred Pottinger to comment in May 1842: 'If the Government does not take some decided steps to recover the affection of the army, I really think a single spark will blow the Sepoys into Mutiny; for the zeal of the Officers is cold and it has been that alone which prevents the spirit hitherto.'[65] Similar warnings were sounded by other officers, notably by Henry Lawrence, and it could be argued that the Mutiny of 1857 proved them right. It could also be maintained that, by his marked partiality for the army, Ellenborough did much to arrest the decline of morale. When he was recalled in 1844 the army officers made clear their support for him and for many years afterwards he remained for the army the ideal Governor-General.

Ellenborough paid a price for his courtship of the army, for the corollary of that romance was his disenchantment with the Civil Service and the Politicals. They were, he claimed, all alike and all exclusively concerned with their own personal advancement.[66] He clashed with his Council, of which his opinion was very low: Prinsep was able but lacked judgement; Bird was honest and experienced but of little value; Nicolls and Casement were useless, although the latter, he conceded, was at least a gentleman. Among other senior officials Robertson and Robert Hamilton (1802–87) in the North-Western Provinces were no good and John Lyall (1811–45), the Advocate-General, he declared, owed his appointment to nepotism, having been given the job by Auckland as a favour to his father, who had then been Chairman of the Court of Directors. The Chief Secretary, Herbert Maddock, he thought unfit for high office.[67] Ellenborough's judgements may not have been all unfounded and in other respects some of the changes which he introduced in the Civil Service were sensible: he advanced some able men and by his reorganization of the Council both increased its responsibilities and gave its members departmental portfolios. But his attitude to his colleagues ensured that his relations with them would be bad and his reforms resented; and also made certain that he would be roughly treated in the British Indian Press.

In the long term Ellenborough looked to the creation of a new basis for Britain in India. Dependence on military power alone was too dangerous and in any case he had no desire that India should be ruled merely for the benefit of the British in India. He himself had, or believed that he had, a genuine affection for India and he regretted that he knew no Indian language. 'For my part,' he wrote,' I really like the people, and I endeavour to make them understand that I do like them and that I am here as much as one of themselves interested in the prosperity of *our* Hindostan, and that the Government is for them also, not solely for my own countrymen.'[68] He wanted to get away from dependence upon the sword and to find new support in the affections of at least some groups of Indians. Partly he hoped to secure the support of a new commercial class by creating opportunities in a vast free trade zone, but more importantly he sought to win the support of the traditional leaders of Indian society. He discussed the creation of a special personal bodyguard, formed from the sons of chiefs and, like Lytton later, of a special college for their education. Ellenborough believed in an aristocratic version of Macaulay's filtration theory; the new loyalty to Britain would percolate downwards through what he thought was the traditional hierarchy of Indian society; and he compared his theory favourably with that of his predecessor, of whom he remarked disdainfully, that he preferred to work through the sons of shopkeepers.[69] In contrast to the increasingly cultivator–orientation of the thinking of Civil Servants, Ellenborough aimed to preserve the position of the traditional aristocracy and to guarantee their territorial possessions. He wholly rejected the growing disposition to favour the annexation of Indian states, reversed the policy of applying more rigorously the doctrine of lapse, and stopped the movement towards closer control of the internal affairs of the states. The new dogmas were no interference and no annexation; like Henry Tucker, Ellenborough regarded recent territorial acquisitions within India as unprofitable and dangerous and believed that if the policy of extending possession were not checked existing British possessions would be put in danger.[70] 'Our true interest', he wrote,

is to preserve what we have in peace, to retain in willing obedience to our reasonable wishes, all the Native States within our Territories and more immediately adjoining them—to have no connection with, no relations, if it were altogether possible to abstain from them, with the Countries further removed as with the Burmese Empire; and with Affghanistan, and to apply whatever surplus Revenue a well directed economy and improved administration might hereafter place at our own disposal, in drawing forth the resources of our dominions and doing everything for a people that can do so little for itself.[71]

In seeking the springs of Ellenborough's strategic thinking we have been led into matters which at first sight seem far removed from the ordinary small change of strategic discussion. But the last passage shows how Ellenborough's reflections on the future of British rule in India helped to shape his strategic conceptions. Ellenborough's hostility to a forward strategy sprang from a deeply pessimistic view of the British position in India. That position was artificial, unstable, and insecure. In the short term it could survive only by the impression of force and in the longer term only by conservatism. Britain must accept the structure of Indian society and work through it and in this way win a degree of toleration which could supplement the ultimate reliance upon force. Survival depended upon restraint everywhere. Set out in this way Ellenborough's views can be seen to bear a close resemblance to those which had dominated an earlier group of British Indian statesmen and which received their clearest expression in the writings of Malcolm. And, of course, this is unsurprising, because through Wellington the link with Malcolm was formed. In Ellenborough's conception it is once again the internal frontier which dominates the view of external strategy, but the internal frontier now fulfils a different role. The view of Malcolm, and it was one which became general, was that because of the danger of disturbance in India foreign infection must be kept at a distance: the view of Ellenborough was closer to that of Charles Metcalfe. Ellenborough thought the patient was too delicate even for Malcolm's prescription and could not be left for even so long as it took to shut the door. Ellenborough in India was like a doctor called to a sick-bed and afraid to move lest the motion should produce convulsions in his patient.

This exposition of Ellenborough's gloomy appreciation enables us to look again with new insight at the contrary, essentially optimistic view of British rule in India, which, under Utilitarian, Evangelical, and empirical inspiration, had become the dominant view of the civil service. The optimistic view was well argued by Herbert Maddock in a minute dated 10 May 1843. Although British rule had been founded on force, Maddock argued, it had, in the course of time, brought many benefits to the people of India through public works, social reforms, etc., and, as a consequence, the majority of the Indian people, particularly peasants, artisans, and merchants, had come to value the good government which Britain provided. To this extent British rule had already come to rest upon opinion, although Maddock, who was by no means the most ardent of the optimists, conceded that ultimately British authority rested upon the continuation of communal divisions within India and on the absence of national feeling.[72] In the context of British India Maddock's view was sanguine; because the masses had no fundamental dislike of foreign rule they were prepared to reward benefits with allegiance. It was also reformist, because the opinion on which Britain rested was that of the masses and not of the traditional leaders, who could be seen to obstruct the formation of the attachment between ruler and worker and who, by implication, must be the sufferers from the extension of British rule. Among the Governor-Generals of the last period of Company rule Bentinck, Auckland, and Dalhousie could all be regarded as leaning towards the optimistic view and Ellenborough, and Hardinge as opposing it. Between the partisans of the empire of opinion and that of the sword there was an unending debate which is fundamental to the appreciation of the strategy of British India.

In practice the different views of the nature of the British position in India could produce varying attitudes towards expansion. With Thoby Prinsep and many of his colleagues the optimistic view could produce a willingness to expand, based upon the conviction that British rule would always confer benefits which would be duly appreciated. With John Lawrence, on the other hand, a similar view led him to eschew expansion beyond the Indian frontiers, while supporting the extension of British rule within. Lawrence believed that a forward strategy consumed resources which were better used to provide benefits which could confirm the hold of British government on the hearts of the Indian people. With Ellenborough the pessimistic view had produced a 'little India' strategy, characterized by the avoidance of external involvement and a mixture of military control and safety-valves within the frontier. Under Lytton the same conservative view produced a different strategic assessment, far nearer to that of Malcolm. A sense of the precarious nature of British rule in India led him to combine a system of safety-valves within India with a forward strategy designed to keep possible enemies at a distance. All these diverse attitudes, however, could be accommodated within a spectrum of perception of the internal frontier; at the one extreme Lawrence, so confident of the solidity of British rule that he ignores the external threat and at the other Ellenborough, so obsessed by the fatal flaws in the British system that he is paralysed in his efforts to construct a strategy to deal with the danger from without.

But at this level strategical analysis is too broad to have much explanatory value in terms of particular events and Ellenborough's Indian career shows how instability of personality makes nonsense of logical categories. In 1842 the smell of danger was so strong as to produce an almost intestinal repugnance towards external entanglement and the greatest trepidation in Ellenborough's attitude towards the Indian states. From 1843 onwards his fears receded and allowed his gross appetite for self-glorification to find freer expression in Sind, Gwalior, the Panjab, and even as far afield as Egypt. Yet still the method of analysis has some value because it is possible also to discern in these later years a growth of optimism about the future of British rule in India; it was at this time that Ellenborough began to shift away from exclusive reliance upon force and towards some reliance upon an opinion to be created through his filtration theory. None the less, in the end Ellenborough's megalomania repudiates rational analysis. While no Governor-General is so consistent as the spectrum approach suggests, with Ellenborough the swings of the pendulum were destructive of all system. So at least his own Cabinet colleagues found when they attempted to control him.

The Conservative Government in England exercised little or no influence upon the resolution of the new pattern of Indian defence. No minister held firm views on Afghanistan and there were no men who combined great talents with a grasp of Indian problems. Neither of the two Presidents of the Board of Control were strong men and they were certainly incapable of controlling Ellenborough. The first, Lord Fitzgerald and Vesir, was appointed to succeed Ellenborough in October 1841 principally because Peel required an Irish peer in the Cabinet who could assist in the consideration of Irish problems, although nothing Fitzgerald was to do for Ireland in the future compared with his involuntary contribution in 1828, when his defeat by Daniel O'Connell at Clare had precipitated Catholic Emancipation. Fitzgerald's ill-health made it difficult for him to rectify his ignorance of India; his eyesight was so bad that he was unable to read for long, a serious disability in a department which received and generated more paper than any other, except the Foreign Office. Ellenborough thought him incapable even at the time of his appointment.[73] In February 1843 Peel complained that Fitzgerald could not control the Court, the first duty of any President, although in truth by that time the Directors were so incensed by Ellenborough's conduct that better men than Fitzgerald might have found the task beyond them.[74] In fact Fitzgerald had much sympathy for the Directors because he had come to share their dislike for Ellenborough and he wrote almost daily to Peel to complain of some fresh enormity. In January 1843 he had asked to be allowed to resign because of Ellenborough's attitude, but Peel would not permit him to do so. By that time Fitzgerald's health had deteriorated to the extent that he could scarcely attend meetings or speak because of pain and he conducted most of his business by letter. More and more of the burden of Indian affairs fell upon an already overloaded Peel and upon Wellington, who frequently advised on dispatches to India, often altering them substantially.

Fitzgerald was succeded, after his death on 11 May 1843, by Lord Ripon, who had been serving as President of the Board of Trade.

Although only sixty-one, Ripon had already enjoyed two previous political careers—as the respectable financial expert, Robinson, and as the ineffectual Prime Minister, Goderich. That he should have accepted his latest humble incarnation gives a clue to the man; mild, reasonable, but generally thought to lack determination—'as cowardly as the most timid worm', according to an unkind critic.[75] He shared with his predecessor ill-health, ignorance of India, and a powerful distaste for Ellenborough. Under him, also, much of the work of the India Board fell upon Peel.

Other members of the Cabinet who were particularly interested in India were Peel, Wellington, Aberdeen and Graham. The first two need no introduction. Peel knew little of India and probably gleaned that little from Henry Tucker. Wellington was almost unassailable in Cabinet or in Parliament when he spoke on military or Indian affairs. Whatever the merits of his views on the former, his opinions on the latter were far out of date. Like his old subordinate, Lord Raglan, some years later, Wellington had a disconcerting habit of regarding the French as the enemy and, although developments during the 1840s made this eccentricity more apposite than it might otherwise have been, it tended to produce a curiously lop-sided view of Indian strategy. More important, however, was his insistence, perhaps impelled by memories of his brother's Indian career and of the Peninsular, on the need to support the man on the spot. His authority and the unswerving loyalty of Hardinge as Secretary of War were of great assistance to Ellenborough. Aberdeen, the Foreign Secretary, was no Palmerston; he lacked his predecessor's force, self-confidence, and interest in India and, although relations with Iran and Russia gave Aberdeen a stake in Indian strategy, the Foreign Secretary never used his position to support any particular plan. The Home Secretary, Sir James Graham, had always taken an interest in India and could have been Governor-General if he had wished. Since he was able to afford an exclusively English political career he refused, but he retained his conviction of the value of India and, with his ability and following, he was a force to be reckoned with, if he chose to exert himself. Few men in British politics aroused such strong feelings as did Graham. His dallyings with both parties caused many to think him dishonest. 'He is an arrant funker and always was', wrote Dalhousie.[76] A letter which Graham wrote to Ellenborough at the time of the latter's appointment to India is peculiarly redolent of the man with his mixture of universal benevolence and pecuniary self-interest: 'By your paternal government', he wrote,

you may alleviate the misery or the sorrows of countless millions and secure the basis of our Empire, which, while we hold it and improve it, may make

England independent of the Commerce of Europe and America; but if we lose it, our glory is departed and the days of our power are numbered.[77]

Graham and Peel shared a similar viewpoint; both judged Indian strategy primarily in the light of the possible repercussions of actions in India upon Parliamentary and public opinion in England; and consequently were the more pleased the less they heard of the question. Like all his predecessors at the India Board, Fitzgerald could not persuade his colleagues to take any real interest in India.[78]

In 1841 the Tory Cabinet leaned towards a permanent withdrawal from Afghanistan. The Conservative leaders had opposed the expedition in 1839 and Peel saw no reason to change his opinion. The news of the Afghan rising confirmed his view of the strategy which he described as 'the most absurd and insane project that was ever undertaken in the wantonness of power'.[79] It was Wellington, however, who formulated the Government's advice to Ellenborough. Wellington recommended that Ellenborough should first secure control of India, withdrawing all forces behind the Satlej and building up the fortresses of northern India. Ellenborough should leave the Panjab alone but try to secure control of Kashimir, which Wellington believed would give control of the Panjab rivers. He advised Ellenborough to retain control of Sind and of the Lower Indus and to preserve a bridgehead across the river at Shikarpur. This more aggressive policy on the lower Indus was revealed later to be the product of his curious fear of France. Mistakenly Wellington believed French influence to be still strong in the Panjab and feared that it might become established in Sind and, through the Indus, linked to French power in northern India. To avoid this possibility he urged the control of Karachi and the maintenance of a strong naval force in the east.[80] The whole scenario bears so striking a resemblance to that displayed by his younger brother in 1802 as to afford a singular demonstration of the persistence of strategic reflexes, wholly detached from reality. Peel, however, was most impressed by the initial plan of defence, which he regarded as a model of understanding, simplicity, and profound sagacity, and which he sent to the Queen.[81] He even took Wellington's French bogey seriously, although Fitzgerald did not.[82]

There is a striking similarity between the views of Wellington and Peel on the one hand and that of Ellenborough on the other, concerning the appropriate course of action in the face of the Afghan peril; all were for pulling back and battening down the hatches. Ellenborough, however, had conceived his own policy independently and, in recommending the Cabinet's advice to him, Peel left the Governor-General full discretion, promising the most liberal interpretation of his actions.[83]

The harmony between India and England began to fade as news of Ellenborough's policy arrived. While the Cabinet were not opposed to eventual withdrawal, they were most unhappy about the manner which Ellenborough had chosen. Despite the advice which Wellington had sent, ministers now felt that to withdraw without avenging the defeat and recovering the prisoners would be very damaging to British prestige. This last issue dominated the entire debate about the withdrawal from Afghanistan throughout 1842.

There was widespread agreement that the Afghan position was not worth the cost of maintaining it; only a few Political Agents, Civil Servants, and Whig politicans contested this view. But everyone recognized that to abandon Afghanistan, even under favourable circumstances, would be a blow to prestige and some men advocated its retention for this reason alone. Outram, for example, argued that to withdraw from Afghanistan without first exacting retribution, would jeopardize British control of India, because the loss of prestige would cause risings which would be expensive to subdue.[84] As always, the cost-accountancy of defence pulled both ways. Even those, like Auckland, who were prepared to abandon Afghanistan without attempting revenge, recognized that there could be very severe repercussions both within India and from a resurgent Islam without. McNeill, in Iran, saw the Afghan disaster as a blow to British prestige throughout Asia and predicted that British diplomats would encounter new difficulties in their relations with newly-confident Asians. In a choice example of sexual racialism, Wellington wrote to Ellenborough of every Muslim heart from Constantinople to Peking, no less, vibrating at the thought of the female prisoners in the hands of Akbar Khan, while his brother Richard capped even that prospect with his injunction to Ellenborough to recover the prisoners, 'especially those of the female sex and of high rank'.[85] In conclusion Wellington wrote:

It is impossible to impress upon you too strongly the notion of the Importance of the Restoration of our Reputation in the East. Our Enemies in France, the United States and wherever found are now rejoicing in Triumph upon our Diasasters and Degradation.
You will teach them that their Triumph is premature.[86]

Whatever the merits of the Wellesleys' assessment of foreign views, they had faithfully reflected a powerful current in Victorian England; the Cabinet feared the tide might sweep their ministry away.

At a meeting on 5 July all members of the Cabinet agreed on the desirability of ultimate withdrawal from Afghanistan. The division came over its timing. Surprisingly, Wellington, supported by Graham, agreed with Ellenborough's decision to withdraw at once; although Wellington was prepared to go far to indulge public opinion, in the last analysis the prisoners were as expendable as other combatants. Supported by the Queen, his colleagues disagreed; before withdrawal they wanted to see the prisoners released and Muhammad Akbar punished.[87] Peel urged Ellenborough to re-occupy Kabul for a time so that withdrawal should appear to be the consequence of a diplomatic settlement which removed the need for British control over Afghanistan, and not the result of military defeat.[88] By August opinion had swung even further towards the views of the majority and Wellington was then the sole advocate of withdrawal.[89] In September Peel wrote to Ellenborough again urging him to make an attempt to rescue the prisoners. The letter was a characteristically exasperating combination of humanitarianism and political cynicism. Even if Ellenborough failed, Peel remarked, 'the unfavourable effect of failure will be greatly diminished if every effort be made to save them.'[90]

The Cabinet recognized that the eventual accomplishment of their wishes was scarcely owing to the efforts of Ellenborough; in private the Governor-General was criticized for his hasty orders for withdrawal in March and his cowardice in thrusting the responsiblity for the advance on Kabul on to the shoulders of Nott and Pollock. There was also agreement that the destruction wrought at Istalif and Kabul before the final evacuation was cruel, wanton, and unnecessary.[91] But once more it was the English political consequences of Ellenborough's actions which concerned the Cabinet; in the strategic implications of the abandonment of Afghanistan they had no interest.

In Parliament too party political prestige and not strategy was the key issue. Both parties had more to bury than to flourish; just as the Conservatives could find little pleasure in the conduct of Ellenborough, so the Whigs were disconcerted by the revelation of the pusillanimity of Auckland, who came out of the affair badly. Greville recalled dining with Auckland and others on 13 September 1842, at which time the former Governor-General had both recovered his nerve and lost his memory, for he advocated the re-occupation of Kabul and the permanent re-establishment of British authority in the area.[92] Hobhouse was unconvinced by Auckland's explanations and believed that Auckland and Nicolls had been unequal to the crisis and that their defeatism had made it more difficult for Ellenborough to act boldly; for this reason the former President would take no part in the debates.[93] In consequence, although there was still strong support on the Whig benches for the 1838 strategy, this could not be easily expressed and Parliamentary discussion focused on minor issues.

The decision to withdraw from Afghanistan was announced in the Queen's Speech at the commencement of the 1843 session. There was no discussion of the policy of this at the time, although Auckland defended his original decision for intervention. Under the leadership of Lansdowne the Whig attack in the Lords concentrated on Ellen-borough's contradictory military orders, but Wellington immediately put a stop to this, by declaring, with all the authority of the victor of Waterloo, that, 'I stand prepared on any day to justify every order for movement, whether one way or the other, that the Governor General has given, from the moment on which he took on him to administer the Govt. of India to the present moment.'[94] Only the irrepressible Brougham had the courage to question that unequivocal declaration and the old Radical promptly alienated whatever support he might have had by criticizing the conduct of British troops and defending that of the Afghans. In the Commons Russell, never the most ardent sup-porter of the 1838 strategy, did not criticize the decision to withdraw.[95]

The publication of the relevant Parliamentary papers, in the middle of February, took from the Whig sails much of what wind was left for the papers clearly showed Auckland's own timorous conduct. As a result the Whigs decided not to oppose the vote of thanks to Ellen-borough and the army, and the resolution passed both Houses on 20 February, encountering opposition only from Joseph Hume and a few Radicals.[96] It was the Radicals again, who took the lead on March 1 when Roebuck brought forward a motion for a Select Committee to examine the original Whig policy of 1838. This was the one Parliamen-tary opportunity for a major debate upon the strategy of Indian defence, a debate which might have taken place in 1838.

The origins of the Radical attack lay in 1841 when David Urquhart published his *Diplomatic Transactions in Central Asia*. Based upon pub-lished Parliamentary papers, this book sought to prove that Palmerston had deliberately provoked the conflict in Iran and Afghanistan in order to promote Russian ambitions in Central Asia! Urquhart's criticisms had been taken up first by Sir Francis Burdett and next by Benjamin Disraeli who in May 1842 brought forward a motion attacking Whig policy in Afghanistan.[97] A second source of inspiration was Bombay, where friends of Burnes published papers which showed that the versions of his dispatches which had appeared in the Parliamentary papers of 1839 were misleading.

The first round of this contest was fought on 23 June 1842 when a motion was introduced by Henry Baillie and seconded by Disraeli, which attacked the Whigs for their garbling of the dispatches and for the financial cost of their policy.[98] Hobhouse gave an able justification of the 1838 policy and produced arguments to deny the financial criticisms. But the main reason for the failure of the demand for the publication of the original dispatches was the attitude of Peel, who in 1842 took the view that publication might jeopardize the good relations then existing between Britain and Russia. Baillie attempted to withdraw his motion, but it was pressed to a division and lost by 75 to 9. In this debate Peel said nothing of Ellenborough's orders for withdrawal.

The principal clash took place in the debate on J. A. Roebuck's motion in March 1843. Equipped with Burnes's dispatches Roebuck launched into a inaccurate account of the origins of the Afghan war and concluded that there had been no need for any action against Russia, but if action there had to be, it should have been by Britain directly in the Baltic or the Black Sea. He was supported by Disraeli and opposed by Russell and Palmerston.[99] Palmerston defended the 1838 policy and the decision to act in Asia and not in Europe. He was quite unrepentant and undisturbed by the laughter which greeted his claims for the triumphs of his own foreign policy. The debate, however, did not proceed beyond the original decision to intervene in Afghanistan and go on to consider the evolution of the Afghan strategy and the decision to withdraw. Peel again opposed on constitutional grounds the demand for the original dispatches and the motion was lost by 189 to 75. Once more, as in 1842, Peel had his own skeletons which he preferred to leave undisturbed. Roebuck did not obtain publication of the ungarbled dispatches until 1859. Neither in Parliament nor in the Press was there any real discussion of the strategic issues. Most papers assumed that the original policy was misconceived and the threat from Russia non-existent.[100]

The unwillingness of any but Young England and the Radicals to discuss strategy meant that the liveliest and most heated debate took place on an issue of no importance whatsoever, namely on Ellenborough's Somnath proclamation. Public opinion on this question had already been excited by the missionary societies which, prompted by the Baptist editor of the *Friend of India*, J. C. Marshman, saw it as a religious question. The Whigs, seeing the opportunity for revenge, tried to persuade the bishops to sponsor a critical motion but failed and Clanricarde was obliged to lead the attack in the Lords. Although Clanricarde coupled with his criticism of the Somnath policy strictures on Ellenborough's proclamation of 1 October 1842 announcing withdrawal, there was no discussion of strategy. The debate turned on the question whether Ellenborough, by deliberately slighting the Indian Muslims, was moving away from the traditional religious impartiality of the Indian Government. The debate in the Commons took a similar course and was chiefly notable for a brilliant and witty speech by Macaulay. All the Indian experts concentrated on the danger of alienating Muslims and there was little reference to wider issues, although Russell, while still defending the 1838 decision, agreed that it was wise to withdraw. The Government won both votes by handsome majorities.[101]

The debates of 1843, like those of 1839, were disappointing; in both years India was essentially a party question and in attempting to extract the maximum party advantage from the problems both parties found it convenient to avoid any discussion of the bases of policy, even had they the knowledge to sustain such a discussion. Nevertheless, it is possible to discern in 1843 a consensus of opinion in favour of withdrawal from Afghanistan. Two factors led to this decision: one, the financial cost, has already been considered; the other, the view that no danger from Russia existed, requires further consideration.

The Conservative Government was much less concerned with any danger from Russia than the Whigs had been and much more willing to accept a policy of general co-operation with that state both in Europe and in Asia. The most obvious example of such co-operation in Asia concerns the Ottoman Empire, although this had, to some extent, been foreshadowed by Palmerston in 1840 to 1841. The policy can also be seen at work in Central Asia, and particularly in Iran.

The Iranian evacuation of Ghuriyan on 31 March 1841 had removed the main obstacle to the resumption of diplomatic relations between Britain and Iran; one of Palmerston's last actions before leaving office was to prepare appropriate instructions for McNeill. These instructions show clearly that Palmerston believed that the British occupation of Afghanistan was to be permanent and that consequently the Iranian alliance was a matter of indifference.

McNeill was instructed first to obtain the signature of Iran to a commercial treaty and this was made a precondition of the restoration of diplomatic relations and the evacuation of Kharag. When this was accomplished McNeill was to insist that Iranian debts to British officers should be paid. Only when these matters were satisfactorily concluded was McNeill to agree to listen to Iranian claims on Britain, which Palmerston assumed would relate to Afghanistan, the political treaty, and the old financial dispute dating back to 1828. To all these McNeill was to say no: Afghanistan was a matter for Britain alone; the political treaty could be left unamended; and the financial claims would not be paid.[102] McNeill wanted to make some concession on the last point as a gesture of goodwill, but Palmerston refused.[103] Iran should be told 'without offence' that Britain was quite indifferent to the Iranian alliance now that she possessed in Afghanistan a much better buffer for the defence of India.[104]

The principal objects of McNeill's mission were soon carried out. He arrived at Tehran on 11 October 1841 and the commercial treaty was signed and ratified by the Shah on 28 October. McNeill then ordered the evacuation of Kharag, which was eventually carried out in the face of a sustained attempt by the Government of India to retain it. Thus relations between Britain and Iran were restored, but they remained at a low level of activity. The logic of Palmerston's policy was that it accepted that British influence in Iran would be greatly exceeded by that of Russia, and Russian influence, which had increased considerably since 1838, continued to expand during the years 1842 to 1844. In the north, particularly around Astrabad, there was an increase in local influence, while at Tehran the new Russian Ambassador, Count Medem, a Courlander, dominated the Iranian ministers.

Russian policy during these years was ambiguous. Official policy, as set out by Nesselrode, was to follow a conciliatory policy towards Britain and to urge Iran to avoid giving offence to that country. Neither Duhamel nor, apparently, Medem were in sympathy with this approach. Duhamel believed that the spread of British influence in Central Asia was inimical to Russian interests and could be employed to stimulate unrest among Muslims within the Russian frontier. Duhamel believed that Simonich and Vitkevich had been right to strive for political influence in Afghanistan and he advocated an aggressive Russian policy in Central Asia, involving the conquest of Khiva, the occupation of Astrabad, and subsidies to Kabul and Qandahar.[105] Although he carried out the official policy, Duhamel continued to hope for the establishment of Iranian suzerainty over Herat.[106] The policy of Duhamel was, in fact, the exact counterpart of that of Palmerston. In the end Nesselrode's patient policy succeeded. Aberdeen took a view different from that of Palmerston. Where Palmerston had pressed for the occupation of Herat, Aberdeen opposed the move; it would provoke a Russian occupation of Khiva. Whereas Palmerston had based his policy on the assumption that a meeting of Russia and Britain in Central Asia was inevitable and should be kept as far away from the Indian frontier as possible, Aberdeen supported voluntary restraint and the preservation of as large a neutral area as possible—the policy of Willock and of Nesselrode himself.[107]

Even before the Afghan disaster the novelties in Aberdeen's

approach were apparent and the collapse of the Afghan position only strengthened his existing desire to replace confrontation in Central Asia by co-operation. Russia was persuaded to restrain Iran from taking advantage of the British difficulties in Afghanistan.[108] With the withdrawal from Afghanistan and from Kharag Britain became dependent upon Russia for the preservation of the independence of Herat from Iran. When, in 1844, it was suspected that Iran was about to renew her attack on Herat it was accepted that Britain could do nothing alone: 'a fresh operation either beyond the Indus or in the Persian Gulph would, under present circumstances, be most impolitic', wrote Ripon.[109]

In consequence the period after 1842 was a time of Anglo–Russian co-operation in Iran: the two powers agreed on the succession to Muhammad Shah; they exerted pressure at Istanbul and Tehran to preserve peace between Iran and the Ottomans and to form the Treaty of Erzerum (1847); and they acted together to prevent fresh Iranian attacks on Herat and Khurasan. In pursuance of the last object they even prevented Iran from checking the Turkoman slave-raids on Iranian territory. In this it was McNeill who took the lead and Medem, who had no objection to an Iranian expedition against Khiva, supported him only because of the general policy of co-operation.[110] Russia was rewarded by the absence of British objections to her gaining new concessions which consolidated her position on the Caspian and in Georgia and Caucasia. As Sheil, who succeeded McNeill in 1842, remarked: 'When England and Russia act in concert in this country, Persia is considerably under the management of those powers for all fair and reasonable purposes.'[111] But the corollary was that without Russia Britain had no influence at all.

The policy of co-operation was also extended to Turkestan, where the seeds had been sown earlier by Shakespear's successful mission for the release of the Russian slaves, and Russia's unsuccessful attempt to obtain the release of Stoddart from Bukhara. The two powers now made a joint attempt to persuade Khiva to release her Iranian slaves and, although nothing was achieved, the will to co-operate was evident.[112] The question arose whether this policy of mutual restraint and practical co-operation could lead on to a general agreement on Central Asia which would define spheres of influence, and establish a neutral zone; in short, whether in the 1840s the system which Russell in 1865 and Clarendon in 1869 tried and failed to secure and which was achieved in 1907 could have been introduced.[113]

In practice neither Britain nor Russia was ready for such a general agreement. Although in theory both Nesselrode and Aberdeen were committed to a large neutral zone, it is doubtful if Russia was prepared to limit her future advance. An approach was made soon after the Conservatives came to power, but Nesselrode refused to discuss the question with the British Minister, the Hon. John Bloomfield, who reported that Russia was only waiting for Britain to withdraw behind the Hindu Kush [*sic*? the Indus] in order to advance her own political and commercial influence into the area.[114] But at that time Britain was still in occupation of Afghanistan and Nesselrode may have merely mistrusted the British approach. Ellenborough took the view that Nesselrode was waiting for the opportunity to discuss the matter directly with Aberdeen, [115] but when in October 1841 Ellenborough tried to discuss the question of Russian co-operation in securing an agreement with Iran which would enable Britain to withdraw from Afghanistan with credit, he found the Russian Ambassador very suspicious of British activities in Turkestan.[116] The awkwardness of the sentence reflects the complexities of the connections.

Although the collapse of the British system in Afghanistan and the end of Conolly's mission, terminated the main causes of Russian suspicions, no agreement followed. The matter was discussed in 1844 when Nicholas I, Nesselrode, and Orlov visited England. It was then made clear that Russia was as suspicious of British activities in the Panjab as she had previously been of Britain in Afghanistan; the Russians were anxious to prevent the annexation of a state the disappearance of which would clearly reduce the extent of the prospective neutral zone. It may well be that the first Sikh war was one of the factors which in 1847 led Russia into her own renewed forward movement into Kazakhstan, a movement which was to last nearly forty years and carry the strategic frontier up to the Oxus and give her control of the whole of Kazakhstan and Turkestan.

The failure to achieve a self-denying agreement demonstrates how frontiers may be more important than strategy. Both in Calcutta and in Orenburg there were strong pressures for expansion, both to protect existing territories and because of certain advantages which attended the annexation of further territories. To have restrained these pressures would have required a major effort by the Governments of Britain and Russia. That they failed to make such an effort does not indicate a preference for a strategy of confrontation over one of co-operation; both Governments vaguely preferred a neutral zone and neither could see substantial advantages to be gained from further expansion that were worth the price of conflict in Europe. Their failure was more than anything else the result of indifference and inefficiency; neither Government really believed that vital issues were at stake either way and neither could effectively control developments on the ground.

There is a marked symmetry in the patterns of Russian and British policies in Central Asia during all these years. Before 1830 neither power had been greatly concerned with the area; both had treated their problems primarily as border problems. During the 1830s each had been led to make deeper penetrations and fears of pre-emption led them to drive still further into more and more exposed positions. Eventually both suffered severe rebuffs— Russia at Khiva and Britain in Afghanistan and both realized that the costs of a forward strategy outweighed the likely benefits. Each therefore resumed a border policy, looking not to a great leap forward, but to steady attrition against their immediate neighbours, Russia against the Kazakhs and Britain against Sind and the Panjab. The British movement will be the subject of Part IV.

PART IV

THE FRONTIER ACHIEVED

Sind and Kalat, 1839–1843

You are well aware that it is the object of His Lordship in
Council that all measures, political and military should be
mainly directed to the one object of permanently securing
free and safe passage upon the communications which
connect Candahar with Sukkur and Somneeanee.

Herbert Maddock to Ross Bell, 17 May 1841.

From 1839 until 1842 British interest in Sind and Kalat was subsidiary
to British interest in Afghanistan and was largely concerned with
maintaining free communications between British India and Afghanistan. The decision to withdraw from Afghanistan in 1842 converted
Sind and Kalat from the status of intermediate stations to that of the
new salients of the British Indian frontier. The question which is of
primary concern is the extent to which the change in the strategic
situation of Sind and Kalat contributed towards the vital decisions to
abandon Kalat and annex Sind.

Auckland had never envisaged a problem of communications.
Under his original 1838 plan Company forces were to be withdrawn
after restoring Shah Shuja to his throne. With the aid of his own forces
and the Contingent it was anticipated that Shuja would be able to
maintain himself against internal and external enemies and that there
would be no need for the regular or urgent passage of troops and
supplies from British India.

In consequence all arrangements for the organization of communications were mere temporary expedients. There was neither centralized political control over the route, different sections of which were
placed under four separate Political Agencies; nor centralized military
control; nor adequate arrangements for the co-ordination of military
and political authority; nor any planned disposition of forces with a
view to securing the route; nor any full consideration of the political
implications of the decisions which were made. All was improvisation
and the character of improvisation stamped British policy during the
years which followed. Because no formal decision to rewrite the 1838
policy was ever taken there was no formal examination of the implications for Sind and Kalat of a permanent British occupation of Afghanistan. Just as British troops were retained in Afghanistan on a short-term

basis with continual short-term extensions, so were those in Sind and Kalat. Only when things went wrong was there an effort to patch up some of the more obvious holes in the system and Britain stumbled insensibly towards a more permanent structure of power in the area.

Four Political Agencies controlled the road from Karachi to Qandahar in 1839. The most southerly of these was that of the Political Agent for Lower Sind whose headquarters were at Haidarabad. This post was held throughout the period by James Outram (1803–63), who replaced Henry Pottinger when the latter resigned in 1839. To the north of Outram's sphere was that of the Political Agent for Upper Sind whose bailiwick included the territories subject to the Amir of Khairpur together with the plain of Kacchi, newly taken from Kalat. His headquarters were at Shikarpur. Lieutenant W. J. Eastwick (1808–1889), Pottinger's former assistant in Sind, who had been put in temporary control, was replaced in 1839 by Ross Bell (d. 1841), a Bengal Civil Servant who had previously held the post of magistrate at Delhi. With Macnaghten and Clerk, Bell was one of the three civilians employed on the frontier; all other men in charge of political matters had a military background. Outram and Bell were independent of each other and separately responsible to the Governor-General, although for certain matters Outram dealt directly with Bombay. Further north was the empire of the Political Agent at Quetta, Lieutenant J. D. Bean, who was responsible to Macnaghten in Kabul. Bean's authority extended over the Bolan Pass itself and over the plain of Shal in which Quetta was situated. Finally, the road from Quetta to Qandahar, including the Khojak Pass, was placed under the superintendence of Lieutenant Bosanquet, who was assisted by a troop of local cavalry, the Achakzay Horse. Bosanquet, whose headquarters were at Qala Abdullah, was under the control of the Political Agent at Qandahar.

Between 1839 and 1841 no major difficulties were experienced at the two extremities of the route. Bosanquet had minor problems in his dealings with the Achakzay tribe of Durranis, but until the 1841 disturbances these did not seriously interfere with the movement of supplies. Outram also had a relatively peaceful sojourn in Lower Sind. The Amirs, after their brief and warlike flourish of resistance in February 1839, accepted their fate and were submissive. Their peaceful habits were encouraged by the conciliatory manner of Outram and by the presence of British forces at Karachi, Tatha, and Bakhar. But even when these garrisons were seriously reduced in 1840, 1841, and again in 1842, in consequence of the need to send reinforcements to Kalat and Afghanistan, the Amirs made no hostile movements, signifying that they had no intention of disputing by force the system thrust upon them in 1839.

The main problems arose at the two intermediate agencies of Shikarpur and Quetta, and each of these will require more detailed examination.

In Upper Sind Bell was virtually supreme. Nominally he was merely an agent, responsible for certain duties within the territory of two independent states, Khairpur and Kabul; but in practice he ignored them both. The Khairpur Amirs had virtually surrendered their claims when they admitted that they could not control the area to the north of Shikarpur[1] and although Bell was supposed to keep in touch with Macnaghten and send reports, accounts, and revenue to Shuja, he did neither.[2] Bell governed Kacchi himself through the agency of a Governor, Sayyid Muhammad Sharif, who, though he held the office of *na'ib* under Shuja, actually took his orders from Bell. Bell claimed that Macnaghten never wrote to him and waxed sarcastic about the Envoy's neglect.[3] Later Macnaghten claimed that although he often wrote to Bell, he never received a reply.[4] Until 1841 the Supreme Government always supported Bell.

Bell was an eccentric. There seems little doubt that he owed his appointment to Colvin, although even the powerful private secretary could not save Bell from the ultimate consequences of his own folly. Bell lived in style; fourteen thousand bottles of beer a year wended their way across seas and deserts to be drunk at his table; and when he set off on tour he made it the particular duty of his deputy to keep him well supplied with fresh vegetables, especially garden peas.[5] Reporting this, his deputy remarked that although he was left in charge of the agency, he was never told anything of the policy which he should pursue. For Bell did not believe in discussing broad issues of policy with his colleagues and subordinates, a habit which no doubt contributed to the strained relations which hung like a miasma around him. The details of one of his more dramatic quarrels are illuminating. Bell complained that troops under the authority of the local military commander, Brigadier Gordon, were offending the inhabitants of the Sakhar area by bullying them and by digging up ancient and venerated tombs and throwing the bones of saints into the river, to the accompaniment of sundry, coarse remarks. In Sind, with its characteristically eclectic Islam of the shrine, this was indeed potentially a serious matter and Bell was right to remonstrate. Gordon, however, took his protest amiss and retaliated by posting guards to prevent Bell from using a house which the agent had borrowed. He also accused Bell of bypassing his authority in military matters. The dispute deepened; words were spoken in public; Bell said Gordon was mad; and a duel was arranged. Fortunately, Gordon did not appear at the prearranged time and the hot-tempered Bell had time to think better of his position. Gordon was subsequently replaced by Brigadier Stephenson.[6] No doubt the heat bore its share of the blame, but the incident reveals the explosive temper and poor judgement of the man who was now called upon to conduct a policy of great delicacy.

The first problem with which Bell had to deal was the hardy perennial of tribal raiding. The Baluchi tribesmen who inhabited the hills to the east of the plain of Kacchi found a profitable target in the supply columns which moved north towards the Bolan. In consultation with the Supreme Government Eastwick had already devised a policy of convoys and occasional punitive expeditions to try to combat this nuisance, but in the longer term Eastwick looked to enlisting members of the plundering tribes to act as guards. This time-honoured practice of setting thieves to catch thieves had been employed elsewhere in India and enjoyed at that time an especial vogue because of Outram's success with it in the Bhil country. As a start a local corps of Baluch levies was raised, although it later appeared that few of the recruits were Baluchis; most were their enemies the Pathans, both local men and two hundred from the Khaibar.[7]

Unsurprisingly, neither the short- nor the long-term policy achieved much success and the Baluchi raiders penetrated the British defences with ease. Bell disbanded all but the Khaibaris on the grounds that the levies were 'incorrigibly mutinous' and asked to be allowed to replace them with imported Afghans or with Baluch Horse under British officers.[8] Auckland refused: he did not want to bring in men from outside and so abandon the policy of conciliation through local enlistment and perhaps he did not want extensive commitments in the area.[9] Under the command of Lieutenant Amiel the levies continued on a reduced and ineffective scale. In February 1840 Bell apparently returned to the original conception with an instruction to Amiel to enlist twenty men from each tribe so as to form a squadron of the Levy for use as frontier police.[10] But Bell himself had little time for long-term conciliation and put his faith in coercion; from the beginning he advocated punitive expeditions and the extension into Baluch territory of direct military control.

Bell was able to put his own policy to the trial in the winter of 1839. His first premature attempt in the summer of 1839 had ended in disaster. He ordered an expedition to be prepared and one detachment of troops lost several men from sunstroke. Bell was obliged to postpone operations until the colder weather made it safe to move troops and in the meantime to resort to the familiar expedient of divide and rule. His efforts to play off one tribe against another only made matters worse, although Bell preferred to blame Mihrab Khan of Kalat for his troubles.[11] Mihrab was destroyed by Willshire in November and the following month Bell was ready to move against the Baluchis. By cutting off their access to the plain he induced the tribesmen to agree to his terms, which involved the surrender of chiefs as hostages and the establishment of several small garrisons of Company troops in the mountains and along lines of communication. Well satisfied with a system which trained military men would have deplored, Bell, who had contracted dysentery, retired to Simla on sick-leave in February 1840, leaving his deputies, Lieutenant E. J. Brown and Lieutenant T. Postans, in charge at Sakhar and Shikarpur respectively.[12]

Bell's optimism was premature. His policy of tying down small packets of troops in isolated garrisons was fundamentally unsound and its weaknesses were revealed when summer returned. The hostile Mari tribe besieged the garrison posted in their capital of Kahan and two attempts to relieve the Kahan force were repulsed with heavy losses, although the garrison eventually extricated itself.[13] Bell returned and began to plan new and still larger campaigns against his Baluchi enemies. But at this moment the Baluch tribal problem was submerged under the much greater problem of the rising which broke out in Kalat itself.

At Quetta Lieutenant Bean's main concern was with the safety of communications between Dadar at the southern end of the Bolan Pass and a position at the western end of the Khojak Pass. This line ran through the provinces of Mastang and Shal, which had been transferred from Kalat to Kabul in 1839. Because Bean was directly under Macnaghten's orders, the influence of Kabul was felt much more in Shal and Mastang than it was in Kacchi. Shal was governed by an Afghan *na'ib*, Muhammad Sadiq Khan Popalzay, and Mastang by a Brahui, Muhammed Khan Sherwani, both of whom held office under Shuja. In addition to his responsibilities in the provinces annexed to Kabul, Bean was also responsible for the conduct of relations with the semi–independent state of Kalat, now ruled by the British nominee, Shah Nawaz Khan. For this latter purpose a British agent, Lieutenant Loveday, who was responsible to Bean, lived at Kalat.

During his first year of authority Bean paid little attention to Kalat and concentrated on communications through the Bolan, where he encountered the same problem of tribal raiding which had beset Eastwick and Bell in Upper Sind. Bean's policy was very similar to that of Eastwick, viz: 'overlooking the past, conciliating the chiefs and enlisting a portion of their retainers in the Bolan Rangers'.[14] But the policy was no more successful above the passes than below. The delightfully named Bolan Rangers, with their delicate blend of exotic and homely associations, were as ineffective as their counterparts, the Baluch Levy. Recruited not from the Brahuis who controlled the Bolan, but from Afghan Kakars from the eastern end of the Shal valley, they were equally self-defeating. Service in the Rangers was popular, not just because of the pay and the lightness of the duties—the men lived at home and never paraded—but because of the opportunity given to the Kakars of entering and plundering the Shal valley.[15] But unlike Bell, Bean did not have the option of direct military coercion for he had no Company forces at his disposal. He was therefore obliged to adopt Bell's temporary expedient of divide and rule more or less as a permanent policy. It was, however, singularly unsuccessful and one morning Bean suffered the mortification of waking up to find himself besieged in Quetta by a tribe with whom he had believed himself to be allied.[16] British officers now contemplated a new approach to the problem of communications, namely control through Kalat.

Between the establishment of Shah Nawaz at the end of 1839 and the summer of 1840 Kalat was largely ignored. Auckland, who, like Hobhouse, had never liked the policy of dismembering Kalat, had accepted the deed and hoped to have nothing more to do with the state. In May 1840 he rejected a proposal by Bean that the Khan should be given help to control his internal enemies, and Lieutenant Loveday, who had been advising Nawaz, was ordered to cease accompanying him on expeditions for the subjection of rebellious chiefs.[17]

There were, apparently, possible advantages to Britain in supporting the Khan's reduction of his enemies, and particularly in bringing under his control the virtually independent province of Las Bayla, which lay in the south-west of Kalat and included the port of Sonmiani. From Sonmiani a commercial route ran north-eastwards through Kalat to Quetta. This route had been traversed with some difficulty by Outram on his return from Afghanistan in 1839.[18] If it could be secured and improved, the Sonmiani route would make possible direct communication between Bombay and Afghanistan via Kalat alone, thus avoiding Sind and the Bolan. Such a route could provide either a replacement for the Sind/Bolan route or a valuable supplement to it. But its adoption would involve a radically different policy towards Kalat because, whereas the Sind/Bolan route could be operated seemingly independently of Kalat, the Sonmiani route would require close control over that state.

Auckland did not accept the plan. His rejection was less a comment upon its strategic merits than a decision to hold to his 1838 plan which had been designed to make any permanent communications arrangements unnecessary, and to enable him to avoid entanglements in Kalat. All he would do was to grant Nawaz an additional loan of £10,000.[19] In consequence Nawaz never achieved anything approaching full control over his own subjects. Quite apart from the semi-independent Brahui tribal confederations, his authority was flouted by erstwhile supporters of the late Mihrab Khan, who collected revenues to maintain their followers. Their figurehead was the youthful Nasir Khan, the only son of Mihrab, and their most prominent leader the former *na'ib* of Mastang, Darogah Gul Muhammad. It was these men who assumed the leadership of the rebellion which broke out in Kalat in the summer of 1840.

Despite the inquiries made subsequently, the true causes of the Kalat revolt remain hidden. No doubt one cause was the financial weakness of the Government of Nawaz, which was crippled by the 1839 Settlement. Most of the land in the remaining central provinces of Kalat was held by Brahui tribesmen on rent-free grants and the rulers of Kalat had always been heavily dependent upon revenues from the now lost crown lands in Kacchi.[20] Under Nawaz the state revenues amounted to less than £5,000 a year and even with British assistance the Khan could not pay for an army powerful enough to enable him to maintain control. Nor could he draw on any natural fund of popular support for he had none; and disaffection among his subjects increased daily. The Brahui chiefs had several causes of complaint. The 1839 harvest in Shal and Mastang had been ruined by the passage of the Army of the Indus and consequent shortages pushed grain prices very high in the following winter. The income of the chiefs was further diminished when, at British instigation, Nawaz reduced tolls on commercial traffic using the Sonmiani route. But their principal cause of complaint and probably the main cause of the rising was the Brahui fear that they would lose the lands which they possessed in Kacchi.

The great Brahui chiefs of Jahlawan and Sarawan possessed lands in Mastang and, more importantly, in Kacchi. These lands were either their own property or were state lands held rent-free in return for military service; only rarely did the chiefs hold written titles. To the Brahui chiefs their lands in Kacchi were as important as the crown lands were to the Khan. The Brahuis lived as nomads pasturing their flocks in the uplands of Kalat and they came down to their lands in Kacchi only in the winter to collect rent, in the form of grain, from the Jat cultivators who worked the land. These grain supplies were vital to the pastoral Brahuis.

Eastwick states that all rent-free grants were resumed after the annexation of Kacchi.[21] This, however, cannot be true, unless they were immediately re-granted to their former holders, for the subject of the future of these lands was under continual discussion throughout 1839 to 1840. At first Macnaghten proposed that while all private and purchased lands could be retained by their owners, all grants for military service should be resumed and re-granted to supporters of Shuja. Bell protested, and misleadingly informed Macnaghten that the Baluchis in Kacchi were permanent residents and that many cultivated their own lands. Although true, this did not apply to the Brahuis who are of major interest to us and whom Bell also wanted to leave in possession of their grants of land. Macnaghten was in principle prepared to allow military holders to retain their grants providing that they continued to perform their military service and if it would be politically dangerous to disturb them, but he asked for more information before reaching a decision.[22] In the meantime, however, Shuja had seen a convenient opportunity to reward his followers at no cost to himself and there arrived in Kacchi a number of recipients of new grants from the Shah and these men demanded that the grants should be honoured. Although Bell refused, the new grantees loudly declared that they would eventually secure their claims.[23] It seems that Bell's assistant, Lieutenant E. J. Brown, may have shared their opinion, for he wrote to Loveday that the favourable terms which had been given to the existing holders in 1839 to 1840 would not be renewed during the following year.[24] A further cause of disquiet to the Brahuis was the activity of the *na'ib*, Muhammad Sharif, who was busily engaged in furthering his own interests.[25]

The situation in Mastang is still more obscure than that in Kacchi. There seems no doubt, however, that Bean was much less able to withstand pressure from Kabul than was Bell. Following Macnaghten's advice, Bean prepared a scheme to resume all holdings in the province, whether private or granted, and to force the holders to pay one-quarter of the produce as revenue. Whether the scheme was put into operation is uncertain; but it is in any case clear that Bean's arrangements for farming the revenues of the province were extremely unpopular and led to extortion.[26] Probably grants were also made to supporters of Shuja. An inquiry later conducted by Lieutenant Wallace, at the instigation of Bell, blamed Macnaghten and Bean.[27] In turn Macnaghten and Bean denied that their revenue arrangements were responsible for the rising and Macnaghten asserted that as far as he knew no grants had been made to the detriment of those who held land under Mihrab Khan. Instead the two Politicals blamed the movement of Bell's troops for the revolt.[28] Auckland, however, believed that the revenue arrangements were at the root of the troubles.[29]

Despite the uncertainty that surrounds the causes of the rising, the evidence points unmistakably towards the role of the men on the spot. At the bottom of the system Afghan and Baluchi agents, barely under the control of the European supervisors, sought their own interests, while the European Political Agents were able to pursue their own paths, independently of each other and of control from above. The affair of Lieutenant Loveday highlights the responsibility which attached to the Political Agent. Loveday was a young man who had been fortunate to obtain a political appointment. Although his compromising support for the ambitions of Nawaz had been partly checked, his conduct did not otherwise receive notice until after the rising. At that time a most curious story was revealed by the complaints of the rebels and the evidence of Charles Masson. Disgusted by the 1838 policy, Masson had thrown up his government appointment, and resumed his private travels. These had taken him to Kalat where he had the opportunity of observing Loveday's behaviour. Masson was subsequently taken prisoner with Loveday during the rising but, unlike the Political Agent, he survived to be arrested by Bean as a spy, and later to tell his story. According to Masson before the rising Loveday had gone mad and sat brooding all day, speaking strangely, pulling the beards and hair of the Kalatis and encouraging his pet bulldogs to attack them. One Kalati was actually killed in this way. Loveday explained to Masson that the Brahuis were only dogs and fit only to be dealt with by dogs.[30] It is fair to say that Eastwick, relying on the testimony of Captain Pontardent, did not believe these stories, but Masson was a reliable witness and had no reason to lie. Auckland believed him.[31] Loveday's principal assistant in Kalat also behaved badly.

The activities of Bell, Bean, and Loveday show how local agents could produce the situation of a general rising which could force their government to modify its policies. Auckland's belief that he could do without a considered political policy in the areas which surrounded his lines of communications was rudely shattered by the Baluchi, Brahui, and Kakar risings of June and July 1840. First the Mari Baluchis attacked Kacchi and the Kakar Afghans attacked Quetta. Then the Sarawan Brahuis of Mastang rose in rebellion and attacked Quetta; when repulsed they joined the equally disaffected Jahlawan Brahuis and took Kalat, putting up Nasir Khan in place of Nawaz. Communications between Shikarpur and Quetta were severed and in consequence the reinforcements which were urgently needed in Afghanistan in September 1840 to counter the threat posed by the return of Dost

Muhammad, could not be sent via Quetta and had to march through the unreliable Panjab. For a time the situation in Upper Sind and Kalat was critical. Bell was helpless; illness had reduced the troops in Upper Sind to 1350 effectives and they could not move because of lack of transport[32] and the summer heat; the defeat at Kahan had damaged morale. Quetta had to be relieved from Qandahar. Only with the coming of the cold weather could Bell, suitably reinforced, begin the task of pacification. Gradually the troops moved northwards clearing Kacchi, Mastang, and Shal. Bell left Kalat alone in the hope that a new political settlement would make military operations unnecessary.[33]

The crisis had thrown the whole 1839 system into the melting-pot. Bell now considered three possible political systems. The first was that Kalat could be nominally annexed to Afghanistan but in reality kept under close British control which would be exercised through agreements negotiated with individual chiefs. Bell rejected this policy on the grounds that it would produce anarchy.[34] He preferred the second possibility of the restoration of Nawaz, but eventually abandoned the idea because of the evidence of Nawaz's unpopularity. The third possibility, which Bell adopted in January 1841, was to recognize Nasir as Khan of Kalat providing that he made some token submission to British authority.[35] But this submission he found impossible to obtain and in July 1841 Bell was still in doubt about what course to adopt when he was dismissed, following direct orders from London. He was already a very sick man when he received his dismissal and on 31 July he died at Quetta.

Bell was replaced by Outram. Outram's appointment had the effect of establishing unified political control over almost the entire length of the southern communications route. Bell had already annexed Bean's empire. Cleverly casting the blame on Macnaghten and Bean for the rising in Upper Sind, he had written privately to Colvin in August 1840, arguing that there would never be a peaceful settlement as long as Bean remained at Quetta and until he himself was given supreme control.[36] Colvin's influence was apparently sufficient and Bell had got what he demanded. Since Outram retained his former powers in Lower Sind the new agent now controlled the entire route as far north as the Khojak pass. With the appointment of Major-General Brooks to the command of all military forces above and below the Bolan in February 1841 a united military command was also brought into being and was continued under his successor, General Richard England. At last it became possible to develop a unified policy for communications.

James Outram had made an early reputation with his settlement of the Bhils and, in consequence, like his contemporary, Colin Mackenzie, carried with him all his life, an aura of great potential. It was a potential which in Outram's case was never fully realized; like John F. Kennedy, he came to personify moral aspiration rather than performance. More by accident that design Outram came to embody the ideals of integrity and honesty and thus acquired the sobriquet of Bayard of India. But he was too self-consciously the *chevalier sans peur et sans reproche*; throughout his career he played assiduously the part of the gallant, selfless hero, carefully fostering his own growing legend with modestly publicized gestures. His later opponent, Sir Charles Napier, said of Outram that he was high-minded and honourable, but that he was by nature a 'partisan'; a man who could work well if he were given his head, but who could not endure control.[37] Although hardly an impartial witness, Napier was an honest one. Outram indeed disliked subordination and to obtain support for the policies which he believed to be right was quite prepared to misrepresent the facts to those who did not understand them. For such a man honour was an invaluable resort when ambition received a check; to resign on a matter of principle was a warmly satisfying experience. Like John Malcolm, Outram was a man whose real importance was misrepresented by legend. He was one of the most notable political strategists to emerge from the Afghan war, and although he was to become enmeshed in controversy during the 1840s and the object of the dislike of Ellenborough and Hardinge, Outram re-emerged under Dalhousie and Canning in the 1850s as a personality almost of the proportions of Malcolm. Physically Outram was insignificant and verbally completely tongue-tied; his great skill was with the pen. 'He sheds his ink as readily as he does his blood', wrote Dalhousie.[38] But in his ruthless determination to seize every opportunity that might advance his own interests, in his literary facility, in his ability to use friends, and above all, in his bold, creative, strategic imagination, Outram was a true disciple of the master-Political and, like Malcolm, he contrived to leave behind him a wholly deceptive image.

Arriving in Sind free from the silken reins of past policies, Outram had no hesitation in deciding that Nasir should be made Khan of Kalat. The more important question was what should be done with the three annexed provinces, which the rebels demanded should be restored to Kalat. Bell had always advocated this action, which would inevitably have swelled his own empire and Loveday and Bean had also come to support the same course. Taking advantage of the rising, Bell announced, without authority, in the autumn of 1840 that the provinces would be restored to Kalat.[39] Macnaghten had opposed him bitterly; the Envoy would accept Nasir in place of Nawaz, but the rest of the 1839 Settlement he wished to preserve.[40] Outram suggested a third possibility which had already won support from Auckland in the autumn of 1840.[41] This was that all three provinces would be taken from Afghanistan but only Kacchi and Mastang restored to Kalat: Shal would be retained by Britain for the time being because of its crucial importance as the main position above the passes along the line of communications; if necessary it would be returned to Afghanistan at a later date.[42] It was on this basis that Outram signed a treaty with Nasir Khan on 6 October 1841.

By the new treaty Shah Shuja retained his nominal suzerainty over the enlarged Kalat; Britain gained control over Kalati foreign affairs; Nasir undertook to be guided by the advice of a British Resident; and Britain retained military control through a provision which gave her the right to station troops anywhere in Kalat.[43] It was a far-reaching step towards firm British control over Kalat; the informal arrangements of 1839 had been found wanting and the logic of events had pushed Britain to assume a position which was beginning to wear an aspect of permanency. Still more important was the retention of Shal, which was in effect annexed to British India, the first new possession beyond the 1838 frontier. What had begun as an attempt to provide a temporary line of communications had progressed to the point where the British position in Baluchistan was beginning to look like a position existing in its own right.

Auckland accepted Outram's policy although he disliked it. Between 1839 and 1841 his own views of Kalat had undergone a complete change. As noted above, his early policy had been wholly negative: Baluchistan was a temporary nuisance to be abandoned as soon as British forces were withdrawn from Afghanistan. The great rising of 1840 had forced Auckland to think again and he had then come to favour a solution very similar to that subsequently embodied in Outram's October 1841 Treaty: namely, the recognition of Nasir as ruler of Kalat under Afghan suzerainty; the restoration of Kacchi and Mastang to Kalat; and the retention of Shal by Britain. But the revolution in his opinions had not stopped there and in 1841 he began to move in the direction of still greater British interference. In this further evolution he was assisted by glowing reports of the popularity of British rule received from his agents in Baluchistan. Among these reports was an elaborate plan submitted by Bell's assistant, Thomas Postans, which called for the economic development of Kacchi under direct British rule, and was supported by arguments based on strategy and humanitarianism.[44] Auckland was impressed: not only could Kacchi become very prosperous but greater control of Kacchi would enable

Britain to control the surrounding tribes. In addition, Auckland had at last begun to turn towards the earlier proposal to develop the Sonmiani route for he was increasingly disillusioned by his experience of the Bolan. Apart from the tribal disturbances which continually threatened and occasionally severed communications, the Bolan was unusable by troops during the hot season and extremely dangerous in the rains; in April 1841 a flash flood cost Skinner's Horse the lives of thirty-three men and a hundred and one animals.[45] As a result of these reflections, and perhaps also in the hope of achieving some success which would compensate for the increasingly obvious failure in Afghanistan, Auckland put forward a new policy in the summer of 1841. He now advocated direct British control over Kalat including its internal administration. Separate agreements should be made with the chiefs and Nasir reduced to a mere puppet.[46] Auckland had curiously anticipated the policy of Robert Sandeman in 1876.

Auckland's latest policy-change had come too late. By the time the recommendations reached him Outram was, or said he was, already committed to the October Treaty with Nasir and that settlement left Nasir considerable power and included no guarantees to the chiefs. Auckland did not attempt to upset the hardly-won peace and contented himself by asking that the British advisor in Kalat should be appointed. This, he hoped, would be sufficient to ensure that Kalat developed along the lines he had laid down.[47]

The movement towards greater British control over Kalat continued in the months which followed. Outram had already appointed a British advisor in Kalat, Captain P. T. French.[48] In December Outram brought forward a further proposal for the extension of his political empire. He proposed that the Qandahar district of Sibi, which was geographically much more closely linked with Kalat than with Qandahar, should be taken from Afghanistan, annexed to Britain, and placed under direct British management.[49] Outram anticipated that Sibi would be capable of considerable development under British rule. But although Auckland supported the proposal, which anticipated the future Lytton/Ripon settlement, it was rejected by London.

The change in British policy in Baluchistan had a dual aspect. In the first place it was a simple recognition that the 1839 policy in Baluchistan had failed. In the second place it was also a recognition that the 1838 Afghan policy had failed. This is true in the most obvious sense that it had proved impossible to withdraw British troops from Afghanistan and therefore that the system of communications which had been adequate for a year would not suffice for the far longer term for which it was now needed. But it is also true in a deeper sense. For the securing of communications alone, even on a more permanent and extended basis, could not have justified Auckland's advocacy of a system of control which made sense only in the context of a permanent British hold on the area; for the proposals for the development of Shal, Kacchi, and Sibi under British management inevitably involved work over many years and rewards over still more. Also, as has been shown in previous chapters, Auckland had come to the conclusion that the Afghan position was untenable; it is difficult to believe that he would plan so elaborate a system of communications with a country which he proposed to abandon. There is a contrast between Auckland's reluctant dragging of his feet in Afghanistan and his eager assumption of greater responsibilities in Baluchistan which demands an explanation.

Auckland's Baluchistan policy in 1841 is only comprehensible on the assumption that communications were no longer the main reason for the British presence in that country. Baluchistan was now coveted for its own sake; the Afghan strategy had failed and Auckland was preparing a fall-back position. It has already been shown how, as early as the spring of 1841, he had begun to identify such a position. He had then placed it on the Indus. In the context of that line of thought it is reasonable to see Baluchistan now assuming the appearance of the principal British salient to the north-west, protecting the main defensive frontier on the Indus, and providing an advanced post for possible future thrusts into Central Asia. The analysis is partly confirmed by recommendations which Auckland made after the news of the rising. In December 1841 and January 1842 he outlined a plan for direct British control of Shikarpur and Kacchi, so as to provide a base from which he could command movement out of either the Bolan or Mulla (Kalat to Kacchi) Passes. In front of this position he wanted an advanced base at Quetta and firm control of Kalat.[50] Even in February 1842, when the crushing blows of the Afghan débâcle led him to sacrifice most of his hopes and to recommend a retreat to the Satlej, the bare bones of the Baluchistan strategy are still visible in a letter which he wrote to Outram. Like Outram, he looked to a main base at Sakhar, a small force at Shikarpur, and the maintenance of British influence in Sind and Kalat. British forces would not be stationed beyond Shikarpur, however, and the defence of Shal, Dadar, and Sibi against any Afghan attack would be left to Kalat. 'I would endeavour', he wrote on the last day of his Governor-Generalship, 'to save at least this much of our late accessions of power from the disasters which have been brought upon them.'[51]

The importance of the new Baluchistan strategy which was worked out between Bell, Outram, and Auckland in the summer and autumn of

1841 must not be underestimated. It was the first major new strategic alternative which had emerged since 1838 and represented a cheaper way of attaining many of the ends which it had been intended to obtain through the 1838 Afghan strategy, with the added benefit that they could be achieved by direct British action. It was the identical strategy which was pursued in various ways by a succession of agents in future years and was realized in 1876 by the establishment of control over Kalat, the introduction of guarantees to the chiefs, and the annexation of Quetta. Within a few years, Sibi too was brought back into the discussion. In 1842 Outram made a major effort to persuade Ellenborough to adopt the new, Kalat strategy immediately.

Ellenborough's decision to abandon Afghanistan left open the question of where the retreat should stop. It has been shown how Rawlinson, supported by Outram, attempted to persuade Ellenborough to hold western Afghanistan alone. The same arguments which had been used to justify that proposal were now brought forward to support the holding of Kalat. A position there, it was argued, would give Britain the opportunity to intervene quickly and decisively at either Herat or Qandahar and would provide an excellent position from which to threaten the advance of any invading army.

Outram's proposals for Baluchistan were originally addressed to Auckland. In February 1842 he suggested that Sakhar and Shikarpur should be held in strength and British influence maintained at Kalat through a Resident and a subsidy. The subsidy would enable Nasir Khan to resist any Afghan attack; ensure the continuation of British influence in the Bolan; and keep open the commercial route through Sonmiani. As a double guarantee Outram proposed that part of the money should be paid directly to the chiefs for military services. Kalat should be enlarged and strengthened by the restoration of Shal and the addition of Sibi. In an interesting echo of Ellenborough's original 1830 strategy Outram wrote that under British influence a strong Kalat could become the agency through which British trade could penetrate Central Asia. These were temporary proposals designed to hold a skeleton position until the present difficulties subsided; in the longer term Outram hoped that Kalat would be given a guarantee of British support against any attack from outside and so eventually be converted into a buffer state and a springboard for the reassertion of British power in Central Asia.[52]

Outram's proposed Baluchistan strategy was discussed by his subordinates in the area. Lieutenant-Colonel Stacy, who had been chiefly responsible for persuading Nasir Khan to accept the British terms in the summer of 1841, supported his chief,[53] but Outram was opposed by

Captain P. T. French, the new agent in Kalat. French recommended the abandonment of Kalat on the grounds that its inhabitants were too barbarous to be trusted. He wrote:

I look on the race forming H.M's subjects as far as my observation goes, as faithless, having no regard for life, no knowledge of morals beyond a ceaseless expression of certain prayers and symbols rude and lawless, ever ready to follow their chiefs to scenes of plunder and bloodshed, and the chiefs scarcely elevated above their followers, equally treacherous and faithless, as much given to lying, as little impressed with any moral obligations, as addicted to rebellion and plunder, fully as rapacious and in fact possessing all the faults of the lower classes without any of their industry . . . Bigotry reigns from end to end and in short a moral leprosy is spread over the people and country.[54]

French's civilized disgust with Baluchistan is interesting because it is symptomatic of a reaction which was common to many who observed directly or indirectly the Afghan disturbances of 1841 and which had its influence on strategic thought. There were several different responses by Britons to acquaintance with the peoples of Central Asia. For a few, like Richard Burton and Edward Eastwick, there was content; the people they saw were certainly different and in many ways not very admirable, but they liked them and saw no reason to try to change them. For some, like Eldred Pottinger, Todd, Conolly, and Postans, there was discontent; they observed practices which they abhorred, but they blamed not the people but their institutions; if the institutions were changed the people had the opportunity of a civilized or even a Christian life: It was Britain's responsibility to give them that opportunity, and so humanitarianism became a justification for expansion. For such men humanitarianism became the major motive for the extension of the imperial frontier; for many others the desire to improve the prosperity of the peoples of Central Asia did not occupy so fundamental a position in their thought but provided an important legitimization of their ambitions. It was a way of winning mass support for British rule and contrasted sharply with the aristocratic system of Malcolm and Ellenborough, which was to find its best-known expression in the work of Lugard in northern Nigeria. But for men like French, experience destroyed idealism and strategic ambition alike. French condemned both the people and the national aristocracy and he made no distinction between men and institutions. In his view the people themselves were morally rotten; the humanitarian mission was not worth the price of defilement; and the best policy for Britain was to shake off the dust of Central Asia entirely. It was a short–lived and bitter reaction, but it played an important part in the decision to withdraw from Central Asia, as it was to play a significant role in the future flight from imperial adventure.

In May 1842 Outram renewed his plans for Kalat in recommendations sent to Ellenborough.[55] He now proposed an annual subsidy of £15,000 (later reduced to £5,000) to Nasir Khan to compensate him for the withdrawal of the pledge of British military protection. Outram also proposed that he should be allowed to hand over to Kalat the two provinces which were under direct British rule, Shal and Sibi.

Ellenborough refused to answer this proposal on the grounds that Outram had no right to make it direct to the Supreme Government. Under his new instructions, all Political Agents had been placed under the orders of the appropriate military commander. In Outram's case this was Nott and, despite the extra delay, Ellenborough demanded that Outram's proposals should be submitted through Qandahar. Outram obeyed but, receiving no reply from Nott who, as usual, was indifferent to anything which did not affect his immediate military movements, proceeded to offer Shal to Nasir Khan on his own responsibility.[56]

Ellenborough now intervened to put an end to Outram's Kalat strategy. Who possessed Shal, the Governor-General asserted, was a matter of indifference to him, but he was determined that Britain should accept no responsibility for its fate.[57] He had decided that Kalat should be completely abandoned and he instructed Outram to inform the Khan that the October 1841 Treaty was abrogated.

British relations with Kalat were not to be terminated as abruptly as Ellenborough had intended. The sequence of events which followed his orders is unclear. Outram had already notified the Khan that Shal would be transferred to his rule and Nasir did resume possession of the province. Now Outram did not inform the Khan that the October Treaty was at an end on the grounds that it would be dangerous to do so until all British subjects were safely out of Baluchistan.[58] This withdrawal was not carried out until the latter part of 1842. General England, returning from Qandahar, withdrew from Quetta in three columns, the last of which did not leave until 1 October, and was required to evacuate the garrisons from Kalat and Kacchi as the column retired to camp at Sakhar on the Indus.

I can find no record that Outram ever informed the Khan that the treaty was at an end and much to suggest that he did not. In all the British discussions which took place in the years which followed no one, including Outram, seemed to know whether the treaty was in force or not. Nasir Khan thought it was, and in 1842 and again in 1843 applied for help under its provisions.[59] Indeed Ellenborough also changed his views on Kalat in the years which followed and although he did not acknowledge the existence of the treaty, he agreed to send the Khan some money, while refusing to send troops. In March 1843, Charles Napier, then commanding in Sind, paid £1,000 to the Khan and at the end of the same year Ellenborough authorized a further payment. At that time Ellenborough argued that the occupation of Sind might have altered the British position in relation to Kalat.[60]

The occupation of Sind did inject a new element into the Kalat problem. The tribes ceased to be a threat to communications and became a threat to the peace of the new border. A new problem of frontier management was created as British officials tried a variety of ways of controlling the tribes. Inevitably, however, the existence of a tribal problem on the frontier caused British officers to look beyond the frontier in an effort to find a solution to their problems there, either by an agreement with Kalat or by advancing the frontier so as to include the tribes within British territory and to be able to deal with them in a different way. In turn the question of tribal management became merged with the problem of forward strategic defence and the way was opened for the re-establishment of British influence in Kalat, when the opportunity was provided by the Crimean war.

Ellenborough's 1842 decision in favour of the total abandonment of Kalat left Shikarpur as the last trans–Indus position which might be retained by Britain. Outram had long been an advocate of the annexation of Shikarpur, a policy which he supported at the time on strategic grounds, but which he later declared to be based upon humanitarian motives. He wished, he wrote, to ameliorate the condition of the people of Sind.[61] This of course was the basis of Postan's argument, in which that agent was supported by another assistant Political Agent, Lieutenant W. S. Terry.[62] Whether it was Outram's real motive is doubtful; his subsequent position as the moral critic of British policy in Sind made it difficult for him to avow any but the most high-minded motives. At all events Outram's views on the desirability of acquiring Shikarpur coincided with those of Auckland, who saw it as a key position in the new system of British bases below the passes, and Auckland gave permission for Outram to negotiate with the Amirs for its purchase.

An opportunity to buy Shikarpur arose in August 1841 when the Amirs offered to trade it for the abolition of their tribute payments.[63] When he heard of this proposal Ellenborough as President of the Board of Control, attempted to stop the transaction on the grounds that it indicated a desire to acquire permanent possessions beyond the Indus,[64] but Auckland rejected his veto on the grounds that the negotiations had already gone too far.[65] In fact Auckland was wrong; the Amirs had had second thoughts and the negotiations could not be completed at that time.

In June 1842 Outram raised the question of Shikarpur again, urging its acquisition for strategic and commercial reasons.[66] Ellenborough, now Governor-General, refused: Ellenborough, who did not consider the argument that the threat of internal disturbances justified a forward policy and who accepted the conventional military view that any invasion must be funnelled through the Panjab, could see no danger on the Lower Indus and therefore no strategic use for Shikarpur. And Shikarpur to him had one overwhelming disqualification—it was situated on the right bank of the Indus. 'I wish to have nothing whatsoever to do with the right bank of the Indus', he wrote, 'except so far as it may be necessary to protect the navigation of the river.'[67]

For Ellenborough had decided that the British withdrawal from Central Asia should stop on the line of the Lower Indus. In coming to this decision he had departed from the strict military view of what constituted the most desirable frontier for British India in that area, namely the desert and not the river, and from his own view as expressed in 1840. He had then written that although the Indus was the logical frontier of British India it was not the best: 'in my opinion the true frontier of India is not the Indus but the Desert.'[68]

Ellenborough's conversion to support of the Indus frontier is accountable by reference to four arguments. The first related to commerce and was essentially a development of his own 1830 arguments which had been put into operation by Bentinck and Auckland; he thought that under British control the Indus could become a great free trade zone which would bring prosperity to the people along its banks.[69] The second linked commerce with strategy; the Indus could provide excellent communications between Britain and the North-Western Provinces of British India and therefore be beneficial in controlling the Panjab.[70] The third argument was that advanced by Wellington and others and represented what one might call the reformed military view: control of the Lower Indus was necessary in order to deny it to France and to threaten the flanks of an enemy who was attacking in the north. But the decisive argument was the fourth, which sprang from the roots of Ellenborough's thoughts on British India: the prestige of the army demanded that retreat should end; if it continued the morale of the army and the confidence of the Indian people in British supremacy might both be shaken. For all these reasons Ellenborough decided to maintain a British position in Sind.

The annexation of Sind was the subject of great debate. Many books and pamphlets appeared at the time and several historians have recently re-examined the controversy.[71] But the entire discussion has been dominated by a moral question: were the Amirs fairly treated? Although I shall comment on that question, it is not my main concern. The question which is relevant to this book is how the annexation of Sind fits into the strategic systems which have been discussed.

It was Outram who inaugurated the series of actions which led to annexation. His own relations with the Amirs had been good. With Auckland's support he had avoided interference in their internal affairs. Apart from a few minor disputes concerning the Indus navigation, the principal matters which had arisen had been the signing of a treaty with the Amir of Mirpur which brought his small state within the framework of the 1839 Treaty system; and the Shikarpur question. It is clear that Outram had no wish to abandon the position that had been built up in Sind and hoped to confirm it by holding Shikarpur. It is probable that it was with a view to bringing pressure to bear on the Amirs to support his negotiations with them over Shikarpur that, in February 1842, he first brought to the notice of Government, certain reports of disaffection, albeit not dangerous, which involved the Amirs.[72]

In May 1842, after further investigation, Outram brought up the question again. He wrote:

I shall have it in my power shortly I believe to expose the hostile intrigues of the Amirs to such an extent as may be deemed by His Lordship sufficient to authorize the dictation of his own terms to the chiefs of Sinde and to call for such measures as he deems it necessary to place British power on a secure footing in these countries.[73]

From his statements in the *Conquest of Seinde* it appears that the measures Outram contemplated were the exchange of the tribute of £35,000 a year for the abolition of the transit duties and *either* Shikarpur and Sakhar *or* Karachi.[74] In purely financial terms the exchange came out about even; Outram was merely proposing to use a threat of punishment for disloyalty in order to force through a carefully calculated and not unreasonable bargain. But he was now to lose control of events and his delicate balance of force was to be totally destroyed by the ambitions of Ellenborough and Napier.

An important element in the concept of prestige which dominated Ellenborough's view of British India was the notion of Britain as the disposer of rewards and punishments. In Afghanistan he had found it difficult to give rein to this element; it was too dangerous and in any case he had found it impossible to lay hands on the arch-criminal, Muhammad Akbar. But in Sind it was possible to deliver a moral lesson to the people of India and to show how Britain could reward the faithful and mercilessly punish the guilty.[75] It was this impulse which first upset Outram's fine computation of advantage.

Ellenborough had seized upon Outram's February revelations. On 6 May he sent Outram a letter to be delivered to any Amir suspected of disaffection, informing him that his territory would be confiscated.[76] Shortly after this he received Wellington's first strategic recommendations concerning the Lower Indus and promptly wrote to Outram again asking him to negotiate a treaty by which the tribute would be abolished in return for the cession of Bhakur, Sakhar, and Karachi, together with some commercial concessions. Shikarpur, he still did not want.[77]

These demands by Ellenborough went beyond those which Outram had hoped to achieve and represented a bargain much more unfavourable to the Amirs. Anticipating opposition, Outram decided to defer any action on the treaty until troops arrived; nor did he deliver Ellenborough's threatening letter.[78] Ellenborough agreed to the postponement.

During the summer of 1842, while waiting for troops to arrive in Sind, Ellenborough increased his demands still further. Believing the ruler of Bahawalpur to be a faithful ally and deserving of reward, he proposed, on 4 June, that the Khairpur Amirs should cede some territory to that ruler.[79] Outram suggested that the district of Sabzalkot, which, with the connected area of Bhuj Bara, was worth £4,500 a year, would be a suitable prize.[80] But it was not enough for Ellenborough who, after further reflection, decided in October 1842 to add to his gift to Bahawalpur and proposed that this addition should take the form of the territory between Rori and the border of Bahawalpur, worth, according to Outram, no less than £8,400 a year. Outram concluded that Ellenborough had made a mistake and reported as much to his new superior, General Sir Charles Napier, on 12 November. He asked Napier to refer the matter back to Ellenborough, but Napier did not do this until 30 January 1843.[81]

The arrival of Napier again transformed the situation in Sind, but before looking at his role it is necessary to review Ellenborough's policy there. The centrality of the Governor-General's concept of rewards and punishments is well illustrated in his letter to Napier of 26 August 1842 in which he invited him to take command of the troops in that country. He would, he wrote, never forgive any breach of faith by the Amirs; if they were disloyal he would 'exact a penalty which shall be a warning to every Chief in India'.[82] In the same letter he emphasized his desire to reward the ruler of Bahawalpur. Why he should have selected Bahawalpur for such favour is unclear, since the Nawab had performed no very obvious services. A writer in the *Edinburgh Review* later suggested that it was because the Nawab had written to Ellenborough in 1830:[83] more probably Ellenborough just wanted someone to reward in the same way as he wanted someone to punish; it was almost accidental that the Nawab and the Amirs drew the parts they were to play in the drama which was preparing. As we have seen, arguments relating to trade and communications were also important in Ellenborough's Sind policy; he suggested the construction of a vast and beautiful caravan-serai at Sakhar.[84] Conventional strategic arguments on the other hand played little part. Although he was prepared to follow Wellington's advice to the extent of retaining control of the Lower Indus, he saw no great importance in this aspect in 1842. 'It is idle to suppose', he wrote to Napier in October, 'that any enemy will ever attempt to invade our territories by the Lower Indus.'[85] In March 1843, after receiving Wellington's strange views on the French menace, Ellenborough changed completely and wrote to Fitzgerald, 'I entirely agree with the Duke in thinking that we must hold the mouth of the Indus or submit to the French hold there.'[86] But by that time Ellenborough was in very deep in Sind and under heavy criticism for his policy and clutched at any argument which could be held to justify his conduct towards the Amirs. He had not sought the position which he had then attained in Sind; his own demands, although going well beyond those of Outram, were still relatively modest. Apart from the territorial changes under his rewards and punishment scheme, he wanted for Britain little more than the legalization and confirmation of the existing British position in Sind through the possession of those towns (Karachi, Sakhar, and Bakhar) which would give him control of the Lower Indus. 'These', he wrote to Napier, 'seem to be the only objects we have in Sind on the supposition that we are to retain our hold on the Lower Indus.'[87]

It was Napier who transformed Ellenborough's limited policy into annexation, and, as several writers have perceived, the reasons for this lay in Napier's own personality. 'Conscience', Napier later remarked to Hobhouse, 'should not wear a red coat.'[88] Napier needed an opportunity. He had demonstrated, during his long military career, powers of ruthless decision, which might have been expected to carry him to the top. Instead he had been left to languish in obscure commands, where ill-health, poverty, and frustration had made him a harsh and bitter man. Why this neglect should have existed is uncertain, but a hint was given by Sir Keith Elphinstone, a man of greatly inferior talents, when he described Napier as a mountebank.[89] Napier was a thrusting, ambitious man and he was resented.

Napier had already given some thought to the problem of the defence of India and had elaborated his views in a memorandum which he wrote while still at Bombay in February 1842. He then envisaged four defensive lines. Of these the most advanced line, that of Kabul, Ghazni, Qandahar (corresponding to the future scientific frontier) should be held for the time being, but possibly abandoned later. The second and main line of defence should be on the Indus and should consist of a series of fortified posts on and beyond the river. Control of the mouth of the river was particularly important. To dominate this line the occupation of the Panjab, and certainly of Sind, was necessary. Behind this main defensive line Napier envisaged the creation of two supporting lines: the first running from Jaisalmer to Lahore and the second from Balmer to Ludhiana.[90] Napier's selection of the Indus as the main line of defence is significant because it was the first purely military appreciation which placed the Indus in that position. Although the reformed military view envisaged control of the lower part of the river, and other modifications contemplated an advanced line on the upper part, yet the weight of military opinion still favoured the Satlej and the desert as the principal defence line. Napier's different view may not be unconnected with the fact that he approached the problem from the point of view of Bombay and not from the usual position of Bengal.

Strategic arguments, therefore, led Napier to regard the occupation of Sind as essential. For him morality pointed the same way: the Amirs were barbarians and their country would be much better off under British rule. The final spur was provided by ambition: the winning of Sind could provide wealth and honour at last. Although, as the traveller, von Orlich, observed, Napier did not anticipate any military action when he arrived at Sakhar in October 1842, the General was fully prepared to take advantage of any loophole which appeared.[91]

Napier was the agent of Ellenborough's policy in Sind. In conformity with his policy of subordinating Political Agents to military commanders the Governor-General ordered Outram to hand over all the evidence of the Amirs' alleged treachery to Napier. Without entering into the detail of previous writers it may be said at once that the evidence was unreliable or related only to minor misdemeanours.[92] Napier, however, accepted it unquestioningly and used it to justify the most sweeping demands. These consisted of the cession of those areas which Ellenborough had previously demanded—Karachi, Sakhar, Bakhar, and Sabzalkot, together with Shikarpur; fuel for steamships using the

Indus; and the replacement of the collective Government of Sind by the rule of a single Amir.

In his turn Ellenborough became more greedy and more ready to abandon his former principles of policy. Although dissatisfied with the evidence of treachery, he adopted the method which he had used successfully in Afghanistan, and passed to Napier the responsibility of judging it. At the same time Ellenborough gave Napier a strong hint to proceed on the assumption that the evidence was correct.[93] Acting on the same assumption he presented a revised list of desiderata. His enlarged territorial demands now included Tatha and Rori, the latter town to be combined with its neighbours, Sakhar and Bakhar, to form a great new commercial and strategic metropolis to be called 'Victoria on the Indus'. The districts of Sabzalkot and Bhuj Bara, together with the territory between Sabzalkot and Rori were to go to Bahawalpur. Shikarpur he still refused, because it was on the right bank of the Indus and because its possession might tempt less prudent Governor-Generals in the future to expand further westwards. Sakhar, of course, was also on the right bank, but Wellington had assured Ellenborough that he needed a bridgehead there. Ellenborough also added a series of demands consistent with his commercial aims and concerned with the navigation of the Indus and the establishment of a uniform currency. In return for all this the Amirs were to be freed from their requirement to pay tribute.[94]

Ellenborough's demands had now risen so high that he began to expect that the Amirs would fight. If they did, he informed Peel, they would be expelled to the right bank of the Indus; no one would regret their departure for they were bad rulers.[95] In fact Ellenborough was coming to believe that no settlement would be permanent until the Amirs had been defeated.[96] Being Ellenborough, however, the prospect of battle aroused mixed feelings; victories he loved, but the prospect of reverses filled him with dread. Left to himself he might have lost his nerve and scaled down his demands. But the matter was now out of his hands.

Napier had been given his head and he welcomed the responsibility. He was in a hurry to dispose of the Sind affair before the hot weather made campaigning too dangerous. Treaties embodying the new proposals were sent to Khairpur and Haidarabad. No discussion was permitted. The Khairpur Amirs agreed, but they were not prompt enough for Napier, who advanced his forces. Frightened, the senior Khairpur Amir, Rustam Khan, fled and Napier immediately replaced him with his brother and rival, Ali Murad, so completing a tradition of British policy which had begun with Ross Bell who had aggravated the quarrel between the brothers. Napier pursued Rustam and his companions into the desert, destroyed a fort, and then turned on Haidarabad. The Haidarabad Amirs also panicked and after signing the treaty they took up arms. Napier defeated them at the battle of Miani in February 1843. Only Sher Muhammad of Mirpur remained. Napier had left him out of the negotiations in the hope that 'in the course of adjusting the treaty, something may occur that will enable Your Lordship to remit his Tribute in exchange for land'.[97] Napier's hopes always possessed a terrifying, self-fulfilling quality that was now once more exemplified. Sher Muhammad, alarmed, fought and was defeated at the battle of Haidarabad (26 March 1843). But even before this decisive engagement Napier had already annexed Lower Sind.

Napier's annexation of the territory of the defeated Amirs left Ellenborough with a dilemma. His previous territorial demands had been limited and he had expressly repudiated even the desirability of acquiring more. Now he had at his disposal the whole of the territories of the Haidarabad Amirs. If his former arguments were to be taken seriously he should have renounced them, but he did not do so: Napier's victory, he declared, left him no choice; the subtle Ali Murad of Khairpur would be suitably rewarded and neighbouring states also given some share, but the remainder of Sind would be British.[98]

As a consequence of his decision to confirm the annexation of Lower Sind Ellenborough posed himself a further embarrassing problem in the form of the territories on the right bank of the Indus. Acquisition of any territory on the right bank, it will be remembered, he had carefully forsworn, on the ground that it might prove too great a temptation to his weaker successors. Alas! Ellenborough himself was not proof against temptation and could not bring himself to surrender it all. With his customary resilience, however, he found a convenient strategic justification to explain the change. 'I consider Rivers to be generally bad boundaries', he wrote, 'They were designed to unite nations and states, not to separate them.'[99] Still he worried about future Governor-Generals and at first wished to limit his gains on the right bank to the positions necessary merely to give him command over the river, lest more should tempt 'some imprudent successor of mine to go further'.[100] But temptation once more proved too strong: Napier produced plans for the development of the right bank through irrigation and Ellenborough accepted these and also the consequential security arrangements which were designed to protect the new colonies from tribal attacks.[101] By such means within a very short time the effective frontier had reached the mountains. The border problem, which was to push Britain towards the new relationship with Kalat which

Ellenborough had spurned, was thus the creation of Ellenborough himself.

The annexation of Lower Sind gave rise to the further problem of justifying the act in the eyes of London. It has been shown that financial considerations played no part in Ellenborough's policy before annexation. The introduction of the financial argument immediately afterwards was clearly an attempt to make the act more acceptable to the Court of Directors. The annexation of Sind, he wrote, provided an opportunity to recover the losses incurred by the wars in China and Afghanistan; Sind would yield a net profit of £500,000 a year.[102] But Ellenborough himself probably never set much store on his own arguments and rightly, for Sind lost money until the end of British India.

The prospect of making the annexation of Lower Sind profitable was a significant factor in the modification which took place after March 1843 in Ellenborough's system of rewards and punishments. The first hint that Ellenborough was coming to believe that generosity might have more than its own rewards appeared early in February 1843 when he wrote to Napier that the gift of Sindian territory to Bahawalpur might be used to advance a British strategic interest, namely, the formation of a line of communication between Sakhar and the British territories on the Satlej through a friendly country.[103] Although the complete annexation of Sind made such a line less necessary, Ellenborough continued to explore the possibilities of gaining new advantages.

The defeat of the Amirs gave Ellenborough the opportunity to extend the recipients of rewards to include states other than Bahawalpur. Partly this extension was inspired by the political desirability of sharing the spoils with his neighbours but partly also by the hope of procuring more general advantages for British commerce. He wrote to Napier: 'My object is to make all the surrounding states derive benefit from your victory, and thus to interest them all in the expulsion of the Amirs. I wish also to make our concessions of territory to these powers conduce to the general freedom of commercial intercourse.'[104]

Thus the rewards ceased to be outright donations and became instead items in a series of bargains with neighbouring states. The bargain with Bahawalpur was particularly favourable because a series of fortunate misunderstandings enabled Ellenborough to secure even greater benefits than he had anticipated. In the first instance he reduced the size of the territory which was to be offered to Bahawalpur, having at last learned how much more valuable it was than he had believed. Some land was kept back to form an *arrondissement* for Rori;

some more to establish an irrigation canal; and yet more to compensate Ali Morad for territory which under the new system he was to cede to the Rajput state of Jaisalmer. In exchange for the remainder of the 'gift' the ruler of Bahawalpur agreed to reduce the duties which he levied on land and river traffic; to provide wells and caravanserais on the road from Bahawalpur to Delhi; and to cede to Britain a strip of land along the Satlej. This last gain made possible a useful modification in the customs line of the North-Western Provinces.[105] In such ways the conquest of Sind served minor purposes of British strategy.

Strategy in the conventional sense had played little part in the conduct of British policy towards Sind. Outram's own initiative, whatever had been the motives of personal ambition which might have underlain it, had been avowedly based upon strategic calculation: his argument was that for the security of British India it was necessary to have military control of Sind, including a position at the mouth of the Bolan, and his recommendations had been carefully designed to secure that end. To aid in the achievement of his objectives he had created a lever which had then been torn from his grasp by Ellenborough and employed for a totally different purpose. Ellenborough was relatively unconcerned about military control of Sind, although the subject was by no means excluded from his calculations. But for him, Sind was essentially the school in which the people of India would be taught a great moral lesson. As John Kaye remarked: 'It was deemed expedient at this stage of the great political journey to show that the British could beat someone, and so it was determined to beat the Ameers of Sindh.'[106] For Ellenborough it was not the needs of the external but the necessities of the internal frontier which condemned the Amirs. But condemned them to what? It was prestige, not material gain, which Ellenborough sought and his proposals would have left the Amirs in the enjoyment of relatively much more than the Marathas had been allowed to retain. Ellenborough's muddle and greed allowed the control of events to be wrested in turn from his hands and grasped by the most resolute of the trio—Charles Napier. Napier's career in Sind provides the most instructive example of what unity of judicial, political, and military power could achieve on the imperial frontier. The Amirs were presented simultaneously with unproven accusations and disproportionate sentences; terrorized first into agreement and then into resistance; and, finally, soundly beaten and dispossessed of all political power. Although the annexation of Sind was consistent with Napier's strategic views, it does not seem that the security of the frontier was the main motive which drove on this complex man. It was personal ambition, contempt for his adversary, confidence in his own civilization, and perhaps the simple pleasure of brutal power, which led him to his complete victory. His share of the Sind prize-money was £70,000.

Although it was not the search for the security of the frontier which had brought about the annexation of Sind, the annexation did create a new strategic situation. Sind was no longer a flexible area of operations, a true strategic frontier in depth, as it had been from 1839 to 1842, but an administrative frontier, a fixed border to be held; the strategic frontier itself must lie beyond.

Napier analysed the new frontier from the viewpoint of strategy in a memorandum written in May 1844.[107] He regarded the line which had been established as a very strong one from the viewpoint of defence. His view of the northern section had undergone some modification since 1842, for he now returned to the traditional military preference for the Satlej frontier over that of the Indus. Nevertheless, he foresaw that eventually Britain would be obliged to conquer the Panjab. The northern frontier, however, had been strengthened by the acquisition of control over Sind, which protected its left flank, which secured the bastion of Bahawalpur (something which could not have been done from the Satlej alone), and which gave control over the Indus communications.

Napier was well content with the frontier of Sind itself. 'Sinde in our hands is a compact, impenetrable and well defined frontier', he wrote. Although he preferred river to mountain frontiers, he found the old Sind frontiers satisfactory enough. Moving northwards from the Arabian Gulf this frontier first followed the line of the Rab river, then that of the Halla mountains, and then ran north to Mithenkot at a distance of some forty miles from the Indus, a total length of four hundred and fifty miles. It was the northern stretch of the frontier, bordering the great plain of Kacchi which Napier was later to discover had serious weaknesses which he had not appreciated when he wrote his memorandum.

There were two possible routes, wrote Napier, by which an invading force might enter Sind,—the Bolan (or Mulla) and the Makran. The former could easily be blocked by virtue of the fact that an enemy issuing into Kacchi would find British forces on both his flanks—at Haidarabad in the south and along the Satlej in the north. Against the prevailing current of strategic thinking, Napier singled out the Makran as the greatest source of danger and recommended the fortification of Karachi to block the route. In this, however, Napier remained isolated; in 1853, when there was speculation about a possible Iranian attack, most writers dismissed the idea of any danger from the Makran. Napier himself seems to have ignored the possible uses of sea power. With regard to the general disposition of troops to meet the danger of invasion, Napier contended that, if he could hold his forces in large concentrations, he would be able to manage with far fewer troops than at present, when they were dispersed in small packets throughout the land. This recommendation, possibly influenced by financial pressure, of course looked at the question only from the viewpoint of foreign invasion; the disposition of troops required to meet tribal raiding or the danger of internal commotion would be somewhat different.

Napier's strategic evaluation was essentially a military justification of a static frontier. Some possible objections to his argument have been indicated, but the main criticism, in the light of previous strategic discussion, is that his system took no account of what had always been the main weapon in the armoury of those who argued for an advanced strategic frontier: namely, the danger that an enemy might take up a position beyond the frontier and use it to provoke disturbances within India; in short, that the real danger lay in the internal frontier. Napier, however, did offer, by implication, an answer to this objection. 'It appears to me,' he wrote:

that there will always be peril to the Company while it leaves Native princes on their thrones within our territories. The people are with us, the Princes and nobles against us, and the people will follow their oppressors because they are not sufficiently independent and civilised to think for themselves.

These words go far to resolve the puzzle of Napier's strategic views. The combination of a close border and a levelling policy in India is unmistakable; Napier was a precursor of John Lawrence. The brutal militarism which seemingly characterizes his policy in Sind is misleading; curiously enough, Napier belongs with Thoby Prinsep and all those Civil Servants who came to form the dominant element in official thinking on India, before the Indian Mutiny shattered their illusions. The core of their view of India was that British rule could be made acceptable to the mass of the Indian people and therefore, by implication, free from the danger of disturbance by foreign infection. If their traditional leaders were removed, the Indian masses could be immunized by good government. The rapid conversion of Napier to confidence in the civilizing mission and its beneficent humanitarian and political results testifies to the speed with which this view reasserted itself after the defeat in Afghanistan. The identification of Napier's view of British India also exposes the immense gulf which separated him from Ellenborough. Because of their association in the conquest of Sind and because both afterwards became the heroes of the British Indian right, it is easy to assume that they were two of a kind. In fact their views on India were entirely different. Ellenborough believed he walked on eggshells and needed the support of a native aristocracy to save him from falling; Napier calmly crushed them in the confidence that he could build something better.

During the course of 1842 the tide of withdrawal from Central Asia had been stemmed and in 1843 it was reversed. Withdrawal had been not only a physical but also a mental process; the defeat in Afghanistan had been a painful blow to self-confidence. In such a situation neither strategic argument, not commercial advantage, nor any other appeal could alone halt the erosion of imperial confidence; something else, a psychological bufferstop, was needed and this was provided by the Indus. We have seen how, over forty years, the Indus had come to seem the predestined frontier of British India. In 1838 Britain had advanced her strategic frontier from the Satlej to the Hindu Kush in a single bound and had acquired control of the Lower Indus almost without noticing it. When it came to withdrawal, however, there was a mental resistance to abandoning 'what all will regard as a proper Barrier, the Indus'.[108] To leave the river which had come to be identified as much with the British Empire in India as it was with the Empire of Alexander, would be to admit the prospect of the same imperial mortality that befell the Macedonian Empire. Prestige impelled Ellenborough to strike his blow there.

Catharsis achieved, the Indus had fulfilled its function; as a frontier it never existed except in Ellenborough's mind. Auckland, Outram, and others had always seen the possession of areas beyond the river, and notably of Shikarpur, as essential; the annexation of Sind purged Ellenborough of his own doubts. And, of course, Ellenborough was proved right; the occupation of the right bank of the Indus set up frontier pressures which did not cease until the frontier was pushed up to Quetta. Yet it is impossible to see how, within the objectives which Ellenborough had set himself, control of the right bank could have been avoided. What is most striking about the Sind affair is the unanimity of view about the need for military control of the country; this is the most notable aspect from the strategic viewpoint and, beside it, the great debate about annexation seems an irrelevance. The truth is that there was no debate about the strategic importance of Sind because there was no division on the subject; all that was left to dispute was the morality of annexation.

In England the debate on Sind was conceived wholly in moral terms. Partly this was because, as we have seen, there was no fundamental division in India about the need for control over Sind but partly also because the defence of India was not a matter of political interest in

Britain. The only two aspects of India which ever moved British politicians to heated debate were finance and morality; the first threatened their pockets and the second allowed them to indulge their passion for humbug. The Sind question brought in both.

The Cabinet's quarrel was not with Ellenborough's objectives in Sind—they accepted that military control over Sind should be retained and that this would require a new legal basis—but with his means.[109] When Fitzgerald first read the evidence of the Amirs' alleged treachery and the demands which Ellenborough and Napier proposed to found upon it he was aghast. He saw at once the possible Parliamentary consequences for the Conservative Government. 'I think it would be almost matter for impeachment if we did not interfere in this matter of the Ameers of Sinde', he wrote to Peel.[110] Like later historians, Fitzgerald took the view that the charges against the Amirs were either unproven or unimportant and concluded that Ellenborough and Napier had simply got up a case to justify their seizure of territory. Fitzgerald issued immediate instructions that Ellenborough should confine his efforts to negotiation and eschew violence. The merits of Ellenborough's objectives he did not discuss.[111] Even Wellington was persuaded to add his private injunction to Ellenborough to be patient and avoid either war or the threat of war. Unlike the situation in the past, wrote Wellington, anything that happened in India now was 'an imperial question' and must be approached with caution.[112]

Of course the Cabinet admonitions arrived too late. 'The course of events', replied Ellenborough, 'has settled the Scinde question.'[113] All that the Cabinet could do was to try to ameliorate the evil consequences to themselves of Ellenborough's immorality. It was in these terms that all but Wellington saw the situation. With a cynicism remarkable even in him the Duke now dubbed as a purely local affair what three months earlier he had described as an imperial question.[114] His strong support for Ellenborough played an important part in softening the expression of the Cabinet's wrath. He forced Fitzgerald to tone down his official criticism of Ellenborough's conduct.[115] The President was disgusted, but he was not able to withstand the authority of the Duke, and Peel gave him little support. Formally the Prime Minister took a strong and elevated moral tone. 'No considerations of temporary convenience', he wrote, 'ought in my opinion to prevent us from making what reparation it may be in our power to make.'[116] In practice it was another story.

Peel's policy in the Sind affair, when he dictated the general lines of the policy of the Board of Control, is comprehensible only in terms of political expediency. He never took the obvious step of recalling Ellenborough because that would have exposed the Government to criticism from within the Conservative Party as well as from without. He limited his efforts to persuading Ellenborough to make some concessions to the fallen Amirs: to restore their sovereignty; to restore their lands; or at least to ameliorate their present condition in some way.[117] These efforts he continued right up to the time of the Parliamentary debates of 1844. He explained the reasons to Ripon: 'the extension to them (the Amirs) of favour and kindness is the only mode by which we can reconcile the public mind here to our policy in Scinde—the only mode by which we can prevent the Ameers from becoming the objects of public commiseration and sympathy—*therefore* dangerous.'[118]

The Prime Minister's appeals for clemency failed to move Ellenborough, but perhaps they served their purpose inasmuch as Peel could be seen to be making some effort. For, simultaneously, Peel bent his energies towards persuading others concerned to accept the annexation. The Cabinet, said Hardinge in 1848, had nearly broken over Sind, and Hardinge himself condemned the annexation as unjust and unprofitable. Since Parliament was already in recess by the time sufficient information to debate the question had arrived Peel could leave the problem of how to deal with that institution over until 1844. The most urgent problem was to draw some of the venom from the outraged fangs of the Directors.

The Court of Directors was totally opposed to Ellenborough's policy in Sind. Already incensed by his Afghan policy and by his contemptuous treatment of the Indian Civil Service, many wanted to recall him. Ellenborough, of course, attributed their opposition to the most selfish motives; Tucker, Bayley, and Lyall were all angry because he would not give jobs to their relatives.[119] But this was unjust. The roots of the opposition in the Court were neither selfish nor strategic. Henry Tucker agreed on the need for military control of Sind and supported not only the occupation of the main towns along the Indus but also Shikarpur and Dadar in advance; although he did have a curious objection to the opening of the Indus which he thought might bring in foreign adventurers and arms.[120] But the basis of his criticism and that of his colleagues was morality and finance.

The Court had become apprised of the moral problem by Outram, who had left India after quarrelling with Napier over his conduct of policy in Sind, returned to England in the early summer of 1843, and commenced an effective propaganda campaign against the Ellenborough/Napier policy. He won many supporters in the Court. The financial problem had been a major issue for some time and in his protracted battles to induce Her Majesty's Government to accept financial responsibility for imperial activities in Asia, Tucker had gained much support among his fellow Directors. It was on the question of finance alone that the Court could be a serious threat to the Government because, if it chose, it would provoke a full Parliamentary inquest, either by forcing the Government to go to Parliament for money or by compelling the President to take them to law to overrule them. So inflamed did the subject become in the early part of 1843 that the Cabinet, which rarely spent time on India, was twice obliged to discuss Indian finances. In the end the verdict went against the Court: Peel had his own financial problems and was reluctant to help India and still more to face the inevitable attack on Indian policy in Parliament, while the Chancellor of the Exchequer, Henry Goulburn, was quite opposed. As Fitzgerald commented, 'it is the genius of his office, and the disposition of every other office to throw all that they can upon the Finances of India.'[121] But the financial cost of the Sind operations was an important issue during the later part of 1843, and against the background of previous discussion provided a significant point of pressure.

The opposition in the Court was a serious matter for the Cabinet. The Directors' financial power, their power to recall the Governor-General, and their ability to influence independent Parliamentary opinion could all be used to embarrass the Government. In the summer of 1843 it was touch-and-go whether the Court could be kept under control; on 29 August a motion condemning Ellenborough's policy actually passed in a Secret Court. But the storm blew itself out; the resolution never became public and the Directors did not go on to recall the Governor-General. The Court of Proprietors carried less weight and their criticisms could be ignored.

Having survived the menace of the Directors Peel found his Parliamentary task much easier. A version of the Sind correspondence, carefully edited to remove Napier's stronger expressions, appeared and by a subtle stroke included papers from as early as 1836. This inevitably put the Whigs on the defensive and divided them from the Radicals. The effects were seen in the main debate which took place on a motion moved by Ashley, which was, said Ripon, 'a piece of sentimentality' directed against the treatment of the Amirs.[122] The amendments moved by Roebuck were directed against Auckland rather than against Ellenborough. The result was confusion and in his speech Hobhouse laid down principles of conduct which amounted to a defence of Ellenborough. Peel bought off a little more opposition with a virtual pledge to do something for the Amirs and another ritual dispatch on their behalf was sent to India. But as a political event the Sind question was over; 'in truth', wrote Ripon in July 1845, 'no one now cares a farthing about the question of the Ameers. It has been superseded by other matters more immediately interesting.'[123] But Ripon spoke too quickly.

As a literary phenomenon the Sind question rumbled on for many years. Sir William Napier justified his brother's policy and Outram, supported by his highly-placed friends at Bombay, who contrived to restore him to political employment, replied in kind. Their paper war and their constant disclosures of secrets embarrassed the authorities in London and Calcutta. 'These Napiers are most inconvenient People in the employment of any Government', complained Wellington.[124] Disgusted by Outram's later political activities in Kolhapur, Hardinge was yet more scathing about the Napiers' enemy. 'The fact is he is not a clever or a prudent man—He is cunning and vulgar in diplomacy—but a bold, enterprizing active Partisan in the field', he wrote.[125] The authorities were unable to check the controversy without publishing material which would cause the 'utmost public mischief' involving much more serious consequences than those affecting Napier and Outram.[126] But while the dispute raged, Sind remained in the public eye, a constant embarrassment. The Napier–Outram quarrel obstructed other policies. It was recognized that Sind should be transferred from Bengal to Bombay, but it was seen to be impossible to place Napier under the Bombay Government.[127] Also Napier was recognized as the best man to replace Sir Thomas McMahon as Commander-in-Chief, Bombay, but it was anticipated that the Court would refuse to appoint him to the post, or at least, decline to make him a member of the Council at that Presidency.[128]

Inevitably the treatment of Sind in the Press was dominated by the personalities involved and by the morality of the treatment of the Amirs. One of the few strategic criticisms was contained in an article in the *Edinburgh Review*, which was largely devoted to the moral question. The author criticized the new trans-Indus frontier on the grounds that it would lead to trouble with the Baluchi tribes; and because of the poor rearward communications; frontier troops would be dependent on either a land route across the desert or a sea route which could be closed by the monsoon. The old frontier was much better because it was screened by the desert and the reliable Rajputs. The writer also questioned the commercial possibilities of the Indus valley.[129]

Peel had met the dangerous combination of morality and politics and survived; Ellenborough did not. His wayward habits eventually provoked the Court beyond endurance and they recalled him in April 1844. But in their final indictment Sind formed only one item and Peel was able to avoid unfortunate repercussions for his own Government.

The curious character of the discussion in England, however, by concentrating on morality to the exclusion of strategy, makes it impossible to decide whether men were all agreed on the desirability of the Indus frontier or whether they cared little about the defence of India. Perhaps both propositions are true.

The Panjab Road,
1838–1841

The plot is thickening and I have no hesitation in asserting my belief that we shall find ourselves in a very awkward predicament, unless we adopt measures for
macademizing the road through the Punjab.

W. H. Macnaghten, 10 April 1840.

The pattern of British relations with the state of Lahore is that of those
with Sind writ large. Before 1838 the Panjab had had a fourfold
importance in British strategic planning. It was important as a frontier
state, as a buffer, as potentially the most dangerous ally of other Indian
states, and as an element in the problem of the Indus communications.
Between 1839 and 1842 all these interests were subordinated to the
single problem of communications with Afghanistan. Although the
Sind/Bolan route had the advantage of being under direct British
military control throughout its course, yet it was inferior to the more
direct route to Kabul through the Panjab, a route which also linked
with the main British bases in the Jamna-Satlej Doab. In times of
urgency or when the Bolan route was closed by climate or disturbances
the Panjab road became of the highest importance.

From the Panjab the route led through Peshawar and the Khaibar
Pass to Jalalabad and thence to Kabul, usually via the Khurd Kabul
Pass. Macnaghten himself controlled the most westerly section of this
route; his subordinate, George Macgregor (1810–83), the Political
Agent at Jalalabad, controlled the central section; while the Khaibar
was the responsibility of Captain F. Mackeson (1807–53), the Political
Agent at Peshawar. Like Macgregor, Mackeson was under the orders
of Macnaghten and reported through him. In consequence less information is available concerning the northern route than about the route
through Sind where all the agents but Bean reported directly to the
Supreme Government. No regular agent was established within the
Panjab proper; the responsible Political Agent had his residence in
British-controlled territory at Ludhiana, where Claude Wade, who was
withdrawn at the beginning of 1840 following Sikh complaints of his
behaviour, was succeeded by George Clerk. For different functions

Wade and Clerk were answerable to the Government of the North-Western Provinces and to the Supreme Government.

That part of the northern route which lay within Afghanistan need not detain us long. The most difficult section was that between Gandamak and Kabul. The tribes which dominated this region, principally branches of the eastern Ghilzays, were controlled by the payment of allowances, nominally in return for their services in guarding the passes, in reality that they might not close them. Supplemented by occasional coercive action the system worked fairly well until October 1841 when the tribes closed the passes following the reduction of their allowances. It was the eastern Ghilzays who were chiefly responsible for the massacre of the Kabul force in January 1842.

The Khaibar Pass was of crucial importance. The pass itself, from Jamrud in the east to Dakka in the west, is about thirty-five miles long. It is dominated by various tribes of which the most important are the Afridis, Wrakzays, and Shinwaris. The Sikhs had had numerous confrontations with these tribes, but the first British encounter took place in 1839. According to the plan for the invasion of Afghanistan a mixed force of Sikhs and Shah Shuja's levies under the leadership of Shahzadeh Muhammad Timur, was to advance to Kabul via the Khaibar in support of the main force which penetrated Afghanistan from the side of Quetta. The Khaibar force was accompanied by Claude Wade who was in political control. Attempts to persuade the tribes to concede an uncontested passage failed and, in July 1839, Wade was obliged to force the pass. In the autumn of 1839 a further clash took place when the Khaibar tribes resisted the passage of the troops returning from Kabul under the command of General Keane.[1]

According to the original plan, the need to make regular use of the Panjab/Khaibar route should have ended with the return of the troops. But the decision to retain part of the British force in Afghanistan meant that the route had to be kept open and more permanent arrangements for its control found. Wade's answer was coercion. He had already established a string of posts through the Khaibar. From west to east these were Dakka, where there was a garrison of irregular troops under the command of a cousin of Mackeson; Ali Masjid, the principal post, located at a point where the pass was only forty feet wide and the cliffs virtually perpendicular; and Lala China, where a party of Yusufzays were placed. These posts seemingly offered a basis for military control which Wade proposed to supplement by political control of the tribes—replacing existing chiefs by new men favourable to Shah Shuja.[2]

Auckland disliked Wade's policy of coercion and preferred the same long-term, cheaper policy which he had ordered to be introduced into Upper Sind, namely the gradual conciliations and civilization of the tribes, particularly through employing them in a new Khaibari corps. For the short term Auckland was content to pay allowances such as the Khaibar tribes had been accustomed to receive from time immemorial. He discovered, however, like most Europeans shopping in Asian bazaars, that the price had risen for him. In former days Shah Shuja had paid £6,000 a year; Dost Muhammad, being poorer, had paid only £1,950. The tribesmen disdained this latter sum when it was offered by Wade and also refused Dr. Lord's offer to double it. In the end they accepted £8,000 a year.[3] In this way the chiefs, who appropriated the allowances, were brought off and organized attacks on the convoys were prevented. Sporadic attacks by groups of tribesmen persisted, however, and other means had to be employed to control their depredations.

Mackeson tried a variety of methods to achieve security through the Khaibar. The garrison posts were maintained, detailed information collected, hostages taken, and the dangerous expedient of setting tribe against tribe introduced when the Afridis were played off against the Wrakzays.[4] This had the common result that eventually, at a critical moment, the two tribes united against their tormentor.[5] In short, Mackeson experimented with most of the methods of tribal control which were subsequently permutated by generations of frontier officials and with similar results. The one policy for which he never had the time was Auckland's policy of gradual conciliation. Like his successors, Mackeson usually veered back towards coercion. Unlike the situation in Upper Sind, however, the necessary troops for this work were rarely available because there was no British base at Peshawar. Only once did Mackeson obtain the opportunity to mount a strong punitive expedition. This occurred in February 1841 when a brigade under the command of Brigadier Shelton passed through the Khaibar on its way to Kabul. Macnaghten seized the chance to launch it against the Sangu Khel division of the Shinwari tribe and Shelton duly laid waste their valley and forced them to make some restitution. The effect was only temporary.

Mackeson had only modest success in his role as guardian of the Khaibar. At ordinary times traffic passed through the Khaibar with small loss; at extraordinary times, when passage was essential, control was lost. In August 1840 the Khaibar was urgently required for communications with Afghanistan: the Bolan was closed and the great crisis of September and October 1840, associated with the return of Dost Muhammad, was about to burst in eastern Afghanistan. But

Mackeson was forced to record that 'our control is now merely nominal'.[6] During the crisis of January 1842, when Jalalabad was under siege, the Khaibar was again closed and the post of Ali Masjid evacuated. Mackeson also failed, as General Pollock discovered to his dismay in 1842, to investigate routes linking Peshawar and Jalalabad which could be used in place of the Khaibar, although several such alternatives existed. Mackeson's policy was essentially and inevitably that of control on the cheap. It was a policy forced upon him by Auckland and derived from Auckland's two assumptions: first, that the presence of British troops in Afghanistan was only a temporary phenomenon; and second, that Britain should not become dependent upon the route through the Panjab. In Peshawar Mackeson was entirely dependent upon the goodwill of the Sikhs, although this circumstance was not wholly disadvantageous to him, for the Sikhs were an easy repository of blame when things went wrong.

Through circumstance Mackeson came to represent not only the British interest in communications through the Panjab but a new frontier interest, not in the old frontier of the Satlej, but in the trans–Indus frontier with Afghanistan. For several years prior to 1838 the Sikhs had been pressing into the tribal area along the Afghan frontier. It was this pressure in the Khaibar sector which had precipitated the fateful clash at Jamrud in 1837. In theory the Tripartite Treaty of 1838 and the restoration of Shah Shuja should have inaugurated a new era of stability on the frontier, but in practice the treaty was too imprecise to delimit Sikh and Afghan interests in the disputed areas. The events of 1838 to 1839 changed the situation in an unexpected manner for in consequence of them the Afghan interest acquired a new and powerful spokesman in the person of Macnaghten, aided by his agents, among whom Mackeson played a prominent part.

Macnaghten became the principal exponent of a policy of hostility towards the Panjab. Partly his attitude derived from an earlier period when suspicions of Sikh designs were stronger. In 1838 he fought hard to exclude the Sikhs from a major role in the new strategy and, like most Britons in India, he undoubtedly looked to the ultimate annexation of Lahore and that sooner rather than later. His position in Afghanistan served to fertilize the seeds of his hostility to the Lahore state. Partly this fresh stimulus derived from the need for speedy communications, partly from frontier disputes and partly from a belief, affected or real, that the Sikhs were fomenting disturbances in Afghanistan. Basically, however, the Afghan strategy made the former Sikh buffer not only unnecessary but also a nuisance, interposed as it was between British India and its new main defensive bulwark. Between 1839 and 1841

Macnaghten sought to destroy the Panjab as an independent state.

The principal spokesman of a pro–Sikh policy was George Clerk, who controlled relations with Lahore from 1839 onwards. Clerk was an able man who, as mentioned previously, had found his way on to the frontier principally as a consequence of a scandal, which still affected his career. In his early life he had had the misfortune to run off with another man's wife and had compounded his error by marrying her. His father disowned and disinherited him and as late as May 1843 the Court of Directors still opposed his election to the Governor-General's Council because of the scandal,[7] although Clerk eventually contrived to live it down and to become Lieutenant-Governor of the North-Western Provinces and twice Governor of Bombay. His early career had been spent largely in the Protected Sikh States and whether in consequence of that experience or by virtue of his temperament his attitudes resembled those of an older generation of British officials. He mistrusted the progressive, social-engineering school of Civil Servants who had become prominent since the time of Bentinck and who were strongly represented in the administration of the North-Western Provinces. When Clerk became Lieutenant-Governor he interrupted the development of the levelling land-revenue policies associated with R. M. Bird, James Thomason, and others. Nor were his morals those of the Evangelicals; to Ellenborough's disgust Clerk was not above exploiting the patronage possibilities open to him as a Lieutenant-Governor.[8] Temperamentally Clerk was a conservative, preferring the situation he knew to one based upon abstract reasoning. This quality of his personality, added to the natural consequences of his position, made Clerk the chief supporter of the Sikh alliance throughout the years 1839 to 1843.

It was while he was deputizing for Wade that Clerk first visited Lahore in April 1839 on an errand intended to arrange for the passage of troops and supplies through Lahore territory. At that time Clerk was unable to accomplish anything because of the illness of Ranjit Singh, who died in June 1839. But the prospective return of the British forces through the Panjab made some agreement with Lahore imperative and in August 1839 Clerk returned to Lahore both to offer British condolences on the death of the Maharajah and to make appropriate arrangements for the return of the troops, as well as to deal with certain commercial matters.[9]

On his second visit Clerk discerned much Sikh concern about the tendency of British policy. Since the death of Ranjit Singh speculation about the prospective break-up of the Panjab had become rife in British

India, where it was widely assumed that the contingency could not be long delayed and must be followed by annexation to the Company. The Sikhs were well aware of this alarming speculation and their fears were enhanced by their realization that the new British position in Afghanistan boded ill for the Lahore state. They feared the creation of a permanent right of way across the Panjab for British troops and supplies. In this situation the slack hand of Ranjit's weak successor, Kharak Singh (*c.* 1801–40), might allow incidents which could lead to war.[10] In fact, in October 1838, real power was taken from Kharak, after the murder of his favourite, Chet Singh, and passed to Kharak's son, Nau Nihal Singh, who was strongly supported by Dhian Singh. Even so Kharak resented his subordination and it became an object with the Nau Nihal faction to prevent the Maharajah seeking British help to restore his authority. Other factions also appealed to Britain: Ranjit's illegitimate son, Sher Singh, offered the Cis-Satlej lands in return for British help, while Kharak's wife, Chand Kaur, offered Kashmir and other territories.[11]

In these circumstances Clerk was pressed to give an assurance that no more British troops would cross the Panjab after the return of Keane's force. Such an assurance was indeed consistent with the original plan and Clerk gave it. Auckland, however, chose to interpret the assurance as signifying merely that the consent of the Sikh Darbar would be asked before further troops were sent across the Panjab.[12] Although Auckland did not propose that the Panjab should form the main route for communications, he wished, nevertheless, in the changed situation, to ensure that the route was available if required. Auckland's interest was still essentially concerned with communications alone.

Macnaghten's views had already come to comprehend more than purely logistical considerations and he now began a verbal onslaught upon the Sikhs which gained momentum during 1840. Macnaghten laid four principal charges against the Sikhs. These were that General Avitabile, the Italian Governor of Peshawar, had taken independent action against the Khaibar tribes; that the Sikhs had failed to make available the five thousand troops which they had agreed to supply under the Tripartite Treaty in return for the £20,000 to be paid by Shuja; that the Sikhs were claiming lands which were Afghan according to the treaty; and that the former Barakzay rulers of Peshawar, who were now feudatories of the Sikhs at Kohat, were actively conspiring against Shah Shuja.[13] All these actions, Macnaghten claimed, demonstrated the hostility of the Sikhs.

None of Macnaghten's charges was worthy of serious consideration.

Avitabile was obliged to protect the citizens of Peshawar and if Mackeson could not control the Khaibar tribes it was not unreasonable that the Sikh Government should take independent action. Mackeson was certainly of little help to Avitabile. On one occasion the British agent claimed from the Sikhs a sum of £4,000, representing the value of plundered property. Subsequently he discovered that the guilty men were Afridis, but instead of withdrawing the claim, he maintained it, for political reasons, meantime refusing to give Avitabile the names of the plunderers so as to prevent the Sikh Governor from taking any action.[14] Avitabile's brutal efficiency did indeed have some success in pacifying the area and together with his hospitality won him some popularity among British officers travelling in the district. One such observer described large treble gibbets at the ends of the city, each decorated with seventeen or eighteen malefactors, and commented' 'I believe there was very little ceremony made with them. If a man looked sulky he was strung up at once, in case he should be disaffected.'[15] Macnaghten's point about the five thousand Sikh troops was sheer casuistry. In 1838 it had been understood that the reference to the Sikh troops was merely a formality to obscure the fact that Shuja was to pay tribute. To supply such a force would have cost the Sikhs three times as much as they received. In any case Macnaghten did not want Sikh troops, at least until he was desperate in November 1841.[16] The frontier issue was debatable. The Sikh claim was certainly justified according to the Persian version of the treaty; the English version left the matter in doubt.[17] The most difficult, and to Macnaghten the most important charge, was that which concerned the Barakzays, whom Macnaghten described as 'the sole cause of the serious disturbances which have prevailed in Affghanistan since His Majesty's accession'.[18] Specifically he claimed that they had aided rebels in Bajaur and that they had sheltered refugee chiefs from Afghanistan. The first charge against the Barakzays was false; they had had no connection with the disturbances in Bajaur. The second charge would have made traditional hospitality a crime.

In truth there was no good evidence against the Sikhs. Even if their feudatories had been intriguing in Afghanistan there was nothing to suggest that the Sikh Government had countenanced their activities. When Clerk pressed him to produce a full statement of the evidence against the Sikhs Mackeson was reduced to constructing an argument from first principles: the Sikhs want Swat, Buner, and Kashmir; therefore they want rebellion in Afghanistan; therefore they must provoke it.[19] Macnaghten admitted that the evidence was slight, but argued that it was dangerous to wait for more evidence before taking action.[20]

It is impossible to avoid the conclusion that the charges against the Sikhs were put forward to justify the actions Macnaghten proposed. He wanted to get rid of the treaty provision for the payment of £20,000 a year by Shuja to the Sikhs; he wanted to force the Sikhs to abandon their frontier claims; and he wanted the Barakzays removed from the frontier. If necessary he would go to war for these demands and if war came it would be welcome, for the Sikh territories west of the Indus could then be annexed to Afghanistan.[21] Presumably the remainder would go to British India. Ironically, Macnaghten's policy, also advocated by T. C. Robertson in Agra, was basically that of Burnes in 1837. Afghanistan, under new management, was a better buffer than Lahore and should be enlarged at Sikh expense. But Macnaghten's charges also served to cloak the weakness of the Afghan position; if the Sikhs could be held responsible for the disturbances in Afghanistan, not only would the Afghan strategy be cleared of an important doubt but some possible blame could also fall from the shoulders of Macnaghten.

Auckland was asked to choose between the arguments of Macnaghten and those of Clerk. Both, he decided later, were guilty of exaggeration, but Macnaghten much more so than his rival.[22] At the time he avoided choosing between them and fixed upon the single issue of communications. Although the annexation of the Panjab might ultimately make communications more secure, a quarrel with Lahore would undoubtedly jeopardize the route in the short term.[23] A war would be expensive and enough money had already gone on defence.[24] Therefore, as long as a reasonably stable government existed in Lahore, such as might preserve the security of the Panjab road, Auckland would seek peace, even if suspicions of Sikh intrigues proved to be justified. 'Even if we catch something of the spirit upon this subject which is felt upon the other side of the Khaibar', he wrote to Robertson in May 1840, 'every exhibition of it should be carefully repressed.'[25] Nevertheless, Auckland made some characteristic concessions to the strong pressures for a harsher policy which were felt not only from Kabul, but from within India and from London, where Hobhouse himself was a keen supporter of the eventual annexation of the Panjab. Auckland decreed that the Lahore Government was to be told to stop Avitabile interfering in the Khaibar. The £20,000 should not be paid to the Sikhs and an attempt should be made to persuade the Sikhs to cancel the relevant clause, which Auckland had never liked. Although at first he was prepared to allow the matter of the disputed frontier claims to go to arbitration, he eventually upheld the Afghan claims, arguing that ownership should depend upon actual possession in 1838. Also, although he had at first been prepared to allow the Barakzays to remain at Kohat, providing they expelled the refugee Ghilzay chiefs, he eventually took a firmer line on this point after one of the Ghilzays had escaped and returned to Afghanistan. After some hesitation Auckland demanded that the Barakzays should be removed from the frontier and their rent-free lands resumed.[26] Clerk was instructed to present these demands to the Sikhs when he visited Lahore in May 1840. Despite his general opinions, Auckland had gone a long way along the road to which Macnaghten had beckoned him. However, Auckland still made the safety of communications the acid test of Sikh intentions. Above all, Clerk was to secure free communications across the Panjab. He was to inform the Sikhs that a refusal to allow convoys to cross their territory would be regarded as an unfriendly act. In effect he was to say 'we heartily desire to be friends. If however our rights are withheld you must expect us as enemies and our enmity will be prompt and vigorous.'[27]

Clerk did not like the instructions he had been given. He disbelieved the charges against the Sikhs and thought that the disturbances in Afghanistan were due to conditions in Afghanistan and not to Sikh action.[28] Accordingly, he saw no merit in pressing Auckland's demands, especially after he received satisfactory assurances from Nau Nihal Singh.[29] Instead he allowed negotiations on the demands to drag on slowly over the succeeding months. The Sikhs agreed to stop Avitabili's interference with the Khaibar tribes, but were reluctant to concede the other demands and Clerk sympathized with their views. He suggested that the territorial question should be left to arbitration, as Auckland had originally proposed, and supported the Sikh desire to retain the clause providing for the payment of £20,000 by Shuja while they agreed not to ask for the money.[30] The most awkward question was still that of the Barakzays. On this point Auckland had now raised his demands still higher and wanted the surrender of the remaining Ghilzay refugees. Without guarantees for the Ghilzays the Sikhs were unwilling to agree to this demand and they wished to retain the Barakzays on the frontier where they were a valuable element in the Sikh system of tribal management; a rising followed their eventual removal. But Auckland, who was willing to let the other demands rest, made this point a test of Sikh sincerity.[31] The evidence against the Barakzays, he asserted inaccurately, was based on 'notorious and undeniable facts.'[32] Accordingly, while on the one hand Auckland rejected Macnaghten's more extreme demands for the march of British troops across the Panjab and for the establishment of a British military base there, on the other, he prodded a reluctant Clerk into taking a firmer line with the Lahore Government.

It was at this moment, in August 1840, that the pressure from Afghanistan was suddenly increased. In the spring of 1840 Macnaghten had employed the bogey of a Russian threat in Turkestan as justification for his arguments for drastic action against the Sikhs; in the summer he utilized the return of Dost Muhammad, an event which he connected with an extensive conspiracy allegedly involving the Barakzays and the Sikh Government.[33] The letters which Macnaghten claimed proved the truth of his contentions were probably forged and by no means convincingly implicated the Sikhs. The danger, however, was imminent and Auckland dared not wait to investigate. He accepted that there was 'clear proof' that the Barakzays were involved and some reason to suppose that the Lahore Government might also be implicated.[34] He began to prepare for a possible war with the Panjab, realizing, however, that a war would prevent him sending the reinforcements across the Panjab which were urgently needed in Afghanistan. Considering the defence of Afghanistan to be more important than a settlement with Lahore, Auckland announced that if the Sikhs would concede an immediate passage he would not ask for more. In the event the Sikhs granted the passage and also withdrew the Barakzays from Kohat and surrendered the Ghilzays. The crisis had passed and Auckland later became satisfied that Macnaghten's alleged proof of Sikh treachery was wholly inadequate.[35]

Undeterred by his failure to bring the Sikh question to a head in the summer of 1840, Macnaghten tried again in November. On 5 November Kharak Singh died and, immediately afterwards, returning from the funeral, his son, Nau Nihal Singh, was killed in an accident. Macnaghten saw his opportunity. Flourishing the standard work by Vattel on international law he argued that the 1838 Treaty was now dissolved and that the Afghan claims could be pressed. In a truly remarkable piece of misrepresentation he concluded: 'It cannot be supposed that in making over to the Maharajah Runjeet Singh and his posterity the countries and places specified in the first article of the Tripartite Treaty Shah Shoojah should have intended to alienate these possessions for ever in favour of a new dynasty.'[36] Setting aside Macnaghten's presumption that Ranjit Singh's dynasty was now extinguished, Shah Shuja had had no say in the 1838 Treaty. He had merely been required to accede to a bargain hammered out between Macnaghten and Ranjit Singh from which Macnaghten now wished to withdraw. As Hobhouse, no Sikh-lover himself, commented when supporting Auckland's sharp rejection of Macnaghten's demands, 'It is rather dangerous having to deal with a diplomatist that goes about with Vattel in one hand and a sword in the other.'[37]

In the Panjab the deaths of Kharak and Nau Nihal Singhs had brought about a new situation. The ability of Nau Nihal had held promise of a stable government, but after his death the Lahore state slipped steadily towards anarchy. A Regency, under the control of Rani Chand Kaur, widow of Kharak, was created for the unborn child of Nau Nihal, but in January 1841 the Regency was overthrown by Sher Singh (1807–43), an illegitimate son of Ranjit Sing. Sher Singh was aided by the Jammu faction and by the European officers in the Panjab, but he owed his elevation primarily to the army which was suitably rewarded and duly encouraged in its new-found ambitions. In opposition to Sher Singh were the leading Sikh chiefs, grouped around the Sindhanwalia family, of which the leading personalities were Lehna Sing, Attar Singh, and their nephews, Ajit and Shamsher Singh. This opposition was led by Rani Chand Kaur until she was murdered in June 1841. Her hoped-for grandchild was either stillborn or murdered. With the loss of its figureheads the Sindhanwalia faction was scattered: Lehna was imprisoned and Attar and Ajit fled to British territory. By the middle of 1841 the Panjab had regained a temporary but uncertain stability. Its eventual disintegration, however, seemed more probable.

Throughout the contest between Sher Singh and Chand Kaur Auckland had remained resolutely neutral. Sher Singh's victory changed the situation, for there seemed no real alternative to him; if Sher Singh were overthrown, anarchy was inevitable. Auckland had to decide whether he would stand back and allow anarchy in the Panjab or whether he would throw British support to Sher Singh in an effort to preserve a stable government in Lahore. If he chose to intervene he had also to settle the price of British aid.

Clerk advised Auckland to intervene to maintain the Lahore state. Clerk saw the Panjab not merely as a staging post on the northern route to Afghanistan, nor even as just a potential threat to the security of the Satlej frontier, but as a valuable buffer state in its own right. As a Hindu buttress on a Muslim frontier a powerful, independent Sikh state was a potential source of great strength to British India.[38] Clerk recommended that Auckland should offer Sher Singh assistance or indeed intervene independently if such action were required to restore order. This could easily be done, he argued on 4 February, with a small force.

Macnaghten urged Auckland to intervene to dismember the Lahore state. In the spring of 1841 the increasing disorders in the Panjab threatened the security of British communications with Afghanistan; at Attock a clash took place involving mutinous Sikh troops and a convoy under the charge of George Broadfoot which was escorting the family of

Shah Shuja from Ludhiana to Afghanistan. Mackeson wished to use this incident to justify the annexation of the territory on the right bank of the Indus to Afghanistan and Macnaghten supported him at least to the extent of demanding Swat and Buner.[39] Despite appearances, it is evident that Macnaghten's Panjab policy was not primarily based upon the need to secure communications, for a demand such as he proposed would have done nothing to safeguard the route to Afghanistan but might well have precipitated a war which would have closed the road. Macnaghten's policy was evidently hinged upon the desirability of strengthening the Afghan buffer at the expense of the Lahore buffer which now presented itself as an alternative. Clerk's solution to the problems presented by the Attock incident was quite different; he would have restored the Barakzay chiefs to Peshawar and employed them, as in the past, to keep order on the frontier.[40]

Once again Auckland refused to accept either the views of Clerk or those of Macnaghten. Whereas Clerk saw the problem of the Panjab in terms of the maintenance of the Hindu buffer and Macnaghten saw it in terms of the development of the Afghan buffer, Auckland obstinately insisted on regarding it primarily from the short-term viewpoint of communications. He considered the right of free passage to have been conceded in 1840 and as long as the road remained open he wanted little else from Lahore—merely some guarantee that the Lahore Government would not interfere in the Protected Sikh States, the abrogation of the 'tribute' article in the 1838 Treaty, a few commercial concessions, and a limitation of the number of foreign officers employed in the Lahore army. He would intervene in the Panjab only in the event of a complete breakdown in the Lahore state which would jeopardize communications. In that event Auckland did envisage a partition of the Panjab in which the Sikh territories on the left bank of the Satlej would fall to Britain and those on the right bank of the Indus to Afghanistan. In this last possibility Auckland inclined towards the views of Macnaghten and Burnes, but he encountered opposition from Herbert Maddock, Thoby Prinsep, and possibly John Colvin who wanted Peshawar to be retained by Britain.[41] It is evident that this latter group were beginning to think of the future not in the Clerk/Macnaghten terms of a choice between Sikh and Afghan buffers, but in terms of a new British frontier in the north-west which should be the first priority in a new scheme of defence. As for the remainder of the Lahore state, lying between the Satlej and the Indus, Auckland envisaged that this would be nominally independent but in practice under British control exercised through a subsidiary force and through British guarantees to the Sikh chiefs.[42] On 18 February Clerk was informed that if the breakdown which he thought to be inevitable and which Auckland thought unlikely did occur he could offer British military assistance to Sher Singh on the terms outlined above, plus a payment of £40,000[43] Auckland made it clear, however, that he did not want to intervene at all.

Clerk misinterpreted his instructions with unfortunate results. In March 1841 he offered British intervention on the onerous terms outlined by Auckland to Sher Singh's agents at Ludhiana. The Sikhs naturally refused the offer, which inevitably served to enhance their suspicions of British intentions. Clerk's unauthorized action in taking the initiative in making the offer gave the false impression that Auckland wanted to intervene, although, quite apart from his own words, the Governor-General's actions, as shown in his attitude to the Attock convoy incident, revealed the contrary. Misled by Broadfoot's exaggerated reports, Auckland at first derived the impression that the situation was so bad as to endanger the communications which were his first priority. Accordingly, Auckland began to make preparations for a war with Lahore in the cold weather.[44] When it subsequently became clear that the situation was not so desperate as he had supposed and after Avitabile had suppressed the mutiny among the Sikh troops, Auckland postponed his war plan and was content to return to distant but friendly relations with Lahore.[45]

Auckland made one intervention in Lahore affairs in 1841 which was not dictated by consideration for communications. This action was intended to check Sikh expansion towards Tibet and was prompted by other British Indian strategic and commercial considerations. The acquisition of the Jammu Hills and of Kashmir had given the Lahore state an interest in Ladakh, which was conquered and completely subdued by Wazir Zorawar Singh Kahluria (1786–1842) between 1834 and 1839. Although nominally representing the Lahore Government, Zorawar was in reality the agent of Gulab Singh of Jammu, and the Lahore Government had virtually no control over his activities. By 1839 Zorawar had made Ladakh into a secure base of operations and in that year he attacked Iskardu in Baltistan (Little Tibet). The following year he turned his attention to the north-east, to western Tibet, which he attacked in force in 1841.[46] This expansion had two objectives, apart from the acquisition of territory and the distant lure of gold. First Gulab wanted to recover control of the shawl wool trade, the weaving of which material had once been the major source of Kashmir prosperity. Sikh exploitation had caused the emigration of weavers and the wool and been diverted to the British-protected state of Bashahr and thence to the plains. Second Gulab wished to be revenged upon the

Chinese whose actions against Sikh traders at Yarkand had damaged the trade of Kashmir.[47]

Before 1841 Britain had paid little heed to Dogra expansion into the hills and appeals from the rulers of Ladakh and Iskardu had been ignored. Only in 1840 had Clerk asked the Lahore Government to divert Zorawar from Yarkand. But the threat to Bashahr now caused Auckland to listen to the repeated warnings of the Political Agents at Sabathu, who had been the principal sources of information on developments on this sector of the northern frontier. Auckland now came to believe that if it were not checked Sikh expansion in the north might not only deprive British India of a valuable trade but would also create a new threat to the security of British India, by forming a direct land link with Nepal. In 1837 to 1838 Auckland had been much exercised in his mind by the frightening prospect of an anti-British coalition of Indian states led by Lahore and Nepal and had viewed contacts between the Gurkhas and the Sikhs with great suspicion. He had no wish to see that putative alliance revived in the form of a direct threat to a vulnerable area of British India's northern frontier.[48] Before Auckland decided what action to take he wanted more information and Clerk dispatched his assistant, Lieutenant Joseph Davey Cunningham (1812–51), to collect information and to try to persuade Zorawar to lift restrictions on trade. While Cunningham's mission progressed, alarm about Sikh activities in the north mounted and Auckland now began to fear that Zorawar's campaign might lead to a Chinese counterstroke which would involve Britain, or even that an alliance between China and Nepal might be formed. Perhaps the vital argument, however, was that advanced by Robertson and his Secretary in the Agra Government, James Thomason (1840–53). The loss of trade might be trifling, they argued, but the loss of prestige if Britain tamely submitted to the injury, would be unbearable.[49] The weight of the arguments clearly indicated that it was the internal frontier, not the external, which was the vital consideration. Accordingly, in October 1841 Auckland instructed Clerk to demand that Zorawar Singh should be withdrawn; if he were not Britain would attack the Panjab.[50]

The Lahore Government gladly agreed to withdraw Zorawar, but it was not the orders of Lahore which brought the Rajput general's career to an end. He was defeated and killed by the Chinese on 12 December 1841, and the Sikh position in the distant hills collapsed. The resultant crisis had important consequences in 1842, for Gulab was anxious to go to Kashmir to re-establish his position in the region just at the time when Britain was anxious for his presence and co-operation at Peshawar, the advanced base for Pollock's army operating against

Afghanistan. In May 1842, however, Gulab was allowed to leave and rebuild his northern empire. A peasant revolt in Ladakh was suppressed and in August 1842 the Chinese army was held by the Sikhs. On 17 September 1842 an agreement between the Sikhs and Chinese virtually restored the position which had existed prior to 1839 by which the Sikhs controlled half of Ladakh directly and half indirectly through its own Raja.[51] The stabilization of the northern frontier therefore owed little to the endeavours either of the British or the Lahore Governments, but represented a compromise between the Jammus and the Chinese. Three points of significance to British policy emerge from the episode, however.

The first consequence was a strengthening of British control over the hitherto neglected Hill States of the northern frontier as a means of diminishing further threats to their security; this was undertaken on the recommendation of Cunningham. The second was a beginning of a process of rethinking British policy towards the Jammus and therefore towards the Panjab. Hitherto the Jammus had been seen as an influential faction in the Lahore Government, possibly hostile towards British influence. Their possessions in the hills had been regarded as a source of their strength in Lahore politics, but not as something of direct concern to Britain. For the first time the Zorawar episode made British policy-makers conscious that what happened in the northern hills could have a direct effect on British India. The first reaction, and that which dominated the 1841 crisis was one of hostility to Jammu ambition. It was Clerk who first began to see that the Jammu position in the hills might be turned to British advantage and to visualize, in the event of the break-up of the Panjab, the emergence of a Dogra Hill State extending through the hills from the Satlej to the Indus. Such a state could provide a second Hindu buffer. In 1842, after the collapse of the Afghan position this concept came to play a role in British thinking. The third point concerns the policy of Auckland towards the Panjab. Auckland's reaction to the Zorawar episode shows the second strand in his thinking about the Panjab. He viewed the Lahore state first and foremost in relation to communications, but he never lost sight of the major problem of British Indian defence, the protection of the internal frontier. For these two he would go to war with the Panjab, but he would not do it for the protection of the external frontier alone or to bolster any strategy designed to provide for defence against an external foe.

Auckland's policy towards the Panjab was essentially negative. As he made clear in November 1841, he still wanted the old alliance with the Sikhs and hoped that any future interference by Britain would be designed to preserve the Lahore state.[52] Nevertheless, by his policy he had contributed to the eventual downfall of Lahore, for if he rejected Macnaghten's policy of partition he had also rejected Clerk's policy of positive intervention. He had contented himself with limiting Sikh expansion—against Sind, against the Afghans, and against the Chinese. Whereas Wade and Clerk understood that the military character of the Lahore state made some outlet for expansion necessary and were prepared to accommodate this need in order to enjoy the advantages of the presence of a powerful Hindu state on the north-western frontier of British India, Auckland deplored Lahore militarism and did all he could to repress it. Inevitably the restrictions imposed by Britain contributed to the inclination of the Sikh army to turn its energies towards the control of the state itself. Even so Auckland might yet have accomplished the change in the character of the Lahore state which he desired by giving full support to the Jammus, but he mistrusted them and gave shelter to their principal rivals, the Sindhanwalias.[53] Nevertheless, positive action was contrary to Auckland's temperament; wherever possible he preferred to let events carry him along.

Auckland was supported in his Panjab policy by the authorities in England, who, however, showed no real enthusiasm for it. In 1841 the Cabinet considered the problem of Lahore and decided to support Auckland's policy of non-intervention as being the only safe course in the circumstances.[54] Hobhouse personally favoured a more active policy and did not believe that the policy of non-intervention could be maintained. Earlier, in November 1840, he had blithely advocated war with Lahore, Nepal, and Oudh.[55] But in his public attitudes Hobhouse was obliged to take account of British Indian means and of public and Parliamentary opinion in England. A more careful assessment was that of the Chairman of the Court, William Butterworth Bayley, who favoured the policy advocated by Maddock and others in India, namely, to withdraw from Afghanistan and take the Panjab instead. Through control of the Panjab Britain would acquire a more efficacious influence in Afghanistan than was conferred by the presence of a military force in that country.[56]

As long as the British position in Afghanistan was maintained the question of communications was the major factor in British policy towards the Panjab. By postponing a decision on the future of the Afghan position in March 1841 Auckland had ensured that the determination of future policy would be left to his successor. Of the three possible lines of development which had been offered to him he had moved steadily away from Macnaghten's proposal to aggrandize Afghanistan. He had never liked it and his diminishing enthusiasm for the Afghan strategy made its adoption highly unlikely. But he had not moved towards Clerk's rival proposal for the reinvigoration of the Hindu buffer strategy. The tendency of his mind had been towards the third possibility—that recommended by Bayley, Maddock, and others—namely, the extension of British control up to and beyond the Indus. But when the Afghan disaster occurred this was still no more than an inclination.

The Hindu Buffer, 1842–1845

The Governor General in Council is convinced that a strong Sikh government as in Runjeet Singh's time, united to us by a common interest in resisting Mahomedan aggression is the most prudent mode of occupying the Punjab instead of advancing the British outposts 300 miles beyond our present Frontier, extending it on one side to the extreme of the Khyber Pass and on the other touching the confines of Chinese Tartary.

> Currie to Broadfoot, 10 September 1845.

The sudden collapse of the Afghan buffer policy at the end of 1841 was the signal for the emergence of a new British policy towards the Panjab. This new policy did not take shape at once for, in the immediate aftermath of the Kabul rising, British policy was governed by short-term considerations only and changes in the military situation continued to affect policy towards the Panjab for some time thereafter. The flighty mind of the new Governor-General, Lord Ellenborough, was also an obstacle in the path of a consistent Panjab policy. But under the guidance of George Clerk, the dominant personality on the North-West Frontier between 1842 and the end of 1843, a coherent view of the Panjab did take shape. Unsurprisingly, this took the form of a desire to preserve the Panjab as a Hindu buffer on a Muslim frontier.

Auckland's first impulse, on hearing of the uprising in Kabul was to seek help where he could. He abandoned the policy of reserve which he had pursued throughout 1841 and declared himself in favour of an 'unimpaired and working intimacy' with the Sikhs and promised full support for the Lahore Government.[1] Under the impact of the full revelation of the extent of the Afghan disaster and in the conviction that it was neither possible nor desirable to restore the Afghan position, Auckland's attitude towards the Panjab changed. The Sikhs were not dependable; to remain at Peshawar was too dangerous; British forces should retire behind the Satlej. Colvin sketched out a possible scenario for what might follow. With British help the Jammus might become established in the hills, from the Jhelum to Peshawar. Britain herself would take the Derajat, that is the southern section of the trans-Indus possessions of Lahore. The Sikh army could be left in control of the remainder of the Panjab, that is, the area between the Satlej and the Jhelum and Indus, and in the course of time a British-controlled subsidiary force could be imposed upon this area. Prinsep would have imposed the subsidiary force on the Sikh area much sooner. Auckland, on the other hand, would have done nothing at all in the Panjab. He appeared to believe that after British troops had withdrawn the Lahore state would collapse between its internal conflicts and the Afghan onslaught which he thought inevitable. A period of anarchy would supervene and Britain would intervene only when this had subsided.[2]

These gloomy speculations in Calcutta had little effect on the actual conduct of British policy towards the Lahore state. These affairs were under the effective control of Clerk who used his own initiative to persuade the Sikhs to help build up a relief force at Peshawar. The Kabul disaster had, of course, only confirmed Clerk in his opinion of the value of the Sikh buffer. He it was who worked to heal the factious divisons at Lahore and in November 1842 effected an apparent reconciliation between Sher Singh and the Sindhanwalia chiefs. It was Clerk and his assistant, Henry Lawrence, who persuaded Gulab Singh to co-operate at Peshawar, promising to confirm him in his hill possessions in the event of the break-up of the Panjab. It was Clerk also who was the originator of the plan to develop the Sikh state by extending it to Jalalabad.

On taking over as Governor-General Ellenborough was strongly attracted by Clerk's plan to extend the Sikh buffer westwards into Afghanistan. Ellenborough hoped to divert Sikh expansion from Tibet to the right bank of the Indus and when it seemed necessary to secure the co-operation of Gulab, even offered to assist the Sikhs against the Chinese in order that they might be able to release troops for service in Afghanistan. Intermittently, although in the end the project came to nothing, Ellenborough supported the Jalalabad plan. He even offered to pay the £20,000 tribute due from Shah Shuja under the 1838 Treaty and the long-withheld Sikh share of the contribution to the Afghan expedition which had unwillingly been made by the Amirs of Sind.[3] But these various expedients all bore the marks of their desperate origin and did not amount to a formed policy. Indeed they contained elements of apparent contradiction, for support for Gulab ran counter to the strengthening of the Sikh state. Not until the withdrawal from Afghanistan was completed at the end of 1842 did Ellenborough feel free to examine British policy towards the Panjab with detachment.

Ellenborough wanted to retain the Sikh alliance as the linchpin of the British strategic system in the north-west.[4] So he declared in

January 1843, and formally he never withdrew from this policy which was recommended alike by Clerk, by the state of Indian finances, and by the considered military view of Wellington and others, which still maintained that the Satlej formed the best military frontier for British India. Ellenborough conceded that events in the Panjab might make this policy unworkable and in these circumstances he would reject both Auckland's final policy of permitting the Panjab to disintegrate into separate states under indirect British control and Clerk's policy of intervention to bolster the Lahore Government. If civil war came to the Panjab Ellenborough contemplated intervention, annexation, and the establishment of the British frontier on the Himalayas.

In the latter part of 1843 events in the Panjab seemed likely to hasten the demise of the Anglo–Sikh alliance. On 15 September the Sindhanwalias slew Sher Sing, Dhian Singh, and Pertab Singh in an attempted *coup*. Led by Sucheit Singh, younger brother of Dhian Singh, and his nephew Hira Singh, son of the murdered Prime Minister, the Jammus rallied, secured army support, and on 17 September struck back at the Sindhanwalias. In the course of three days nearly one thousand men were killed and a new government emerged under the nominal rule of the infant Dalip Singh (1838–93), allegedly the son of Ranjit Singh. Real power was in the hands of the new First Minister, Hira Singh, who ignored the claims of two other supposed sons of Ranjit Singh, Peshaura Singh (1818–45) and Kashmira Singh (1819–44), because they were too old for him to control. The main threat to Hira's power came from the army, which was now the true arbiter of power in the Panjab and increasingly conscious of this fact.

These events precipitated a reassessment of British policy. Clerk was no longer in direct control of relations with Lahore; in June 1843 he had been promoted to head the Agra Government and at the end of the year returned to England. With no great confidence in the wisdom of his choice Ellenborough chose to replace him Lieutenant-Colonel A. F. Richmond, a soldier who had distinguished himself in Afghanistan and thereby secured the favour of Ellenborough. A man of considerable personal charm, Richmond was indecisive, and knew nothing either of diplomacy or of Indian languages. He was, wrote James Abbott, his subordinate, 'the mildest and kindest of men but cautious in the extreme.'[5] Richmond became wholly dependent upon his subordinates, notably upon Joseph Cunningham. Through the influence of Cunningham and others the ideas of Clerk remained a persistent element in British strategic thought. Richmond, however, could not claim the authority which Clerk had won and Ellenborough began to look elsewhere for advice. The Governor-General was immediately attracted by the analysis propounded by a French adventurer in the service of the Lahore state, General Ventura. Ventura predicted the break-up of the Lahore state, the independence of the Jammus in the hills and of the Governor Mulraj in Multan, the recovery by the Afghans of the right bank of the Indus, and Sikh rule only in the rump of the Lahore state.[6] In this situation Ellenborough envisaged, rather in the manner of the Auckland scenario which he had earlier rejected, that Britain would establish a protectorate over each of the separate successor states.

There was an ambiguity about Ellenborough's Panjab policy in the autumn of 1843. In letters to various correspondents at this time he emphasized different points so as to give the impression that he contemplated almost any action, or even no action at all. But amid the confusion which was such a feature of his public intellectual processes it is possible to detect a steady drift towards acceptance of the ultimate desirability of annexation as the answer to the Panjab problem. One important factor in pointing him in this direction was the annexation of Sind. Possession of the Lower Indus was both an incentive and a means to the control of its northern tributaries; Multan was now within his grasp. The occupation of Sind had thrust forward the left flank of the British defensive position in north-western India and thereby drawn attention to the situation on the right flank. Wellington, although he had argued strongly in favour of the Satlej frontier, endorsed this line of thought by urging Ellenborough to push the military frontier in the hills as far westwards as possible in order to protect the right flank of the Satlej position. Ellenborough employed this military refinement to open the path to a major expansion of British India. Britain could not occupy the Panjab plains without occupying the hills because to omit the latter precaution would expose the entire British right flank. Therefore if Britain were obliged to intervene in the Panjab she must take hills and plains. This, however, would be too much to digest, Ellenborough informed Wellington, and in his official dispatch on the subject to Richmond, Ellenborough employed for the time being the military argument as one in favour of the traditional policy of preserving the Panjab buffer. The Lahore state was the most convenient neighbour for British India; the alternative was to place the western frontier against that of the Afghans and the northern frontier on the summit of the Himalayas: There were no other stopping-places once the Satlej had been passed.[7] Nevertheless, Ellenborough's hesitation was merely tactical and in a letter to Ripon at the Board of Control the Governor-General made it clear that the advance of the frontier would ultimately be necessary and was even desirable:

if it be our fate to remain the Paramount Power in India it is our fate to have the Indus, or rather the chain of mountains beyond the Indus, and the Himalaya as our *ultimate* boundary. This may not happen next year or the year after, but it will happen and the period cannot be very far removed.[8]

During the early months of 1844 Ellenborough leaned more and more obviously towards the goal of a speedy and comprehensive settlement with the Panjab. 'The termination of the present state of things in the Punjab is essential to the security of British power in India', he informed Queen Victoria in April 1844.[9] But it was clear that Ellenborough was no longer governed by purely Indian considerations; his leaping ambition had begun to dictate the shape of his future policies and he was already looking beyond the Panjab to Egypt, 'that Country which has ever been the ultimate object of my Desires'.[10] Egypt he proposed to annex, after a struggle with France, in 1847 to 1848.[11] His timetable was planned. The Panjab, including Peshawar and Kashmir, would be annexed in December 1845, by which time, 'I should have an army with which I could march to the Dardanelles'. British rule in India would then be secured by making Victoria Empress of India—'without that nothing is secure. We must give a natural Position to the Chiefs of India, who will be ennobled in their own opinion by becoming the feudatories of an Empire.' This act would be followed by the conquest of Egypt, and Ellenborough added menacingly, 'perhaps I may have seen in a vision something even beyond this.'[12] As was the case in Sind, Ellenborough's policy towards the Panjab cannot be comprehended in conventional, limited strategic terms, but must be seen as part of a total vision composed of elements of great insight and of megalomania.

One event which had played a significant part in the sudden escalation of Ellenborough's perception of possibilities was the victory over Gwalior in January 1844. The causes of the Gwalior war need not be considered here; it is sufficient to note that it blew up suddenly and was not connected with events elsewhere. Ellenborough, however, later rationalized it as part of his plan for dealing with the Panjab:

The insulated transaction, the movement on Gwalior was a movement upon a field of battle extending from Scinde through the Punjab even to the frontiers of Nepal. Every movement which might eventually have become necessary towards the Sutlej was altogether paralysed by the position of that army: it was essential to our safety that it should be removed.[13]

The argument seems sensible and has been accepted by subsequent historians. It was not, however, the cause of the Gwalior war and

provides another illustration of the way in which the strategic imagina-
tion may be stretched to explain disconnected events. For the effect of
Ellenborough's argument was not merely to justify the Gwalior war by
reference to the Panjab strategy, but to impel him towards a particular
Panjab strategy in order to justify his justification of the Gwalior affair.
Taken in conjunction with his strengthening of the frontier with the
Panjab by the construction of new fortifications and cantonments, the
formation of arsenals, and the increases both in the total size of the
army and of the forces stationed in the area of the frontier, the Gwalior
episode serves to confirm the impression that Ellenborough was moving rapidly towards a settlement with the Lahore state.

Such indeed was the impression derived by the Cabinet in London,
which had observed the evolution of Ellenborough's views with mount-
ing horror. The policy of the Cabinet, founded upon strategy, finance,
and on the European *rapprochement* with Russia, was to leave the Panjab
alone and hope that it would maintain itself.[14] But from the moment the
withdrawal from Afghanistan was accomplished ministers began to
tremble at the successive revelations of the Governor-General's imperial whims. Fitzgerald was terrified lest the great army which Ellenborough had assembled to welcome the returning troops should be
transformed into an army of invasion and even Peel breathed a sigh of
relief when it was eventually disbanded and 'the chance of yielding to
temptation with regard to the occupation of the Punjaub is thereby
diminished.'[15] Alarm revived in the Cabinet when the direction of
Ellenborough's thought became more apparent, and the Governor-
General was repeatedly urged to be cautious. In the light of this feeling,
Ellenborough's eventual recall by the Court of Directors, embarrassing as it was to the Government, could not have been wholly unpleas-
ing to ministers. Nor indeed was his recall an unmitigated disaster
for Ellenborough. His successor, Sir Henry Hardinge, commented
after his arrival in India that 'as the Punjab was to be forbidden
fruit, I really think he was glad to be relieved, for he could only have
existed in the excitement of preparing for and directing future conquests.'[16]

The Cabinet's hostility towards Ellenborough's projected Panjab
adventures was partly based, as mentioned in chapter 12, upon the
improved relations with Russia. During the visit of Nicholas I and
Nesselrode to England in 1844 conversations ranged over all issues
between the two countries. The Russians emphasized their opposition
to the annexation of the Panjab. Nesselrode remarked to Peel that while
he, the Emperor, and Count Orlov all desired a cordial understanding
with Britain:

there is a powerful party in Russia attached to a French alliance—and that party was strengthened by our apparent desire to extend our Northern Frontier in India, that they took pains to impress the Russian public with a belief that there was no assignable limit to the progressive aggrandisement of our Indian Empire—and that Russia and England must ultimately, and at no remote period come into hostile contact on that account.[17]

The similarity between the Russian argument and that which Palmerston had utilized in his talks with Brunnow in 1840 is obvious. One is tempted to believe that the demon Jorkins had re-entered the field of international diplomacy. Bluff or not, the argument had the effect of strengthening the Conservative Government's antipathy to military adventure in the Panjab. At the root of that hostility was a feeling for public opinion. Peel spelled out the Cabinet's view in November 1844. When the recalled Governor-General had returned to England Peel had offered him the Post Office with a seat in the Cabinet. Ellenborough rejected the offer contemptuously and drove Peel to comment to Hardinge that the former ruler of India misjudged his position. There was no public interest in his Indian victories.

He will not infect the people of this country with the love of military glory. If you can keep peace, reduce expense, extend commerce and strengthen our hold on India by confidence in our justice, kindness and wisdom, you will be received here on your return with acclamations a thousand times louder, and a welcome infinitely more cordial than if you have a dozen victories to boast of, and annex the Punjaub to the overgrown Empire of India.[18]

The choice of Sir Henry Hardinge as Governor-General was a prudent and calculated political move. As a friend of Ellenborough, Hardinge's selection demonstrated that the Directors were not to be permitted to dictate policy to the Government. Hardinge was also a close associate of Wellington and an intimate of Peel, at least to the extent that the cold Prime Minister had intimates. Indeed Peel did not want to lose Hardinge from the Cabinet, where he was a pillar of strength at the War Office, and had earlier been relieved when Hardinge abandoned his appointment as Commander-in-Chief in India because of the illness of his wife. Despite Hardinge's dashing military background the new Governor-General was no military adventurer; like many senior officers, his instincts were pacific and he was more conscious of the limitations of military power than were civilians like Ellenborough. Hardinge's especial talents lay in organizing armies, not in original, political or strategic thought. Peel could be confident that the new Governor-General would struggle ardently for peace against the pressures of British Indian opinion and the apparent logic of the unfolding drama in the Panjab.

The political situation in the Panjab worsened during the course of 1844, after the temporary improvement which had led Britain to recognize Dalip Singh as Maharajah in March 1844. But the factious divisions were unbridged and even the Jammus no longer held together; Sucheit Singh was killed in rebellion against his nephew in March 1844 and a gulf opened between Hira and Gulab. Hira's quarrel with the Sikh chiefs became more bitter and in May 1844 Attar Singh Sindhanwalia was killed. The Lahore army became yet more self-assertive. Hira strove to maintain control over the army and the chiefs by reducing the size of the army, resuming rent-free tenures, and using Hill troops as a counterpoise to the Sikh soldiers of the Khalsa. In the end he contrived only to unite his enemies against himself and on 21 December 1844 was overthrown by an uneasy coalition of Sikh chiefs and the army under the leadership of Rani Jind Kaur (d. 1863) and her brother, Jawahar Singh (d. 1845).

Before this event Hardinge had already taken one important step in framing his policy towards the Panjab by the appointment of George Broadfoot (1807–45) to replace Richmond as Political Agent. As the Lahore situation developed, Richmond's deficiencies became more obvious; in May 1844 he contrived to appear to be a supporter of the Sindhanwalia faction. Richmond was kicked upstairs to replace George Pollock in the lucrative Lucknow Residency. The appointment of Broadfoot to the leading position in frontier policy-making provides a suitable opportunity to review the important changes whch had taken place in the engine-room of British Indian strategy.

It had been remarked that the opening of the Afghan war coincided with, or precipitated a general change in the personnel and pattern of British Indian frontier political representation. The close of that war saw a similar change. Of those who had played a leading role in the policy of the Afghan war, Macnaghten, Burnes, Lord, Bell, and three of the ill-fated Conolly brothers were dead, the last and ablest, John Conolly, having died in captivity. Of those who had survived the war, Todd had been disgraced and returned to his regiment; Outram, who was to rise to a position of great influence during the 1850s, was presently under the cloud of his great controversy with the Napier brothers; Rawlinson languished in rewarding obscurity in Iraq; George Macgregor, who had incurred Ellenborough's disfavour through his conduct with Pollock, was, like Frederick Mackeson, in temporary oblivion, although destined to return to influence as assistant to Sir

Frederick Currie in Lahore; and Leech, ambition extinguished, was content to live out his last months quietly as agent at Ambala.

In place of those whom Afghanistan had unhorsed three new groups had risen to prominence in the political system. One group was composed of those military officers who had won the favour of Sir Charles Napier, who was now a lonely dictator in Sind. But Napier's influence, while it guaranteed this group employment in Sind, equally denied them influence in Bombay, where everything to do with Sind was regarded with repugnance. So E. J. Brown and A. R. Rathborne never secured the influence on policy that they sought and it was some years before John Jacob and his followers of the Sind school—men like William Merether and Henry and Malcolm Green—rose to challenge the pre-eminence of their Panjab frontier rivals.

It was the second group, composed of officers and officials associated with the Panjab, which rose to predominance during the years immediately after the end of the Afghan war. Clerk and his subordinates, including Henry Lawrence and Joseph Cunningham, were the architects of Pollock's redeeming victory, untainted by Macgregor's alleged efforts to pervert it, and they emerged from the struggle into high favour. All of them were pro-Sikh both by policy—believing that the existence of an independent Hindu state in the north-west was a source of strength to British India—and by inclination—admiring the virtues of courage, self-reliance, and discipline which they discerned in the Sikh community. As mentioned before, the inspiration of this view, George Clerk, was able to dominate frontier policy until his retirement to England at the end of 1843 following an accident. Under his successor at Ludhiana, Lieutenant-Colonel A. F. Richmond, real power belonged to Joseph Cunningham who served as private secretary to the Political Agent.[19] Cunningham's frontier influence, however, did not long survive the passing of Richmond, for he was himself quickly removed by Broadfoot. Cunningham was to achieve a final and lasting notoriety as an influential critic of British policy towards the Panjab. The leadership of the Clerk school really devolved upon Henry Lawrence, but Lawrence was cast into lucrative purgatory in Nepal and had to wait until 1846 to assume the frontier purple. In the meantime it was the turn of the third group of men who had been thrown up by the Afghan débâcle.

The third group was composed of the Ellenborough men. Their background was military, their regimental service much longer than that of the traditional Political. They recommended themselves to Ellenborough partly by their military distinction and partly by their previous innocence of the corruption of political work. Some of them, like Richmond, turned out to be poor appointments, but others revealed startling political abilities. Most prominent among these were Ellenborough's private secretary, Henry Marion Durand (1812–71) and George Broadfoot. Durand does not concern us here, although it may be noted that he became a powerful figure in political discussions during the 1850s and 1860s. But in 1844 to 1845 it was George Broadfoot who was to play a dominant role on the north west Frontier.

Broadfoot was that formidable phenomenon, the intellectual soldier. He had studied his profession deeply and had endeavoured to understand the political arena within which it functioned. A poor man, lacking influence, he had striven to win a reputation in Afghanistan. In 1841, escorting Shuja's family across the Panjab his belligerence had almost precipitated a war, but his real fame was acquired at Jalalabad, where he had been the chief inspiration of the resolute defence. This achievement had won him Ellenborough's regard and the post of Commissioner at Moulmein from which place Hardinge recalled him in September 1844 to replace Richmond on the frontier. It may well be that Broadfoot owed his appointment to the recommendations of Ellenborough and of his friends at Calcutta, notably Thoby Prinsep and Charles Cameron, the Law Member of the Supreme Council, but the immediate reason for his selection was a memorandum on Jalalabad which he had written and which so impressed Hardinge that the new Governor-General decided to give him the preference over Henry Lawrence, who also enjoyed powerful support in Government.[20] Hardinge was not entirely sure he had made the right choice, thinking Broadfoot might be 'too prone to war', but after meeting the new agent, decided that Broadfoot was sufficiently discreet.[21] Hardinge's first doubts, however, never quite left him and his admiration for Broadfoot was always tempered by a lurking feeling that his agent was insufficiently convinced of the merits of the pacific policy recommended by Hardinge and his colleagues in London. 'He was a little too warlike, but invaluable', was Hardinge's final summing up of Broadfoot.[22] Hardinge's doubts were not shared by Broadfoot; the post was exactly what he wanted and some clue to his motives may be gathered from a letter written by a friend who declared his hope of seeing Broadfoot Governor of the Panjab.[23]

Broadfoot took charge of the frontier agency on 1 November 1844 and immediately began to sweep away the system which had prevailed under Richmond. One feature of this system had been Richmond's dependence on his interpreters. The role of the interpreters in the history of British India is as dark as it is in the Ottoman Empire. For the most part they worked in the shadows of the stage and the sources rarely permit their influence to be identified. Yet in India, as in the Ottoman Empire, their influence was of crucial importance, as is witnessed on the rare occasions when evidence of their extensive influence over their superiors and of their dealings, corrupt or innocent, with those with whom they negotiated, floats to the surface. The influence of Nubkissen on Clive is well known; Charles Napier described his interpreter as one of the four conquerors of Sind; the curious role of Mulla Sadiq and his family in Aden emerged through reverberating scandals; and efforts at concealment failed to hide all the activities of Mohan Lal in Afghanistan. At Ludhiana there is evidence that Cunningham's favourite Indian interpreter, Bakshallah Khan, was dishonest and that other Indian employees of the agency possessed great influence.[24]

Broadfoot aimed to control everything himself. Cunningham was packed off to be Political Agent at Bahawalpur and some of the subordinate Indian officials were dismissed. Knowing Persian and Urdu well and even a little Panjabi, Broadfoot was able to dispense with interpreters and to conduct his own correspondence with Lahore and his own negotiations with the Lahore agents at Ludhiana. No correspondence was seen by anyone but Broadfoot and his personal assistant, R. N. Cust (1821–1907). Broadfoot also kept his thoughts on policy to himself; unlike Richmond, who wrote private letters constantly to his subordinate British agents, Broadfoot wrote almost nothing to his lieutenants. At the same time the new agent kept strict control over his assistants; they were ordered to recall all their own native agents from the Panjab and forbidden to correspond with persons in the Panjab or in Afghanistan without Broadfoot's permission. Broadfoot habitually burned all the intelligence which he himself received from the Panjab, arguing that if it were filed, the native employees of the Residency would be able to discover the identity of Broadfoot's informants and, by making this known to the Sikhs, perhaps endanger the lives of Broadfoot's correspondents.[25] Some of Broadfoot's most important recommendations, for example those relating to the Cis-Satlej Sikhs, were supported by accounts of verbal submissions by unidentified Lahore notables.

Broadfoot's new system gave him a virtual monopoly over the supply of information to his own Government. In September 1845 Hardinge remarked that the Supreme Government knew little more of Panjab affairs than did London because it was wholly dependent on the Political Agent.[26] Nor was Hardinge able to obtain information from elsewhere. In November 1845 he found James Thomason, now Governor-General of Agra and the senior Civil Servant in the north-west,

quite unwilling to venture an opinion on Panjab affairs.[27] It was not
that Hardinge was entirely happy with the information which he
received from Broadfoot, who wrote few official dispatches, preferring
to employ the device of private letters to the Foreign Secretary,
Frederick Currie (1799–1875). In January 1845 Hardinge complained
of the irregularity of Broadfoot's dispatches and in September complained that Broadfoot had failed to send him copies of his correspondence with the Lahore Government or to supply sufficient facts on
which his proposals could be judged.[28]

Broadfoot was extremely sensitive to criticism. In the summer of
1845 there were rumours that George Clerk might return from England
to take charge of the frontier. Broadfoot's reaction was to bear down
more severely on the Lahore Government; the rumours, he complained, caused the Sikh ministers to address him disrespectfully and
even to refuse to have dealings with him on the grounds that he was not
in full control. Hardinge found it necessary to urge his agent to be less
sensitive and to pay less attention to gossip, arguing that Broadfoot
exaggerated the mischief caused by the rumours. The episode did,
however, cause light to be shed on the darker areas of policy-making.
Broadfoot claimed that the rumour of his replacement by Clerk originated with Mohan Lal, who was then in London. Mohan Lal had been
attached to the Ludhiana agency, but had taken himself off to London
without permission. In consequence, his pay had been stopped, but the
London authorities ordered the Indian Government to refund the lost
salary and also paid Mohan Lal a considerable sum in compensation
for losses suffered by the Indian agent in Afghanistan. There is no
doubt that this generosity was intended to shut Lal's mouth, for
Burnes's old companion had evidence that Macnaghten and John
Conolly had ordered him to arrange the murder of various Afghan
chiefs and the East India Company did not want this discreditable
information to become known. Peel was disgusted by the whole affair
but decided to keep his hands clean and his mouth closed. While in
London Lal had collected information and opinions and relayed them
to his brother-in-law, an East Indian named Hodges, whom Broadfoot
had dismissed from the agency for misconduct. Hodges passed on Lal's
news to the *Delhi Gazette*, on which newspaper he had friends, to the
Lahore agents at Ludhiana, and to Kashmiri Brahmin friends of
Mohan Lal at Lahore.[29]

Such was George Broadfoot and the milieu in which he worked. The
man was able and ambitious, sensitive and secretive. He was as hospit-
able as an unmarried British Indian officer could be, but he had few
friends and several powerful enemies. Unsurprisingly, Cunningham

hated him; Henry Lawrence disliked him; and George Macgregor, who may have been reminded of his own less than distinguished performance at Jalalabad, could not bear to be in the same room as Broadfoot. But Broadfoot was the mainspring of British policy towards the Panjab during the year before the first Anglo-Sikh war. In his general political views Broadfoot stood nearer to Ellenborough than to Hardinge. To the former he wrote as follows, shortly after taking up his appointment:

All rational men in the Punjab fear a general war with us; and we shall seek to avoid offence; and on our side, though there is in general a desire for war, yet the considerations I find in one of your Lordship's letters to my predecessor are weighty indeed; for war here should be no half measure; that would but prolong and double every evil. We must go to the top of the Himalayas or stop in a false position; but once across the Punjab, we enter on that great mass of unmixed Mahomedanism which extends from the Indus to the Mediterranean. To this we must sooner or later come; but whatever we do we cannot stop, and going on in such conditions is only just less ruinous than stopping.[30]

Hardinge had assumed office on 23 July 1844, but the first statement of his maturing views on the Panjab came in a letter to Ripon of 8 January 1845 in which he discussed the Lahore revolution of December 1844 which had brought about the fall of Hira Singh and induced various Sikh chiefs to make new approaches to Britain in the hope that the paramount power in India would intervene to restore order and preserve their position. Hardinge then rejected intervention but claimed that he could not be indifferent to what happened in the Panjab for one supreme reason—the condition of the Indian army.[31]

The possible effects of the example of Sikh military insubordination upon the British Indian Army was the first and the most enduring of the factors which impelled Hardinge to intervene in the Panjab. Ellenborough had made the restoration of the morale of the Indian Army his prime objective and had elected to accomplish this by rewards, encomiums, medals, and easy victories. At the time of his departure from India he thought that he had succeeded in his aim and that his army (if not its Commander-in-Chief, Sir Hugh Gough (1779–1869)) was fit for any duty, although he still wished to postpone a Panjab settlement partly on the army's account. Ellenborough was, concerned about the example of the mutinous Sikh troops. It was more dangerous to British India than the Sikh army in the field, he informed Victoria.[32] From the beginning of his rule Hardinge contemplated the Indian Army with suspicion and its sepoy element with outright mistrust. The Indian Army, he declared soon after his arrival, needed quite.

Accordingly, the army factor was at first a factor militating against intervention in the Panjab, but in January 1845 Hardinge, retaining his diagnosis, reversed his conclusions; the condition of the army now became an argument for intevention in the Panjab.

Shortly before Hardinge arrived in India a succession of mutinies took place in Bengal sepoy regiments. At the time this ebullition of indiscipline was attributed to the regiments being ordered for service in Sind and Hardinge accepted this explanation. But about the beginning of January, General Ventura advanced another theory; the mutinies had been fostered by Sikh emissaries. Ventura's motives are themselves a matter of interest. Like other foreign officers in the Panjab, he had been dismissed by Hira Singh and wanted to take his wealth out of India. But much of his fortune was derived from lands in the Jamna–Satlej Doab, which he held on a grant from the Lahore Government and which he feared might be withdrawn. British intervention in the Panjab would safeguard Ventura's fortune.

Hardinge accepted Ventura's explanation and its implication. The Lahore army represented a threat to British India both because of the direct incitement to the Company's sepoys to mutiny and because of the example of successful mutiny which it provided. The Company's sepoys received seven rupees a month; in consequence of their demands the pay of the Sikh soldiers had risen to eleven and a half rupees in 1842 and to fourteen in December 1844. The sepoys of the Bengal Army were well aware of the disparity in rewards. In a metaphor no less striking for being mixed, Hardinge wrote that 'this wonderful instrument of our power in India may be seduced by the contagion of what is daily passing under their eyes.'[33] The affair of the incitement to mutiny, Hardinge thought, was too explosive an issue to be dealt with by inquiries through the usual army channels, for the news that such an inquiry was being made would inevitably become public and if the sepoys became conscious of a general alarm the danger might be increased. Accordingly, on 12 January 1845, Hardinge put the matter into the hands of Broadfoot, who was instructed to collect information about the attitude of the Company's sepoys and about conditions in the Sikh army.[34]

Hardinge's fears concerning the loyalty of the Company's sepoys were not widely shared. Most Indian Army officers would have resented the imputation on the fidelity of their troops if they had known that it was made and many civilians would have agreed with them. Frederick Currie, who was privy to Hardinge's fears, believed that the Governor-General exaggerated the dangers and Currie was confident that the sepoys would remain faithful.[35] It may well be, as the Indian

Mutiny of 1857 appears to suggest, that the doubts held by Hardinge and by officers like Henry Lawrence were well founded, and it may be that Broadfoot's prompt agreement with Hardinge represented his genuine feelings. Broadfoot had, he declared, for some time considered the question to be 'the most important in our relations with the Panjab'.[36] But Hardinge's argument and action were also most convenient for Broadfoot. In the future the army factor was to provide Broadfoot with a crucial weapon, to be used at the appropriate time. His use of this argument will be discussed later; here it is sufficient to note that although little was heard of the possibility of mutiny during the following months, it remained a powerful influence on Hardinge's mind and in the autumn of 1845 became a critical factor in his decision to intervene. From September 1845 onwards, Peter Nicholson, Broadfoot's deputy at Firuzpur and a man previously encountered in Ghilzay land, provided a stream of vague and unsubstantiated reports of Sikh efforts to suborn the loyalty of the Bengal sepoys. These reports made a particular impact on Hardinge because of their coincidence in time with his much questioned action in restoring the punishment of flogging in the Bengal Army in October 1845.[37] Right until the outbreak of war Hardinge remained concerned about the possibility of mutiny. On 3 December 1845 he informed Ripon that when he first received reports that the Sikhs were advancing towards the Satlej he was convinced that they would not attempt a crossing unless they were sure that they would be joined by the Company's sepoys. Hardinge determined to destroy the Sikh army *panchayat* (soldiers' council) system because it was a danger to British security.[38]

Broadfoot's reference to 'that great mass of unmixed Mahomedanism' lying to the west of the Indus directs attention to the second new factor which shaped Hardinge's Panjab policy. The Afghan war had revived those fears of Muslim political rivalry which had fallen into abeyance during the previous years, and in Clerk's strategic system the Sikh buffer policy had been a central element in the search for security by virtue of its separation of the dangerous Islamic component in British India from the menacing, independent Muslim peoples beyond the Indus. Lahore could fulfil this function only so long as its Government was strong enough to hold the Empire of Ranjit Singh together; if that Empire crumbled the trans-Indus territories might once more pass under Afghan control and the whole of the predominantly Muslim, western Panjab might follow suit. Auckland, during his last years of office, and Ellenborough, during his first year, had contemplated this prospect with a sense of being helpless to do much about it. Ellenborough, even in his last year, had not finally decided on the importance to be attached to this prospective danger. Hardinge had no such doubts and it was the prospect of the re-establishment of Muslim power on the right bank of the Indus which became another of the factors bending him away from his original intention to avoid intervention in the Panjab.

The evolution of Hardinge's views on the Muslim question can be traced from their first mention in a letter to Ripon dated 23 January 1845. 'The Government of the Punjab must be Sikh or British', he stated. The old device of the subsidiary alliance would not answer because Britain would incur all the obligations of defending the Panjab without the benefit of its resources; also Oudh and Haidarabad provided gloomy examples of the working of that system. Nor would a Rajput government headed by Gulab Singh survive because the hill peoples were too weak to dominate the plains. Finally, the vital point in this context, no Muslim government could be permitted to exist at Lahore because its presence would endanger the British position in Upper Sind and would excite Muslims throughout India.[39] In this letter there was no mention of the specific problem of an Afghan occupation of Peshawar and the trans-Indus lands and, indeed, a fortnight later, Hardinge confessed that, like his predecessors, he could see no way in which he could provide against this eventuality.[40] But by August he had altered his views on this central point. The occasion was the rebellion of Peshaura Singh, one of the excluded sons of Ranjit Singh, who seized the Indus fort of Attock in July 1845, declared himself to be ruler of the Panjab, and offered Peshawar to the Afghans. Hardinge's reaction was quick and strong. Peshawar he now declared to be a vital position guarding the Khaibar Pass and, in Afghan hands, it would become an indispensable base for further operations in the Panjab. Worse, if Muhammad Akbar, the unpunished villain of Britain's Afghan débâcle, became established as Governor of Peshawar, his name would arouse the Muslims of the Indus and of Rohilkhand as well.[41]

Despite his new-found realization of the importance of Peshawar, Hardinge did not yet see its fate as a motive for British annexation, for he still shrank from the prospect of military operations conducted at so great a distance from the Satlej frontier. Rather the Peshawar problem was another reason for keeping alive a strong, independent Sikh Government. It was Broadfoot who seized upon the Peshawar question and turned it into a fresh argument for annexation. There was, he reported a disposition in Lahore, to make Peshawar over to Sultan Muhammad Khan Barakzay, its former ruler, and not to Dost Muhammand Khan of Kabul. Plainly such a proposal, if true, was no more than a projected return to the former Sikh policy, accepted by Clerk, of controlling the frontier through a Barakzay vassal. Broadfoot claimed, quite inaccurately, that such a move would be no different from making Peshawar over to the ruler of Kabul. He contended that the Lahore Government would endeavour to carry out the transfer before Britain could conquer Peshawar, thus presenting the paramount power with an accomplished fact. No Barakzay, said Broadfoot, should be permitted to rule at Peshawar.[42]

The third new element in the Panjab puzzle which emerged during the course of 1845 was that of the Cis-Satlej Sikhs. The antecedents of this problem wound back to 1809 when Minto had established a British protectorate over the area and ended Ranjit Singh's efforts to unite all the Sikhs under his rule. However, Minto's act had left a problem in the form of the position of the Cis-Satlej Sikh territories which had previously submitted to Ranjit Singh, and during subsequent years there were frequent disputes over sovereignty involving Britain and Lahore. While the Delhi Residents retained undivided authority there was a unity of approach on the British side, but the separation of the conduct of relations with Lahore from those with the protected Sikh States led to a division between Wade and Murray. Wade's sympathies for Lahore opened the way in 1827 to a compromise favourable to the Lahore state; Ranjit Singh was left in control of all those Sikh principalities over which he had established control prior to Ochterlony's intervention in 1809, other than Firuzpur, which was excluded from the Lahore orbit because of its supposed military value. This compromise reflected the growing British conviction that the state of Lahore constituted a valuable element of stability on the north-west frontier and, although occasionally criticized, the settlement was substantially maintained during the pre-eminence of Wade and Clerk, even though the latter thought that the agreement was a mistake and that it would have been better if Britain had controlled all the area on the left bank of the Satlej.[43]

At the beginning of 1845 the 1827 compromise was challenged by Currie and Broadfoot. In the course of 1844 the situation in the Cis-Satlej territories had caused increasing concern as disputes between Lahore and Britain multiplied. Richmond and Cunningham were thought to have been too ready to allow merit to the contentions of the Lahore Government and from the beginning Broadfoot took a harder line, rejecting the claims of the Lahore Government and himself intervening more decidedly in the affairs of the Protected Sikh States. Firmness was necessary, claimed Broadfoot, because the Cis-Satlej Sikhs had become much more restive since the defeats suffered by

Britain in Afghanistan. It was Currie, however, who was the instigator
of the major challenge to the Lahore position. On 19 January 1845 he
advised Broadfoot that the most important question at issue was that of
the Cis–Satlej districts which belonged to Lahore under the 1827
compromise: should they be regarded as family or as state property?
Currie was inclined to think they were in the former category and
therefore liable to lapse to Britain, but he wanted Broadfoot's opinion
before he brought the matter before the Supreme Council.[44]

Once more Broadfoot seized the opportunity presented to him to
force a stronger policy on his Government. In March he challenged the
right of the Lahore Government to administer their districts on the left
bank of the Satlej and early in April submitted a long report in which he
claimed that the Lahore possessions were family property and also that
they were covered by the British protectorate in the same way as the
independent territories. The 1827 compromise was a concession
granted to Ranjit Singh for his lifetime and had expired with the
Maharajah. The Satlej frontier was impermeable.[45]

Hardinge adopted the view of Currie and Broadfoot. Following the
lines of Broadfoot's argument he reported to Ripon that 'our Protected
Sikhs since the Cabool disaster and the imprudence of borrowing small
sums of money from the Chiefs, indicating want of resources as well as
adverse fortunes in war, had taken up the notion, that we were in a state
of weakness and decay.'[46] Accordingly, he supported Broadfoot's
firmer policy towards the Cis-Satlej Sikhs and also his arguments
concerning the Lahore districts which Hardinge recommended should
be resumed by Britain.

In London Ripon had been following Sikh affairs closely and
shrewdly. When, by implication, Hardinge raised the possibility of
annexation in his letter of 23 January 1845 Ripon was quick to infer the
the possible consequences for British India of a shift in its centre of
gravity towards the north-west. If the Panjab were annexed, he argued
in an interesting anticipation of the direction of subsequent developments, it would be desirable to create a fourth Presidency from Sind,
Lahore, and the Satlej–Jamna Doab and to transfer the Supreme
Government from Calcutta to Delhi. He also foresaw the need for
railways to speed up the movement of troops and supplies.[47] More
clearly than Hardinge he also perceived that war was probable and that
Britain would be obliged to decide on the future of the Panjab. Ripon,
however, found it difficult to interest his Cabinet colleagues in these
matters. He found them unwilling to offer Hardinge any advice at all:
Wellington proposed, and Peel agreed, that everything should be left to
the Governor-General's discretion; and Ripon was obliged to content

himself with transmitting private generalities, principally to the effect that the Cabinet wanted peace, and more in the hope of strengthening Hardinge's determination to resist British Indian pressures for war than because he felt the Governor-General needed any urging. 'Pray keep us out of a War and a Conquest', he wrote. If Hardinge was forced to intervene in the Panjab he should limit his demands to the Cis-Satlej districts of Lahore and an indemnity.[48]

It may be observed that Ripon wanted the Cis–Satlej districts even before he received Hardinge's recommendations to resume them. Nevertheless, in accordance with his and the Cabinet's general attitude, he wished to be sure about the legality of the Indian Government's proposal, especially as consequential action could lead to war. In that event the question of legality would have an important bearing upon the reception of the news in England. Ripon consulted George Clerk, who was still in London, on the merits of the proposals. Clerk's opinion gave Ripon pause, for while the former Political Agent conceded that the Cis–Satlej districts would be a very useful acquisition by Britain, he was sceptical about the morality of the proposed proceedings, and suggested that behind the new policy lay a desire to control Lahore 'because there is nothing else to do'.[49] The picture of idle militarism which this comment conjured forth in Ripon's mind was sufficient to cause the President to warn Hardinge that he should be careful not to give the impression that he was manufacturing new or untenable grounds for doing someting which he wanted to do for other reasons. Like Clerk, Ripon wanted the Cis–Satlej territories, but not through the dubious back door of the doctrine of lapse. It would be better, he wrote, to demand them as a payment in equity for the trouble and expense to which the anarchy in Lahore had put British India and he warned Hardinge not to act without Cabinet consent.[50]

Clerk and Ripon had delivered their opinions before receiving Broadfoot's lengthy paper on that subject and when he studied that document a month later some of Ripon's apprehensions were removed. Broadfoot had been careful to avoid giving the impression that the legal claim had been disinterred for the occasion, but instead had based the demand for the Cis–Satlej territories on the very grounds indicated by Ripon: namely, the recent proceedings of the Lahore Government. Accordingly, despite his own lingering legal doubts, Ripon gave Hardinge *carte blanche* in the matter of the Cis–Satlej Sikhs, hoping that the affair might not lead to war, and indeed rather naïvely supposing that it might even make the continuance of peace more likely by removing a fruitful cause of dispute between the two Governments.[51]

In the meantime the earlier opinion of Clerk and Ripon had reached

India and had produced a noteworthy reaction. Hardinge had sent Ripon's letter of 23 May enclosing Clerk's detailed criticisms of Broad-foot's policy to Broadfoot, who proceeded to answer them. Clerk's criticisms fell into two classes. The first class comprised detailed critic-isms of Broadfoot's policy towards the Lahore possessions on the left bank of the Satlej, and these Broadfoot answered in detail. The second class is more interesting for it included Clerk's objections to the general drift of British policy towards Lahore. In essence Clerk contended that there had been no material change in the Panjab since 1841 and that the change had occurred in British policy, which, freed from former constraints, was now at liberty to indulge in aggression against Lahore. Broadfoot's response to this latter charge provides an excellent illustra-tion of the power which the frontier agents derived from their monopoly of information. He disposed of Clerk's opinion, founded on fifteen years' experience, simply by stating that Clerk's information was already out of date. The situation in the Panjab had changed materi-ally. Although there had been disorders at Lahore during the period of Clerk's frontier rule, the Lahore Government had been able to retain control and those who directed its fortunes had been well disposed towards the British connection. But since the murder of Sher Singh in September 1843, one month before Clerk had left Agra for Calcutta and England, the situation had been profoundly modified. The Sikh chiefs had lost all their power and now 'almost to a man they are eager for an English invasion' and for British protection for their lives and property. Real power had passed to the army the character of which was com-pletely altered; formerly it had been a mercenary instrument in the hands of Ranjit Singh; now it had become a national institution repres-enting 'the most permanent and a highly influential body of the com-munity—the cultivating landholders', a group which was profoundly anti–British. The army was governed not by its officers but by *pan-chayats* or councils of ordinary Sikh soldiers, and it was these *panchayats* which commanded the actions of the Lahore Government.[52] In short, the Sikh army had become not a praetorian guard but a New Model Army.

It is useless to inquire whether Broadfoot's picture of the Lahore army was a correct one. It is the one which has been adopted by all recent writers on the subject, but this cannot be a matter of choice because Broadfoot's monopoly of information has ensured that his picture is the only one for which substantial evidence survives.[53] Cer-tainly the army was mutinous and certainly there were *panchayats*, but whether Broadfoot was right in what he said of the nature of their power and the implications of it is uncertain. What is plain is that the theory was admirably adapted to Broadfoot's purpose for it enabled him to reject the opinions of the man who was both his most prominent rival and the foremost upholder of the Sikh alliance, and to drive home an argument which he knew would have a profound impact upon Hardinge and which, because of the secrecy concerning the matter (which Hardinge had ordered and Broadfoot had contrived) could not readily be contradicted by anyone, including Broadfoot's own subordinate agents. Hardinge did indeed accept Broadfoot's view that Clerk's ideas were outdated and he informed Ripon that he did not want Clerk back in India; it was rumoured, he remarked, that Clerk would prefer to return to Agra rather than resume his post on the Supreme Council because of his wife's social position.[54]

By the summer of 1845 the three main arguments luring Hardinge towards intervention in the Panjab had all been deployed: the danger of an army mutiny, the menace of a Muslim conspiracy, and the unrest of the Cis-Satlej Sikhs. Ventura and Currie had played their part in introducing these arguments, but they had all been cultivated by Broadfoot. All were those arguments which most affected the innocent mind of the Governor-General. Hardinge wanted neither war nor expansion, merely peace within his own frontiers. The most striking features of all of these arguments is that they indicated that peace within the British frontiers could be obtained only through war with the Panjab; all were concerned with one or another aspect of the internal enemy. The single argument which never appealed to Hardinge was that by a war with the Panjab he might improve the external frontier. Hardinge had no desire for the Indus frontier; like all military authorities, he preferred the Satlej—'a better barrier, than the more circuitous frontier, formed by the present limits of the Lahore state'. The Lahore frontier was three times longer and would bring Britain into direct contact with the Muslim tribes of Central Asia: it was also more distant from Calcutta and from the main recruiting area for the Indian Army in Oudh.[55] Against these disadvantages the benefits to be derived from using the Indus for communications weighed little: and 'the commerce on the Indus, except from the Punjaub, is nothing and only exists in Lord Palmerston's speeches.'[56]

By September 1845 Hardinge, on his own admission, was almost the only man in India who believed that a war with Lahore could still be avoided, and indeed, one of the few who wished to avoid it.[57] The Indian Press wanted it; the Army wanted it; his Council and the Civil Service thought it inevitable.[58] In fulfilment of a decision reached in June, Hardinge set off for the frontier to investigate the situation for himself, thereby reversing his previous decision not to undertake such a journey lest it should alarm the Sikhs. Hardinge was in a familiar trap: to prepare for war might frighten the Lahore state into hostilities; not to do so might invite attack and endanger the security of British India. While trying to avoid too ostentatious military preparations, Hardinge had steadily strengthened his forces on the frontier, continuing the process begun by Ellenborough. Hardinge had doubled the number of troops to forty thousand and increased the number of guns in the north-west by half to nearly a hundred. The vulnerable garrisons at Firuzpur and Ludhiana had been made stronger and baggage animals assembled along the whole line of communications from the Ganges to the Satlej. Boats had been brought up to Firuzpur ready to form a bridge across the river.

Still Hardinge continued to proclaim the pacific policy which had been instilled into him by his colleagues in London and which he had defended in India. From both a military and a political view, he repeated to Broadfoot, the best arrangement was a strong Sikh Government in the Panjab. British power in India was already over-extended, more territory was not needed, and the Cabinet wanted peace. It is this last point which casts just a shadow of a doubt upon Hardinge's plausible edifice of argument in support of his policy. It was, he reiterated to Broadfoot, essential to be able to demonstrate to London that, if peace proved ultimately too difficult to preserve, the Indian Government had done all in its power to prevent its decomposition.[59] Such evident consciousness of the audience raises suspicions in a cynical mind and such were evidently held by Peter Nicholson who doubted whether the Government was sincere in its pacific protestations, speculated whether peace might not be merely for appearance's sake, and inquired of Broadfoot whether he should not pursue a more aggressive policy. Broadfoot's reproof may also have been for appearances.[60] The vagueness of Hardinge's reasons for his visit to the frontier also cause doubts about his desire for peace, in view of his previous remarks upon the subject. Partly he wanted to study the problem for himself, and to talk to the reticent Broadfoot. Partly he hoped to bring the Sikhs to order. In August he explained that he intended to threaten to cancel the 1809 Treaty on the grounds of the unfriendly behaviour of the Sikhs.[61] More precisely he may have intended to exclude the Sikhs from their possessions on the left bank of the Satlej. The evidence is slight, but the possibility must exist that by the late summer Hardinge had come to the conclusion that his policy, however desirable in theory, was unworkable in practice, but that he would not declare this conclusion, and sturdily maintained that his former policy was still the right one.

Broadfoot had spent the summer of 1845 in Simla whither he had retired in May for his health's sake. At the beginning of June he had suffered a bad fall from a horse and injured his head, an incident to which Hardinge was inclined to attribute what he thought to be a deterioration in Broadfoot's judgement during the following months. Broadfoot's policy, however, was still consistent with the views he had always held. But the agent was increasingly worried about his own position, fearing that he might after all be replaced by Clerk. He informed Hardinge that the Sikh Darbar was reluctant to deal with him because of reports that he had no authority and that Hardinge himself was bound hand and foot by instructions from England. Broadfoot needed something to break the stalemate.

At the end of August 1845 Broadfoot reported an important new development. For many months approaches had been made by Sikh chiefs who sought British assistance. In January 1845 Broadfoot had been instructed not to reply to these overtures; in accordance with the policy of non–intervention, Britain was to do nothing which might be construed as offering aid to any party at Lahore.[62] Hasrat suggests that Broadfoot had ignored this instruction and that the agent had sought to persuade Mulraj, the Governor of Multan, to desert the Sikhs in the event of war, while Broadfoot's assistant, Peter Nicholson, had attempted to win over Mulla Ahmad of Kashmir.[63] But the key figure on the Lahore side was Gulab Singh. Ever since that Jammu disaster of September 1843 Gulab had contemplated the dissolution of the Lahore state and had bent his efforts to securing his own position in the hills. It became clear to him, however, that without outside help he could not free himself from the control of Lahore. As early as March 1844 he had sounded the British Government about the possibility of the recognition of his independent authority in the hills but had been given no encouragement.[64] In January 1845 he had tried again, offering not only that he would not oppose a British capture of Lahore but also a sum of £500,000. In February he even offered the co-operation of his hill troops in the attack on Lahore. Hardinge had steadfastly rejected all these overtures and in April 1845 Gulab was forcibly reconciled with the Lahore Government by the Sikh army. Still he continued to hope for British aid and in August 1845 repeated his February offer, specifying the assistance of fifty thousand hill troops. Gulab now added that the Darbar intended to make war in the cold weather and that the Sikh chiefs hoped to provoke British intervention in the expectation that it would lead to the destruction of the Sikh army and the establishment of a protectorate or subsidiary alliance. Broadfoot commented that several chiefs wanted to make terms for themselves but were deterred by fear of betrayal.[65]

Hardinge was disturbed by this dispatch from his agent and complained that Broadfoot had failed to supply sufficient information to enable Government to judge the merits of his arguments; there was too much speculation and too few facts. But in any case Hardinge declined to intervene in the Panjab in order to establish a subsidiary alliance or a protectorate, or to assist Gulab and the Sikh chiefs—the Sikhs, he remarked, formed only one-sixth of the population of the Lahore state.[66] But although Hardinge repeated his preference for an independent Sikh state and his antipathy to an advance beyond the Satlej, it is plain that Broadfoot's information about the attitude of the Sikh chiefs had made the success of Hardinge's policy much less likely and had struck a body-blow at the whole strategic concept on which it was ultimately founded. For, notwithstanding Hardinge's remark about the size of the Sikh population of the Panjab, it was only as a Sikh, or at least as a Hindu state that Lahore made any sense in British strategy. If the Sikh chiefs themselves did not think the Lahore state could survive in independence then Hardinge would be obliged to look again at the only possibility which he had apparently left open, that is annexation.

In the end it was the Sikhs who brought on the first Sikh war. In Lahore the Chief Minister, Jawahar Singh, despairing of controlling the army, which now consumed two-thirds of the state revenue, and unable to reach agreement with Hardinge, decided to precipitate a war and dispose of the army by sending it against the British. The army leaders recognized the trap and refused to move unless the notables led them.[67] On 27 September 1845 soldiers killed Jawahar, nominally in retribution for the death of Peshaura Singh. Suspicious of the chiefs and ministers the army then sought to control them more closely, notably in their communications with the British. Just as it began to seem that the army had successfully intervened to prevent war, the army decided after all to fight. For reasons which are unclear, on 24 September that same brigade which a few days earlier had complained of Jawahar's hostility to the British demanded to be led against Firuzpur.[68] No further move took place, however, until 18 November when the Sikhs announced their intention to make war, agreed on a plan of operations, and set 23 November for their march. Even then there was hesitation and delay and the possibility of a change of mind. But early in December the Sikhs moved up to the Satlej and on 12 to 13 December they crossed the river, making war certain.

In his criticism of British policy towards Lahore, Joseph Cunningham blamed British military preparations for the Sikh decision to attack; it was these, he believed, which finally tipped the balance.[69] It may indeed have been fear which drove the Sikh army to its fatal resolution, but it is difficult to see how Hardinge could have done less than he did. Sensitive as he was to possible Parliamentary criticism, and advised by Broadfoot that the Sikhs would not fight, the Governor-General delayed acting as long as he could. The most economical tactic would have been a pre-emptive strike. By renouncing this measure he surrendered the initiative to the Sikhs and was forced to keep his main forces back from the frontier until he could determine the point on which the main Sikh attack would fall, meantime strengthening the Ludhiana and Firuzpur garrisons sufficiently to enable them to hold out until help arrived. 'I have not allowed a man of our force to be moved', he informed Peel on 4 December, when he reaffirmed his belief that there would be no war. By then, however, Hardinge was worried by reports that Hindus in British territory were ready to join the Sikhs in a general rising against British rule and concerned about the effect of discussion of such possibilities upon the loyalty of the sepoys.[70] Not until 5 December did Hardinge order his main force to move up to the frontier and he did not set it in motion until 8 December. Only on 10 December did he order all forces to concentrate on Firuzpur, which was, by that time, clearly indicated as the danger point. However, when the Sikhs finally crossed the Satlej Hardinge was ready and on 13 December he issued a declaration of war and proclaimed the Cis–Satlej districts annexed to British India.

The Panjab of the
Politicals, 1846–1847

This Hindoo state has another opportunity afforded to it if
re-establishing its government and at the same time, of
securing the tranquillity of the frontier, and I hope, of all
India . . . Personally I may regret that it has not been my
fate to place a British standard on the banks of the Indus. I
have taken the less ambitious course, and I am consoled
by the reflexion that I have acted right for the interests of
England and India.

Henry Hardinge, December 1846.

The policy of the Hindu buffer, which had reigned supreme in official
orthodoxy since 1842 and to which Hardinge had clung with such
determination, despite the efforts of others to undermine and overthrow it, was effectively destroyed by the first Sikh war. The policy was
not, however, officially buried for more than two years, until the second
Sikh war finally demonstrated that it was unviable. In the meantime
Hardinge made an effort to re-establish it in a considerably modified
form. The reasons for Hardinge's attempt, and the causes of his failure,
form the subject matter of this chapter.

The details of the war need not be examined except in so far as they
contributed to the evolution of Hardinge's policy. The first inconclusive encounter at Mudki on 18 December was succeeded by the bloody
battle of Firuzshah (21–22 December) in which the British forces
gained the field but little else, and at a heavy cost. Bruised and battered
the main British force then squatted on the banks of the Satlej throughout the whole of January awaiting further reinforcements before ven-
turing across the river. On 28 January 1846 the situation of the British
forces was considerably eased by the remarkable victory of Sir Harry
Smith (1787–1860) at Aliwal, where, having collected various bodies of
detached troops under the nose of the enemy, he destroyed the Sikh
force which had remained on the left bank of the Satlej, leaving the
Sikhs only a tiny bridgehead at Sobraon, and thereby freed the British
garrisons along the river line and opened communications with
Meerut. Duly reinforced, the main force was able to defeat the Sikh

army at the destructive and decisive engagement of Sobraon (10 February), cross the river, and open the way to peace negotiations at Kasur on 15 February.[1]

The unhappy weeks that elapsed between the battles of Firuzshah and Sobraon were decisive for the evolution of British policy in the Panjab. By excluding the possibilities of a protectorate and of a subsidiary alliance, Hardinge had effectively narrowed down the choice to annexation or the retention of an independent Sikh state. Although opinion in Britain was hostile to annexation, Hardinge had been given a free hand and in the circumstances annexation would have been accepted by all and applauded by many. Hardinge's eventual decision in favour of retaining an independent Sikh state was partly in deference to London opinion but primarily the consequence of his appreciation of the military situation in January 1845.

During the December battles, out of 5,500 European troops engaged, almost 2,000 had become casualties. Sepoy losses were much slighter; only 1,200 out of 11,000 engaged. But Hardinge had no confidence in his sepoy troops and judged the strength of his forces by reference to the European element. Further reinforcements were available to him in Sind and the Lower Provinces, but these could not be employed before late March, when the spring floods would make the Panjab rivers a serious obstacle and the advent of the hot weather would make campaigning extremely hazardous. In short, Hardinge had grave doubts about whether he had a force sufficient to subdue the Panjab, particularly if, as he supposed would be the case, Sikh resistance became more obdurate when it became plain that annexation was intended. Also he lacked siege-equipment with which to pry the Sikhs out of the forts of Lahore, Amritsar, and Govindgarh, if they should occupy them; and he lacked cavalry with which to pursue the Sikhs if they withdrew. If therefore, as seemed likely, a war for the annexation of the Panjab would be prolonged into the winter of 1846 to 1847, various undesirable results might follow: the Afghans might take Peshawar and there could be uprisings within India. It was this last possibility which especially exercised the minds of his Councillors in Calcutta, led by Herbert Maddock, and although Hardinge later contended that Maddock exaggerated the danger from the internal enemy and cited Thomason, Sleeman, and others in support of his own views, there seems little doubt that the Governor-General's confidence was not so great in January 1846.[2] Certainly Hardinge believed that if British arms had suffered another reverse the Cis-Satlej Sikhs would have joined their co-religionists, so severing his communications. He informed Ripon that an advance to Lahore might endanger the safety of

British India.[3] These military arguments pointed towards a speedy negotiated solution.

In his dilemma Hardinge had no one to whom he could turn with real confidence. Broadfoot and Nicholson had been killed at Firuzshah and the Acting Political Agent, Captain Mills, lacked the experience and authority to rise above a purely executive role. Hardinge's principal source of political advice was his secretary, Frederick Currie, for whose opinions Hardinge had great respect, but Currie was a civilian and Hardinge saw the problem primarily in military terms. And there lay his greatest anxiety: he had no confidence whatsoever in his Commander-in-Chief, Sir Hugh Gough (1779–1869), or in the Commander-in-Chief's staff and he could find no quick way to replace them. Just as Elphinstone's incompetence had served to restrain Macnaghten in Afghanistan, so that of Gough acted as a brake upon both Ellenborough and Hardinge.

Hardinge announced his intended policy in a letter to Ripon dated 3 February, the same day on which Smith rejoined the main force after Aliwal and one week before the victory of Sobraon. Hardinge plumped for a weakened, but still independent Sikh state at Lahore, its army disbanded and reorganized, deprived of the Cis–Satlej lands (already annexed by Britain) and of the hills, wherein an independent Rajput state would be founded as contemplated in Hardinge's proclamation.[4] The only possible choice to head the Rajput state was, of course, Gulab Singh, whose latest approach to Britain after Firuzshah had not been wholly rebuffed, and who, as the new Chief Minister of Lahore, was ideally placed to procure a favourable negotiated settlement.[5] But the creation of an independent hill State was not merely a device to buy off Gulab as has sometimes been implied; it was a positive and long-contemplated element in the emerging British strategy. Hardinge's plan was modified in the more favourable situation after Sobraon in two ways, both to the detriment of the Sikh state. First, he proposed to transfer Kashmir from Lahore to Gulab Singh and second, he added the Jalandhar Doab (the stretch of territory lying between the Satlej and the Beas) to the British gains from the war.

The transfer of Kashmir was intended to weaken the Sikhs still further and to strengthen the new hill State of Gulab Singh which was seen as a counterbalance to Lahore. 'A Rajpoot State independent of the Sikhs on the right flank of our Beas frontier would strengthen us and weaken the Sikhs,' wrote Hardinge.[6] Later, he added that the transfer of Kashmir to the Rajput state would be useful in opposing Afghan claims.[7] In effect, in the new system there would be two anti-Muslim Hindu buffers, although there was about them an aura of ambiguity for they were also intended to neutralize each other. Hardinge did not reveal his intentions by demanding Kashmir directly, lest the demand should cause a prolongation of the war, but asked for an indemnity of £2 million which he was confident that the Lahore Government could not pay. Then, subsequently, he reduced his demand by £1 million for Kashmir and £500,000 for the Jalandhar Doab. Kashmir he sold to Gulab for £500,000 down and another £500,000 to pay later, although he later reduced this to £250,000 when Gulab agreed to relinquish certain territories on the right bank of the Beas which Hardinge required for better protection of the new British frontier.[8]

The annexation of the Jalandhar Doab was also intended to weaken the Lahore state by depriving it of valuable territory: 'a diminution of strength of such a war-like nation on our weakest frontier, seems to me imperatively required', wrote Hardinge.[9] It had another purpose of serving as an example to others throughout Asia that aggression would be punished. Most interesting, however, were the strategic reasons which inclined Hardinge to take the Jalandhar Doab. The war had demonstrated to him that the much praised Satlej frontier was unsatisfactory. It was too long and it presented grave problems of communications; the east-west course of the upper Satlej had allowed the Sikh force at Phillaur to threaten the main axis of Hardinge's communications, the route from Karnal to Firuzpur. Possession of the line of the Beas would shorten the frontier; screen Ludhiana and Rupar, which could therefore be used as supply depots; and would place the British forces only thirty-five miles from Amritsar and in a position to threaten the Sikh capital itself.[10]

Hardinge, recent contrary assertions notwithstanding, believed or claimed that he had secured the best military frontier for British India.[11] He had remedied what appeared to him to be the deficiencies of the Satlej frontier and he did not want the Indus frontier, partly because it would have meant the sacrifice of the Hindu buffer, but even more because of the problems of communications and finance which its possession would raise. Because of the flooding of the five great Panjab rivers communications would be disrupted between May and October. In consequence, Hardinge argued, each of the garrisons in each of the four Doabs as well as that at Peshawar would require to be of sufficient strength to support itself. The cost of garrisoning the Panjab he estimated at £1·7 million and the revenues of the remaining independent territory at £0·7 million. Taking into consideration the existing deficit of £1 million in British Indian finances Hardinge concluded that 'we could not shoulder the burden of annexation on financial grounds'.[12]

It is reasonable, however, to decline to accept Hardinge's arguments at face value, for many of them were elaborated subsequently in reply to severe criticism of his moderation in India and because of his fears that the incoming Whig Government in London might overturn his new system. Some of his arguments were expansions of points he had made before the war in defence of the Hindu buffer policy; such were the arguments concerning the Hindu buffer itself, the problems of communications, his general contention that British India was already overgrown, and his supposition that annexation of the Panjab would alarm other Indian states, themselves so valuable as safety-valves within the British system. Other arguments were more novel, such as his rather contradictory argument that without the presence of a powerful enemy the British Indian army would degenerate into a militia dangerous to the state. Some of his arguments, notably that relating to the cost of garrisoning the Panjab, could have been fairly easily demolished by anyone who cared to examine his assumptions and figures. While it may well be true that Hardinge attached some weight to each of these arguments, they do constitute a rationalization after the event. As argued above, expediency counted for more than long-term strategic calculation during the crucial period from January to March 1846. This observation can be supported by reference to statements which Hardinge made to James Hogg and to Ripon. To Hogg he wrote that from the viewpoint of personal ambition he would have liked to have annexed everything up to Peshawar, but to do so was not practicable.[13] And to Ripon he claimed that one of the advantages of his settlement was that it would allow annexation to be easily accomplished if it were so desired.[14]

Hardinge's settlement, which was formalized by the Treaties of Kasuri (9 March 1846) with the Lahore Government and Amritsar (16 March 1846) with Gulab Singh, was inherently unstable. In the first place, as noted earlier, there was a contradiction in the notion of two Hindu buffers, each counterbalancing the other. Second, there was a contradiction between the concept of Lahore as a state strong enough to be a useful buffer for British India and yet weak enough not to present a danger to British India. Hardinge, advised by Currie, who was thought to have been the principal architect of the settlement, had endeavoured to strike a balance: to reduce the power of Lahore so that it could not be a formidable enemy, while leaving it sufficient resources to be able to survive on its own. In fact the two British planners had tipped the balance too far towards weakness. The Lahore Government could not stand alone without British military and financial support. More than half the revenues of the former state had gone to Britain and to Gulab. With the meagre resources left the Lahore Government not only had to

maintain order but also to carry out a massive and unpopular reorganization; the remains of the old army had to be disbanded and a
new and smaller force formed. In consequence of the evident inability
of the Lahore Government to carry out these tasks unaided Hardinge
was compelled to agree, against the advice of his military counsellors,
who feared a repetition of the Kabul disaster, to leave a British garrison
at Lahore until the end of the year. The effect of this decision, as at
Kabul, was to transfer real power to the British Resident.

Broadfoot's death at Firuzshah created a temporary vacuum on the
frontier which enabled Hardinge and Currie to construct a settlement
which did not arise from the activities of the Political Agents. Contemplating Broadfoot's body, his personal assistant, Robert Cust,
remarked that there lay the main cause of the war.[15] Cust did not
explain the reason for a view which was shared by Cunningham,
George Clerk, and others. But its real justification surely resided in
Broadfoot's information monopoly position and in his ambition. Saunders Abbott recalled that when the news of the Sikh crossing of the
Satlej was first received Broadfoot turned to him in delight. ' "If we live
through this, Abbott", he said, "we are both made men." '[16] No doubt
Broadfoot was right and had he survived he would have been Resident
or Commissioner at Lahore with the eventual prospect of a seat on the
Supreme Council or a Governorship. But a Sikh bullet cut him down
and the prizes went elsewhere.

Of Broadfoot's senior assistants, Leech had died in September 1845,
and Nicholson had been killed at Mudki. At Firuzshah died D'Arcy
Todd, the former British representative at Herat. Hardinge was prejudiced against Cunningham whom he regarded as too pro-Sikh and
whom he sent to Bhopal. Mills and Abbott lacked sufficient experience
and Edward Lake, Cust, and P. A. Vans Agnew were all too junior to
succeed their former master. Hardinge was therefore obliged to go
outside the Ludhiana agency to find a new agent to take charge at
Lahore. The outstanding candidate was Henry Lawrence, a man of
unquestioned ability, unclouded reputation, undoubted knowledge of
the Sikhs, and useful and influential friends. Lawrence had already
been summoned from his Nepal Residency after Broadfoot's death and
had assisted Currie in the negotiation of the Treaties of Kasuri and
Amritsar.

The brothers Lawrence form the last and greatest of the frontier
political groups with which we are concerned. On the frontier were
three brothers. The oldest, George Lawrence, had served in Afghanistan as Military Secretary to Macnaghten and was now to serve in a
series of influential positions on the north-west frontier, rising to take

charge of the Rajasthan agency during the Mutiny. The second, Henry, became in 1846, as British Resident at Lahore, the builder of the new British policy in the north-west. Henry rapidly secured the allegiance of the younger Political Agents in the area, men like Edward Lake and Herbert Edwardes, and recruited new men who were thus initiated into the developing tradition of frontiersmanship. But Henry was not to reap the full rewards of his great position. Hardinge respected Henry's integrity and energy, but sometimes doubted his judgement and thought him inferior to Broadfoot. The Governor-General wanted to replace him with Currie. Currie's failings were to be exposed during the second Sikh war and Henry's second opportunity arrived but, as will be observed, Hardinge's successor, Dalhousie, liked neither Henry's policies nor his manners and preferred his brother, John. It was therefore to John Lawrence that the ultimate prize of the Panjab fell and, as his predecessors had foreseen, it was a post which could make a man. It made John Lawrence Governor-General. It would be a dull and insensitive historian who, contemplating the glistening careers of the Lawrences, did not allow his thoughts to stray back to another band of frontier brothers who once seemed to be clothed in anticipation in the imperial purple. When the Afghan strategy was in the ascendant and Macnaghten at the helm, it was the Conolly brothers who had seemed fated to dominate the frontier during the next generation and who blossomed under the patronage of their relative. But the Afghan strategy killed three of them before it finally collapsed and a fourth brother was later murdered by Moplahs. Frontier agents could make and unmake strategy or strategic fashion, but realities and blind chance could make and unmake them.

   Henry Lawrence was quick to stamp the impression of his strong personality on his new appointment. The nominal ruler of the reduced Lahore state was the eight-year-old Dalip Singh. His mother, Jind Kaur, was Regent, the Chief Minister was Lal Singh, and the army commander was Tej Singh. The last two were suspected of having betrayed the Sikh forces to the British during the war, but although they had made approaches to British agents before the war, there seems no sure evidence of any collusion during the hostilities. Certainly there is no reason to doubt their desire to establish an independent state at Lahore. According to the Treaty of Kasuri, British intervention in the internal affairs of Lahore was forbidden, unless it was requested, but the Lahore Government was powerless to evade British control. From the beginning the Lahore ministers were forced to act at Lawrence's bidding; in April 1846 when a riot took place at Lahore, following a cow-killing incident, Lawrence forced a reluctant Lal Singh to arrest the Brahmin ringleader. In December 1846 Lal Singh was removed because of his opposition to British interference and replaced by a Council of four. The change enabled Lawrence to rule the Panjab through his own agents and through the Brahmin ministers at Lahore, men who had no independent source of influence such as might enable them to withstand British pressure. The Sikh element was also diminished in the reorganized Lahore army which was principally recruited from Muslims and Hindus.

British intervention was exercised to various ends. It was employed first to carry out the provisions of the treaties. The Darbar was reluctant to transfer the hill territories, Kashmir and Hazara, to Gulab Singh and the Muslim majority in Kashmir also resented the imposition of Rajput rule. The Muslim Governor, Shaikh Imam al-Din, sought British support for the independence of Kashmir and defeated Gulab's troops when they invaded the province, but Lawrence declined to modify the settlement in so important a particular and placed himself at the head of the unwilling Sikh troops which were sent to enforce the transfer. With the help of a British force the rebel resistance was overcome. It was for encouraging Kashmiri resistance that Lal Singh was removed from power.[17] British interference was also used to bring Multan under closer control by Lahore. The great Governor of Multan, Sawan Mul, had been murdered in 1844 and was succeeded by his son Mulraj. Mulraj's hopes of independence had been frustrated in the 1846 Settlement and he soon found himself under pressure to pay more revenue to the Central Government. Lawrence intervened to negotiate a settlement by which Mulraj retained the Governorship from which Lal Singh had sought to remove him, but surrendered control of certain districts. The subsequent British attempt to replace Mulraj by a Governor who would be under complete British control was the direct cause of the second Sikh war. Yet another example of British interference is the Kangra episode. The Sikh garrison at Kangra in the north-east Panjab refused to surrender and Lawrence intervened to dictate harsh terms of surrender and almost provoked a siege. Hardinge was critical of Lawrence's conduct in this affair.[18]

It was soon evident that the system contemplated by Hardinge in March 1846 would not work in the Panjab any more than that contemplated by Auckland had worked in Afghanistan in 1839 and for the same reasons: the local Government was too weak and the British agents too interventionist. By December it was plain that the reformed and weakened Lahore Government could not do without the British troops which were due to be withdrawn in that month. As a condition of the retention of these troops the Lahore Government was obliged to accept a new treaty (Bhairowal, 16 December 1846) according to which British troops were to remain until 1854 and during that period the administration would be effectively placed in the hands of the Resident, who would choose ministers himself.

Hardinge accepted the change in policy with great reluctance. He had wanted to withdraw the British forces from Lahore believing their presence there to be too expensive, too distracting, too dangerous because of the problems of communications, deleterious to the troops concerned because of the distance from their homes in Oudh and because of the constant reminder of mutiny afforded by the sight of the former Khalsa soldiers around them, and prejudicial to his hopes for an independent Sikh Government.[19] But Hardinge shrank from the alternative of annexation and was therefore obliged to do whatever was necessary to bolster up his chosen system. A fortnight after his strong condemnation of the idea of retaining troops at Lahore beyond December 1846 he was compelled to accept the general opinion that it was impossible to withdraw them. Forced to make a virtue out of necessity he then claimed advantage for the new system which 'would enable the Government to govern the Punjab up to Peshawar more easily and cheaply than on any other terms'.[20] It was better than annexation: 'It is in reality annexation brought about by the supplication of the Sikhs without entailing upon us the present expense and future inconvenience of a doubtful acquisition.'[21] A further alleged merit of the new system was that it would give the Government in Britain time to think about the best policy for the Panjab. Hardinge was in fact well aware that the eventual decision might be for annexation. Without confessing that his judgement had been defective he himself could not espouse that alternative and was compelled by that convention which demands that we should always be right to argue against it. But he knew that his revised system had made the final step to annexation an easier one and even had the effrontery to claim as a further advantage for it that it facilitated a policy which he condemned. 'My successor', he remarked in an exceptionally unfortunate prophecy, 'may march to Peshawar without losing 100 men, whenever the true policy and real interest of Her Majesty may render such a step politic and proper.'[22]

In Hardinge's mind financial and strategic factors yet tipped the balance against annexation as a solution to the problems of the Panjab. Unobtrusively contradicting his own claims for the popularity of the new system in the Panjab he maintained that his high estimates of troops required to hold down the Panjab were still valid and continued to calculate the net cost at £1 million. From the strategic viewpoint he persevered in his opinion that the Sikh buffer was still required to insulate British India from contact with the Afghans. He rejected a proposal by Henry Lawrence to form a movable column for use in Bannu and to build a fort on the right bank of the Indus, on the grounds that the Sikh army would be unequal to maintaining these commitments and that the duty would fall upon Company troops which were unsuited to the work; above all, British India could not afford a reverse on the frontier. 'A Sikh mistake on the Indus is of no importance', he wrote, 'a British reverse howr. small wd. vibrate thoughout India, aye through Asia . . . Every skirmish agt. our arms with the Caffres [in South Africa] is joyfully proclaimed in the Native Press: the same of New Zealand.'[23]

It was therefore the internal enemy who once more dominated Hardinge's thinking about the external frontier. For the external frontier Hardinge had no fear. A Russian threat never entered his calculations and even the Afghan threat was dismissed in 1847. It would take the Afghans years to recover from anarchy, he argued. In March 1847 he wrote, 'there is no external enemy that can give the Govt. any real inconvenience. Nepal would be troublesome but soon ended.'[24] In July 1847 Hardinge summarized the frontier situation for Queen Victoria in a letter which, allowing for his natural desire to present his work to his Queen in the most favourable light, yet displays the principles of his strategic thought.

Your Majesty's Eastern Empire has this remarkable feature of unity and strength which renders it almost impenetrable against any external aggression. From Karrachee to Singapore the Frontier is 6000 miles in extent with no harbour except Bombay. The land frontier is also rather more than 6000 miles in extent from Karrachee by the Sutledge, Thibet and Nepal down to Singapore, with no entrance into India, except for the Khyber and Bolan passes. The latter opening into Scinde is of no importance.

Thus Your Majesty's Eastern Empire, embracing a circumference by land and sea of 12000 miles, cannot be assailed by any External Enemy which need give the Government of India any uneasiness . . .

As regards internal dangers there is no native power remaining able to face a British army in the field. The people are peaceful and the only dangers could come from mishandling of the Indian army in time of peace or interference with religious prejudice.[25]

The remarkable resemblance which existed between the situation in Afghanistan during the years 1839 to 1841 and that in the Panjab from 1846 to 1848 is nowhere better exemplified than in the spectacle of real power being exercised increasingly by the British Resident at the centre and by his assistants working through local Governors in the provinces. Many of those employed in the Panjab had served their political apprenticeship on the frontier during the period of the Afghan war and now re-emerged from the temporary oblivion to which Ellenborough had consigned them. Lawrence's chief assistant at Lahore was George Macgregor, Macnaghten's former assistant at Jalalabad. At Hazara was James Abbott, who had blotted his copybook at Khiva, and at Peshawar was George Lawrence, Macnaghten's former Military Secretary. Lawrence's principal rival for the Lahore post had been Frederick Mackeson, formerly assistant to Wade and then to Macnaghten at Peshawar. Mackeson was given charge of the Cis-Satlej Sikhs as a consolation prize, but was well placed to play a major part in frontier policy in 1848 to 1849. Henry's younger brother, John, a civil servant, was put in charge of the Jalandhar Doab, to which R. N. Cust was also assigned. Another civil servant employed on the frontier was P. A. Vans Agnew (1822–48) at Lahore but the great majority of the younger political assistants were recruited by Henry Lawrence from the traditional source of Political Agents—ambitious Indian army officers. Such were Herbert Edwards (1819–68) and Edward Lake (1823–77), H. B. Lumsden (1821–96), W. S. R. Hodson (1821–57), who had been served in Afghanistan where he had met George and Henry Lawrence, N. B. Lumsden (1821–96), W. S. R. Hodson (1821–57), who had been introduced to Henry Lawrence by their mutual friend, James Thomason, F. R. Pollock (1827–99), and Reynell Taylor (1822–86). These and others were employed in various capacities—as political assistants, as officers seconded to reorganize the Lahore army, and even on private missions until official employment became available. In 1847 Lumsden was employed to form the Guides, a force which provided Lawrence with a useful reconnaissance and small striking-force under his own control. British influence was strongest in the trans–Indus districts. There George Lawrence, James Abbott, Herbert Edwardes in Bannu, John Nicholson, and others on special missions built up a new basis of British influence among the Muslim peoples of the frontier. These agents had direct access to the Resident and were able to ensure the selection of governors of their choosing. The system which had seemed completely discredited by the events of 1841 to 1842 had now achieved new peaks of influence.

The first Sikh war led to a change in the locus of British Political Agency. With the exception of the brief usurpation of its position by the Kabul agency between 1839 and 1841, Ludhiana had been the centre of British frontier thinking and action for twenty years. With the establishment of the Lahore Residency the nerve-centre was at once shifted further westwards and the agent in the Cis–Satlej states lapsed into a position similar to that of Political Agents in other Indian states, suffering the fate of the past Residents of Lucknow, Ujjain, and Delhi. But although the dominance of Lahore under the new system was evident, it was also apparent that its place would eventually be taken by Peshawar for the transcendent importance of that city under the new state of affairs was clear; it was with George Lawrence that the Afghans opened communications in 1847. Thus the reign of Lahore was to be brief and even in the period between the two Sikh wars the shape of the last evolution of British frontier strategy, which was to make Peshawar, after 1849, the nerve-centre of the final apotheosis of the Political Agency system, was apparent.

The Lahore system, so rapidly created and staffed by so many young, able, energetic, and ambitious officers, generated its own dynamism. It was the Political Agency system which demanded more and more interference, even against the principles of its director. Some years later Henry Lawrence confessed to John Kaye, the historian, that

Looking back on our Regency career, my chief regrets are that we did so much. I and my assistants laboured zealously for the good of the country and the good of the people of all ranks, but we were ill supported by a venal and selfish Durbar, and were gradually obliged to come forward more than I wished and to act directly when I desired to do so only by advice.[26]

It might have been Macnaghten writing of Afghanistan. And just as it had done to Macnaghten, the logic of events pushed Lawrence further. There is little doubt that by the time he was obliged to leave India for his health at the end of 1847 the Resident had come to see the situation in the Panjab as inherently unstable and to regard annexation as ultimately inevitable.[27]

The shadow of London had played a considerable part in moulding Hardinge's policy towards the Panjab. It was his fears of the attitude which the Cabinet might take which had led him to restrain Broadfoot and the same fears continued to worry him up to and even beyond the outbreak of war. Immediately before the first bloody battle of Mudki he asked, 'Will the people of England consider an actual invasion of our frontier a justification of war?'[28] Although it seems probable that it was his doubts about Britain's military capacity to defeat both Lahore and internal risings which mainly decided him against annexation, it seems likely that his persistent worries about attitudes in England towards such an expansion of the Indian Empire also played their part in his final decision to preserve the state of Lahore.

The influence of London was exercised indirectly through general restraint upon Hardinge and not directly through Cabinet directions concerning the policy which he was to pursue. As has been shown, the Cabinet had rejected Ripon's proposal to set out general guidelines for Hardinge in advance, with the result that the war was over and the settlement framed before ministers had time to act, even if they had wished to do so.

The first news of the war reached London about 6.0 p.m. on Thursday 5 February, two days after Hardinge, on the Satlej, had outlined his intended settlement. Characteristically, *The Times* received the first information and the Government was left to wait for the dispatches. Even when they arrived there was little solid news in them beyond the bare fact of the Sikhs having crossed the Satlej, because Hardinge sent neither letter nor dispatch for three weeks. Not until the end of December did Hardinge send Ripon his first detailed narrative of events. His own personal comments he put into a private letter to Peel in which he set out his desperate worries about the competence of his Commander-in-Chief.

Despite the assumed optimism of his official dispatch, the situation was critical, Hardinge reported, and the army and British rule in India were in great peril so long as Gough remained in charge. Gough was a brave and honourable officer, an excellent divisional commander, but quite unsuited to the charge of an army in the field. He was an incompetent strategist, a poor tactician, had no capacity for administration, and his staff was very bad. Gough's imprudence had placed the army in a critical positon at Firuzshah. Hardinge confessed that he had thought of sending for Sir Charles Napier from Sind, believing him to be the best man to take over from Gough. As it was, said Hardinge, with Gough as Commander-in-Chief, he was obliged to proceed with great caution, for 'at this extremity of the Empire a defeat is almost the loss of India.'[29] It was this sombre, even despairing letter which destroyed the early optimism which had distinguished the reaction of ministers to the news of the war and brought the Cabinet together on 24 February to discuss the problems of the Panjab.

The immediate need was to give Hardinge the military and financial help which he required. There was no problem about military reinforcements; the Government was willing to supply at India's expense all the Queen's troops that Hardinge wanted. The financial question, however, indicated the limitations on British help. To meet the costs of the war Hardinge needed cash and it seemed improbable that he could borrow enough in India at the existing rate on government loans of 4 per cent. Some commentators blamed the dismal military performance for the reluctance of investors to lend money, although Hardinge, not surprisingly, preferred to blame general economic conditions. Because of the size of the existing financial deficit in India, Hardinge did not want to raise the rate of interest to 5 per cent to attract funds, but proposed to borrow £2 million from the British Treasury. But the Treasury refused and all the Cabinet would do was to authorize a 5 per cent loan in India and this Hardinge was reluctantly obliged to accept. Hardinge had forgotten the prime condition of the existence of Britain's Indian Empire, namely that it should not cost Britain anything.

The critical problem which the Cabinet had to resolve was that of political and military leadership. The Cabinet immediately appointed Sir George Arthur, the Governor of Bombay, as prospective successor to Hardinge in the not unlikely event of the Governor-General's death, thereby superseding Herbert Maddock, the President of the Bengal Council, who would normally have become acting Governor-General. Maddock nearly resigned when he heard of the matter, but the Cabinet were confident that Arthur was the better man for a military emergency. A more crucial problem, however, was that of command of the British Indian Army. Ellenborough, now restored to the Cabinet as First Lord of the Admiralty, declared India to be in mortal peril, bombarded Ripon with plans of defence, and urged that Sir Charles Napier should be appointed Commander-in-Chief. This proposal threatened to precipitate a constitutional crisis because the Court of Directors, who would willingly have co-operated in getting rid of Gough, would not have in his place a man they detested and who returned their dislike with interest. Ellenborough, perhaps seeing an opportunity for personal revenge, would have coerced the Directors with an Act of Parliament, but, as Ripon remarked, 'to undertake such a change under the actual circumstances of the Government at home, would be a very tender affair indeed, and not to be decided in an afternoon.'[30]

Ripon's allusion was to the weakness of the Conservative Cabinet since Peel's announcement in November 1845 of his intention to repeal the Corn Laws and it exposes another important constraint limiting the ability of the Cabinet to control India. While a strong Ministry could, if it wished, dictate policy to the British Indian Government, strong ministries were unusual in Britain at this time and a weak Ministry risked losing the support of independents and even of its own supporters if it attempted to dictate to Calcutta or to the Court of Directors. British Governments had to contend both with the Indian interest and with the more general conviction that India was a valuable possession not to be hazarded for political ends. British Governments, therefore, preferred that the Indian Government should accept responsibility for its own policies and it frequently suited them that the Governor-General should belong to the opposition party, for that fact would tend to reduce criticism of the Indian Government which might injure the Ministry. This natural inclination to avoid responsibility for Indian affairs had its effect during the 1846 Panjab affair as in other episodes.

The Conservative Cabinet wanted a device which would enable them to dispose of Gough quietly, both out of consideration for his personal feelings and to avoid presenting political capital to their opponents. It took them two weeks before a suitable legal procedure was found by which Hardinge was left in command and Gough was to be sent down to Calcutta with a polite letter from the invaluable Wellington to salve his pride.[31] Ripon proposed to compensate Gough with a peerage, but Peel indignantly refused; a peerage was a quite inappropriate reward for a man who was being dismissed for incompetence, he remarked in his old-fashioned way.[32]

Ministers spent more time on the Gough affair than on any other aspect of Panjab policy and the reason is plain; like the affair of the Kabul prisoners in 1842, it was political dynamite. In the past, Parliament had demonstrated that it could give short shrift to a government which appointed and maintained an incompetent general who threw away the lives of British soldiers. And the Conservative Government was on singularly weak ground in respect of Gough, for it had already been warned of his failings. Gough should not have had the post of Commander-in-Chief, but had been given it by Wellington as a consolation prize for losing the command at Madras through no fault of his own. Gough's poor performance in the Gwalior war had led Ellenborough to question his suitability, but nothing had been done to find a replacement, although the Cabinet received a further warning in the summer of 1845. As the war clouds gathered over the frontier, Hardinge's Council, led by Herbert Maddock, wrote privately, without Hardinge's knowledge, to the Chairman of the Court, Sir Henry Willock, warning of the dangers of leaving Gough to command against the Sikhs. Hardinge did not stop his colleagues but, by refusing to act with them, prevented the Council from taking the matter up officially. Willock informed Ripon who in turn asked Wellington's advice on 7 October. But Wellington expressed his confidence in Gough and nothing could be done in the military field against the Duke's advice. The upshot was that the Government had a good deal to hide in the affair of Gough.

The charges against Gough were that he had little idea of strategy, or of the organization of armies, that his chosen staff was incompetent, and that his battlefield tactics were crude and costly. The first three charges were much the more serious against a Commander-in-Chief, but it was the last charge of tactical ineptitude which attracted greater attention and it was on this point that Wellington stood up for Gough. Gough had a predilection for charging the enemy with the bayonet and tended to regard artillery preparation as a wasteful decoration; his critics favoured a much longer period of softening up the enemy by artillery bombardment. It is impossible at this distance to deliver a verdict on which was right, the more so since one of the alternatives was purely hypothetical, but it is fair to say that Gough's critics were partly led astray by experience of easy victories over undisciplined troops who lacked artillery. As Wellington himself had discovered at Assaye, where his losses were proportionately higher than those suffered by Gough, cheap victories against a resolute, skilled, well-disciplined and well-equipped foe were not to be had, and in 1845 the Sikh artillery and infantry was comparable in all but size to the best European armies. Nevertheless, the impression remains that Gough mishandled his battles. Even Wellington regarded Mudki as a defeat, but with admirable phlegm he asserted that the Government should put a good face on it and order the Park and Tower guns to be fired in celebration of a victory.[33]

Only when the Gough affair was out of the way did the Cabinet feel able to consider Panjab policy. Little was to be gleaned on this subject from the Court of Directors, which was never consulted about policy and which, in any case, was divided; the Chairman, Willock, wanted nothing west of the Satlej, while the Deputy, Sir James Hogg, wanted everything east of the Indus. In consultation with George Clerk, who left for India at this time, Ripon drew up a proposal to annex the Panjab as far west as the Ravi, that is including Lahore, Amritsar, and Govindgarh. The area west of the Ravi was to be a protectorate, but, being Muslim, should not be administered directly. The hills should also become a British protectorate. Ripon later revived his former notion of joining the newly-annexed territory with Sind and the Jamna–Satlej Doab to form a fourth Presidency and moving the seat of government to the north-west. Wellington opposed the last suggestion on the grounds that the capital should be on the coast at Calcutta.[34] The possibility of moving the capital of British India to the north-west was one frequently mooted and the continuing sensitivity of the north-western frontier, which had compelled successive Governor-Generals to give much of their attention to the area, was a major argument for the move; since Amherst's tour in 1826 to 1827 the Governor-Generals had spent more than half their time on tour in the north-west.[35]

Ripon wanted the Cabinet to consider his draft proposal and to advise Hardinge on the policy which he should follow in the Panjab, but Peel refused on the grounds that the British Government had insufficient information and suggested that Hardinge should be asked to report to the Cabinet and given authority to make any provisional arrangement.[36] This suggestion was tantamount to leaving the decision to Hardinge, for it was impossible to postpone a decision on the Panjab for the required length of time. Peel also suggested that Ripon's draft should be circulated and members of the Cabinet invited to submit their own views; then, if so desired, the draft could be sent to Hardinge merely as points for his consideration. Ripon was unhappy with this arrangement, which seemed an evasion of responsibility, and thought Hardinge entitled to receive, at least in the form of a private letter, some statement of the principles which ministers would like to see embodied in a settlement of the Panjab.[37] Nevertheless, he was obliged to do as Peel wished and to circulate the draft. Only Ellenborough chose to submit an alternative draft: namely that the Jalandhar Doab should be annexed, Gulab made independent in the Hills, and the remainder of the Lahore state converted into a protectorate on the Cis–Satlej model, that is broken up into a number of small princely states. The Cabinet considered the two drafts on Saturday 21 March and ministers endorsed Peel's view, refusing to authorize Ripon to advise Hardinge what policy he should pursue. The general opinion, Ripon reported when he sent Hardinge copies of his own and Ellenborough's memoranda, was that everything should be left to Hardinge's decision.[38]

The news of Hardinge's victory at Sobraon, his terms for peace, and the opening of peace negotiations reached London on 1 April. In the light of the Cabinet's decision there was little Ripon could do but give his immediate approval. Indeed Hardinge's news was generally received with delighted relief; the Governor-General had not gone as far as Ripon had hoped, but his proposals were very satisfactory.[39] 'There is but one feeling in this Country as to your conduct,' he wrote. 'Everybody of whatever party, admires every part of your conduct.'[40] Hardinge had indeed extricated his colleagues from a potentially embarrassing situation.

The Conservative Cabinet made no further attempt to advise Hardinge on general policy. Wellington offered some constructive comments on the maintenance of military communications in the Panjab, Ripon expressed disquiet about the prospect of Peshawar falling into Afghan hands, and there was general unease concerning the morality of the deal with Gulab Singh, which looked uncommonly like bribery.

Nevertheless, there was no attempt to fetter Hardinge. Even so, the Governor-General remained acutely sensitive to the opinions of London and reacted in a hurt manner to the outdated and discarded suggestions which Ripon had sent to him on 24 March. Ripon, Hardinge complained, had changed his opinions considerably, while for Ellenborough's interventions the Governor-General felt real bitterness.[41] Ellenborough had not only sent advice to Hardinge but also to his military commanders and had criticized Hardinge's military dispositions in his letters to them. Hardinge remarked that Ellenborough even cherished the delusion that the sepoys would have fought well for him because they knew that Ellenborough had confidence in them.[42]

In summary, the authorities in London had little influence on the Panjab Settlement, as little as on the Afghan or Sind Settlements earlier. The Court of Directors cancelled itself out and the Cabinet refused responsibility. Although Ripon, Ellenborough, and possibly Wellington would have liked to advance the British defensive frontier to the Indus, they did not agree on the means and the majority of the Cabinet did not wish to concern itself with strategy. Nor was it especially worried about the international repercussions. In October 1845 Brunnow had expressed dark doubts about Russia's reception of the news of any possible British advance into the Panjab. Peel and Aberdeen had endeavoured to allay the Russian Ambassador's fear and had warned Hardinge accordingly.[43] But when the news of the war arrived in London the Russian reaction became a matter of insignificance. As in 1842 to 1843 the main matters which concerned ministers were those which seemed likely to have adverse consequences in Parliament: namely, anything smacking of a desire for war and conquest, which were thought to be immoral and unprofitable; and anything reflecting upon the Cabinet's competence as opposed to that of the Indian Government. Gough and Gulab Singh were the weak points in the Government's armoury and the object was to keep them quietly hidden and to put a good face on the affair. With the help of Hardinge and Wellington the Ministry was successful and when the Conservative Government did fall in June 1846 it was over the Corn Laws and not over Lahore.

The Panjab Annexed

For many years the bare mention of the possible acquisition of the dominions of Runjeet Singh kindled a fever of expectancy in the minds of the English in India. Their imaginations grasped the grand idea of a country of inexhaustible wealth, whose annexation to our own territories would supply a general remedy for all our financial diseases.

J. W. Kaye, 1853.

Throughout this book the process of imperial expansion has been seen as one of interaction between individuals, groups, and institutions placed in a particular relationship to each other in a bureaucratic system by historical circumstance and conversing through the special language of strategy. Within that system of relationships there is no rule of precedence to dictate that one or another level should predominate in the formation of policy, any more than in a motor car one can say that the petrol pump is more important than the carburettor or either of more consequence than the pistons. Yet human systems are not wholly analogous to mechanical systems; and within the former, weight is continually redistributed according to situations produced both by outside logic and by the vagaries of human personality. What is here termed outside logic confers upon the frontier agent the advantage of a virtual monopoly of information and upon the Cabinet power of ultimate decision; it also provides a role for all intermediate authorities. The extent to which the opportunities provided by outside logic are exploited depends in large part upon personality. The development of British policy towards the Panjab during the years 1839 to 1849 provides an instructive illustration both of the strength of the intermediary role of the Governor-General, forming as he did the keystone in the arch connecting Britain and India, and of the impact of personality upon its exploitation. It was the apprehension of an indecisive man, rather than strategic conviction, which led Auckland to lean away from the Panjab policy recommended by Macnaghten; first fear, then megalomania which determined the attitudes of Ellenborough; uncertainty and lack of self-confidence which induced Hardinge to permit Broadfoot and the Cabinet to exercise such influence over his policy during the first eighteen months of his rule, and accident, combined with a peculiar obsession with one facet of the problem, which obliged him eventually to select his own new system; and it was the strength and self-confidence of Dalhousie which shaped the final dénouement in 1848 to 1849.

Dalhousie succeeded Hardinge as Governor-General in January 1848. Beyond question he was an outstanding man, probably the greatest of all the men sent by Britain to administer India. Physically insignificant, ordinary in conversation, unexciting as a letter-writer, uninterested in external display, he would have seemed nondescript but for the extraordinary power of his mind, the certainty of his judgement, and the facility of his execution. He was a superb adminis-trator. He could read quickly, form a sound opinion, and support it with careful arguments designed to smother all objections; a Dalhousie minute wrapped up its subject as neatly as a spider enfolds its prey. Like Richard Wellesley, Dalhousie was prone to melancholia; a fatal kidney disease provided a physical foundation for his ill-health. Like Wellesley too he was vain, but only in respect of the glory of his family, and Dalhousie avoided the personal absurdities which charac-terized the career of his predecessor.

Dalhousie sought and accepted the post of Governor-General partly through family pride (his father had been Commander-in-Chief in India); partly for money (his £5,000 a year would not support his earldom); and partly because his hopes in English politics had been disappointed. He had served Peel diligently at the Board of Trade and in the House of Lords, where he had carried the greatest burden of Government business, but he did not feel that he had been adequately rewarded and was quite bitter about Peel and others among his col-leagues. The break-up of the Conservative Party in 1846 left him with few prospects, and India, although he detested the thought of life there, offered him an opportunity to achieve fame and handsome rewards. To the Whigs he was a most suitable candidate for the chief post in India because his appointment served not only as an olive branch towards their political opponents but also as a means of muzzling Peelite criticism if anything went wrong in India. The Whigs certaintly knew little of Dalhousie at the time of his appointment, although his qualities later commanded the admiration of Hobhouse who had been back at the Board of Control since the summer of 1846.

Dalhousie's expansionist record has led some writers to see expan-sion as a fixed principle of his mind. This view is erroneous; Dalhousie was an administrator who took each problem as it came. If his judgement frequently favoured annexation this was because of his inclination to believe that 'whate'er is best administered is best'. British administration was better than Indian administration and should prevail if no good reason opposed itself to the transfer. Although this policy found support within the Civil Service, there is no reason to suppose that the Governor-General was unduly influenced by his fellow Councillors or by his subordinates. Much of Dalhousie's time was spent on tour away from his Council to whom he confided the details of Bengal adminstration. His relations with the Councillors were good, apart from some differences with the Law Member, John Bethune (1801–51), and a decisive clash with his second Commander-in-Chief, Sir Charles Napier, who resigned. Dalhousie's relations with London were also good. He disliked Hobhouse, who 'addressed me as no gentleman would address his gamekeeper',[1] but concealed his dislike and worked well with the Whig President. And although he disliked the Court of Directors as an institution, because it acted as a screen for the clerks who wrote the dispatches and who 'fancy themselves the hidden springs by which this Empire is in reality moved',[2] he got on well with the Directors as individuals.

Hardinge's Panjab Settlement did not long survive its author's departure. The attempt to establish effective British rule in Multan provoked a rising in April 1848 which spread to the Sikh troops in that town and resulted in the murder of the two British representatives, Vans Agnew and Lieutenant William Anderson, who had been sent to take over the government of Multan. Dalhousie's response to this episode has led to some debate among historians. Dalhousie could have chosen either to take risks in order to suppress the Multan outbreak quickly in the hope of sealing it off, or to wait until the autumn made campaigning safer, with the danger that the insurrection would become general throughout the Panjab. Dalhousie chose the latter alternative and had been accused of deliberately delaying action in the hope that the rising would spread and so justify annexation.[3]

The evidence does not support the view that Dalhousie wished to create a situation in which annexation became the obvious course. He hoped that the Hardinge system would work because he believed the Sikh buffer policy to be strategically the most desirable arrangement and because of the financial objections to annexation. His decision to wait until autumn was not really his decision at all, although he took full responsibility for it, but an endorsement of the recommendations of Sir Frederick Currie, acting Resident in Lahore, and of Sir Hugh Gough, still the Commander-in-Chief.

Currie's initial reaction was to regard the troubles at Multan as a minor disturbance and to send Sikh troops to deal with them. Subsequently, on hearing that the former Governor of Multan, Mulraj, was involved in the disturbances, Currie alerted the British movable column, which Hardinge had ordered to be stationed at Lahore to deal with such contingencies, to prepare to march to Multan. Afterwards, when he heard of the full extent of the disturbances, of the murder of Vans Agnew and Anderson, and of the desertion to the rebels of the Sikh troops and chiefs who had accompanied the British officers, Currie decided to retain the column at Lahore. At this point Currie anticipated a series of disasters, including a mutiny of other Sikh troops, a rising by the Cis–Satlej Sikhs, and an Afghan occupation of Peshawar. He even imagined an extensive conspiracy against British rule involving Muslims, Hindus, and Sikhs, and extending from Lahore to Delhi. Currie's instinct was to batten down hatches and to hang on at Lahore until help could arrive. In his advice to Dalhousie, however, Currie laid greatest stress on the factor of the weather which, he said, made military movements very dangerous: the heat could slay four British soldiers out of five as they marched to Multan, the hottest place in India; and the rains in July would disrupt all communications. In addition no siege-equipment was available to take Multan. Gough agreed with this analysis and added that he could not supply troops for Multan because, on the advice of Hardinge that no dangers were to be expected, he had dismissed all the carriage animals kept by his supporting force on the Satlej at Firuzpur.

Dalhousie gave full support to Currie in each successive decision. Dalhousie was unhappy in so doing for he anticipated strong criticism from England because he was not acting sufficiently vigorously. Also he understood the dangers of delay—that the insurrection might engulf the whole Panjab. Yet it is difficult to see that he had any option but to accept the views of those on the spot who declared that the dangers of premature action were even greater. Political considerations did not enter into Dalhousie's decision; he did not want annexation—'we do not, and ought not to desire the country', he wrote on 11 May, 'We have in my opinion every reason for wishing it to remain an independent and a friendly power.'[4] Punishment of the guilty there must be for the sake of British prestige: if the Lahore Government was loyal the Governor-General would limit his revenge to those at Multan; but if the Sikh Government was proved to be implicated he would impose an unspecified national retribution upon the Lahore state.[5] Dalhousie maintained these views throughout May and June 1848.

While official British policy was to imitate the action of the hedgehog until autumn, a local Political Agent in the trans-Indus districts, Herbert Edwardes, had decided to play the role of the fox. Raising a force of Pathan irregulars and in alliance with the ever-faithful Nawab of Bahawalpur, Edwardes marched on Multan. Dalhousie doubted the military safety of this expedition and had much stronger doubts about its political repercussions when it was reported that Edwardes, with Currie's approval, had offered terms to Mulraj. The Governor-General was strongly opposed to bargaining with a traitor and was still more annoyed with the unauthorized action of a subordinate officer in so binding his Government.[6]

Dalhousie's critics have taken his reproof of Edwardes and Currie as evidence of his alleged desire to prolong the crisis in order to justify annexation. Once more the charge cannot be sustained. Dalhousie's objection to Edwardes's policy was in accordance with the fundamental point of Dalhousie's stance—the maintenance of British prestige—a point which ultimately proceeds from the concept of the internal frontier. It was prestige, not appetite for expansion, which led him to demand that ultimate negotiation with the Lahore Government should be reserved to himself.[7] Dalhousie believed that Edwardes was acting from weakness in offering his concession; when he learned that Edwardes had crossed the Indus and defeated Mulraj on 18 June the Governor-General was delighted. If Edwardes could capture Multan in the face of the opinion of Gough that the task was impossible without a large siege-train, supported as that opinion was by Currie and by Dalhousie himself, the Governor-General would be delighted, despite the blow to his own dignity and judgement.[8]

Edwardes's success was the first blow to Dalhousie's confidence in the judgement of his Resident and his Commander-in-Chief. On 9 July his confidence was still more shaken by the receipt of an announcement by Currie that, after all, he had decided to send the movable column to Multan to assist in the siege.[9] Dalhousie had backed his subordinates completely in May when they had argued that such a move was impossible and thereby laid himself open to possible criticism from London. Now, in July, although nothing had changed, they announced that the expedition was possible after all. Seemingly, Currie was as wrong about the weather as he was in his prognosis of a general insurrection. Dalhousie's feelings must have been similar to those of the Emperor who discovered he had no clothes. Because of Currie's previous arguments Dalhousie had refused Gough's request for an immediate increase in the Indian army, arguing that if nothing could be done until October there was no point in incurring needless expense until nearer the time. Now Dalhousie lacked the forces which might be required to support the move on Multan. If Currie's present arguments were right Dalhousie greatly regretted that he had not acted to suppress the rebellion in early May. So, although he again backed Currie's judgement, from this time onwards the new Governor-General began to rely more upon his own judgement which told him that the May policy had been correct.[10]

It was early in August that the balance of Dalhousie's opinion swung in favour of annexation. In May and June he had hoped for an early settlement, more or less continuing Hardinge's system. At the beginning of July he seems to have been undecided, for he pleaded illness to Hobhouse as an excuse for postponing any discussion of future plans.[11] But on 4 August he wrote to his friend, Couper, that the Sikh army was traitorous to a man, that the Lahore Government was impotent, and that Hardinge's policy had broken down. There could be no real peace without annexation which must be the inevitable end of the affair.[12] In a letter to Hobhouse dated 15 August the Governor-General set out his reasoning in greater detail. If, as Dalhousie believed would happen, it was proved that there had been a general conspiracy against British authority, there was no option but to annex the Panjab. If no general conspiracy were proved to have existed there would be four possible courses of action: to leave the existing system intact and limit retribution to Mulraj and those found guilty of participation in the disturbances; to follow this course and to annex Multan as well; to punish the guilty, annex Multan, and then withdraw from the Panjab; or to annex the whole. Dalhousie judged that the first two were unacceptable; the concept of the Hindu buffer was the most desirable for British India but the policy of maintaining an independent Panjab was unviable—the materials for a Sikh Government did not exist, and the financial burden on Britain was too great. The third option was unworkable because of problems of communications. The best solution was annexation: 'to subvert that Govt., to abolish that army, and to convert into a British province the Raj of the Punjab'. This would ensure the punishment of the guilty, the recovery of expenditure, and 'it affords us the only means of securing the tranquillity of our frontier and safety of our subjects.' The only major objection to annexation was financial. Working from figures provided by the former Secretary to the Board of Revenue, now Foreign Secretary, Sir Henry Elliot (1808–53), Hardinge had estimated the net loss on the annexation of the Panjab at £1 million per year. Dalhousie now challenged these figures. By resumptions of rent-free grants the Panjab revenues could be increased by £500,000 while the expense of garrisons could be continually reduced as the Sikh troops were disarmed, and their forts destroyed. The estimates of the cost of administration could be lowered if a simple, rough and ready system were introduced.[13]

The events of the following six months confirmed Dalhousie in his approval of annexation. The rebellion did spread. In the Hazara territory, the local British agent, James Abbott, convinced of the existence of a general Sikh conspiracy, decided to raise Muslim irregular troops and to attack the Sikh Governor of Hazara, Sardar Chattar Sing Attariwala, a man for whom Abbott had a personal dislike. If Chattar Singh were indeed contemplating rebellion, Abbott's action turned the balance. Chattar Singh's rebellion was shortly followed by that of his son, Raja Sher Singh, the commander of the hitherto loyal Sikh troops engaged in the siege of Multan. The British column under General William Whish (1787–1853) was forced to raise the siege of Multan and this reverse to British arms was followed by further outbreaks of revolt including one at Peshawar, seized by Chattar Singh on 3 November.

The operations of Edwardes and Abbott suggest that a fundamental change in British policy had been wrought by the experience gained in the trans-Indus districts since 1846. The British agents who had taken over the government of these areas under the Lawrentian system had imbibed the impression that British rule was welcomed by the Muslim subjects of the Lahore Government. Accordingly, they did not hesitate to employ Muslim troops against the Sikhs. One effect of this policy may well have been to drive the Sikhs into hostility to British rule. But a more important implication concerns the possibility of annexation. For whereas Hardinge had seen the Sikhs in the manner of Clerk as a valuable communal bulwark insulating Britain from contact with the wild Muslim peoples of the frontier, Dalhousie was led by the reports of his agents to see the Sikhs not as a buffer, but as an unwelcome obstacle standing between Britain and Muslims who craved the benefits of British rule. The people of the three western Doabs, he wrote to Hobhouse on 15 August, are largely Muslim and eager for British rule. Thus crumbled the strategic orthodoxy of twenty years.

The spread of the war seemed to corroborate Dalhousie's opinion in favour of annexation. 'I can see no escape from the necessity of annexing this infernal country', he wrote to Couper on 18 September.' I shall avoid annexation to the last moment; but I do not anticipate that it can be avoided.'[14] The news of the defection of the Sikh troops at Multan dispelled any remaining doubts which he might have held. 'The rebellion of the Sikh nation has at last become open, flagrant, and universal', he wrote to Hobhouse on 1 October. There was no choice but to fight and to annex. Until this was accomplished 'there will be no peace for India—no security for our frontiers—no release from anxiety—no guarantee for the tranquillity and improvement of our own provinces.'

Dalhousie ordered a substantial increase in the size of the army and the assembly of a force at Firuzpur.[15]

The second Sikh war was uncomfortably like the first. Dalhousie wanted Gough to move cautiously until Multan had surrendered and the Commander-in-Chief had been able to unite his forces with the seventeen thousand now under Whish at Multan so as to form an overwhelming army for the conquest of the Panjab. This strategy was also that recommended by Wellington. But Multan did not fall until January 1849 and early in November 1848 Sir Hugh Gough's force of twenty-one thousand men and sixty-five guns began to cross the Ravi. On 26 November and 2 to 3 December Gough fought his Mudkis—two inconclusive engagements at Ramnagar and the Chenab—and then, on 13 January 1849 repeated the horrors of Firuzshah at the village of Chilianwala, on the banks of the Jhelum. In consequence of this last engagement Gough was forced to retire to the Chenab, where, reinforced by the Multan troops, he contrived his Sobraon—a decisive victory at Gujarat (21 February 1849).

Similar events had decided Hardinge in favour of a negotiated settlement, but the progress of the campaign served only to increase Dalhousie's determination to annex the Panjab. The reverses to British arms required to be revenged and to be seen to be revenged in the most signal fashion—by annexation. The peace of the internal frontier also required annexation and this argument from the internal frontier was especially reinforced by the developments which took place at Peshawar. At Peshawar Chattar Singh had decided to seek a deal with the Afghans: in return for their help against the British onslaught which he foresaw, he offered to deliver the district of Peshawar to the Afghans. This was not of course a new conception. Something like it had been feared by Britons in 1845 and 1846 and in July 1848 Mulraj had offered Peshawar to Dost Muhammad, but the Afghan ruler had refused what Mulraj was in no position to deliver. Chattar Singh's offer was a different proposition and Dost Muhammad responded by sending troops. However, after occupying Peshawar, Chattar Singh made over the district not to Dost Muhammad, but to the old Sikh protégés, the Barakzay Sardars, Sultan Muhammad Khan and Pir Muhammad Khan.[16] Despite this rebuff, Dost Muhammad's forces did take action in support of the rebels and fifteen hundred fought at Gujarat. One son was sent to take possession of Bannu and Dost Muhammad himself visited Peshawar to lay claim to Kashmir, the Darajat, and Hazara and also took some part in the siege of Attock. In addition the Kabul ruler urged the Sardars of Qandahar to march on Sind. In short, Dost Muhammad took action to register and support his claims, but stopped short of any all-out commitment to the rebel Sikhs. Presumably his best hope was an agreement with Britain which would have permitted him to retain Peshawar in some capacity.

The prospect of an Afghan occupation of Peshawar came to occupy an influential position in Dalhousie's calculations. 'Hitherto this had not been the case. Unlike Hardinge and Ripon, for whom the safety of Peshawar had been an important objective in their plans for a Panjab settlement. Dalhousie had not given any prominence to the future of that frontier city until he received the news that it had been made over to the Afghans. Even then he adopted no immediate fixed opinion concerning the disposition of Peshawar itself, providing that it was under some form of British control. But he was adamant that he could not tolerate its forcible acquisition by Dost Muhammad; the Afghan ruler must be evicted first, although at the beginning of January 1849 Dalhousie did not exclude the possiblity of a subsequent agreement within him.[17] The Governor-General repeated this view at the beginning of February: 'we cannot *with safety*, permit a Mahommedan power, raising the Cry of Islam, to seize by force territories under our protection.'[18]

At root Dalhousie's objection to Dost Muhammad was not his presence in Peshawar, but the fact that his presence had come about in opposition to Britain. The question was essentially one of prestige. The eyes of India were on the Panjab and they had witnessed British military reverses which had destroyed the general conviction of British superiority. Dalhousie made this point clear and in so doing clarified the basic principle of his Panjab and Indian strategy in a letter written before he received news of the victory at Gujarat. The quotation is long, but it repays study for it is a clear statement of one of the fundamental arguments in the long debate on Indian defence.

Above all the Ameer of Cabul, proclaiming himself the Apostle of Islam and calling on all Mussulmans to join in a Holy War against the Feringhees, has joined the inveterate enemies of his people in order to combined (*sic*) attack on us. *There is a Mahomedan invasion from the West.*

This is no question of provinces. This is a direct appeal to Mahomedan India. If you do not boldly meet this invasion, crush it and eject the invader, and *hold as your own* every foot of the territory which has been forcibly taken by the Mussulman from under the protection of Britain, you will be considered as having been worsted; you will assuredly encourage hopes of restored supremacy in the minds of Mahomedan states and people here in India; where hostility is now dormant perhaps, but where it is not, and never will be extinct. You will lay the first hand on the fabric of your own power in India; and you will take the first step towards retiring some day from it.

I regard this now as a question of national self-preservation. If the national supremacy is fully vindicated in the eyes of the native powers now, I apprehend nothing in the future. If not—if this Mahomedan invasion be submitted to, if concession or compromise be made—if anything be done wh. shall appear to fall short of full assertion of absolute superiority now over this enemy, and of maintenance of it hereafter, I believe in my conscience it will be the beginning of misfortunes and of dangers to this Empire. War beyond the Khyber, let me add, I never contemplate.[19]

This important letter constitutes a justification for the annexation of the Panjab by reference to the internal enemy. Dost Muhammad was nothing—he could easily be defeated or even, under different circumstances, be allowed to remain in Peshawar. Unlike Hardinge, Dalhousie did not base his argument for the occupation of Peshawar upon the need to exclude the external enemy. He based himself four-square on the need to vindicate British prestige; the rout of a Muslim adversary would quash any Muslim discontent within India. It is true that no direct connection between the expulsion of the Afghans and the annexation of the Panjab existed; although London had cautioned Dalhousie about annexation, no one had told him not to expel the Afghans and in theory he could have driven them out and yet evolved some other system short of annexation for the Panjab. But Dalhousie had made the connection by his insistence that British vindication required that Peshawar should be held as her own. Plainly, to hold Peshawar must involve the military occupation of the Panjab and therefore the extinction of the independent Sikh state. Of Dalhousie's four options only annexation was compatible with holding Peshawar. The connection between expulsion and annexation was implicit and accounts for the way in which Dalhousie laboured the apparently uncontroversial point about expulsion. That Dalhousie had decidedly discarded the whole basis of the Sikh buffer strategy is revealed in the first paragraph of the letter; far from operating as a Hindu breakwater designed to stem the Muslim tide, the Sikhs had joined with the Afghans against Britain.

Peshawar therefore had become a powerful argument for the annexation of the Panjab and one which could be used to quell the opposition to annexation which had appeared in London. It could be represented as a new factor in the equation and consequently employed to support the argument that the situation had changed sufficiently to invalidate Hobhouse's caution against precipitate action which was sent on 24 November 1848. It is indeed interesting that Dalhousie avoided the once popular, although now discredited financial argument for annexation, and did not use the argument of the external enemy, although this had once appealed so strongly to Hobhouse and to Palmerston. This latter argument was used by others at the time, notably by George

Campbell (1824–92), a young Civil Servant who was to enjoy a notable career, not least as a controversial writer on British India. Campbell argued that for the defence of India against Russia the mountains formed a far better strategic frontier than did the Satlej. 'With our outposts at the mouths of the passes (in those hills) it is absolutely and definitely impossible that any power can obtain entrance—whereas on the Sutlej we have no defence and the slightest alarm must be the signal for a preliminary contest—a Punjab war or a Kabul expedition'[20] But perhaps wisely in view of the good relations which then obtained between Britain and Russia in Europe and which ensured that such arguments would not be so well received in England as they had been in 1838 to 1839 or as they would be four years later, Dalhousie ignored these arguments, to which he evidently attached no importance, and based himself essentially on the tried ground of the internal enemy, an argument which, in the context of the greater value set on India in Britain, was much more weighty than it had once been. For Dalhousie the real connection between Peshawar and the Panjab lay in the same motive which had driven Auckland into Afghanistan and Ellenborough into Sind; the need to teach India a moral lesson.

The resounding victory at Gujarat opened the way to Dalhousie's final victory. A quick advance to Peshawar followed. The Afghans melted away into the Khaibar. 'Dost Mahomed came like a thief and he has run away like a coward', Dalhousie remarked.[21] On 29 March 1849, without waiting for authority, Dalhousie proclaimed the annexation of the Panjab. On 7 April he sent a defiant dispatch to London, written, he stated, 'in heat, haste, dust and influenza', listing his reasons for annexing the great new province and virtually daring Hobhouse to reverse his decision. It was 'just, politic and necessary', he informed Couper, 'The deed I have done is for the glory of my country, the honour of my sovereign, the security of her present subjects, and the future good of those whom I have brought under her rule.'[22]

Dalhousie had accomplished the annexation of the Panjab with cool determination. At the outset he had held no preconceived views and, new to India and nervous of the responsibility thrust upon him so quickly, he was content to adopt the advice of his experienced advisors. Within three months he had learned to distrust his subordinates and to rely upon his own judgement. It then became plain to him that the Hardinge system had broken down and that annexation was the most sensible course open to him. In the succeeding months his determination to carry annexation through, even against the opposition of London, hardened. Annexation was primarily the solution indicated by pragmatism, but it was supported by the one general strategic concept which influenced the Governor-General; the connection between British prestige and the control of the internal enemy. This conviction of the empirical and strategic rightness of annexation sustained him and also led him to draw still greater resolution from the military reverses of December and January, reverses which caused Maddock to gloom about a likely coalition against Britain and Gough to lose his nerve and to hint to Dalhousie, as he had to Hardinge three years before, that on military grounds it would be unwise to press ahead with annexation.[23] Few things became Dalhousie more than the courage with which he rejected this suggestion and ordered his Commander-in-Chief to crush the Sikhs in the next battle. Annexation, he informed Gough, was essential in order to recreate the impression of British power in India.[24]

Curiously enough, Dalhousie's settlement, like that of Hardinge, was achieved without undue benefit of Political Agency. Just as the death of Broadfoot had left Hardinge without close political guidance at a crucial time, so the absence of Henry Lawrence, who did not return from England until the early months of 1849, gave Dalhousie more freedom. Currie, whom Hardinge had admired so much, was a Secretariat man, not a Political Agent, and out of place at Lahore, where his assistants knew him, in terms reminiscent of those once applied to Macnaghten, as 'Old Rosy'. In any case Currie was shut up in Lahore and Dalhousie's mind was made up before he left Calcutta. On the frontier Dalhousie found a suitable political instrument in Frederick Mackeson, whom he employed as his agent with Gough, and Mackeson may well have been partly responsible for Dalhousie's emphasis upon the importance of Peshawar.

By the time that Henry Lawrence arrived in Dalhousie's camp on 1 February, the Governor-General required no political advice. Even so Lawrence sought to change Dalhousie's mind. Lawrence had forgotten the doubts about Hardinge's system which he had voiced while in the Panjab and now became an ardent supporter of an independent Lahore. The Resident condemned Currie and his former subordinates for their conduct during his absence. Even when Dalhousie persuaded Lawrence to admit that the behaviour of the Sikhs justified annexation Lawrence continued to dispute the expediency of the act. Eventually Dalhousie shut him up, informed him that whether it was expedient or not, annexation was necessary, and said that if Lawrence would not carry it out, someone else would be put in his place. Lawrence grudgingly gave way at this, although even then he vainly attempted to issue a proclamation promising the most lenient terms. In the same words with which Hardinge had dismissed Cunningham, Dalhousie wrote that Lawrence was 'plus Sikh que les Sikhs' and determined to reduce the great Political Agent from the Potentate which he considered himself to be, to a mere Resident.[25] Lawrence had met his match and the great age of the Politicals had passed its zenith.

The role of Government in England once more provides a convincing demonstration of the insignificance of the Cabinet's part in Indian affairs. The Whig Government of Lord John Russell was not strong, for it lacked a working majority and was vulnerable to coalitions of its enemies on several issues. One such issue was India, for on that the opponents of the Whigs could readily unite for they had little to divide them in their attitudes to that dependency. Dalhousie's position as a Conservative appointed by Whigs offered some reassurance to the Government, but equally Dalhousie might blame the Cabinet for lack of support if things went wrong. This possibility introduced an element of caution into Hobhouse's dealings with Dalhousie. Another issue which was relevant to the attitude of the Government was that of the defence of Britain itself, on which subject the Cabinet was divided. Particularly since the famous Pritchard affair, which had revived the possibility of war with France over distant Tahiti, Palmerston and Clarendon had pressed for increased spending on defence to provide for a better navy, arsenals, dockyards, fortifications, and a militia. Accepting the possibility of a French invasion Russell supported these arguments in a memorandum dated 10 January 1848. Palmerston threatened to resign if the Government would not find £100,000 for a militia. Russell's February budget proposals provided for a sharp increase in income tax partly to pay for this force, but the Commons rejected his proposals and the February Revolution in France temporarily removed the urgency from the debate on the national defences.[26] But the spread of the 1848 revolutions in Europe and the possibilities that Ireland might become the scene of violent revolution and that Britain herself might not be immune from infection continued to engage the public interest and to trouble the Government. These concerns ensured that attention was diverted from India.[27] The defence problem also revived ancient worries about the possible drain on British military resources which India could become.

In opposition the Whigs had been thought to be in favour of the annexation of the Panjab and Ripon and Hardinge had feared that they would try to reverse the 1846 Settlement when they came to power.[28] Hobhouse had indeed long looked forward to the annexation of the Panjab and Palmerston saw it as a step made necessary by the requirements of the external frontier. If, as Hardinge claimed, the Khaibar was the main gate to India, we should occupy it ourselves, the Foreign Secretary remarked in 1847. In terms reminiscent of 1838 he argued that Iran had become a mere advanced post for Russia and that Afghanistan could easily fall into the same position.[29] In power, however, the Whigs were content to let sleeping dogs lie. Hardinge's settlement was allowed to stand, although the Bhairowal modifications were welcomed. Most members of the Cabinet, Hobhouse recorded, thought that annexation was ultimately inevitable. Auckland commented that the Regency would not work and that it would encourage delusive hopes of eventual independence.[30]

In the light of the foregoing paragraph it might have been thought that the Whigs would have welcomed the excuse to annex which the Multan uprising provided and that they might have supported Dalhousie to the hilt. Such, however, was not the case. One reason for their pusillanimity was the strength of the opposition to annexation which persisted in expert circles. Hardinge and Henry Lawrence, both then in London, were strongly opposed to taking the Panjab and, from his retirement in the Isle of Wight, they were joined by Sir Claude Wade. As usual, the Court of Directors was divided, although a majority favoured annexation, but the Chairman, Sir James Lushington (1779–1859), was an opponent. Annexation therefore would be a controversial step and Hardinge's attitude made it likely that strong criticism could be expected from the Conservative benches, on which Ellenborough had decided to appear as an opponent of annexation. The most important reasons for the Government's reluctance to espouse annexation, however, arose within the Cabinet itself.

The British Government was slow to accept that a crisis had occurred in the Panjab. When Hobhouse first received news of the Multan outbreak in June, Hardinge quickly reassured him that the news could not possibly be true and that there was no fear of a revolt.[31] As further news contradicting this assertion was received, an unbashed Hardinge, strongly supported by Lawrence, continued to supply similar anodynes: the outbreak would be confined to Multan and put down as soon as the weather permitted. Ellenborough was disturbed by the progress of events and wrote to Wellington who persuaded Hobhouse to bring the matter before Russell. But others were quick to ridicule Wellington's fears: Hardinge informed Hobhouse that the Duke was mistaken, while begging his confidant not to report his remark to Wellington; a Colonel Rowan assured Hobhouse that the Duke 'was a little the worse for wear'[32] while Grey (the former Howick) was outspoken about the visible decay of Wellington's intellect, angrily asserting that Wellington's Indian advice was as bad as his advice about the Kaffir war which had cost the country half a million and involved military preparations more suitable to war with France 'instead of beating bushes for savages'.[33] And even Wellington, like other experts in England, believed that Dalhousie's military preparations, let alone Gough's much larger demands, were excessive.[34]

Comforted by this Panglossian advice and reassured by the not alarming news from India, Hobhouse continued to enjoy his summer in optimistic mood. September was spent on holiday in Scotland and it was not until he returned to his home at Erle Stoke on 5 October that he was brought sharply down to earth by Dalhousie's letter of 15 August in which the Governor-General proposed to annex the Panjab. Hobhouse wrote to India the next day accepting that Hardinge's system had failed Hobhouse himself evidently favoured annexation, having in no way abated his former opinion in favour of that course. As early as 6 July, when the question seemed academic since he believed that the Multan outbreak was insignificant, Hobhouse had suggested that Dalhousie would find annexation the only course of action if there was a war.[35] But he then assumed that an indemnity would cover the affair.[36] Now on October 6 Hobhouse informed Dalhousie that he favoured the Governor-General's solution of annexation and recorded his conviction that an independent Panjab 'was incompatible with the present advanced position of our Empire' and the attempt to maintain it would only provoke fresh frontier troubles.[37]

After consultation with others Hobhouse was obliged to modify his advice to Dalhousie, however, and to warn the Governor-General against annexation. Henry Lawrence, for whose judgement Hobhouse had great admiration, opposed annexation but supported permanent occupation, a move which, Lawrence claimed, he had always supported, an admission which casts some doubt upon the determination with which he had sought to implement Hardinge's old policy.[38] Russell agreed with Lawrence that annexation was undesirable, but either did not feel that the matter was particularly important or, like his predecessor, mistrusted his ability to control events at a distance, for he added a crucial qualification. Hobhouse should inform Dalhousie that the general feeling in London was opposed to annexation, but he should add a reassurance that if Dalhousie felt obliged to take an important step (a phrase which in this context must refer primarily to annexation) without authority, he could rely upon the Government's placing a favourable construction upon his conduct.[39] Hobhouse wrote to Dalhousie to this effect on 23 October. 'Annexation, immediate annexation', he informed Dalhousie, 'is not looked upon favourably at Home.' But 'any measure short of that would, however, I believe, be well received . . . complete subjection, without the name, if such a result can be achieved'. Russell's reassurance, however, which Hobhouse carefully relayed, effectively took any force from the warning.[40] That such a letter was sent following conversations between Russell and Hobhouse suggests either a disinclination to be bothered with Indian problems or a notion that opposition to annexation might be circumvented by this device. It is a curious fact that at the two-day Cabinet meeting of 24 to 25 October, when ministers reviewed their policies over a range of problems, India was not mentioned.

Hobhouse's letter of 23 October had been in form a private response to Dalhousie's private analysis of the situation and it was not until 22 November, when he received Dalhousie's official proposal (of October) for annexation, that Hobhouse was obliged to abandon his informal approach to the matter and to begin a series of consultations with Russell, Grey, Auckland, Lushington and others. The Chairs were persuaded to ask for there Queen's regiments as a reinforcement for India; they were not shown that part of Dalhousie's dispatch which referred to annexation lest they made difficulties. Russell, who reported that the Queen favoured annexation, appeared not to regard the Panjab as a matter over which it was worth disturbing his unsteady Government. Auckland inclined to a pacific approach and raised a quaint and chivalrous objection to annexation on the score of Dalip Singh's youth. But the real opposition to Dalhousie came from Grey who, as he grimly reminded Hobhouse, had come very near resignation in 1838, when the Cabinet approved the Kabul expedition.[41] Grey demanded a Cabinet meeting to discuss the matter and in the meantime set out his total opposition to annexation: he wanted to blow up all forts in the Panjab, disarm the population, and quit the land for good. Auckland and Hobhouse agreed that this was absurd and Russell endeavoured to sooth Grey by saying that annexation had not been decided on and that no Cabinet was necessary. In the light of this reassurance given to Grey it was of course impossible that Dalhousie should be told to go ahead and on 24 November Hobhouse, who favoured 'the complete reorganization of the Provinces with everything short of annexation'[42] wrote to Dalhousie advising against annexation and asking him to wait until he had full control over the Panjab before reaching a final decision. In this letter Hobhouse also posed an embarrassing but highly relevant question which struck at Dalhousie's whole original argument: how could the Lahore Government be held responsible for the situation when, under the Bhairowal Treaty, Britain had full power in the Panjab?[43]

The problem of the Panjab was at last raised in Cabinet on 6 December when it was agreed that before the Cabinet pronounced on the question of annexation Hobhouse should circulate the relevant

papers. Soon after this step the question of what policy should be
pursued towards the Panjab was driven from the minds of ministers by
a much more explosive matter, namely, the conduct of Gough. Like the
Conservatives in 1846, the Whigs in 1849 were obsessed by the problem
presented by Gough's military failings. Although the effect of the
Gough affair upon the evolution of Panjab policy was essentially negative, tending as it did to divert attention from the greater problems of
the future government of that province, the matter of the Commander-
in-Chief is most important for the insight which it provides into the
constraints upon the Indian policy of the British Government.

The Gough affair blew up in the second half of January 1849. News
of the first indecisive action at Ramnagar reached London on 21
January and two days later Hobhouse informed the Cabinet that it
would be necessary to replace Gough (and also Whish who was blamed
for the withdrawal from Multan). Grey immediately burst into a rage
and accused Hobhouse of retaining Gough in his command despite his
previous record. Hobhouse agreed that he was technically responsible,
but pointed out that the decision had been Wellington's and claimed
that 'the conditions of our Government are such that in military
matters we should give way to the D[uke] of W[ellington] and I had
done so.'[44] But Hobhouse was unfair in shifting the whole blame on to
Wellington.

The great difficulty which Hobhouse and Wellington had found in
securing a replacement for Gough had been in obtaining agreement
upon a successor. The single outstanding candidate was Charles
Napier. Napier said Wellington, was like himself when he was in India,
'"a puissance" his name alone is a power—and in times of difficulty
could do what no other man could'.[45] But the Court of Directors would
not have Napier at any price. Napier's part in the annexation of the
unwanted Sind, his controversy with Outram, his quarrel with the
Bombay Government, and his expressed contempt for the Directors
themselves,—all made him unacceptable to the Court and to the
influential James Weir Hogg in particular. Shortly after his return to
office Hobhouse had sought to persuade the Chairs to accept Napier,
but had been told that the General would not obtain a single vote in the
Court. And although the Government could override the Court and
appoint Napier as Commander-in-Chief, only the Court make him a
Member of Council. Since Wellington would not propose any other
candidate the deadlock was complete and the Whig Government was
trapped between two institutions, neither of which did they wish to
offend.

When the news of the Multan outbreak had reached London in the summer of 1848 Wellington had revived his suggestion that Napier should be sent out to India as Commander-in-Chief. Russell had lazily agreed, but Hobhouse had not dared to mention that controversial name to the Court. Hobhouse himself was anxious to get rid of Gough and in September suggested that the Commander-in-Chief should be compelled to retire 'by a little gentle violence'. The big problem, however, was to find a successor; Hobhouse knew of no one who was both fit for the job and acceptable to the Court.[46] In November Hobhouse reported that there were Press complaints that Napier had not been sent out, but commented that there was no prospect of Napier's appointment following his recent 'most scandalous attack' upon Hogg and on the Indian Governments generally.[47] In January 1849 Wellington and Russell revived the proposal to appoint Napier, but Hobhouse again demurred because of fear of the Court's hostility. In fact, on 27 January Hobhouse did sound the Chairs on the subject, but Lushington told him not to put forward the name of Charles Napier, and Russell and Wellington agreed that it was of no use, the more readily since Napier had informed Wellington that in the circumstances he did not wish to go. An alternative candidate would have to be found.

The search for an alternative Commander-in-Chief had begun on 23 January and the results were scarcely creditable to Britain's military reputation. Sir Frederick Adam (1781–1853), a veteran of the Peninsular and Waterloo, who had been suggesting himself for months, was not given serious consideration. Wellington first suggested Lord Seaton (1778–1863), although he did not think much of his conduct in Canada (when he suppressed the revolution in 1838–1839). Russell did not want Seaton who, he said, was 72 years old. The matter became increasingly urgent as Parliamentary criticism of Gough's competence began to develop. Little was said of the Panjab in the Queen's Speech, but Brougham and Ellenborough attacked the Commander-in-Chief, and George Thompson, the Radical Member of Parliament who was a familiar thorn in the flesh of the Board of Control, put down a motion which was later withdrawn. Wellington next suggested Sir George Napier (1784–1855), Charles's younger brother who had served as Governor of the Cape. George Napier was accepted by the Chairs on 2 February and ministers breathed a sigh of relief, which was rudely dissipated when George Napier, who was then at Nice, refused the appointment because of a bladder complaint. On 15 February Hobhouse began a new round of consultations. In another effort to persuade the Chairs to accept Sir Charles Napier, Wellington himself offered to talk to them, but Lushington declined the offer, saying that although Wellington might persuade him, he (Lushington) could never persuade the Court. The Deputy Chairman, General Archibald Galloway (?1780–1850), took a different view, however, and informed Hobhouse that he thought that the Court might yet be persuaded to accept Napier, but Lushington doused that little flame of hope by remarking that if the other Directors heard what Galloway had said, then the Deputy's otherwise automatic elevation to the office of Chairman in April would not take place.[48]

The search for a successor to Gough continued. On 18 February Russell, having consulted Hardinge, suggested the names of Seaton and of Sir William Gomm (1784–1875), whose name had also previously been mentioned, while another possible candidate considered at this time was Sir Harry Smith, the hero of Aliwal, the single outstanding military success of the first Sikh war. Wellington approved Smith's military abilities, but two conclusive objections were made to his appointment: he would have to be replaced at the Cape of Good Hope; and he had acquired a reputation as a foolish talker. When the Court rejected Seaton on 22 February, Gomm's was the only name left and a letter offering him the appointment was immediately dispatched. Gomm's hour, however, had not yet come. On 3 March the Indian mail brought the news of the disaster at Chilianwala. Gough was universally condemned in the Cabinet and the Court. On the following day Hobhouse had a significant interview with John Delane (1817–79), the youthful but formidable editor of *The Times*. Delane said that Charles Napier should replace Gough and when Hobhouse informed him that Gomm had already been appointed Delane declared that Sir William was incompetent. In Jamaica, said Delane, Gomm's silliness had reached such proportions that his most foolish sayings were collected in a book entitled *Gommeriana*. He promised Hobhouse the full support of public opinion if Napier were appointed.[49] Profoundly disturbed by the prospect of the Government's choice to redeem the defeat of Chilianwala figuring in the Press as a latter day Justice Shallow, Hobhouse went straight round to see Lord Fitzroy Somerset at the Horse Guards, confessed his doubts about Gomm, and tried in vain to persuade Somerset to go instead. Some time later the same day Charles Greville called to see Hobhouse and reported that Wellington was more than ever convinced of the need for Napier.

The foregoing events were decisive in securing the appointment for Napier. On 5 March Hobhouse and Russell agreed that Napier must go to India and the two immediately went to see Wellington, who promised to explain the situation to the unfortunate Gomm, before they went on to interview the Chairs. Russell informed the Chairmen flatly that Napier was to be appointed Commander-in-Chief. Lushington accepted the Governmemt's right to make this appointment, but explained that the Court would not appoint Napier to the Council. If that were so, replied Russell, the Court would be guilty of gross dereliction of duty. In fact Lushington was wrong; the Court backed down: Wellington persuaded Napier to accept the post; Russell announced the appointment in the Commons on 6 March; and the following day the Court appointed Napier Commander-in-Chief and Member Extraordinary of the Bengal Council. There was not a dissenting voice in England, wrote Hobhouse. In Bombay, however, the Commander-in-Chief, Sir Willoughby Cotton, resigned in a huff at being passed over, thus creating a vacancy for Gomm, who received the Bombay post as a consolation prize but never took it up, for within a year he succeeded Napier as Commander-in-Chief.[50]

The importance of the episode of the appointment of a successor to Gough does not reside in the appointment itself for the Court's feelings had been sacrificed in vain—the war was already won when Napier arrived and the conqueror of Sind was not a success as a peacetime Commander-in-Chief and resigned at the end of 1850. The importance lies in the revelation of the scale of priorities of ministers. The appointment of a Commander-in-Chief was the unavoidable responsibility of the Government and a military defeat in the Panjab which could be attributed to the incompetence of Gough would surely be laid at the door of the Cabinet. The weak Russell Government could hardly have survived the furore. Public feeling, wrote Hobhouse, was even higher than at the time of the Kabul massacres, 'so much so, that if we ourselves had been slow to act, which we were not, we should have been compelled by the pressure from without, to take some decisive and immediate step'.[51] To secure the services of the man who was universally acclaimed as Britain's greatest fighting General was to demonstrate the Government's competence. This was an issue which quite transcended the muddied arguments about the future of the Panjab. It was the extreme political sensitivity of the issue which induced Hobhouse to take Cabinet advice and to rebuke Dalhousie for complaining (in his letter of 22 January) that his wish to have Gough replaced had been ignored by the Government. No such demand had been made by Dalhousie, complained Hobhouse; if it had been made Gough would have been replaced immediately. The President went on to suggest that in trying to cast the blame on the Whig Government Dalhousie was playing politics and behaving in a manner unworthy of a public servant.[52] The episode drives home the lesson derived from the story of the Kabul prisoners; for the Cabinet the important thing was not to succeed, but to be seen to be trying hard. It was in the same spirit that

Dalhousie was sent two more European regiments which he did not want and could not afford. But the Government had their reward when the vote of thanks in April 1849 went off well.

During the interregnum imposed upon discussion of the future of the Panjab by the Gough affair there had been a significant drift of opinion in favour of annexation. Public opinion, initially favourable to annexation, had swung against this solution during the early months of 1849, but after the news of Chilianwala reached England the tide of opinion ran more strongly still in the opposite direction. On 4 April Hobhouse reported that ministers still discussing the question of annexation, but that Russell had told him the previous day that half measures would not do; it must be annexation or complete withdrawal. As the majority of ministers certainly excluded the abandonment of the Panjab, this statement by Russell was effectively a declaration in favour of annexation. Hobhouse remarked: 'if we resolve to annex we must annex up to the Khyber Pass, and Peshawar must be one of our principal military stations.'[53] Nevertheless, Hobhouse yet sought to leave the question open; he insisted that the decision must be reserved to the Cabinet and mentioned that Russell had particularly said that he trusted there would be no mistake on this subject. Hobhouse's carefully prepared Blue Book omitted Dalhousie's dispatch recommending annexation and everything else which might appear to commit the Government regarding their future policy towards the Panjab.[54]

Hobhouse's attempt to maintain his options on future Panjab policy failed and the decision was made in India not in London. The swing in public opinion in Britain did not influence Dalhousie's decision, but it helped to obtain acceptance for annexation. Hobhouse himself was taken aback when he first heard of what Dalhousie appeared to have done and could hardly believe the news was true. He admitted that he himself favoured annexation, but thought that Dalhousie had been too quick off the mark and that the move required more preparation: 'I should prefer that whatever you do should be backed by Leadenhall St. and all Downing Street, which, with a little patience and fair management, I have no doubt it will be', he wrote to Dalhousie.[55] But he was needlessly cautious, as he admitted a fortnight later. He and Russell were confident that the Cabinet and Court would accept annexation.[56] And so it was. After all, Grey did not resign, and the Court, having swallowed Sir Charles Napier, found the Panjab a much milder draught.

The annexation of the Panjab accomplished and accepted, it remained for Dalhousie to devise suitable systems of military and political control. In the organization of a military system Wellington played a significant and valuable role. The criticisms of him which were quoted earlier were ill founded; the second Sikh war brought out the best in the Duke. The Gough affair showed how willingly he placed his unassailable reputation and immense influence at the service of a Government composed of his political opponents. And his penetrating analysis of the military campaign in the Panjab showed the continued quality of his military judgement despite his eighty years. As early as the beginning of July 1848, almost alone in England, he correctly foresaw the seriousness of the Multan outbreak and urged the dispatch of Napier and of reinforcements of European troops, although the Cabinet did not agree to send out three additional European regiments until the end of November. His strategic recommendations—first to reduce Multan and then to combine the forces of Whish and Gough before launching offensive operations—were correct, as were his pertinent criticisms of Gough's operations. And his military foresight matched the political gaze of Dalhousie. Long before the campaign was over Wellington had turned his attention to the problems of control. From March onwards he sent Dalhousie painstaking advice about the size and disposition of garrisons and the problems of communications. Even the details and costs of the construction of bridges were carefully prescribed and estimated.[57] With changes of detail, the main principles of Wellington's recommended system, including the maintenance of a large disposable force in the Panjab and the creation of excellent all-year-round communications throughout the Panjab and with British India, were adopted. The system was thoroughly vindicated in 1857 when the Panjab became the arsenal by means of which northern India was reconquered from the mutineers.

The new administrative system in the Panjab was Dalhousie's own creation. He rejected Ellenborough's wild advice to make Napier the supreme military and political authority in the Panjab and fought off Napier's independent attempt to take control. Without apparently risking a grave clash with London he could not shake off Henry Lawrence, as he would have wished, but he controlled the former Resident by carefully harnessing him with two Civil Servants, Charles Mansel (1806–86), a financial expert, and John Lawrence, to form the Punjab Board of Administration, which introduced the simple, non-regulation system which Dalhousie had envisaged in the interests of economy, but which was subsequently considered to have many additional merits. Dalhousie confessed that he would not have employed the device of the Board if he had had more confidence in Henry Lawrence and saw the system as a stopgap until Henry resigned and the Governor-General could insert his chosen subordinate, John Lawrence, into the Panjab with full powers.[58] That day came in 1853.

The creation of a civilian Government in Lahore marked the close of an era in the development of the system of frontier Political Officers. Their usefulness and their importance were by no means at an end. Peshawar in the northern sector (supplemented for a time by Kashmir) together with Shikarpur and later Quetta in the southern sector of the western frontier became the headquarters of networks of frontier agents whose activities ranged all along the frontier from Gilgit to Makran. The politicals remained the principal source of information and a continued fount of political and strategic ideas. They were to play a major part in future British relations with Tibet, Chinese Central Asia, Dardistan, Afghanistan, Kalat, the Gulf, Iraq, Arabia, and many other countries. They continued to serve as Residents in Indian states and they were the main engineers of frontier management. But their role in the second half of the nineteenth century was not identical with that in the first, although the precise nature of the change is difficult to express, other than by the vague observation that the supreme importance in the history of British expansion which they once had appears diminished in the later period. Partly this change may be explained by the post-Mutiny military reorganization which altered career prospects in the Army. After the Mutiny the Quartermaster-General's Department became an important centre for the collection of information and the dissemination of strategic ideas. Partly the change was the consequence of the greater control which was exercised over the agents through the expanded machinery of government, by the creation of new layers of subordinate authority on or near the frontier, and through the development of imperial communications. But perhaps the principal reason for their changed role was that with the annexation of the Panjab, British dominance over the Indian subcontinent was virtually complete, while the Mutiny was the cause of the termination of the last major internal security problem. In other words, the particular concatenation of circumstances which the Politicals had been able to exploit so successfully had departed. The external enemy alone was sufficient to establish the myth of the Great Game, but on its own it was not adequate to maintain a process of expansion comparable to that which had characterized the period which had passed.

Conclusion

Between 1798 and 1849 Britain had experimented with several strategies for the defence of India. The first was that of the Iranian buffer. It has been suggested that British India was not seriously inclined towards that strategy even when the 1801 Treaty with Iran was negotiated; that British lack of interest was subsequently made clear by Barlow; and that after Minto's brief flicker of enthusiasm in 1807 to 1808 British Indian interest in the Iranian buffer finally and completely lapsed. With but few exceptions, from 1808 onwards the rulers of British India regarded the Iranian alliance as an expensive and unwanted albatross which had been hung round their necks by the Government of Britain; an encumbrance which stood in the way of a more reliable, independent strategy in the Gulf. This attitude endured throughout the period with which we have been concerned and persisted for almost all the nineteenth century until Lord Curzon, under the pretence of asserting an ancient British Indian wisdom, injected a quite novel concept of the importance of Iran to the defence of India.

It has also been argued in this book that the British Government was not really interested in the strategy of the defence of India by means of an Iranian buffer state, although it chose to present its Iranian policies in that form. On the contrary, the evidence shows that the principal concern of British Foreign Secretaries from the time of Wellesley onwards was to avoid the possibility of serious dispute with Russia over Iran; Britain's European interests were always placed first. The only zealous and abiding adherents of the Iranian buffer strategy were the members of the British mission in Tehran, who were occupationally committed to that strategy. It was the Ministers in Tehran who continually agitated the prospective danger to India from the alleged growth of Russian influence in Iran and who defined the manner in which that danger would be made manifest through an Iranian occupation of Herat. And to Herat they continued to point, notwithstanding the apparent indifference of the Government of India to their warnings. From September 1846 onwards, Justin Sheil, McNeill's successor, argued that Iran was sinking inexorably under Russian control and pressed for action to restrain Iranian ambitions in the direction of

Herat. His efforts led to an Anglo–Iranian agreement concerning
Herat in 1853 (about which the British Indian Government was not
consulted) and those of his successor to the Anglo–Iranian war of 1856
to 1857, a war for which the Indian Government had no stomach and
which was fought at the behest of the Cabinet chiefly to vindicate
British prestige at a time when this could be done without fear of
Russian intervention.

The second strategy considered was that of the Afghan alliance,
which Wellesley had spurned in 1799, with which Minto had flirted in
1809, and Bentinck even more distantly in 1834, and which had been
the subject of all the hopes and disappointments of 1838 to 1842. The
Afghan strategy had appeared to offer to the British Indian authorities
some chance of relief from the vexations of the Iranian alliance, with its
Russian complications, and, in its original conception of a friendly
understanding deriving from mutually beneficial trade had seemed
well within the resources of India. Even in its metamorphosis of 1838 it
was still within the capacity of Indian finance. The experience of 1839 to
1842, however, showed that all the calculations were wrong. The
Afghan alliance did not free British India from the restrictions imposed
by the Iranian and Russian connections and, even in the modest form
demanded by Auckland, it cost more than British India was prepared
to pay. In the mighty concept of Macnaghten and his lieutenants in
Afghanistan it was far too great a burden; nor could it sustain the
ambitious purposes to which Palmerston attempted to bend it in the
interests of his European policies. The bitter experience of 1841 to 1842
left a mark on British Indian thinking; the failure in Afghanistan, even
though it was partly avenged, was long held to have severely damaged
British prestige and thereby given strength to the internal enemies of
British rule. Britons were very reluctant to become involved in
Afghanistan again.

British India, however, found it impossible to abstain from all
connection with Afghanistan. Pressure was applied from London by a
Government which was uneasy about the state of the Iranian alliance
and which foresaw possible dangers from Russian activity as the Crimean conflict drew nigh. Pressure also came from the Political Agents
on the frontier. The annexation of Sind and the Panjab had converted
Kalat and Afghanistan into neighbours of British India and Political
Agents found it impossible to separate their policies towards the tribes
along their frontiers from the question of relations with the Governments in Kalat and Kabul. The tasks of tribal management, they
believed, would be made much easier by a suitable agreement with the
rulers of those states; some spirited and undaunted souls even favoured

setting them aside and annexing their states. Just as the mission in Tehran was the main prop of the Iranian buffer strategy, so the frontier agents were the leading proponents of the creation of buffer states in Kalat and Afghanistan, or of variants of these strategies. From Herbert Edwardes to Gēorge Roos-Keppel, the Commissioners in Peshawar were the chief advocates of British influence in Afghanistan; while John Jacob and his successors in Upper Sind recommended the establishment of British influence in Kalat.

Dalhousie bowed to this pressure and concluded agreements with Kalat in 1854 and Afghanistan in 1855. The agreements were innocuous enough in themselves, but they pointed the way towards the British advance to Quetta in 1876 and the assumption of close control over Kalat, and to the revival of interest in the Afghan buffer strategy. The arguments of strategy and border management had intertwined and what the latter could not in themselves justify the former could legitimate in the eyes of England. The Afghan Treaty of 1855 and the rather stronger agreement of 1857 insensibly committed Britain to the idea of a united Afghanistan and from that point it was an easy matter to conceive of Afghanistan as a buffer state. For long the Indian Government resisted this conclusion, seeing itself in no way committed to the support of any particular form of government in Afghanistan, but at the end of the 1860s this attitude began to change and during Lord Lytton's Viceroyalty an attempt was made to dictate the policies and nature of the Afghan Government. In his decision to embark upon the second Afghan war Lytton was strongly influenced by considerations of prestige, an argument inseparably connected with the control of the internal enemy within British India; and in his policies which led up to the war he was encouraged by a British Cabinet for reasons deriving from European politics. Despite the advantages of shorter lines of communication, Lytton's attempt to secure close control over Afghanistan foundered. He had offended against British moral principle and British Indian financial independence and prestige. Thereafter Britain settled for a modest degree of influence in Afghanistan, exercised through nominal control over Afghan foreign relations and through a subsidy. The effort of Curzon to increase British control over Afghanistan met with little or no success. From 1880 until 1919 the Afghan buffer policy operated at a low level of efficiency and only within the framework of Anglo-Russian co-operation over frontier demarcation. When the British bridle was rejected by Afghanistan in 1919 the Indian Government was quick to agree to abandon what was felt to be an outdated and unsuitable device for perpetuating British influence.

That some British influence in Afghanistan was required was therefore acknowledged in British India, but it was also generally accepted
that the influence must of necessity be modest under normal circumstances. Lytton's experiment confirmed the experience of Auckland; a
more positive influence was not worth the heavy price which was
demanded. The possibility remained, of course, that under abnormal
circumstances Britain might demand a much greater degree of control.
But these abnormal circumstances envisaged a Russian invasion of
Afghanistan as a preliminary to an attack upon British India and,
despite the attention devoted to this possibility in military circles
during the later nineteenth century, it was still regarded as but a remote
contingency by most political strategists, to whom the principal peril
remained that of externally-induced, internal unrest. And, although it
was customary to discuss Afghanistan in conventional buffer terms, it is
doubtful if this was the true light in which that country appeared to
British India; rather Afghanistan was a state on a sensitive border, a
possibly disruptive factor in the delicate business of tribal management, or at least a convenient scapegoat for its failures; and a country
whose policies bore directly upon the internal enemy. Much the same
might be said of Kalat. There too British agents mixed strategy and
tribal management in their recommendations and there too there is
good reason to believe that it was the day to day problems of border
control which loomed larger than the more glamorous, eye-catching
prospects of the clash of empires in the remote wastes of Central Asia.

From this brief and sceptical review of the Iranian and Afghan buffer
systems we are led back towards the leading strategy of British Indian
defence— the control of India itself. It has been argued in this book that
the chief concern of the Indian Government was with the internal
enemy and that this concern focused its attention upon the subcontinent itself, upon the states and peoples within and immediately contiguous to its borders. In the period from 1765 to 1818 we observed an
almost uninterrupted search for secure frontiers for the British possessions, a search which ended in the achievement of a continuous land
frontier and the destruction of the power of the principal Indian states.
After 1818 the problem of the internal enemy did not disappear; the
enemy merely changed his shape but continued in various guises to
haunt the rulers of British India. The decision in favour of the Afghan
strategy in 1838 was framed largely with the internal enemy in mind,
althoug it may appear that Auckland was deluded by rumours. Even
before the Afghan strategy collapsed Auckland and his Council were
already planning a return to something much nearer to the traditional
strategy of British India; the reduction of the Afghan commitment, the

strengthening of British control within India, and the improvement of the immediate frontier. The subsequent movements into Sind and the Panjab were influenced not by broad notions of their relevance to an external enemy—the new frontier was regarded as inevitable but undesirable—but by the importance of demonstrating British power to the internal enemy. The power of that enemy was massively demonstrated in the Indian Mutiny of 1857, the greatest crisis of British India, and the internal enemy continued in its aftermath to dominate considerations of British strategy.

It should not be supposed that the analysis upon which the buffer strategy had been based was rejected by British India. The abandonment of Afghanistan in 1842 did not mean that the Indian Government had ceased to believe that an external enemy could exercise a maleficent influence upon the internal enemy; on the contrary, British Indian strategists continued to find evidence of outside instigation in ebullitions of domestic discontent. The withdrawal from Afghanistan merely signified that British India could not afford the price of insulation at the rates charged in 1839 to 1842. Instead, British India opted for something nearer to the strategy of Charles Metcalfe: control of the internal enemy by conciliation, judicious coercion, and by the strict maintenance of the appearance of unassailable British power—that is through insistence upon the psychological factor of prestige.

Conciliation of the internal enemy under Ellenborough and Lytton was conciliation of the aristocracy; under Dalhousie it was conciliation of the cultivator through good, efficient government. Dalhousie's system was most clearly exhibited in what was universally regarded as the most sensitive and dangerous province of British India—the newly-acquired Panjab. His principal agent was John Lawrence, with whose name the policy of abstention from external entanglements and concentration on domestic improvement was to be most closely associated. Lawrence's policy was essentially that summed up by Lord Northbrook in 1898 when he told the Indian Currency Committee that 'the safety of India depended upon the land revenue being easy'. Northbrook's formulation was perhaps a little too negative; Lawrence certainly believed in raising revenue to spend for military purposes and was also willing to lay out money for public works when some positive return could be seen, more particularly if benefits flowed to the cultivating class. But the broad implication of Northbrook's remark sums up the view of a large body of British Indian opinion which was represented by Lawrence and endorsed by those whose careers were formed in his shadow.

It would be wrong to conclude that Lawrence and his followers did not believe that danger to India might not materialize as a consequence of the effect upon the Indian mind of the advance of Russia. They shared the view expressed above that their policy was the best that India could afford. Good government might not work, but there was certainly nothing else that British India could do with its available revenues. If Russia were to be stopped this would have to be through the action of the British Government in London. They recognized that Britain would be unlikely to go to war with Russia to try to stop her advance in Central Asia, but they hoped that some agreement might be negotiated between the two powers.

We have seen how the idea of an Anglo–Russian agreement grew during the period studied. The possibility was indicated by the role of British agents in Iran during the Napoleonic struggle and revived by subsequent Anglo-Russian co-operation in that country, notably in the matters of the succession to Fath Ali in 1834 and the restoration of Anglo-Iranian relations in 1841. In Turkestan, too, we witnessed the elements of joint action and the way of formalizing it was sketched by men as various as Arthur Conolly and Auckland. In the 1840s discussions were held between British and Russian ministers, although there was then no will to come to agreement. From the time of Auckland onwards an Anglo-Russian agreement became a favourite project of Governor-Generals; only Lytton and Curzon were resistant to the notion, at least on the terms which they thought were available. Following the Russian advance in Turkestan during the 1860s the idea was given a new impetus by John Lawrence and pursued by his successor, Mayo, through the mission of Douglas Forsyth to St. Petersburg in 1869, and through the subsequent Clarendon–Gorchakov discussions. Although these negotiations did not provide a final settlement, the project was revived after the interlude of the second Anglo-Afghan war by Alfred Lyall and pressed by Dufferin. The Government in Britain was slow to respond to this pressure from India and only when the bill for the alternative policy of fortifying British India against a Russian attack was presented by Curzon and Kitchener did London look more favourably upon an agreement which was also recommended by developments in Europe. The Anglo–Russian agreement of 1907 was a partial fulfilment of the British Indian strategy first delineated by Auckland in 1841.

We may now compare the view of Britain and British India concerning the defence of India. The British Indian strategy may be summarized as follows: concentrate resources within India; combine strict military control with good government; maintain British prestige; abstain from involvements in areas outside India; and leave the prob-

lem of Russia to London. The attention undeservedly captured by
Lytton and Curzon has obscured this traditional strategy, which was
well developed by 1849 and which prevailed in the following period.
The strategy of the Government in London differed at almost every
point. The British Government scarcely understood what was meant
by the internal enemy, usually opposed the reduction of the Indian
states, and frequently abstracted European troops for use elsewhere.
For thirty years the British Government obliged the Indian Government to maintain an Iranian alliance which it did not want, frowned
upon any action by the Indian Government against Iran, disapproved
British India's attempts to improve its position in the Gulf, forced the
Company into an Iranian war which it disliked, and thereafter maintained an involvement with Iran which was unwanted by India, cul-
minating in the 1919 Agreement which the Indian Government
opposed. Notwithstanding its protestations, London's attitude was
governed throughout not by the needs of India but by its fluctuating
attitude to Russia. On Afghanistan there was less difference between
the two Governments in practice, although the British Government
never understood India's border problems and misleadingly conceived
the problem in strategic terms. Perhaps the greatest difference was the
resolute refusal of the British Government to pursue systematically the
prospect of an agreement with Russia until the European situation
inclined it towards this solution.

The division between British interests in Europe and India which is
reflected in the strategic debates of British India continued until the
end of British rule in India. The gap was bridged throughout by the
device the origins of which we have studied. This was the special
language of the strategy of the external enemy, like Esperanto, an
artificial language, constructed to facilitate communication, but possessing the appearance rather than the substance of that resource.
Within that strategic language the morpheme of the internal enemy
bound the various parts of the British Indian structure together and the
morpheme of the external enemy linked British India with Europe.

We may now reconsider and elaborate the strategic model which
was outlined in the Introduction. In the evolution of British Indian
strategy the role of the Government in England was mainly negative.
By far the most notable exception concerns Ellenborough's important
initiative at the India Board in 1830, which launched the new Indus
policy. In general, however, the British Government's contribution
was principally to impose limits upon British Indian strategy, limits
which were related to Britain's European interests, to the availability of
British resources, and to the attitudes—bellicose, pacific, economic,

and humanitarian—of the British public, Press, and Parliament. The British Government's efforts to use British India in a more positive sense as an arm of British policy were interesting but of lesser importance and their true significance is in the area of diplomatic bluff; the hidden army was neither hidden nor an army, or at least an army that Britain could use to real effect. By and large the weight of the Indian Government was also cast towards restraint; the devil it knew was usually preferred to the devil it did not know and it was always conscious of the weakness of its resources and the great strength of the internal enemy. That same combination of limited resources and a feared foe could, however, spur it to major initiatives; frightened weakness had its own expansionist logic.

In the period with which we have been concerned the true motor of imperial expansion was provided by the Political Agents. Characteristically, the Political had local problems on his section of the imperial frontier. In order to satisfy his superiors he must solve these problems, or, like Macnaghten in Afghanistan, find some plausible pretext for not solving them. Usually he was ambitious and sought to extend his responsibility in hopes of greater reward and promotion. Commonly he was a man of ability and energy and wished to achieve some great thing for the satisfaction its accomplishment would bring. Frequently he was drawn on by a spirit of adventure. Occasionally he was driven by moral impulse to deliver some portion of suffering humanity from an evil and to be the agent of civilization, or even of God's purpose. About the springs of action of many of these men we can only speculate. We would do well to remember, however, that these were not ordinary men, but men who had pushed themselves forward from a highly competitive environment in which the ordinary restraints upon human conduct were already weakened and who found themselves in strange, lonely, and responsible situations. They had, and they knew they had, an opportunity to mould the future given to very few. If I have laboured their deceptions and stressed the gulf which separated their professions from their actions it is not to denigrate their achievements but rather to place them in a different perspective which may indeed serve to make those achievements more remarkable.

To master his local problems the Political required an additional allocation of resources which he was unable to secure for his local purposes alone. In order to justify his demand for extra resources he had to obtain a higher priority for his area. This he did by arguing that its strategic importance was undervalued, either in terms of existing strategic postulates or, more commonly, in terms of a new strategic system for which he hoped to win acceptance. In his effort to persuade his superiors of the justice of his arguments the Political enjoyed advantages in the form of a virtual monopoly of information, whether geographical or political. In these circumstances a skilled propagandist like P. B. Lord, John Malcolm, or George Broadfoot could produce a powerful argument which could not readily be dismissed by his superiors. Most decisions are ninety-five per cent information and only an especially determined gambler will dare to ignore the information supplied to him, even if it runs counter to his own ideas. The calculated courage and self-confidence of Dalhousie in his decisions to disregard the advice of Currie, Gough, and later Henry Lawrence stand out as singular demonstrations of the rare willingness of the supreme authority to use its power. Of course, information accumulated from a variety of sources enabled superiors to counter the arguments of local agents and, as the raw frontier situation stabilized and time moved on, the burden of past information digested into experience and precedent operated as a greater and greater restraint upon the freedom of the Political. Nevertheless, the frontier agent could always produce a new body of information which completely invalidated the accumulated wisdom of the past. Thus Herbert Edwardes and his colleagues argued that Britons could rule Muslims much better than Sikhs could, and weakened the long-held view that the Sikhs were necessary intermediaries on the north-west frontier. And, in the most striking demonstration, George Broadfoot's new account of the Sikh army in 1845 completely dissolved the apparently entrenched opinions of the supporters of the Hindu buffer policy. It was this comparative helplessness of governments in the face of the frontier officers' monopoly of information which was graphically described by that continual source of political wisdom, Lord Salisbury, when he wrote, at a later period when it was soldiers rather than Politicals who menaced the imperial peace: 'It is always open to the military authorities to discover in the immediate vicinity of the area to which your orders confine them, some danger against which it is absolutely necessary to guard, some strategic position whose invaluable qualities will repay ten times any risk or cost that its occupation may involve. You have no means of arguing against them.' He might have been writing of Lord or Pottinger in northern Afghanistan.

And yet, of course, as the careers of Lord and Pottinger show, the Political Agent did not always get his way. Reality intruded and dissolved Lord's fantasy in the most violent way. The fate of D'Arcy Todd at Herat was of a different order; his arguments were skilfully constructed and at different levels appealed to Macnaghten in Kabul and Palmerston in England. Todd failed, however, to strike a chord in the fearful heart of Auckland and he paid the price for his failure. Opportunities for expansion occcur often, but they do not last long; if one element in the official hierarchy is sufficiently stubborn the action may be frustrated and the chance lost. In similar fashion Malcolm's Gulf strategy, for which he had won the support of Minto, was lost because of the persistence of Harford Jones; so Burnes's Afghan strategy failed in 1837 to 1838 because of the hostility of Claude Wade; and so Macnaghten and Rawlinson failed in certain of their aims because of the opposition of Keith Elphinstone and William Nott. Successful propaganda for a strategic theory often takes more time than is available. As Thomas Hardy wrote of Clym Yeobright in *The Return of the Native*: 'A man should be only partially before his time: to be completely to the vanward in aspiration is fatal to fame . . . Successful propagandists have succeeded because the doctrine they bring into form is that which their listeners have for some time felt without being able to shape.'

The constraints therefore were very real. If a Political Agent pitched his demands too high his government might close down his position rather than pay the alleged price of maintaining it. At a grander level the same proposition could also apply to India itself. At least until the 1830's no Governor-General could take it for granted that he would always be supported in the actions he thought necessary; and even after 1830 it is doubtful if Britons would have agreed to defend India at any cost. In 1905 Lord Esher remarked that a series of disasters comparable to those which had befallen Russia in the Far East would raise an overwhelming party in Britain to argue that India was not worth a shilling on the income tax or the lives of fifty thousand men. India could not be allowed to become a permanent charge upon Britain. The condition of being the brightest jewel was that India should also be the cheapest, and the difference between a jewel and a millstone was as small as that which Mr. Micawber discovered to lie between happiness and misery. British India's cherished freedom of action depended upon its financial independence; accordingly, defence should cost no more than India could afford. Hence the strong objections of Indian Governments to any attempts to involve British India in strategic concepts and operations for which India could not pay.

From the diplomatic doubts of British Governments, through the sentimental humanitarianism of Parliamentary critics and the bureaucratic forms of Indian Governments, to the military caution of the generals and the financial worries of British India the limitations on the freedom of the Politicals were considerable. A budding strategy had to make its way through the minefields of established authority, justify itself with different arguments at different levels, and endure through changing circumstances. The most successful strategies were those which had the widest appeal and were the most difficult to refute; the strength of the information which supported them was less important than the absence of the information which would destroy them.

Of all strategies which we have reviewed, some appeal more to British and some to British Indian audiences. The only strategy which linked all elements in the diverse hierarchies was the strategy based on the theory of externally-induced, internal disaffection which I have placed largely to the credit of John Malcolm. It offered something to everyone and was virtually irrefutable; to this day no one can say whether it had any objective value as a diagnosis and prognostication of British India's perils. It was an intellectual triumph and it worthily endured in one form or another, through Pan-Islamism and Bolshevism to Japanese Pan-Asianism, until British rule in India came to an end.

Notes to pp 24–579

CHAPTER 1, THE FORMATION OF THE ANGLO-IRANIAN ALLIANCE, 1798–1810

[1] Malcolm to Kirkpatrick, 7 May 1800, AM 13707, f.248.

[2] E. R. Ingram Ellis, 'British Policy towards Persia and the Defence of British India, 1789–1807' Ph. D. London, 1968, 57–8.

[3] Mornington to Dundas, 28 Feb. 1798, *Minutes and Correspondence of Marquess Wellesley* (ed. M. Martin) 5 vols., 1836 (hereafter *Wellesley Despatches*), i, 17.

[4] Mornington to Dundas, 24 Oct. 1798, ibid., i, 306.

[5] Mornington to Duncan, 5 Feb. 1799, ibid., i, 428.

[6] Jones to Dundas, 1 Mar. 1789, KC 9211.

[7] Jones to Willis (pte.), 2 Dec. 1799, KC 9212.

[8] Manesty to Malcolm, 7 Mar. 1800, AM 13707, f.215.

[9] Wellesley to SC, 28 Sept. 1801, *Wellesley Despatches*, ii, 578.

[10] Jones to Willis (pte.), 23 Jan. 1801, KC 9213.

[11] Jones to Willis (pte.), 18 Apr. 1800, KC 9212.

[12] Ingram, *Two Views of British India*, Bath, 1970, 211.

[13] Malcolm to Manesty (pte.), 28 Mar. 1800, AM 13707, f.223.

[14] Malcolm to Henry Wellesley, 17 Dec. 1799, AM 13707, f.139.

[15] Malcolm to Manesty (pte.), 19 Feb. 1800, AM 13707, f.211.

[16] Mornington to Dundas, 29 Nov. 1799, Ingram, *Two Views*, 211.

[17] Dundas to Mornington, 18 Mar. 1799, *Wellesley Despatches*, i, 608.

[18] Dundas to Mornington, 9 Oct. 1799, Ingram, *Two Views*, 186–7.

[19] Jones to Willis (pte.) 9 Feb. 1800, KC 9212.

[20] Malcolm to Wellesley, 6 May 1800, FRP 22,233. The point is discussed by Ingram Ellis, op. cit., 66, 361–2. See also his article, E. Ingram, 'A Preview of the Great Game in Asia–II: The Proposal of an Alliance with Afghanistan 1798–1800', *MES* 9 (1973), 157–74.

[21] Mornington to Duncan, 13 Feb. 1799, *Wellesley Despatches* i, 432–3.

[22] Duncan to Mehdi Ali Khan, 18 July 1799, FRP 21.

[23] SC to GGC, 10 Sept. 1800, BDSLI 2; Ingram Ellis, op. cit., 85–6.

[24] C. Pasley, Memo., 7 July 1805, FRP 24.

[25] GGC to SC, 28 Sept. 1799, BSL 4, 83–102.

[26] Kirkpatrick to Malcolm, 10 Oct. 1799, HM 511.

[27] Kirkpatrick to Malcolm, 13 July 1800, HM 511; Malcolm to Wellesley 20 Feb. 1801, FO 60/1; see also A. T. Wilson, 'Unpublished Despatches of John Malcolm', *JCAS* 16 & 17 (1929–30) and Kaye, *Life of Malcolm*, i, 144.

[28] GGC to SC, 26 Aug. 1802, BSL 4, 483–91; see also Alfred Spencer (ed.), *Memoirs of William Hickey*, 4 vols., London, 1925, iv, 261–3.

[29] Ingram Ellis, op. cit., 280.

[30] H. Jones-Brydges, *His Majesty's Mission to Persia*, London, 1834, ix.

[31] Lovett to SC, 10 Nov. 1803, SLV 9.

[32] Pasley, Memo., 7 July 1805, FRP 24.

[33] Lovett to Manesty, 1 Dec. 1803, FRP 24.

[34] Lovett to Manesty (pte.), 2 Dec. 1803, FRP 24.

[35] Manesty to Jones, 13 July 1804, BomPC 382/3, 9 Feb. 1805, 292.

[36] Manesty to Wellesley, 2 Feb. 1804, FRP 24.

[37] Manesty to Wellesley, 31 July 1804, FRP 24.

[38] The principal source for Russo–Iranian relations during this period is the massive collection

of documents published under the title *Akty, Sobrannye Kavkazskoj archeologicheskoj komissiej* (AKAK), 8 vols., Tiflis, 1866–78. Selected documents from this collection are included with other documents in *Vneshnyaya Politika Rossii* (*VPR*), Series 1, 8 vols., Moscow, 1960–72. Recent monographs in Russian concerning this topic include A. R. Ioannisyan, *Prisoedinenie Zakavkaz'ya k Rossii i mezhdunarodnye otnosheniya v nachale XIX stoletiya*, Erivan, 1958, and M. A. Igamberdyev, *Iran v mezhdunarodnykh otnosheniyakh pervoj treti XIX veka*, Samarkand, 1961. The most detailed account in English is still that of J. F. Baddeley, *Conquest of the Caucasus*, 1906. See also D. M. Lang, *Last Years of the Georgian Monarchy 1658–1832*. New York, 1957, and *Modern History of Georgia*, London 1962.

[39] Manesty to Wellesley, 21 Feb. 1804, FRP 24.
[40] Manesty to Addington, 18 Apr. 1804, FRP 24.
[41] Manesty to Drummond, 18 Apr. 1804, FRP 20.
[42] Manesty to Shawe (pte.), 12 June 1804, AM 13704, f.58.
[43] Manesty to Shawe (pte.), 15 June 1804, AM 13704, f.58.
[44] Shawe to Manesty (pte.), 14 Mar. 1804, AM 13704, f.19.
[45] See correspondence in AM 13704, f.48 et seq.
[46] Manesty to Wellesley (pte.), 5 July 1804, 18 July 1804, and 31 July 1804, FRP 24.
[47] Edmonstone to William Ramsay, 9 July 1804, FRP 24.
[48] GGC to SC, 2 Sept. 1806, BSL 9.
[49] See M. E. Yapp, 'The Establishment of the East India Company Residency at Baghdad 1798–1806', *BSOAS* 30 (1967), 332.
[50] See H. Jones-Brydges, *H. M. Mission to Persia*, 32–3; President in Council, Bombay, Minute on Persia, 9 Dec. 1805, BomPC 382/10, 10 Dec. 1805, 4756–5014; see also the vast collection of information in BomPC 382/14, 25 Feb. 1806.
[51] Jones-Brydges, *H. M. Mission*, 38.
[52] Spencer (ed.), *Hickey*, iv, 360–2.
[53] BPSC 382/23 2 Dec. 1806 8339. On Franco-Iranian relations during this period see V. J. Puryear, *Napoleon and the Dardanelles*, Los Angeles, 1951; Alfred de Gardane, *Le mission du Général Gardane en Perse*, Paris, 1865; Ange de Gardane, *Journal d'un voyage dans la Turquie d'Asie et la Perse, fait en 1807 et 1808*, Paris and Marseilles, 1809; H. Déherain, *La vie de Pierre Ruffin*, 2 vols., Paris, 1929; E. Driault, *La politique orientale de Napoléon 1806–8*, Paris, 1904. Fath Ali did not pin all his hopes on French help; in August 1806 he approached the Russian C.-in-C. General I. V. Gudevich, but the basis for negotiation proposed by the Russians was unsatisfactory to Iran and Fath Ali broke off the contacts with Russia in the expectation that he would achieve better results following a French intervention. (see *VPR*, iv, 600).
[54] Barker to Jones, 25 July 1805, BomPC 382/8, 4 Oct. 1805, 3421; Jones to Grant, 6 Sept. 1805, BomPC 382/9, 12 Nov. 1805, 4211; Jones to Castlereagh, 14 Oct. 1805, BomPC 382/11, 27 Dec. 1805, 5413; Reza Quli's letter is in BomPC 382/13, 21 Jan. 1806, 412.
[55] GGC to SC, 20 Aug. 1806, BSL 9.
[56] GGC to CD (Pol. Dept.), 14 Jan. 1807; Robert Dundas to Canning, 20 Aug. 1807, FO 60/1; SC to GGC, 79/14 Feb. 1812, BDSLI 4.
[57] Jones-Brydges, *H. M. Mission*, xi.
[58] Text in Gardane, op. cit., 71.
[59] Ibid., 32.
[60] Champagny to Gardane, 29 Oct. 1807, quoted Puryear, op. cit., 229.
[61] Stuart, Memo., 23 June 1806, FO 60/8.
[62] Jones, Memo., 7 Jan. 1807, FO 60/1.
[63] Malcolm, Journal, 25 June 1810, M188.
[64] A. Wellesley to Malcolm, 23 Feb. 1807, Wellington (ed.), *Supplementary Despatches and Memoranda of Wellington*, 15 vols., 1858–72, iv, 590–2; Kaye, *Life of Malcolm*, 2 vols., 1856, i, 374.
[65] Dundas to Minto, 3 July 1809, M172.
[66] Jones-Brydges, *H. M. Mission*, 16.
[67] Inglis to Jones (pte.), 21 June 1807, KC 5949.
[68] Inglis to Jones (pte.), 8 Sept. 1807, KC 5577.
[69] Jones to Dundas (pte.), 16 June 1808, in A. T. Wilson, 'Melville Papers' *JCAS* 16 (1929), 36.
[70] SC to GGC 28/, 1 June 1807, BDSLI3.
[71] Dundas to Canning (pte.), 20 Aug. 1807, FO 60/1; Canning to Jones, draft no. 2 of 21 Aug. 1807, FO 60/1; see also copy in Melville Papers 1071, f.55.
[72] SC to Jones, 8 Sept. 1807, FO 60/2.

[73] SC to GGC, 24 Sept. 1807, BDSLI 3.

[74] Dundas to Canning, 6 June 1807, Canning Papers 99A.

[75] Canning to Jones 1/, 28 Aug. 1807, FO 60/1.

[76] SC to GC, Bombay, 24 Sept. 1807, BDSLI 29, 60.

[77] Jones-Brydges, *H. M. Mission*, 356.

[78] Inglis to Jones (pte.), 26 May 1807, KC 5572.

[79] Inglis to Dundas (pte.), 22 July 1807, KC 5574.

[80] C. H. Philips, *The East India Company 1784–1834*, Manchester, 1940, 144–9.

[81] *Lord Minto in India, 1807–14* (ed. Countess of Minto), 1880, 51.

[82] GGC to SC, 26 Sept. 1807, BSL 10.

[83] *Minto in India*, 53 et seq.

[84] Minto to Dundas, Nov. 1807, quoted *Minto in India*, 55–6.

[85] *Minto in India*, 100.

[86] GGC to SC 343/, 15 Feb. 1808 and 345/, 31 Mar. 1808, BSL 10; see also G. J. Alder, 'Britain and the Defence of India—the Origins of the Problem, 1798–1815', *JAH* 6 (1972), 20.

[87] Malcolm to Elliot (pte.), 28 June 1807, M182.

[88] Spencer (ed.), *Hickey*, iv, 363.

[89] Malcolm, Memo., 26 July 1807, M182; Malcolm to Elliot (pte.), 24 July 1807, M183.

[90] Malcolm to Elliot (pte.), 27 Oct. 1807, M182.

[91] Malcolm to Edmonstone, 12 Aug. 1807, M182.

[92] Malcolm to Minto, 23 Nov. 1807, M181.

[93] GG to Malcolm, Summary of Instructions, 30 Jan. 1808, AM 37285, f.32.

[94] Minto to Malcolm (pte.), 31 Jan. 1808, AM 13748, f.58.

[95] AM 37285, f.35; see also *Minto in India*, 111–12.

[96] Edmonstone to Malcolm, 11 Mar. 1808, AM 37285, f.42.

[97] GGC to SC 346/, 3 May 1808, BSL 10.

[98] Malcolm to Minto (pte.), 8 June 1808, AM 37285, f.20.

[99] Malcolm to Wellesley (pte.), 23 Feb. 1808, AM 13748, f.62.

[100] Sir John Malcolm, *History of Persia*, 2 vols., London, 1815, i, ix.

[101] E. Thompson, *Making of the Indian Princes* Oxford, 1943, 39.

[102] M. E. Yapp, 'Two British Historians of Persia', in B. Lewis and P. M. Holt (eds.), *Historians of the Near and Middle East*, London, 1962, 343–56.

[103] Malcolm to Minto (pte.), 26 Feb. 1809, M186.

[104] GGC to SC, 3 May 1808, BSL 10.

[105] Malcolm to Minto (pte.), 1 May 1808, AM 37285, f.45.

[106] Malcolm to Pasley, 18 May 1808, AM 37285, f.50.

[107] Ibid.

[108] GGC to SC 345/, 31 Mar. 1808, and 346/, 3 May 1808, BSL 10.

[109] Malcolm to Minto (pte.), 20 Aug. 1808, M182.

[110] Minto to Malcolm, 21 July 1808; Minto to Hewitt, 30 July 1808; *Minto in India*, 114.

[111] See Abdul Amir Amin, *British Interests in the Persian Gulf*, Leiden, 1967.

[112] W. Eton, 'Second Observations on a Plan of Communications by Harford Jones', 17 May 1796, AM 41767.

[113] Malcolm to Mornington, 26 Feb. 1800, FRP 22, 53; Malcolm to Manesty, 19 Feb. 1800, AM 13707, f.211.

[114] Jones to Malcolm, 10 Oct. 1800, FRP 23; Jones to Griffith, 27 Nov. 1800, KC 9213; Manesty to Malcolm, 23 June 1800, AM 13707, f.361; Kirkpatrick to Malcolm, 13 July 1800, AM 13706, f.77.

[115] Malcolm to Minto (pte.), 5 June 1808, 6 June 1808, M182.

[116] This is the view held by A. Majumdar, 'Lord Minto's Administration in India, etc.', D. Phil. Oxon. 1962, 87. I encountered this valuable work after this chapter was drafted. Majumdar's conclusions are broadly similar to mine but his judgements of Minto and Malcolm are much more favourable to those worthies.

[117] Cp. Minto to Malcolm, Note of Instructions, *c*. Aug. 1808, AM 37285, f.117.

[118] Jones-Brydges, *H. M. Mission*, 138.

[119] Jones to Minto, 28 Apr. 1808, FO 60/1; Jones to SC, 30 Apr. 1808, SLV 7; Jones to Minto, 13 May 1808, FO 60/1.

[120] Malcolm to Minto (pte.), 23 Dec. 1808, M182.

[121] Jones to Minto, 30 Oct. 1808 and 1 Nov. 1808, FRP 25, 47, 63–5.

[122] Malcolm to Minto (pte.), 26 Feb. 1809, M186; Jones to Dundas 1/, 11 Jan. 1809, SLV 7.

[123] Jones-Brydges, *H. M. Mission*, 128.

[124] J. Morier, *Journey Through Persia*, London, 1812, 161.

[125] Malcolm to Minto (pte.), 13 Feb. 1809, M186.

[126] Malcolm to Minto (pte.), 8 Dec. 1808, M182; cp. also Malcolm to Minto (pte.), 19 Dec. 1808, M182.

[127] Malcolm to Minto (pte.), 23 Dec. 1808, M182.

[128] Malcolm to Minto (pte.), 10 Dec. 1808, M182.

[129] Malcolm to Minto (pte.), 5 Jan. 1809, 6 Jan. 1809, M186.

[130] Jones-Brydges, *H. M. Mission*, 196–7; extract of a letter to Lt. John Briggs, 17 May 1809, M184.

[131] Jones to Dundas, 16 Mar. 1809, SLV 7.

[132] Treaty enclosed in Jones to Canning 4/, 16 Mar. 1809, FO 60/2; see also Aitchison, *Treaties*, xii, 46.

[133] Minto to Jones, 30 Jan. 1809, FRP 26, 239.

[134] Malcolm to Minto (pte.), 22 Mar. 1810, M188.

[135] Ja'afar Ali, Memo., FO 60/6.

[136] Minto to Jones, 26 Oct. 1809, FO 60/3.

[137] Minto to Malcolm, 26 Oct. 1809, FO 60/3.

[138] Pasley to Malcolm (pte.), 10 Feb. 1809, M186.

[139] Malcolm to Minto (pte.), 10 Apr. 1810, M188.

[140] Malcolm to Minto (pte.), 31 May 1810, M188.

[141] Anonymous letter from a member of Jones's mission, 28 Jan. 1810, M188.

[142] Jones to Minto, 1 Jan. 1810, FO 60/3.

[143] Jones to Canning 2/, 2 Jan. 1810, FO 60/3; Jones to Minto, 30 Jan. 1810, FO 60/3.

[144] A. Trollope, *Phineas Redux*, World's Classics, ii, 188.

[145] Malcolm to Minto (pte.), 11 May 1810, M186.

[146] Malcolm to Jones (pte.), 15 July 1810, FO 60/3.

[147] Malcolm to Wellesley (pte.), 7 Jan. 1810, AM 13748, f.80.

[148] Jones to SC 12/, 24 June 1810, FO 60/3; Malcolm to Minto (pte.), 1 July 1810 and journal enclosed.

[149] Sidmouth to A. Wellesley, 9 June 1808, Wellington, *Supplementary Despatches*, iv, 597.

[150] Dundas to Minto, 3 July 1809; Dundas to Minto, 1 Sept. 1810, M172.

[151] SC to Jones, 4 Nov. 1809, FO 60/2; Bathurst to Jones, 6 Nov. 1809, FO 60/2.

[152] Wellesley to Jones, 22 Mar. 1810, FO 60/3; SC to GGC, 6 May 1810, BDSLI 3.

[153] Minto to Dundas (pte.), 20 Apr. 1810, M377.

[154] Minto to Dundas (pte.), 6 Nov. 1810, M377.

[155] Pottinger, *Travels in Baloochistan*, London, 1816, 212.

[156] J. MacDonald Kinneir, *A Geographical Memoir of Iran*, London, 1813.

[157] Jones to Willis (pte.), 23 Jan. 1801, KC 9213.

[158] SC to GGC, 6 May 1810, BDSLI 3.

[159] SC to GGC 79/, 14 Feb. 1812, BDSLI 4.

[160] Edmonstone to Elphinstone, 17 June 1809, HM 657, 445.

[161] Malcolm to Jones (pte.), 15 July 1810, FO 60/3.

[162] A. Tripathi, *Trade and Finance in the Bengal Presidency 1793–1833*, Calcutta, 1956, 119.

[163] Morier, op. cit., 121.

[164] Memo., for Auditor's Office of India Board, 29 May 1823, FO 60/23.

CHAPTER 2, THE CONSUMMATION OF THE ALLIANCE, 1810–15

[1] Jones to Dundas 14/, 17 July 1809, SLV 7.

[2] Malcolm to Jones (pte.), 15 July 1810, FO 60/3.

[3] Jones-Brydges, *H. M. Mission*, 340.

[4] Sir Robert Ker Porter, *Travels in Georgia, etc.* 2 vols., London, 1821–2, ii, 506–7.

[5] Morier, *Journey Through Persia*, 282.

[6] Jones-Brydges. *H. M. Mission*, 314–8.

[7] Ibid., 269–76.

[8] Sir R. Adair, *Peace of the Dardanelles*, 2 vols., 1845, ii, 191.

[9] Jones to Minto, 18 May 1809, FO 60/2.

[10] Jones to Adair, 12 Feb. 1810, FO 60/3.

[11] Adair, op. cit., ii, 98.

[12] Igamberdiev, op, cit., 145.

[13] *VPR*, v, 94.

[14] See Tormasov to Abbas Mirza, 23 Dec. 1809/ 4 Jan. 1810, *VPR*, v, 333–6.

[15] Jones to Bathurst 8/, 27 Mar. 1810, FO 60/3.

[16] Jones to Bathurst 13/, 27 May 1810, FO 60/3.

[17] Aspinall (ed.), *Later Correspondence of George III*, 5 vols., Cambridge, 1962–70, v, 499.

[18] Chairs to Dundas, 22 Feb. 1810, FO 60/4.

[19] F. A. Wellesley (ed.), *Diary and Correspondence of Henry Wellesley, First Lord Cowley, 1790–1846*. London, n.d., 38. On Ouseley's life see the memoir by the Revd. James Reynolds in Sir Gore Ouseley, *Biographical Notices of Persian Poets*, London, 1846.

[20] Ouseley to Wellesley (pte.), 7 Feb. 1810, AM 37285, f.233. For Ouseley's motives in seeking the post see Ouseley to Wellesley (pte.), 1 June 1812, AM 37285, f.280.

[21] George III to Ouseley, 13 July 1810, FO 60/4.

[22] Ouseley, op. cit., li–lii.

[23] Ouseley to Wellesley 2/, 26 Sept. 1810, FO 60/4.

[24] Ouseley to Wellesley (pte.), 23 Jan. 1811, AM 37285, f.252.

[25] Ouseley to Jones 1/, 15 Jan. 1811, FO 60/6.

[26] Ouseley to Jones, 25 Mar. 1811, FO 60/6.

[27] Ouseley to Wellesley 3/, 21 Apr. 1811, FO 60/6.

[28] Their journals, but for that of Gordon, are in FO 60/7. See also Sir William Ouseley, *Travels in the East*, 3 vols., London, 1819 and J. P. Morier, *Second Journey Through Persia*, London, 1818.

[29] Ouseley to Wellesley 12/, 30 Nov. 1811, FO 60/6.

[30] Aberdeen to Hamilton, 10 Feb. 1812, AM 37285, f.278.

[31] G. Ouseley, op. cit., xci.

[32] Jones to Wellesley 23/, 24 July 1810, FO 60/3.

[33] Wellesley to Ouseley, Dec. 1810, FO 60/4.

[34] Ouseley to Jones 2/, 1 Mar. 1811, FO 60/6.

[35] Ouseley to Wellesley (pte.), 21 Apr. 1811, AM 37285, f.256.

[36] Ouseley to Wellesley 4/, 4 May 1811 and enclosures, FO 60/6.

[37] Ouseley to SC 3/, 30 June 1811, FO 60/6.

[38] Ouseley to Wellesley (pte.), 23 Aug. 1811, AM 37285, f.264.

[39] Sheridan to Jones (pte.), 24 Feb. 1812, KC 9017; cp. Cormick to Jones (pte.), 22 Aug. 1811, KC 9011.

[40] Ouseley to Wellesley (pte.), 29 Dec. 1811, AM 37285, f.276.

[41] Ouseley to Smith, 4 Jan. 1812, FO 60/6.

[42] Ouseley to Wellesley 8/, 27 Oct. 1811, FO 60/6.

[43] Ouseley to Minto 13/, 6 Oct. 1811, FO 60/6.

[44] Malcolm to Jones (pte.), 15 July 1810, FO 60/3.

[45] Morier, *Journey*, 30.

[46] Morier, *Second Journey*, 210–12.

[47] Minto to Malcolm, Notes on instructions, *c*. Aug. 1808, AM 37285, f.117.

[48] Malcolm to Minto, 18 Dec. 1809, AM 13748, f.98.

[49] Malcolm to Jones (pte.), 15 July 1810, FO 60/3.

[50] Ouseley to Wellesley (pte.), 21 Apr. 1811, AM 37285, f.256.

[51] Igamberdiev, op. cit., 157–8.

[52] S. Lane-Poole, *Life of Stratford Canning*, 2 vols., 1888; and in rebuttal see F. Ismail, 'The Ottoman Empire and the Great Powers 1805–21', Ph.D. London, 1975.

[53] Ouseley to Wellesley (pte.), 25 Aug. 1812, AM 37285, f.290.

[54] Morier to Ouseley, 6 Oct. 1812, FO 60/7; see also Morier, *Second Journey*, 217.

[55] Ouseley to Castlereagh (pte.), 30 Dec. 1812, FO 60/7.

[56] Ouseley to Wellesley (pte.), 18 Jan. 1813, AM 37285, f.305.

[57] Ouseley to Castlereagh 9/, 10 July 1813, FO 60/8.

[58] Ouseley to Rtishchev, 16 July 1813, FO 60/8.

[59] Ouseley to Castlereagh 15/, 28 Sept. 1813, FO 60/8.

[60] Ouseley to Wellesley (pte.), 30 Oct. 1813, AM 37285, f.309. For the Russian documents concerning the treaty negotiations see *AKAK*, v, 722–47; a facsimile of the treaty is in *VPR*, 403–27.

[61] Ouseley to Wellesley (pte.), 1 June 1812, AM 37285, f.280.

[62] Ouseley to Castlereagh 33/, 24 Dec. 1812, FO 60/7.

[63] Ouseley to Castlereagh, 1 Sept. 1814, FO 60/9.

[64] Ouseley to Castlereagh 2/, 16 Feb. 1814, FO 60/9.

[65] Ouseley to Castlereagh, 1 Sept. 1814, FO 60/9.

[66] Cp. Ouseley to Liston (pte.), n.d. c. Sept. 1813, Liston MSS., NLS 5620. (I am indebted to Dr F. Ismail for this reference.)

[67] Ouseley to Wellesley (pte.), 15 Apr. 1815, AM 37285, f.317.

[68] Ouseley to Hamilton (pte.), 4 Apr. 1815, FO 60/10.

[69] *Private Journal of the Marquess of Hastings* (ed. Bute), 2 vols., 1851, i, 140.

[70] Buckinghamshire to Castlereagh, 23 Aug. 1812, FO 60/5.

[71] See the unsigned and undated memo. comparing the treaties in FO 60/8.

[72] Bathurst to Ouseley 1/, 28 Apr. 1814, FO 60/9.

[73] Bathurst to Ouseley 4/, 28 Apr. 1814, FO 60/9.

[74] Ellis to Buckinghamshire, 8 July 1814, FO 60/9.

[75] Ouseley to Morier, 19 Sept. 1819, FO 60/14.

[76] Morier and Ellis to Castlereagh 1/, 21 Aug. 1814, FO 60/9; a translation of the bond is enclosed in this dispatch.

[77] Morier and Ellis to Castlereagh 4/, 30 Nov. 1814, FO 60/9.

[78] GCBC 9, 91–115.

[79] Jones to Dundas 8/, 2 May 1809, SLV 7.

[80] Minto to Ouseley, 3 Feb. 1811, FO 60/6.

[81] Italinsky to Nesselrode 2/, 14 Oct. 1815, *VPR*, viii, 541–5.

[82] Rumyantsev to Alexander I, 27 June/9 July 1813, *VPR*, vii, 293–4.

[83] A. R. Ioannisyan, *Prisoedinenie Zakavkaz'ya k Rossii i mezhdunarodnye otnosheniya v nachale XIX stoletiya*, Erivan, 1958.

[84] T. E. Colebrooke, *Life of Mountstuart Elphinstone*, 2 vols., 1844, i, 225–9.

[85] SC to GGC, 24 Sept. 1807, BDSLI 3; SC to GGC, 2 Oct. 1809, BDSLI 3.

[86] SC to GGC 68/, 7 July 1810, BDSLI 3.

CHAPTER 3, THE MIDDLE AGE OF AN ALLIANCE, 1815–35

[1] J. Planta to Ouseley (pte.), 30 Oct. 1817, FO 60/12/Pt 2.

[2] Morier and Ellis to Castlereagh 5/, 30 Nov. 1814, FO 60/9.

[3] Morier, *Second Journey*, 390.

[4] SC to GGC 125/, 1 Oct. 1818, BDSLI 5.

[5] Mirza Abu'l Hasan Khan to Castlereagh, 6 June 1816, FO 60/11.

[6] Walpole to Castlereagh 41/, 5 Sept. 1814, FO 65/94.

[7] Cathcart to Castlereagh 66/, 9/21 Nov. 1816, FO 65/104.

[8] Nesselrode to Lieven. 14 Apr. 1816, quoted Igamberdiev, op. cit., 181.

[9] Willock to Castlereagh 3/, 8 June 1816, FO 60/11.

[10] Baddeley, op. cit., 100–4; Igamberdiev, op. cit., 178–86; B. P. Balayan, *Mezhdunarodnie otnosheniya Irana 1813–1828*, Erivan, 1967, 33–55.

[11] Castlereagh to Willock 1/, 24 Mar. 1818, FO 60/13.

[12] Willock to Canning, 13 Feb. 1825, FO 60/25.

[13] Willock to Castlereagh 12/, 25 May 1818, FO 60/13.

[14] Willock to Hamilton (pte.), 18 Aug. 1818, FO 60/13.

[15] Mirza Abu'l Hasan Khan, Memo., 8 Dec. 1819, FO 60/14.

[16] Willock to Planta (pte.), 10 July 1821, FO 60/21.

[17] Willock to Hastings, 24 Sept. 1821, FO 60/21.

[18] See M. E. Yapp, 'The Control of the Persian Mission, 1822–36', *University of Birmingham Historical Journal*, 7 (1960).

[19] Canning to Wynn (pte.), 19 Dec. 1822, FO 60/21.

[20] Canning to Wynn (pte.), 24 Oct. 1826, FO 60/29.

[21] Swinton to Macdonald, 18 Mar. 1825, enc. in Willock to Canning, 3 July 1825, FO 60/25.

[22] GGC to SC, 25 Mar. 1826, FO 60/29.

[23] McNeill to Lockhart (pte.), 17 Oct. 1824, Lockhart MSS. 925, III, f.43; The story is too good to omit but it is suspiciously close to an announcement by one of the wives of Shuja al-Dawla; see Luke Scrafton, *Reflections on the Government of Indostan*, London, 1763, 78.

[24] Extract of a letter from Willock, 13 July 1828, FO 60/30.

[25] Macdonald to Swinton, 22 Feb. 1825 enc. in Willock to Canning 14/, 3 July 1825, FO 60/25.

[26] Canning to Wynn (pte.), 6 Oct. 1825, FO 60/26.

[27] On Russo-Iranian relations during this period see B. P. Balayan, *Mezhdunarodnie otnosheniya Irana, 1813–28*, Erivan, 1967. On the Iranian decision see Hamid Algar, *Religion and State in Iran 1785–1906*, California University Press, 1969.

[28] Macdonald to Swinton, n.d. FRP 39, 584.

[29] Macdonald to Wynn, 29 Sept. 1826, FRP 39, 713.

[30] Canning to Wynn (pte.), 9 Oct. 1826, FO 60/29. On Wynn see Gwynneth Evans, 'Charles Watkin Williams Wynn 1775–1850', M. A. Bangor, 1935.

[31] Canning to Wellington, 22 Nov. 1826; Wellington, *Despatches, Correspondence*, etc, 8 vols., London, 1867–80, iii, 467.

[32] Malcolm to Wellington, 12 Dec. 1826, in Kaye, *Life of Malcolm*, ii, 454–5.

[33] Canning to Wynn (pte.), 17 Jan. 1827, Canning Papers 78A.

[34] Lieven, Memo., 26 Feb. 1827, FO 65/ 168.

[35] Baddeley, op. cit., 176.

[36] Text in Martens, *Recueil*, 22, 564; See discussion in Balayan, op. cit., 218–34. A recent account using Persian sources is Kamran Ekbal, *Der Briefwechsel Abbas Mirzas mit dem britischen Gesandten MacDonald Kinneir, (1825–1828)*, Freiburg, 1977.

[37] Macdonald to Swinton, 3 July 1828, FRP 43, 563.

[38] Macdonald to Sterling, 9 July 1828, FRP 43, 599.

[39] Macdonald to Sterling, 27 Mar. 1828, FRP 43, 439.

[40] SC to GGC 199/, 27 Oct. 1829, BDSLI 7.

[41] McNeill to Campbell, 30 June 1832, ESL 43 27/, 18 Dec. 1832.

[42] Macdonald to Auber, 5 Jan. 1830, FRP 45, 1. His poor judgement as a second had once nearly killed his principal, Mountstuart Elphinstone, in a duel. See F. D. Drewitt, *Bombay in the Days of George IV*, London, 1907, 226–33.

[43] Macdonald to Malcolm (pte.), 17 June 1829, EM D556/1.

[44] Macdonald to SC, 10 Mar. 1830, BSC 358 8/, 8 July 1830.

[45] Malcolm to Bentinck (pte.), 17 May 1829, EM D556/1.

[46] Macdonald to Bentinck (pte.), 13 Aug. 1829, EM D556/1.

[47] Bentinck to Ellenborough (pte.), 26 Aug. 1830, BM. This letter is printed in C. H. Philips (ed.), *The Correspondence of Lord William Bentinck*, 2 vols., Oxford, 1977, i, 501–3. Many other letters in the Bentinck MSS. which are referred to in this book may be found in the Philips edition.

[48] Auber to Bentinck (pte.), 7 July 1831; 17 July 1832; Sir Robert Campbell to Bentinck (pte.), 20 July 1831; CD to GGC, 20 July 1831, BM.

[49] Draft dispatch CD to GGC, BM.

[50] Hyde Villiers to Auber, 24 Oct. 1832, GCBC, 234.

[51] Auber to Macaulay, 15 Dec. 1832, GCBC, 234; final draft in BM.

[52] Auber to Bentinck (pte.), 11 July 1832, BM.

[53] Bentinck to Auber (pte.), 15 Dec. 1832, BM.

[54] Bentinck to Ellenborough (pte.), 16 Jan. 1831, EM D556/1.

[55] Clare to Bentinck (pte.), 28 Dec. 1831, BM.

[56] Metcalfe, Minute, 9 Nov. 1828, in Kaye, *Metcalfe Papers*, 245–48.

[57] Ilchester (ed.), *Lady Holland to Her Son, 1821–45*, London, 1946, 78.

[58] (Emily Eden) *Miss Eden's Letters* (ed. Violet Dickinson), London, 1919, 133.

[59] SC to GGC 181/, 7 Nov. 1828, BDSLI 7. For the correspondence between Wellington and Ellenborough concerning drafts of the dispatch see Wellington to Ellenborough (pte.), 9 Oct. 1828, PRO 30/9/4/Pt. 2/5, and Wellington, *Despatches, Correspondence* v, 117–19.

[60] Ellenborough to Wellington (pte.), 18 Oct. 1829, PRO 30/9/4/Pt.1/1; SC to GGC 199/, 27 Oct. 1829, BDSLI 7.

[61] SC to GGC 202/, 7 Dec. 1829, BDSLI 7.

[62] SC to GGC 182/, 2 Dec. 1828, BDSLI 7.

[63] Ellenborough to Wellington (pte.), 18 Oct.1829, PRO 30/9/4/Pt.1/1.

[64] Ellenborough to Wellington, 15 Oct. 1829, PRO 30/9/4/Pt.1/1.

[65] Macdonald to SC 3/, 10 Mar. 1830, FRP 45, 21; Macdonald to Ellenborough (pte.), 7 Mar. 1830, PRO 30/9/4/Pt.4/9.

[66] Ellenborough to Abbas Mirza, 14 July 1830, FO 60/32/4.

[67] SC to GGC 226/, 4 Oct. 1830, BDSLI 7.

[68] Campbell to Ellenborough (pte.), 23 Nov. 1830, ESL 39, 32/9, 5 Aug. 1831.

[69] Campbell to Ellenborough (pte.), 26 Nov. 1830, FRP 45, 355.

[70] Campbell to Macnaghten, 24 Apr. 1834, ISC 2 & 3/, 11 Mar. 1835.

[71] Campbell to Ellenborough, 20 Nov. 1830, BSC 361/, 4/, 27 May 1831.

[72] Campbell to Sec. GG, 6 Nov. 1831, BSC 365, 3/, 12 Mar. 1832; Campbell to Sec. GG, 4 Dec. 1831, BSC 367 2/, 30 July 1832.

[73] Campbell, Journal 1833, BSC 380, 3/, 8 May 1834.

[74] Shee to Campbell (pte.), 31 Jan. 1832, FRP 47, 129; Shee to Campbell (pte.), 1 Feb. 1832, FRP 47, 149; Shee to Campbell (pte.), 8 Apr. 1832, EM D/556/2.

[75] McNeill to Campbell, 28 Nov. 1832, FRP 47, 759; See also *Memoir of Sir John McNeill GCB, 1795–1883*, by his Granddaughter, London, 1910, 157–61.

[76] McNeill to Campbell, 21 Dec. 1832, BSC 374, 17/, 23 May 1833.

[77] Campbell to Bentinck, 10 Feb. 1833, BSC 374, 18/, 23 May 1833.

[78] Gerard to Trevelyan, 3 June 1834, ISC 1, 5/, 26 Aug. 1834. The importance of Herat was previously indicated by Arthur Conolly who visited the city in 1830. See A. Conolly, *Journey to the North of India*, 2 vols., London, 1834. See also the discussion in chapter 6 below and Court's Narrative in G. W. Forrest (ed.), *Selections from the Travels and Journals preserved in the Bombay Secretariat*, Bombay, 1906, 8–9.

[79] Prinsep to Campbell, 7 Nov. 1831, BSC 363, 7/, 2 Dec. 1831.

[80] Palmerston to Durham 24/, 31 Aug. 1832, FO 65/200.

[81] G. O. Trevelyan, *Life of Macaulay*, 2 vols., London, 1876, i, 387.

[82] Memo. dated between March and August 1832 in FRP 48.

[83] Grant to Palmerston (pte.), 25 Nov. 1833, GCBC (1) 2, 7.

[84] On trade see M. E. Yapp 'British Policy in Central Asia 1830–43;, Ph.D. London, 1959, nn. 67–8; and Charles Issawi, 'The Tabriz–Trebizond Trade 1830–1900', *IJMES*, 1, 18–27.

[85] Palmerston to Fraser, 4 Dec. 1833, FO 60/33.

[86] Memo. n.d., FRP 48.

[87] Cp. Palmerston to Grant (pte.), 3 Nov. 1833, FRP 48.

[88] SC to GGC 284/, 8 Feb. 1834, BDSLI 8.

[89] Bligh to Palmerston 14/, 28 Jan. 1834, FO 65/213.

[90] Campbell to Palmerston, 9 Apr. 1834, FO 60/34.

[91] Campbell to R. Campbell, 7 Apr. 1834, EM D556/1.

[92] Campbell, Journal, FRP 52, 590–2.

[93] Memo. of a conversation between Riach, Fraser, and the *Qa'im maqam*, 25 Feb. 1835, FO 60/38.

[94] Campbell to Macnaghten, 20 Feb. 1835, FRP 52.

[95] Campbell to Backhouse 2/, 12 Mar. 1835 and enclosures FRP 52, 179.

[96] Count Simonich, 'Précis historique de l'avènement de Mahomed Schah au trône de Perse', dated Warsaw, 1841, in Archives of the Institut Vostokovedenie, Leningrad, 1/6/1, ff.105–7; A. H. Layard, *Early Adventures*, 2 vols., London, 1887, i, 251–9; Lady Sheil, *Life and Manners in Persia*, London, 1856, 344..

[97] Campbell, Journal, FRP 52, 594.

CHAPTER 4, THE COLLAPSE OF THE IRANIAN BUFFER, 1835–8

[1] Kaye, *Memorials of Indian Government*, London, 1853, 266; Kaye, *Life of Tucker*, London, 1854, 490–5.

[2] Fraser's reports are summarized in a memo. by William Cabell, 18 Dec. 1834, FO 60/35; Fraser's opinions are in his memos. dated 8 June 1835 and 23 June 1835, FO 60/38.

[3] Fraser, Memo., 8 June 1835, FO 60/38.

[4] Fraser to Palmerston, 28 Dec. 1836, FO 60/44.

[5] Ellenborough, Diary, 113, PRO 30/12/28/5.

[6] Draft instructions to Ellis, *c.* March 1835, FO 60/26; Ellis, Memos., 20 May 1835, 28 May 1835, 5 June 1835, FO 60/37. Final instructions Palmerston to Ellis, 25 July 1837, FO 60/36.

[7] Ellis, Memo., 20 May 1835, FO 60/37.

[8] Ellis, Memo., 28 May 1835, FO 60/37.

[9] Palmerston to Hobhouse (pte.), 22 June 1835, AM 46915, ff.7–9.

[10] Palmerston to Hobhouse (pte.), 5 July 1835, AM 46915, ff.15–16.

[11] Palmerston to Hobhouse (pte.), 17 July 1835, AM 46915, ff.17–18.

[12] Ellenborough to SC, 20 Dec. 1834, PRO 30/12/29/Pt.2/7.

[13] Wellington to Ellenborough (pte.), 8 Jan. 1835, PRO 30/12/29/Pt.1/4.

[14] Riach to Campbell (pte.), 10 Oct. 1835, EM D556/1.

[15] Riach to Campbell (pte.), 25 Nov. 1835, EM D556/1.

[16] Ellis to Palmerston (pte.), 12 Nov. 1835, FO 60/37; Simonich, 'Précis', ff.118–9.

[17] Riach to Campbell (pte.), 23 Feb. 1836, EM D556/1.

[18] Ellis to Palmerston 16/, 20 Nov. 1835, FO 60/37.

[19] Ellis to Palmerston (pte.), 12 Nov. 1835, FO 60/37.

[20] Ellis to Palmerston (pte.), 21 Nov. 1835, FO 60/37.

[21] Ellis to Palmerston 5/, 15 Jan. 1836, FO 60/40.

[22] Ellis to Palmerston 2/, 8 Jan. 1836, FO 60/40.

[23] Ellis to Palmerston 23/, 25 Feb. 1836, FO 60/40.

[24] Ellis to Palmerston 33/, 10 Apr. 1836, FO 60/40.

[25] Ellis to Mirza Masud, 29 Apr. 1836, FO 60/40.

[26] Ellis to Palmerston (pte.), 25 Nov. 1836, FO 60/41; for the text of the firman see Aitchison, *Treaties* xii, 60.

[27] Ellis to Palmerston (pte.), 15 Nov. 1835, FO 60/37.

[28] Palmerston to Russell (pte.), 1 Oct. 1838, PRO 30/22/3.

[29] McNeill to Aberdeen, 9 Mar. 1842, FO 60/86.

[30] *Memoir of McNeill*, 188.

[31] Palmerston to McNeill 5/, 2 June 1836, FO 60/42; drafts of political and commercial treaties are enclosed. See also McNeill's memos., Sept. 1835, 9 Oct. 1835, 18 Oct. 1835 (FO 60/38), March 1836, 14 Apr. 1836, 21 May 1836 (FO 60/43).

[32] McNeill, memo., 12 Feb. 1833, BSC 374, 22/, 23 May 1833.

[33] McNeill, memo., with Palmerston's comments, 21 May 1836, FO 60/43.

[34] McNeill, memo., March 1836, FO 60/43.

[35] Palmerston to Hobhouse (pte.), 23 May 1836, HM 833, 185.

[36] McNeill, memo., 8 Jan. 1835, BSL (1) 22, 535.

[37] Palmerston to McNeill 18/, 13 June 1836, FO 60/42.

[38] A. Colvin, *John Russell Colvin*, Oxford, 1911.

[39] SC to GGC 334/, 25 June 1836, BDSLI 9.

[40] Hobhouse to Palmerston (pte.), 19 July 1836, HM 833, 193.

[41] Hobhouse to Auckland, 15 Dec. 1836, HM 837, 114.

[42] Hobhouse to Auckland, 31 Dec. 1837, HM 838, 278.

[43] For further discussion of this episode see chapter 8 below.

[44] Simonich, 'Précis', ff.215–16.

[45] Ibid, f.108.

[46] McNeill to Hobhouse (pte.), 28 Feb. 1837, HM 838, 55.

[47] McNeill to Palmerston (pte.), 27 Feb. 1837 and 5 May 1837, BP; *Memoir of McNeill*, 205.

[48] McNeill to Palmerston 26/, 2 May 1837, FO 60/49.

[49] McNeill to Palmerston 15/, 24 Feb. 1837, FO 60/48; McNeill to Palmerston 26/, 2 May 1837, FO 60/49.

[50] McNeill to Palmerston 15/, 24 Feb. 1837, FO 60/48.

[51] Simonich, 'Précis', f.154.

[52] McNeill to Auckland, 30 May 1837, HM 841, 251; McNeill to Palmerston 31/, 30 June 1837, FO 60/49.

[53] Simonich, 'Précis', ff.156–70.

[54] Milbanke to Palmerston 17/, 15 July 1837, FO 65/235.

[55] McNeill to Palmerston 3/, 30 June 1837, FO 60/49.
[56] McNeill to Palmerston 33/, 30 Dec. 1836, FO 60/43.
[57] McNeill to Palmerston 15/, 24 Feb. 1837, FO 60/48.
[58] McNeill to Auckland (pte.), 4 July 1837, FO 60/41.
[59] Macnaghten to McNeill, 21 Nov. 1836, ISC 5, 25/, 21 Nov. 1836.
[60] Macnaghten to McNeill, 10 Apr. 1837, ESL 46, 58/3, 10 Apr. 1837.
[61] Auckland to McNeill (pte.), 15 Sept. 1837, AM 37692, f.3.
[62] McNeill to Palmerston 54/ 29 July 1837, FO 60/50.
[63] McNeill to Palmerston (pte.), 31 Aug. 1837 BP; McNeill to Palmerston 84/, 2 Oct. 1837, FO 60/51.
[64] McNeill to Palmerston 97/, 27 Nov. 1837, FO 60/51.
[65] McNeill to Palmerston 95/, 25 Nov. 1837, FO 60/51.
[66] Cp. Melbourne's speech of 22 Feb. 1841, *Hansard* III, 56, col.764.
[67] Simonich, 'Précis', f.179.
[68] McNeill to Palmerston 105/, 15 Dec. 1837, FO 60/51.
[69] McNeill to Palmerston 12/, 23 Feb. 1838, FO 60/56.
[70] McNeill to Palmerston 16/, 28 Feb. 1838, FO 60/56.
[71] McNeill to Auckland (pte.), 5 Mar. 1838, *Memoir of McNeill*, 205.
[72] Burnes to Macnaghten, 6 Mar. 1838, ESL 49, 39/5, 5 Apr. 1838.
[73] Auckland to Hobhouse (pte.), 9 Apr. 1838, AM 36472, f.234.
[74] Milbanke reported that the Tsar had informed the Iranian Ambassador at Erivan that he would recall Simonich if the deserters were not returned within a month. (Milbanke to Palmerston 63/, 23 Nov. 1837, FO 65/235). The issue had been an important one since the early part of the century and had played a crucial part in the tragedy of Griboyedev's mission. The Russian Government feared that the example of profitable desertion might infect the discontented troops in the Caucasus. The situation resembles that of Britain and Lahore in 1845.
[75] Simonich, 'Précis', f.197.
[76] McNeill to Palmerston 25/, 12 May 1838, FO 60/57.
[77] McNeill to Fraser (pte.), 10 May 1838, FO 60/37.
[78] Simonich, 'Précis', ff.189–90.
[79] Nesselrode to Pozzo di Borgo, 23 Feb./5 Mar. 1839 enc. in Clanricarde to Palmerston, 25 Mar. 1839, FO 65/256.
[80] Simonich, 'Précis', ff.193–5.
[81] Clanricarde to Palmerston 19/, 4 Feb. 1839, FO 65/251.
[82] Simonich, 'Précis', f.197.
[83] Simonich to Nesselrode, 23 Oct./4 Nov. 1838, quoted P. G. Kotlyar 'Russko–Afghanskie Otnosheniye, etc.', *Uchenie Zapiski Istoriya Vostoke II* 33, Tashkent, 1962, 79.
[84] McNeill to Palmerston (pte.), 17 May 1838, FO 60/57.
[85] Simonich, 'Précis', f.200.
[86] McNeill to Palmerston 30/, 25 June 1838, FO 60/58.
[87] McNeill to Mrs. McNeill, *c.* Sept. 1838, *Memoir of McNeill*, 231.
[88] McNeill to Fraser (pte.), 16 May 1838, FO 60/37.
[89] Mulla Rashid to Dost Muhammad, Dec. 1837, BP.
[90] McNeill to Burnes, 13 Mar. 1837, EM 633, f.18.

CHAPTER 5, THE FRONTIER OF BRITISH INDIA, 1765–1830

[1] Quoted S. N. Sen, *Anglo-Maratha Relations, 1772–85*, Calcutta, 1961, 118; see also C. C. Davies, *Warren Hastings and Oudh*, Oxford, 1929, 241.
[2] GGC to SC, 13 July 1804, BSL 6, 225.
[3] See P. Nightingale, *Trade and Empire in Western India 1784–1806*, Cambridge, 1970.
[4] Duncan to Minto, 8 Feb. 1808, M337.
[5] T. E. Colebrooke, *Life of Mountstuart Elphinstone*, 2 vols., London, 1844, i, 179–81; see also Sir G. W. Forrest, *Selections from the Minutes and other Official Writings of the Hon. Mountstuart Elphinstone*, London, 1884. The long memorandum in HM. 512, 47, et seq. is also useful. Elphinstone's first instructions are in Edmonstone to Elphinstone, 19 Aug. 1808, HM 657, 1.

[6] Edmonstone to Elphinstone, 29 Aug. 1808, HM 657, 57.

[7] Edmonstone to Elphinstone, 5 Dec. 1808, HM 657. Colebrooke dates these instructions 11 Dec. 1808, Colebrooke, op. cit., i, 193.

[8] Edmonstone to Elphinstone, 19 Aug. 1808, HM 657, 1.

[9] Mountstuart Elphinstone, *An Account of the Kingdom of Caubul*, 2 vols., London, 1815.

[10] Edmonstone to Elphinstone, 6 Mar. 1809, HM 657, 189.

[11] Forrest, op. cit., 27.

[12] Elphinstone to Edmonstone, 19 Mar. 1809, HM 657, 255; and 22 Mar. 1809, 221; Edmonstone to Elphinstone, 15 Apr., 1809, HM 657, 231.

[13] Minto to Ouseley, 3 Feb. 1811, FO 60/6; Benjamin Jones, Memo., 10 Feb. 1813, HM 511.

[14] Elphinstone to Minto, 28 Mar. 1809, HM 657, 367.

[15] Edmonstone to Elphinstone, 13 May 1809, HM 657, 359.

[16] SC to GGC 80/, 6 Mar. 1812, BDSLI 4.

[17] B. J. Hasrat, *Anglo-Sikh Relations 1799–1849*, Hoshiarpur, 1968, 39–6; see also P. E. Bhatta, 'The East India Company's Policy Towards the Sikhs 1764–1808', *JIH* (1945).

[18] Hasrat, op. cit., 48–50.

[19] Mian Bahir Faroogi, *British Relations with the Cis-Sutlej States*, Lahore, 1941, 3; see also V. J. Kiernan, *Metcalfe's Mission to Lahore 1808–9*, Lahore, 1943.

[20] Countess of Minto (ed.), *Lord Minto in India, 1807–1814*, London, 1880, 158.

[21] Hasrat, op. cit., 68.

[22] Minto, op. cit., 147.

[23] J. W. Kaye, *Life of Metcalfe*, 2 vols., London, 1854, i, 249 et seq.

[24] Ibid., i, 268.

[25] Hasrat, op. cit., 29.

[26] A. Majumdar, 'Lord Minto's Administration in India', 216–17; see also G. J. Alder, 'Britain and the Defence of India', *JAH* 6 (1972).

[27] Faroogi, op. cit., 8; Minto, op. cit., 154.

[28] Metcalfe to Edmonstone, 11 Dec. 1808, quoted Majumdar, op. cit., 231.

[29] S. R. Bakshi, *British Diplomacy and Adminstration in India 1807–13* Delhi, 1971, 145.

[30] Hasrat, op. cit., 102.

[31] Ochterlony to Lushington, 5 May 1810, quoted K. N. Panikkar, *British Diplomacy in North India*, New Delhi, 1968, 113.

[32] Edmonstone to Ochterlony, 13 June 1809, *Ludhiana Agency Records*, ii, 123–6.

[33] See Fauja Singh Bajwa, *The Military System of the Sikhs*, Delhi, 1964.

[34] Dundas to Minto (pte.), 3 Sept. 1810, M172.

[35] SC to GGC 75/, 18 Sept. 1811, BDSLI 4.

[36] The most recent account of the Pindaris is M. P. Roy, *Origin, Growth and Suppression of the Pindaris*, New Delhi, 1973.

[37] For Hastings's assessment of the frontier see *The Private Journal of the Marquess of Hastings* (ed. Bute) 2 vols., London, 1851, i, 293–301.

[38] R. J. Bingle, 'The Governor-General, The Bengal Council and the Civil Service, 1800–1835,' in P. Robb and D. Taylor (eds.) *Rule, Protest, Identity*, 1978, 1–27.

[39] Metcalfe, Minute, Dec. 1814, in E. Thompson, *Life of Metcalfe*, London, 1937, 154–60.

[40] *Hastings's Private Journal*, i, 54 and *passim*.

[41] On these events see H. T. Prinsep, *A Narrative of the Political and Military Transactions of British India under the Administration of the Marquess of Hastings, 1813–18*, London, 1820, 144–5; K. S. Mehta, *Lord Hastings and the Indian States*, Bombay, 1930, 29; B. Ghosh, *British Policy Towards the Pathans and the Pindaris in Central India 1805–18*, Calcutta, 1966, 167–8; and C. H. Philips, *The East India Company*, 214–6. The most readable account of the period is still E. Thompson, *The Making of the Indian Princes*, Oxford, 1943.

[42] Memo. on Cutch 1802–16, HM 503, 1–92; W. T. Money, Memo., HM 503, 539–64.

[43] Minute, 26 Jan. 1821, *Bombay Gazetteer, Cutch*, Bombay, 1880, 261.

[44] H. Burton, *Scinde; or the unhappy valley*, 2 vols., London, 1851, i, 202.

[45] Nightingale, op. cit., 158; Sir James Craig, Memo., c. 26 Sept. 1798; *Wellesley Despatches*, ii, 671.

[46] Mornington to Duncan, 7 Apr. 1799, *Wellesley Despatches*, i, 518.

[47] Quoted R. A. Huttenback, 'The French Threat to India and British Relations with Sind, 1799–1809', *EHR* (1961), 598.

[48] On Seton's Mission to Sind and other aspects of Minto's policy towards that state see Bakshi, op. cit., 36–43; Majumdar, op. cit., 308–28; K. Thairani, *British Political Missions to Sind*, London, 1973, S. K. S. Singh, 'Seton's Mission to Sind 1808', *JIH* 29 (1951), 231–2; and B. Jones, Memo., 10 Feb. 1813, HM 511.

[49] T. E. Colebrooke, *Life of Mountstuart Elphinstone*, 2 vols., London, 1844, i, 221.

[50] C. Masson, *Travels, etc.*, 3 vols., London, 1842, i, 462–71.

[51] Huttenback, op. cit., 600.

[52] H. Pottinger, *Travels in Baloochistan and Scinde*, London, 1816.

[53] Colebrooke, op. cit., i, 218–25.

[54] S. Bhattacharya, *The Rajput States and the East India Company*, New Delhi, 1972, 127–9.

[55] Metcalfe to Warden, 29 July 1820, quoted M. S. Mehta, *Lord Hastings and the Indian States*, 212; see also Kaye, *Life of Malcolm*, ii, 332.

[56] James Burnes, *Narrative of a Visit to the Court of Sinde*, Edinburgh, 1831.

[57] Malcolm to Pottinger (pte.), 2 Feb. 1828, HM 734, 62.

[58] G. Rawlinson, *Memoir of Sir Henry Rawlinson*, London, 1898, 57.

[59] R. N. Cust, Memo., 5 Mar. 1846, AM 40129, f.101.

[60] Malcolm, Minute, Oct. 1830, PRO 30/9/4/5/2.

[61] Colvin to Pottinger, 17 June 1838, AM 37693, f.46.

[62] K. N. Panikkar, *British Diplomacy in North India*, New Delhi, 1968.

[63] Ochterlony to Stewart, 13 Apr. 1821, quoted Panikkar, op. cit., 74–5; see also H. C. Batra, *The Relations of Jaipur State with the East India Company (1803–1858)*, Delhi, 1958, 65–7.

[64] N. K. Sinha and A. K. Dasgupta (eds.), *Selections from the Ochterlony Papers, 1818–25*, Calcutta, 1964, 305.

[65] Batra, op. cit., 83.

[66] Quoted Kaye, *Life of Metcalfe*, ii, 27.

[67] A. T. Ritchie and R. Evans, *Lord Amherst*, Oxford, 1894, 138, 145.

[68] See Ram Pande, *Bharatpur up to 1826*, Jaipur, 1970.

[69] J. W. Kaye, *Lives of Indian Officers*, 2 vols., London, 1847, ii, 80–1.

[70] Batra, op. cit., 128–45.

[71] On Wade see Sir C. M. Wade, *Narrative of the Services of Sir Claude Wade*, Ryde, 1847.

[72] Quoted Hasrat, *Anglo-Sikh Relations*, 112.

[73] Fane, Memo., 30 May 1837; Fane to Metcalfe, 8 Apr. 1837; Fane to Auckland, 26 Sept. 1836, ESL 47, 21/, 20 Dec. 1837.

[74] Fane to Auckland, 7 May 1839, ESL 58, 124/18, 11 July 1839.

[75] GGC to SC 21/, 20 Dec. 1837, SLI (1) 23, 192; see also Auckland, Minute, 14 June 1837, AM 37691, f.16.

[76] Dundas to Mornington, 9 Oct. 1799, in Ingram, *Two Views*, 186–7.

[77] Blair to Dundas, 17 Dec. 1807, M172.

[78] Seemingly, James Rennell (1742–1830) the best-known contemporary geographer of India, who was employed as Cartographer of the East India Company, also wrote a memorandum (*c.* Dec. 1807) on the practicability of a French invasion of India via Central Asia, but I have not been able to find this study. See Aspinall, *Later Correspondence of George III*, iv, 663. In 1808 a pamphlet written by 'A Late Resident of Blagulpore' proposed the line of the Indus as the main defensive position for British India.

[79] A. Wellesley to Dundas, 20 Apr. 1808; Wellington, *Supplementary Despatches*, iv, 592–601.

[80] SC to GGC 43/, 2 Mar. 1808, BDSLI 3.

[81] G. J. Alder, 'Britain and the Defence of India'.

[82] Colebrooke, op. cit., i, 225–9.

[83] Philips, *East India Company*, 268.

[84] Canning to Moira (pte.), 30 Aug. 1816, Canning Papers 99A.

[85] Ellenborough, *Political Diary*, ii, 123–5.

[86] The progress of the official discussion is considered in subsequent chapters.

[87] *United Services Journal*, 7 (1831).

[88] *Quarterly Review*, 53 (Feb. 1835), 19.

[89] *Quarterly Review*, 61 (Jan. 1838), 96 et seq.

[90] *Edinburgh Review*, 71 (July 1840).

[91] Hardinge to Hobhouse, 2 Sept. 1846, AM 36475, f.26.

CHAPTER 6, THE INDUS AND BEYOND, 1830–8

[1] SC to GGC 208/, 12 Jan. 1830, BDSLI 7.

[2] Ellenborough to Bentinck (pte.), 12 Jan. 1830, BM.

[3] SC to GGC 182/, 2 Dec. 1828, BDSLI 7.

[4] Ellenborough, *Political Diary*, ii, 29–37.

[5] Ellenborough, op. cit., ii, 149–50. For Wellington's views see Ellenborough to Malcolm, 18 Dec. 1829, PRO 30/9/4/Pt.5/2; and Ellenborough to Macdonald (pte.), 23 Dec. 1829, PRO 30/9/4/Pt.1/4.

[6] Ellenborough to Chairs, 15 Jan. 1830, PRO 30/9/4/Pt.4/1.

[7] Heytesbury to Aberdeen 9/, 18 Jan. 1830, FO 65/185.

[8] Ellenborough, op. cit., ii, 88.

[9] Macdonald to SC, 11 Mar. 1830, BSC 358 8/, 8 July 1830.

[10] *Blackwoods Magazine*, 130 (Sept. 1827).

[11] Malcolm to Ellenborough (pte.) and enclosure, 1 July 1830, PRO 30/9/4/Pt.5/7; Malcolm, Minute, 4 July 1830, BSC 358 3/, 20 Aug. 1830.

[12] Bentinck to Ellenborough (pte.), 1 June 1830, BM.

[13] Stewart, Memo., 22 June 1830, PRO 30/9/4/Pt.5/1.

[14] Bentinck, Minute, 29 Jan. 1832, BSC 2/, 6 Aug. 1832; see Auckland Colvin, *Life of John Russell Colvin*, Oxford, 1911, 62.

[15] Quoted Bonamy, Memo., BSC 358 7/, 14 Oct. 1830.

[16] Malcolm to Ellenborough (pte.), 28 Apr. 1830, PRO 30/9/4/5/2.

[17] Bonamy, Memo.

[18] Malcolm, Minute, 9 Aug. 1830, BSL(1), 23, 113.

[19] Metcalfe, Minute, 25 Oct. 1830, BSC 358 4/, 14 Oct. 1830.

[20] Ellenborough to Fitzgerald (pte.), 16 Jan. 1843, PRO 30/12/77.

[21] Bentinck to Ellenborough (pte.), 1 June 1830, PRO 30/9/4/Pt.2/2.

[22] Burnes, Report, 12 Sept. 1831, BSC 363 3/, 25 Nov. 1831; see also A. Burnes, *Travels to Bokhara*, 3 vols., London, 1834, vol. 3.

[23] The reports of Trevelyan, Conolly, and others are in BSC 363 4–15/, 25 Nov. 1831; see also A. Conolly, *Journey to the North of India*, 2 vols., London, 1834.

[24] Ravenshaw, Memo., 23 Aug. 1831 BSC 363, 3/, 25 Nov. 1831.

[25] GGC to SC, 19 Nov. 1831, BSL(1) 23, 347.

[26] BSC 374 4–8/, 6 June 1833.

[27] Bentinck, Minute, 1 June 1833, ESL 44, 14/4, 6 June 1833.

[28] Metcalfe to Bentinck, 9 Oct. 1831, quoted E. Thompson, *Life of Metcalfe*, London, 1937, 284–5.

[29] Metcalfe, Minute, 2 June 1833, ESL 44, 16/4, 6 June 1833.

[30] BSL(1) 22, 479.

[31] McNeill, Memo., 8 Jan. 1835, BSL(1) 22, 535.

[32] Kaye, *Life of Tucker*, 495–6.

[33] SC to GGC 318/, 7 Mar. 1835, BDSLI 9; see also H. Ellis, Memo. on GGC to SC, 2 July 1832, BSL(1) 22, 121.

[34] Adam to Ochterlony, 2 Aug. 1815, *Ludhiana Agency Records* 2, 460–2.

[35] Swinton to Ochterlony, 30 June 1821, Sinha and Dasgupta (eds.), *Ochterlony Papers*, 171.

[36] Macnaghten to Wade, 13 Dec. 1832, BSC 371 2/, 21 Jan. 1833.

[37] Shuja to Bentinck (recd. 21 Sept. 1833), ISC 1 1/, 9 Oct. 1834.

[38] Macnaghten to Wade, 13 Dec. 1832, BSC 372 41/, 19 Mar. 1833.

[39] Pottinger to Masson (pte.), 3 Oct. 1833, EM 631, f.5.

[40] GGC to SC, 19 Nov. 1831, BSL(1) 23, 347; Bentinck to Pottinger (pte.), 3 Nov. 1831; and Bentinck to R. Campbell (pte.), 15 Dec. 1831, EM D556/1.

[41] H. T. Prinsep, *Origins of the Sikh Power*, Lahore, 1847, 139.

[42] GG to SC, 2 July 1832, BSL(1) 22, 135; text in Aitchison, *Treaties* vii, 354; see also W. Pottinger to Clare, 14 Feb. 1832, 17 Feb. 1832, 28 Mar. 1832, PRO 30/12/26/1; and W. Pottinger to Macnaghten, 22 Feb. 1832, BM. K. Thairani, *British Political Missions to Sind*, Orient Longmans, 1973, 61–71, contains a good account of the negotiations.

[43] Clare to Bentinck (pte.), 22 Dec. 1831, 28 Dec. 1831; Macnaghten to Bentinck (pte.), 26 Dec.

1831, BM; Prinsep, op. cit., 126–32; for Wade's negotiations see references in M. E. Yapp, 'British Policy in Central Asia', Ph.D. London, 1959, 120.

[44] Prinsep, op. cit., 133.

[45] Clare to Bentinck (pte.), 28 Dec. 1831, BM.

[46] SC to GGC 242/, 29 July 1831, BDSLI 8; see also Ellis, Minute, n.d., BSl(1), 23, 161.

[47] Bentinck to R. Campbell (pte.), 15 Dec. 1831, EM D556/1.

[48] Macnaghten to Pottinger, 10 Oct. 1833, BSC 377 14/, 10 Oct. 1833.

[49] Pottinger to Trevelyan, 24 June 1834, ISC 1 2/, 18 July 1834; Pottinger to Macnaghten, 4 Aug. 1834, ISC 1 5/, 2 Sept. 1834; Macnaghten to Pottinger, 5 Sept. 1834, ISC 1 2/, 5 Sept. 1834; text in Aitchison *Treaties* vii, 322.

[50] Text in Aitchison, *Treaties*, i, 233; Bahawalpur treaty, ibid., i, 39. For a description of the negotiations see GGC to SC, 5 Mar. 1833, BSL (1) 22, 593.

[51] Bentinck to Pottinger (pte.), 25 Feb. 1834, BM.

[52] Trevelyan, Minute, 2 July 1836, ESL 44, /3, 26 Sept. 1836.

[53] Greville, *Memoirs* (ed. Reeve), 8 vols., London, 1888, vi, 260–2.

[54] Auckland, Minute, 4 May 1836; Robertson, Minute, 20 Apr. 1836; Fane, Minute, 6 May 1836, ESL 45, 27/3, 26 Sept. 1836.

[55] Macnaghten to Ellis, 20 June 1836, AM 37690, f.8.

[56] Thairani, op. cit., 83.

[57] Hasrat, *Anglo-Sikh Relations*, 138.

[58] Metcalfe to Auckland (pte.), 15 Oct. 1836, AM 37689, f.39.

[59] Auckland may also have been influenced by a report which worried Palmerston in 1834–5, to the effect that France might establish a protectorate over the Panjab. (Palmerston to Hobhouse (pte.), 2 Nov. 1835, AM 46915, f.33–5.)

[60] GGC to SC 4/, 28 Nov. 1836, BSL(1) 23, 25; Auckland to Metcalfe (pte.), 7 Oct. 1836, AM 36473, f.91. Hasrat's interpretation of Auckland's policy is based upon a mistaken reading of this last letter, for he attributes to Auckland statements quoted by Auckland from a letter from Metcalfe.

[61] Colvin to Pottinger (pte.), 1 Sept. 1836, AM 37690, f.5.

[62] Auckland, Minute, 23 Sept. 1836, ISC 5 17/, 3 Oct. 1836; Macnaghten to Pottinger, 26 Sept. 1836, ibid., 19.

[63] Auckland to Hobhouse (pte.), 7 Oct. 1836, AM 36473, f.91.

[64] Macnaghten to Wade, 26 Sept. 1836, ISC 5 18/, 3 Oct. 1836.

[65] Pottinger to Macnaghten, 10 Dec. 1836, ESL 46, 15/3, 10 Apr. 1837.

[66] Pottinger to Macnaghten, 23 Mar. 1838, ESL 53, /5, 20 Feb. 1839; text in Aitchison *Treaties*, vii, 363. Pottinger was appointed Resident at Haidarabad with Captain P. M. Melville as his assistant, although Melville's wife forced the latter to decline his appointment.

[67] E. R. Kapadia, 'The Diplomatic Career of Sir Claude Wade', M. A. London, 1938, 207–8; this neglected thesis is particularly valuable for Anglo–Sikh relations in 1836.

[68] Auckland to Carnac (pte.), 20 Sept. 1836, HM 837, 313; Burnes's instructions are in Macnaghten to Burnes, 5 Sept. 1836, ESL 45, 21/3, 26 Sept. 1836; cp. Auckland, Minute, 19 Aug. 1836, AM 37709, f.98.

[69] Auckland to Hobhouse (pte.), 26 Aug. 1836, AM 36473, f.79.

[70] Wade to Macnaghten, 11 Dec. 1836, ESL 46, 42/9, 5 Aug. 1837.

[71] Auckland to Hobhouse (pte.), 9 Apr. 1837, AM 37691, f.12.

[72] N. K. Sinha, *Ranjit Singh*, Calcutta, 1945, 94–100.

[73] Wade to Macnaghten, 12 Apr. 1837, ESL 46, 14/9, 5 Aug. 1837.

[74] Wade to Macnaghten, 23 June 1837, ESL 47, 27/22, 27 Dec. 1837.

[75] Wade to Macnaghten, 9 July 1837, ibid., 81.

[76] Wade to Macnaghten, 21 Aug. 1837, ibid., 81.

[77] Wade to Macnaghten, 21 Sept. 1837, ESL 48, 28/4, 21 Feb. 1838.

[78] Macnaghten to Burnes, 15 May 1837, ESL 46, 18/9, 15 May 1837.

[79] Burnes to Masson (pte.), 2 June 1837, EM 633, f.7.

[80] Burnes to Colvin (pte.), 12 May 1837, EM 633, f.7.

[81] Burnes to Macnaghten, 8 June 1837, ESL 47, 92/22, 27 Dec. 1837.

[82] Burnes to Dost Muhammad, 23 June 1837, ESL 46, 88/9, 5 Aug. 1837.

[83] Burnes to Masson (pte.), 6 Aug. 1837, 4 Sept. 1837, EM 633, f.40, 45.

[84] Auckland, Minute, 9 Sept. 1837, AM 37691, f.125.

[85] Macnaghten to Burnes, 11 Sept. 1837, ESL 47, 13/15, 9 Oct. 1837.

[86] Auckland to Loch (pte.), 11 July 1837, AM 37691, f.40.

[87] Colvin to Burnes (pte.), 26 July 1837, AM 37691, f.57.

[88] Colvin to Wade (pte.), 14 Aug. 1837, AM 37691, f.88.

[89] Burnes to Macnaghten, 10 Sept. 1837, ESL 48, 49/4, 21 Feb. 1838.

[90] Wade to Macnaghten, 25 June 1837, ESL 47, 58/22, 27 Dec. 1837.

[91] Masson to Wade, 5 June 1837, ESL 47, 58/22, 27 Dec. 1837.

[92] C. Masson, *Narrative of Various Journeys in Baloochistan*, etc., 3 vols., London, 1842, iii, 455–6.

[93] Dost Muhammad to the Sirdars of Qandahar, 25 Oct. 1837, ESL 48, 57/1, 8 Feb. 1838.

[94] Burnes to Macnaghten, 5 Oct. 1837, ESL 48, 29/1, 8 Feb. 1838.

[95] Burnes to Captain Jacob (pte.), 29 Oct. 1837, SC (NAI), 34/43, 28 Sept. 1842.

[96] Burnes to Holland (pte.), 30 Oct. 1837, SC (NAI), 17/43, 28 Sept. 1842.

[97] Burnes to Macnaghten, 31 Oct. 1837, ESL 48, 57/1, 8 Feb. 1838.

[98] Burnes to Macnaghten, 22 Dec. 1837, ESL 48, 111/1, 8 Feb. 1838.

[99] Burnes to Holland (pte.), 9 Jan. 1838, SC (NAI), 2/43, 28 Sept. 1842.

[100] Quoted *IA Russkaya Starina* 1880, 8, 789.

[101] Simonich, 'Précis', ff.156–7.

[102] Instructions to Vitkevich, 14 Mar. 1837, *AKAK* 8, 964–94.

[103] P. S. Kotlyar 'Russko-afganskie otnosheniya v seredine XIX–nachalo XX v. i anglo-russkoe sopernichestvo na srednom vostoke', *Uchenye Zapiski Istoriya Vostoke* 33 (1962), 75.

[104] P. E. Moseley, 'Russian Policy in Asia 1838–9', *SR* 14 (1936), 670.

[105] Senyavin to Duhamel, 1 Aug. 1839, *Russkij Arkhiv*, 1885, 5, 81.

[106] Letters enclosed in Burnes to Macnaghten, 22 Dec. 1838, ESL 48, 77/1, 8 Feb. 1838.

[107] Vitkevich to Simonich, 24 Nov. 1838, in A. L. Popov, 'Bor'ba za sredneaziatiskij platsdarm', *Istoricheskie Zapiski*, 1940, 206; cp. Vitkevich to Simonich, 17 Apr. 1838, BP.

[108] Wade to Macnaghten, 13 Jan 1838, ESL 48, 100/1, 8 Feb. 1838.

[109] Mulla Rashid to Dost Muhammad, n.d., BP.

[110] Burnes to Auckland (pte.), 23 Dec. 1837, ESL 48, 105/1, 8 Feb. 1838.

[111] Wade to Macnaghten, 7 Nov. 1837, ESL 48, 32/1, 8 Feb. 1838.

[112] Macnaghten to Burnes, 20 Jan. 1838, ESL 48, 106/1, 8 Feb. 1838.

[113] Macnaghten to Burnes, 20 Jan. 1838, ESL 48, 106/1, 8 Feb. 1838.

[114] Colvin to Burnes (pte.), 7 Feb. 1838, in Colvin, op. cit., 98.

[115] Wade to Macnaghten, 21 Dec. 1837, ESL 48, 80/1, 8 Feb. 1838.

[116] Macnaghten to Burnes, 20 Jan. 1838, ESL 48, 106/1, 8 Feb. 1838.

[117] Burnes to Kohundil Khan, 22 Feb. 1838, ESL 49, 27/5, 5 Apr. 1838.

[118] Burnes to Macnaghten, 26 Jan. 1838, ESL 49, 5/4, 7 Mar. 1838.

[119] Masson, op. cit., iii, 469.

[120] Burnes to Macnaghten, 25 Apr. 1838, ESL 49, 8/11, 22 May 1838. This account of the last weeks of Burnes's mission is based upon his official dispatches and differs considerably from the account written by his companion. Mohan Lal, some years after the event. (See Mohan Lal, *Life of Dost Mohammed Khan*, 2 vols., London 1846, i, 310–11) Lal depicts Dost Muhammad as having demanded British help to make himself master of Afghanistan and to oust Ranjit Singh from Peshawar. Burnes's dispatches are consistent with Masson's account.

[121] Leech to Burnes, 12 May 1838, ESL 50, 46/18, 13 Aug. 1838; Todd, memo., n.d., ESL 50, 47/18, 13 Aug. 1838.

[122] Wade to Macnaghten, 21 Aug. 1837, ESL 47, 81/22, 27 Dec. 1837; Mackeson to Wade, 6 Mar. 1838, ESL 49, 5/5, 5 Apr. 1838; Ranjit Singh to Wade, Aug. 1837, ESL 47, 81/22, 27 Dec. 1837; Ranjit Singh to Burnes, (recd. 25 Nov. 1837), ESL 48, 98/1, 8 Feb. 1838; Masson, op. cit., iii, 461.

[123] Auckland to Loch (pte.), 11 July 1837, AM 37691, f.40.

[124] Auckland to Hobhouse (pte.), 9 Feb. 1839, AM 37695, f.69.

[125] Auckland to Hobhouse (pte.), 3 May 1838, AM 36473, f.243.

[126] Colvin to Burnes (pte.), 21 Jan. 1838, AM 37692, f.91.

CHAPTER 7, HAMLET AT SIMLA

[1] GG to SC, 27 Apr. 1838, BSL(1) 23, 404.

[2] Auckland to Hobhouse (pte.), 23 Aug. 1838, 15 Nov. 1838, AM 36473, ff.304, 339.

[3] Auckland to Kamran Shah, 1 May 1838, ESL 49, 7/9, 1 May 1838.

[4] Auckland, Minute, 12 May 1838, ESL 49, 12/11, 22 May 1838.

[5] Auckland to Hobhouse, 3 May 1838, AM 36473, f.243.

[6] Auckland to McNeill, 30 Mar. 1837, AM 37690, f.77. McNeill's letter to Auckland of 22 Jan. 1837 is in FO 60/48.

[7] Wade to Macnaghten, 12 July 1837, ESL 47, 44/22, 27 Dec. 1837.

[8] J. Hume, *Selections from the Writings of Henry Torrens with a Biographical Memoir*, 2 vols., Calcutta, 1854.

[9] Wade to Macnaghten, 1 Jan. 1838, ESL 48, 87/1, 8 Feb. 1838.

[10] Macnaghten to Wade, 20 Jan. 1838, ESL 48, 108/1, 8 Feb. 1838.

[11] Burnes to Macnaghten, 26 Jan. 1838, ESL 49, 5/4, 7 Mar. 1838.

[12] Burnes to Macnaghten, 17 May 1838, ESL 50, 5/18, 13 Aug. 1838.

[13] Torrens to Burnes, 1 June 1838, ESL 50, 6/18, 13 Aug. 1838.

[14] Torrens to Macnaghten, 15 May 1838, ESL 49, 13/11, 22 May 1838.

[15] Torrens to Macnaghten (pte.), 27 May 1838, AM 37693, f.9; 1 June 1838, f.16; 12 June 1838, f.37; Colvin to Pottinger (pte.), 13 June 1838, AM 37693, f.38; Colvin, op. cit., 107–10.

[16] Auckland to Macnaghten (pte.), 1 June 1838, AM 37693, f.15.

[17] 'Case of Sir William Macnaghten', PSL B107 (IOR).

[18] Burnes to Holland (pte.), 21 Mar. 1839, SC (NAI), 8/43, 28 Sept. 1842.

[19] J. Broadfoot to Mrs. Bayley, 24 June 1842, in W. Broadfoot, *Career of Major Broadfoot*, London, 1888, 120–1.

[20] Hobhouse, Diary, 26 Aug. 1842, AM 43744.

[21] Burnes to Jacob (pte.), 19 Sept. 1839, SC (NAI), 37/43, 28 Sept. 1842.

[22] Cp. W. Macnaghten to E. Macnaghten, 5 Apr. 1840, Macnaghten Papers.

[23] Hasrat, *Anglo-Sikh Relations*, 86.

[24] Macnaghten to Torrens, 4 June 1838, 8 June 1838, 11 June 1838, ESL 50, 21, 24, 29/ 18, 13 Aug. 1838.

[25] Lala Sohan Lal Suri, *Umdat-ut-Tawarikh* (trans V. S. Suri), Delhi, 1961, 460–1.

[26] Macnaghten to Torrens, 20 June 1838, ESL 50, 35/18, 13 Aug. 1838.

[27] Macnaghten to Torrens, 23 June 1838, ESL 50, 38/18, 13 Aug. 1838.

[28] Clerk to Maddock, 5 Apr. 1842, ESL 85, 30/3, 21 Apr. 1842.

[29] Suri, op. cit., 495.

[30] Macnaghten to Torrens, 17 July 1838, ESL 50, 59/18, 13 Aug. 1838.

[31] Auckland to Hobhouse (pte.), 3 June 1838, AM 36473, f.249.

[32] Auckland to Macnaghten (pte.), 12 June 1838, 27 June 1838, AM 37693, f.57; Colvin to Macnaghten (pte.), 12 June 1838, 30 June 1838, AM 37693, ff.37, 64.

[33] Auckland to Minto (pte.), 10 July 1838, M645.

[34] Auckland to Hobhouse (pte.), 12 July 1838, AM 36473, f.304; cp. Todd to Burnes, 23 June 1838, ESL 50, 4/18, 16 July 1838. Todd arrived at Simla from Herat on 20 July.

[35] Kaye, *History of the War in Afghanistan*, 3 vols., London, 1857, i, 312–5.

[36] Cp. the stories told to Beresford, EM 708, 353–7.

[37] Hume, op. cit., i, xxxviii–lv.

[38] EM 638, ff.7–9.

[39] EM C130, 4 (18 Nov. 1838).

[40] *Miss Eden's Letters* (ed. Violet Dickinson) London, 1919, 302; also Emily Eden to Minto (pte.), 25 Aug. 1839, M645.

[41] Council to Auckland, 5 Sept. 1838, ESL 52, 3/23, 24 Sept. 1838.

[42] Colvin, op. cit., x.

[43] GG to SC, 13 Aug. 1838, BSL(1) 23, 500.

[44] See references in Yapp, 'British Policy', 172.

[45] *Miss Eden's Letters*, 314–5.

[46] See Yapp, op. cit., 173. On Jaipur see H. C. Batra, *The Relations of Jaipur State with the East India Company (1803–1858)*, Delhi, 1958.

[47] Auckland to Prinsep (pte.), 8 July 1838, AM 37693, f.80.

[48] Emily Eden to Minto (pte.), 17 Sept. 1838, M645.

[49] Colvin to Prinsep (pte.), 8 July 1838, AM 37693, f.84.

[50] Colvin to Macnaghten (pte.), 12 July 1838, AM 37693, f.96.

[51] Auckland to Hobhouse (pte.), 12 July 1838, AM 36473, f.304.

[52] Auckland to Hobhouse (pte.), 19 Sept. 1838, AM 36473, f.319.
[53] Auckland to Fane, 30 Sept. 1838, ESL 52, 111/23, 24 Sept. 1838.
[54] Auckland to Hobhouse (pte.), 15 Nov. 1838, AM 36473, f.338.
[55] Hume, op. cit., xlviii.
[56] Macnaghten to Mackeson, 23 July 1838, ESL 50, 64/18, 13 Aug. 1838. Draft treaty enclosed (No. 66).
[57] Auckland to Prinsep (pte.), 8 July 1838, AM 37693, f.80.
[58] Mackeson to Macnaghten, 16 Aug. 1838, 18 Aug. 1838, 23 Aug. 1838, 26 Aug. 1838, 7 Sept. 1838, 9 Sept. 1838, ESL 52, 59, 60 & 65–8/23, 24 Sept. 1838.
[59] Mackeson to Macnaghten, 16 Aug. 1838, ESL 52, 59/23, 24 Sept. 1838.
[60] Colvin to Mackeson (pte.), 8 Jan. 1839, AM 37695, f.12.
[61] Mackeson to Torrens, 23 Jan. 1839, ESL 58, 1230/18, 11 July 1839 (PC).
[62] Cotton to Ellenborough (pte.), 3 Jan. 1839, PRO 30/12/26/1.
[63] Wade to Macnaghten, 6 Aug. 1838, ESL 52, 9/23, 24 Sept. 1838.
[64] Macnaghten to Pottinger, 26 July 1838, ESL 50, 67/18, 13 Aug. 1838.
[65] Colvin to Pottinger (pte.), 12 July 1838, AM 37693, f.100.
[66] Colvin to Pottinger (pte.), 11 Sept. 1838, AM 37694, f.44.
[67] Pottinger to Macnaghten, 13 Aug. 1838, ESL 52, 83/23, 24 Sept. 1838.
[68] Macnaghten to Pottinger, 6 Sept. 1838, ESL 52, 84/23, 24 Sept. 1838.
[69] Pottinger to Macnaghten, 27 Aug. 1838, ESL 52, 87/23, 24 Sept. 1838.
[70] Macnaghten to Pottinger, 20 Sept. 1838, ESL 52, 88/23, 24 Sept. 1838.
[71] Macnaghten to Burnes, 6 Sept. 1838, ESl 52, 88/23, 24 Sept. 1838.
[72] Burnes to Pottinger, 25 Oct. 1838, ESL 56, 310/18, 11 July 1839 (PC).
[73] Pottinger to Burnes, 29 Oct. 1838, ESL 55, 162/18, 11 July 1839 (PC).
[74] Pottinger to Masson (pte.), 16 Sept. 1838, EM 631, f.166.
[75] Pottinger to Burnes, 22 Nov. 1838, ESL 55, 164/18, 11 July 1839 (PC).
[76] Burnes to Torrens, 25 Dec. 1838, ESL 56, 291/18, 11 July 1839 (PC). Copy of treaty in ESL 53, 7/4, 13 Mar. 1839 and Aitchison, vii, 363.
[77] Pottinger to Maddock, 6 July 1839, ESL 60, 4/32, 19 July 1839.
[78] Pottinger to Eastwick, 13 Jan. 1839, ESL 53, 9/4, 13 Mar. 1839.
[79] Pottinger to Torrens, 13 Feb. 1839, ESL 57, 705/18, 11 July 1839 (PC). Copy of draft treaty dated 5 Feb. 1839 in ESL 53, 11/4, 13 Mar. 1839.
[80] Auckland to Hobhouse (pte.), 9 Feb. 1839, AM 36473, f.419.
[81] Auckland to Keane (pte.), 18 Jan. 1839, AM 37695, f.37.
[82] Torrens to Pottinger, 19 Nov. 1838, ESL 52, 5/31, 31 Dec. 1838.
[83] Colvin to Macnaghten (pte.), 10 Feb. 1839, AM 37695, f.65.
[84] Colvin to Pottinger (pte.), 9 Mar. 1839, AM 37695 f.109; Maddock to Pottinger, 11 Mar. 1839, ESL 53, 13/4, 13 Mar. 1839. Draft treaty enclosed (No. 12).
[85] Auckland to Pottinger (pte.), 2 Aug. 1839, AM 37696, f.220.
[86] Colvin to Pottinger (pte.), 15 Aug. 1838, AM 37694, f.14.
[87] Pottinger to Auckland, 21 Jan. 1839, ESL 58, 1102/18, 11 July 1839 (PC).
[88] Macnaghten to Mihrab Khan, 11 Feb. 1839, ESL 58, 1107/18, 11 July 1839 (PC).
[89] Macnaghten to Burnes, 18 Mar. 1839, ESL 58, 1212/18, 11 July 1839 (PC); Burnes to Macnaghten, 30 Mar. 1839, ESL 60, 59/25, 26 Aug. 1839 (PC); Burnes to Macnaghten, 2 Apr. 1839, ESL 54, 10/13, 9 May 1839.
[90] Macnaghten to Maddock, 5 Apr. 1839, ESL 54, 8/13, 9 May 1839.
[91] Macnaghten to Maddock, 25 Dec. 1839, ESL 64, 13/2, 13 Jan. 1840.
[92] Bell to Maddock, 5 Nov. 1839, HM 798, 603.
[93] Macnaghten to Maddock, 11 Apr. 1839, ESL 60, 21/25, 26 Aug. 1839 (PC).
[94] Bean to Maddock, 23 Nov. 1839, ESL 63, 9/53, 19 Dec. 1839.
[95] Memo., 9 May 1840, ESL 69, 5/63, 8 June 1840.
[96] Burnes to Macnaghten, 2 Apr. 1839, ESL 54, 10/13, 9 May 1839; cp. Masson, *Travels in Kalat*, London, 1843, 92–3.
[97] Macnaghten to Maddock, 5 Apr. 1839, ESL 54, 8/13, 9 May 1839.
[98] Muhammad Husayn to Mihrab Khan, ESL 69, 20/64, 8 June 1840.
[99] These letters were sent in Macnaghten to Maddock, 6 Apr. 1839, but are absent from the enclosures. Two are in ESL 60, 21/25, 26 Aug. 1839 (PC). In an accompanying letter to Macnaghten dated 10 Apr. 1839 Burnes argues that they are genuine.

[100] Letters in ESL 69, 20/64; 8 June 1840; cp. Masson, *Kalat*, 97–100, 107–9.
[101] Colvin to Sutherland (pte.), 8 Dec. 1839, AM 37697, f.174.
[102] Maddock to Macnaghten, 29 Apr. 1839, ESL 54, 11/13, 9 May 1839; Auckland to Macnaghten (pte.), 25 May 1839, AM 37696, f.27.
[103] Bell to Maddock, 14 Nov. 1839, HM 798, 608.
[104] SC to GGC 521/, 11 Oct. 1839, BDSLI 11.
[105] Torrens to Macnaghten, 8 Dec. 1838, ESL 52, 3/29, 14 Dec. 1838; see also Auckland to Keane, 8 Dec. 1838, ibid., 4.
[106] Hobhouse to Auckland (pte.), 17 Feb. 1839, HM 839, 98.
[107] SC to GGC 27/, 18 Feb. 1839, BDSLI 10.
[108] Macnaghten to Maddock, 8 May 1838, ESL 63, 3/51, 12 Dec. 1839.
[109] Maddock to Macnaghten, 12 Sept. 1839, ESL 63, 8/51, 12 Dec. 1839.
[110] ESL 63, 8/51, 12 Dec. 1839.
[111] Auckland to Todd (pte.), 11 Jan. 1839, AM 37695, f.19.
[112] Auckland to Macnaghten, 15 June 1839, AM 37696, f.91.
[113] Auckland, Minute, 20 Aug. 1839, ESL 59, 3/26, 22 Aug. 1839; Auckland to Macnaghten (pte.), 4 Aug. 1839, AM 37696, f.222.
[114] Colvin to Bell (pte.), 13 Dec. 1839, AM 37697, f.27.

CHAPTER 8, LONDON AND CENTRAL ASIA, 1838–9

[1] Palmerston to McNeill (pte.), 2 July 1837, in *Memoir of Sir John McNeill*, 199.
[2] McNeill to Palmerston (pte.), 1 Dec. 1837, BP.
[3] Sheil, Memo., 7 Mar. 1838, FO 60/61.
[4] Palmerston to McNeill, 12 Feb. 1838, BP; see also Palmerston to Hobhouse (pte.), 9 Feb. 1838; AM 46915, f.71.
[5] Hobhouse to Auckland (pte.), 13 Feb. 1838, HM 838, 290.
[6] McNeill to Palmerston 12/, 23 Feb. 1838, FO 60/56.
[7] Hobhouse to Palmerston (pte.), 17 Apr. 1838, AM 36469, f.11; for the views of Sheil see his memos. dated 7 Mar. 1838, 28 Nov. 1838, FO 60/61, and Sheil to Palmerston, 13 Apr. 1838, AM 36469, f.5.
[8] Palmerston to McNeill (pte.), 14 Apr. 1838, BP; cp. Palmerston to Hobhouse (pte.), 14 Apr. 1838, AM 46915, f.77.
[9] Hobhouse to Auckland (pte.), 14 Apr. 1838, HM 838, 316.
[10] SC to GGC 384/, 10 May 1838, BDSLI 9.
[11] Palmerston to Hobhouse (pte.), 9 May 1838, AM 46915, f.79.
[12] Hobhouse to Auckland (pte.), 9 May 1838, HM 838, 295.
[13] Cp. the original draft of SC to GGC, 10 May 1838 in HM 838, 327 with that actually sent (n. 10 above). This dispatch is completely misrepresented by Auckland Colvin, (Colvin, op. cit., 116–8) in his attempt to argue that Hobhouse was responsible for the Afghan policy.
[14] Palmerston to McNeill 24–7/, 18 May 1838, FO 60/55.
[15] Palmerston to Hobhouse (pte.), 20 May 1838, AM 46915, f.83.
[16] Palmerston to Hobhouse (pte.), 21 May 1838, AM 46915, f.85.
[17] Palmerston to Hobhouse (pte.), 21 May 1838 (second letter of this date), AM 46915, f.86; Hobhouse's reply is on the reverse. Melbourne's agreement to a modification of the dispatch recorded in Palmerston to Hobhouse (pte.), 22 May 1838 7.0 p.m., AM. 46915, f.88.
[18] Palmerston to McNeill 29/, 21 May 1838, FO 60/55.
[19] Kaye, *War in Afghanistan*, i, 284.
[20] Palmerston to McNeill, 22 May 1838, BP.
[21] SC to GGC 12/, 4 June 1838, BDSLI 10.
[22] Hobhouse to Auckland (pte.), 9 June 1838, HM 838, 364.
[23] Hobhouse to Grant (pte.), 10 May 1838, HM 838, 301.
[24] Palmerston to Hobhouse (pte.), 18 June 1838, HM 838, 397.
[25] Palmerston to McNeill (pte.), 23 June 1838, BP.
[26] Hobhouse to Auckland (pte.), 2 July 1838, HM 838, 411.
[27] Palmerston to Hobhouse (pte.), 27 July 1838, AM 46915, f.103; Palmerston to McNeill 39/, 27 July 1838, FO 60/55.

[28] Hobhouse to Auckland (pte.), 4 Aug. 1838, HM 838, 414.

[29] Palmerston to McNeill (pte.), 10 Aug. 1838, BP.

[30] Palmerston to Hobhouse (pte.), 25 Aug. 1838, AM 46915, f.105.

[31] Grant to Hobhouse (pte.), 4 June 1838, HM 838, 198.

[32] Hobhouse to Melbourne (pte.), 25 Aug. 1838, HM 838, 453.

[33] Hobhouse to Palmerston (pte.), 25 Aug. 1838, HM 838, 453.

[34] Comment by Hobhouse on Burnes to Macnaghten, 2 June 1838, ESL 50, 51/18, 13 Aug. 1838.

[35] Palmerston to Hobhouse (pte.), 27 Aug. 1838, AM 46915, f.107.

[36] Melbourne to Hobhouse (pte.), 28 Aug. 1838, HM 838, 450.

[37] Palmerston, memo., 29 Aug. 1838 on a letter from Quli Reza Mirza 1 Aug. 1838, BP.

[38] Palmerston to Hobhouse (pte.), 27 Sept. 1838, AM 46915, f.123.

[39] Russell to Howick (pte.), 30 Sept. 1838, Grey MSS; Melbourne to Hobhouse (pte.), 24 Sept. 1838, HM 838, 440.

[40] Palmerston to Hobhouse (pte.), 26 Sept. 1838, AM 46915, f.119.

[41] Hobhouse to Palmerston (pte.), 29 Sept. 1838, HM 838, 440.

[42] *The Girlhood of Queen Victoria* (ed. Esher), 2 vols., London, 1912, 7 Oct. 1838.

[43] Hobhouse to Auckland (pte.), 27 Oct. 1838, HM 838, 464. On the Cabinet decision see a pencilled note by Hobhouse, AM 36469, f.44.

[44] Palmerston to Minto (pte.), 16 Oct. 1838, MP ELL/218.

[45] Russell to Hobhouse (pte.), 14 Oct. 1838, HM 838, 444; Palmerston to Russell (pte.), 1 Oct. 1838 in R. Russell (ed.), *The Early Correspondence of Lord John Russell*, 2 vols., London, 1913, ii, 222.

[46] Melbourne to Spring Rice, 12 Oct. 1838, in W. M. Torrens, *Memoirs of Viscount Melbourne*, London, 1890, 463, see also *Girlhood of Victoria*, ii, 147.

[47] Howick to Russell, 8 Oct. 1838, 18 Oct. 1838, PRO 30/22/3; see Webster, *Foreign Policy of Palmerston*, ii, 475. Palmerston's reference is presumably to the *Bounty* mutineer who founded a theocracy on the island of Pitcairn..

[48] See their letters to Hobhouse in HM 839, 53–4.

[49] *Girlhood of Victoria*, ii, 63.

[50] Melbourne to Russell (pte.), 13 Oct. 1838; Russell to Howick (pte.), 14 Oct. 1838, Grey MSS.

[51] Palmerston to McNeill 57/, 12 Oct. 1839, FO 60/55.

[52] SC to GGC 1/, 24 Oct. 1838, BDSLI 10. See also the correspondence with Russell and Melbourne in HM 838, 459–65. A draft of the dispatch dated 27 Oct. 1838 with queries is in AM 36469, f.144.

[53] Hobhouse to Auckland (pte.), 27 Oct. 1838, HM 838, 477.

[54] SC to GGC 32/, 5 Nov. 1838, 5/, 4 Dec. 1838, BDSLI 10; Hobhouse to Auckland (pte.), 1 Oct. 1838, HM 838, 20.

[55] Hobhouse to Palmerston (pte.), 17 Dec. 1838, HM 839, 57.

[56] SC to GGC 1/, 24 Oct. 1838, 6/, 21 Dec. 1838, BDSLI 10.

[57] Hobhouse to Auckland (pte.), 1 Nov. 1838, HM 838, 492.

[58] Palmerston to Hobhouse (pte.), 31 Oct. 1838, AM 46915, f.135.

[59] Note on Maddock to Macnaghten, 28 Dec. 1840, ESL 74, 7/4, 21 Jan. 1841.

[60] *Girlhood of Victoria*, ii, 258.

[61] Hobhouse to Auckland (pte.), 5 Dec. 1838, HM 839, 19.

[62] Hobhouse to McNeill (pte.), 6 Jan. 1839, HM 839, 79.

[63] P. E. Moseley, *Russian Diplomacy and the Opening of the Eastern Question*, Cambridge (Mass.), 1934, 85; see also F. S. Rodkey, 'Conversations on Anglo-Russian Relations in 1838', *EHR* 50 (1935), 120.

[64] Palmerston to Hobhouse (pte.), 29 Oct. 1838, AM 46915, f.133; cp. Palmerston to Melbourne (pte.), 31 Oct. 1838 in Torrens, op. cit., 464.

[65] Cp. C. J. Bartlett, *Great Britain and Sea Power, 1815–53*, London, 1963, 109, 120–2; also Palmerston to Minto (pte.), 13 Nov. 1838, MP ELL/218.

[66] Simonich, 'Précis', f.210.

[67] McNeill to Palmerston (pte.), 3 Jan. 1839, FO 60/69.

[68] McNeill to Palmerston (pte.), 3 Dec. 1838, FO 60/60.

[69] Sheil to SC, 12 Feb. 1839, FO 60/70; Sheil, Memo., 15 Feb. 1839, FO 60/65.

[70] Sheil. Memo., 20 July 1838. FO 60/61; Simonich, 'Précis', f.173.

[71] Palmerston to Sheil (pte.), 2 June 1841, BP.

[72] Comte de Sercey, *Une ambassade extraordinaire: La Perse en 1839–40*, Paris, 1928, 28.

[73] Sercey, op. cit., 247. The French mission was little more than an aristocratic jaunt; it included one count, two marquesses, and four viscounts. More interestingly, among the interpreters was one M. Outrey, *fils*, thus providing a link with Jaubert and Gardane, who employed his father.

[74] Farrant to J. Campbell (pte.), 18 Mar. 1841, EM 556/1.

[75] Palmerston to Nesselrode 18/, 26 Oct. 1838, FO 65/243.

[76] Nesselrode to Pozzo di Borgo, 20 Oct. 1838, FO 65/207.

[77] Harold T. Cheshire, 'The Expansion of Imperial Russia to the Indian Border', *SR* 13 (1934, 85.

[78] Clanricarde to Palmerston 52/, 25 May 1839, FO 65/252; see also Brunnow to Aberdeen (pte.), Feb. 1843, AM 43144, f.40.

[79] Palmerstone to Hobhouse (pte.), 14 Nov. 1838, AM 46915, f.137.

[80] Palmerston to Pozzo di Borgo, 20 Dec. 1838, FO 65/247.

[81] Nesselrode to Pozzo di Borgo, 29 Jan. 1839, FO 65/256.

[82] P. E. Moseley, 'Russian Policy in Asia', 670.

[83] P. E. Moseley, *Russian Diplomacy*, 22.

[84] Nesselrode to Pozzo di Borgo, 5 Mar. 1839, FO 65/256.

[85] Haji Mirza Aghasi to Nesselrode, 25 Apr. 1839, enc. in Sheil to Palmerston 39/, 5 June 1839, FO 60/66.

[86] Palmerston to Clanricarde 124/, 15 Aug. 1839, FO 65/250.

[87] Wellington to Hill, n.d. *c.* Dec. 1838, PRO 30/12/26/1.

[88] Hobhouse to Auckland (pte.), 19 Feb. 1839, HM 839, 98.

[89] Cabell, Memo., 14 Feb. 1839, AM 36474, f.103.

[90] Hobhouse, Diary, 29 May 1842, AM 43744.

[91] See H. Temperley and L. M. Penson, *A Century of Diplomatic Blue Books, 1814–1914*, London, 1966.

[92] Palmerston to Hobhouse, 6 Oct. 1836, FO 60/46.

[93] Hobhouse to Auckland (pte.), 4 Dec. 1839, HM 839, 248.

[94] Hobhouse to Auckland (pte.), 16 Sept. 1839, HM 839, 183.

[95] Lushington to Hobhouse (pte.), 20 Oct. 1838, HM 836, 41; Hobhouse to Auckland (pte.), 16 Mar. 1839, HM 839, 109; Hobhouse to Jenkins (pte.), 3 Dec. 1839, HM 836, 99.

[96] Willock to Palmerston (pte.), 1 Dec. 1838, FO 60/63.

[97] Tucker, Memo., 29 Jan. 1839 in Kaye, *Memorials of Indian Government*, 266. See also ibid., 261, 282, and Kaye, *Life of Tucker*, 497–516.

[98] *India under Ellenborough* (ed. Colchester), London, 1874, 1.

[99] Wellington, Memo., 21 Nov. 1838, HM 839, 15; see also Greville, op. cit., v, 101–2; Torrens, *Melbourne*, 465.

[100] Wellington to Hill, n.d. *c.* Dec. 1838, PRO 30/12/26/1.

[101] Wellington to Lansdowne, 3 Nov. 1838, Torrens, op. cit., 465.

[102] Peel to Wellington (pte.), 26 Jan. 1839, in C. S. Parker, *Peel*, 3 vols., London, 1891–9, ii, 373.

[103] See Graham to Russell [26 Mar. 1839], AM 40318, f.143. (The cataloguer has wrongly ascribed this letter to April 1838.)

[104] Hobhouse to Auckland (pte.), 19 Feb. 1839, HM 839, 98.

[105] Kaye, *Memorials*, 266.

[106] *Edinburgh Review*, 71 (July 1840), 327.

[107] *Quarterly Review*, 64 (June 1839), 145.

[108] *Times*, 26 Oct. 1838, 29 Oct. 1838, 1 Nov. 1838, 13 Dec. 1838, 17 Dec. 1838, and 25 Dec. 1838.

[109] SC to GGC 91/, 8 July 1839, BDSLI 10.

[110] Hobhouse to Palmerston (pte.), 10 July 1839, HM 839, 101.

[111] Hobhouse to Auckland (pte.), 16 Mar. 1839, HM 839, 184.

[112] Hobhouse to Auckland (pte.), 16 Sept. 1839, HM 839, 184.

[113] Palmerston to Hobhouse (pte.), 10 July 1839, AM 46915, f.171.

[114] Palmerston to Minto (pte.), 31 Oct. 1839, MP ELL/218.

[115] Hobhouse to Auckland (pte.), 4 Dec. 1839, HM 838, 248.

CHAPTER 9, AFGHANISTAN, 1839–41

[1] Auckland to Hobhouse (pte.), 21 Dec. 1839, AM 36474, f.188; Auckland to Macnaghten (pte.), 7 Dec. 1839, AM 37697, f.12.

[2] Macnaghten to Auckland (pte.), 1 Sept. 1841, ESL 81, 64/109, 22 Dec. 1841.

[3] Macnaghten to Maddock, 13 Jan. 1840, ESL 66, 3/15, 17 Feb. 1840.

[4] Macnaghten to Maddock, 6 Jan. 1841, ESL 74, 49/13, 19 Feb. 1841.

[5] Warburton to Lawrence, 5 Aug. 1841, ESL 80, 29/88, 21 Oct. 1841.

[6] Macnaghten to Maddock, 8 Apr. 1841, ESL 78, 54/58, 8 July 1841.

[7] Macnaghten to Maddock, 10 June 1841 & enc., ESL 79, 74/68, 20 Aug. 1841; Macnaghten to Maule, 8 May 1840, ESL 69, 16/72/, 6 July 1840; Macnaghten to Maddock, 7 Aug. 1841, ESL 80, 47/79, 20 Sept. 1841.

[8] Trevor, Report, 31 Aug. 1840, ESL 73, 5/140, 19 Dec. 1840.

[9] Auckland to Macnaghten (pte.), 29 Oct. 1840, AM 37702, f.48.

[10] Macnaghten to Keane, 27 Feb. 1839, ESL 60, 6A/25, 26 Aug. 1839 (PC).

[11] Roberts to G. Lawrence, 7Mar. 1840, ESL 68, 6/32, 16 Apr. 1840.

[12] K. Elphinstone to J. Elphinstone, 3 Sept. 1841, EM F/89/3/8.

[13] Auckland to Macnaghten, 15 Jan. 1841, AM 37703, f.92.

[14] Anquetil to Macnaghten, 9 Sept. 1841, ESL 80, 25/96, 20 Nov. 1841.

[15] Memo. on Shuja's forces, PRO 30/12/32 Pt. 1/2.

[16] See 'Disturbances in Eastern Afghanistan, 1839–42', *BSOAS* 25 (1962), 499–523; 'Disturbances in Western Afghanistan, 1839–41', *BSOAS* 26 (1963), 288–313; and 'The Revolutions of 1841–2 in Afghanistan', *BSOAS* 27 (1964), 333–81.

[17] Cotton to Auckland (pte.), 5 Dec. 1840, HM 546, f.116.

[18] Elphinstone to J. B. Elphinstone, 2 Sept. 1841, EM F/89/3/5.

[19] Burnes to J. Burnes, 1 May 1842, quoting letter from Alexander Burnes of 1 Apr. 1841, SC (NAI), 30/43, 28 Sept. 1841.

[20] H. Havelock, *Narrative*, etc., 2 vols., London, 1840, ii, 227–29.

[21] Wade to Auckland (pte.), 31 Jan. 1839, AM 36473, f.431.

[22] J. H. Stocqueler, *Memorials of Afghanistan*, Calcutta, 1843, 71.

[23] Lord to Macnaghten, 15 Mar. 1840, ESL 69, 19/64, 8 June 1840.

[24] Macnaghten to Lord, 30 Mar. 1840, ESL 69, 19/64, 8 June 1840.

[25] [E. B. Eastwick] *Dry Leaves from Young Egypt*, London, 1849, 56.

[26] H. C. Rawlinson, 'Journal of a Journey from Quetta to Qandahar, 1840' (29 Apr. 1840), RM.

[27] Macnaghten to Rawlinson (pte.), 3 Feb. 1841, RM.

[28] Macnaghten to Maddock, 6 June 1839, ESL 59, 20/20, 15 July 1839.

[29] Leech to Macnaghten, 7 Apr. 1840, ESL 70, 41/78, 27 July 1840.

[30] Leech to Macnaghten, 19 May 1840, ESL 69, 73/72, 6 July 1840.

[31] Leech to Macnaghten, 3 Jan. 1840, ESL 68, 21/29, 14 Apr. 1840.

[32] Leech to Macnaghten, 18 Jan. 1840, ESL 68, 21/29, 14 Apr. 1840; Leech to Macnaghten, 8 Feb. 1840, ESL 68, 21/44, 8 May 1840.

[33] Macnaghten to Leech, 13 Mar. 1840, ESL 68, 21/44, 8 May 1840.

[34] Macnaghten to Leech, 15 Feb. 1840, ESL 68, 21/29, 14 Apr. 1840.

[35] Auckland to Hobhouse (pte.), 15 Aug. 1840, AM 36474, f.338.

[36] Leech, Suggestions for the government of Afghanistan, 1 May 1840, ESL 70, 2/95, 11 Sept. 1840.

[37] Leech to Macnaghten, 9 May 1840, ESL 69, 42/72, 6 July 1840.

[38] Leech to Magnaghten, 3 Apr. 1840, ESL 69, 22/64, 8 June 1840.

[39] Nicholson to Macnaghten, 27 Apr. 1840, ESL 69, 38/72, 6 July 1840.

[40] Macnaghten to Maddock, 5 May 1840, ESL 69, 38/72, 6 July 1840.

[41] Torrens to Macnaghten, 15 June 1840, ESL 69, 39/72, 6 July 1840.

[42] Colvin to Macnaghten (pte.), 15 June 1840, AM 37700, f.53.

[43] Nicholson to Lynch, 5 July 1840, ESL 70, 20/99, 13 Sept. 1840.

[44] Rawlinson to Macnaghten, 20 Jan. 1841, ESL 71, 4/19, 21 Mar. 1841.

[45] Macnaghten to Rawlinson, 20 Feb. 1841, ESL 78, 53/58, 8 July 1841.

[46] Nicholson, Statement, 13 Aug. 1840, ESL 71, 46/112, 16 Oct. 1840; Macnaghten to Rawlinson (pte.), 26 Aug. 1840, RM.

[47] Leech to Macnaghten, 17 June 1840, ESL 70, 120/85, 10 Aug. 1840.

[48] Macnaghten to Rawlinson (pte.), 25 June 1841, RM.

[49] Macnaghten to Rawlinson (pte.), 29 June 1841, RM.

[50] Macnaghten to Rawlinson (pte.), 1 July 1841, RM.

[51] Macnaghten to Rawlinson, 14 July 1841, ESL 79, 67/68, 20 Aug. 1841.

[52] Macnaghten to Rawlinson (pte.), 25 Dec. 1840, RM.
[53] Macnaghten to Rawlinson, 23 June 1840, ESL 70, 102/85, 10 Aug. 1840.
[54] Macnaghten to Rawlinson (pte.), 18 Sept. 1840, RM.
[55] Macnaghten to Rawlinson (pte.), 13 Dec. 1840, RM.
[56] Rawlinson to Macnaghten, 14 Oct. 1840, ESL 76, 95/41, 24 May 1841.
[57] Rawlinson to Eastwick (pte.), 6 Mar. 1841, EM 731 F/18/1,333.
[58] Rawlinson 'Report on the Dooranee Tribe', in C. M. Macgregor, *Central Asia Part II. Afghanistan*, Calcutta, 1871, 840.
[59] Macnaghten to Maddock, 6 June 1839, ESL 59, 20/20, 15 July 1839.
[60] Elliot to Rawlinson, 29 Jan. 1841, ESL 75, 15A/19, 21 Mar. 1841.
[61] Macnaghten to Rawlinson (pte.), 7 July 1841, RM.
[62] Macnaghten to Rawlinson (pte.), 29 Dec. 1840, RM.
[63] Rawlinson to Macnaghten, 11 Mar. 1841, ESL 77, 6A/47, 9 June 1841.
[64] Macnaghten to Rawlinson (pte.), 26 Apr. 1841, RM.
[65] Rawlinson to Elliot, 10 Sept. 1841, ESL 80, 17A/88, 21 Oct. 1841.
[66] Rawlinson to Macnaughten, 22 Mar. 1841, ESL 77, 66/47, 9 June 1841.
[67] Macnaghten to Rawlinson (pte.), 4 Jan. 1841, RM.
[68] Macnaghten to Rawlinson (pte.), 24 Feb. 1841, RM.
[69] Macnaghten to Rawlinson (pte.), 7 Feb. 1841, RM.
[70] Macnaghten to Rawlinson (pte.), 28 Feb. 1841, RM.
[71] Macnaghten to Maddock, 12 July 1841, ESL 79, 44/68, 20 Aug. 1841; Macnaghten to Rawlinson (pte.), 2 Aug. 1841, ESL 81, 64/109, 22 Dec. 1841.
[72] Macnaghten to Colvin (pte.), 17 Aug. 1841, ESL 81, 64/109, 22 Dec. 1841.
[73] Macnaghten to Rawlinson (pte.), 1 Aug. 1840, RM.
[74] Macnaghten to Rawlinson (pte.), 2 July 1841, RM.
[75] Macnaghten to Rawlinson (pte.), 4 July 1841, RM.
[76] Macnaghten to Rawlinson (pte.), 29 June 1841, RM.
[77] Macnaghten to Rawlinson (pte.), 15 July 1841, RM.
[78] Macnaghten to Rawlinson (pte.), 24 July 1841, RM.
[79] Note by Burnes on a conversation with Shah Shuja, ESL 70, 35/99, 13 Sept. 1840.
[80] Elphinstone to J. B. Elphinstone, 5 Apr. 1841, EM F/89/3/7.
[81] Burnes to Macnaghten (pte.), 7 Aug. 1840, ESL 71, 65/112, 16 Oct. 1840.
[82] Macnaghten to Torrens, 10 Aug. 1840 and Macnaghten's comments on Burnes to Macnaghten, 7 Aug. 1840, ESL 71, 65/112, 16 Oct. 1840.
[83] Burnes to Wood, Feb. 1841, in J. Wood, *A Journey to the Source of the River Oxus*, London, 1872, ix–x.
[84] Burnes to Holland (pte.), 6 Sept. 1840, SC (NAI), 17/43, 28 Sept. 1842.
[85] Torrens to Macnaghten, 5 Oct. 1840, ESL 71, 66/112, 16 Oct. 1840.
[86] Hobhouse to Auckland (pte.), 4 Feb. 1840, HM 839, 269; Hobhouse, comments on Macnaghten to Maddock, 13 Jan. 1840, ESL 66, 3/15, 17 Feb. 1840.
[87] Palmerston to Hobhouse (pte.), 12 Dec. 1840, AM 46915, f.241.
[88] Palmerston to Auckland (pte.), 24 Dec. 1840, BP; Palmerston to Hobhouse (pte.), 12 Dec. 1840, AM 46915, f.241.
[89] SC to GGC 694/, 31 Dec. 1840, BDSLI 13.
[90] Hobhouse to Carnac (pte.), 4 Dec. 1840, HM 839, 469.
[91] Auckland, Minute, 19 Mar. 1841, ESL 75, 3/23, 22 Mar. 1841.
[92] Nicolls, Minute, 10 Nov. 1840, ESL 74, 3/11, 15 Nov. 1841.
[93] Hobhouse to Auckland (pte.), 4 Apr. 1841, HM 840, 82.
[94] Burnes to Jacob (pte.), 25 Apr. 1841, SC (NAI), 38/37, 28 Sept. 1841.
[95] Colvin to Macnaghten (pte.), 21 Mar. 1841, AM 37704, f.70.
[96] On this discussion see Kaye, *War in Afghanistan*, ii, 140–9. Kaye used Nicoll's MS. diary, but his account confuses the discussion of the Afghan position with the simultaneous but separate discussion of the Herat problem.
[97] *Miss Eden's Letters*, 320.
[98] Prinsep, Minute, 1 Mar. 1841, ESL 75, 5/23, 22 Mar. 1841.
[99] *Edinburgh Review*, July 1840, 327 et seq.
[100] Torrens to Macnaghten, 6 July 1840, ESL 69, 4/77, 11 July 1840.
[101] *Hansard* III, 61, (11 Mar. 1842), cols. 428–9.

[102] GGC(Finance Dept.) to SC, 20 Mar. 1840, BSL(1) 25, 217.

[103] Memo., 7 Sept. 1841, PRO 30/12/32/Pt. 1/2.

[104] Tucker, Memo., to Aberdeen, 18 Mar. 1842, FO 60/93.

[105] Memo. on army increases, 8 Sept. 1841, PRO 30/12/32/ Pt. 1/2.

[106] Kaye, *Life of Tucker*, 511–16.

[107] Auckland to Low, (pte.), 1 Apr. 1841, AM 37704, f.116.

[108] Auckland, Minute, 30 Sept. 1841, AM 37713, f.124.

[109] Auckland, Minute, 28 Dec. 1841, AM 37713, f.140.

[110] Auckland, Minute, 2 Jan. 1842, AM 37713, f.139.

[111] Auckland to Macnaghten (pte.), 30 Apr. 1841, AM 37705, f.36; See also Auckland to Macnaghten (pte.), 21 Aug. 1841, AM 37706, f.55.

[112] Colvin to Macnaghten (pte.), 28 June 1841, AM 37705, f.138.

[113] Macnaghten to Maddock, 6 Jan. 1841, ESL 74, 49/13, 19 Feb. 1841.

[114] Maddock to Macnaghten, 17 May 1841, ESL 77, 13/47, 9 June 1841; see also Auckland to Macnaghten, 16 June 1841, AM 37705, f.124.

[115] Maddock to Macnaghten, 25 Oct. 1841, ESL 80, 24/96, 20 Nov. 1841.

[116] Macnaghten to Colvin (pte.), 1 Sept. 1841, ESL 81, 64/109, 22 Dec. 1841.

[117] Macnaghten to Maddock, 28 Aug. 1841, ESL 80, 35/88, 21 Oct. 1841.

[118] E. Hobsbawm, *Bandits*, London, 1969, 79–80.

[119] Macnaghten to Rawlinson (pte.), 16 June 1841, RM.

[120] Macnaghten to Auckland (pte.), 5 Sept. 1841, ESL 81, 64/109, 22 Dec. 1841.

[121] Burnes to Holland (pte.), 6 Nov. 1839, SC (NAI), 11/43, 28 Sept. 1842.

[122] Macnaghten seems to have believed that, as Governor of Bombay, he might be given special responsibility for Afghanistan. (Burnes, Diary, 8 Sept. 1841, quoted Mohan Lal, Memo. 29 June 1842, ESL 88, 24/32, 17 Aug. 1842.)

[123] Macnaghten to Rawlinson (pte.), 4 Jan. 1841, RM.

CHAPTER 10, THE BOUNDARIES OF AFGHANISTAN

[1] Macnaghten to Lord, 20 Aug. 1839, ESL 60, 11/38, 19 Sept. 1839.

[2] William Moorcroft and George Trebeck, *Travels in the Himalayan Provinces of Hindostan, etc.*, 1819–25, 2 vols., London, 1838, i, xlvi–l.

[3] Lord to Macnaghten, 30 Aug. 1839, ESL 64, 42/2, 8 Jan. 1840. For accounts of Lord's previous visit to Kunduz see J. Wood, *A Journey to the Source of the River Oxus*, London, 1872; A. Burnes, *Cabool*, Lahore, 1961, 127–55; and A. Burnes, R. Leech, P. B. Lord, and J. Wood, *Reports, etc.* Calcutta, 1839.

[4] Macnaghten to Lord, 2 Oct. 1839, ESL 64, 7/6, 13 Jan. 1840.

[5] Lord to Macnaghten, 3 Nov. 1839, ESL 64, 1/6, 13 Jan. 1840.

[6] Lord to Macnaghten, 6 Jan. 1840, ESL 66, 6/21, 16 Mar. 1840.

[7] Pottinger to Macnaghten, 7 July 1839, ESL 60, 6/33, 19 Sept. 1839; Pottinger to Macnaghten, 3 Dec. 1839 and memo., ESL 64, 20/6, 13 Jan. 1840.

[8] Macnaghten to Maddock, 31 Oct. 1839, ESL 63, 3/11, 1839 (SC); Macnaghten to Maddock, 15 Jan. 1840, ESL 66, 4/21, 16 Mar. 1840; Kaye, *War in Afghanistan*, ii, 42–5.

[9] Lord to Macnaghten, 22 June 1840, ESL 70, 3/88, 11 Aug. 1840.

[10] Maddock to Macnaghten, 26 Dec. 1839, ESL 64, 21/7, 13 Jan. 1840.

[11] Macnaghten to Maddock, 15 Jan. 1840, ESL 66, 4/21, 16 Mar. 1840.

[12] Maddock to Macnaghten, 17 Feb. 1840, ESL 66, 5/21, 16 Mar. 1840.

[13] Lord to Macnaghten, 2 Mar. 1840; Lord to Macnaghten, 28 Mar. 1840; ESL 69, 3 & 2/64, 8 June 1840.

[14] R. Burslem, *A Peep into Toorkisthan*, London, 1846.

[15] N. A. Khalfin, 'Britanskaya ékspansiya v Srednej Azii v 30–40–kh gg. xix v. i missiya Richmonda Shekspira', *Istoriya SSSR*, 1953, 103–112.

[16] Macnaghten to Maddock, 15 June 1840, ESL 70, 41/85, 10 Aug. 1840.

[17] Macnaghten to Lord, 14 May 1840, ESL 69, 20/72, 6 July 1840.

[18] SC to GGC 558/, 26 Dec. 1839, BDSLI 11.

[19] Torrens to Macnaghten, 29 May 1840, ESL 68, 4/54, 4 June 1840.

[20] SC to GGC 651/, 17 Aug. 1840, BDSLI 13.

[21] Lord to Macnaghten, 10 Aug. 1840, ESL 71, 3/112, 16 Oct. 1840.

[22] See M. E. Yapp, 'Disturbances in Eastern Afghanistan 1839–42', *BSOAS* 25 (1962), 508–14, where further references are given..

[23] Cotton to Auckland (pte.), 2 Oct. 1840, HM 546, f.8.

[24] Macnaghten to Maddock, 1 May 1841, ESL 77, 17/47, 8 June 1841.

[25] Garbett to Macnaghten, 17 Feb. 1841, ESL 75, 29/19, 21 Mar. 1841.

[26] Roberts to Auckland and enclosures, 30 Sept. 1840, PRO 30/12/32/Pt.1/2; Garbett to Douglas, 17 Apr. 1840, ESL 69, 46/64, 8 June 1840; Garbett to Douglas, 4 July 1840, ESL 70, 52/99, 13 Sept. 1840.

[27] Macnaghten to Pottinger, 29 May 1841, ESL 78, 72/58, 8 July 1841.

[28] Pottinger to Macnaghten, 14 Jan. 1839, ESL 58, 1248/18, 11 July 1839 (PC).

[29] Todd to Macnaghten, 31 May, 1839, ESL, 62, 316/34, 14 Nov. 1839 (PC).

[30] Auckland to Hobhouse (pte.), 14 July 1839, AM 36474, f.104.

[31] Pottinger to Macnaghten, 18 May 1839, ESL 62, 277/34, 15 Nov. 1839 (PC).

[32] Pottinger to McNeill, 25 Jan. 1839, ESL 58, 1101/18, 11 July 1839 (PC).

[33] Pottinger to Macnaghten, 3 Feb. 1839, ESL 54, 15/13, 9 May 1839.

[34] Auckland to Kamran Shah, 21 Jan. 1839, ESL 54, 13/13, 9 May 1839.

[35] Colvin to Burnes (pte.), 17 Jan. 1839, AM 37695, f.34.

[36] Auckland to Macnaghten (pte.), 28 Feb. 1839, AM 37695, f.87; Maddock to Macnaghten, 8 Mar. 1839, ESL 54, 10/13, 8 May 1839.

[37] Macnaghten to Todd, 15 May 1839, ESL 60, 17/33, 19 Sept. 1839. On the life and character of Todd see Kaye, *Lives of Indian Officers*, ii, 209–74.

[38] Macnaghten to Maddock, 11 June 1839, ESL 60, 10/26, 19 Sept. 1839 (PC).

[39] Todd to Macnaghten, 2 Oct. 1839, ESL 63, 3/11, 1839 (SC); see also J. Login, 'Memorandum on the Political Relations of the English Mission with Herat 1837 to 1841', in J. P. Ferrier, *Caravan Journeys*, London, 1857, 522–34.

[40] Copy in Todd to Macnaghten, 13 Aug. 1839, ESL 61, 3/36, 14 Oct. 1839.

[41] Todd to Macnaghten, 2 Oct. 1839, ESL 63, 3/11, 1839 (SC).

[42] Yar Muhammad to Asif al-Dawla, 11 Oct. 1839, ESL 79, 23/71, 20 Aug. 1841.

[43] Macnaghten to Maddock, 30 Nov. 1839, ESL 63, 10/11, 17 Dec. 1839 (PC); see also Macnaghten to Maddock, 31 Oct. 1839, 15 Nov. 1839, ESL 63, 3 & 7/11, 1839 (SC).

[44] Auckland to Hobhouse (pte.), 21 Dec. 1839, AM 36474, f.188.

[45] Maddock to Macnaghten, 13 Jan. 1840, ESL 64, 20/7, 13 Jan. 1840.

[46] Maddock to Macnaghten 5 Dec. 1839, ESL 63, 8/11, 1839 (SC); Auckland to Macnaghten (pte.), 7 Dec. 1839, AM 37697, f.12.

[47] Todd to Macnaghten, 22 Oct. 1839, ESL 63, 10/11, 1839 (SC).

[48] Todd to Macnaghten, 16 Nov. 1839, ESL 64, 20/7, 13 Jan. 1840.

[49] Todd to Macnaghten, 13 Feb. 1840, ESL 68, 3/40, 20 Apr. 1840.

[50] Todd to Macnaghten, 26 Feb. 1840, ESL 68, 2/49, 11 May 1840 (map enclosed).

[51] Conolly to Macnaghten (pte.), 16 Nov. 1840, ESL 75, 4/34, 22 Apr. 1841.

[52] Macnaghten to Todd, 18 Sept. 1840, ESL 72, 47/124, 16 Nov. 1840.

[53] Hobhouse to Auckland (pte.), 4 Dec. 1839, HM 839, 248.

[54] SC to GGC 521/, 26 Dec. 1839, BDSLI 11.

[55] Palmerston to Hobhouse (pte.), 20 Feb. 1840, AM 46915, f.204.

[56] Hobhouse to Auckland (pte.), 29 Feb. 1840, HM 839, 282.

[57] Melbourne to Hobhouse (pte.), 28 Feb. 1840, HM 839, 309.

[58] Russell to Hobhouse (pte.), 29 Feb. 1840, HM 839, 310.

[59] SC to GGC 577/, 29 Feb. 1840, BDSLI 12.

[60] Auckland to Hobhouse (pte.), 10 July 1840, AM 36474, f.328.

[61] Hobhouse to Auckland (pte.), 4 June 1840, HM 839, 363.

[62] Todd to Macnaghten, 22 Oct. 1839, ESL 63, 10/11, 1839 (SC).

[63] Auckland to Palmerston (pte.), 16 Feb. 1840, AM 37698, f.25.

[64] Todd, Journal, ESL, 79, 6/3/71, 20 Aug. 1841.

[65] Todd to Macnaghten (pte.), 15 June 1840, ESL 79, 3/71, 20 Aug. 1841.

[66] Todd to Macnaghten (pte.), 5 Apr. 1840, ESL 79, 3/71, 20 Aug. 1840.

[67] Todd to Macnaghten, 5 Aug. 1840, ESL 71, 8/108, 16 Oct. 1840.

[68] Macnaghten to Maddock, 17. Feb. 1841, ESL 75, 7/19, 21 Mar. 1841.

[69] Todd to Macnaghten (pte.), 20 Jan. 1841, ESL 79, 3/71, 20 Aug. 1841; Macnaghten to Rawlinson (pte.), 8 Mar. 1841, RM.

[70] Todd to Macnaghten, 4. Feb. 1841, ESL 75, 9B/19, 21 Mar. 1841.

[71] Todd to Macnaghten (pte.), 22 Feb. 1841, ESL 75, 6/35, 22 Apr. 1841.

[72] Todd, Memo., *c.* 20 Aug. 1841, ESL 79, 3/71, 20 Aug. 1841.

[73] Riach to McNeill, 6 Sept. 1841, enc. in McNeill to Palmerston 14/, 2 Oct. 1841, FO 60/78.

[74] McNeill to Aberdeen 43/, 2 Dec. 1841, FO 60/79.

[75] McNeill to Aberdeen 57/, 31 Dec. 1841, FO 60/79.

[76] Saunders to Rawlinson, 24 Feb. 1841, ESL 75, 33/34, 22 Apr. 1841; H. Johnson to G. Lawrence (pte.), 24 Feb. 1841, RM.

[77] K. Elphinstone to J. B. Elphinstone, 5 Apr. 1841, 3 Sept. 1841, EM F89/3/8.

[78] Auckland to Hobhouse (pte.), 22 Apr. 1841, AM 36474, f.481; Auckland to Palmerston (pte.), 20 Mar. 1841, BP.

[79] Robertson to Bayley, 19 Apr. 1841; Carnac to Hobhouse (pte.), 1 Apr. 1841, HM 843, 123; Prinsep, Minute, 21 Mar. 1841, ESL 75, 5/23, 23 Mar. 1841.

[80] SC to GGC 675/, 2 Nov. 1840, BDSLI 13; SC to GGC 624/, 31 Dec. 1840, BDSLI 13; Hobhouse to Auckland (pte.), 4 Dec. 1840 HM 839, 462. For the views of the Court see Bayley to Hobhouse (pte.), 25 Nov. 1840, HM 836. 177.

[81] Palmerston to Hobhouse (pte.), 2 Feb. 1841, FO 60/82.

[82] See letters in HM 840, f.263. The Cabinet discussion must have been very perfunctory. In a private letter to Hobhouse dated 3 June 1841 (AM 46915, f.263) Palmerston states that Morpeth and Baring were agreeable to taking Herat, but did not recall the matter being discussed in Cabinet. Palmerston suggested that Hobhouse should send the relevant papers to Lansdowne, Clarendon, and Normanby, presenting the matter as one agreed by Melbourne and Russell. The evidence thus suggests that Palmerston and Hobhouse pushed the decision through a largely indifferent Cabinet..

[83] SC to GGC 746/, 4 June 1841, BDSLI 14.

[84] Palmerston to Hobhouse (pte.), 1 June 1841, HM 840, 179.

[85] See minutes by Auckland, Nicolls, Casement, Bird, and Prinsep, 18–20 Aug. 1841, ESL 79, 14/68, 20 Aug. 1841.

[86] SC to GGC 785/, 4 Sept. 1841, BDSLI 15; Ellenborough Memo., 15 Sept. 1841, PRO 30/12/28/1.

[87] Sheil, Memo., 30 Nov. 1841, McNeill, Memo., 30 Nov. 1841, FO 60/79.

[88] Aberdeen to Rothesay 22/, 15 Feb. 1842, FO 65/279.

[89] Aberdeen to McNeill 13/, 24 Feb. 1842, FO 60/85.

[90] Macnaghten to Rawlinson (pte.), 15 Sept. 1840, RM.

[91] Macnaghten to Auckland (pte.), 28 July 1840, in Kaye, *War in Afghanistan*, ii, 56.

CHAPTER II, THE LIMITS OF FORWARD DEFENCE: TURKESTAN, 1839–42

[1] See *Istoriya uzbekskoi SSR*, Tashkent, 1955–6.

[2] See *Istoriya kazakhskoi SSR*, vol. 1. Alma Ata, 1957; also N. G. Apollova, *Ékonomicheskie i politicheskie svyazi Kazakhstana s Rossiej*, Moscow, 1960.

[3] *Istoriya turkmenskoj SSR*, Ashkhabad, 1957; Yu.. E. Bregel, *Khorezemskie Turkmeni v XIX veke*, Moscow, 1961.

[4] F. Nazarov, *Zapiski o nekotorykh narodakh i zemlyakh srednei chasti Azii*, Moscow, 1968 (first published St. Petersburgh, 1821).

[5] N. Murav'ev, *Puteshestvie v Turkmeniyu i Khivu v 1819 i 1820, etc.*, Moscow, 1822; (English trans. Lockhart, *Journey to Khiva*, Calcutta, 1881).

[6] T. G. Tukhtametov, *Rossiya i Khiva v kontse XIX—nachale XX veka*, Moscow, 1969, 12–13.

[7] S. Z. Zimanov, *Politicheskij stroj kazakhstana kontsa XVIII i pervoj poloviny XIX vekov*, Alma Ata. 1960, 227–8.

[8] *Istoriya turkmenskoj SSR*, i, part 2, 99–100.

[9] *Istoriya kazakhskoy SSR*, i, 601; see also *Voprosy Istorii Kazakhstan XIX—nachale XX veka*, Alma Ata, 1961.

[10] *Istoriya turkmenskoj SSR*, i, part 2, 72.

[11] V. V. Grigor'ev (ed.) *Zamechaniya maiora Blankennagelya, 1793–4*, St. Petersburg, 1858; V. V. Grigor'ev (ed.), *Khrisanoa mitropolita novopatrasskago o stranakh srednej Azii, etc.*, Moscow, 1861; F. S. Efremov, *Strantsvovanie nadvornogo sovetnika Efremova v Bukharii*, St. Petersburg, 1794; E. S. Kajkalov, *Karavan–zapiski vo vremya pokhoda v Bukhariyuo rossijskogo karavana pod voinskim prikrytiem v 1824–1825* (3 vols. in 1), Moscow, 1827; G. Meyendorff, *Voyage d' Orenburg à Bukhara fait en 1820*, Paris, 1826; and *Russian Missions into the Interior of Asia*, London, 1823.

[12] Tukhtametov, op. cit., 10.

[13] On the trade routes see Yeames to Palmerston 12/, 31 Dec. 1830, FO 65/188; and Durham to Palmerston 90/, 17 May 1837, FO 65/234.

[14] Yeames to Aberdeen, 15 Feb. 1830, FO 65/188.

[15] *Istoriya turkmenskoj SSR*, i, part 2, 103 et seq.

[16] On the fair at Nizhni Novgorod see Bligh to Palmerston 51/, 9 Sept. 1835, FO 65/213; Milbanke to Palmerston 67/, 25 Dec. 1837, FO 65/235 and copy of *St. Petersburg Gazette* enclosed; and Durham to Palmerston 144/, 10 Sept. 1836, FO 65/225. On the Volga trade see Clanricarde to Palmerston 48/, 22 Dec. 1838, FO 65/244.

[17] This account is based upon documents transmitted to the British Embassy in St. Petersburg by a spy in the Russian Ministry of Finance. See in particular Karelin to General Cherkin, 25 July 1836 in 206/, 19 Dec. 1836; Karelin to Count Caucrine, 1 July 1836 in 63/, 8 Apr. 1837, FO 65/234; Rhodofiniken to Caucrine, 14 Aug. 1837 in 33/, 9 Sept. 1837, FO 65/235; Questions by Tsar to Council and answers in 35/, 30 June 1838, FO 65/242; Caucrine, Memo., 72/, 20 July 1838, FO 65/252; Milbanke to Palmerston 42/, 25 July 1838, FO 65/242; Clanricarde to Palmerston and enclosures 12/, 21 Jan. 1839, FO 65/251; JBK to Caucrine, 2 Mar. 1839 in 31/, 1 Apr. 1839, FO 65/251.

[18] On the Khivan expedition see I. N. Zakharin, *Graf V. A. Perovskij i ego zimnij pokhod v Khivy*, St. Petersburg, 1901. The first version of Zakharin's book was published at St. Petersburg in 1898 and the second, revised version takes account of criticisms made of the first edition and also includes a life of Perovsky. Part two deals with the expedition. See also A. G. Serebrennikov, *Sbornik materialov dlya istorii zavoevaniya turkestanskogo kraya*, Tashkent, 1908. Vols. 1 (1908) and 2 (1912) deal with Perovsky's expedition and contain important documents. Finally, see M. Ivanin, *Opisanne zimnego pokhoda v Khivu v 1839–40*, St. Petersburg, 1874.

[19] Nesselrode, Memo., 1839, quoted in Moseley, 'Russian Policy in Asia', 670.

[20] Serebrennikov, op. cit..

[21] Copy in Bloomfield to Backhouse, 17 Dec. 1839, FO 65/253.

[22] W. H. Dennie, *Personal Narrative, etc.*, (ed. W. E. Steele) Dublin, 1843, 98–9.

[23] Todd to Abbott, 22 Dec. 1839, ESL 66, 8/21, 16 Mar. 1840; 'Sketch of a Journey from Herat to Khiva and St. Petersburgh', by Captain J. Abbott (enc. in SC to GGC 659/, 4 Sept. 1840, BDSLI 13; J. Abbott, *Narrative of a Journey to Khiva*, London, 1856.

[24] N. A. Khalfin, 'Britanskij ékspansiya v Srednij Azii, etc.', *Istoriya SSR 1956*, 2. English summary in *CAR* 7 (1958), 386.

[25] Bell to Robertson, 26 May 1840, HM 798, 220.

[26] Macnaghten to Maddock, 9 May 1840, ESL 69, 69/72, 6 July 1840.

[27] Auckland, Minute, 7 June 1840, AM 37700, f.20; the wording is, of course, intended as a reply to Palmerston's first use of the phrase 'the Cossack and the Sepoy' in his letter to Hobhouse of 14 Feb. 1840 and first noted by P. Guadella, *Palmerston*, London, 1926, 225.

[28] Auckland to Hobhouse (pte.), 21 Dec. 1839, AM 36474, f.188.

[29] Auckland to Willshire (pte.), 20 Dec. 1839, AM 37697, f.46.

[30] Maddock to Macnaghten, 20 Jan. 1840, ESL 64, 8/2, 22 Jan. 1840 (SC).

[31] Auckland to Macnaghten, 13 Apr., 1840, AM 37699, f.110.

[32] Maddock to Macnaghten, 13 Apr. 1840, ESL 68, 3/34, 15 Apr. 1840.

[33] GGC to SC 34/, 15 Apr. 1840, BSL(1) 25, 251.

[34] Auckland to Hobhouse (pte.), 15 Aug. 1840, AM 37701, f.16.

[35] Prinsep, Minutes, 7 June 1840, ESL 69, 6/62, 8 June 1840, and 14 Aug. 1840, ESL 70, 6/92, 15 Aug. 1840.

[36] Auckland to Hobhouse (pte.), 11 June 1840, AM 36474, f.294.

[37] Bird, Minute, 29 May 1840, ESL 69, 4/62, 8 June 1840; Colvin to W. Bayley (pte.), 11 June 1840, AM 37700, f.34.

[38] Palmerston to Hobhouse (pte.), 14 Feb. 1840, BP.

[39] Clanricarde to Palmerston 17/, 24 Feb. 1840, FO 65/260.
[40] SC to GGC 575/, 29 Feb. 1840, BDSLI 12.
[41] Hobhouse to Auckland (pte.), 4 Feb. 1840, HM 839, 269.
[42] Palmerston to Clanricarde 13/, 24 Jan. 1840, FO 65/258.
[43] Palmerston to Clanricarde 50/, 24 Mar. 1840, FO 65/258; cp. Webster, *Foreign Policy of Palmerston*, ii, 748–9.
[44] On the discussions see also Hobhouse to Auckland (pte.), 29 Feb. 1840 and 4 Apr. 1840, HM 839, 282 and 320.
[45] Palmerston to Auckland (pte.), 4 July 1840, BP.
[46] Brunnow to Duhamel 12/24 Nov. 1840, FO 65/267; cp. Webster, op. cit., ii, 875.
[47] Nesselrode to Brunnow 16/, 28 Apr. 1840, FO 65/267; handed to Palmerston, 11 May 1840.
[48] Khan Huzrat to Nicholas I in Bloomfield to Palmerston 35/, 25 July 1840, FO 65/261.
[49] Palmerston to Hobhouse (pte.), 25 May 1840, AM 46915, f.212.
[50] Hobhouse to Palmerston (pte.), 27 May 1840, HM 839, 362; Hobhouse to Auckland (pte.), 27 May 1840, HM 839, 363.
[51] Palmerston to Auckland (pte.), 4 July 1840, BP; Hobhouse to Palmerston (pte.), 9 Aug. 1840, HM 840, 2.
[52] SC to GGC 634/, 2 July 1840, BDSLI 13.
[53] Hobhouse to Palmerston (pte.), 19 Aug. 1840, FO 65/268.
[54] Palmerston to Hobhouse (pte.), 31 Aug. 1840, FO 65/268.
[55] Todd to Macnaghten, 15 May 1840; Todd to Shakespear, 13 May 1840; Shakespear to Todd, 13 May 1840, ESL 69, 69/72, 6 July 1840.
[56] Quoted G. Morgan 'Two Forgotten Missions', *History Today*, July 1975, 495–502 (500).
[57] For Shakespear's mission see Shakespear to Todd (pte.), 14 June 1840, AM 36474, f.316; Shakespear to Todd, 13 June 1840, ESL 70 3/92, 15 Aug. 1840; 4 July 1840, 7 July 1840, 13 July 1840, 17 July 1840, 18 July 1840, 12 Aug. 1840, 14 Aug. 1840, ESL 72, 6–10/120, 11 Nov. 1840; 8 Oct. 1840, ESL 74, 8/13, 19 Feb. 1841. Shakespear published an account of his journey in *Blackwood's Magazine*, 51 (1842).
[58] Bloomfield to Palmerston 93/, 24 Oct. 1840, FO 65/262.
[59] A. G. Serebrennikov, *Sbornik etc.*, 3, Tashkent, 1912, deals with Nikiforov's mission to Khiva.
[60] Hobhouse to Auckland (pte.), 14 Dec. 1840, HM 839, 462.
[61] Peacock, Memo., 12 Feb. 1839, AM 36470, f.87.
[62] Conolly, Memo., enclosure to SC to GGC, 24 Jan. 1839, BDSLI 10 (dispatch loose and unnumbered).
[63] Kaye, *Lives of Indian Officers*, ii, 74.
[64] SC to GGC, 24 Jan. 1839, BDSLI 10; cp. original draft sent to Palmerston, FO 60/70.
[65] Hobhouse to Auckland (pte.), 9 Feb. 1839, HM 839, 95.
[66] [Eastwick] *Dry Leaves*, 98–100.
[67] GGC to SC 23/, 22 Mar. 1841, BSL(1) 26, 113.
[68] Auckland to Conolly (pte.), 30 Nov. 1839, AM 37697, f.7.
[69] Rawlinson, Memo., 3 June 1838 enc. in McNeill to Palmerston 39./ 1 Aug. 1838, FO 60/58.
[70] Kaye, *Lives of Indian Officers*, ii, 88–91.
[71] Macnaghten to Conolly, 10 Apr. 1840, ESL 68, 3/46, 3 May 1840.
[72] Conolly, Memo., 14 June 1840, ESL 70, 37/85, 10 Aug. 1840.
[73] Burnes to Macnaghten (pte.), 16 Apr. 1840, in Kaye, *Lives*, ii, 71–5.
[74] Macnaghten to Conolly, 5 Sept. 1840, ESL, 4/120, 11 Nov. 1840.
[75] Auckland to Burnes (pte.), 7 June 1840, AM 37700, f.18.
[76] Colvin to W. B. Bayley (pte.), 12 May 1840, AM 37699, f.83.
[77] Torrens to Macnaghten, 26 Oct. 1840, ESL 72, 5/120, 11 Nov. 1840.
[78] Bayley to Macnaghten, 11 & 12 May 1840, ESL 68, 12 May 1840 (S).
[79] Auckland to Hobhouse (pte.), 11 & 12 May 1840, AM 36474, f.28.
[80] Torrens to Macnaghten, 6 July 1840, ESL 69, 79/72, 6 July 1840.
[81] Conolly to Macnaghten (pte.), 16 Nov. 1840, ESL 75, 4/34, 22 Apr. 1841.
[82] Conolly to Macnaghten, 26 Dec. 1840, ibid., 4B.
[83] *Encyclopaedia of Islam*, first edition, s.v. Khwarazm.
[84] See n. 79 above.
[85] Maddock to Macnaghten, 28 Dec. 1840, ESL 74, 7/4, 21 Jan. 1841.
[86] Maddock to Macnaghten, 12 Apr. 1841, ESL 75, 4C/34, 22 Apr. 1841.

[87] Shah Muhammad Popolzay, Narrative enc. in Pollock to Maddock, 20 June 1842, ESL 87, 59/22, 8 July 1842.

[88] Rawlinson to Nott, 25 Apr. 1842, ESL 87, 68/22, 8 July 1842.

[89] Palmerston to McNeill 25/, 18 May 1838, FO 60/50; McNeill to Stoddart, 31 July 1838 enc. in 35/, 31 July 1838, FO 60/58.

[90] J. Grover, *The Bokhara Victims*, London, 1845.

[91] Lord to Wade, 21 July 1839, ESL 63, 3B/37, 16 Dec. 1839 (PC).

[92] Khan-i Mulla, Statement, ESL 70, 50/99, 13 Sept. 1840.

[93] Conversation between Macnaghten and Sayyid Reza, 18 June 1840, ESL 70, 37/85, 10 Aug. 1840; Macnaghten to Maddock, 22 June 1840, ibid., 46; Macnaghten to Torrens, 31 July 1840, ESL 70, 50A/99, 13 Sept. 1840; Burnes to Macnaghten, 6 May 1841, ESL 78, 3/58, 5 Feb. 1841.

[94] Queen Victoria to Khan Huzrat, 30 June 1840, in SC to GGC 684/, 30 Nov. 1840, BDSLI 13.

[95] Macnaghten to Maddock, 10 Dec. 1840, ESL 74, 15B/13, 19 Feb. 1841.

[96] Macnaghten to Maddock, 7 May 1841; Maddock to Macnaghten, 7 June 1841, ESL 77, 3C & 3D/47, 9 June 1841.

[97] Stoddart to Todd, 26 Jan. 1841, FO 60/81.

[98] Stoddart to Palmerston, 21 Aug. 1841, FO 60/82.

[99] Stoddart to Palmerston, 10 July 1841, FO 60/82. Buten'ev made a further unsuccessful attempt to secure Stoddart's release before his own departure. On the Russian mission see N. Khanikov, *Opisanie bukharskogo khanstva*, St. Petersburg, 1842; N. Khanikov, *Bokhara* (trans. Bode), London, 1846; A. Lehmann, *Reise von Orenburg nach Bukhara*, St. Petersburg, 1842; M. Solov'ev, *Éxpeditsiya v Bukharu v 1841–1842 gg., pri uchastii naturalista A. Lemena*, Moscow–Leningrad, 1936.

[100] Stoddart to Conolly, 22 June 1841, FO 60/82.

[101] Conolly to J. Conolly, EM 490, 47.

[102] Conolly, Memo., 27 Mar. 1842, FO 60/89.

[103] See Hobhouse's comment on Macnaghten to Maddock, 10 Dec. 1840, ESL 74, 15B/4, 21 Jan. 1840.

[104] SC to GGC 699/, 29 Jan. 1841 BDSLI 14.

[105] Clanricarde to Hobhouse (pte.), 9 Dec. 1840, HM 840, 13.

[106] Auckland to Macnaghten (pte.), 23 Apr. 1841, AM 37705, f.16.

[107] Quoted Webster, op. cit., ii, 748–9.

[108] Palmerston to Auckland (pte.), 4 July 1840, BP.

[109] Palmerston to Auckland (pte.), 20 Jan. 1841, BP.

[110] Auckland to Palmerston (pte.), 21 Apr. 1841, BP.

CHAPTER 12, AFGHANISTAN ABANDONED, 1841–2

[1] Report of Assistant Surgeon Campbell, 26 July 1841, EM F89/3/7; see also K. Elphinstone to J. B. Elphinstone, 21 Aug. 1841, EM F 89/3/5.

[2] Auckland to Macnaghten, 21 Aug. 1841, AM 37706, f.55.

[3] Broadfoot to W. Elphinstone, EM F89/3/7.

[4] Broadfoot, Report, Oct. 1841, EM F89/3/7.

[5] Elphinstone, Memo., Dec. 1841, ESL 86, 38/14, 17 May 1842.

[6] Burnes to Cotton (pte.), 1 Aug. 1841, PRO 30/12/11.

[7] G. A. Berkeley to Maddock, 1 Feb. 1843, ESL 91, 2/8, 16 Feb. 1843 (PC).

[8] Auckland to Nicolls (pte.), 1 Dec. 1841, AM 37706, f.197.

[9] Maddock to Residents, 16 Dec. 1841, ESL 81, 59/109, 22 Dec. 1841; Auckland to Sleeman (pte.), 14 Jan. 1842, AM 37707, f.102; see also Kaye, *War in Afghanistan*, iii, 12–13.

[10] Colvin to Macnaghten (pte.), 26 Sept. 1841, AM 37706, f.95; Auckland to Cotton (pte.), 20 Oct. 1841, AM 37706, f.125; Auckland to Ellenborough, 22 Dec. 1841 AM, 37707, f.48.

[11] Auckland to Macnaghten (pte.), 6 Dec. 1841, AM 37706, f.202.

[12] Prinsep, Minute, 7 Feb. 1842, ESL 83, 68/16, 19 Feb. 1842.

[13] Maddock to Clerk, 10 Feb. 1842, ESL 83, 27/16, 19 Feb. 1842; Colvin to Clerk (pte.), 9 Feb. 1842, AM 37707, f. 155. cp. note by Auckland in GGC to SC, 19 Feb. 1842, BSL (1) 27, 129. For a defence of Auckland's actions during the crisis see J. A. Norris, *The First Afghan War, 1838–1842*, Cambridge, 1967, 383–90.

[14] Aberdeen to Heytesbury (pte.), 2 Oct. 1841, AM 43238, f.12.

[15] Parker, *Peel*, ii, 575–6.
[16] Auckland to Minto (pte.), 23 Dec. 1841, M646.
[17] Hobhouse, Diary, 26 Aug. 1842, AM 43744.
[18] Ellenborough, letter, 21 Nov. 1840, PRO 30/12/16/1.
[19] Kaye, *Memorials of Indian Government*, 282.
[20] Willock, Memo., 4 Sept. 1841, AM 40462, f.12.
[21] Sir G. Murray, Memo., 19 Oct. 1841, PRO 30/12/11.
[22] Palmerston to Hobhouse (pte.), 7 Sept. 1841, AM 46915, f.265.
[23] Ellenborough to Murray (pte.), 11 Sept. 1841, PRO 30/12/8.
[24] Ellenborough to Aberdeen (pte.), 6 Oct. 1841, AM 43198, f.26.
[25] Ellenborough, Speech to Directors, 3 Nov. 1841, PRO 30/12/11.
[26] Ellenborough to Wellington (pte.), 26 Oct. 1841, PRO 30/12/28/12.
[27] Ellenborough to Ripon (pte.), 23 Mar. 1844, PRO 30/12/77.
[28] GGC to Nicolls, 15 Mar. 1842, ESL 84, 54/25, 22 Mar. 1842.
[29] Maddock to Nott, 19 Apr. 1842; Ellenborough to Nicolls, 19 Apr. 1842, ESL 85, 1–4/4, 22 Apr. 1842.
[30] Maddock to Pollock, 28 Apr. 1842, ESL 86, 7/10, 17 May 1842.
[31] Pollock to Maddock, 13 May 1842, ESL 92, 34/, 9 May 1843; Kaye, *War in Afghanistan*, ii, 198–201 implies that Ellenborough suppressed this letter and thus accounts for its late arrival in England. In his acknowledgement to Pollock, dated 11 July 1842, the Chief Secretary, Maddock, states that Pollock's original never reached him and that the duplicate has 'only lately been received'. This, however, also leaves unexplained why Maddock's reply and the duplicate were not sent to England by the August 1842 mail.
[32] Pollock to Maddock, 19 May 1842, ESL 86, 39/15, 8 June 1842.
[33] GG to SC, 16 Aug. 1842, BSL(1) 27, 699; Ellenborough to Pollock, 23 July 1842, ESL 88, 7/29A, 16 Aug. 1842; Ellenborough to Nott, 4 July 1842, ESL 87, Enc. to 24A, 8 July 1842; Ellenborough to Nott, 10 July 1842, ESL 88, 2/29A, 16 Aug. 1842.
[34] Kaye, *War in Afghanistan*, iii, 285.
[35] On these operations see C. R. Low, *Life of Sir George Pollock*, London, 1873; and J. H. Stocqueler, *Memoir of Sir William Nott*, 2 vols., London, 1854.
[36] Maddock to Pollock, 1 June 1842, ESL 86, 44/15, 8 June 1842.
[37] Maddock to Pollock, 28 Apr. 1842, ESL 86, 5/10, 17 May 1842.
[38] Rawlinson, Journal, 16 Sept. 1842, RM..
[39] W. Broadfoot, *Career of Major George Brooadfoot*, 55, 66.
[40] GGC to SC 32/, 17 Aug. 1842, BSL(1) 27, 731.
[41] Pollock to Maddock, 24 Oct. 1842, ESL 90, 30/52, 19 Nov. 1842.
[42] Hasrat, *Anglo-Sikh Relations*, 212.
[43] Clerk to Maddock, 15 Jan. 1842, ESL 82, 18 Jan. 1842 (Agra).
[44] Clerk to Maddock, 10 Feb. 1842, ESL 84, 20/25, 22 Mar. 1842.
[45] Clerk to Maddock, 23 Apr. 1842, ESL 86, 64/14, 17 May 1842.
[46] GG to SC, 17 May 1842, BSL(1) 27, 471; Ellenborough to Wellington (pte.), 7 June 1842, PRO 30/12/28/12; Ellenborough to Clerk (pte.), 22 June 1842, PRO 30/12/81.
[47] Clerk to Maddock, 23 Apr. 1842, ESL 86, 89/14, 17 May 1842.
[48] Maddock to Clerk, 27 May 1842, ESL 88, 98/15, 8 June 1842; Maddock to Clerk, 22 July 1842, 29 July 1842, 29 July 1842, ESL 88, 79 & 81/32, 17 Aug. 1842; Ellenborough to Clerk (pte.), 21 July 1842, PRO 30/12/81.
[49] Clerk to Maddock, 19 July 1842, 31 July 1842, ESL 88, 80 & 85/32, 17Aug. 1842.
[50] Maddock to Clerk, 29 July 1842, 8 Aug. 1842, ESL 88, 81, 86 & 87/32, 17 Aug. 1842; Maddock to Clerk, 23 Aug. 1842 ESL 89, 85/38, 17 Sept. 1842.
[51] GG to SC 48/, 19 Oct. 1842, BSL(1) 27, 873; Rawlinson, Journal, 27 Oct. 1842, RM.
[52] Rawlinson to McNeill (pte.), 11 Dec. 1841, AM 43238, d.329.
[53] Rawlinson to Nott, 23 Apr. 1842, Rawlinson to Hammersley, 10 May 1842, ESL 86, 133/15, 8 June 1842; Rawlinson to Outram (pte.), 11 Apr. 1842, 3 May 1842, 12 June 1842, PRO 30/12/62.
[54] [Eastwick] *Dry Leaves*, 56–7.
[55] Outram to Maddock, 3 May 1842, ESL 86, 86/14, 17 May 1842; Outram to Sutherland (pte.), 20 Dec. 1841, PRO 30/12/16/1; F. J. Goldsmid, *James Outram*, 2 vols., London, 1881, i, 260–1.
[56] Ellenborough to Wellington (pte.), 17 May 1842, PRO 30/12/28/12.

[57] Maddock to Nott, 25 June 1842, ESL 87, 76A/22, 8 July 1842.
[58] Ellenborough to Napier, 25 Oct. 1842, ESL 90, 110/52, 19 Nov. 1842.
[59] Ellenborough, Proclamation, 1 Oct. 1842 in J. H. Stocqueler, *Memorials of Afghanistan*, Calcutta, 1843, 278–9.
[60] SC to GGC 25/, 28 Mar. 1843, BSL(1) 28, 211.
[61] Ellenborough to Peel (pte.), 21 Feb. 1842, AM 40471, f. 119; Ellenborough to Nicolls (pte.), 5 Mar. 1842, PRO 30/12/32/Pt.1/6.
[62] Maddock to Willoughby, 13 June 1842, ESL 87, 4/20, 8 July 1842.
[63] Ellenborough to Wellington (pte.), 4 Oct. 1842, PRO 30/12/28/2.
[64] J. Greenwood, *Narrative etc.*, London, 1844, 293.
[65] Pottinger to R. Haughton, 29 May 1842 in J. C. Haughton, *Char-ee-Kar*, London, 1879, 39.
[66] Ellenborough to Fitzgerald (pte.), 17 May 1842, PRO 30/12/77.
[67] Ellenborough to Fitzgerald (pte.), 27 Dec. 1842, PRO 30/12/77.
[68] Ellenborough to Fitzgerald (pte.), 19 Feb. 1843, PRO 30/12/77.
[69] Ellenborough to Fitzgerald (pte.), 28 Apr. 1843, PRO 30/12/77.
[70] Ellenborough, Memo., 27 Apr. 1842, PRO 30/12/31/10.
[71] Maddock to Clerk, 27 Apr. 1842, ESL 86, 58/14, 17 May 1842.
[72] Maddock, Minute, 10 May 1843, ESL 92, 16/, 12 May 1843 (PC).
[73] Ellenborough, Diary, 21 Oct. 1841, EP 28.
[74] Parker, *Peel*, ii, 579.
[75] *Letters of Princess Lieven*, ed. L. G. Robinson, London, 1907, 115; On Ripon see W. D. Jones, *'Prosperity' Robinson*, London, 1967.
[76] *Private Letters of Dalhousie*, 327; On Graham see J. T. Ward, *Sir James Graham*, London, 1967.
[77] Graham to Ellenborough (pte.), 10 Oct. 1841, PRO 30/12/28/8.
[78] Fitzgerald to Peel (pte.), 3 Feb. 1843, AM 40463, f.78.
[79] Peel to Tucker (pte.), 26 Mar. 1842, in Parker, *Peel*, ii, 580.
[80] Wellington to Fitzgerald (pte,), 11 Oct. 1842, PRO 30/12/8; see also Wellington to Fitzgerald (pte.), 6 Apr. 1842, PRO 30/12/28/3.
[81] Peel to Arbuthnot (pte.), 5 Apr. 1842, in Parker, *Peel*, ii, 535.
[82] Peel to Fitzgerald (pte.), 14 Oct. 1842, AM 40462, f.256; Fitzgerald to Ellenborough (pte.), 3 Nov. 1842, PRO 30/12/8.
[83] Peel to Ellenborough (pte.), 6 Apr. 1842, AM 40471, f.177.
[84] Outram to Clerk (pte.), 19 May 1842, in Goldsmid, op. cit., i, 250–1.
[85] Wellesley, Memo., 4 July 1842, PRO 30/12/26/2.
[86] Wellington to Ellenborough (pte.), 30 Mar. 1842, PRO 30/12/28/13.
[87] Fitzgerald to Ellenborough (pte.), 6 July 1842, PRO 30/12/42.
[88] Peel to Ellenborough (pte.), 6 July 1842, AM 40471, f.193.
[89] Peel to Fitzgerald (pte.), 13 Jan. 1843, AM 40463, f.32.
[90] Peel to Ellenborough (pte.), 24 Sept. 1842, AM 40471, f.227.
[91] Fitzgerald to Ellenborough (pte.), 31 Jan. 1843, PRO 30/12/42.
[92] Greville, *Memoirs*, v, 102.
[93] Hobhouse to Palmerston (pte.), 20 May 1843, BP.
[94] *Hansard* III, 66, col. 32; cp. Fitzgerald to Ellenborough (pte.), 4 Feb. 1843, PRO 30/12/42.
[95] *Hansard* III, 66, col. 98.
[96] Fitzgerald to Ellenborough (pte.), 4 Mar. 1843, PRO 30/12/42.
[97] Hobhouse, Diary, 31 May 1842, AM 43744.
[98] *Hansard* III, 66, col. 435.
[99] See Hobhouse to Ellenborough (pte.), 4 Mar. 1843, PRO 30/12/42. Hobhouse, who was abroad, refused to return to England for the debate despite Palmerston's urging. (See Palmerston to Hobhouse (pte.), 3 Feb. 1843, 9 Mar. 1843, AM 46915, ff.275, 277.
[100] e.g. *Standard* 28 Nov. 1842, *Times* 7 Jan. 1843.
[101] *Hansard* III, 67, cols. 513 et seq. & 581 et seq.
[102] Palmerston to NcNeill 3/, 31 July 1841, FO 60/77.
[103] McNeill, Memo., 1 Apr. 1841, FO 60/78.
[104] Palmerston to McNeill 10/, 10 Aug. 1841, FO 60/77.
[105] Moseley, 'Russian Policy', 670.
[106] Duhamel to Nesselrode, 22 Nov. 1841 enc. in Rothesay to Aberdeen 9/, 12 Jan. 1842, FO 65/280.

[107] Aberdeen to McNeill 6/, 22 Jan. 1842, FO 60/85.

[108] McNeill to Aberdeen, 25 Jan. 1842, FO 60/86.

[109] Ripon to Ellenborough (pte.), 6 Mar. 1844, PRO 30/12/42.

[110] Rothesay to Aberdeen, 47/, 22 Mar. 1842, FO 65/280.

[111] Sheil to Canning, 29 Oct. 1842 enc. 2 in Sheil to Aberdeen 77/, 29 Oct. 1842, FO 60/91.

[112] Rothesay to Aberdeen 47/, 22 Mar. 1842, FO 65/280; Nesselrode to Brunnow 4/, 16 Sept. 1842, FO 65/287.

[113] See A. P. Thornton, 'The Central Asian Question' and 'Afghanistan in Anglo-Russian Relations 1868–1873', in *For the File on Empire*, London, 1968, 134–69.

[114] Nesselrode, Memo. 1844, in *Cambridge History of India*, vi, 404; Brunnow to Aberdeen (pte.), Am 43144, f.125; Rothesay to Aberdeen 119/, 27 Dec. 1842, FO 65/283; Bloomfield to Aberdeen 62/, 25 Sept. 1841, FO 65/272.

[115] Ellenborough to Aberdeen (pte.), 6 Oct. 1841, AM 43198, f.26.

[116] Ellenborough, Diary, 31 Oct. 1841, EP 28.

CHAPTER 13, SIND AND KALAT, 1839–43

[1] Eastwick to Macnaghten, 7 Apr. 1839, ESL 58, 1214/18, 11 July 1839 (PC).

[2] Macnaghten to Torrens, 26 June 1840, ESL 70, 88/85, 10 Aug. 1840.

[3] Bell to Bean (pte.), 23 Sept. 1840, HM 797, 146.

[4] Macnaghten to Rawlinson (pte.), 28 Feb. 1841, RM.

[5] [Eastwick] *Dry Leaves*, 78, 97–8.

[6] Bell to Colvin (pte.), 7 June 1839, HM 798, 36.

[7] H. T. Lambrick, *John Jacob of Jacobabad*, London, 1960, 38; see also idem, 'Lt. Amiel and the Baluch Levy', *Journal of the Sind Historical Society*, 2(1936).

[8] Bell to Maddock, 13 Oct. 1839, ESL 66, 82/9, 10 Feb. 1840.

[9] Maddock to Bell, 24 Oct. 1839, ESL 64, 4/8, 13 Jan. 1840.

[10] Bell to Postans, 24 Feb. 1840, HM 797, 435.

[11] Bell to Maddock, 21 July 1839, HM 798, 435.

[12] Bell to Maddock, 8 Feb. 1840, ESL 66, 40/23, 16 Mar. 1840; H. T. Lambrick, *Jacob*, 40–51; [John Jacob] *Memoir of a First Campaign in the Hills North of Kutchee*, London, 1852; Bell to Stevenson (pte.), 21 Feb. 1840, HM 797, 78.

[13] Bell to Postans, 31 May 1840, HM 797, 578; C. R. Williams, *The Defence of Kahun*, London, 1880.

[14] Bean to Bell, 5 July 1839, ESL 65, 177/, 8 Feb. 1840.

[15] Outram to Sutherland (pte.), 18 Sept. 1841, HM 797, 226.

[16] Bean to Maddock, 5 June 1840; Bean to Torrens, 24 June 1840, 2 July 1840, ESL 70 9, 20 &27/91, 11 Aug. 1840.

[17] Maddock to Bean, 18 May 1840, ESL 69, 4/63, 8 June 1840.

[18] J. Outram, *Rough Notes of the Campaign in Sinde and Afghanistan in 1838–9*, London, 1840.

[19] Maddock to Bean, 9 June 1840, ESL 64, 9/13, 13 Jan. 1840.

[20] Bell to Maddock, 14 Nov. 1839, HM 798, 169.

[21] [Eastwick], *Dry Leaves*, 117.

[22] Macnaghten to Maddock, 10 Apr. 1840, ESL 70, 28/78, 27 July 1840.

[23] Bell to Colvin (pte.), 10 Oct. 1840, 12 Oct. 1840, HM 798, 271–3.

[24] Brown to Loveday (pte.), 17 June 1840, HM 797, 114.

[25] Brown to Loveday (pte.), 2 July 1840, HM 797, 119; [Eastwick] *Dry Leaves*, 116.

[26] See Bean to Macnaghten, 11 Mar. 1840, ESL 69, 48/64, 8 June 1840.

[27] Wallace to Bean, 19 May 1841, ESL 78, 11/57, 8 July 1841.

[28] Macnaghten to Maddock, 1 June 1841, ISC 22/, 13 Sept. 1841; and 4 July 1841, ISC 89/, 2 Aug. 1841.

[29] Maddock to Macnaghten, 2 Aug. 1841, ISC 90, 2 Aug. 1841.

[30] C. Masson, *Kalat*, London, 1843; Masson, Statement, EM 638, f. 1; EM 642, f. 104; Masson to Jephson (pte.), 11 Mar. 1841, EM 636, f.41.

[31] [Eastwick] *Dry Leaves*, 161; Auckland to Carnac (pte.), 26 Mar. 1841, AM 37704, f.98; Colvin to Bell (pte.), 5 Mar. 1841, AM 37704, f.50.

[32] Bell to Stevenson (pte.), 6 June 1840, HM 797, 385.

[33] Bell to Bean (pte.), 26 Oct. 1840, HM 797, 464. The best account of these operations is in J. Buist, *Operations in Scinde and Afghanistan*, Bombay, 1843.

[34] Bell to Colvin (pte.), 23 Apr. 1841, HM 798, 316.

[35] Bell to Auckland (pte.), 4 Jan. 1841, HM 798, 288.

[36] Bell to Colvin (pte.), 21 Aug. 1840, HM 798, 218.

[37] Napier to Ellenborough, 9 Apr. 1843, ESL 93, 40/32, 28 Aug. 1843.

[38] Dalhousie to Couper, 9 Apr. 1858, *Private Correspondence*, 413.

[39] Bell to Bean (pte.), 23 Sept. 1840, HM 797, 146; Loveday to Bean, 30 July 1840, ESL 70, 20/101, 11 Sept. 1840; Bean to Macnaghten, 4 Aug. 1840, ibid.

[40] Macnaghten to Maddock, 15 May 1841, ESL 78, 3/5, 8 July 1841.

[41] Torrens to Bell, 11 Sept. 1840, ESL 70, 21/101, 11 Sept. 1840; Auckland, Minute, 19 Oct. 1840, AM 37702, f.21.

[42] Outram to Maddock, n.d., ESL 81, 10/99, 20 Nov. 1841.

[43] Text of treaty in ESL 81, 10/99, 20 Nov. 1841. Negotiations were conducted by Lt. Col. L. R. Stacy; see L. R. Stacy, *Narrative, etc., 1840–2*, London, 1848.

[44] Postans, Memo., 31 July 1841, ESL 80, 11/87, 21 Oct. 1841. For Postans's views see also T. Postans, *Personal Observations on Sinde*, London, 1843.

[45] J. H. Stocqueler, *Memorials of Afghanistan*, appendix 3, xxxvii.

[46] Auckland to Hobhouse (pte.), 7 Aug. 1841, AM 37705, f.150; Auckland to Outram (pte.), 3 Sept. 1841, AM 37706, f.71.

[47] Maddock to Outram, 8 Nov. 1841, ESL 81, 11/99, 20 Nov. 1841.

[48] Outram to French (pte.), 16 Oct. 1841, HM 797, 542.

[49] Outram to Maddock, 1 Oct. 1841, ESL 82, 17/7, 22 Jan. 1842.

[50] Auckland to Outram (pte.), 5 Jan. 1842, AM 37707, f.87; Auckland to Ellenborough (pte.), 22 Dec. 1841, ibid., f.48; Colvin to Outram (pte.), 15 Dec. 1841, ibid., f.215.

[51] Auckland to Outram (pte.), 28 Feb. 1842 in Goldsmid, op. cit., i, 242–3; see also Auckland, Minute, 28 Feb. 1842, ESL 84, India Financial Secret No. 1 of 1842 (located between Nos. 21 amd 22).

[52] Outram to Colvin (pte.), 2 Feb. 1842, 6 Feb. 1842, ESL 86, 116/15, 8 June 1842.

[53] Stacy to Durand (pte.), 5 May 1842, PRO 30/12/11.

[54] French, Memo., n.d. ibid..

[55] Outram to Maddock, 8 May 1842, ESL 86, 116/15, 8 June 1842.

[56] Outram to Maddock, 8 July 1842, ESL 88, 101/32, 17 Aug. 1842.

[57] Maddock to Nott, 13 July 1842, ESL 88, 96/32, 17 Aug. 1842.

[58] Outram to Maddock, 25 Aug. 1842, ESL 89, 105/38, 17 Sept. 1842.

[59] Napier to Maddock, 17 Nov. 1842, ESL 90, 62/62, 20 Dec. 1842; Napier to Ellenborough, 19 Sept. 1843, ESL 94, 15/63, 21 Nov. 1843 and encs.

[60] Ellenborough to Napier, 23 Oct. 1843, ESL 94, 16/63, 21 Nov. 1843.

[61] J. Outram, *Conquest of Scinde, A Commentary*, 2 vols., London, 1846, 32–3.

[62] Postans, Memo., 31 July 1841, ESL 80, 11/87, 27 Oct. 1841; Terry to Outram, 20 Aug. 1841, ibid.

[63] Outram to Maddock, 21 Aug. 1841, ESL 80, 5/87 27 Oct. 1841.

[64] SC to GGC 794/ 25 Oct. 1841, BDSLI 15.

[65] GGC to SC, 22 Jan. 1842, BSL(2) 10.

[66] Outram to Maddock, 20 June 1842, ESL 88, 113/32, 17 Aug. 1842.

[67] Ellenborough to Napier, 25 Oct. 1842, ESL 90. 111/52, 19 Nov. 1842.

[68] Ellenborough, letter, (pte.), 21 Nov. 1840, PRO 30/10/16/1.

[69] Ellenborough to Napier, 4 Nov. 1842, ESL 90, 111/52, 19 Nov. 1842.

[70] GG to SC 53/, 26 June 1843, BSL(1) 419.

[71] The best recent study is H. T. Lambrick, *Sir Charles Napier and Sind*, Oxford, 1952, which contains a good guide to the literature on this subject. See also R. A. Huttenback, *British Relations with Sind 1799–1843*, Berkeley and Los Angeles, 1962.

[72] Outram to Willoughby (pte.), 22 Feb. 1842; Outram to Colvin (pte.), 27 Feb. 1842, ESL 84, 86 & 89/25, 22 Feb. 1842.

[73] Outram to Maddock, 8 May 1842, ESL 86, 116/15, 8 June 1842.

[74] Lambrick, *Napier*, 32–3; see also *Calcutta Review*, 6 (1846), 578.

[75] Ellenborough to Napier, 13 Oct. 1842, ESL 90, 85/62, 20 Dec. 1842.

[76] Maddock to Outram, 6 May 1842, ESL 89, 59/14, 17 Aug. 1842.

[77] Maddock to Outram, 22 May 1842, ESL 86, 126/15, 8 June 1842; cp. Ellenborough to Wellington (pte.), 7 June 1842, PRO 30/12/28/12.

[78] Outram to Maddock, 21 June 1842, ESL 88, 114/32, 17 Aug. 1842.

[79] Maddock to Outram, 4 June 1842, ESL 86, 13/15, 8 June 1842.

[80] Outram to Maddock, 26 June 1842, ESL 88, 118/32, 17 Aug. 1842.

[81] Outram, *Conquest of Scinde*, i, 43-4.

[82] Ellenborough to Napier, 26 Aug. 1842, ESL 89, 65/38, 17 Sept. 1842.

[83] *Edinburgh Review*, 160 (April 1844), 476.

[84] Ellenborough to Napier, 14 Nov. 1842, ESL 90, 12/52, 19 Nov. 1842.

[85] Ellenborough to Napier, 25 Oct. 1842, ESL 90, 111/52, 19 Nov. 1842.

[86] Ellenborough to Fitzgerald (pte.), 22 Mar. 1843, PRO 30/12/77.

[87] Ellenborough to Napier, 8 Oct. 1842, ESL 93, 11/14/32, 22 Aug. 1843.

[88] Quoted Hobhouse, Diary, AM 43752, f.66. On Napier and his brothers see the writings of Priscilla Napier, notably *The Sword Dance*, London, 1971.

[89] Elphinstone to J. Elphinstone, 3 Sept. 1841, EM F89/3/8.

[90] Napier, Memo., 18 Feb. 1842, PRO 30/12/32/Pt.1/2.

[91] L. von Orlich, *Travels in India etc.* (trans. Lloyd), 2 vols., London, 1845, i, 123; Napier to Ellenborough, 17 Oct. 1842, ESL 90 17/5, 19 Nov. 1842.

[92] The evidence is contained in the enclosures to Napier to Ellenborough, 17 Oct. 1842, ESL 90, 115/52, 19 Nov. 1842 and is summarized and analysed in Lambrick, *Napier*.

[93] Ellenborough to Napier, 24 Nov. 1842, ESL 90, 64/62, 20 Dec. 1842.

[94] Ellenborough to Napier, 25 Oct. 1842, 3 Nov. 1842, 4 Nov. 1842, 14 Nov. 1842, ESL 90, 111, 113, 117, 127/52. 19 Nov. 1842.

[95] Ellenborough to Peel (pte.), 15 Nov. 1842, AM 40471, f.255.

[96] Ellenborough to Wellington (pte.), 18 Dec. 1842, PRO 30/12/28/12.

[97] Napier to Ellenborough, 8 Dec. 1842, ESL 90, 84/62, 20 Dec. 1842.

[98] GG to SC 52/, 19 Nov. 1842, BSL(1) 27, 969.

[99] Ellenborough to Napier, 6 Mar. 1843, ESL 92, 23/17, 13 Mar. 1843.

[100] Ellenborough to Napier, 8 Mar. 1843, ESL 92, 28/17, 13 Mar. 1843.

[101] Ellenborough to Napier, 12 June 1843, ESL 92, 11/33, 26 June 1843; Napier to Ellenborough, 9 July 1843, 19 Sept. 1843, PRO 30/12/61; Ellenborough to Peel (pte.), 29 May 1843, AM 40471, f.310.

[102] GG to SC, BSL (1) 28, 419; Ellenborough to Wellington (pte.), 22 Apr. 1843, PRO 30/12/28/12; Ellenborough to Fitzgerald (pte.), 22 Apr. 1843, PRO 30/12/77.

[103] Ellenborough to Napier, 9 Feb. 1843, PRO 30/12/14/3.

[104] Ellenboorugh to Napier, 8 Mar. 1843, ESL 92, 28/17, 13 Mar. 1843.

[105] Ellenborough to Napier, 3 Mar. 1843, ESL 92, 11/17, 13 Mar. 1843; Ellenborough to Napier, 12 June 1843, ESL 92, 11/53, 26 June 1843; Ellenborough to Napier, 19 Sept. 1843, PRO 30/12/77.

[106] *Calcutta Review*, 1 (1844), 231.

[107] Napier, Memo. 19 May 1844, ESL 96, 84/38, 10 June 1844.

[108] Colvin to J. Colvin (pte.), 22 Dec. 1841, AM 37707, f.64.

[109] Fitzgerald to Peel (pte.), 3 Feb. 1843, AM 40483, f.78; Wellington to Ellenborough (pte.), 14 Feb. 1843, PRO 30/12/28/13.

[110] Fitzgerald to Peel (pte.), 4 Feb. 1843, AM 40463 f.84.

[111] SC to GGC 917/, 4 Feb. 1843, BDSLI 17; Fitzgerald to Peel (pte.), 5 Feb. 1843, PRO 30/12/42.

[112] Wellington to Ellenborough (pte.), 4 Feb. 1843, PRO 30/12/28/13.

[113] Ellenborough to Fitzgerald (pte.), 22 Mar. 1843, PRO 30/12/77.

[114] Fitzgerald to Peel (pte.), 1 May 1843, AM 40463, f.269.

[115] SC to GGC 928/, 6 May 1843, BDSLI 17; Fitzgerald to Peel (pte.), 5 May 1843, AM 40463, f.275.

[116] Peel to Fitzgerald (pte.), 13 Apr. 1843, AM 40463, f.229.

[117] SC to GGC 929/3 June 1843, BDSLI 17.

[118] Peel to Ripon (pte.), 9 Feb. 1844, AM 40465, f.180.

[119] Ellenborough to Peel (pte.), 19 Feb. 1844, AM 40472, f.137.

[120] Kaye, *Memorials of Indian Government*, 313, 326.

[121] Fitzgerald to Ellenborough (pte.), 2 Apr. 1842, PRO 30/12/77.

[122] Ripon to Ellenborough (pte.), 4 Feb. 1844, PRO 30/12/42.
[123] Ripon to Hardinge (pte.), 7 July 1845, AM 40873, f.26.
[124] Wellington to Ripon (pte.), 7 July 1845, AM 40873, f.26.
[125] Hardinge to Peel (pte.), 8 Mar. 1845, AM 40474, f.231.
[126] Ripon to Hardinge (pte.), 24 June 1846, AM 40877, f.155.
[127] Hardinge to Hobhouse (pte.), 19 Sept. 1846, 22 Oct. 1846, AM 36475, ff.43, 87.
[128] Ripon to Wellington (pte.), 17 Aug. 1845, AM 40872, f.155.
[129] *Edinburgh Review*, 160 (April 1844), 476.

CHAPTER 14, THE PANJAB ROAD, 1838–41

[1] For accounts of these events see Shahamat Ali, *Sikhs and Afghans*, London, 1849; W. Barr, *Journal etc.*, London, 1844; W. Hough, *Review of Operations, etc.*, Calcutta, 1849; H. Havelock, *Narrative, etc.*, 2 vols., London, 1840; R. H. Kennedy, *Campaign on the Indus*, 2 vols., London, 1840. See also C. M. Macgregor (ed.), *Gazeteer of the North West Frontier of British India*, 3 vols., Calcutta, 1873.
[2] Wade to Maddock, 21 Dec. 1839, ESL 64, 14/5, 13 Jan. 1840.
[3] Mackeson to Macnaghten, 7 Dec. 1839, ESL 64, 3/9, 13 Jan. 1840.
[4] Mackeson to Macnaghten, 8 Mar. 1840, 13 Mar. 1840, ESL 70, 2/8, 10 Aug. 1840.
[5] Mackeson to Macnaghten, 6 Oct. 1841, ESL 80, 13/96, 20 Nov. 1840.
[6] Mackeson to Macnaghten, 12 Aug. 1840, ESL 72, 56/124, 16 Nov. 1840.
[7] Fitzgerald to Peel (pte.), 3 May 1843, PRO 30/12/42.
[8] Ellenborough to Ripon (pte.), 25 Nov. 1843, PRO 30/12/77.
[9] Maddock to Clerk, 20 Aug. 1839, ESL 59, 4/25, 22 Aug. 1839.
[10] Auckland to Hobhouse (pte.), 25 Sept. 1839, AM 36474, f.132.
[11] Barkat Rai Chopra, *Kingdom of the Punjab 1839–45*, Hoshiarpur, 1969, 41 & 145.
[12] Clerk to Maddock, 14 Sept. 1839, ESL 61, 3/38, 4 Nov. 1839; Maddock to Clerk, ibid., no. 4.
[13] Macnaghten to Wade, 10 Nov. 1839, ESL 64, 12/5, 13 Jan. 1840; Macnaghten to Maddock, 13 Mar. 1840, ESL 68, 6/45, 8 May 1840; Macnaghten to Maddock, 22 Apr. 1840, 26 Apr. 1840, 3 & 16/60, 6 June 1840.
[14] Mackeson to Macnaghten, 10 May 1840, ESL 69, 41/72, 6 July 1840.
[15] J. Greenwood, *Narrative etc.*, London, 1844, 152–3.
[16] Clerk to Maddock, 15 May 1842, ESL 86, 79/15, 8 June 1842.
[17] Clerk to Maddock, 28 Sept. 1839, ESL 64, 5/5, 13 Jan. 1840.
[18] Macnaghten to Torrens, 5 Aug. 1840, ESL 71, 54/112, 16 Oct. 1840.
[19] Mackeson to Clerk, 25 June 1840, ESL 70, 3/7(S), 18 Sept. 1840.
[20] Macnaghten to Torrens, 5 Aug. 1840, ESL 71, 54/112, 16 Oct. 1840.
[21] Macnaghten to Maddock, 13 May 1840, ESL 69, 3/77, 11 July 1840; Auckland to Hobhouse (pte.), 11 & 12 May 1840, AM 36474, f.280; Kaye, *War in Afghanistan*, ii, 48.
[22] Auckland to Hobhouse (pte.), 20 Nov. 1840, AM 36474, f.371.
[23] Auckland to Carnac (pte.), 27 June 1840, AM 37700, f.67.
[24] Colvin to Macnaghten (pte.), 13 June 1840, AM 37700, f.45.
[25] Auckland to Robertson (pte.), 5 May 1840, AM 37699, f.45.
[26] Auckland to Clerk (pte.), 22 Mar. 1840, AM 37698, f.85; Auckland to Clerk (pte.), 15 May 1840, AM 37699, f.94; Maddock to Clerk, 4 May 1840, ESL 68, 9/45, 8 May 1840; Maddock to Clerk, 15 May 1840, 25 May 1840, Torrens to Clerk, 5 June 1840, 5, 15 & 40/60, 6 June 1840; Colvin to Clerk (pte.), 2 June 1840, AM 37700, f.11.
[27] Colvin to Clerk (ptc.), 20 May 1840, AM 37699, f.104.
[28] Clerk to Maddock, 18 July 1840, ESL 70, 2/7, 18 Sept. 1840 (S); cp. Macnaghten to Torrens, 13 Sept. 1840, ESL 72, 54/124, 16 Nov. 1840.
[29] Clerk to Auckland (pte.), 23 May 1840, AM 36474, f.304.
[30] Clerk to Torrens, 19 Aug. 1840. ESL 70, 3/7, 18 Sept. 1840 (S).
[31] Colvin to Clerk (pte.), 12 June 1840, AM 37700, f.39.
[32] Torrens to Clerk, 3 Aug. 1840, ESL 70, 115/85, 10 Aug. 1840.
[33] Macnaghten to Torrens, 19 Aug. 1840, 22 Aug. 1840, 24 Aug. 1840, ESL 71, 6, 7&8/112, 16 Oct. 1840.
[34] Auckland to Clerk (pte.), 7 Sept. 1840, AM 37701, f.111.

[35] Auckland to Robertson (pte.), 12 Nov. 1840, AM 37702, f.74.

[36] Macnaghten to Maddock, 26 Nov. 1840, ESL 74, 51/4, 21 Jan. 1841.

[37] Note on Maddock to Clerk, 2 Nov. 1840, ESL 72, 4/123, 16 Nov. 1840.

[38] Clerk to Macnaghten, 14 Mar. 1841, ESL 75, 23 Mar. 1841 (Agra). Advocates of the Sikh buffer strategy commonly referred to Lahore as a Hindu state, regarding Sikhism as a useful variant of Hinduism. I have employed the phrase 'Hindu buffer' because it expresses the vital point, namely that Lahore was in opposition to Islam, the prevailing religion of the north-west. It was rarer, although not unknown, for writers to indicate that Sikhism was also strongly differenti-ated from Hinduism, a feature which was considered to be of lesser importance, although one which was not without value. No writers that I have encountered ever alluded to the possibility that Sikhism could become a dangerous link between Islam and Hinduism.

[39] Mackeson to Macnaghten (pte.), 20 Apr. 1841, ESL 76, 12 May 1841 (Agra).

[40] Clerk to Mackeson, 30 Apr. 1841, ESL 76, 12 May 1841 (Agra).

[41] Colvin to Macnaghten (pte.), 10 Apr. 1841, AM 37704, f.132.

[42] Auckland to Clerk (pte.), 15 Feb. 1841, AM 37704, f.5; Colvin to Clerk (pte.), 16 Feb. 1841, AM 37704, f.11.

[43] Maddock to Clerk, 18 Feb. 1841, ESL 74, 17B/12, 18 Feb. 1841; cp. Maddock to Clerk, 26 Feb. 1841, ESL 75, 7/20, 21 Mar. 1841.

[44] Maddock to Clerk, 29 Mar. 1841, ESL 75, 57/31, 22 Apr. 1841.

[45] Auckland to Hobhouse (pte.), 7 July 1841, AM 37705, f.150.

[46] On these events see C. L. Datta, *Ladakh and Western Himalayan Politics 1819–1848*, New Delhi, 1973; and B. S. Singh, *The Jammu Fox*, Southern Illinois University Press, 1974.

[47] Cunningham to Clerk, 30 July 1842, ESL 89, 114/38, 17 Sept. 1842; Cunningham, Report, ESL 87, 120/23, 8 July 1842.

[48] Auckland to Clerk (pte.), 30 June 1841, AM 37705, f.139; Auckland to Hobhouse (pte.), 7 July 1841, AM 37705, f.150; Auckland to Hobhouse (pte.), 20 Aug. 1841, AM 37706, f.41.

[49] Datta, op. cit., 163.

[50] GGC to SC, 21 Oct. 1841, BSL(2) 10.

[51] K. C. Khanna, 'Anglo-Sikh Relations 1839–49', Ph.D. London, 1932, 177–9.

[52] Auckland to Ellenborough (pte.), 20 Nov. 1841, AM 37706, f.175.

[53] Auckland to Clerk (pte.), 30 June 1841, AM 37705, f.139.

[54] Hobhouse to Auckland (pte.), 4 Apr. 1841, HM 840, 82.

[55] Hobhouse to Auckland (pte.), 4 Nov. 1840, HM 839, 450.

[56] Bayley to Hobhouse (pte.), 11 Jan. 1841, HM 836, 184.

CHAPTER 15, THE HINDU BUFFER, 1842–5

[1] Maddock to Clerk, 3 Dec. 1841, ESL 81, 38/109, 22 Dec. 1841.

[2] Colvin to Clerk (pte.), 9 Feb. 1842, AM 37707, f.155 (with note by Auckland).

[3] Maddock to Clerk, 27 Apr. 1842, 3 May 1842, ESL 86, 58&22/14, 17 May 1842; GG to SC 14/, 17 May 1842, BSL (1) 27, 495.

[4] GG to SC 6/, 20 Jan. 1843, BSL(1) 28, 67.

[5] S. A. Abbott, Memo., AM 40129, f.81.

[6] Bikrama Jit Hasrat, *Anglo-Sikh Relations 1799–1849*, Hoshiarpur, 1968, 225.

[7] Ellenborough to Wellington (pte.), 20 Oct. 1843, PRO 30/12/28/12, f.106; Thomason to Richmond, 10 Oct. 1843, ESL 94, 24/37, 21 Oct. 1843.

[8] Ellenborough to Ripon (pte.), 18 Oct. 1843, PRO 30/12/77.

[9] Ellenborough to Queen Victoria (pte.), 21 Apr. 1844, PRO 30/12/28/11.

[10] Ellenborough to Hardinge (pte.), 15 Apr. 1844, AM 40474, f.134.

[11] Ellenborough to Peel (pte.), 22 July 1844, AM 40472, f.229.

[12] Ellenborough to Hardinge (pte.), 15 Apr. 1844, AM 40474, f.134.

[13] Ellenborough to Ripon (pte.), 4 July 1844 in B. J. Hasrat (ed.), *The Punjab Papers*, Hoshiarpur, 1970, 76.

[14] SC to GGC 924/, 3 Apr. 1843, BDSLI 17.

[15] Peel to Fitzgerald (pte.), 15 Mar. 1843, AM 40463, f.166.

[16] Hardinge to Peel (pte.), 1 Aug. 1844, AM 40474, f.144.

[17] Peel to Hardinge (pte.), 4 Oct. 1844, AM 40474, f.168; cp. Peel to Ellenborough (pte.), 7 June 1844, AM 40472, f.208.

[18] Peel to Hardinge (pte.), 6 Nov. 1844, AM 40474, f.172.

[19] Broadfoot, *Career of Major George Broadfoot*, 192–3.

[20] Ibid., 409.

[21] Ibid., 235–6.

[22] Hardinge to Ripon (pte.), 2 Jan. 1846, AM 40875, f.18.

[23] Broadfoot, op. cit., 235.

[24] R. N. Cust, Memo., 5 Mar. 1887, AM 40129, f. 105. For Cust's views see also his *Memoirs of Past Years of a Septuagenarian*, London 1904, and *Linguistic and Oriental Essays*, London, 1906.

[25] Broadfoot, op. cit., 246, 257.

[26] Hardinge to Ripon (pte.), 8 Sept. 1845, AM 40873, f.274; cp. Hardinge to Peel (pte.), 23 Oct. 1845, AM 40475, f.41.

[27] Hardinge to Ripon (pte.), 5 Nov. 1845, AM 40874, f.196.

[28] Hardinge to Ripon (pte.), 6 Sept. 1845, AM 40873, f.266.

[29] Hardinge to Ripon (pte.), 20 Sept. 1845, AM 40873, f.330.

[30] Broadfoot to Ellenborough (pte.), 18 Nov. 1844, in Hasrat (ed.), *The Punjab Papers*, 78.

[31] Hardinge to Ripon (pte.), 8 Jan. 1845, AM 40871, f.24.

[32] Ellenborough to Queen Victoria, 20 Mar. 1844, in Hasrat, *Anglo-Sikh Relations*, 236–7.

[33] Hardinge to Ripon (pte.), 23 Jan. 1845, AM 40871, f.85.

[34] Broadfoot, op. cit., 257–9.

[35] Ibid., 268.

[36] Ibid., 271.

[37] Hardinge to Ripon (pte.), 30 Sept. 1845, AM 40873, f.346.

[38] Hardinge to Ripon (pte.), 3 Dec. 1845, AM 40474, f.271.

[39] Hardinge to Ripon (pte.), 23 Jan. 1845, AM 40871, f.85.

[40] Hardinge to Ripon (pte.), 7 Feb. 1845, AM 40871, f.188.

[41] Hardinge to Ripon (pte.), 8 Aug. 1845, AM 40873, f.151; Hardinge to Peel (pte.), 18 Aug. 1845, AM 40475, f.19.

[42] Broadfoot, op. cit., 326.

[43] Clerk to Ripon (pte.), 22 May 1845, AM 40872, f.126.

[44] Broadfoot, op. cit., 269–70.

[45] Ibid., 302; see also Hasrat, *Anglo-Sikh Relations*, 259–60.

[46] Hardinge to Ripon (pte.), 13 May 1845, AM 40872, f.104.

[47] Ripon to Hardinge (pte.), 7 Mar. 1845, AM 40871, f.301.

[48] Ripon to Hardinge (pte.), 24 Mar. 1845, AM 40871, f.345.

[49] Clerk to Ripon (pte.), 22 May 1845, AM 40872, f.124.

[50] Ripon to Hardinge (pte.), 23 May 1845, AM 40872, f.132.

[51] Ripon to Hardinge (pte.), 7 July 1845, AM 40873, f.32; SC to GGC 1100/, 5 July 1845, BDSLI 18. This dispatch superseded that of 1 July 1845 (no. 1099) in which Hardinge was given permission to assume the temporary administration of the Cis-Satlej territories, paying over the revenues to Lahore, without prejudice to the permanent solution.

[52] Broadfoot to Hardinge, 29 Aug. 1845, 9 Sept. 1845, AM 40129, ff.66, 75.

[53] Fauja Singh Bajwa, *Military System of the Sikhs*, Delhi, 1964; cp. Barkat Singh Chopra, *Kingdom of the Punjab 1839–45*, Hoshiarpur, 1969, 362–414; Hasrat, *Anglo-Sikh Relations*, 229–39.

[54] Hardinge to Ripon (pte.), 18 Aug. 1845, AM 40873, f.187.

[55] Hardinge to Ripon (pte.), 23 Jan. 1845, AM 40871, f.85.

[56] Hardinge to Peel (pte.), 8 Sept. 1845, AM 40475, f.33.

[57] Hardinge to Ripon (pte.), 30 Sept. 1845, AM 40873, f.346.

[58] Hardinge to Ripon (pte.), 20 Sept. 1845, AM 40873, f.330.

[59] Hardinge to Broadfoot, 14 June 1845, in Broadfoot op. cit., 312–3; cp. Hardinge to Emily Hardinge, 20 Feb. 1845: 'Come what may we shall have a case that will bear a House of Commons scrutiny', quoted Datta, op. cit., 100.

[60] Broadfoot, op. cit., 366–7.

[61] Hardinge to Ripon (pte.), 15 Aug. 1845, AM 40873, f.179.

[62] Currie to Broadfoot, 13 Jan. 1845, quoted Chopra, op. cit., 362.

[63] Hasrat, *Anglo-Sikh Relations*, 253–4.

[64] Datta, op. cit., 64, 98; Hasrat, 'British Policy Towards the State of Lahore 1842–49', in *The Research Bulletin (Arts) of the University of the Punjab*, 33, 1962, History (1), 10.

[65] Broadfoot, op. cit., 330; Hasrat, *Anglo-Sikh Relations*, 254–5.

[66] Hardinge to Ripon (pte.), 8 Sept. 1845, AM 40873, f.270; cp. GGC to SC, 8 Sept. 1845, AM 40873, f.280; Edwardes to Broadfoot, 10 Sept. 1845, AM 40873, f.296; Hardinge to Broadfoot (pte.), 11 Sept. 1845, in Hasrat (ed.), *Punjab Papers*, 90–1.

[67] Chopra, op. cit., 407–8.

[68] Ibid., 416.

[69] J. D. Cunningham, *History of the Sikhs*, London, 1849.

[70] Hardinge to Peel (pte.), 4 Dec. 1845, AM 40475, f.72.

CHAPTER 16, THE PANJAB OF THE POLITICALS, 1846–7

[1] There are many accounts of the Sikh wars. A competent modern study is Hugh Cook, *The Sikh Wars*, London, 1975. A more popular, but sound work on the first war is D. Featherstone, *At Them with the Bayonet*, London, 1968.

[2] Hardinge to Ripon (pte.), 5 May 1846, AM 40876, f.167.

[3] Hardinge to Ripon (pte.), 19 Jan. 1846, AM 40875, f.22.

[4] Hardinge to Ripon (pte.), 3 Feb. 1846, AM 40875, f.58.

[5] B. S. Singh, *The Jammu Fox*, 109–12.

[6] Hardinge to Ripon (pte.), 19 Feb. 1846, AM 40875, f.78.

[7] Hardinge to Ripon (pte.), 18 Mar. 1846, AM 40875, f.281.

[8] Hardinge to Hogg (pte.), 19 Apr. 1846, AM 40876, f.58.

[9] GG to SC, 19 Feb. 1846, AM 40875, f.80.

[10] Hardinge to Ripon (pte.), 4 Mar. 1846, AM 40875, f.176.

[11] For a contrary view see E. R. Crawford, 'The Sikh Wars 1845–9', in B. Bond (ed.), *Victorian Military Campaigns*, London, 1967, 49.

[12] Hardinge to Hobhouse (pte.), 2 Sept. 1846, AM 36475, f.9.

[13] Hardinge to Hogg (pte.), 19 Apr. 1846, AM 40876, f.58. Admittedly this is what Hardinge knew that Hogg would like to hear.

[14] Hardinge to Ripon (pte.), 9 May 1846, AM 40876, f.201.

[15] AM 40129, f.108.

[16] S. A. Abbott, Memo., AM 40129, f.89.

[17] H. Edwardes and H. Merivale, *Life of Sir Henry Lawrence*, London, 1873, 395–409.

[18] Hardinge to Ripon (pte.), 7 June 1846, AM 40877, f.88.

[19] Hardinge to Hobhouse (pte.), 2 Sept. 1846, AM 36475, f.9.

[20] Hardinge to Hobhouse (pte.), 19 Sept. 1846, AM 36475, f.51.

[21] Hardinge to Hobhouse (pte.), 5 Apr. 1847, AM 36475, f.219.

[22] Ibid.

[23] Hardinge to Hobhouse (pte.), 2 May 1847, AM 36475, f.271.

[24] Hardinge to Hobhouse (pte.), 5 Mar. 1847, AM 36475, f.201.

[25] Hardinge to Queen Victoria, 27 July 1847, AM 36475, f.343.

[26] Kaye, *Lives of Indian Officers*, ii, 297.

[27] cp. Edwardes and Merivale, op. cit., 410–14.

[28] Cust, Memo., AM 40129, f.101.

[29] Hardinge to Peel (pte.), 30 Dec. 1845, AM 40475, f.82.

[30] Ripon to Peel (pte.), Tuesday [3 Mar. 1846], AM 40466, f.370.

[31] See correspondence in AM 40875 and 40466.

[32] Peel to Ripon (pte.), 28 Feb. 1846, AM 40466, f.376.

[33] Hobhouse, Diary, 3 Oct. 1847, AM 43751, f.29.

[34] Ripon to Hardinge (pte.), 4 June 1846, AM 40877, f.12.

[35] Hardinge, Memo., 7 June 1846, AM 40877, f.39.

[36] Peel to Ripon (pte.), 10 Mar. 1846, AM 40466, f.392.

[37] Ripon to Peel (pte.), 12 Mar. 1846, AM 40875, f.264.

[38] Ripon to Hardinge (pte.), 23 Mar. 1841, AM 40875, f.326.

[39] Ripon to Hardinge (pte.), 6 Apr. 1846, AM 40876, f.14.

[40] Ripon to Hardinge (pte.), 7 May 1846, AM 40876, f.181.

[41] Hardinge to Ripon (pte.), 9 May 1846, AM 40876, f.203.
[42] Hardinge to Ripon (pte.), 24 June 1846, AM 40877, f.137.
[43] Peel to Hardinge (pte.), 26 Oct. 1845, AM 40475, f.67.

CHAPTER 17, THE PANJAB ANNEXED

[1] There is no good modern study of Dalhousie. See Sir W. Lee–Warner, *Life of Dalhousie*, 2 vols., London, 1904.
[2] *Private Correspondence of Dalhousie* (ed. Baird), London, 1910, 27.
[2] Ibid., 84.
[3] Sita Ram Kohli, *Sunset of the Sikh Empire*, London, 1967, 146–9; Hasrat, *Anglo-Sikh Relations*, 305–9.
[4] Dalhousie to Hobhouse (pte.), 11 May 1848, AM 36476, f.77.
[5] Dalhousie to Hobhouse (pte.), 4 May 1848, AM 36476, f.68.
[6] Dalhousie to Hobhouse (pte.), 2 June 1848, AM 36476, f.90.
[7] Dalhousie to Currie (pte.), 28 May 1848, HM 855, 103.
[8] Dalhousie to Hobhouse (pte.), 3 July 1848, AM 36476, f.138.
[9] Dalhousie to Hobhouse (pte.), 10 July 1848, AM 36476, f.150.
[10] Dalhousie to Hobhouse (pte.), 7 Aug. 1848, AM 36476, f.163.
[11] Dalhousie to Hobhouse (pte.), 1 July 1848, AM 36476, f.131.
[12] *Private Correspondence*, 29–30.
[13] Dalhousie to Hobhouse (pte.), 15 July 1848, AM 36476, f.183.
[14] *Private Correspondence*, 33.
[15] Dalhousie to Hobhouse (pte.), 1 Oct. 1848, AM 36476, f.245. This letter is misdated 8 Oct. in Hasrat (ed.), *The Punjab Papers*, 188–90.
[16] Hamid ud-Din, 'Dost Muhammad and the Second Sikh War', *Journal of the Pakistan Historical Society*, 2 (1954), 280 et seq.
[17] Dalhousie to Hobhouse (pte.), 4 Jan. 1849, AM 36476, f.311.
[18] Dalhousie to Hobhouse (pte.), 7 Feb. 1849, AM 36476, f.372.
[19] Dalhousie to Hobhouse (pte.), 21 Feb. 1849, AM 36476, f.393.
[20] Quoted Kohli, op. cit., 191.
[21] Dalhousie to Hobhouse (pte.), 7 Apr. 1849, AM 36476, f.497.
[22] *Private Correspondence*, 62–3.
[23] Gough to Dalhousie (pte.), 9 Feb. 1849, AM 36476, f.412.
[24] Dalhousie to Gough, 13 Feb. 1849, AM 36476, f.414.
[25] Dalhousie to Hobhouse (pte.), 6 Mar. 1849, AM 36476, f.420.
[26] D. Southgate, '*The Most English Minister*', London, 1966, 308–10.
[27] Hobhouse, Diary, AM 43752, ff.103–4.
[28] Hardinge to Ripon (pte.), 20 Apr. 1847, AM 40877, f.256.
[29] Palmerston to Russell (pte.), 9 June 1847, in Ashley, *Life of Palmerston 1846–65*, i, 23–5.
[30] Hobhouse, Diary, AM 43749, f.63.
[31] Hobhouse, Diary, AM 43752, f.101; Hobhouse to Dalhousie (pte.), 24 June 1848, HM 859, 20.
[32] Ibid., f.119.
[33] Hobhouse, Diary, AM 43753, f.2.
[34] Hobhouse to Dalhousie (pte.), 7 Aug. 1848, HM 859, 35.
[35] Hobhouse to Dalhousie (pte.), 6 July 1848, HM 859, 28.
[36] Hobhouse to Dalhousie (pte.), 7 Aug. 1848, HM 839, 35.
[37] Hobhouse to Dalhousie (pte.), 6 Oct. 1848, HM 839, 55.
[38] Hobhouse, Diary, AM 43753, f.44.
[39] Ibid.
[40] Hobhouse to Dalhousie (pte.), 23 Oct. 1848, HM 859, 60.
[41] Hobhouse, Diary, AM 43753, f.59.
[42] Ibid., f.58.
[43] Hobhouse to Dalhousie (pte.), 24 Nov. 1848, HM 859, 76.
[44] Hobhouse, Diary, AM 43753, f.81. cp. Hobhouse to Dalhousie (pte.), 24 Jan. 1849, HM 859, 100.

[45] Hobhouse, Diary, AM 43751, f.42.

[46] Hobhouse to Dalhousie (pte.), 20 Sept. 1848, HM 859, 53.

[47] Hobhouse to Dalhousie (pte.), 7 Nov. 1848, HM 859, 68.

[48] Hobhouse, Diary, AM 43753, f.102. Hobhouse's diary is the principal source for this episode. For Napier's view see Sir W. Napier, *Life of Sir Charles Napier*, 4 vols., 1857, iv, 147–54, and for the dispute with Sir James Hogg, 107, 112–13.

[49] Ibid., f.115.

[50] Hobhouse to Falkland (pte.), 24 May 1849, HM 859, 167.

[51] Hobhouse to Dalhousie (pte.), 7 Mar. 1849, HM 859, 121.

[52] Ibid., also Hobhouse to Dalhousie (pte.), 7 June 1849, HM 859, 168.

[53] Hobhouse to Dalhousie (pte.), 4 Apr. 1849, HM 859, 141.

[54] Hobhouse to Dalhousie (pte.), c. 24 Apr. 1849, HM 859, 146.

[55] Hobhouse to Dalhousie (pte.), 7 May 1849, HM 859, 155.

[56] Hobhouse to Dalhousie (pte.), 24 May 1849, HM 859, 163.

[57] Wellington to Dalhousie (pte.), 5 Mar. 1849, AM 36476, f.449; Wellington to Dalhousie (pte.), 2 June 1849, AM 36477, f.2. Hobhouse wrote of two earlier military appreciations by Wellington, dated 7 Jan. 1849 and 22 Jan. 1849, 'They are very extraordinary productions; equal in my humble opinion, to anything which has appeared in his published dispatches.' (Hobhouse to Dalhousie (pte.), 7 Feb. 1849, HM 859, 105.)

[58] Dalhousie to Hobhouse (pte.), 25 May 1849, AM 36476, f.554.

Bibliography

NOTE ON MANUSCRIPT SOURCES

Official Documents

In the Public Records Office I used the following series FO 60 (Persia), FO 65 (Russia), and FO 78 (Turkey). The reference shows where appropriate, sender, recipient, dispatch number followed by an oblique stroke (/), series and volume number.

In the Commonwealth Relations Office Library (India Office Records) I used a number of series, of which the principal are listed in the note on abbreviations. The series used throughout were the Boards Drafts of Secret Letters to India and Bengal and India Secret Letters. References to these series follow the pattern of those employed for Foreign Office Records. The Bengal and India Secret Letters were supplemented by the Consultations and Enclosures, of which I have usually preferred the latter, which were arranged to be read in conjunction with the covering dispatch. References to the Consultations show the date of the consultation and the volume number. References to the Enclosures (ESL) are to be read as follows: sender, recipient, date of letter, series, volume number, enclosure number, oblique stroke (/) dispatch number, date of dispatch. Occasional use has been made of Bombay records for which a similar system has been employed. Considerable use has been made of the Factory Records Persia and the Persian Gulf series, but the system of referencing used for this and other series calls for no particular comment. Full information on these series may be obtained from the various lists published by the India Office Library. Collections used in the Home Miscellaneous Series are mentioned separately below under *Private Papers*. Since I originally collected material from the India Office Records many series have been renumbered under the heading Letters, Political and Secret (LP & S). As it is quite easy to connect the new and old numbers I have not troubled to alter my references.

Private Papers

In the British Library the following collections were used: Aberdeen, Auckland, Broadfoot, Broughton, Dalhousie, Harford Jones, Peel, Ripon, and Wellesley. AM has been preferred to the customary Add.MS. because it is shorter.

In the Commonwealth Relations Office (India Office Library) the following collections were used: Auckland, Lyall, and Robertson (D552), Beresford (C70–2), Campbell (D556), Conolly (B29,D161), Eastwick (F18/1), Elphinstone (D128–9,E91–2,F89), Forster (B14), Griffith (D159), Masson (E161–2 and others), Moorcroft (D236–54, and others), Peers (E125), Strange (D358), West (D160). References are prefixed by EM. In some cases the old catalogue numbers of the collections have been used. In the Home Miscellaneous Series the following collections were used: Bell, Broughton, Cotton, Malcolm, Sale.

In the Archives of the Institute of the Peoples of Asia (Leningrad) I used the memoir by Count Simonich, 'Précis historique de l'avènement de Mahomed Schah au Trône de Perse'. I am informed that this has now been published.

In the Leeds City Archives I consulted the Canning Papers (by courtesy of Lord Harewood).

In the National Library of Scotland I used the following collections: Lockhart, Melville, Minto.

In the National Library of Wales I consulted the following collections: Boultibrooke, Coed-y-Maen (Wynn Papers), Kenchurch Court.

In the National Maritime Museum I used the Minto Papers.

In Nottingham University Library I consulted the Bentinck Papers.

In the Public Records Office I used the following collections of private papers: Colchester, Ellenborough, Russell.

In the Library of the Royal Geographical Society I examined the papers of Henry Rawlinson.

Two collections of papers in private hands were used by me. One, the Palmerston Papers, now in the care of the British Library, was then in the possession of the late Lady Mountbatten at Broadlands in Hampshire. In referring to these documents I have adopted the same style as the late Sir Charles Webster. The second collection, referred to as Macnaghten Papers, consists of some letters in the possession of Sir Antony Macnaghten, and was made available to me through the kind intervention of Mr A. I. Macnaghten, formerly of the British Council.

PRINTED WORKS

Parliament

For Parliamentary Debates the following have been used: *Cobbett's Parliamentary Debates*, *Parliamentary Debates*, *Parliamentary History*, and *Hansard* Series I and III. Details of Parliamentary Papers used may be found in the footnotes.

Contemporary Newspapers and Periodicals

Annual Register
Asiatic Journal
Blackwoods Magazine
Calcutta Review
Edinburgh Review
English Review
Friend of India
Quarterly Review
The Times
United Services Journal
Westminster Review.

PRINTED BOOKS AND ARTICLES
(Where unstated the place of publication is London)

Abbott, A., *Afghan War, 1839–42* (ed. C. R. Low), 1879.
Abbott, J., *Narrative of a Journey to Khiva*, 1856.
Adair, Sir R., *Peace of the Dardanelles*, 2 vols., 1845.
Aitchison, C. U., *Treaties, Engagements and Sanads*, 12 vols., Calcutta, 1932.
Aitken, E. H., *Gazetteer of Sind*, Bombay, 1907.
Akhmedzhanov, G. A., *Anglijskia Ekspansiya na Srednom Vostoke, 1840–50*, Moscow, 1960.
Alcock, T., *Travels, 1828–9*, 1831.
Alder, G. J., 'Britain and the Defence of India—the Origins of the Problem, 1798–1815', *JAH* 6 (1972).
—— 'The Key to India? Britain and the Herat Problem, 1830–1863', Part 1, *MES* 10 (1974).
Algar H., *Religion and State in Iran 1785–1906*, California University Press, 1969.
Ali, B. Sheik, *British Relations with Haidar Ali (1760–1782)*, Mysore, 1963.
Ali, S., *Sikhs and Afghans*, 1849.
Allen, I. N., *Diary of a March*, 1843.
Amin, A. A., *British Interests in the Persian Gulf*, Leiden, 1967.
Apollova, N. G., *Ékonomicheskie i politicheskie svyazi Kazakhstana s Rossiej*, Moscow, 1960.
Argyll, George Douglas, *The Afghan Question 1841–79*, 1879.
Ashley, E., *Life of Palmerston, 1846–1865*, 2 vols., 1876.
—— *Life of Palmerston*, 2 vols., 1879.
Aspinall, A., *Three Early Nineteenth Century Diaries*, 1952.
—— (ed.) *Later Correspondence of George III*, 5 vols., Cambridge, 1962–70.
Atkinson, J., *Expedition into Afghanistan*, 1842.
Avery, P. W., 'An Enquiry into the Outbreak of the Second Russo-Persian War, 1826–28', in C. E. Boswell, (ed.), *Iran and Islam*, Edinburgh, 1971.

Babakhodzhaev, M. A., *Bor'ba Afganistana za nezavisimost', 1838–1842*, Moscow, 1960.
Baddeley, J. F., *Conquest of the Caucasus*, 1906.
Baird, J. S. A., (ed.), *Private Letters of Dalhousie*, 1910.
Bajwa, Fauja Singh, *Military System of the Sikhs*, Delhi, 1964.
Bakshi, S. R., *British Diplomacy and Administration in India, 1807–13*, New Delhi, 1971.
Balayan, B. P., *Mezhdunarodnye otnosheniya Irana, 1813–22gg.* Erivan, 1967.
Banerjee, I. B., 'Nao Nihal Singh and the Nepalese Mission to Lahore', *PIHRC* 22 (1945).
Barr, W., *Journal*, 1844.
Batorskij A. A., 'Proekty ékspeditsij v Indiyu, predlozhennykh Napoleonom Bonapartom imperatoram Pavlu i Aleksandru I v 1800 i 1807–1808 gg.' in *Sbornik geograficheskikh, topograficheskikh i statisticheskikh materialov po Azii*, St. Petersburg, 1886, 23.
Batra, H. C., *Relations of Jaipur State with the East India Company (1803–1858)*, Delhi, 1958.

Bell, H. F. C., *Palmerston*, 2 vols., 1936.

Bellasis, *Honourable Company*, 1952.

Bentinck Correspondence (*see* Philips, C. H.).

Beurmann, E., *Afghanistan*, Darmstadt, 1842.

Bhatta, P. N., 'East India Company's Policy Towards the Sikhs, 1764–1808', *JIH* 24 (1945).

Bhattacharya, S., *Rajput States and the East India Company*, New Delhi, 1972.

Bingle, R. J., 'The Governor General, The Bengal Council and the Civil Service, 1800–1835', in P. Robb and D. Taylor (eds.), *Rule, Protest, Identity*, 1978, 1–27.

Blacker, V., *Memoirs of Operations During the Mahratta War of 1817, 1818 and 1819*, 1821.

Boileau, A. H. E., *Tour through Western Rajputana*, Calcutta, 1837.

Bond, B. (ed.), *Victorian Military Campaigns*, 1967.

Bombay Gazetteer, vol. 5, Cutch, Bombay, 1880.

Borozdna, V., *Kratkoe opisanie putashestviya*, St. Petersburg, 1821.

Boulger, D. C., *Lord William Bentinck*, Oxford, 1892.

Bregel, Yu. E., *Khorezmskie Turkmeni v XIX veke*, Moscow, 1961.

Broadfoot, W., *Career of George Broadfoot*, 1888.

Broughton, Lord, *Recollections of a Long Life*, 6 vols., 1909–11.

Bruce, H., *Life of Napier*, 1885.

Brydges, Sir Harford Jones, *Dynasty of the Kajars*, 1823.

—— *His Majesty's Mission to Persia, 1807–11*, 1834.

—— *Brief History of the Wahauby*, 1834.

Buckland, C. E., *Dictionary of Indian Biography*, 1906.

Buist, G., *Operations in Scinde and Afghanistan*, Bombay, 1843.

Bulwer, H. Lytton, *Palmerston*, 3 vols., 1870–4.

Burnes, A., *Travels to Bokhara*, 3 vols., 1834.

—— *Cabool*, 1842 (reprinted Lahore 1961).

—— (with Leech, Lord, and Wood) *Reports etc.*, Calcutta, 1839.

Burnes, J., *Visit to the Court of Sind*, Edinburgh, 1831.

Burslem, R., *A Peep into Toorkisthan*, 1846.

Burton, R., *Scinde*, 2 vols., 1851.

—— *Scinde Revisited*, 2 vols., 1877.

Bute (ed.), *Private Journal of the Marquess of Hastings*, 2 vols., 1851.

Butler, S., *Eldest Brother*, 1973.

Cambridge History of India, vols. 5 and 6, Cambridge, 1929.

Campbell, George, *Memoirs of My Indian Career*, 2 vols., 1893.

Castlereagh, *Memoirs and Correspondence of Castlereagh* (ed. Londonderry), 12 vols., 1848–53.

Cecil, Lord D., *Lord M.*, 1954.

Chaudhuri, C. B., *Civil Disturbances During the British Rule in India, 1765–1857*, Calcutta, 1955.

Cheshire, H. T., 'Expansion of Russia to the Indian Border', *SR* 13 (1934).

Chopra, B. R., *Kingdom of the Punjab 1839–45*, Hoshiarpur, 1969.

Chopra, G. L., *Punjab as a Sovereign State 1799–1839*, Lahore, 1928.

Colchester, Lord (ed.), *Indian Administration of Lord Ellenborough*, 1874.

Colebrooke, Sir T. E., *Mountstuart Elphinstone*, 2 vols., 1844.
Collection of Papers Regarding the Course of the Indus, Calcutta, 1843.
Collett, H., *Gazetteer of Khiva*, Calcutta, 1973.
Colvin, Sir A., *John Russell Colvin*, Oxford, 1911.
Conolly, A., *Journey to the North of India*, 2 vols., 1834.
Cook, H., *Sikh Wars*, 1975.
Costello, D. P., 'Griboedov in Persia in 1820: Two Diplomatic Notes', *Oxford Slavonic Papers*, 5 (1954).
—— 'The Murder of Griboedov', *Oxford Slavonic Papers*, 8 (1958).
—— 'A Note on the Diplomatic Activity of A. S. Griboyedov by S. V. Shostakovich', *SR* 40 (1961–2).
Cotton, J. S., *Mountstuart Elphinstone*, Oxford, 1896.
Crawley, C. W., 'Anglo-Russian Relations 1815–40', *CHJ* 3 (1929).
Cunningham, J. D., *History of the Sikhs*, Calcutta, 1904.
Cust, R. N., *Memoirs of Past Years of a Septuagenarian*, 1904.
—— *Linguistic and Oriental Essays*, 1906.

Dalhousie Correspondence (*see* **Baird**).
Datta, C. L., *Ladakh and Western Himalayan Politics 1819–48*, New Delhi, 1973.
Davies, C. C., *Warren Hastings and Oudh*, 1939.
—— *Private Correspondence of Lord Macartney*, 1950.
Davis, H. W. C., *Great Game in Asia*, 1926.
Déherain, H., *La Vie de Pierre Ruffin*, 2 vols., Paris, 1929.
Dennie, W. H., *Personal Narrative* (ed. W. E. Steele), Dublin, 1843.
Driault, E., 'La Mission de Gardane en Perse 1807–9', *RHM* 4 (1900).
—— *La politique orientale de Napoléon: Sebastiani et Gardane*, Paris, 1904.
—— *La question d'Orient*, Paris, 1921.
Drouville, C., *Voyage en Perse 1812–13*, 2 vols., Paris, 1819.
Dunbar, J., *Golden Interlude*, 1955.
Dupré, A., *Voyage en Perse 1807–9*, 2 vols., Paris, 1819.
Durand, H. M., *First Afghan War*, 1879.
Durand, H. Mortimer, *Henry Marion Durand*, 2 vols., 1883.

[Eastwick E. B.] *Dry Leaves From Young Egypt*, 1849.
Eastwick, W. J., *Speeches*, 1862.
Eden, E., *Up the Country* (ed. Thompson), 1937.
—— *Miss Eden's Letters* (ed. F. Dickinson), 1919.
Edwardes, H. B., *A Year on the Punjab Frontier*, 2 vols., 1851.
—— *Memorials of Sir Herbert Edwardes*, 2 vols., 1886.
—— (and Merivale, H.), *Life of Sir Henry Lawrence*, 1873.
Efremov, F. S., *Strantsvovanie nadvornogo sovetnika Efremova v Bukharii*, St. Petersburg, 1794.
Ekbal, K., *Der Briefwechsel Abbas Mirzas mit dem britischen Gesandten Macdonald Kinneir (1825–1828)*, Freiburg, 1977.
Ellenborough, Lord, *Political Diary 1828–30* (ed. Colchester), 2 vols., 1881.
Elphinstone, M., *Caubul*, 2 vols., 1815.
Epitome of Correspondence regarding our relations with Afghanistan and Herat, 1863.
Erickson, A. B., *Public Career of Sir James Graham*, 1952.

Esher, Lord (ed.), *Girlhood of Queen Victoria 1832–40*, 2 vols., 1912.
Eton, W., *Survey of the Turkish Empire*, 1799.
Evans, G. de L., *Designs of Russia*, 1828.
—— *On the Practicability of a Russian Invasion of British India*, 1829.
Eversmann, E. (ed.), *Reise von Orenburg nach Buchara*, Berlin, 1823.
Eyre, V., *Military Operations*, 1843.
—— *Portraits of the Cabul Prisoners*, 1843.

Fane, H. E., *Five Years in India*, 2 vols., 1842.
Faroogi, M. B. A., *British Relations with the Cis-Sutlej States*, Lahore, 1941.
Featherstone, D., *At Them With the Bayonet*, 1968.
Feiling, K., *Warren Hastings*, 1954.
Ferrier, J. P., *Caravan Journeys*, 1857.
—— *History of the Afghans*, 1858.
Flandin E. and Coste, P., *Voyage en Perse 1840–1*, 2 vols., Paris, 1851.
Forbes, A., *Afghan Wars*, 1892.
Forrest, Sir G. W., *Life of Lord Roberts*, 1914.
—— (ed.), *Selections from the Minutes etc., of Mountstuart Elphinstone*, 1884.
Forster, G., *Journey from Bengal to England*, 2 vols., 1798.
Fortescue, Sir J., *History of the British Army*, 13 vols., 1902–30.
Fowler, G., *Three Years in Persia*, 2 vols., 1841.
Francklin, W., *Observations on a Tour from Bengal to Persia 1784–7*, 1792.
Fraser-Tytler, Sir W. K., *Afghanistan*, 1953.
Frazer, J. B., *Journey to Khorasan 1821–2*, 1825.
—— *Travels in Persia*, 1826
—— *History of Persia, Afghanistan and Baloochistan*, 1834.
—— *Persian Princes*, 2 vols., 1838.
—— *Winter's Journey*, 2 vols., 1838.
—— *Travels in Koordistan*, 2 vols., 1840.
Fredericks, P. G., *Sepoy and the Cossack*, 1972.
Furber, H., *Henry Dundas, 1742–1811*, 1931.
—— (ed.), *Private Record of an Indian Governor Generalship*, Cambridge (Mass.), 1933.

Gankovskj, Yu. V., *Imperiya Durrani*, Moscow, 1961.
Gardane, Alfred de, *Mission du Général Gardane*, Paris, 1865.
Gardane, Ange de, *Voyage dans la Turquie et la Perse 1807–8*, Paris and Marseilles, 1809.
Garrett, H. L. O., and Chopra, G. L., *Events at the Court of Ranjit Singh 1810–17*, Lahore, 1939.
—— and Grey, L., *European Adventurers of Northern India, 1785–1849*, Lahore, 1929.
Gene, J. B. D., *Un fourrier de Napoléon vers l'Inde*, Paris, 1915.
Ghorbal, S., *Beginnings of the Egyptian Question and the Rise of Mehemet Ali*, 1928.
Ghosh, B., *British Policy Towards the Pathans and the Pindaris in Central India 1805–18*, Calcutta, 1966.
Gleason, J. H., *Genesis of Russophobia in Great Britain*, Cambridge (Mass.), 1950.

Gleig, G. R., *Life of Sir Thomas Munro*, 3 vols., 1830.
—— *Memoirs of Warren Hastings*, 3 vols., 1841.
—— *Sale's Brigade in Afghanistan*, 1846.
Goldsmid, Sir F. J., *James Outram*, 2 vols., 1880.
Gordon, P., *Fragment of a Journal of a Tour through Persia in 1820*, 1833.
Greville, C. F., *Memoirs* (ed. Reeve), 8 vols., 1888.
Grenville, *Mss. of J. B. Fortescue preserved at Dropmore*, 10 vols., 1892–1927.
Griffin, Sir L. H., *Punjab Chiefs*, Lahore, 1865.
—— *Ranjit Singh*, Oxford, 1892.
Griffiths, W., *Journals* (ed. McClelland), 6 vols., Calcutta, 1847–54.
Grigor'ev, V. V. (ed.), *Khrisanoa mitropolita novopatrasskago o stranakh srednej Azii, poseshchennikh im v 1790 godakh*, Moscow, 1861.
—— (ed.), *Zamechaniya maiora Blankennagelya 1793–4*, St. Petersburg, 1858.
Grover, J., *Bokhara Victims*, 1845.
Guadella, P., *Palmerston*, 1926.
Gupta, P. C., *Baji Rao and the East India Company, 1796–1818*, 1939.

Hambly, G. R. E., 'Aga Muhammad Khan and the Establishment of the Qajar Dynasty', *RCAJ* 50 (1963).
—— 'An Introduction to the Economic Organisation of Early Qajar Iran', *JBIPS* 2 (1964).
Hamid ud-Din, 'Dost Muhammad and the Second Sikh War', *JPHS* 2 (1954).
Hardinge, H., *Viscount Hardinge*, Oxford, 1891.
Harlan, J., *Memoir*, Philadelphia, 1842.
—— *Central Asia*, 1939.
Hasrat, B. J., 'British Policy Towards the State of Lahore 1842–49', *Research Bulletin (Arts) of the University of the Punjab*, 33 (1962).
—— 'Anglo-Sikh Relations. British Political Missions to the Court of Ranjit Singh 1800–1838', ibid., 48 (1965).
—— *Anglo-Sikh Relations 1799–1849*, Hoshiarpur, 1968..
—— (ed.), *The Punjab Papers*, Hoshiarpur, 1970.
Hassnain, F. M., *British Policy Towards Kashmir (1846–1921)*, New Delhi, 1974.
Hastings (*see* Bute).
Haughton, J. C., *Char-ee-Kar*, 1879.
Havelock, H., *Narrative*, 2 vols., 1840.
Hinde, W., *George Canning*, 1973.
Holdsworth, A. H. (ed.), *Campaign of the Indus*, 1840.
Hollingberry, W., *Journal during the British Embassy to Persia in 1799, 1800 and 1801*, Calcutta, 1805.
Holmes, Sir T. R., *Sir Charles Napier*, 1925.
Hopkins, D., *Dangers to British India from French Invasion*, 1808.
Hoskins, H. L., *British Routes to India*, 1928.
Hough, W., *Narrative*, 1841.
—— *Review of Operations*, Calcutta, 1849.
Hughes, A. W., *Gazetteer of Sind*, 1876.
Hume, J., *Selections from the Writings of H. W. Torrens*, 2 vols., Calcutta, 1854.
Hunter, W. W., *Brian Houghton Hodgson*, 1896.

Huttenback, R. A., 'The French Threat to India and British Relations with
   Sind 1799–1809', *EHR* 76 (1961).
—— *British Relations with Sind, 1799–1843*, California University Press, 1962.

Igamberdyev, M. A., *Iran v mezhdunarodnykh otnosheniyakh pervoj treti XIX veka*,
   Samarakand, 1961.
Imlah, A. H., *Lord Ellenborough*, Cambridge (Mass.), 1939.
India and Lord Ellenborough, n.d.
India, Great Britain and Russia, 1838.
Ingram, E., 'The Defence of British India I: The Invasion scare of 1798', *JIH*
   48 (1970).
—— (ed.), *Two Views of British India*, Bath, 1970.
—— 'The Defence of British India II. Elphinstone's Mission to Kabul', *JIH*
   49 (1971).
—— 'An Aspiring Buffer State: Anglo-Persian Relations during the Third
   Coalition 1804–1807', *HJ* 16 (1973).
—— 'A Preview of the Great Game in Asia', Parts 1–4, *MES* 9 (1974) and 10
   (1974).
—— 'The Rules of the Game. A Commentary on the Defence of British India
   1798–1829', *JICH* 3 (1975).
Ioannisyan, A. R., *Prisoedinenie Zakavkaz'ya k Rossii i mezhdunarodnye otnosheniya v
   nachale XIX stoletiya*, Erivan, 1958.
Issawi, C., 'The Tabriz–Trebizond Trade 1830–1900', *IJMES* 1 (1960).
Istoriya kazakhskoj SSR, Alma Ata, 1957.
Istoriya turkmenskoj SSR, Ashkhabad, 1957.
Istoriya uzbekskoj SSR, Tashkent, 1955–6.
Ivanin, M., *Opisanne zimnego pokhoda v Khivu v 1839–40*, St. Petersburg, 1874.

Jackson, Sir K. A., *Views in Afghanistan*, 1841.
[Jacob, J.] *First Campaign in the Hills North of Kutchee*, 1852.
Jaubert, P. A., *Voyage en Armenie et en Perse 1805–6*, Paris, 1821.
Jones, Harford (*see* Brydges).
Jones, W. D., *'Prosperity' Robinson*, 1967.
Jourdain, A., *La Perse*, 5 vols., Paris, 1814.

Karelin, G. S., 'Puteshestviya po kaspijsckomu moryu', *ZRGO* 10 (1883).
Kajdalov, E. S., *Karavan-zapiski vo vremya pokhoda v Bukhariyu rossijskogo karavana
   pod voinskim prikrytiem v 1824 i 1825 godakh*, 3 vols., Moscow, 1827.
Kaye, Sir J. W., *Selections from the Papers of Lord Metcalfe*, 1845.
—— *War in Afghanistan*, 2 vols., 1851.
—— *Memorials of Indian Government*, 1853.
—— *Administration of the East India Company*, 1853.
—— *Life of Henry St George Tucker*, 1854.
—— *Life of Metcalfe*, 2 vols., 1854.
—— *Life of Malcolm*, 2 vols., 1856.
—— *War in Afghanistan*, 3 vols., 1857.
Kelly, J. B., *Britain and the Persian Gulf 1795–1880*, Oxford, 1968.
Kennedy, R. H., *Campaign on the Indus*, 2 vols., 1840.

Kessler, M. H., *Ivan Viktorovich Vitkevich 1806–39*, Washington, 1960.
Khalfin, N. A., 'Britanskaya ékspansiya v Sredni Azii, etc.', in *Istoriya SSSR*, 1958 (English version in *CAR* 6 (1958)).
—— 'Anglijskaya ékspansiya v Afganistane i osvoboditel'naya bor'ba afganskogo naroda v pervoj polovine XIX veka', in *Nezavisimij Afganistan*, Moscow, 1958, 180–218.
Khanikov, N., *Bokhara* (trans. Bode), 1846.
Kiernan, V. G., *Metcalfe's Mission to Lahore, 1808–9*, Lahore, 1943.
Kinneir, J. M., *Geographical Memoir of Iran*, 1813.
Kohli, S. R., *Sunset of the Sikh Empire*, 1967.
Kotlyar, P. S., 'Russko-afganskie otnosheniya v serednine XIX–nachale XX v.i anglo-russkoe sopernichestvo na srednom vostoke', *Uchenye Zapiski. Istoriya Vostoka II*, 33, Tashkent, 1962.
Kotzebue, M., *Journey to Persia in 1817*, 1819.
Krishen, I., *Historical Interpretation of the Correspondence of Sir George Russell Clerk 1831–43*, Lahore, 1952.

Labouchere, J. D., *Gazetteer of Ajmere*, Calcutta, 1875.
Lahore Political Diaries 1846–9, 4 vols., Lahore/Allahabad, 1909—11.
Lambrick, H. T., 'Lt. Amiel and the Baluch Levy', *JSHS* 2 (1936).
—— *Sir Charles Napier and Sind*, Oxford, 1952.
—— *John Jacob of Jacobabad*, 1960.
Lane-Poole, S., *Life of Stratford Canning*, 2 vols., 1888.
Lang, D. N., 'Griboedov's Last Year in Persia', *ASR* 7 (1948).
—— *Last Years of the Georgian Monarchy 1658–1832*, New York, 1957.
—— *Modern History of Georgia*, 1962.
Lawrence, G., *Forty Three Years in India*, 1874.
Layard, A. H., *Early Adventures*, 2 vols., 1887.
Lee Warner, Sir W., *Life of Dalhousie*, 2 vols., 1904.
—— *Native States of India*, 1910.
Lehmann, A., *Reise von Orenburg nach Bukhara*, St. Petersburg, 1842.
Low, C. R., *Life of Pollock*, 1873.
—— *History of the Indian Navy, 1613–1863*, 2 vols., 1877.
Ludhiana Agency Records, 1808–15, Lahore, 1911.
Ludhiana Gazetteer, Lahore, 1888–9.
Lumsden P. S., and Elsmie, G. R., *Lumsden of the Guides*, 1900.
Lushington, H., *A Great Country's Little Wars*, 1844.

Macgregor, C. M., *Gazetteer of Afghanistan, Central Asia II*, Calcutta, 1871.
—— *Gazetteer of Persia*, Calcutta, 1871.
—— *Gazetteer of the North West Frontier of British India*, 3 vols., Calcutta, 1873.
—— *Gazetteer of Beloochistan*, Calcutta, 1875.
Mackintosh, R. J., *Memoirs of Sir J. Mackintosh*, 2 vols., 1836.
Maclean, F., *Person From England*, 1958.
McNeill, J., *Progress of Russia in the East*, 1836.
Mahajan, J., *Annexation of the Punjab*, Allahabad, 1949.
Malcolm, Sir J., *History of Persia*, 2 vols., 1815.
—— *Memoir of Central India*, 2 vols., 1824.

——*Political History of India*, 2 vols., 1826.

——*Sketches of Persia*, 2 vols., 1828.

Malleson, G. B., *Herat*, 1880.

Marshman, J. C., *Memoir of Sir Henry Havelock*, 1870.

Masson, C., *Journeys in Balochistan, Afghanistan and the Panjab*, 3 vols., 1842.

——*Kalat*, 1843.

Matheson, C., *Henry Dundas*, 1933.

Meer Izzut Ullah, *Travels in Central Asia 1812–13* (trans. Henderson), Calcutta, 1872.

Meerza, H. R. H. Najaf Koolee, *A Residence in England*, 2 vols., 1971.

Mehta, M. S., *Lord Hastings and the Indian States*, Bombay, 1930.

Memoir of Sir John McNeill by His Granddaughter, 1910.

Meyendorff, G., *Voyage d'Orenburg à Boukhara fait en 1820*, Paris, 1826.

Mill, J., *History of British India*, 10 vols., 1858.

Minto. *Lord Minto in India 1807–14* (ed. Countess of Minto), 1880.

Misra, G. S., *British Foreign Policy and Indian Affairs, 1783–1815*, 1963.

Mohan Lal, *Journal*, Calcutta, 1834.

——*Life of Dost Mohammed*, 2 vols., 1846.

——*Travels*, 1846.

Moorcroft, W. and Trebeck, G., *Travels in the Himalayan Provinces of Hindustan*, 2 vols., 1838.

Morgan, C., 'Myth and Reality in the Great Game', *Asian Affairs*, 60 (1973).

——'Two Forgotten Missions', *History Today* (1975).

Morier, J., *Journey Through Persia*, 1812.

——*Second Journey Through Persia*, 1818.

Morier, R. N., *Memoir on the Countries about the Caspian and Aral Seas* (trans. from the German of Carl Zimmerman). 1840.

Morison, J. L., *Alexander Burnes to Lord Roberts*, 1936.

Morris, M. W., *First Afghan War*, 1878.

Moseley, P. E., *Russian Diplomacy and the Opening of the Eastern Question 1828–9*, Cambridge (Mass.), 1934.

——'Russian Policy in Asia 1838–9', *SR* 14 (1936).

Murav'ev, N., *Puteshestvie v Turkmeniyu i Khivu v 1819 i 1820 godakh*, Moscow, 1822 (English trans. Lockhart, *Journey to Khiva*, Calcutta, 1871).

Nair, L. R., *Sir William Macnaghten; a correspondence relating to the Tripartite Treaty*, Lahore, 1942.

Napier, Sir W., *Conquest of Scinde*, 1845.

——*History of Sir C. Napier's Administration of Scinde*, 1847.

——*Life of Sir Charles Napier*, 4 vols., 1857.

Narrative of the Events in Afghanistan between 2 Nov. 1841 and Sept. 1842, Calcutta, 1864 (sometimes called a *Quondam Captive's Narrative*).

Nash, C. (ed.), *History of the War in Afghanistan*, 1843.

Nazarov, F., *Zapiski o nekotorykh narodakh i zemlyakh srednej chasti Azii*, St. Petersburg, 1821. (reprinted Moscow, 1968).

New, C. W., *Durham*, Oxford, 1929.

Nightingale, P., *Trade and Empire in Western India 1784–1806*. Cambridge, 1970.

Nijjar, B. S., *Punjab under the Sultans (1000–1526 AD)*, Delhi, 1968.
—— *Punjab under the Great Moghuls*, Bombay, 1968.
Norris, J. A., *First Afghan War, 1838–42*, Cambridge, 1967.
Notes Relative to the Late Transactions in the Mahratta Empire, 1804.
Nott's Brigade in Afghanistan 1838–1842. The Private Diary of an Officer, Bombay, 1880.

Osborne, W. G., *Court and Camp of Runjeet Singh*, 1840.
Ouseley, Sir G., *Biographical Notices of Persian Poets*, 1846.
Ouseley, W., *Travels in the East*, 3 vols., 1819.
Outram, J., *Rough Notes of the Campaign in Sind and Afghanistan*, 1840.
—— *Conquest of Scinde*. A Commentary, 2 vols., 1846.

Pande, R., *Bharatpur up to 1826*, Jaipur, 1970.
Panigrahai, D. N., *Charles Metcalfe in India 1806–35*, Delhi, 1968.
Panikkar, K. N., *British Diplomacy in North India*, New Delhi, 1968.
Parihar, G. R., *Marwar and the Marathas (1724–1843)*, Jodhpur, 1968.
Parker, C. S., *Peel*, 3 vols., 1891–9.
—— *Life of Sir James Graham*, 1907.
Parkinson, H. N., *Trade in the Eastern Seas 1793–1813*, 1937.
—— *War in the Eastern Seas 1793–1815*, 1954.
Parry, E. J. (ed.), *Aberdeen-Lieven Correspondence*, 1938–9.
Pashuto, V. T., 'Diplomaticheskaya deyatleno'st' A. S. Griboedova', *IZ* 24 (1947).
Pearse, H., *Life of Viscount Lake*, 1908.
Peel, G. (ed.), *Private Letters of Sir Robert Peel*, 1920.
Pellew, G., *Life of Sidmouth*, 3 vols., 1847.
Pelly, L., *Views of General Jacob*, 1858.
Perkins, J., *Eight Years Among the Nestorians*, Anderson U.S.A., 1843.
Petrov, G. M., 'Novye materialy ob ubijstve A. S. Griboedova', *Uchenye Zapiski Instituta Vostokovedeniya*, 8 (1953).
Philips, C. H., *East India Company 1784–1834*, Manchester, 1940.
—— (ed.), *Correspondence of David Scott*, 2 vols., 1951.
—— (ed.), *Correspondence of Lord William Bentinck*, 2 vols., Oxford, 1977.
Popov, A. L., 'Bor'ba za sredneaziatskij platsdarm', *IZ* 10 (1940).
Popova, O. I., *Griboedov-diplomat*, Moscow, 1964.
Popowski, J., *Rival Powers in Central Asia* (trans. Brabant), 1893.
Porter, R. K., *Travels in Georgia*, 2 vols., 1821–2.
'Poslantsi iz Afghanistana v Rossiyu v 1833–36 gg.', *Russkaya Starina*, 8 (1880).
Postans, T., *Personal Observations on Sinde*, 1843.
Pottinger, H., *Travels in Baloochistan and Scinde*, 1816.
—— *Account of Events in Upper Sindh and Cutchee 1839–1841*, Bombay, 1845.
Prinsep, H. T., *Political and Military Transactions of British India 1813–18*, 1820.
—— *Runjeet Singh*, Calcutta, 1834.
—— *Origins of the Sikh Power*, Lahore, 1847.
Puryear, V. J., *Napoleon and the Dardanelles*, Berkeley, 1951.

Rait, R., *Life of Sir Hugh Gough*, 2 vols., 1903.

Rajputana Gazetteer, 3 vols., Calcutta, 1879–80.

Rawlinson, G., *Life of Sir Henry Rawlinson*, 1898.

Rawlinson, Sir H., *England and Russia in the East*, 1875.

R. C. M., *Journal of a Tour in Persia 1824–5*, 1828.

Recollections of a First Campaign West of the Indus, by a Bengal Officer, 1845.

Reid, S. J., *Life of Durham*, 1906.

Ritchie, A. T. and Evans, R., *Amherst and the British Advance Eastwards to Burma*, Oxford, 1894.

Roberts, P. E., *India under Wellesley*, 1929.

Robinson, L. G., *Letters of Princess Lieven*, 1902.

Rodkey, F. S., 'Conversations on Anglo-Russian Relations in 1838', *EHR* 50 (1953).

Ross of Bladenburg, *Marquess of Hastings*, Oxford, 1897.

Ross, C., *Cornwallis Correspondence*, 3 vols., 1859.

Rosselli, J., *Lord William Bentinck*, 1974.

Rousseau, J.-B. J., *Extrait d'un itineraire en Perse par la voie de Baghdad*, Paris, 1813.

Roy, M. P., *Origin, Growth and Suppression of the Pindaris*, New Delhi, 1973.

Rozhkova, M. K., *Ékonomicheskie svyazi Rossii so Srednej Aziej*, Moscow, 1963.

Russell, R., *Early Correspondence of Lord John Russell*, 2 vols., 1913.

Russian Missions into the Interior of Asia, 1823.

Sale, Lady F., *Journal*, 1843.

Sale, R. H., *History of the War* (ed. C. Loch), 1843.

Sarkar, Sir J., *Fall of the Mughal Empire*, 4 vols., Calcutta, 1932–50.

—— *Mahadji Sindhia and North Indian Affairs 1785–94*, Bombay, 1936–7.

Scheidemann, J. L., 'Paul's Plan of 1801', *JIH* 35 (1957).

Schiemann, T., *Geschichte Russlands unter Kaiser Nikolaus I*, 4 vols., Berlin, 1904–9.

Schwartz, B. (ed.), *Letters from Persia 1828–55*, New York, 1942.

Scott, A. F., *Scinde in the Forties*, 1912.

Seaton, Sir T., *Cadet to Colonel*, 2 vols., 1866.

Selections from the Bombay Government Records 17: Memoirs on the River Indus, Bombay, 1855.

Sen, S. N., *Anglo-Maratha Relations 1772–85*, Calcutta, 1961.

Sen, S. P., *French in India 1763–1816*, Calcutta, 1958.

Sercey, Comte de, *Une ambassade extraordinaire. La Perse en 1839–49*, Paris, 1928.

Serebrennikov, A. G., *Sbornik materialov dlya istorii zavoevaniya turkestanskogo kraya*: vols. 1–3, St. Petersburg, 1908–12.

Shadwell, Gen. L. (ed.), *Life of Colin Campbell*, 2 vols., Edinburgh and London, 1881.

Shand, A. I., *General John Jacob*, 1900.

Sheil, Lady, *Life and Manners in Persia*, 1856.

Shore, C. J., *Memoirs of the Life of Lord Teignmouth*, 2 vols., 1843.

Shostakovich, S. V., *Diplomaticheskaya deyatel'nost' A. S. Griboedova*, Moscow, 1960.

Singh, B. S., *The Jammu Fox*, Southern Illinois University Press, 1974.
Singh, S. K., 'Seton's Mission to Sind 1808', *JIH* 29 (1951).
Sinha, N. K., *Ranjit Singh*, Calcutta, 1945.
—— and Dasgupta A. K. (eds.), *Selections from the Ochterlony Papers (1818–25)*, Calcutta, 1964.
Skrine, F. H., *Expansion of Russia 1815–1900*, Cambridge, 1903.
—— and Ross, E. D., *The Heart of Asia*, 1899.
Smith, Sir H., *Autobiography*, 1901.
Smyth, C., *Reigning Family of Lahore*, 1847.
Solov'ev, M., *Ékspeditsiya v Bukharu v 1841–2 gg., pri uchastii naturalista A. Lemena*, Moscow-Leningrad, 1936.
Southgate, D., 'The Most English Minister', 1966.
Spencer, A. (ed.), *Memoirs of William Hickey*, 4 vols., 1925.
Stacy, L. R., *Narrative 1840–2*, 1848.
Stapleton, A. G., *Life of Canning*, 3 vols., 1831.
—— *Official Correspondence of Canning*, 2 vols., 1887.
Steinbach, H., *The Punjaub*, 1846.
Stirling, E., *Political State of the Countries between Persia and India*, 1835.
Stocqueler, J. H., *Fifteen Months Pilgrimage Through Persia*, 2 vols., 1832.
—— *Memorials of Afghanistan*, Calcutta, 1843.
—— *Sir William Nott*, 2 vols., 1854.
Strachey, Lady (ed.), *Memoirs of a Highland Lady*, 1898.
Strange, G. le (ed.), *Lieven–Grey Correspondence*, 1890.
Sundley, Lord, *Lieven–Palmerston Correspondence*, 1913.
Suri, L. S. L., *Umdat ut-Tawarikh* (trans. V. S. Suri), Delhi, 1961.
Sykes, Sir P., *History of Afghanistan*, 2 vols., 1940.

Taucoigne, M., *Journey to Persia and Residence at Tehran*, 1820.
Taylor, W., *Scenes and Adventures in Afghanistan*, 1842.
Temperley, H. W. V., *Foreign Policy of Canning 1822–7*, 1925.
—— *England and the Near East; the Crimea*, 1936.
—— (and Penson, L. M.), *Century of Diplomatic Blue Books*, 1966.
Terent'ev, M. A., *Istoriya zavoevaniya Srednej Azii*, 4 vols., St. Petersburg, 1906.
Theirani, K., *British Political Missions to Sind*, 1973.
Thompson, E., *Life of Metcalfe*, 1937.
—— *Making of the Indian Princes*, Oxford, 1943.
Thorn, W., *Memoir of the War in India 1803–6*, 1818.
Thornton, A. P., *For the File on Empire*, 1968.
Thornton, E. (ed.), *Gazetteer of the Countries on the North West of India*, 2 vols., 1844.
Timianov, Yu., *Death and Diplomacy in Persia*, 1938.
Tod, J., *Rajasthan*, 2 vols., Madras, 1873.
Torrens, W. M., *Memoirs of Melbourne*, 1890.
Tripathi, A., *Trade and Finance in the Bengal Presidency, 1793–1833*, Calcutta, 1956.
Triulhier, M., *La Route de Teheran à Meched en 1807*, Paris, 1847.
Trotter, J. M., *Gazetteer of Bokhara*, Calcutta, 1873.
Trotter, L. J., *Auckland*, Oxford, 1893.

Urquhart, D., *Diplomatic Transactions in Central Asia 1834–9*, 1841.

Varma, B., *English East India Company and the Afghans (1757–1800)*, Calcutta, 1968.

Verete, M., 'Palmerston and the Levant Crisis 1832', *JMH* 24 (1952).

Victoria, Queen, *Letters of Queen Victoria 1837–61* (ed. Benson and Esher), 3 vols., 1908.

Vigne, G. T., *Ghuzni, Kabul and Afghanistan*, 1840.

Vneshnyaya politika Rossi, (VPR) 1800–1815, 8 vols., Moscow, 1960–72.

Wade, Sir C. M., *Narrative of Services*, Ryde, Isle of Wight, 1847.

Ward, J. T., *Sir James Graham*, 1967.

Waring, E. S., *Tour to Shiraz*, 1807.

Watson, R. G., *History of Persia, 1800–58*, 1866.

Webster, Sir C. (ed.), *British Diplomacy 1813–15*, 1921.

—— *Foreign Policy of Castlereagh, 1815–22*, 1947.

—— *Foreign Policy of Palmerston, 1830–41*, 2 vols., 1951.

Weller, J., *Wellington in India*, 1972.

Wellesley, F. (ed.), *Diary and Correspondence of Henry Wellesley, First Lord Cowley*, n.d.

Wellington. *Despatches, Correspondence, etc.* (ed. J. Gurwood), 12 vols., 1837–9.

—— *Supplementary Despatches and Memoranda* (ed. Wellington), 15 vols., 1858–72.

—— *Despatches, Correspondence, etc., 1819–32* (ed. Wellington), 8 vols., 1867–80.

Wilberforce-Bell, H., *History of Kathiawad*, 1916.

Williams, C. R., *Defence of Kahun*, 1880.

Wills, C. U., *British Relations with the Nagpur State in the Eighteenth Century*, Nagpur, 1926.

Wilson, Sir A. T., 'Melville Papers: Unpublished Despatches of John Malcolm', *JCAS* 16 & 17 (1929–30).

—— *Bibliography of Persia*, Oxford, 1930.

—— *Persian Gulf*, 1954.

Wolff, J., *Narrative of a Mission to Bokhara*, 1845.

Wood, J., *Journey to the Source of the Oxus*, 1872.

Woodman, D., *Himalayan Frontiers*, 1969.

Yapp, M. E., 'Control of the Persian Mission 1822–36', *University of Birmingham Historical Journal*, 7 (1960).

—— 'Two British Historians of Persia', in B. Lewis and P. M. Holt (eds.), *Historians of the Near and Middle East*, 1962.

—— 'Disturbances in Eastern Afghanistan 1839–42', *BSOAS* 25 (1962).

—— 'Disturbances in Western Afghanistan 1839–41', *BSOAS* 26 (1963).

—— 'Revolutions of 1841–2 in Afghanistan', *BSOAS* 27 (1964).

—— 'Establishment of the East India Company Residency at Baghdad 1798–1806', *BSOAS* 30 (1967).

Younghusband, C. J., *Story of the Guides*, 1908.

Zakha'rin, I. N., *Graf V. A. Perovskij i ego zimnim pokhod v Khivu*, St. Petersburg, 1901.

Zimanov, S. Z., *Politicheskij stroj Kazakhstana kontsa xviii i pervoj poloviny xix vekov*, Alma Ata, 1960.

Zimmermann, C., *Geographische Analyse der Karte von Inner Asien*, Berlin, 1841.

—— *Der Kriegs Schauplatz in Inner Asien*, Berlin, 1842.

THESES CONSULTED
(University of London unless otherwise stated)

Adamiyat, F., 'Diplomatic Relations of Persia with Britain, Turkey and Russia, 1815–30', Ph.D., 1949.

Chopra, G. L., 'Punjab as a Sovereign State, 1799–1839', Ph.D., 1923.

Ellis, R. Ingram, 'British Policy Towards Persia and the Defence of British India, 1798–1807', Ph.D., 1968.

Evans, Gwynneth, 'Charles Watkin Williams Wynn, 1775–1850', M. A. Bangor, 1935.

Holmes, J., 'Administration of the Delhi Territory, 1803–32', Ph.D., 1955.

Ismail F., 'Ottoman Empire and the Great Powers, 1805–21', Ph.D., 1975.

Kapadia, E. R., 'The Diplomatic Career of Sir Claude Wade', M.A. 1938.

Khanna, K. C., 'Anglo-Sikh Relations, 1839–49', Ph.D., 1932.

Lunger, A. J., 'Economic Background of the Russian Conquest of Central Asia', Ph.D., 1953.

Majumdar, A., 'Lord Minto's Administration in India (1807–13) with special reference to his Foreign Policy', D.Phil., Oxford, 1962.

Shadman, S. F., 'The Relations of Britain and Persia, 1800–15', Ph.D., 1939.

Yapp, M. E., 'British Policy in Central Asia, 1830–43', Ph.D., 1959.

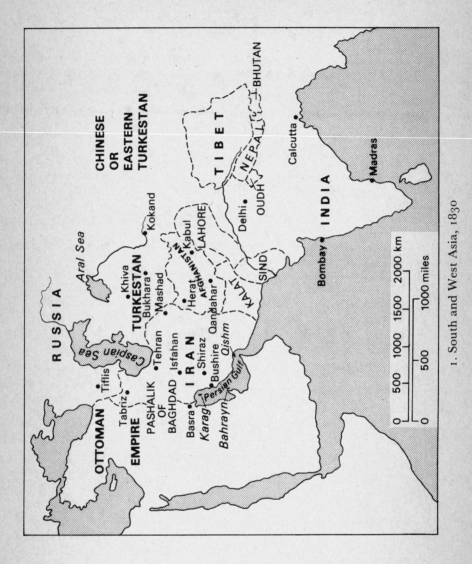

1. South and West Asia, 1830

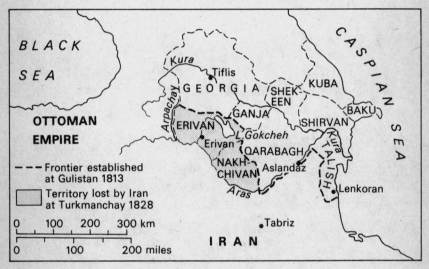

2. The Russo-Iranian Frontier, 1804–1828

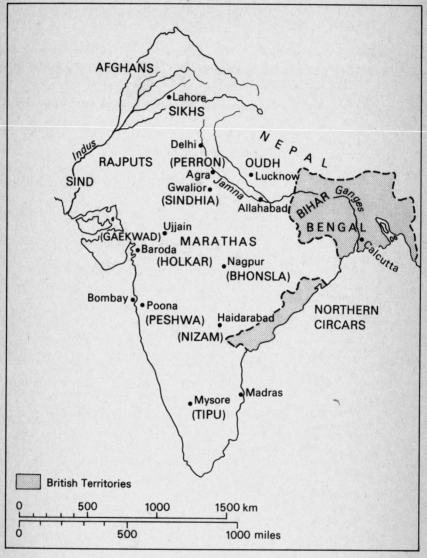

AFGHANS

•Lahore
SIKHS

Indus

RAJPUTS

Delhi•
(PERRON)

N E P A L

OUDH

•Lucknow

Agra•
Gwalior•
(SINDHIA)

Jamna

Allahabad•

BIHAR   *Ganges*

BENGAL

•Calcutta

SIND

Ujjain
•
(GAEKWAD)

MARATHAS

•Baroda
(HOLKAR)

•Nagpur
(BHONSLA)

Bombay•
  •Poona
(PESHWA)

Haidarabad•
(NIZAM)

NORTHERN
CIRCARS

•Mysore
(TIPU)

•Madras

British Territories

0   500   1000   1500 km

0   500   1000 miles

3. India in 1798

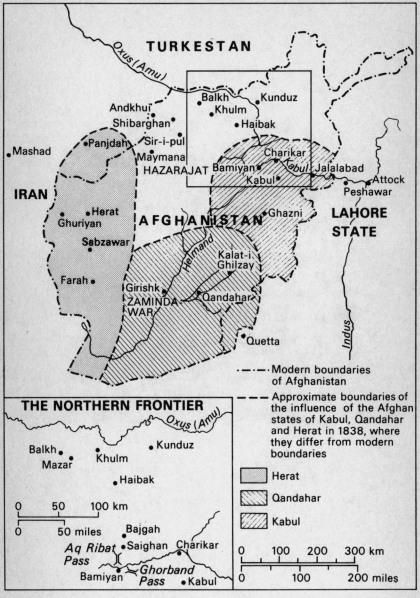

4. Afghanistan, 1838–1842

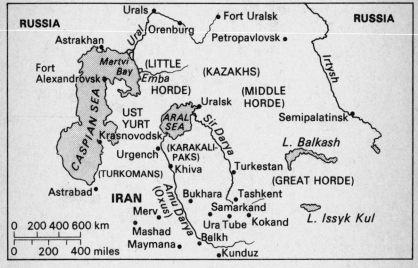

5. Turkestan

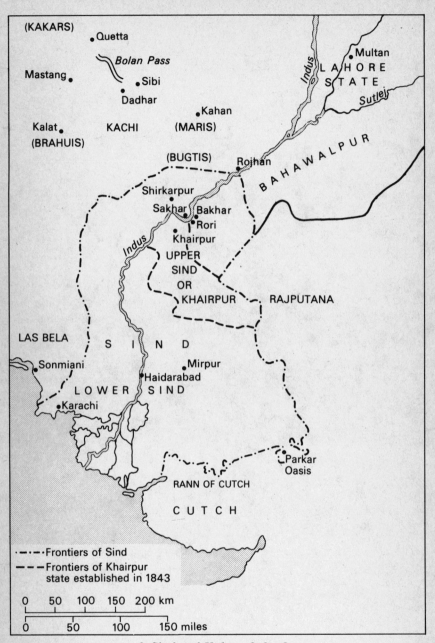

6. Sind and Kalat, 1838–1843

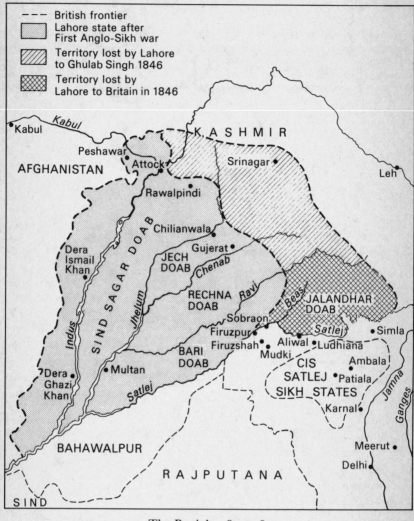

7. The Panjab, 1839–1849

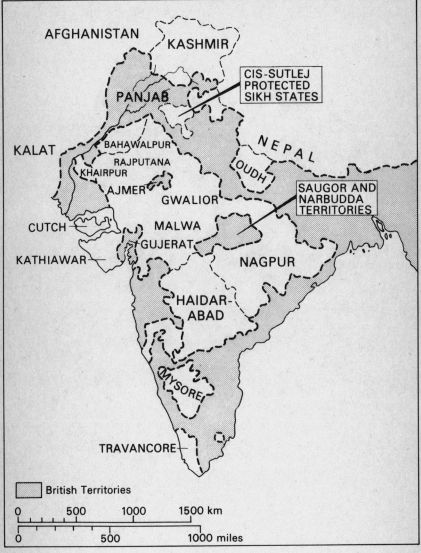

8. India in 1849

Acknowledgments

'Look! We have come through!' So D. H. Lawrence expressed what many authors feel when they take up their pens to write at last the traditional acknowledgments. And as this frail craft, laden with information and comment, gilded with a little entertainment and, doubtless, sorely holed by error, is launched upon the seas, I would like to remember those who helped the vessel and its builder to come through.

In the bibliography I have noted the libraries and other depositories of materials where I have worked and my thanks are due and willingly offered to their staffs. If, at this sentimental moment, I might single out one for its particularly grateful memories it would be the pleasing confusion of the old India Office Library in King Charles Street, before the long shadow cast by Burgess and Maclean ended the scholar's freedom to wander unhindered among those enthralling stacks and to explore enchantedly the warehouses of the minds of those who lived, moved and had their being among them. Oh my Burtons! Oh my Hills of long ago!

Books and documents form one part of the historian's stock; another is constituted by his reflections upon them. And reflection does not take place in isolation but is constantly fashioned and stimulated by the society of students and colleagues. I have been fortunate indeed in enjoying the privilege of working in the University of London History School and in the School of Oriental and African Studies for the past quarter of a century. I would like to register my thanks to all those who have made these years such pleasant and fruitful ones. In relation to this book, however, three of my colleagues must be mentioned by name, even at the cost of preventing them from reviewing it. I was lucky enough to be guided in my original research by Professor Sir Cyril Philips. Only his students know what scholarship lost through the demands made upon his administrative skills; his gentle comments provided enduring food for thought. Professor W. G. Beasley read the original version of this book, no mean feat, for, I am ashamed to confess, it was twice as long as the present volume. I profited greatly from his sound advice. And when hope dwindled and energies faltered I could always rely upon the steady support of my old friend, Dr B. N. Pandey.

Neither materials nor reflection would avail without the aid of those who translate manuscripts into books. To Joan Oliver and her colleagues and to Ruth Cranmer for help with typing; to Chris Brown and especially to Frances Kelly for making the vital connection with my publishers; and to Ivon Asquith, his colleagues at the Oxford University Press, and the anonymous readers whose excellent advice they sought and from which I benefited much: to all these my sincere thanks.

M. E. Yapp

Index